496

IN THE LION'S COURT

Derek Wilson came to prominence thirty years ago, after graduating from Cambridge, with *A Tudor Tapestry: Men, Women and Society in Reformation England*. This was followed by several critically acclaimed and bestselling books, such as: *Rothschild: A Story of Wealth and Power*, *Sweet Robin: Robert Dudley Earl of Leicester*, *Hans Holbein: Portrait of an Unknown Man* and, most recently, *The King and the Gentleman: Charles Stuart and Oliver Cromwell 1599–1649*. He has also written and presented numerous radio and television programmes. Now, after three decades of study and reflection he returns to those themes he first explored in *A Tudor Tapestry*.

More details can be found on his website:
www.derekwilson.com

IN THE
LION'S COURT

Power, Ambition and Sudden Death
in the Reign of Henry VIII

———

DEREK WILSON

PIMLICO

Published by Pimlico 2002

2 4 6 8 10 9 7 5 3 1

First published in Great Britain by Hutchinson, 2001
Pimlico edition 2002

Pimlico
Random House, 20 Vauxhall Bridge Road,
London SW1V 2SA

Random House Australia (Pty) Limited
20 Alfred Street, Milsons Point, Sydney
New South Wales 2061, Australia

Random House New Zealand Limited
18 Poland Road, Glenfield,
Auckland 10, New Zealand

Random House South Africa (Pty) Limited
Endulini, 5A Jubilee Road, Parktown 2193, South Africa

The Random House Group Limited Reg. No. 954009
www.randomhouse.co.uk

A CIP catalogue record fo this book
is available from the British Library

ISBN 0-7126-6529-3

Printed and bound in Great Britain by
Bookmarque Ltd, Croydon, Surrey

'You often boast to me that you have the king's ear and often have fun with him, freely and according to your whims. This is like having fun with tamed lions – often it is harmless, but just as often there is fear of harm. Often he roars in rage for no known reason, and suddenly the fun becomes fatal.'

Thomas More

CONTENTS

LIST OF ILLUSTRATIONS

1st section

Solomon and the Queen of Sheba, Hans Holbein the Younger, c.1534. (The Royal Collection © 2000, Her Majesty the Queen Elizabeth II.)

The Field of Cloth of Gold (at Hampton Court), artist unknown. (The Royal Collection © 2000, Her Majesty the Queen Elizabeth II.)

'The King' and 'The Pope' from *The Dance of Death*, Hans Holbein, c.1523–6.

Henry VIII, c.1537, after Hans Holbein. (Walker Art Gallery, National Museums & Galleries on Merseyside.)

Thomas Howard, 3rd Duke of Norfolk, 1540, Hans Holbein. (The Royal Collection © 2000, Her Majesty the Queen Elizabeth II.)

Cardinal Thomas Wolsey as founder of Cardinal (later Christ Church) College, Oxford, Sampson Strong. (Christ Church College, Oxford.)

Effigy of Bishop Wainfleet in Winchester Cathedral. (The Dean and Chapter of Winchester.)

Christina of Denmark, Duchess of Milan, 1538, Hans Holbein. (National Gallery, London.)

2nd section

Thomas More, 1527, Hans Holbein. (Copyright The Frick Collection, New York.)

Henry VIII, King of England (with his daughter Princess Mary and William Somers, the Jester), Hans Holbein. (Hulton Getty.)

Anne de Clèves, reine d'Angleterre, 1539, Hans Holbein. (Photo RMN.)

A Lady: Portrait of an Unknown Lady (inscribed Anna Bollein Queen), c.1530, Hans Holbein. (The Royal Collection © 2000, Her Majesty the Queen Elizabeth II.)

The Light of the World, Hans Holbein.

German woodcut of the deluge, 1524.

INTRODUCTION

There were lions in London. Thomas More, born and bred in the City, knew them well. They were the 'King's Beasts', housed in the Tower menagerie, and a major tourist attraction. Did More take Erasmus and other visiting foreign scholars to look at these awesome, savage creatures prowling around their semicircular enclosure in the Barbican or Lion Tower? Was he a spectator at any of the bloody displays occasionally mounted when mastiffs or bears were matched unequally with these wild royal animals? What is beyond doubt is that this is what he had in mind when he likened the court of Henry VIII to a lion pit in which the magnificent and deadly king of beasts held sway. Sharing with the King in all the sumptuous diversions of palace life could be fun but 'often he roars in rage for no known reason, and suddenly the fun becomes fatal'.

More knew, as anyone close to the Tudor monarch knew, that life at court was precarious. The monolithic personality of King Harry and its impact on the men and women who shared his life are the ingredients in a saga of unending fascination. It has become commonplace for those wishing to understand the reign to focus on the 'Six Wives'. The tragic comings and goings of three Catherines, two Annes and a Jane, summed up in the mantra

> Divorced, beheaded, died,
> Divorced, beheaded, survived

have suggested a simple résumé of the second Tudor's reign. This has always seemed to me inadequate, not because it 'reduces' history to a sequence of personal relationships – history is nothing if it is not a chronicle of human interaction – but because it does not get to grips with the real issues over which the nation's leaders quarrelled, fought and died in the first half of the sixteenth century.

That is why, in this book, I propose a different set of relationships which I believe offers a much more illuminating approach to the court and government of Henry VIII. I can even suggest an alternative mortuary mnemonic, though admittedly one which may not come quite so trippingly off the tongue:

> Died, beheaded, beheaded,
> Self-slaughtered, burned, survived.

Such were the exits of the six men most closely involved with the King in the governance of the 'empire' of England between 1509 and 1547. Thomas Wolsey was an accused traitor on his way to the block when a kinder death intervened. Thomas More and Thomas Cromwell, whose convictions and policies could scarcely have been more different, both perished beneath the headsman's axe. Thomas Howard, Duke of Norfolk, would have met the same end had the King's own death not brought him an eleventh-hour reprieve. Thomas Wriothesley, Earl of Southampton, and Thomas Cranmer, Archbishop of Canterbury, though outliving the monarch, perished as a direct result of that faction war of ambitions and ideologies which rumbled on after 1547. Wriothesley succumbed to poison of either body or mind in the aftermath of a failed coup. Cranmer went to the stake as a heretic at the insistence of Mary Tudor, who was very much the daughter of the father she hated. Manifestly, the atmosphere at Henry's Council table was no healthier than that within his bed.

The goings-on at the court of King Harry have fascinated generations of historians, students, novelists, playwrights, film directors and armchair enthusiasts, and that for many reasons. Not least among them is the feeling that we know the main occupants of this *petit-monde*. Whereas the personnel of earlier royal households are mere names or stiff-visaged icons, thanks to the incomparable genius of Hans Holbein, we can people the chambers and corridors of early Tudor Greenwich and Whitehall with men and women whose faces are familiar. The belief that, therefore, we 'know' them may be illusory but it is none the less powerful for that. 'Proud' Wolsey, 'saintly' More, 'scheming' Cromwell, 'slippery' Wriothesley, 'innocent' Cranmer and 'arrogant' Howard are stereotypes which, as we shall see, evaporate under the arc lights of research but those very stereotypes do provide us with a basis for closer observation.

Then there is the high drama of events crowded into these years: the stage-managed splendour of the Field of Cloth of Gold; the struggle for the divorce; More's wit as he knelt before the headsman; the dissolution of the monasteries – history's largest single act of nationalisation; the Pilgrimage of Grace, which came perilously close to toppling the throne; the sudden striking-down of Cromwell, the man who had made his master the richest prince in Christendom.

Over all these momentous happenings looms the larger-than-life figure of Henry VIII, powerful and capricious yet always an enigma. For how should we view him: as a lazy opportunist with no clear policies of his own, or as a wily puppet-master manipulating his creatures according to a script of his own devising, or as a vicious tyrant, ready to sacrifice everything and everyone to the security of the dynasty, or as a giant among kings, who inspired loyalty and genuine affection among his servants, or as the worst kind of self-indulgent megalomaniac – Junker Heinz, who, in the words of Luther, 'will be God and does whatever he lusts'?

Mention of the German monk brings us to the final and, for me, the most compelling argument for telling the story of Henry VIII and his six Thomases: it forms a tiny part of the greatest upheaval in European history before the French Revolution, the socio-politico-religious volcanic eruption we call the Reformation. Tiny it may be, as a single-cell culture is tiny by comparison with the organism from which it is taken, but placing such a sample under the microscope increases our knowledge of the whole living tissue. In the following pages I have pared off a sliver from the macrocosm of European Reformation politics so that the reader can observe, I hope with fascination, the antigens and antibodies striving and manoeuvring within it and then proceed to arrive at a clearer prognosis of the state of the whole. Just as diseases and disorders within the body result from the interaction of microbes, so the great movements of history only happen because of the conflicts and congresses of individuals. They can only adequately be understood by sampling significant personal relationships.

I have referred to the similarity of councillors and queens but we may not drive the comparison too far: a wife and a minister were clean different things. For one thing, ministers were easy to acquire and much easier to dispose of than wives. Few Renaissance monarchs were served by a more talented and industrious assemblage of advisers than was Henry VIII. None was more profligate in discarding those same able and loyal officials. A more fundamental distinction was that, unlike wives, whose influence could only ever be subtle and indirect, ministers were involved in the origination and implementation of policy. That was their function: they existed so that the sovereign could be master in his own house and yet be spared the very unkingly drudgery of day-to-day administration. Therein lay the rub, for there was no rule-of-thumb method of balancing the power of the ruler and the freedom of the servant. Niccolò Machiavelli enunciated the problem with his customary naked objectivity:

> when you see that a minister is thinking more about himself than about you . . . never can you rely on him; because he who has your existence in his hands should never think of himself but of his prince . . . the wise prince, in order to keep the minister good, always has him in mind, honours him, makes him rich . . . gives him his share of honours and offices, so that the minister sees he cannot stand without the prince . . . When . . . the ministers and the princes . . . are of such a sort, they can have faith in each other; and when it is otherwise, always the outcome is harmful either to the one or to the other.'[1]

Henry had no need of such advice; he knew instinctively how to extract the utmost from his apparatchiks. His presence overawed them and there was nothing assumed or manufactured about his massive personality. From ebullient, bonhomous youth to petulant, irascible old age he inspired genuine awe, respect, affection and fear within his household. It was not just the sheer power to reward hugely and punish devastatingly that the King possessed which obliged councillors to weigh carefully their words and actions. Henry VIII was no mere capricious monster who made or broke men at a whim; nor was he an empty-headed sybarite, who gave himself to pleasure and left others to do the work. Henry possessed a lively mind and, when he chose to employ it, he could grasp clearly the intricacies and implications of any proposed policy. He could be manipulated; he was susceptible to flattery and he always tended to be more interested in what would bring him immediate advantage than in the achievement of long-term objectives. Yet, at any moment, his intellectual curiosity or (more devastatingly) his enigmatic conscience might suddenly be aroused and when that happened a minister had to be skilled in explaining, convincing and persuading.

If, under cover of magnifying the Tudor regime, a royal servant was pursuing his own agenda – even though he might be convinced that his and the King's interests were in perfect harmony – he was venturing on to marshy ground. The six Thomases were not holograms who took shape only as and when Henry called them into being but who otherwise had no reality. They belonged to complex networks of kith, kin, ideology and clientage and were themselves made up of no less intricate interwefts of piety, political principle and personal ambition. Importuning the King on behalf of themselves and dependants was a constant of their activity. Attempting to move him to their understanding of the nation's weal was a responsibility they accepted. Forming alliances and introducing protégés to the royal entourage were the accepted means of achieving their objectives and outmanoeuvring their rivals.

All this was the stuff of court politics as it might have existed in any European principality at any time in the mid-centuries of the second Christian millennium. But this was not 'any time'. This was an epoch of tumultuous and self-conscious change throughout western Europe, a battlefield where new ideas exploded without warning, bringing down seemingly solid edifices, where the cohorts of martialled principle were locked in merciless confrontation, leaving their victims dead or maimed on the won and lost ground. Tudor England, no less than its neighbours, underwent this destabilising metamorphosis. Never had the kingdom experienced such rapid change. In the past, baronial wars, harvest failures and plagues had all had devastating effects – some within living memory – but they had been but temporary dislocations of a way of life that was as regular as the cycle of seed time and harvest and the feasts and fasts of the

Church's year. The opening decades of the sixteenth century witnessed an almost wanton tearing-up of ancient social and political landmarks in response to new ways of thinking about and exercising power.

As the Tudor governmental revolution increased in efficiency so the authority of local magnates – ecclesiastical and lay – declined. Never again would baronial alliances be able to offer effective resistance to the centralised state. Customary roles were also changing at the heart of government. The bishops and hereditary peers who traditionally made up the royal Council and headed the household offices were being replaced by a band of common-law logic-choppers, who introduced a new intrusiveness into government – sending snooping commissioners around the shires and obliging clergy to register details of their parishioners' private lives. They were examples of a new breed of graduate emerging from the universities and the Inns of Court, their heads stuffed with unconventional and revolutionary ideas. Some of those ideas originated in Germany where a renegade monk was snuffling around like a wild boar in the ecclesiastical vineyard and uprooting old certainties. Within a decade of the name 'Martin Luther' becoming widely known in England his disciples were creating havoc throughout the land. Pulpits and market crosses became the launch pads for rival propagandas. Wilder elements began to take the law into their own hands 'stripping the altars' of images which enslaved the people to old superstitions and a grasping papal regime.

Worse followed swiftly: 'reformation', long since urged by ardent churchmen of both radical and orthodox stamp, was endorsed by the King. The English Church was cut loose from its centuries-old Roman moorings. The people were ordered to work on what had always been regarded as holy days. Processions and pilgrimages were banned. Literate parishioners were encouraged to read for themselves the English Bible, newly set up by royal command in every church. Familiar, impressive landmarks disappeared from the countryside as monasteries tumbled into dust or were converted into fine houses for a new class of jumped-up merchants, lawyers and property speculators grown rich on the spoils of the dispossessed religious. Many of the new landowners and some of the old brought a new ruthless efficiency to the management of their estates; throwing fences around meadows long regarded as common; turning deaf ears to the demands of unwritten custom.

It was inconceivable that members of the Tudor élite could remain indifferent to these interconnected revolutions. According to their personal convictions, the framers of policy saw it as their duty to encourage or balk further reform. Whether or not self-interest coloured their perceptions, they could and did enpanoply their actions with the showy trappings of religious conviction, institutional reform, age-hallowed custom or devotion to their royal liege lord. Inevitably, therefore, personal and group rivalries were the stuff of day-to-day politics. Council members maintained their own clientage networks for gathering information and recruiting support. They paid and received 'pensions' (bribes). They maintained agents in the households of the royal ex-queens and princesses. They sent men abroad on private missions. They had their own hotlines to foreign embassies. They insinuated kith and kin into the private apartments of the King and the reigning queen. Above all, they tried to second-guess Henry Tudor's chameleon moods and take advantage of them. In their relationships with each other, each of them was manoeuvring for personal advantage. The velvet cloak of cordial correspondence between the Thomases, preserved in state and private archives, conceals the poniards of hatred and mistrust held beneath.

The 'English Reformation' and the 'Reign of Henry VIII' have been the subjects of numerous studies over the past half-century. This field of academic endeavour has been dignified by the work of masters of the stature of Pollard, Elton, Dickens, Scarisbrick, Haigh, Duffy, Starkey and MacCulloch and also by others, scarcely less distinguished, who have illumined the subject with discoveries in local archives and observations on specialist aspects of Tudor life. It would be nonsensical for a work of popular synthesis like mine not to draw thankfully on the labours of such scholars. But I do presume to offer a corrective to the academic methodologies which sometimes bemuse the ordinary reader. On the one hand we find the minimalist who reduces the complex symphony of a great age to a few notes discovered in parish registers or family letters. On the other hand we discover experts who rewrite the score according to their own theories, seeking to convince us, for example, that the Reformation did or did not have its roots in the people, or that Henry was essentially reactive or proactive.

Recent decades have seen the production of excellent biographies of key characters – Marius on More; Gwyn on Wolsey; MacCulloch on Cranmer; Ives on Anne Boleyn; Loades on John Dudley. These, again, are splendid contributions to our understanding of the period. But they, too, by their very excellence, have their drawbacks. They are magnifying glasses which enlarge their subjects and by enlarging distort them. They are like those medieval pictures of kings and courtiers in which the most important characters are drawn twice or thrice the size of their companions.

There is room, and I am bold enough to say, there is *need* for books like *In the Lion's Court* which complement these other approaches. By looking at the lives of six very different men and their relations with each other and the King I believe we keep three intertwined facts at the forefront of our minds. Fact one: history is shaped by ideas, beliefs and principles. Fact two: those ideas, beliefs and principles are mediated and distorted by individuals who are a prey to clashing passions and interests. Fact three:

what emerges is muddled and untidy, and defies neat classification by the organising minds of historians.

To understand the complex of relationships which did so much to shape the history of England in the first half of the sixteenth century we must do more than examine again the meanders and rapids of policy; we must look afresh at the lives of those whose beliefs, self-interest and animosities forced policy into the channels it took. And we must go further back to consider the influences which shaped those men. In the following pages the careers of the six Thomases will be described in parallel – their family and social origins, their education, their pathways to the royal Council chamber, their occupancy of the siege perilous, and the tragedies which, one by one, overwhelmed them.

Sir Walter Ralegh was scathing on the relationships between Henry VIII and his principal officers of state:

> if all the pictures and patterns of a merciless prince were lost in the world, they might all again be painted to the life out of the story of this king. For how many servants did he advance in haste (but for what virtue no man could suspect) and with the change of his fancy ruined again, no man knowing for what offence? To how many others of more desert gave he abundant flowers, from whence to gather honey and in the end of harvest burned them in the hive?[2]

Ralegh, who was languishing in the Tower when he wrote those words, knew all about the fickleness of kings and was certainly soured by the experience. But his opinion has been a colourful strand in the woven verdict of history. It is a verdict we need to scrutinise afresh. To understand the six Thomases is to understand in a wholly new way the most formative period of our national story.

PART ONE:

1499

If . . . we are to call any age golden, it is beyond doubt that age which brings forth golden talents in different places. That such is true of this our age he who wishes to consider the illustrious discoveries of this time will hardly doubt.

Marsilio Ficino, 1492[1]

The night before his last Advent sermon, 1492, he beheld in the middle of the sky a hand bearing a sword, upon which these words were inscribed: *'Gladius Domini super terram cito et velociter.'* He heard many clear and distinct voices promising mercy to the good, threatening chastisement to the wicked, and proclaiming that the wrath of God was at hand. Then, suddenly the sword was turned towards the earth; the sky darkened; swords, arrows, and flames rained down: terrible thunderclaps were heard; and all the world was a prey to war, famine, and pestilence. The vision ended with a command to Savonarola to make these things known to his hearers, to inspire them with the fear of God, and to beseech the Lord to send good shepherds to His Church, so that the lost sheep might be saved.

P. Villari, Life and Times of Savonarola[2]

CHAPTER 1

A Question of Identity

It was the end of time; it was the beginning of time. For those who knew their almanacs or listened to the apocalyptic rhetoric of fiery preachers the approach of the year 1500 had a doom-laden significance. *Fins de siècles* always possessed a special interest for men and women who knew that the world ticked to the rhythm of an inexorable divine clock but at the conclusion of this particular century the consciousness of standing on the threshold of a new epoch was particularly strong. Ever since the twelfth-century monk Joachim of Fiore had prophesied the imminence of creation's third and final age, star watchers and interpreters of human affairs had been writing the script for the inauguration of the Janus era which would be both the beginning of the end and the end of the beginning. Now, as the world reached the halfway point of the second Christian millennium, a multiplication of momentous events seemed to be hastening mankind towards a decisive turning point.

Christian civilisation was on the march. Constantinople, its eastern bastion, may have fallen to the forces of Islam in 1453, but Sultan Mehemed, the 'Conqueror', was long dead and his empire under increasing pressure. In the West the year 1492 – Anno 7000 in the Byzantine calendar and long prophesied as the date for Armageddon – brought the end of a centuries-old culture conflict as the Moors were expelled from Spain. The decade ended on a flurry of maritime activity associated with the names of Columbus, Dias, Da Gama, Cabot, Ojeda, Vespucci and Cabral, which, as geographers believed, made the whole of Asia vulnerable to the Gospel and commercial exploitation.

Yet, what was this Christendom poised to extend its boundaries so dramatically? Visionaries proclaimed it to be nothing but a ship of fools. Such was the title of both a book and a painting presented to the world at this very fulcrum moment in human destiny and whether we read Sebastian Brant's impassioned derision:

> The whole world lives in darksome night,
> In blinded sinfulness persisting,
> While every street sees fools existing

or gaze upon Hieronymous Bosch's boatload of doomed merrymakers, the message is the same: the madness of sin has possessed all sorts and conditions of men. From pope to peasant, from emperor to eremite, from monk to merchant, from priest to prostitute and pederast, the denizens of a supposedly Christian society wallow insanely in pride, gluttony, avarice, fornication and warmongering, while from despairing saints the cry is torn, 'How long, O Lord, how long?'

There was, of course, nothing new about denunciations of sin and exhortations to righteousness. If it were possible to gauge such things we should probably discover that Europe was no more or less a sink of iniquity than it had been for centuries. What *was* new was the prowling abroad of an intense, rampant, questing spirituality. Ardent souls were seeking, perhaps as never before, a meaningful faith-life for themselves and their society. Gospel revivalism surfaced in scores of different ways: renewed monastic asceticism; increased traditional devotion at altars, shrines, chantries and pilgrimage sites; publication of vernacular catechisms and holiness manuals for the growing number of literate men and women (Thomas à Kempis's *Imitation of Christ* received its first English translation in 1503); a plethora of lay communities for those who wished to be in the world but not of it; translation and colportage of Bible fragments – some clandestine, some officially blessed – many illustrated with affecting woodcuts and loaded glosses (the equivalents of the sensationalising photography and banner headlines of today's tabloids); clandestine heretical networks comprised for the most part of artisans, harmless in themselves but corporately a sufficient irritant to justify sporadic investigation and attempts at suppression.

All these contributed to and were nourished by a ragout of popular attitudes, comprising confusion about what the Church actually taught, superstitious adherence to religious externals, scepticism and a growing indignation with the power – spiritual and temporal – exercised by the clergy. In this world, through tithes, fees, indulgence sales and papal taxation, the priestly caste battened on men's material goods and, in the next world, through their privileged access to the court of heaven, they held a lien over the souls of believers and their departed loved ones. Yet, as the common gossip ran in alehouse, marketplace and royal ante-chamber, the ecclesiastical establishment exhibited few of those virtues of humility, self-control and charity to which its members exhorted the laity. Men in the upper levels of society who received their information along diplomatic, political and mercantile supply lines knew just how bad things were at all levels of the Church, right to the very top.

Corruption had reached new depths with the scandalous regime of the Borgia Pope, Alexander VI, but the Lord had chastised him through the French army of Charles VIII which rampaged through Rome in 1494. At least, such was the spin put on this shocking event by the Florentine apocalypticist Girolamo Savonarola, and Charles was not the only one to believe that God had raised him up to be the Last Emperor, the scourge of the Antichrist, the harbinger of the Age of Gold. His invasion of papal territory and his demand for a general council to reform the Church amounted to a swordpoint demonstration that Vatican power, expressed through excommunication, interdict and inquisition, was on the wane. National rulers were demanding greater control over the ecclesiastical institutions within their boundaries and they did not lack for scholars whose scriptoria were stuffed with theological justifications.

What was sauce for the goose was sauce for the goslings. Criticism, invective and ribaldry directed against inadequate clergy and the religious whose lives were less than exemplary were the stuff of common culture and had been for generations, but as the year 1500 drew near scepticism was more widespread than ever before. It was strongest among those who cared most. Devout clergy and laity, idealistic students and indignant preachers urged the need for reform and there were those whose passionate concern convinced them of the divine judgement about to come crashing down on God's disobedient people.

O prostitute Church, thou hast displayed thy foulness to the whole world, and stinkest unto Heaven. Thou hast multiplied thy fornications in Italy, in France, in Spain, and all other parts. Behold, I will put forth my hand, saith the Lord, I will smite thee, thou infamous wretch; my sword shall fall on thy children, on thy house of shame, on thy harlots, on thy palaces, and my justice shall be made known. Earth and heaven, the angels, the good and the wicked, all shall accuse thee, and no man shall be with thee; I will give thee into thy enemy's hand . . . O priests and friars, ye, whose evil example hath entombed this people in the sepulchre of ceremonial, I tell ye this sepulchre shall be burst asunder, for Christ will revive His Church in His spirit.[3]

So Savonarola thundered from the pulpit of Florence's *Duomo* and many throughout Europe not cursed with the gift of prophecy shared a gut feeling that things could no longer be suffered to continue as they were. Such conviction was not stifled with the deaths of both Savonarola and his unlikely champion in 1498 – the one crushed by the Vatican machine, the other expiring in apoplectic rage on a pile of urine-soaked straw.

The most effective group of critics at the turn of the century and in the years which followed was a Christendom-wide band of brothers known to historians, but known inadequately,* as 'Christian humanists'. These

*Inadequately because, being scholars, these thinkers of new thoughts were united as much by their disagreements as by those ideas they held in common. There was no Christian humanist 'agenda' beyond rejection of traditional scholastic method. Thus humanists would be found among the most radical advocates of reform and among those who sought to silence them.

members of Europe's intellectual avant-garde were the draughtsmen of a redeemed society. Like visionary architects aspiring to raise innovative cityscapes upon the rubble of decayed slums, they sought to sweep away the wasteful belligerence of princes, the corruption of churchmen, the exploitation of landowners and all the ills to which their world was prey and to raise a beautiful and magnificent new order in which peace, justice and humanity should prevail. The foundation of this brave new world was to be, in a word, education. A new generation of society's leaders, instructed in the wisdom of the ancients and, more especially, in the lively oracles of God as contained in Holy Scripture, would effect the transformation for which the humanists longed.

It was a century and a half since Petrarch had attacked the traditional teaching methods of the universities which equated learning with intellectual conviction based on the study of hallowed proof texts: 'This prattling of the dialecticians will never come to an end; it throws up summaries and definitions like bubbles, matter indeed for endless controversies.'[4] Petrarch and his Italian followers were largely concerned with rediscovering the 'virtues' advocated by classical authors through a return to the original texts, as opposed to comparative studies of what later authorities had written about them. It was only a matter of time before radical scholars applied the same principles to the teaching and learning of Christian doctrine. And it was only a matter of technology before this novel approach became the basis for revolution. The invention of printing with movable type, the most stupendous development in human communication between the appearance of the scriptorium and that of the Internet, delivered scholars from their semi-isolation in Europe's centres of higher learning and unleashed an excitement at the ready exchange of ideas equivalent to that which now gives a buzz to surfers on the World Wide Web.

Christian humanists were angry with and scornful of a Church hierarchy which had colluded in the obfuscation of the Gospel and which, therefore, bore much of the responsibility for the appalling state of contemporary society. They aimed to reform the educational system by a study of original Greek, Latin and Hebrew texts, especially the books of the Bible, by producing new translations purified from mistaken readings and scribal errors, by expounding ancient wisdom in ways which spoke to the heart and the will as well as the intellect, and by making this 'New Learning' as widely available as possible. Some even went so far as to advocate that ploughboys should learn to read so that they could study the Bible in the vernacular. They doubted not that this evangelical revival, once begun, would permeate and reform the whole of society.

That may strike the modern cynic as naïve but the Christian humanists were no bunch of irresponsible junkies shooting up on some ideological narcotic which made a harsh world suddenly seem cosily pink and furry at the edges. The past bore frequent testimony to the *bouleversant* power of Holy Scripture on the lives of individuals and communities, and the immediate future would confirm the brightest dreams (or darkest nightmares) of those who knew how devastating could be the unsheathed 'sword of the Spirit which is the word of God'. The great monastic reforms of the Middle Ages, no less than the ebullition of heresies such as Lollardy and Waldensianism, had been inspired by the rediscovery of New Testament truths. Examples were legion of individual conversions wrought by the bursting of biblical light into lives darkened by ignorance and sin. A fourteenth-century Archbishop of Armagh was far from alone in being able to testify, 'I used to think that I had penetrated to the depths of your truth with the citizens of your heaven, until you, the solid truth, shone upon me in your Scriptures, scattering the cloud of my error and showing me how I was croaking in the marshes with the toads and frogs.'[5] If God had enlightened groups and individuals sporadically throughout history, what might he not do in the dawning new age through the words of the Bible widely available to devout scholars and dynamically expounded by a new breed of preachers? The man acknowledged as the leader of the humanist revolt, and whom we shall now meet, enthusiastically prophesied that whole nations 'sworn to idolatry, by a sudden change of life, shall embrace the teachings of true piety'. What the humanists were proposing was an effective, interiorised and essentially lay religion which could be followed outside the cloister and did not depend ultimately upon those means of grace in which the institutionalised Church held a monopoly. It is difficult for us to comprehend the zeal and joy with which this vision was embraced by educated Latin-speakers throughout western Christendom and, beyond them, by humbler men and women who saw for themselves a new destiny not dominated by a monolithic ecclesiastical establishment.

Of course, not everyone in 1499 was aware that society was trembling on the brink of change. Most people were preoccupied most of the time with the usual mundane pursuits of making a living, making a career, making love, making friends and making enemies. Nevertheless this was one of those ages which was self-conscious and introspective. When people lifted their eyes to the horizon they did see lightning flashes and lurid clouds. The world in which Henry VIII and his six Thomases grew up was one in which the pious dreamed new dreams, the learned thought new thoughts and the powerful dared new deeds. It is this which gives significance to a mundane event in the middle of 1499.

On a summer's morning in the last year of the fifteenth century a witty young man about town, a crotchety Dutch scholar and an eight-year-old boy held a brief, learned conversation in a fine Kentish house. This is the earliest recorded meeting between the future King Henry VIII and Thomas

More, the first of six remarkable men who shared the same 'chrysten' name and were to share the privileges and perils of power beneath the Crown when the little boy at Eltham Palace became the most capricious tyrant ever to occupy the English throne. The third member of this ad hoc symposium was Desiderius Erasmus of Rotterdam and we only know of this event, trivial in itself, because he wrote an account of it a quarter of a century later when the twists and turns of time rendered it worthy of record. The brief encounter in the summer of 1499 has possessed a curiosity value for later generations because it brought together for the first time the scholar who more than any other championed the new ideas that were to devastate English society, the Prince who would give those ideas legal force and the lawyer who would die resisting them.

The man who took his friend to visit the royal children in the summer of 1499 was twenty-one years of age and about to enter his fourth year at Lincoln's Inn. On the face of it he had just about everything going for him: a comfortable home; a father who was an ambitious, prominent barrister well able to pull the strings necessary to establish his son in the same profession; the best education money could buy; and he already had valuable contacts in high places (not many citizens of London enjoyed access to royal palaces). Better than all these, he possessed the qualities and talents necessary to make the most of his material advantages: a brilliant analytical mind; a ready wit; a conscientious application to study; a natural gift for acting; and an ability to make friends.

More's progress through the law's nursery was at this time proceeding rapidly. The combination of his own talents and his father's influence (John More was a senior member of Lincoln's Inn) set him on the fast track to qualification as a barrister, which took less favoured mortals upwards of ten years.

He attended lectures delivered by 'readers' who were so called because they expounded from the great medieval standard works but by 1499 he was sufficiently well versed in the texts to become a reader himself at one of the Inns of Chancery (Furnival's). He took an increasingly prominent part in the 'moots', the debates on points of law arising from current cases. At Westminster Hall he was allowed to assist the pleading barristers. The lofty and already ancient building was divided by partitions into several enclosures or courts where the justices of King's Bench heard criminal or other cases affecting the Crown, those of Common Pleas determined civil actions and those of Exchequer dealt with revenue matters. More may also have accompanied, out of term, the justices who went on circuit to preside over civil and criminal cases in the provinces.

There was, as there always is, more to student life than dry books and dryer expounders of books. London offered a host of diversions to young men with long purses or indulgent parents. The narrow, gorged streets of the capital were abustle with taverns, cook shops, brothels and the unscrupulous hawkers of fashion accessories, bawdy ballads, cheap ale and sundry items 'fallen off the back of a wagon'. They were the battle-ground for affrays between bands of students and apprentices. In Smithfield a prodigal away from home could find horse races and wrestling bouts to waste his substance on, while for the more energetic there was archery on Bunhill or Finsbury Fields or the 'beastly fury and extreme violence' of football. The City corporation and the livery companies provided public spectacles in the form of pageants, processions, mystery plays and bonfires. And the inns themselves had an annual routine of banquets, plays and seasonal revels.

Few of these youthful delights entrapped Thomas More for he was incapable of abandoning himself to pleasure. This was not because he lacked a sense of humour; he was an accomplished, if cynical and some-times cruel, wit with a penchant for detached irony and the barbed shaft fired from an emotional distance. Nor was the young More an introvert. As a child and later at Oxford he took part in dramatic performances and wrote scenes of his own – valuable early experiences for a barrister. If More eschewed the rumbustious and carnal delights of his peers it was because his early training and his own inclinations steered him in the direction of spiritual and intellectual delights.

An enquiring mind and an acute sense of filial duty had been the twin goads of More's early development. It must have become evident at a very early age that the boy was very bright (perhaps even a prodigy) and this can only have encouraged the ambition that his father had for Thomas's success. John More decided that his son should follow his own profession. More senior seems to have been a hard parent even by the standards of the day and the adolescent entertained no thoughts of rebellion. On the contrary, he stifled his own interests in obedience to his father's wishes. He was a natural scholar and at Oxford became intoxicated with the mingled wine of ancient wisdom and new methods of study. Left to his own devices he would have chosen an academic career which would almost of necessity have involved him in taking holy orders.

More was a devout son of the Church deeply touched by that yearning for holiness which was a mark of the age. In young Thomas it took the form of asceticism, self-control and burning indignation against Christian leaders who did not follow the same rigid life code. It also produced guilt induced by metaphysical dualism. As an adolescent with very normal urges, he felt his soul torn by the opposed magnetisms of flesh and spirit. In later years he described an erotic adventure he went through at the age of sixteen. He fell in love with an anonymous 'Elizabetha' but, as he proudly recorded, he was able to hold his passion in check so that the relationship remained *sine crimine*. All fleshly desires were sinful and so he kept his body under control. By the age of eighteen he had taken to wearing a hairshirt next to his skin.

He exercised the same self-abnegation in relation to his career. John More had no intention of seeing his son become a scholar-priest and so he removed Thomas from Oxford after two years. The boy submitted and dutifully embarked on his legal studies. But not without inner conflict. The student More had acute tensions to resolve. The divine law enjoined a Christian man to honour his father and mother and this Thomas did by submitting to his parents' wishes. Becoming the successful lawyer John More wanted his son to be would mean the acquisition of wealth and status and immersing himself in the affairs of this world. But the perfect law also required the believer to love God above all others, with heart, mind, soul and strength. Supposing these two could not be reconciled? How could Thomas, who longed to devote himself to contemplation and the study of holy things, justify involvement in the world of human frailty and litigation? Where a man's treasure is there will his heart be also. More's intense internal conflict cannot have been very different from that experienced by another law student only a few years later. Martin Luther resolved his difficulty by disobeying his father and entering the cloister. The curse of it was that, unlike the German reformer, More was ambitious, a trait he, perhaps, inherited from his parents. When writing to humanist friends he sometimes did 'protest too much' his indifference to wealth, fame, position and influence but his actions belied this disavowal. The very profession he was entering was a self-conscious brotherhood of proud practitioners who were striving to increase their importance to Crown and State, and thereby, their wealth and prestige.

The nervous system of the body politic through which the king exercised control over subjects great and small and which also linked them with each other was the common law. Englishmen have always been schizophrenic in their attitude towards the courts and those who practise there. By nature litigious, they are yet suspicious of being taken for a ride by grasping barristers and solicitors, and are easily persuaded that the legal system provides only 'rich men's justice'. The compass needle of public opinion swings between the Gilbertian Lord Chancellor's assertion that 'the law is the true embodiment of everything that's excellent' and Mr Bumble's complaint, 'the law is a ass – a idiot'.

At the end of the fifteenth century fluctuation between these poles was even more erratic. In a largely illiterate age members of the legal profession constituted the only well-educated body of men in the country. They were certainly more learned than the bulk of the parish clergy who were not noted for that devotional study which might minister to their own souls' health and the good of their flocks. Their 'conning skill' earned them a basic respect which had not changed since Chaucer had described his Man of Law.

The Sergeant of the *Canterbury Tales* was cautious and wise and, though he was wealthy and acquisitive and 'seemed busier than he was', the poet did not begrudge him his success:

> In term-time he could cite all the cases and judgements
> That from the time of King William had occurred.
> By reference to them he could make a point
> So convincingly that no-one could fault his interpretation,
> And every statute he could recite by heart.[6]

But this certainly did not mean that ordinary folk were satisfied with the workings of the courts, as a mid-century chronicler complained:

> The law is like unto a Welshman's hose,
> To each man's leg that shapen is and mete;*
> So maintainers† subvert it and transpose,
> Through might it is full low laid under feet.[7]

The courts had inevitably suffered from the dislocation of the times. The king's justice at local level and even in the capital was frequently sabotaged by the bribing of juries, intimidation of witnesses and the 'springing' of jailed suspects, and it was not only the cynical and the socially challenged who regarded the law as something of a joke. At the same time the only advice that could be given to a dedicated grumbler was, 'If you know of a better 'ole, go to it.'

The courts did, after all, offer to poorer people the only possibility of protection from those who, 'through abundance of riches wax more insolent, headstrong and rumbustious'.[8] At the turn of the sixteenth century Englishmen resorted to litigation with remarkable alacrity: every year around 3,000 new suits were introduced into the central courts alone and we would need to multiply that by a three-figure factor to appreciate just how many cases were being heard at any one time throughout the realm. Since the entire population was no more than 2 million, it is clear that going to court was a part of life's routine and not a special, awe-inspiring occasion. The local assizes were the preservative of the social contract, dealing with a range of civil and criminal matters from market pickpocketing to the maintenance of bridges; from assault and affray to commercial fraud.[9] For all its faults, the common law, often referred to as the 'glory of the middle ages', was the guarantor of the people's freedoms.

Important as it was to the king's subjects, the law was vital to Henry. If he was to extend and enforce Crown control throughout his realm the means available to him were the legal system and main force. The latter was always expensive and could carry the risk of failure and for these

---

*'Mete' = 'well-fitting'.
†'Maintainer' = one who supports a suit in which he is not involved.

reasons the first Tudor avoided it whenever possible. By contrast, he relied increasingly on those who, because of their study and application of ancient custom, were, theoretically at least, independent of all vested interests, including the Crown. In the localities he widened the magistrates' boundaries of juridical competence. This did not, of itself, wrest power and influence from the major landholders but, by enhancing the prestige of the gentry, who were dependent for office on the king, it enabled central government to widen political roadways into those fastnesses where people had hitherto 'known no king but a Percy' or a Stanley or a Courtenay, and in that they were assisted in their deliberations by circuit judges, their decisions were enwrapped in the dignified mantle of ancient custom.

At the centre common lawyers had also claimed positions of influence. The royal Council, whose members were always drawn from the ranks of the bishops and the nobility, invariably included a few legal experts. Though socially inferior, they were no mere clerks or recorders of proceedings; their knowledge of precedent earned them the right to be listened to. About the time that our story begins Henry VII drew together a special group of advisers known as 'the King's Council Learned in the Law'. His principal interest in so doing was to seek out new ways in which he could further exploit traditional legal processes but his commitment to statute and case law and his desire to rescue the courts from the clutches of overmighty subjects indicate that Henry VII was at one with his people in questing the holy grail of undisputed authority. More immediately, the King's respect for the legal profession accelerated a process already in motion which ensured that gentlemen of the law would play an enhanced and more creative role in the affairs of the nation. It is, therefore, not surprising that three of our six Thomases were students of common law. We certainly shall not understand where they were 'coming from' without an acknowledgement of their ideological fundament. Common lawyers were members of a highly self-conscious and self-regarding brotherhood.

> Law may . . . be described as that which is the Art of the Good and the Just, in virtue of which they call us priests. For a priest is by etymology said to be one who gives or teaches holy things, and, because human laws are said to be sacred, hence the ministers and teachers of the law are called priests.[10]

Although his more important works did not begin to be printed until the reign of the second Tudor, it is conventional to look to Sir John Fortescue, the Lancastrian Chief Justice of the King's Bench who died in 1476, for an understanding of the law and the way its practitioners perceived it on the cusp of the sixteenth century. Lawyers saw themselves as an élite marked out by learning just as the nobility were distinguished by land ownership and feudal right, and the clergy by the grace of orders. Indeed, as Fortescue claimed, there was a holy parallel between Law and Church. For where did justice flow from if not the throne of God? Custom law was the channel conveying it to the people and lawyer were charged with the solemn task of keeping that channel clear. The implicit overlapping of identity and authority between priest and lawyer was not merely academic. There was increasing rivalry between officials of secular and ecclesiastical courts. Laymen and particularly lawmen were frequently frustrated by the fact that clergy were subject only to their own systems of justice; whatever felonies they were charged with, they could claim the privilege of trial in an episcopal or archiepiscopal court, where penalties were largely thought of in terms of spiritual penance rather than restitution to victims or punishment exacted on body or purse. The exponents of competing systems were constantly sniping at each other. For example, when, shortly before the meeting of More, Erasmus and Prince Henry at Eltham, the Bishop of Winchester's steward refused to allow one John Wykys the benefit of a common law counsel in the episcopal court, the defendant was encouraged by his affronted adviser to take the matter up with the Lord Chancellor, the highest judicial authority in the land. Every such clash was like fresh oxygen to the smouldering but still green kindling of English anticlericalism. Law students, according to Fortescue, even exceeded many members of the spirituality in pursuit of one activity which was supposed to be the clergy's exclusive preserve: 'On the working days most of them apply themselves to the study of the Law and on the holy days to the study of Holy Scripture.'[11] Doubtless Fortescue exaggerated but there is no doubt that the Bible was making a noteworthy impact on that expanding class of educated laymen of whom the lawyers made up a sizeable contingent.

In Fortescue's robust apologetic it was not only ecclesiastical and baronial authorities who were obliged to show due deference to common law. Its very ancientness proclaimed its superiority over all other systems. It had been established, pure and entire, in 'Albion' by a band of heroes returning from the Trojan Wars, led by one Brute and therefore antedated not only Roman law (the basis of most continental legislation) but also those systems which drew their inspiration from the Christian Gospel. Simply put, it was on a par with the Mosaic law as being a near-perfect expression of the mind of God. Even kings were subject to it. Monarchs did not rule by right of conquest nor could they exercise power arbitrarily.

> . . . just as the head of the body physical is unable to change its nerves or to deny its members proper strength and due nourishment of blood, so a king who is the head of the body politic is unable to change the laws of that body, or to deprive that same people of their own substance uninvited or against their wills.[12]

Parliamentary statutes, framed by King, Lords and Commons were the vertebrae which made up the backbone of the common law; precedent and judicial interpretation were the ligaments attaching it to the social skeleton. Any attempt to interference with this physical framework, which alone guaranteed the security of freeborn Englishmen, must of necessity cripple the whole body. Such an exalted concept did not, of course, go unchallenged in practice. Much of the history of the next two centuries could be told in terms of a power struggle between the common law and its rivals – royal prerogative, baronial authority and canon law. But throughout the revolutionary years we shall chronicle, when old truths were being questioned and ancient institutions undermined, the common law renewed its strength and it did so largely because its commitment to equity and custom struck chords which resonated deep within the national psyche.

Nothing illustrates this more clearly than the role the professional training institutions had already come to occupy within the educational system by the end of the fifteenth century. The Inns of Chancery and the Inns of Court, where future barristers and judges learned their craft, were situated in the London suburbs between the City and Westminster and students could enjoy the numerous diversions offered by the one and the practical experience provided by the other. Boys (they usually began in their mid-teens) destined for a legal profession spent a couple of years absorbing the basics of the craft at one of the ten Inns of Chancery before going on to an associated senior inn to complete their studies. As well as learning statutes and past rulings by heart, they attended cases being tried in the various courts operating in Westminster Hall. But the education offered at the inns extended far beyond specialist training. They were parallel to the colleges of Oxford and Cambridge and had their own curricula: in addition to legal studies instruction was given in history, theology, music and courtly accomplishments. Increasingly the sons of noblemen, gentlemen and wealthy merchants were sent to the inns to complete their education. The inns became, in effect, expensive – very expensive – finishing schools where the rich, the fashionable and the upwardly mobile sent their boys to obtain a grounding in the arts of civilised behaviour. Young men who emerged from this system were equipped to take up posts in the royal household, to become cultured and efficient managers of inherited estates, to represent their class and local interests in parliament or to serve temporal or spiritual lords in administrative capacities. The little community living and learning in the hostels clustered between Holborn and Fleet Street were, thus, a microcosm of society's 'better sort'; an exclusive gathering together of young men with connections and pretensions; a nursery of the nation's leaders. A young man reared in this social hothouse hoped to develop into a luxuriantly successful man of affairs making his mark in commerce, politics or land, as well as in the law.

It was in order not to be seduced by dreams of wealth and power that the dichotomous Thomas More sought the inspiration of the religious life to which he knew he could not abandon himself. For a period of four years while he was a member of the inns he lodged in the outer part of the northern suburbs, a mere stone's throw from the lawyers' quarter. Here was to be found a literal 'holy huddle' of buildings: the House of the Salutation of the Mother of God at Smithfield, the Priory of the Knights of St John of Jerusalem and the Priory of St John at Clerkenwell. It was to the first of these monastic establishments, a house of Carthusian monks, commonly called the Charterhouse, that More was especially attracted. Here he found respite from the sordid disputes of the courts and the raucous carousings of his less mature colleagues. A great historian of English monasticism thus describes the London Charterhouse:

> Lying as it did at the edge of the city, with its orchards and gardens running up among the town houses of the great, the Charterhouse could scarcely fail to be a centre of religious influence. The solemn devotion of the liturgy, the contrast between the silence and austerity there and the noisy, restless, ambitious and sordid whirl of the city streets, the presence within its walls of a number of men of gentle birth and high abilities, attracted to its gatehouse many of the *âmes d'élite* of the time, and facilities seem to have been given for those in need of spiritual direction to visit and confess themselves to the priests, and even to make a prolonged stay in the guest quarters.[13]

The effect of this ascetic community on More was profound. The Carthusians attached special importance to silence, manual labour and the strict suppression of sexual desire. They were the last religious to maintain the severer forms of mortification such as self-flagellation. More loved dearly the holy brothers and sisters who remained true to the ideal life which he knew he could never attain, just as he was scathing of those who brought the monastic institution into disrepute by succumbing to worldly temptations. His later vitriolic attacks on Luther often centred on the German's marriage to a former nun (the heretic was 'an open incestuous lecher, a plain limb of the devil, and a manifest messenger of hell') and they tell us more about the author's repressed sexuality than they do about the object of his hatred.

This was the later More – a bigot, a fanatic, a man whose piety led him into such impious actions as vulgar abuse, lying and persecution. Hagiographers have always found it difficult to reconcile this character with the one described by Erasmus as a man *omnium horarum* (conventionally translated as a man 'for all seasons' but more accurately implying 'a good companion at any time of day), a good-natured, intelligent fellow, moving easily among monks, scholars, lawyers, and courtiers and well known among the City's fashionable élite. It used to be argued that the transformation took place in later life: the eager reformer became the violent reactionary who repented of his earlier enthusiasm for radical thinking when he saw the excesses to which that thinking had led. This is simplistic. More never really changed, except to become further convinced of his core beliefs. As a young man he shared the idealism of the humanists who believed that the world (and, specifically, the Church) could be altered for the better; that men could be educated out of foolish superstitions and brought to a clearer understanding of the Bible whose simple truth had been obscured by centuries of academic over-painting. However, he was always a 'yes, but' man in his response to spiritual and intellectual radicalism. His love affair with the institutional Church touched the deepest levels of his being. He was passionate about its age-hallowed doctrines, its routines of ritual, its orderliness, its hierarchy which, like Jacob's ladder, linked earth and heaven, the security which only the sacraments could bring to the aspiring soul desperately trying to free itself from the strangling, anaconda coils of the world, the flesh and the devil. We need to understand clearly this inner conflict before we consider the friendship between the man of the world who had a hankering for the religious life and the monk who escaped the cloister and resisted all attempts to draw him back within its confining walls.

One friend and close contemporary of Thomas More was William Blount, Baron Mountjoy who, unusually among the nobility of this time, also had a passion for scholarship. William was still a minor when his father died and so he had more freedom to pursue his own interests than might have been the case had he been subjected to the conventional training of a soldier-courtier. His search for the best teachers of the day took him to Paris where he became a pupil of Desiderius Erasmus. The man from Rotterdam was at this time a struggling peripatetic in his early thirties who was just beginning to make his name among the younger intelligentsia as a devastatingly witty critic of the religious establishment. Fresh-minded students like Blount applauded wildly when Erasmus castigated the learned professors of the old school whose subtle arguments were so much mud in the pool of Gospel Christianity: 'They exhaust the mind by a certain jejune and barren subtlety, without fertilizing or inspiring it . . . they disfigure theology.' He was merciless in his denunciation of Christian conduct as exemplified by the 'professionals'. Like More he longed for the Church to display to the world a sincere, uncorrupted faith. Unlike More, he had, as an Augustinian monk, seen that Church's organisation from within and the experience had made him profoundly cynical:

[Priests] insist that they've properly performed their duty if they reel off perfunctorily their feeble prayers which I'd be greatly surprised if any god could hear or understand . . . the priests who call themselves 'secular' push the burden [of piety] on to the 'regulars', and they pass it on to the monks; the less strict monks shift it on to the stricter orders, and the whole lot of them leave it to the mendicants; and from there it goes to the Carthusians, amongst whom alone piety lies hidden and buried, hidden in fact so well that you can scarcely ever get a glimpse of it . . .[14]

Young Lord Mountjoy was excited by the teacher who made such outrageously daring pronouncements and urged him to come to England. Erasmus was no less delighted with his young pupil, for Blount was impressionable, rich and influential, as he explained to a friend, 'He is a young man of great authority with his own folk.' Erasmus's assessment of his patron's importance was only a slight exaggeration. Few families rode higher in the esteem of Henry VII than the Blounts. William's uncle, Sir James Blount, was a trusted servant of Richard III who had deserted to Henry Tudor during the latter's exile, crossed the Channel with him and fought beside him at Bosworth Field. William, who succeeded to the family title and lands in 1485, was sometime attached to the household of Prince Henry (in the years to come Blount was trusted by the King with various very sensitive posts) and the boy, who had a genuine love of learning, developed a great affection for the young man who could bring exciting stories and sparkling apophthegms out of his stored knowledge of the classics. Thus it was that tutor and tutee were both satisfied that they had made a great 'catch' when they travelled to London in May 1499.

Naturally, Mountjoy wanted to show off the celebrity to his scholarly friends and Thomas More was among those who travelled downriver to Blount's mansion at Greenwich to be introduced. They hit it off immediately and Erasmus was soon affirming to a correspondent in his rather flowery language that nature had never fashioned anything 'gentler, sweeter and happier than the character of Thomas More'. Much of the later adulation of More is based on the picture painted in Erasmus's letters. That means we must be cautious about taking it at face value. The Dutch reformer remains one of the world's most brilliant correspondents. Even in translation, his prose is witty, incisive, elegant and perceptive. His collected epistles are a glass through which we observe in great detail the international world of Renaissance humanism. But it is a glass which has its striations and impurities. One of them – perhaps the most distorting – is flattery. Flowery praise of friends, colleagues, patrons and associates was a sixteenth-century epistolary convention but Erasmus raised it to the level of an art form. When he was writing to or about More he was lavish in his praise and his motives were those of friendship, ambition and mutual support. It was axiomatic that writers 'puffed' each other to patrons and prospective patrons and Erasmus never failed to commend the Englishman to those who might advance his career. That does not mean that he was insincere; he was genuinely impressed (though not over-impressed) by More's classical scholarship and his commitment to humanist principles. At the same time Erasmus recognised in the London lawyer someone with whom he might do well to maintain good relations. More had friends in high places and was clearly destined, himself, for greater things. As a wandering scholar always pleading poverty, Erasmus could not afford to ignore any channel through which he might receive financial help and, over the years, he worked assiduously to maintain good relations with several influential Englishmen, including Thomas More. It was he, rather than More, who strove hardest to keep the friendship alive and, though it would be foolish to deny the genuine bond between the two men, it would be equally mistaken to regard them as soulmates.

It was during a convivial scholarly gathering at Lord Mountjoy's that the suggestion was made of a gentle walk to Eltham Palace to present Erasmus to the King's younger children. We only have the great scholar's reminiscence to identify this as an impromptu visit and the actual details suggest that Erasmus's memory may have been faulty or that he preferred to put his own gloss on his encounter with the Prince. The fact is that the meeting proved an embarrassment to him. When young Henry, as host, received his guests, More, in obedience to polite convention, presented a little literary offering, which must indicate that he had spent some hours preparing for the trip to Eltham. Erasmus was mortified because he had no gift to offer. Either he had not been warned or he was not sufficiently versed in the demands of court etiquette. His discomfort was compounded during dinner, which the guests took seated in the great hall where Henry and his sisters were waited upon, although at a lower table. The Prince sent a message that he would be graciously pleased to receive a few lines from the celebrated scholar's pen and, on his return to Lord Mountjoy's, Erasmus had to burn the midnight oil concocting some suitably adulatory verses. Nevertheless, he was considerably impressed by England and particularly the intellectual freedom and the wealth of radical academic activity he discovered on his first visit. He was at pains to maintain his contacts with friends and potential patrons and when, in 1509, the self-assured little Prince of Eltham became king, Erasmus lost no time in returning to place his talents at the disposal of a young Renaissance monarch of whom all his English friends had high hopes.

CHAPTER 2

Walking the Tightrope

If we are to understand the kind of England ruled over by the first two Tudors and the problems confronting the new dynasty a brief digression at this point is inevitable. A late fifteenth-century chronicler lamented:

> . . . in divers parts of this realm, great abominable murders, robberies, extortions, oppressions and other manifold maintenances, mis-governances, forcible entries . . . affrays, assaults be committed and done by such persons as either be of great might, or else favoured under persons of great power, in such wise as their outrageous demerits as yet remain unpunished, insomuch that of late divers persons have been slain, some in Southwark, and here nigh about the City, and some here at Westminster Gate, no consideration [being] taken . . . that your high presence is had here at your palace of Westminster, nor that your high court of Parliament is here sitting . . .[15]

Thomas More emerged from the womb in 1478 into a nation at war within itself. None of those among whom he grew up could remember a time when it had been otherwise. Major battles between Yorkist and Lancastrian factions had only occurred sporadically since 1455 but the cauldron of instability from which arose the noxious fumes of rebellion, rivalry and civil unrest had been bubbling ever since the accession to the throne of a weak-minded minor in 1422 had enabled territorial magnates to exercise local control through corrupt administration, perversion of justice and thuggery. The House of Commons' complaint of 1472, quoted above, was far from being a unique document. Parliaments, individuals and corporations frequently petitioned the king for redress of grievances suffered at the hands of over-mighty subjects. At about the time of More's birth the prayer of a Norfolk gentlewoman was, 'God in his holy mercy give grace that there may set a good rule and a wise [one] in the country in haste',[16] and most people throughout the country would have given a loud 'Amen' to her plea.

What those who thought about such things desired was strong government, legitimate government and untroubled succession. Neither

27

Yorkists nor Lancastrians had been able to deliver all three. After the disastrous reign of Henry VI, Edward IV gave England a dozen years of relative peace but he was succeeded by a minor who disappeared, along with his brother, in the Tower. The usurping Richard III suffered his greatest disaster when his only son died at the age of eight. When Henry Tudor took the crown by right of conquest in the year that Thomas More celebrated his seventh birthday there was no guarantee that his rule would be any more effective nor his dynasty any more secure than those of his predecessors. Henry and his queen were blessed with eight children but only two of their sons survived infancy and Arthur, the heir, was of a weak (probably consumptive) constitution. Other claimants watched from the wings and were sometimes propelled on to the stage by their powerful backers. In this year of 1499, in which our story begins, the troublesome pretender Perkin Warbeck was hanged at Tyburn.

Throughout the realm little kings who had grown accustomed to virtual autonomy in their own regions and to exercising real power in national politics had a vested interest in preventing central authority from becoming too strong. When William Caxton wrote a preface to his printing of Malory's *Morte D'arthur* in the year of Bosworth he had clearly in mind the clashing interests and ambitions of contemporary noblemen. He urged them

> to see and learn the noble acts of chivalry, the gentle and virtuous deeds that some knights used in those days, by which they came to honour, and how those who were vicious were punished and after put to shame and rebuke, humbly beseeching all noble lords and ladies, with all other estates of whatsoever estate or degree they be that shall see and read in this said book . . . that they take the good and honest acts in their remembrance and follow the same . . . Do after the good and leave the evil and it shall bring you to good fame and renown.[17]

The story itself was an allegory for the times, sadly chronicling, as it did, the break-up of the Round Table fellowship and the end of the Arthurian dynasty as a result of feuding among the knights.

Henry VII's first responsibility was to stay alive long enough to pass the crown to a legitimate heir of mature years. His second responsibility was to ensure that no forces existed within the country powerful enough to challenge the succession. That involved weeding out potential rivals and winning the loyalty of those who might otherwise be disaffected. His third responsibility was to establish an efficient, centralised administration based on sound finance. He met all these obligations and established a dynasty which occupied the throne for a hundred and seventeen years and seven months.

Yet the Tudor hold on power was always precarious. The personalities and remarkable achievements of Henry's son and younger granddaughter tower over the England of the sixteenth century – which also happened to be the most formative century of the millennium – but the very successes of Henry VIII and Elizabeth I tend to dazzle our eyes and prevent us from seeing just what an unhealthy horticultural specimen the Tudor family tree was. It had to survive the accessions of a sickly minor, and a barren woman and it eventually withered when the last sovereign refused to become a cutting for grafting on to a foreign stock. Only by keeping in mind the insecurity of the dynasty and the political disasters which could result from the weaknesses of the hereditary principle can we fully understand Henry VIII's matrimonial misadventures, his sporadic paranoia and the attraction for malcontents of a rival ancient line which would return the nation to the 'old' ways.

The Yorkist tree was as prolific of male fruit as the Lancastrian was bereft. In 1485 there were no less than seven nephews of Edward IV who, if they chose and if they were able to attract support, could have challenged for the crown. One died in a failed insurrection in 1487. The King already had another, Edward, Earl of Warwick, safely in the Tower of London and, for good measure, managed to get him indicted for plotting with Warbeck and beheaded in 1499. Within a couple of years another, William, was incarcerated in the Tower and two of his brothers had fled abroad to avoid the same fate.

No one understood better than Henry the implications of potential rivals living under the protection of foreign princes. Between the ages of fourteen and twenty-eight he had been a guest of Duke Francis of Brittany, who had resisted the blandishments and outwitted the whiles of Edward IV aimed at getting the outlaw into his clutches. Now it was Henry's turn to employ ambassadors and secret agents to lay hands on the Yorkist renegades. Internal security was an important aspect of the King's foreign policy. Being no more than a bit player in the drama of Christendom politics, it took him years of hard negotiation to bring to fruition marriage treaties with Spain and Scotland, and to do so without alienating France, or involving England in costly military adventures overseas. However, potential rivals still lurked in foreign courts and continued to maintain contact with barons who might raise armies from among their own retainers if ever the time seemed propitious for revolt.

Breaking the power of the magnates was, therefore, as essential a plank of domestic policy as restricting the runagates' freedom of movement was of foreign policy. Henry employed a two-pronged attack to inhibit the ability of the nobles to wage war: he extracted large sums of money from them and he obliged them to cut down the numbers of their armed retainers. He had to begin cautiously but the more successful his policies became the tighter he turned the screw: 'the king's grace . . . was much set to have many persons in his danger [i.e. under his control] at his pleasure, spiritual men as well as temporal men, wherefore divers and many persons were bound to his grace or to others to his use in great sums of money, some by recognizances and some by obligations.'[18] Recognisances and obligations were bonds taken by the King to ensure certain conditions of behaviour which might vary from being constantly in attendance at court (and therefore under royal scrutiny) to not alienating land without Henry's permission or even remaining within a geographically prescribed area. Such exactions came as a profound shock to the leading families of the realm, three-quarters of whom were hammered by the King's financial officers. But these imposts were not the only financial encroachments from which they suffered. Henry's agents were set to collect all feudal dues owing to the Crown with a ruthless efficiency which had been totally lacking throughout the preceding decade of administrative chaos. It is, therefore, no wonder that Henry VII gained a reputation as the 'miser king'. Men made wry jokes about him. They said, for example, that he kept a 'little black book' in which he noted every minor misdemeanour which he could turn to advantage. One day his pet monkey got hold of the offending volume and tore it to shreds, to the King's tearful rage and the secret jubilation of the court.

The second Thomas whom we must now meet had followed a more hazardous route to royal favour. In the year that More and Erasmus visited Eltham, Thomas Howard's father, the Earl of Surrey, was admitted to the inner circle of Henry VII's Council. His had been a long campaign for rehabilitation; fourteen years before, at the start of the reign, he had been in the Tower awaiting execution for treason.

The Howards were *arrivistes* but, like most social climbers, they claimed pedigree. Thomas's grandfather, John Howard (*c.* 1430–85), was a Norfolk gentleman who was second cousin on his mother's side to the last of the great Mowbray Dukes of Norfolk and he could, through a tortuous genealogical route meander his lineage back to Edward I. Through the disturbed mid-century decades he staked his family's fortunes on the Yorkists and the gamble paid off: he received lands and honours at the hands of Edward IV, made an advantageous marriage, was raised to the peerage, admitted to the Council and, by 1483, was the most influential landholder in East Anglia. Then, while reaching for the ripest fruit at the top of the tree, he fell – fatally.

It was inevitable that John should throw in his lot with Richard, Duke of Gloucester, in his schemes to usurp the crown from Edward's young sons, the 'Princes in the Tower'. Howard and Gloucester were old comrades in arms and were further bound together by mutual self-interest. Richard wanted the throne; Howard coveted the Mowbray lands and titles. The key to their relationship and to Howard's role in Richard III's seizure of power was the Tower of London. Control of the fortress was vital: here the Princes' uncle gathered his supporters, controlled the royal Armoury and

Treasury and disposed of those who threatened his supremacy. For several crucial weeks in the summer of 1483 the man placed in control of the Tower was John Howard.

This is not the place to rehearse again the gruesome events surrounding the accession of the last Plantaganet king but those that relate to Thomas Howard's ancestry are instructive about his family's dynastic instincts and their relationship to the Crown. Thomas's grandfather had been conspicuously loyal to Edward IV and in the faction fighting following the King's death in April it may well have seemed to him the most natural course of action to back Gloucester's claim to be Protector of the realm: someone had to act quickly and firmly if widespread disorder and the threat of civil strife were to be avoided. But he was certainly not motivated by disinterested loyalty. On the day that Richard's regency was declared (13 May) John Howard was appointed privy councillor and steward of the Duchy of Lancaster. It seems likely that he was also put in charge of the Tower of London at the same time. The previous Constable, the Marquess of Dorset, had fled to sanctuary at Westminster and Richard needed to install without delay someone he could trust implicitly. As soon as the Tower was secure the boy-king, Edward V, was lodged there and within a month he was joined there by his brother.

This is the point at which sinister overtones may first be detected in the story. Lord Howard took a leading role in persuading the Queen to deliver her ten-year-old son out of sanctuary into the care of his uncle. He had a very personal interest in little Richard. After the death of John Lord Mowbray in 1475 his lands and titles had been bestowed by Edward IV on his younger son, who became Duke of York and Norfolk. Thus, in 1483, only this boy stood between Howard and the inheritance he believed to be rightfully his. In the same way the lives of Richard and his brother constituted the only barrier between Gloucester and the crown. Did the two men draw the obvious conclusion? According to early chroniclers the Howards' direct involvement in the maleficent scheming of the Protector was now stepped up several degrees. Gloucester's first priority was to purge the Council of dissidents opposed to his seizure of power of whom the most influential was William Hastings, the Lord Chamberlain. A meeting was fixed for 13 June and Sir Thomas Howard, John's only son, was despatched to summon Hastings from his town house. According to the early recorder who improved on the bare narrative:

> This Sir Thomas, while the lord Hastings stayed awhile communing with a priest whom he met in Tower Street, broke the lord's tale, saying to him merely, 'What my Lord, I pray you come on. Wherefore talk you so long with that priest? You have no need of a priest yet,' and laughed upon him, as though he would say, 'You shall have need of one soon.' But little whist the other what he meant . . .[19]

31

No sooner had the councillors sat at their table than Richard denounced Hastings as a traitor, had him bundled out to Tower Green and there despatched immediately, a piece of builders' timber serving as a makeshift block (the first of seven private state executions to take place within the walls of the Tower). This had the effect of overawing the Council which now acquiesced in those moves necessary to achieve Richard's plan to grasp the crown. Within days the young princes were declared illegitimate and Edward V's signature on a document dated 17 June is the last piece of historical evidence that he was still alive. An Italian visitor to England noted, 'After Hastings was removed, all the attendants who had waited upon the king were debarred access to him. He and his brother were withdrawn into the inner apartments of the Tower proper, and, day by day began to be seen more rarely behind the bars and windows till at length they ceased to appear altogether.'[20]

The mysterious fate of Edward IV's sons gave rise over the centuries to a piranha tankful of conspiracy theories. The extent of Howard involvement in their assassination depends on the date of that event and this is simply unknown. Thomas More's notoriously flawed (if we judge it as an exercise in objective historiography) *History of King Richard III* told the story of the murder of the princes in detail. It was self-evidently an attempt to blacken the name of Richard III but may it also have aimed to exculpate the Howards who were then (*c.* 1515) riding high in royal favour? More set the direful deed within the constableship of Sir Thomas Brackenbury, who was appointed to command the Tower on 17 July 1483 (Brackenbury had been killed at Bosworth and so could not contest the allegation) and the names of John Howard and his son do not feature in his narrative. If More was wrong and the boys were already dead by mid-July then it would be impossible for John Howard not to have been involved. There is certainly circumstantial evidence that could be made to point towards his collusion in royal infanticide. His household accounts show him to have bought two bags of lime in June – possibly an innocent purchase but one which could be invested with sinister significance by a clever prosecution lawyer.

What is more telling is the remarkable increase in trust which Richard suddenly reposed in Howard. Like every insecure tyrant, Gloucester was always looking about him for signs of treachery and eager to encourage generously those he believed he could rely on. When, on 26 June, he publicly proclaimed himself king by assuming the chair of state in the court of King's Bench at Westminster Hall he was supported on his left hand by the Duke of Suffolk, his brother-in-law, but in the place of honour on his right stood Baron Howard. The new monarch immediately began handing out rewards to his supporters. John Howard, obviously by pre-arrangement, was created Duke of Norfolk, with a large tranche of Mowbray lands to support the dignity. His son, Thomas, became Earl of Surrey. There was no revocation of the Act of Parliament of 16 January

1478 by which the Mowbray estates had been allocated to Prince Richard. Should we infer from this that the title to the dukedom and its lands had recently become vacant? And is it purely coincidence that More's account of Richard III's crimes written a generation later and totally ignoring the Howards' participation in them should have been undertaken at precisely the time that the dukedom was again restored to John's son?

No speculation is necessary to record the mutual dependence of Richard III and the Duke of Norfolk. The King showered rewards on his henchman: within days of receiving the coronet, the golden rod and the cap of maintenance, Howard was appointed Earl Marshal, Admiral of England, Ireland and Aquitaine and Steward of the Household and he received considerable grants of land. At the coronation on 6 July he carried the crown and featured prominently in all the ceremonial of the great event, so much so that he provoked the jealousy of the Duke of Buckingham, which may have contributed to the latter's fatal rebellion in the autumn. For his part, Norfolk remained totally loyal to his royal benefactor. In August 1485, when news reached him that Henry Tudor had landed in England, Howard summoned his East Anglian retainers to come to his standard at Bury St Edmunds. Friends warned him that the pragmatic course was to stay out of the conflict:

> Jack of Norfolk, be not too bold,
> For Dickon, thy master, is bought and sold.

But Howard refused to countenance disloyalty and marched his host across country to Leicester to join the royal army. At Bosworth he led the vanguard and was cut down fighting valiantly in the thick of the mêlée. Thomas Howard, Earl of Surrey, was carried wounded from the field and, a few days later, found himself back in the Tower, not as a privileged courtier, serving in the palace buildings, but lodged as a prisoner with as little prospect of survival as the royal Princes had enjoyed.

But Henry VII was too shrewd to destroy the Howard clan. None of Richard's captains suffered – in their persons. The new King had no desire to scare his more powerful subjects into concerted opposition nor to cast away seasoned soldiers who had demonstrated their loyalty to the previous regime. His technique was to maintain a close watch on members of the nobility and to put them under financial pressure. Thomas Howard was attainted for treason which meant that his life and goods were forfeit to the Crown. He was stripped of his titles and most of his estates and kept under confinement at the King's pleasure.

Henry was pleased to restore Howard's liberty after three and a half years. Early in 1489 the forty-five-year-old warrior's attainder was reversed, his earldom and some of his patrimonial lands were restored and he was given an opportunity to redeem himself. Shortly afterwards, Henry

Percy, Earl of Northumberland, upon whom the King relied to keep order in the North, was killed in a minor insurrection and Henry despatched Surrey to Yorkshire in charge of the vanguard of a retributionary force. Howard grasped his chance: he surprised the rebels by appearing suddenly in their midst and made short work of suppressing what was little more than a small-scale local uprising. He dealt summarily and very demonstratively with their ringleaders. John à Chamber, the principal offender, was strung up at York on 'a gibbet set on a square pair of gallows' with his accomplices suspended from 'the lower story round about him'. It was an impressive spectacle to present to the King who arrived a couple of days later. Henry responded by appointing Surrey to Northumberland's office of Deputy Warden of the North Marches (Percy's heir being still a minor).

Surrey discharged his duties with vigour, intelligence and careful reference to the wishes of his royal master. He is always quoted as the textbook example of medieval magnate turned royal official but it would be a mistake to see this metamorphosis as something pre-planned in the devious mind of Henry Tudor. In fact, Northumberland's death was very fortuitous for both the King and Surrey. Henry was able to separate two baronial families from their traditional followers. Young Henry Algernon Percy was brought south to be reared at the royal court and his sisters married off to men the King could trust. Thomas Howard was well distanced from his East Anglian tenants and retainers, and his elder sons, Thomas and Edward, were also attached to the Tudor household to learn loyalty to the new regime and to act as hostages for their father's good behaviour. For Surrey his appointment was a swaying rope ladder of opportunity – not without its dangers but the only means of hauling himself and his family back to the eminence from which they had fallen. He was, in effect, a little king throughout the habitually troublesome border region. Technically the deputy of Prince Arthur, Henry's elder son, Surrey presided over a 'royal' court and had a council to help him administer the region. Judge, general, bureaucrat and diplomat, he was responsible for maintaining law and order, suppressing dissent, collecting revenues and keeping the uneasy peace with James IV across the border. He acquitted himself well and earned his sovereign's gratitude. Part of the price he paid was not seeing his children grow up.

Lord Thomas Howard was twelve years old at the time of the battle of Bosworth Field, old enough to feel the sudden disgrace into which his family had been plunged and certainly old enough to miss the company of his father and the excitement of life at the royal court. Lady Howard took her six surviving children to the rural obscurity of her manor at Ashwelthorpe, south-west of Norwich. She must have felt keenly her humiliation and anxiety and these will have been conveyed to her eldest son, now *de facto* head of the family. Then came the summons to him and his younger brother Edward to attend the King.

The court where Thomas passed the rest of his teenage years was not the dreary ménage of a niggardly, miserly monarch. Contrary to the popular image of him which has survived, Henry VII did know how to enjoy himself and was prepared to spend money in so doing. It was important for him to keep a glittering court, especially as he was deliberately attempting to raise his profile among European monarchs. He created a bright aura around himself, determined to demonstrate to observers at home and abroad that he was much more than 'top baron' among a squabbling crew of uncultured feuding feudalists. He was well aware of the changing fashions of royal lifestyle throughout Renaissance Europe. Thus he was the last reigning sovereign to use the Tower of London as a principal residence. Changing canons of taste and comfort, as well as newly emerging political realities rendered the gaunt, draughty, cavernous chambers of the fortress's palace complex increasingly obsolete. The international *haut monde* were providing themselves with residences having smaller, warmer private rooms and public ones made grand by wide windows, carved wainscots and moulded ceilings. Downriver from the capital Henry extended an old house, Placentia, into the sumptuous palace of Greenwich. Almost equidistant from Westminster by water to the west he rebuilt the royal residence of Sheen (destroyed by fire in 1497) and renamed it Richmond and he modernised Baynard's Castle, built originally to safeguard the western approach to the City. Piety and the desire to make artistic statements combined in several religious foundations and ecclesiastical buildings, of which the Henry VII Chapel at Westminster Abbey survives (as he intended) as a permanent memorial. The King employed Italian and Netherlandish artists and craftsmen to help create the image he desired and commissioned more royal portraits than any of his predecessors. We should be cautious about making too much of this; portraiture was the cinderella of the arts, valued by patrons for pragmatic rather than aesthetic reasons. When Henry VII was contemplating marriage to the widowed Queen of Naples his emissaries were instructed to bring back as accurate an impression as possible of the lady's charms. Not only were they to get close enough to judge the 'sweetness' of her breath, they were also to secure the services of a painter to

draw a picture of the visage and semblance of the said young queen as like unto her as it can or may be conveniently done. Which picture and image they shall substantially note and mark in every point and circumstance so that it agree in similitude and likeness as near as it may [be] possible to the very visage, countenance and semblance of the said queen. And in case they may perceive that the painter at the first or second making thereof hath not made the same perfect to her similitude and likeness or that he hath omitted any feature or circumstance either in colours or other proportions of the said visage, then they shall cause the same painter or some other the most coning painter that they can get so often times to renew and reform the same picture till it be made perfect and agreeable in every behalf with the very image and visage of the said queen.[21]

However, when it came to projecting his own 'very image' he was happy to encourage the art of the flatterer, as, for example, in the representation of himself and his family with St George and the Dragon still to be seen at Windsor.

Henry was no Maecenas but he was embarrassingly aware that his island realm was widely considered as being beyond the cultural pale. Benvenuto Cellini referred dismissively to 'those beasts of Englishmen', but Erasmus, having arrived with no very great expectations, was so surprised and impressed with the state of scholarship he discovered that he told a friend that England was but little inferior to Italy in that regard. The first Tudor was intent on enhancing the prestige of himself and his kingdom. His backing of the Genoese mariner John Cabot in his quest for a North Atlantic route to Asia (when our story opens England was waiting with waning hope for news of the expedition which had set out the previous year) was purposefully imitative of Ferdinand and Isabella's support for Columbus. He was aware of the possibilities of the printing revolution. He continued the patronage extended by Edward IV and Richard III to William Caxton whose *Fayts of Armes and Chivalry* (translated from the French) was, by royal permission, dedicated to Prince Arthur and came off the Westminster press in 1489, to be followed two years later by *Fifteen Oes and other Prayers*, commissioned by Queen Elizabeth.

But Henry's court was not that of a scholar – rather that of a businessman with a keen eye for PR. In the day-to-day conduct of palace life and in the celebration of special events the King took his own pleasure and also set about impressing all who came within the royal ambit. He enjoyed hunting, hawking, archery, tennis and playing cards and he spent large sums on jewellery. However, the banquets, revels, pageants and tournays that punctuated the life of the household were carefully considered displays more for the benefit of others than for his own pleasure. During Henry's reign tournaments became more elaborate, following the European pattern, and there was a growing interest in the romance of chivalry. This was part of the prevailing culture in princely courts but it also connected the new dynasty with ancient glory and tradition. When Queen Elizabeth was expecting her first child Henry conveyed her to Winchester, the old capital steeped in myth and history, and when the baby, to his great delight, turned out to be a boy he was christened Arthur. This event and every other which secured the succession and enhanced the permanence of the Tudor line were marked with spectacular public celebrations which increased in splendour and ingenuity as the years passed. The birth of a second son (Henry) in 1491, the installation of Arthur as Prince of Wales in the same year, and the creation of Henry as Duke of York in 1494 were all marked with feasts, pageants and feats of arms.

This was the routine into which the Howard boys fitted. They began as pages, waiting at table upon the great personages of the household, running errands and carrying out a variety of chores. They learned court etiquette the hard way, being beaten when they failed to employ the proper modes of address or display the appropriate body language to their betters. They received the education appropriate to the sons of a loyal nobleman – Latin, rhetoric, logic, music, arithmetic and the martial arts of swordplay and mounted combat which set their class apart from lesser men.

The most important event in the life of the younger Thomas Howard was his marriage. During the reign of Richard III when the Howards were, briefly, the second most important family in the land, Thomas had been betrothed to Edward IV's third daughter, Anne. Any thought of uniting the Howards and Plantagenets was, of course, put on hold during the years when Surrey was proving his loyalty to the new regime. So, it is a measure of his success in commending himself to Henry Tudor that the marriage was allowed to proceed in 1495. Thomas thus became related to the King, for Anne was the Queen's sister. This union brought the Howards little in terms of property – the bride had no inheritance of her own – but the prestige more than made up for the lack of acreage and the negotiators of the marriage settlement ensured that the couple were able to set up home in a style suitable to their station. Whether there was any more than a commercial-political arrangement involved here we cannot know. Thomas and Anne were similar in age (Thomas had celebrated his majority in 1494) and had been much in each other's company for several years, for Anne was one of the Queen's attendants. However deep their affection for each other was, Thomas and Anne now left the court and divided their time between homes in Suffolk and at Lambeth.

Henry Tudor looked to the young bloods of noble houses to fulfil their traditional military role and Thomas Howard's chance to show his worth came in 1497. If scanty extant records can be relied on, Surrey's eldest son gave little evidence of skill or ability in the tiltyard. His name does not figure among the lists of combatants in any of the celebratory jousts of the period. However, he was expected to turn out, suitably accoutred and accompanied by his own paid troops, in defence of the realm. In the spring of 1497 the cross-border sparring between Surrey and James IV's military leaders reached a stage at which Henry VII decided to provide the Earl with some extra muscle. He despatched a force under the leadership of the highly experienced general and diplomat Baron Daubeney, to link up with Surrey's men for a punitive expedition into Scotland. Thomas and Edward

Howard were among the commanders who set off up the Great North Road. They did not get very far. The independent-minded men of the far West chose this moment to launch one of their periodic revolts and Daubeney had to be diverted from his original purpose to deal with it.

The first stirrings of the Cornish Rebellion were felt in the Lizard as a protest against taxation to pay for the remote Scottish campaign. Inspired by local orators, a group of ordinary countrymen set off for the capital to present their grievances but as they marched, with the support and assistance of towns and villages through which they passed, their numbers were swelled by a medley of men drawn from all ranks of society. Each had his own reasons for discontent. Some were Yorkists who had never been reconciled to the new regime. Some were supporters of the pretender to the throne, Perkin Warbeck. As they marched across the southern counties the demonstrators became an army, perhaps 15,000 strong. Amazingly, they were in Kent before King Henry became really alarmed and despatched messengers scudding northwards to recall his prime troops. He sent his family to the safety of the Tower and joined with Daubeney to confront the rebels at Blackheath, scarcely a mile from the royal palace of Greenwich. The 'Battle of Blackheath' took place on the morning of 17 June. Despite the courage and commitment of the rebels and the genuine alarm their march had created in the government, the clash of arms was no contest: 'being ill-armed, and ill-led, and without horse or artillery, [the insurgents] were with no great difficulty cut to pieces and put to flight'.[22] Some 200 rebels were killed in this inglorious fracas at the cost of no more than a score of the King's men. Immediately afterwards Henry dubbed as knights upwards of thirty men who had figured prominently in the action. The Howards were not among them.

Daubeney now had to be sent to Cornwall to deal with Perkin Warbeck's supporters but the young Howards resumed their northward march to join their father. James IV, taking advantage of Henry's distraction, had crossed the border to lay siege to the Bishop of Durham's (Richard Fox) castle at Norham, which guarded the vale of the Lower Tweed. As soon as he received the necessary reinforcements, Surrey, accompanied by Bishop Fox, hurried to relieve the fortress and chase the Scots back into their own country. There, he retaliated by attacking and taking Ayton Castle, under the nose of King James, who watched from high ground nearby. The chivalric Stuart offered to settle the dispute in hand-to-hand combat with Lord Howard to which Surrey responded that he would happily fight the King at a later date but that now he was on his master's business and not to be deflected. It was left to Fox to negotiate a truce and, after a few days during which his army had to endure being lashed in their tents by torrential rain, Surrey withdrew to the greater comfort of Berwick. But not before he had made good Henry VII's omission: he knighted his two sons at Ayton.

If the new distinction pleased Thomas there was that about it that soured his satisfaction: he had to share it with his younger brother. This was yet one more proof of an infuriating truth that over the years had been forced upon him. Ever since boyhood he had been overshadowed by Edward, who was four years his junior. Edward was as ebullient and outgoing as Thomas was taciturn. He made friends easily and was popular at court. More importantly, he had already begun to make a military reputation for himself. As early as the age of fourteen Edward had seen military action. In 1492, pursuing his policy of ingratiating himself with the potential enemies of France, Henry had committed a seaborne force of 1,500 men, under the leadership of Sir Edward Poynings, to help the Emperor Maximillian suppress a revolt among his Netherlands subjects. Poynings carried out a successful siege of the port of Sluys, then sailed down the coast to where Henry VII was, in person, leading an attack on Boulogne. Like many of Henry's foreign sorties this was more in the nature of a threat than a wholesale military action and it brought about a negotiated settlement but the English forces were able to claim a 'victory'. As for Edward Howard, it brought him to the attention of the King as a promising young captain eager to put his sword at the disposal of his sovereign. The teenage soldier was able to return to court with martial tales to tell his friends and admirers and exploits to brag about. How his elder brother, yet to be blooded, reacted we can only speculate. Thomas had to wait five years for his military prowess to be recognised – and even then he had to share the honour with Edward.

However, the family had given fresh proof of their dedication to the house of Tudor and their long period of apprenticeship in government was coming to an end. After 1497 Bishop Fox conducted long negotiations with James IV which, in 1499, resulted in the fractured bones of peace being reset and splinted by the promise of marriage between James and Henry's daughter, Margaret. Surrey's responsibilities in the North were now divided among others and he was recalled to court. He had long been a member of the 'Council', which simply meant that he was one of over 200 advisers upon whom Henry called as and when the need arose, but now he became one of the very few noblemen to be admitted to the inner circle of clerics, lawyers and administrators who could claim to have any share in government. His status was confirmed two years later when he was appointed Treasurer, one of the great offices of state. His elevation seems to have done nothing to bring his eldest son into prominence. Thomas and Anne apparently lived quietly overseeing their country manors and bringing up children, none of whom survived beyond the age of eleven. However, there were important matters to attend to in East Anglia. Slowly, by purchase and by royal grant, the Howards were rebuilding the old Mowbray empire, determined to become what, briefly, they had been under Richard III: great landed magnates with a regional power base.

CHAPTER 3

The Life of the University and the University of Life

We may conveniently take together the early history of the next three Thomases because they shared two important characteristics: Thomas Wolsey, Thomas Cranmer and Thomas Cromwell came from obscure families and rose to positions of power and intimacy with the King. This tells us something about the openness of Tudor society. In all ages advancement depends on a combination of ability, ambition and patronage (whom you know) and the early sixteenth century was certainly no less socially stratified than its predecessors but the spread of literacy, the decline of feudal obligation, the growth of mercantile wealth and the challenge of new ideas about 'common weal' were blurring old distinctions. That said, it is no contradiction to note that Wolsey and Cranmer (or their parents) chose the one recognised environment within which men of humble origin could achieve wealth and status – the Church.

Thomas Wolsey may very well have seen Thomas Howard during the years of his childhood and youth and he will certainly have been familiar with the family and their clients. The two men were exact contemporaries and Wolsey grew up in Ipswich, a town surrounded by Howard properties, most notably the manor of Stoke-by-Nayland a dozen miles to the south-west, where Thomas Howard took his bride to live in 1495, and the great fortress of Framlingham as many miles to the north-east which Surrey was able to reclaim and make his principal residence after his restoration to full favour.

Robert Wolsey, who was variously recorded as being a butcher and an innkeeper, was a townsman of modest means who possessed property in the parishes of St Nicholas and St Mary Stoke and who could afford to send his son to Oxford. Ipswich was a place where an industrious tradesman could prosper. In 1499 its determinedly independent burgesses were preparing to celebrate the three hundredth anniversary of their charter, granted by King John in 1200, which meant that, as a corporate entity, they were legally defended from interference by East Anglia's powerful magnates, the Mowbrays, De la Poles, De Veres and Howards. And they were rich. The half-timbered town houses and magnificent

Perpendicular churches which are a part of Suffolk's architectural heritage still bear testimony to the commercial boom of the fifteenth century. Ipswich and its environs boasted several merchants, landowners and entrepreneurs who were the equivalent of today's 'fat cats'. They had, since 1350, transformed a failing wool-exporting region into one of Europe's leading centres of textile production. Average incomes had risen fourfold over the century and there were several families whose projection into the ranks of the super rich had been phenomenal. Most of the region's trade passed through the port of Ipswich on its way to the Continent and that meant that enterprising townsmen at all levels had the opportunity to build successful businesses.

Robert Wolsey, if we can make any intelligent guesses based on the scanty information available, seems to have learned the value of diversification. Perhaps he started out as an innkeeper satisfying the thirst of those who spent market days in hard bargaining, and providing well-swept chambers for foreigners who came to Ipswich on business. The time came when he was able to invest in land and graze a few sheep. This enabled him to become a wool merchant in his own right and to provide the customers at his table with fresh lamb and mutton. It was an obvious step from there to set up his own butcher's shop or stall. We can easily imagine such an upwardly mobile tradesman rearing his children to appreciate the virtues which go to the making of a self-made man, and striving to give them a better start in life than he had enjoyed.

We do not know whether Robert and his wife, Joan, had any other surviving children. None are mentioned in the taverner's will of 1496 but that is not conclusive. We would expect Robert to have trained up his eldest son to take over the family business before providing for other siblings to make their own way in the world. Setting Thomas on an ecclesiastical career may have been the conventional start given to a younger son or it may reflect genuine piety on the part of parent or child.

One fact may be safely deduced: Thomas Wolsey gave early evidence of intellectual ability. While still a child, he was selected as a promising pupil by the fellows of Magdalen College, Oxford, for their recently founded school. No explanation has been discovered for this move, which is rendered doubly strange by the fact that Ipswich possessed its own ancient grammar school of high repute, which was well supported and endowed by the mercantile community. Perhaps Thomas Wolsey did spend some time at this local institution. Certainly he had an affection for it; when he was at the height of his power he devised great plans for it which, had they come to fruition, would have made Ipswich School one of the best in the land. A tentative link can be made between the two establishments. The Bishop of Norwich took a close interest in the East Anglian establishment and he also had in his gift four free places per annum at Magdalen College School. Ever on the lookout for bright pupils, the diocesan (James Goldwell, sometime principal Secretary of State to Edward IV) might have selected the innkeeper's son as worthy of the best education available.

The influence of Magdalen College and School, where Wolsey spent the next twenty years, was formative. Both institutions were founded by one of the splendid episcopal statesmen of the fifteenth century, William Wainfleet, Bishop of Winchester and Lord Chancellor of England. It would be going well beyond the bounds of the evidence to suggest that Wolsey modelled himself on the great churchman but there are striking parallels in the careers of the two men and Wainfleet, highly venerated by members of his college, cannot have failed to be an inspiration to a scholar who had definite ambitions. One of young Thomas's most vivid experiences occurred in July 1483, when Bishop Wainfleet, an impressive figure with wide eyes and a shock of age-bleached hair, entertained Richard III and his court in sumptuous state at Magdalen. It was probably the Ipswich boy's first sight of royalty in all its dazzling splendour – the fine clothes, the ceremonial, the profusion of dishes served from gold and silver vessels, the musicians playing the latest airs from France and Italy, the overall impression of luxury and refinement – and, at the very least, it showed Wolsey a world which it would be highly desirable to enter.

But there was much more to Wainfleet than the typical medieval political prelate. He was a highly dedicated patron of learning. Eton, Winchester, King's College, Cambridge, New College, Oxford and the grammar school he founded at his home town of Wainfleet, Lincolnshire, all benefited from the Bishop's generosity with money and energy. However, Magdalen was his principal contribution to the world of education. He founded the college in 1458 for the study of philosophy and theology and particularly for the equipping of the Church to eradicate heresy. The university authorities, who at this very time were in the process of building and equipping the divinity schools, were extremely twitchy about the attraction unorthodox doctrines held for inquisitive young minds. The catastrophic impact of John Wycliffe, more than half a century before, was still an embarrassment to the Oxford magisters. Wainfleet was well aware of the need for vigilance and was at pains to acquire the best academic brains to staff his new foundation, for, in 1457, he had taken part in the age's most celebrated heresy trial against Bishop Reginald Pecock.

Pecock's mistake had been in fighting radicalism with radicalism. Instead of simply asserting that the Church was the repository of divine truth and could not err, he had attempted to disprove the tenets of Lollardy on philosophical and rational grounds. His books were burned by irate vigilantes, not because he upheld diabolical teachings such as the inefficacy of pilgrimages and prayers for the dead or because he rejected the doctrine of the mass, but because he encouraged seekers after truth to think for themselves and accepted the possibility, though only for the sake of argument, that the Pope and the doctors of the Church were fallible. Men studying for university degrees were expected to explore thesis and hypothesis, to employ their God-given reason, to open their minds to all knowledge, but they had to be wedded to the conviction that no truths honestly and prayerfully arrived at could contradict *the Truth* as defined by the Church. Wainfleet's Magdalen was a coach set on a journey to a known destination – the defence of orthodoxy – but some of the new drivers latterly taken aboard interpreted academic freedom more liberally. The excursion became a mystery tour and one which many passengers found stimulating and exciting. Wolsey was one of the students who experienced this novel radicalism.

What exponents would soon be calling the New Learning began as an educational reform movement. What was 'new' was the subjects, techniques and pedagogic principles introduced to university teaching, which took their inspiration from that 'humanism', long dominant in the academic centres of Italy, but only now drifting over the Alps. This humanism was defined long ago by Jacob Burckhardt:

> Now, as competitor with the whole culture of the Middle Ages, which was essentially clerical and was fostered by the Church, there appeared a new civilisation, founding itself on that which lay on the other side of the Middle Ages. Its active representatives became influential because they knew what the ancients knew, because they tried to write as the ancients wrote, because they began to think, and soon to feel, as the ancients thought and felt.[23]

Those who brought the New Learning to Oxford had no intention whatsoever of challenging traditional theology; they would have been appalled at any such suggestion. Yet that, in the fullness of time, was the end result of their novel approach to study.

Humanism was a different organism from scholasticism, the system of study hitherto prevailing in the schools. They shared common DNA elements but with crucial variations. Study of Scripture, the Fathers and classical authors were the fundamental genetic elements in all classrooms but, whereas the old schoolmen based their teaching around age-hallowed commentaries and convoluted disputation over doctrinal minutiae, the reformers insisted on going back to the original texts so that students could discover for themselves a civilised and pious pattern of living untrammelled by traditional interpretations and barren logic-chopping. And it was their conviction that education *was* about equipping men for the good life that fired up the advocates of the New Learning. The more outspoken of them castigated the old ways as barbarous and irrelevant and, as corruption in the Church painfully demonstrated, not spectacularly conducive to righteousness. They presented their students with original Latin and Greek texts and taught them both languages (as opposed to the debased Latin which had all too often prevailed in the schools) so that they could fully appreciate the wisdom of the ancients, learn from their moral precepts and develop an elegant written style of their own.

It is significant that humanism developed in the ducal courts and independent universities of northern Italy. Just as the education offered in the Inns of Court was suitable for lawyers and laymen who would be prominent in commerce and administration, so that available in the city states equipped rulers, merchants and officials who aimed to lead a civilised and civilising life. It was not a clerically dominated regimen; rather it affirmed that intellectual, moral and cultural attainment were just as much a layman's prerogative. Indeed, it was vital that particularly those responsible for creating a just society should be reared in the principles of the New Learning, as Plato had pointed out two millennia before:

> . . . the idea of good . . . is indeed the cause . . . of all that is right and beautiful, giving birth in the visible world to light, and . . . being the authentic source of truth and reason . . . anyone who is to act wisely in private or public must have caught sight of this . . . [24]

Henry VII certainly grasped the importance of the modernistic approach to learning. He staffed the educational establishments of his sons almost entirely with Oxford scholars committed to the new ways and others brought over from the Continent.

When Erasmus paid his first visit to Oxford in the autumn of 1499 he found

> so much humane learning, not of the outworn, commonplace sort, but the profound, accurate, ancient Greek and Latin learning, that I now scarcely miss Italy . . . When I hear my Colet, I seem to hear Plato himself. As for Grocyn, who is not amazed at his complete mastery of disciplines? What is sharper than the judgment of Linacre, what higher, what more refined? . . . Now why should I recite the rest of the catalogue? It is amazing to see how thickly this standing grain of ancient letters now ripens to harvest. [25]

The Dutch scholar was describing an intellectual generating plant which had been humming with increasing cerebral electricity for two decades – precisely those decades when Thomas Wolsey had been living there. William Grocyn, the most venerable member of this brotherhood of illuminati, was a divinity reader at Magdalen from 1481 to 1488 and the college was proud of his immense erudition. When Richard III paid his visit in 1483 it was Grocyn who was put up to participate in a disputation for his entertainment. More importantly, the Magdalen man is the first known to have given lectures on Greek (though he may have been anticipated in this by Cornelio Vitelli, a visiting Italian scholar). Thomas Linacre, who was a veritable polymath, studied at Oxford from 1480 to 1485 and was widely acclaimed as an elegant Latinist and formidable Greek scholar, travelled to Italy where he graduated MD from Padua and spent some time as a member of the 'academy' of Lorenzo the Magnificent before returning to teach at his alma mater, become physician and tutor to Prince Arthur and, later, to found England's first professional body of medical practitioners. John Colet studied and taught, probably at Magdalen, between 1483 and 1493 before making the Italian tour which had become virtually obligatory for all true devotees of the New Learning. Ever a serious-minded theologian, wary of being lured into falling in love with classical authors for their own sakes, he returned as a preacher and teacher of vivacious freshness and stunning originality. The public lectures he gave on the Epistle to the Romans in 1497 became a high-standing landmark in the terrain of English religious life and one to which later commentators seeking the origins of the Reformation would look back. The innovative style and content of Colet's erudition drew large, excited crowds of students, teachers and townsmen, including several who found in his exposition support for their own far from orthodox opinions.

These were the outstanding names in Erasmus's 'catalogue' but there were many other scarcely less remarkable scholars to whom he alludes. William Lily, a godson of Grocyn, studied at Magdalen from 1486 to 1490, pilgrimaged to the classical shrines of the Latin world and was later selected by Colet as high master of his mould-breaking St Paul's School. William Latimer, fellow of All Souls, was a friend and travelling companion of Grocyn and Linacre and was worthily numbered among the lights of learning in his time. John Holt, yet another Magdalen man, was a distinguished grammarian who served as usher at the college school before being summoned to the royal court as a tutor to Prince Henry. John Skelton, the poet, who also shared in the education of the future king, was reckoned an Oxford wit but his serrated verse in later years did not hesitate to slice into the careers of one-time friends and contemporaries like Lily and Wolsey.

Such were the men who set the tone in the Oxford of Thomas Wolsey's formative years. He heard them lecture and preach. He thrilled to the intellectual cut and thrust of their disputations. He enjoyed the subtle viciousness and in-jokes which then, no less than now, were essential elements of donnish affectation. He revelled in the mealtime camaraderie of fellow academics. Erasmus has left us a description of one such dinner at Magdalen to which Wolsey might well have been a party:

It was a meal such as he liked, and afterwards frequently pictured in his

Colloquies: cultured company, good food, moderate drinking, noble conversation. Colet presided. On his right hand sat the prior Charnock of St. Mary's College . . . On his left was a divine whose name is not mentioned, an advocate of scholasticism; next to him came Erasmus, 'that the poet should not be wanting at the banquet'. The discussion was about Cain's guilt by which he displeased the Lord. Colet defended the opinion that Cain had injured God by doubting the Creator's goodness, and, in reliance on his own industry, tilling the earth, whereas Abel tended the sheep and was content with what grew of itself. The divine contended with syllogisms, Erasmus with arguments of 'rhetoric'. But Colet kindled, and got the better of both . . .[26]

At this point Erasmus, perceiving that the debate had become too serious for the dinner table, turned it into an easier channel with a lightweight tale. Biographers have never failed to point out Thomas More's participation in the Colet circle of English humanists in Oxford and London but it is not always made clear that Wolsey had a far greater exposure to these influences. The lawyer spent only two years at university; the future cardinal had two decades in Oxford and, not only in Oxford, but at Magdalen which was, clearly, the hub of the New Learning wheel.

Magdalen Grammar and Song School, founded in 1479, provided education for choristers employed in the chapel whose numbers were augmented by fee-paying pupils. The headmaster there when Wolsey arrived was John Anwykyll who quickly established his humanist credentials by introducing his young charges to the works of Cicero, Horace, Quintilian and other classical exemplars and maintaining their interest with *vulgaria* (passages for translation from Latin into English or vice versa) likely to catch their interest, such as this schoolboy's lament:

. . . at five o'clock I must go to my book by moonlight and leave sleep and sloth behind, and if our master has to wake us up he brings a rod instead of a candle. Now I leave those pleasures that I once enjoyed [i.e. at home]. Here nothing is preferred but scoldings and beatings . . . I would tell more of my misfortunes but, though I have leisure to speak, yet I have no pleasure, for the telling of them makes my mind more heavy.[27]

Anwykyll was commended by the Magdalen fellows for 'a new and most useful form of grammar, conceived and prescribed by him for the school'.[28] No less enlightened was Anwykyll's assistant from 1487, John Starbridge. He was the author of several textbooks and treatises on teaching method and the pattern he subsequently established at Banbury School became a widely copied model.

With such stimulating and innovative pedagogues to guide him

Wolsey's must have been a pleasant introduction to formal education. It is scarcely surprising that he elected to proceed from the school to the college. After taking his first degree he returned to the song school as headmaster and also served as college bursar while studying for his B.Th. Wolsey was never an outstanding scholar but he enjoyed the company of erudite men and loved the intellectual freedom of academe. In later years he not only became a generous patron of education; he also showed a great distaste of harrying unorthodox thinkers for their opinions.

By 1499 Thomas Wolsey was twenty-seven years of age and, much as he relished the life of Oxford, the time had come to move on. He chose the obvious path of ecclesiastical preferment and took holy orders. The academic world provided him with many useful contacts among the rich and powerful and it was Thomas Grey, Marquess of Dorset, who gave him his first foothold on the ladder to greatness. Grey, a stepson of Edward IV, had subsequently proved his loyalty to Henry Tudor, most recently in helping to suppress the Cornish Rebellion. Wolsey taught Grey's sons in Oxford and by this means came to the attention of the Marquess who now appointed him to the valuable benefice of Limington near Ilchester, in Somerset, where, for the moment we must leave him.

Aslockton is, and was, a tiny village a dozen or so miles east of Nottingham on the edge of the fens. It was this place, little more than a hamlet and without a parish church of its own, that was the cradle of the architect of the Church of England. Thomas Cranmer was the second son born into a minor gentry family in 1489. The Cranmers were typical elements of an intermarried subculture of landed families able to boast more of their ancient lineage than their current wealth. By the time Thomas was born they had been established for three generations in the substantial manor house which once stood near where the Victorians belatedly built a place of worship. In a stretch of country not dominated by any noble house it fell to the local squirearchy, the Cliftons, Markhams, Willoughbys, Cranmers *et al.*, to keep the peace and maintain the fabric of rural society. The imposing abbey of Welbeck, mother house of the Premonstratensian order in England, was a major landowner and the abbot exercised some of the functions of a temporal lord, joining those who, through their tenantry and cousinage, exercised day-to-day control and upon whom the Tudor regime increasingly relied.

The Cranmers had close relations with Welbeck. When Thomas senior made his will in 1501 two members of the house were among the witnesses and the abbot was nominated to supervise the execution, probably because the eldest son, and principal beneficiary, John Cranmer, was still a minor. It may well have been the monastic influence which set John's siblings upon religious careers. Alice was directed to a nunnery and the other boys, Thomas and Edmund, were destined for Cambridge and ecclesiastical preferment. In 1499 all this was still in the future. Young Thomas was a child, experiencing the joys and pains of childhood. The pleasures included learning from his father those athletic pursuits appropriate to a gentleman – archery, hawking and hunting – and the boy became an expert horseman. Less enjoyable by far was his introduction to education at an unidentified grammar school where he later recalled being put to 'a marvellous severe and cruel schoolmaster'. Before he reached his thirteenth year his father was dead and not long after that, Thomas left home for Cambridge, where he would spend the next twenty-six years.

The college for which he had been entered was yet another of many new foundations. The steady growth of the two universities was milestoned by, on average, one new college every decade between 1450 and 1510. Jesus, Cambridge, opened its doors to students in 1496 when John Alcock, Bishop of Ely, commandeered the buildings of an ailing nunnery to create a new temple of learning. Alcock was another of those exemplary medieval ecclesiastics who, like Wainfleet, was a statesman-bishop but dedicated much of his time and material resources to works of piety and, especially, to the encouragement of education. But Jesus was not another Magdalen, a postern gate for the admission of the intellectual Renaissance. This may have been due, in small measure, to its semi-seclusion on the outskirts of the town by the meadows edging the lower river. The fenland mists and the searing Siberian winds were disincentives to too much coming and going. But in truth Cambridge lacked a New Learning heart. Devotees of purified classical studies there certainly were but not in any concentrated nucleus which could identify itself as a 'school' or 'movement'. Radical theology and philosophy would not take over the university for another two or three decades but when they did the results would be devastating. At the turn of the century the Jesus preparing to receive a fourteen-year-old boy from Nottinghamshire was a safe storehouse of conventional knowledge and methodology.

Thomas Cromwell obtained his basic education in the university of life. Not for him a foundation well-laid by assiduous parents and influential patrons. His home was a positive disincentive to material progress, save that it thrust him upon his own resources and made him early develop the thick skin and quick wit which enabled him to force his way to the very pinnacle of political power.

Thomas was born about the time that Henry Tudor emerged victorious from Bosworth Field, the youngest son of Walter Cromwell who, like Robert Wolsey, was an entrepreneurial dabbler. The family lived at Putney where Walter ran an alehouse and managed to combine this with keeping some kine on a small acreage, dressing hides and blacksmithing. He must have been a strong man and surviving court records testify that he was certainly a rough one. He was convicted for a variety of crimes including drunkenness, assault, fraud, overgrazing the common and selling sub-standard ale. There were several 'chancers' like Walter Cromwell who were drawn to the environs of the rapidly expanding metropolis, determined to make a killing by fair means or foul. Some of them, as is the way of the world, prospered. Walter seems to have been one of them. We know that he managed to engineer very respectable marriages for his two daughters (from one of whom Oliver Cromwell would be descended).

With such a role model it is not difficult to imagine the sort of wild and indisciplined youth his son grew into, and Thomas in later years acknowledged that he had been a tearaway. It is also easy to envisage the circumstances which would have made home life intolerable for the teenager. Not long after our story opens Thomas took off for the Continent where, according to the fragments of story and fable that have survived, he managed to cram several adventures into the next few years. For the moment we must take our leave of him serving in a French army, perhaps in the capacity of page to some Gallic knight.

We have now met Thomas the lawyer, Thomas the nobleman, Thomas the cleric, Thomas the scholar and Thomas the jack of all trades. We must defer making acquaintance with Thomas the courtier for, in 1499, he would not be born for another six years.

Before we leave the last months of the fifteenth century we should record one more event whose awesome significance none at the time could have guessed. In May 1499 Henry VII and his people joyfully celebrated the crowning achievement of the King's foreign diplomacy: the proxy marriage of Prince Arthur to the youngest daughter of Ferdinand and Isabella of Spain, known as Catherine of Aragon.

PART TWO:

1509

He cherished justice above all things; as a result he vigorously punished violence, manslaughter and every other kind of wickedness whatsoever. Consequently he was greatly regretted on that account by all his subjects, who had been able to conduct their lives peaceably, far removed from the assaults and evil doing of scoundrels. He was the most ardent supporter of our faith, and daily participated with great piety in religious services . . . But all these virtues were obscured latterly by avarice, from which he suffered. This avarice is surely a bad enough vice in a private individual, whom it forever torments; in a monarch indeed it may be considered the worst vice since it is harmful to everyone, and distorts those qualities of trustfulness, justice and integrity by which the State must be governed.

Polydore Vergil on Henry VII[1]

CHAPTER 4

A Lawyer's Life

This day marks the limit of our slavery, the beginning of our freedom, the end of sadness, the source of joy . . . Now the people, freed, run before their king with bright faces. Their joy is almost beyond their own comprehension. They rejoice, they exult, they leap for joy and celebrate their having such a king. 'The King' is all that any mouth can say.

Ten years after Thomas More had made a literary gift to the eight-year-old Duke of York at Eltham he penned a Latin poem welcoming that same boy to the English throne. By its suitably overblown flattery he sought to draw himself to the attention of Henry VIII on the occasion of the new king's coronation in the spring of 1509. There was nothing remarkable about the adulation the lawyer/scholar lavished on the royal boy who had grown into a princely paragon in the ten years since their first recorded encounter. Scores of other subjects, inspired by loyalty and/or the desire to win favour, addressed encomiums to the new monarch and most or all of these adulatory offerings doubtless went unread by a king who had little love for desk work and, with his accession, had several more exciting things on his mind.

But there was another, darker, aspect to the poem and one which was to cause More much anxiety in the future. The author used his coronation ode to reflect, very unflatteringly, on the reign which had just ended:

The nobility, long since at the mercy of the dregs of the population, the nobility, whose title has too long been without meaning, now lifts its head, now rejoices in such a king, and has proper reason for rejoicing. The merchant, heretofore deterred by numerous taxes, now once again ploughs seas grown unfamiliar. Laws, heretofore powerless – yes, even laws put to unjust ends – now happily have regained their proper authority. All are equally happy. All weigh their earlier losses against the advantages to come. Now each man happily does not hesitate to show the possessions which in the past his fear kept hidden in dark seclusion. Now there is enjoyment in any profit which managed to escape the many sly clutching hands of the many thieves. No longer is it a criminal offence to own property which was honestly acquired (formerly it was a serious offence). No longer does fear hiss whispered secrets in one's ear, for no one has secrets either to keep or to whisper. Now it is a delight to ignore informers. Only ex-informers fear informers now.[2]

This went beyond required convention. It went beyond the high praise which might draw More to the new King's attention. It was an eruption of that anger and indignation which always bubbled beneath the surface of More's psyche, ready to burst forth in barbed humour, elegant satire or (in later years) vulgar vituperation. More was convinced that, in his latter years, Henry VII had lapsed into tyranny. This conviction, based on personal experience, observation of contemporary events, reflection on Greek and Roman precedents and earnest discussion with his scholarly friends, eventually emerged in *Utopia*, where the late King's policies are described under the careful fiction of the kind of advice that *might* be given to a *hypothetical* ruler by unprincipled advisers.

One advises crying up the value of money when he has to pay any and crying down its value below the just rate when he has to receive any . . . Another councillor reminds him of certain old and moth-eaten laws, annulled by long non-enforcement, which no one remembers being made and therefore everyone has transgressed. The king should exact fines for their transgression, there being no richer source of profit nor any more honourable than such as has an outward mask of justice! Another recommends that under heavy penalties he prohibit many things and especially such as it is to the people's advantage not to allow. Afterwards for money he should give a dispensation to those with whose interests the prohibition has interfered . . . Another persuades him that he must bind to himself the judges, who will in every case decide in favour of the king's side . . . a pretext can never be wanting for deciding on the king's side. For him it is enough that either equity be on his side or the letter of the law or the twisted meaning of the written word or, what finally outweighs all law with conscientious judges, the indisputable royal prerogative!

All the councillors agree and consent to the famous statement of Crassus: no amount of gold is enough for the ruler who has to keep an army. Further, the king, however much he wishes, can do no wrong; for all that all men possess is his, as they themselves are, and so much is a man's own as the king's kindness has not taken away from him. It is much to the king's interest that the latter be as little as possible, seeing that his safeguard lies in the fact that the people do not grow insolent with wealth and freedom. These things make them less patient to endure harsh and unjust commands, while, on the other hand, poverty and need blunt their spirits, make them patient, and take away from the oppressed the lofty spirit of rebellion.[3]

There could scarcely be a clearer summary of the policies pursued by Henry VII and his Council Learned in the Law.

Over the previous ten years More had given much thought to what constitutes good and bad government. He had come to some very definite conclusions. 'Tyranny is always a violent and fearsome thing', he wrote in his first published book, a joint translation into Latin of some of the *Dialogues* of Lucian of Samosata which he undertook with Erasmus and which was printed in Paris in 1506. More was obsessed by tyranny, a characteristic his co-author noted and commented on years later. This was for him a matter of much more than academic interest. It is tempting to speculate on the psychological forces operating in the life of such a complex, driven character. The man whom Erasmus described as 'good-natured' and of 'an exceptionally charming disposition' was also a man of intense hatreds and this can only be because he wrestled in the very depths of his being with the conflicting interests of conscience, personal inclination, authority, duty and obedience. He faced up to the demands of an overbearing parent, the dictates of an awesome, holy God, the imperatives of his own carnal nature, the teachings of the Church, and the requirements of the law. We can only guess at the nature of those inner struggles but we see clearly their results: his asceticism, his indignation at the moral laxity of many clergy, his determination not to repeat the harsh regimen of his father when bringing up his own children and his insistence on the limitations of sovereign sway. More studied what classical authors, such as Suetonius and Tacitus, had to say on the abuse of power and distilled much of their wisdom into his own most famous writings, *The History of Richard III* and *Utopia*. Like all good humanists, he believed that the ancients were superior guides to the conduct of contemporary affairs, and reflection on political realities occupied much of his leisure time until defence of the Church Catholic became a greater priority.

While the old King breathed More dared not voice his criticism. Anyone venturing to comment on the conduct of rulers was walking on spongy ground and no free speech stepping stones existed by means of which he might safely cross. In the reign of the first Tudor a man who had opinions to air had to guard his pen and his tongue. Throughout the realm magistrates, government officers, courtiers wishing to curry favour, informants who made a precarious living from tale-telling and grudge-bearing neighbours were ever ready to accuse the incautious of lese-majesty. On 25 April 1508 information was laid before the Council against John Bray, Prior of the house of Austin canons at Shouldham, Norfolk, for uttering these 'treasonous' words: 'I marvel the King's grace thus polleth us [i.e.

levies swingeing taxes]. I had liefer [i.e. I would rather] than we should be thus polled that yon gentleman beyond the sea, Edmund de la Pole [the senior Yorkist claimant], should come in, and I would spend with him my body and my goods.'[4] The security of Crown and realm provided adequate justification for proceeding against such seemingly harmless grumblers and few would have challenged the government's need for vigilance. A political commentator certainly needed circumspection – a virtue More held in spades.

He judged that it was safe to comment on the writings of a scurrilous, second-century wit; that it was safe to denigrate the ruler vanquished at Bosworth; that it was safe to theorise on law and sovereignty in the context of a fictional island state. Anything beyond that was risky. However, once the late King was safely interred in the splendid chapel he had created at Westminster, More's indignation could no longer be held in check. He may have calculated on the animosity that had grown up between Prince Henry and his father but, even so, the opinions expressed by an otherwise cautious lawyer were indiscreet and they later came back to haunt him. A decade later Erasmus, without the author's permission, included More's June 1509 address to the new King in a collection of the Englishman's writings (*Ipigrammata clarissimi disertissimique viri Thomae Mori . . .,* Basle, 1518). Immediately, a rival scholar pounced on More's apparent disloyalty to the Tudor regime. When social and political context changes, words can take on a new meaning and More was alarmed that Henry VIII, who had been happy to receive his admirer's praises in 1509, might now read between the lines and take offence at what he found there. It is probably no coincidence that More broke off his work on *The History of Richard III* at the same time and also abandoned a projected study of the reign of Henry VII (see, pp. 158f).

More had personal reasons for being disenchanted with the first Tudor. One was frustrated ambition. In the early years of the new century he had established a reputation as a man of piety, wit and learning and one of the brightest exponents of the law. He enjoyed a growing practice as a successful barrister and in the capital he was a member of one of the most remarkable informal academies of eager and gifted scholars ever to come together. In effect, Oxford had moved to London. William Lily was teaching in the capital. In 1501 William Grocyn was appointed to the living of St Lawrence Jewry, a 'fair and large' church right at the heart of the City and not a hundred yards from Guildhall. Thomas Linacre set up as a doctor in London, probably soon after the death of Prince Arthur, to whom he was attendant physician, in 1502 and rapidly established a fashionable practice which included men about the court such as William Warham and Bishop Fox as well as Colet, More, Lily and others of his scholarly friends. John Colet became Dean of St Paul's in 1504 and within months citizens were flocking to the cathedral to be enthralled by sermons and lectures delivered by Colet himself and his learned friends. And there were others who were intimate with the London intelligentsia and who also moved in more exalted circles. Lord Mountjoy had entered fully into his inheritance in 1499 and was considered as a 'Maecenas' by several exponents of the New Learning. Richard Whitford, Mountjoy's chaplain, left his household in 1501 to take up service with Bishop Fox and, in 1507, entered Syon House at Isleworth, near the royal palace of Richmond. The Brigittine house, compared by one historian to Port-Royal, the later home of Jansenism, was a generator of intellectual and devotional vigour which exercised considerable influence among the rich and powerful. Christopher Urswick, an old and intimate friend of the King and his mother, became rector of Hackney in 1501 and was a friend and patron of members of the Colet circle.

More conscientiously exploited all his contacts in an effort to win patronage. The bar has frequently been a nursery for those coveting political and or showbiz fame and More, if not the first, was certainly one of the most celebrated advocates who graduated from law to a position of national prominence. His first public appearance was in the pulpit of Grocyn's church. In 1502 he delivered, we are told to an enraptured audience, a series of lectures on Augustine's *De Civitate Dei*. Later events imposed a curious irony on the location of More's first success. St Lawrence Jewry was a church loosely connected with the Boleyn family and, as the speaker's eyes moved over his hearers (standing or seated on stools they had brought with them) they may have occasionally rested on the monument created to the memory of Sir Geoffrey Boleyn, Lord Mayor of London and great-grandfather of the lady whose marriage to Henry VIII would be the occasion of his own downfall. The following year More composed a eulogy on the recently deceased Queen Elizabeth and, in lighter vein, wrote a verse comedy entitled *A Merry Jest how a Sergeant would Learn to Play the Friar*, which was played before the King during some grand civic or Inns of Court celebration.

In the latter part of 1505 Erasmus returned to England at the earnest invitation, as he claimed, of Mountjoy and 'the entire scholarly community'.[5] Almost immediately More was involved with him in the translation of Lucian's *Dialogues*. Each part of the work was separately dedicated to some prominent English notable in order to draw the widest possible attention to the editors. Erasmus was assiduous in puffing his collaborator. Commending More to Richard Whitford, he described him as

> so full of eloquence that he could not fail to carry any argument, even with an enemy . . . nature never created a livelier mind, or one quicker, more discerning, or clearer – in short, more perfectly endowed with all the talents – than his; and his intelligence is matched by his power of

expression. Moreover, he has an exceptionally charming disposition and a great deal of wit; yet the wit is good-natured; so you could not find him lacking in a single one of the qualities needed by a perfect barrister.[6]

Doubtless More returned the compliment when writing of Erasmus to his contacts in high places. Copies of the scholar's works were sent to Thomas Ruthall, the King's Secretary, to William Warham, recently become Archbishop of Canterbury and Lord Chancellor, and, doubtless to several other habitués of the court.

Yet despite all the efforts made by and on behalf of Thomas More he was not taken up by the King or by any member of his close entourage. It is an eternal truth that success depends not on what you know but on who knows you and neither More nor his Dutch friend had yet made the all-important breakthrough. Erasmus seems to have been promised a benefice but nothing ever came of it. There is a distinct sting in the tail of some flattering comments he made to Mountjoy in 1508: 'you have won the favour of the most intelligent king whom not only your own age but even the annals of antiquity ever saw, and who is also (a very great virtue in a prince) most chary in choosing whom he would cherish'.[7] Henry VII might secure the services of fashionable humanists for his son's household but he was little inclined to dip into the royal treasury to encourage and support the wider spread of the New Learning.

More resented this lack of royal recognition but, by the middle of the century's first decade, his life was far from unsatisfactory. He became a married man and a man of property. He and his father jointly bought land at North Mimms, Hertfordshire. The acquisition of 'a place in the country' was a sound and conventional move for upwardly mobile Londoners; it was a good investment, it conveyed status and it provided entrée to a new élite. Mixing in rural society brought Thomas into contact with, among others, Sir John Colt, a gentleman of substantial means whose residence lay a few miles away across the Essex border at Roydon. Within a few months a marriage had been organised for him with Colt's seventeen-year-old daughter, Jane. Like most such arrangements this was basically a business contract, entered into with hard-headed calculation. More's bride was ten years his junior, young, healthy, sexually desirable and likely to be good at childbearing. William Roper, his earliest biographer, notes, and notes approvingly, that his father-in-law's inclination lay towards one of the younger Colt girls but took Jane to spare her the embarrassment she might feel at being passed over in favour of one of her sisters. His wife brought with her a handsome dowry and More was able to lease from the Mercers' Company an impressive and commodious London dwelling. The Old Barge on the corner of Bucklersbury and Walbrook in the very centre of the City would have been described by a sixteenth-century estate agent as a decidedly 'des res'. It was 'a manor or great house' of considerable antiquity, a 'great stone building . . . on the south side of [Bucklersbury] which of late time hath been called the Old Barge, of such a sign hanged out, near the gate thereof'.[8] The residence, which comprised several private and public rooms and domestic offices arranged round an inner courtyard, proclaimed that its occupant was a man of substance.

Thither resorted all More's scholarly friends to enjoy the lawyer's hospitality and engage in witty, erudite converse. Erasmus and other visitors spoke highly of the agreeable atmosphere in the More household and the Dutch scholar spent two very productive periods as a guest chez More. Yet there are conflicting reports about the jovial host of Bucklersbury. Erasmus will not hear a word said against him: 'he is of so rare a courtesy and charm of manners that there is no man so melancholy that he does not gladden . . . From his boyhood he has loved joking, so that he might seem born for this, but in his jokes he has never descended to buffoonery, and has never loved the biting jest.'[9] Erasmus likened his friend to Democritus, the fourth-century BC Greek philosopher, who retired to the tranquillity of a garden near his native Abdera from where he railed at the follies and vanities of mankind. While the inner circle found More's ready wit highly diverting, for others it was rather tiresome. The chronicler Edward Hall (who cannot have known More much before 1520 and who was an apologist for Henry VIII who had dismissed More from office and had him executed) concluded, 'I cannot tell whether I should call him a foolish wise man or a wise foolish man, for undoubtedly he beside his learning had a great wit, but it was so mingled with taunting and mocking that it seemed to them that best knew him, that he thought nothing to be well spoken except he had ministered some mock in the communication.'[10] Erasmus, himself, found it necessary to defend the brand of humour that he and his friend shared and which not all appreciated: 'if someone censures the lives men live in such a way that he does not denounce a single person by name, tell me if he appears to bite and worry mankind, or rather to teach and admonish them'.[11]

Was Erasmus, who, whether praising or denigrating, never did so by half measures, being objectively honest when he described More as no exponent of the biting jest? More's mind was a telescopic sight which saw issues in clear detail and could not help identifying human frailties and absurdities, while his tongue was the automatic rifle which fired devastating *mots* at the discerned target. But did he know when to stop, when superior, donnish cleverness had arrogantly stridden across the boundary into bad taste? More's tragedy was that he could never be, like Erasmus, the detached satirist for whom style was all. Whether as barrister, courtier, politician or polemicist, he had to be involved because he felt deeply. Just as, when dealing with heretics, he could not control his passions, so when confronted by 'the oppressor's wrong' 'the proud man's contumely' or 'the insolence of office' – evils he was powerless to redress – his soul cried out in protest which found its expression in ridicule. Bitterness is the brother of frustration. Their first cousin is cruelty and More could be exquisitely cruel.

His attitude towards his 'dear little wife' as he condescendingly described her in her epitaph is a case in point. Jane came to him as an unsophisticated country girl with few of the accomplishments necessary for the consort of a lawman, savant and prominent citizen. According to a story told by Erasmus which many biographers believe to have been based on the life of the Mores, Thomas set about dinning into the poor girl literature, philosophy, music and theology until her head ached and she screamed with the pressure of it all. More had to enlist the aid of his father-in-law to bring Jane to a due submission. Even then he could not resist making her simplicity the butt of jokes told to his clever friends who visited the couple in Bucklersbury. Given More's revulsion at his own sexual appetite it is no wonder that his rage should be channelled into verbal sallies against the 'trap' that was woman. Anger and indignation fuelled much of his erudite ribaldry against 'wickedness in high places'.

This picture of the well-to-do More, successful and settled in his comfortable new home, is difficult to square with the insistence of Roper that Thomas and his father were under a cloud and, in these very years, experiencing the King's ruthlessness at first hand. Roper tells us that More was elected to the House of Commons in 1504 and that during his brief membership of that assembly he opposed the King's request for a grant of taxation, to such good effect that the house denied Henry his revenue. The King was furious that he had been frustrated by 'a beardless boy' and expressed his displeasure by throwing old John More into prison until he had paid a £100 fine. He also sent Bishop Fox to persuade Thomas into an apology, an entreaty which Richard Whitford, the Bishop's chaplain, urged More to resist. Thus fortified, the outspoken lawyer stood his ground but deemed it prudent to leave the country.

Roper, who was eight years old when all this is supposed to have happened, was More's devoted son-in-law and was, we may imagine, repeating a favourite family story which had become embellished with frequent retelling. His manuscript was designed to be read within a small circle of friends and relatives and its principal objectives were to counter the hostile official press that 'More the traitor' had suffered and the black legend of 'More the persecutor' which was current in Protestant circles. He had certain conscious objectives in narrating, in the way he did, the events of 1504, which have no corroboration in contemporary documents. He wanted to draw attention to More's oratorical skills and to demonstrate that his father-in-law's determination to put principle above the desire to curry royal favour was not a character trait that only emerged in the 1530s. He introduced Richard Whitford into the story because, in the 1550s, the elderly priest was a pivotal figure in the Catholic community in London, living in the household of Lord Mountjoy (the grandson of More's friend) and writing a number of highly acclaimed devotional manuals.

In the absence of evidence to support or contradict Roper's account any assessment of it must be based on a critique of its plausibility in relation to what we *do* know of More's activities in the latter years of Henry VII's reign. The author's description of the twenty-six-year-old barrister as a 'beardless boy' can only have been included for effect and warns us to approach the rest of the narrative with caution. The story of More's 'flight' from the King's wrath is certainly untrue. The only recorded foreign travel he undertook was a brief visit to the universities of Paris and Louvain in 1508 – four years after his supposed altercation with the King. It can easily be explained as a sabbatical in which he emulated the travels of his scholarly friends and took the opportunity to strengthen ties with humanist circles abroad. In the years between 1504 and 1508 there is no suggestion that the More family were in disgrace. Thomas, as we have already seen, was actively courting the patronage of men in the royal circle. The only recorded event featuring More *père et fils* is the joint purchase of property in Hertfordshire, which suggests a steady increase in the family's standing and prosperity, rather than any sudden reversal. Furthermore, Thomas's marriage took place only a few months after his supposed disgrace and we may reasonably doubt whether an Essex gentleman would have been eager to ally his house with a family under the cloud of royal disfavour.

This does not necessarily mean that Roper's story is a fabrication, either on the part of the author or his family sources. Rather, it suggests that he may have been at fault in constructing a coherent narrative out of unconnected events. Thomas More could have been a member of Henry VII's last parliament in 1504, although young to be selected by the London electors. The seeking of such an honour would certainly fit in with what we know of More's thrusting ambition and the pressure of his father. The Commons of that parliament certainly did resist the King's claim to levy certain taxes by right of prerogative and Thomas may have added his voice to those of his colleagues. John More may, at some stage, have come within reach of Henry's avaricious grasp – many subjects did. It is wholly probable that, during the backstairs political negotiations over the King's finances, Richard Fox, the Lord Privy Seal, would have attempted to lean on some MPs – he would scarcely have been doing his job if he had not. More and Whitford may have had, at some time, a discreet conversation during which, as Roper reported, the Bishop's chaplain intimated that his master was a complete politique, who would not hold back from murdering his own father if it would please the King. All these 'maybes' do not add up to a direct confrontation between Thomas More and Henry VII but the fact that the suggestion could be put on record during the reign of Henry's granddaughter, when circumspection might still have been wise, that More had always been somewhat at odds with the Tudor regime does provide a degree of credibility to the impression that More was prepared to include the old King among his catalogue of tyrants.

There were two elements in his critique. Neither was novel and neither was unique to More. The first was that Henry VII impinged on the wealth and liberty of his subjects: merchants were crippled by swingeing taxes; nobles were placed under heavy financial obligations to the Crown; all men of substance were hindered in the open enjoyment of their possessions by the fear of attracting the attention of royal spies. This was no more than the common perception of Henry VII. Polydore Vergil, the contemporary historian, after lauding all the King's virtues, admitted that they

> were obscured latterly by avarice, from which he suffered . . . surely a
> bad enough vice in a private individual [but] . . . in a monarch . . . it may
> be considered the worst vice since it is harmful to everyone, and distorts
> those qualities of trustfulness, justice and integrity by which the State
> must be governed.[12]

This was a common complaint against medieval and Renaissance rulers (and not only against them; what modern political party seeking election does not promise voters to reduce the burden of taxation imposed by the existing government?), although certainly justified in the case of the late King.

The other grievance to which More drew attention in his panegyric was also part of the stock-in-trade of political commentators: the King did not rely on the counsel of the great territorial magnates. Ever since Magna Carta and before, the barons had campaigned for influence in and power over national affairs, and the first Tudor had made the Crown strong by putting them firmly in their place. Many ordinary subjects felt the benefit of central control over regional tyrants but the belief persisted, by no means only among the nobility, that civil rights were best protected when the realm's leading landowners were permanently represented, not only in the (sporadically summoned) upper house of parliament, but also in the Council. In 1536 a group of rebels took Henry VIII to task over this very issue: the King, they said, had excluded great men from the number of his most trusted advisers in favour of upstarts like Cromwell and Cranmer. Henry's angry rejoinder is instructive. It asserted the King's right to choose his own advisers and went on:

> . . . as touching the beginning of our reign, where ye say so many
> noblemen were councillors, who were then councillors I well
> remember, and yet of the temporalty I note none but two worthy calling
> noble: the one Treasurer of England [Thomas Howard], the other High

Steward of our house [George Talbot, Earl of Shrewsbury]. Others, as the Lord[s] Marney and Darcy, [were] but scant well-born gentlemen, and yet of no great lands, till they were promoted by us . . .[13]

The necessity for some inner circle of royal advisers who would be representative of the political realm and exercise a restraining influence over the monarch was a theme taken up by several commentators throughout the reign (e.g. Thomas Elyot in *Pasquil the Plain* and *Image of Governance*, Thomas Starkey in *A Dialogue between Reginald Pole and Thomas Lupset*).

The obvious fear of those who looked back not only at Henry VII's regime but also to the Woodville ascendancy at Edward IV's court was that if the King excluded from his regular deliberations those who should, as of right, be included it was in order to replace them with worthless royal favourites whose only interest was feathering their own nests, or, worse still, with yes-men who would pander to the monarch's baser instincts. This, latter, Henry VII had done, in the eyes of his critics, by relying on the advice of Empson and Dudley and others of the Council Learned in the Law.

Although More was singing the same song as all reactionary and unoriginal political commentators, his thinking on the subject of kings and councillors did run deeper. Political theory was a constant in the rarefied atmosphere of Christian humanist debate. Scholars confronted the reality of corruption in high circles – wilful monarchs, time-serving advisers and sycophantic courtiers – and looked to the Gospel and classical models for theoretical remedies. They had to be cautious; men living under totalitarian regimes must guard what they write about those in power and garb their naked critiques in wit, erudition and cautious obfuscation. In *Utopia* More would do just that. His most famous book was an airing, largely in dialogue form, of the principles which might govern an ideal state which – nudge, nudge; wink, wink – could never actually exist. No one could seriously claim that he was thrusting a revealing lamp into the dark places of Tudor government. More was working on *Utopia* by 1514 but its main themes had engaged his mind since before the inauguration of the new reign.

One of the 'original' ideas he and his scholar-friends debated was the feasibility of introducing another category of royal advisers into the routine of government. Five weeks after Henry VIII's accession Mountjoy wrote euphorically to Erasmus about the change of regime. He referred to a recent conversation with the young King: '. . . when he said that he wanted to be a more accomplished scholar, I remarked, "We do not expect this of you; what we do expect is that you should foster and encourage those who are scholars." "Of course," he replied, "for without them we could scarcely exist." What better remark could be made by any?'[14]

Mountjoy was cross-referencing the aspirations of the young monarch to the current scholarly debate on Plato's theory of the philosopher-king. In the Athenian's ideal state rulers would be drawn from a class of men specifically educated for that role and supported by the counsel of wise advisers. When More came to discuss *his* model commonwealth he debated at some length whether the Utopian pattern, in which all holders of public office were drawn from a scholarly élite, could be translated into reality. Should disciples of the New Learning seek admission to the Council, where their insights would inform policy and serve the common weal or should they remain outside the sycophantic world of the royal court? By gaining positions of influence could they really change for good the disposition of the King or would their scholarly integrity inevitably become corrupted by power? Here we see that tension which More felt strongly between political ambition and academic detachment.

CHAPTER 5

A Fair Beginning

There is no blueprint for kingship. Each succeeding monarch can only establish that style of rule which flows from personality, training and experience. Where there is a stable dynasty, succession inevitably entails both transition and transformation and if the change in style is dramatic (as, for instance, in 1815 or 1901) subjects will be more aware of the latter than the former. In 1509 everyone who knew the Tudors, father and son, could be forgiven for believing that, after a quarter of a century of drab despotism, the sun had at last broken through the overspread of grey cloud. Age had given way to youth; tight-fisted piety to jovial bonhomie; oppression to liberalism. There was probably no one in court or capital who conceived or applied the idea that a king might 'smile and smile and be a villain'. Henry VIII was certainly jovial. He acknowledged as much in the lyrics of a song he delighted to sing while accompanying himself on the lute:

> Pastance* with good company
> I love and shall until I die
> Grudge who will, but none deny,
> So God be pleased this life will I
> For my pastance,
> Hunt, sing, and dance,
> My heart is set;
> All goodly sport
> To my comfort
> Who shall me let?
>
> Youth will needs have dalliance,
> Of good or ill some pastance;
> Company me thinketh best
> All thoughts and fancies to digest,
> For idleness

*'Pastance' = pastime.

Is chief mistress
Of vices all;
Then who can say
But pass the day
Is best of all?

Company with honesty
Is virtue – and vice to flee;
Company is good or ill
But every man hath his free will.
The best I sue,
The worst eschew;
My mind shall be
Virtue to use;
Vice to refuse
I shall use me.

Everything about the young man who came to the throne in April 1509, two months before his eighteenth birthday, was on a lavish scale. He was broad-chested and tall by the standards of the day – a figure whose sheer physical presence was imposing. He dressed with a luxuriantly careless grace; his clothes in the French taste and his fingers heavily beringed. He was curly-headed and fresh-featured – 'angelic' his flatterers inevitably dubbed him. He loved to sing and dance and to compose his own lyrics. He was an eager, extrovert young man with many passions and enthusiasms who could as easily play Lancelot the chivalric lover, Alexander sitting at the feet of Aristotle or Roland the perfect Christian knight. Even when allowance is made for the flattery of courtiers and ambassadors, it is clear that Henry was no mean athlete. In the hunting field, the tiltyard, the butts and the tennis court his stamina and skill proved more than a match for most of his companions and combatants. It is Henry's well-attested sporting successes that give the clearest evidence of what was the spinal cortex of his character. Prowess, fitness and enthusiasm will carry a player so far; to be outstanding a man needs an overpowering will to win. Henry's will was adamantine.

It had been hardened by bitterness nursed in solitude. The precocious child of 1499 had, within four years, been thrice bereaved. His mother died early in 1503. Within six months Margaret, the only sibling close to him in age, was carried off to Scotland as the bride of James IV. Yet more significant was the news brought to Henry in April 1502 that his brother had wasted unto death in his marcher palace at Ludlow. Significant, not because Henry was close to the sickly Arthur, who was five years his senior, but because the Tudors' only grasp upon the throne of England was now concentrated in his person. Suddenly the young Prince's life became 'cabined, cribbed, confined, bound in'. Henry VII learned how to guard and preserve his resources and his only son was now his most precious resource. Spasmodically the King contemplated remarriage as an insurance policy which might provide him with more sons but he never followed through on any matrimonial project and focused his attention instead on keeping the Prince safe from everything that conceivably might harm him.

Young Henry passed his teenage years in subjection to his careworn and prematurely aged father and the matriarch of the family, his grandmother, Lady Margaret Beaufort, Countess of Richmond. It is a constant for heirs to the throne to be nagged by their elders regarding their private and public lives. Charles I suffered it from his father as did George IV from his. Victoria was constantly on at Bertie about his association with gamblers and ne'er-do-wells and today's tabloids keep us well informed of the tensions within our present royal family. Prince Henry suffered in precisely the same way. His grandmother was a lady of awesome piety who, without actually entering a nunnery, subjected herself to a strict religious regime of daily devotion and applied her fortune to the encouragement of godly learning. Her Rasputin was John Fisher, Bishop of Rochester (from 1504), not in all truth a sinister figure, but one who, as Lady Margaret's confessor and closest adviser, exercised enormous influence over her and her household and, by extension over her grandson, for it was she who, after the demise of Queen Elizabeth, had closest charge of the upbringing of the heir to the throne. On her deathbed, knowing full well Henry's predilection for worldly vanities, she earnestly counselled the young man to take Fisher for his principal councillor.

The Bishop was an ascetic and a scholar. Like More, Colet and the circle of Oxford humanists, he was committed to educational reform. While never venturing out of the safe, warm abode of the Roman Catholic establishment and the traditional spirituality and doctrines which gave it its comforting appearance of permanence, he did open the door to the New Learning, even to the extent of learning Greek when in his late fifties. Fisher passed on to the Queen Mother his zeal for raising the intellectual standards of the clergy and this zeal became the key which unlocked the coffers of royal bounty. Under his direction Lady Margaret endowed new divinity professorships at both universities. Oxford's educational pioneers hoped to benefit still further from her patronage but Fisher persuaded her that her duty lay not there, nor in Westminster Abbey, which she proposed to extend lavishly. He claimed the lion's share of Lady Margaret's wealth for his own alma mater. If any single individual deserves the title 'Father of Cambridge University' it is John Fisher. He became Chancellor in 1504 and held the post until his death in 1535. During his early years he personally established lectureships in Greek and Hebrew and persuaded Lady Margaret not only to make princely endowments to Jesus and

Michaelhouse (later absorbed into Trinity) and set up a vernacular preachership for the townspeople, but also to found the new colleges of Christ's and St John's. It is largely thanks to Fisher that Cambridge took over from its rival the leadership of the New Learning and, ironically, went on to become the academic centre of that religious radicalism that the Bishop of Rochester loathed and died resisting.

Three months after Henry VII died his mother followed him to the grave. It was the end of an age but the new King did not wait for the final curtain before he started rearranging the set. Within hours of assuming power he began making drastic policy changes. On day two he arrested Richard Empson and Edmund Dudley, the leading members of the Council Learned in the Law. Symbolically he rejected his father's rapacity by scapegoating the old King's 'evil councillors' and this act prefaced a rehabilitation of others who had been out of favour in recent years. On day six Henry surprised everyone by announcing his intention of marrying Catherine, his brother's widow. Negotiations had been in hand to unite the heir to the throne with Eleanor of Savoy as part of a grand dynastic schema which would link England with the powerful Habsburgs. Now, Henry put his own stamp on foreign policy by announcing that he would seek a papal dispensation to wed the Spanish Princess, five and a half years his senior, who had been in a state of harassed limbo since Arthur's death. The decision was also an act of defiance to Lady Margaret, who heartily loathed her granddaughter-in-law. An even more pointed demonstration of his animosity towards the pious matriarch occurred soon after her death when Henry tried to frustrate the Countess's will by diverting funds designated for St John's into projects of his own. Only the tenacity of Bishop Fisher, backed by the law, blocked the young King's imperious intent. Henry never took kindly to opposition, so it is no surprise that Fisher's career now came to a full stop. Throughout the remaining quarter-century of his life he received no further ecclesiastical preferment and could only look on while new men in favour, like Wolsey, Cuthbert Tunstall (London), Nicholas West (Ely), William Atwater (Lincoln) and John Clerk (Bath and Wells) were appointed to senior bishoprics. There was certainly no question of Henry taking the intransigent, other-worldly cleric for his spiritual adviser.

Fisher was, however, a member of the Council the new King inherited from his father, a body which assumed greater importance than usual in the early years of the reign because of Henry's inexperience and his dis-inclination to become embroiled in the minutiae of government. There were two groups of men close to the King. The Council continued to be that ill-defined body of ecclesiastics, lawyers and nobles who had served Henry VII. The other, equally unformalised, grouping consisted of the King's chosen companions, the leading figures of his court, for the most part young men who shared his passions for the tilt, the chase and the dance.

Many years later, Sir William Paulet, who became one of the century's great political survivors, referred to a formal debate which supposedly took place at court, led by two great officers of the household – John de Vere, Earl of Oxford, a veteran general and councillor and long-time friend of the late King, and Edward Stafford, Lord Buckingham, England's only non-royal duke. The subject was nothing less than the 'handling' of the young monarch: should he be tutored in the mysteries of policy and administration or encouraged to devote himself to the creation of a magnificent, cultured court and leave the details of government to his Council? Not surprisingly, the court elders opted for the latter alternative.[15]

Such a discussion, if, indeed, it took place in the form described by Paulet, would be wholly understandable. Henry VIII was technically under age when he assumed the crown. There was never any question of a regency: England in 1509 enjoyed the luxury of an undisputed succession with no royal uncles waiting in the wings to grasp the political initiative. Nevertheless, the burdens of supreme office were heavy and could well absorb those energies the young King needed to devote to his important representative role. The realm was fortunate in having as monarch an Adonis, a paragon, a glittering prince who loved display and could parade before the whole of Europe the splendours of a renascent England. His advisers had no wish to shut him up in the Council chamber and the counting house. The dynasty needed good PR. It was essential for the King and his entourage to be magnificent and to be seen to be magnificent.

However, the deliberations will not have been conducted in a spirit of wholly disinterested concern for the well-being of king and country. Its instigators may well have been stung into action by certain alarming initiatives taken by the headstrong young ruler within hours of coming into his own (see pp. 79f). They will have been concerned for continuity of policy and the avoidance of confusion likely to arise from any sudden lurches, particularly in the conduct of foreign affairs. Although there were certainly some ways in which they wanted to encourage young Henry's inclination to abandon his father's conduct of government, their primary concern was for the preservation of the *status quo*, and the restoration of power to the representatives of the baronage.

In terms of Council personnel, continuity was more evident than change. Certainly the disbandment of the odious Council Learned in the Law (see below) was dramatic and hailed as harbinger of better days to come but the inner core of the Council still consisted mainly of senior clergy and household officers. The dominant personalities were William Warham, Archbishop of Canterbury, and Richard Fox, Bishop of Winchester. As in the temporal, so in the spiritual sphere titles, while carrying responsibilities, were more important as signifying prestige, honour and usefulness to the King. Warham was Lord Chancellor as well as primate, and Fox combined the office of Lord Privy Seal with his ecclesiastical position. These men, together with the bishops of Durham, Norwich and Rochester who frequently attended meetings, were the intellectual backbone of the Council. Of the lords temporal the only one who had firmly established himself by the beginning of the new reign was Thomas Howard, Earl of Surrey. When he was appointed to the treasurership in 1501 he became one of the three principal officers of state. This had nothing to do with his competence in matters financial, since the actual work was done by the Under-Treasurer, Sir John Cutt, and his staff. It indicated that Howard had been promoted from the general group of magnates whose members might be summoned at the King's pleasure to deliberate on matters of national importance, to the body of permanent advisers. Surrey's experience as a diplomat, soldier and a practical man of affairs made him a valuable contributor to debate, and the relative peace of Henry VII's latter years meant that he was not absent on campaign and could concentrate on strengthening his position at the centre of power.

A few other magnates, according to the King's later remembrance, were immediately admitted to his government. One was George Talbot, Earl of Shrewsbury. Almost a generation separated him from Surrey but he was an up-and-coming member of the establishment who had proved himself through military and diplomatic service and his appointment as Lord Steward of the Household at the beginning of the new reign must have been an obvious step for one already prominent in national affairs. Two other noblemen were immediately appointed to household office by the young King: Edward Stafford, Duke of Buckingham, became Lord Constable and Charles Somerset, Lord Herbert, was made Lord Chamberlain (in confirmation of a grant made a few months earlier). Sir Henry Marney (who now became Vice Chamberlain) and Thomas, Lord Darcy, seem to fall into the same category. They were men of middle years well versed in Tudor administration. Marney became an assiduous attender of the Council but Darcy, appointed Warden of the East Marches in 1509, was seldom in London and therefore rarely present. By advancing such men to his inner counsels Henry VIII might be regarded as simply continuing his father's policy of building up a 'new' nobility of men rewarded for their loyalty and worthy to take a major share in government. The truth is not so simple.

Neither, unfortunately is it easy to determine. The study of the composition and functions of the royal Council in the early sixteenth century is a bosky wood in which one gropes uncertainly among speculations and fragmentary evidence. While some noblemen appear to have achieved a place at the Council board which they might have considered their due by right of birth or faithful service, others, such as Thomas Grey, Marquess of Dorset, who had been *persona non grata* with Henry VII, were now also promoted.

The records of attendance are incomplete but there is no doubt about the identity of the most active councillors. Warham normally chaired the meetings. Fox, Surrey, Shrewsbury, Herbert and Marney were among the more permanent members and were soon joined by royal favourites such as Dorset and Charles Brandon. What is quite clear is that Thomas Howard, Earl of Surrey, was regarded as the leading temporal lord in the government.

Henry very rarely presided at Council meetings. If he agreed with the greybeards' assessment of his role it was because he was hugely enjoying his new-found freedom and power. It was 'party time', to be spent, as Queen Catherine reported to her father, King Ferdinand of Spain, 'in continual festival'.[16] The description of a progress south and west of London in 1510 indicates the typical royal routine: the King filled his days energetically with

shooting [archery], singing, dancing, wrestling, casting of the bar [throwing a heavy baton of wood or iron], playing at the recorders, flute, virginals, and in setting of songs, making of ballads, and did set two goodly masses, every of them five parts, which were sung oftentimes in his chapel and afterwards in divers other places. And when he came to Woking, there were kept both jousts and tournays. The rest of this progress was spent in hunting, hawking and shooting.[17]

But the King was not entirely motivated by self-indulgence. He was a natural showman who delighted to flaunt himself before the court, foreign visitors (who would, of course, report back to their own sovereigns) and his people at large. But he also understood, perhaps instinctively, the importance of what we would today call 'image' and his commitment to visual propaganda was, in itself, a policy statement: here was a monarch who was determined to play a major role in European affairs and who, unlike his father, was 'upfront' about his intentions. Most of the pageantry was public. When the court was on progress local people would gather to watch the 'quality' hunting, enjoying al fresco banquets or indulging in various high-spirited revels.

The tournay was the most lavish court spectacle and Henry's army of ingenious writers, producers, stage managers and artisans raised this chivalric passage of arms to new heights of sumptuousness and complexity. The celebrations accompanying the coronation were of eye-opening lavishness and originality but they were as nothing compared with those which marked Henry's exuberant public rejoicing over the birth of a male heir eighteen months later. At the start of the two-day tournay the entrance of the four knights who appeared as challengers to the royal champions was spectacular in the extreme. They were concealed within a huge pageant cart decorated as a forest of which trees, grass and flowers were made of green velvet, green damask, and silk of divers colours, satin and sarcenet. In the midst of this forest was a castle standing, made of gold, and before the castle gate sat a gentleman freshly apparelled, making a garland of roses for the prince. This forest was drawn, as it were by strength of two great beasts, a lion and an antelope, the lion flourished all over with damask gold, the antelope was wrought all over with silver of damask, his beams or horns and tusks of gold: these beasts were led with certain men apparelled like wild men or woodwoses [mythical savage forest dwellers], their bodies, heads, faces, hands, and legs, covered with green flushed silk. On either of the said antelope and lion sat a lady richly apparelled, the beasts were tied to the pageant [cart] with great chains of gold, as horses be in the cart. When the pageant rested before the queen, the forenamed foresters blew their horns, then the device or pageants [cart] opened on all sides, and out issued the aforesaid four knights, armed at all pieces, every of them a spear in his hand on horseback with great plumes on their heads, their basses and trappers [i.e. horse coverings] of cloth of gold, every of them his name embroidered on his bass and trapper.[18]

As with major sporting events at all times, participants and audiences entered fully into these games – sometimes too fully. The final event of the coronation tournay, a battle between two mounted 'armies', had to be broken up, with great difficulty, by royal guards when the fighting became too hot. As for the 1511 celebrations, they ended in scenes reminiscent of the mobbing of 1960s pop stars. Excited Londoners broke through the barriers, grabbing souvenirs from pageant trappings, mobbing the richly apparelled ladies and gentlemen, tearing off items of clothing and even ripping gold ornaments from the clothes of the laughing King, who treated the riot as a great joke.

The official charged with the not inconsiderable task of organising these events was the Earl Marshal, an honour bestowed on Thomas Howard senior at the beginning of the reign. In all matters of chivalric protocol he relied on the royal heralds, the officers of the College of Arms, an ancient body reconstituted by Richard III in 1483. The importance of this body in a highly stratified society can hardly be overemphasised. It possessed more than ceremonial significance and extended far beyond the allocation and verification of armorial devices to be carried in battle and the mock-battle of the joust; although this could become a matter of life and death as Surrey's grandson discovered when, in defiance of the heralds, he quartered the arms of Edward the Confessor with his own and was sent to the block for his presumption (see pp. 493f). The heralds kept genealogical tables and were highly knowledgeable about the great families of the land and their labyrinthine interconnections. They were called upon to decide matters of precedence and inheritance and upon their verdict could hang not only a man's prestige but also his wealth and his prospects for making an advantageous marriage. Heralds, like lawyers and scholars, possessed a specialist expertise potentially valuable to the Crown and their profession was an avenue leading to royal favour and patronage. They not infrequently became trusted couriers and diplomats and the senior members of the college enjoyed unrestricted access to the royal household. The perquisites of office were considerable. The following fees and gifts are recorded for the time of Richard II and, though undoubtedly modified over the succeeding century, they would still have been impressive in the early sixteenth century:

at the coronation of the king, a bounty of £100; when the king first displayed his banners, 100 marks; when the king's son was made a knight, 40 marks; when the prince and a duke first display their banners, £20; if it be a marquis, 20 marks; if an earl, £10; if a baron, 5 marks of silver crowns, or 15 nobles; and if a knight bachelor, newly made a banneret, 3 marks, or 10 nobles; when the king is married, the said Kings of Arms and heralds to have £50; when the queen has a child christened, a largess at the queen's pleasure, or of the lords of the council, which was sometimes £100, and at others 100 marks, more or less; and when she is churched, such another largess; when princesses, duchesses, marchionesses, countesses, and baronesses have a child christened, and when they are churched, a largess suitable to their quality and pleasure; as often as the king wears his crown, or holds royal state, especially at the four great festivals of Christmas, Easter, Whitsuntide, and All Saints, to every one of the three Kings of Arms present when the king goes to the chapel to mass, a largess at the king's pleasure; when a maiden princess, or daughter of a duke, marquis, earl, or baron is married, there belongs to the said Kings of Arms, if present, the upper garment she is married in; if there be a combat within lists, there belong to the Kings of Arms, if present, and if not to the other heralds present, their pavilions; and if one of the combatants is vanquished, the Kings of Arms and heralds who are present shall have all the accoutrements of the person so vanquished, and all other armour that falls to the ground; when subjects rebel, and fortify any camp or place, and afterwards quit the same, and fly, without a battle, there appertain to the said Kings of Arms and heralds who are present all the carts, carriages, and tool left behind; and, at new Year's Tide, all the noblemen and knights of the court used to give the heralds New Year's gifts.[19]

Senior heralds were also courted by ambitious *arrivistes* eager to provide themselves with noble ancestry and this was a ready source of income for less scrupulous officers prepared to stretch a genealogical point and 'discover' some ancient connection which no one was in a position to challenge. The senior herald, Garter King of Arms, in 1509 was Sir Thomas Writh or, as he preferred to be known, Sir Thomas Wriothesley (pronounced Wrisley).

One would expect family pride to be strong among people whose business was bound up with matters of heredity and so it was with the Wriothesleys. Sir Thomas created for himself a very impressive pedigree running back, on his father's side, through a succession of heralds to the time of King John and, on his mother's, involving direct descent from Henry I. This can be discounted but what is obvious is that heraldry was very much the family business. Thomas's father, Sir John Writh, was Garter King of Arms under Edward IV and Richard III and was the first holder of that office to be the head of the new College of Arms, a fact commemorated in the college's own arms which, except for colour, were identical with Writh's. On John's death in 1504 Henry VII wished to promote his old friend and seasoned diplomat, Roger Machado, currently Clarenceux King of Arms and Richmond King of Arms (the King's personal herald) to the top job but Machado (a Frenchman by birth) declined on the grounds of age and infirmity. It was under these circumstances that Thomas, John Writh's younger son, and, at that time, a mere pursuivant (the lowest rank in the college) was unexpectedly promoted over the heads of all other members of the college. He had come into a considerable inheritance (his father having married very well) and it is possible that money changed hands.

Having acquired his new dignity, Thomas lost no time in emphasising his own importance. He changed his name from Writh to Wriothesley in order to establish a connection with a more ancient house and, as well as concocting a spurious family tree, built himself a stylish residence in the fashionable suburb of Cripplegate which had the unusual feature of a chapel in the attic called *St Trinitatis in Alto* (Holy Trinity on High). So that there would be no mistaking the ownership of this fine edifice he named it Garter House. Thomas was obviously a very 'pushy' man and it is not surprising to learn that he and Machado were frequently at odds over their respective areas of jurisdiction. Thomas had an elder brother, William, who, at the time of their father's death, was appointed Rouge Croix Pursuivant and Windsor Herald in 1509 but it was Thomas who became the acknowledged leader of the family and prominent in all the ceremonial occasions of the years 1504–34.[20]

However, it was William who provided the family tree with its most illustrious branch. He married the daughter of a London goldsmith and by her had two sons and four daughters who survived infancy. Evidence that the Wriothesleys moved in exalted circles may be deduced from the baptism of the younger boy, Edward, in 1509. His godfathers were Edward Stafford, Duke of Buckingham and Henry Algernon Percy, Earl of

Northumberland. Nevertheless, it is his elder brother who interests us. On St Thomas's Day (21 December) 1505 William's first son was born and named after the apostle. Thus, the last of our six Thomases makes his appearance. He came into a family right at the centre of English court life and it may not be too fanciful to envisage that among his earliest memories might have been that of being held aloft within the enclosure reserved for court officials and their families to see the brave knights and horses in their gaudy liveries thundering up and down the tiltyard at Westminster in February 1511.

CHAPTER 6

Council and Councillor

The glamorous, thronging world of the royal household was a loadstone which attracted members of all the nation's leading families. In the recent past many great men had learned to keep well away from the centre of royal power. More's friend, Lord Mountjoy, had been counselled by his father not to 'desire to be great about princes, for it is dangerous' and the old man spoke for many of his generation. Young Mountjoy acted in concert with many of *his* generation by ignoring this advice. Henry VIII's court was crowded with noble scions, scholars, lawyers, merchants and adventurers jostling to attract the attention and win the favour of the King or Queen or those close to them. The pulsating nebula of the household was binuclear; its two power centres were the Council and the Chamber. Ensuring that the Council was served by responsible men and men of substance kept royal favourites away from the main organ of government; it did not stop the King having favourites or being influenced by them. Thus, the King's 'gang' existed as an alternative and sometimes a rival source of policy. A generation gap now existed between the sovereign's body of partly inherited, partly chosen professional advisers and his wholly chosen group of companions. Peer pressure was a potent force in Henry's life and it did not confine itself to the macho exploits of hunting field, tiltyard and boudoir. Councillors might hope that the King would be preoccupied by 'pastance with good company' but they would be naïve to suppose that the good company would leave politics to their elders and betters. The tensions this could create are well illustrated by the relationships between the Howards in the first years of the reign.

The Earl of Surrey, well established at the centre of court and Council life, continued to work at securing the future of the Howard dynasty. His choice of spouses for his children displays an acute awareness, not only of where wealth and prestige were to be found, but also of the changing patterns of royal favour. In 1501 he married one daughter, Elizabeth, to Thomas Boleyn who, besides being one of the Howards' wealthier Norfolk neighbours, was a descendant of the Butler earls of Ormonde and popular with Henry VII. The elder Howard girl, Muriel, had been bestowed upon John Grey, Viscount Lisle, a son of the Marquess of Dorset

The Howards and their fatal Tudor contacts

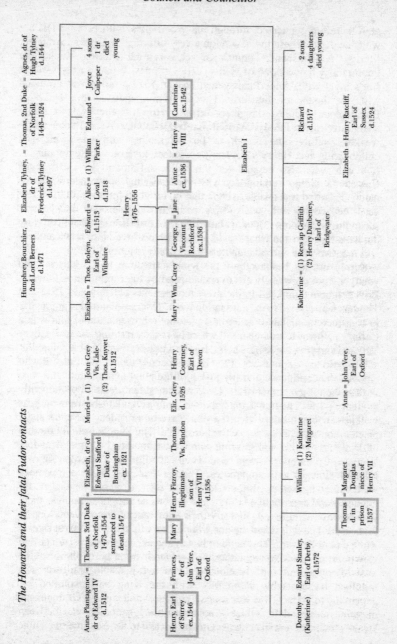

(and therefore connected, through the Woodvilles, with Edward IV) but when he died early in the new reign a very different match was arranged. Muriel's new husband, Thomas Knyvet, was a parvenu but, much more importantly, he was one of Henry VIII's cronies. When Surrey's eldest son's royal wife, Anne Plantagenet, died in 1512 a union was arranged with the house of Stafford: Thomas junior married the Duke of Buckingham's eldest daughter. Edward Howard, the swashbuckling adventurer of the family, married purely for money. Alice Parker was a wealthy widow old enough to be his mother and was well past childbearing age; Henry's stepson was, in fact, his exact contemporary. A rich wife was also bagged for the feckless Edmund Howard. Joyce Culpeper's family commanded vast estates in the south-east. Unfortunately, Edmund was unable to capitalise on his good fortune. Within a few years he and his wife were living with his eldest brother and he was surviving on handouts from his father. What Lord Howard could certainly not have foreseen and what would probably have saved him much anxiety was that two of his granddaughters would marry Henry VIII.

Surrey did his best to draw the King's attention to his heir but the younger Thomas was always overshadowed by the rumbustious Edward. Both brothers competed in the great tournaments of 1509 and 1511 and Thomas won a prize in the coronation joust. Thomas featured prominently in court ceremonial and the earliest pictorial representation of him is in a College of Arms tournament roll where he is shown riding ahead of Henry VIII and carrying the King's helm. But he was too young to be a councillor and too old to be a member of the King's peer group. It was Edward who enjoyed the confidence and friendship of the playboy monarch, and was, in fact, the only member of the Howard clan to feature at all prominently in Henry's life. The new King appointed him a standard-bearer which, as well as carrying a salary of £40 a year, gave him residence at court and a place in the regular routine of the household. The King's little fellowship of drinking, gaming and sporting companions included Charles Brandon, William Compton, Edward and Henry Guildford, Thomas Knyvet, Edward Howard and, sometimes, Thomas Boleyn. These companions were rather like elder brothers to Henry; men to whom he looked for guidance and approbation at the same time as he sought to impress them with his own adulthood. In 1509 their ages ranged from twenty-one to thirty-two. The oldest and the one whom Henry held in the highest esteem was Edward Howard. This band of funsters were, according to the age and viewpoint of the observer, either high-spirited young heroes who set the tone of a youthful and vivacious court or irresponsible braggarts who indulged an unseemly familiarity with the King and exploited his generosity to extract from him money, sinecures and land grants. Incidents occurred almost daily which emphasised the generation gap between Henry's mentors and his chums. On one occasion, for example, the Duke of Buckingham discovered his sister *in fragrante delicto* with William Compton and whisked her away from the court. However, when Henry got to hear of it, it was not the King's friend who was censured but Buckingham. He received the rough edge of the King's tongue for his 'interference' (perhaps Henry felt he owed his Groom of the Chamber a favour: in a tiltyard passage of arms between them in 1510 Compton had almost been killed).

Yet, of more concern to the greybeards of the Council was the influence of the royal companions on policy. Henry's peremptory decision to marry his brother's widow was, doubtless, a declaration of his intention to take charge of his own destiny but it was also the first indication of his determination to take sides in the European power struggle and to resume the ancient feud with France. A few weeks later he flew into a rage on learning that the Council, in his name, had written to Louis XII ensuring him of England's friendship. It soon became obvious that Henry was set upon military adventure across the channel. Enmity with France meant rousing the sleeping giant of the 'auld alliance' and the risk of war on two fronts. This was a dramatic reversal of Henry VII's policy of avoiding all unnecessary costly conflict and most of the Council were against it. Not so the King's bosom companions, especially Edward Howard.

Age had not cooled the young man's passion for martial adventure and that passion had fired enmity between father and son. Edward had grown up in the border country where generations of reiver incursions had sustained longstanding, bitter feuds. Mistrust and hatred of the Scots were in his gut and he longed for a showdown with the perfidious James IV. In 1511 Bishop Fox received a report that the younger Howard, 'marvelously incenseth the king against the Scots, by whose wanton means his grace spendeth much money and is more disposed to war than peace'. Surrey, who had an intricate knowledge of Anglo-Caledonian affairs and a commitment to maintaining peace, was irritated by his son's behaviour. He was even more angry when Henry, stirred by his friend's ardour, turned a deaf ear to counsels of caution. The same report spoke of the Earl being received by the King with 'such manner and countenance . . . that on the morrow he departed home again and yet is not returned to court'.[21]

The Council now had a new problem – or, rather, they had not fully solved an older one. They had agreed the role the King was to play in government but had not sufficiently taken on board the reality that the change of reign demanded from them a revision of their own priorities. Were they there to do the King's bidding or to execute policies they knew to be in the best interests of the kingdom? If Henry chose to dig in his heels on an issue, as he did on Anglo-French relations, how far did his senior advisers dare go in resisting him? Throughout the first sixteen months of the reign the councillors were confronted with a powerful object lesson.

Another of Henry VIII's immediate actions on assuming the throne was to order the arrest of Edmund Dudley and Richard Empson. The leading members of the old Council Learned in the Law were thrown into the Tower and languished there from April 1509 to August 1510. It was some months before a sufficiently convincing legal fiction could be found for the indictment of two men whose only crime had been carrying out their master's wishes with too much efficiency and ingenuity. At last they were charged with constructive treason in that they had gathered their armed retainers in London during Henry VII's last illness and (in the words of the indictment against Dudley) had, 'falsely, feloniously and treacherously conspired, imagined and compassed how and in what manner he, with a great force of men and armed power might hold, guide and govern the [new] king and his council against the wishes of the king'.[22] They were, of course, found guilty by the special commissions appointed to try them and a bill of attainder was brought into parliament (though never passed) in January 1510. The two wretched 'conspirators' then languished in prison throughout the spring and summer before, eventually, being sent to the block on 18 August.

The scapegoating of Empson and Dudley is usually attributed to Henry's desire to win popularity and signify his distancing himself from his father's draconian financial measures. The King certainly had these motives but they do not fully explain the significance which the fate of the two ministers held for some of those most closely involved. There was a very pointed message in the precise words of the indictment, to 'govern the king and his council against the wishes of the king'. Thomas Howard and his colleagues might well, when thinking of the prisoners in the Tower, have reflected that there, but for the grace of God, went they. No member of Henry VII's Council had protested against the King's exactions. Doubtless all of them, in the uncertain days surrounding the passing of the crown to a minor, had taken the precaution of ensuring that their town houses were well guarded. The very first power Henry VIII displayed was the power to destroy highly placed servants who failed to do his bidding. It was a power he would exercise frequently and to devastating effect in the years ahead. As they gathered round the Council board largely left to their own devices in deciding matters of state, Surrey and his colleagues were conscious that their comfortable security was an illusion which would be exposed if they wandered too far outside the perimeter of the royal will. No wonder Surrey was angry at his son's irresponsible and dangerous stirring of the King's xenophobia.

It is not difficult to understand how, under these circumstances, personality clashes began to appear among the royal advisers. Polydore Vergil records that when Henry attended the Council to preside over a debate on policy towards France most of those present were against military intervention. Rumours were soon flying around of divisions within the Council. One that reached Lord Darcy on the Scottish border spoke of a disgruntled Bishop Fox finding himself isolated by a new aristocratic clique led by Howard and Talbot which was trying to draw Buckingham and Northumberland into an alliance against the ecclesiastical majority. Whether this indicated a serious attempt by the nobles to regain the upper hand or was simply a temporary spat between individuals, it is clear that old-established working relationships were coming under pressure in the changed circumstances of the new reign.

The originator of the report sent to Fox about divisions within the Howard family was Thomas Wolsey. As he reached his late twenties the master of Magdalen School had decided that Oxford was no place for an ambitious young cleric. Determined like so many others to enter the service of the monarch, he used the patronage of the Marquess of Dorset and Henry Deane, Bishop of Salisbury, both of whom were prominent at court as stepping stones to the origin of all advancement. When he obtained the benefice of Limington, near Ilchester, Somerset, he was obliged, under university statutes, to relinquish his fellowship and other appointments at Magdalen but his unearned income provided him with the leisure to pursue his career plans more aggressively. It is unlikely that he spent any time in the rural obscurity of Somerset; he would have followed the prevailing custom of instituting a curate to perform his parish duties for about £5 p.a. Very soon after this (April 1501) Deane was elevated to the archbishopric of Canterbury and he appointed Wolsey to be one of his chaplains.

William Deane, the second senior ecclesiastic upon whom Wolsey had the opportunity to model himself, was an impressive figure. He first appears in the records as a reforming prior of the house of Austin canons at Llanthony, near Gloucester. His administrative abilities were soon recognised by the King and Deane served Edward IV and Henry VII in a variety of diplomatic and executive offices in Church and State. As Bishop of Bangor (1496–1500) he embarked on the restitution of a cathedral and diocese which had lain devastated for the greater part of a century since the rising of Owen Glendower. As a man of great industry, clear principles and fearless defence of justice Deane strongly commended himself to Henry VII, so much so that, on Deane's appointment to Canterbury, the King made a unique gesture which was noted with no little amazement by contemporaries. It was customary for the monarch to pocket all diocesan revenues paid during an interregnum and this constituted a significant addition to the Treasury. Not only did Henry secure Deane's rapid election to the archbishopric, he also restored all the temporalities and the profits which had accrued since the death of the previous incumbent.

As chaplain, Wolsey accompanied Deane as he assiduously went about his temporal and spiritual affairs. The Archbishop travelled to Edinburgh with Fox and Howard to negotiate the marriage of Princess Margaret and James IV. He presided at the magnificent wedding of Prince Arthur and

Catherine of Aragon. He rebuilt the archbishops' manor house at Otford. All these activities initiated Wolsey into the daily routines of a royal minister and a prince of the Church. They also meant that his face was seen around the court. He was beginning to be known by the right people. Then, in February 1503, Archbishop Deane died.

Wolsey's career could, at this point, have suffered a setback. However, his court connections stood him in good stead. The next man of consequence to be impressed by the young cleric's abilities was Sir Richard Nanfan, courtier, diplomat and governor of Calais. His four years as chaplain to his new patron involved duties on both sides of the Channel and gave Wolsey first-hand knowledge of Anglo-French affairs. In all probability he acted as a courier or deputy for Nanfan who spent an increasing amount of his time on his Worcestershire estates. By the time of his employer's death in January 1507 he had drawn sufficient attention to himself at court to be awarded a royal chaplaincy. Wolsey's work for the King was a continuation of the duties he had performed for Nanfan. He travelled on diplomatic and fact-finding missions and during the last months of the reign he was sending reports from Scotland and the Low Countries.

In April 1509 death once again deprived him of a patron but by now Wolsey had become adept at selling himself. He had learned that an excellent recipe for advancement consisted of the following ingredients: bonhomie, industriousness, agreeing with his employer, a clear mind for digesting information and a facility for making clear and concise reports. These are the qualities that mark the good senior civil servant in all ages – the man or woman who can stamp his or her own personality on a department while being officially the mouth and hands of a ministerial superior. Wolsey's very agreeableness and efficiency flattered those for whom he worked and enhanced their reputations. The court of the new King was crowded with place-seekers. The men who stood out from the throng did so largely by force of personality and Thomas Wolsey's personality was massive.

Was it also Machiavellian? Did he deliberately set out to become the greatest man in the land, even Henry's evil genius? There is always a temptation to attribute stunning success to some simple cause – a massive stroke of luck, a scheming nature, a cunningly devised game plan. In Wolsey's case hostile chroniclers accused him of manipulating an impressionable prince and fomenting court faction for his own ends. A grasper of main chances Wolsey certainly was. That he was hugely ambitious there can be no doubt. Manifestly he possessed the wit and determination to outmanoeuvre his opponents. And in the end he became corrupted by power. Yet if we want to understand how the royal chaplain of 1509 became the Cardinal Lord Chancellor and *ipse rex* of 1515 we must not allow ourselves to be dazzled by the popular representation of the later Wolsey. The only near-contemporary portrait shows, in side view, a seemingly portly, fleshy, middle-aged man resplendent in ecclesiastical scarlet and this has become the basis for the image of the proud, overindulgent prelate which has survived the centuries. Just as we still see Henry VIII through Holbein's eyes – massive, standing four square, hands on hips, the very personification of power – so we envisage the overweight, overdressed Cardinal as he was portrayed by the anonymous limner. The impression has become augmented for us by those who wrote in the white heat of the Reformation for whom Wolsey was the very embodiment of a haughty, venal and worldly Roman Catholic hierarchy. In reality, just as there is no evidence that Wolsey was particularly fat (and a drawing of a younger Wolsey, though admittedly later, presents a more sympathetic picture), so there is nothing to support the notion that he entered Henry VIII's service as a ruthless, self-seeking schemer. The Wolsey phenomenon is better understood in terms of a complex interplay of factors – talent, patronage, Henry's personality and the politics of the royal household.

We have already rehearsed the main qualities of the King's chaplain. Wolsey was an extrovert whom it was difficult to ignore. In character he had more in common with the King's rumbustious companions than with some of the other solemn-faced clerics of the chapel royal. But he possessed what Henry's playfellows did not – a sophisticated education. He spoke the language of the New Learning, and not without sincerity. He had a rare appreciation of painting, music, poetry and architecture and would become the age's most prodigious patron. He had mastered the niceties of European politics. In fact, he was on the way to being *l'uomo universale* of the Renaissance. Few could fail to be impressed by the charm and erudition of Thomas Wolsey, certainly not a young king seeking men of taste and learning who would be an adornment to his court.

His next step on the gilded staircase to power does not seem immediately very impressive. He became the royal Almoner, a position suddenly available by the death of the incumbent in September 1509. Technically, the job entailed the distribution of largesse on behalf of the King and dealing with the multitude of supplicants who applied for it. In reality there were underlings to deal with such mundane business. What mattered about this and other household posts was that they secured daily attendance upon the King. From thereon in it was up to the office holder to make of it what he would. He might use it to enrich himself with benefices and ecclesiastical sinecures. In the sixteenth century the almonership was often a stepping stone to bishoprics. The King also might use his almoner in whatever ways he chose, as, for example, messenger, diplomat or intermediary. Wolsey used to the full the opportunities provided by this very flexible position. Thanks to the King's character such opportunities were legion: there was a surfeit of royal chores which Henry did not want to undertake. The ever-willing Wolsey was always on hand to lift these burdens on to his own broad shoulders. In a surprisingly short space of time he became the supreme go-between. Councillors, nobles, ambassadors, household officers – anyone whom the King could not be bothered to deal with directly – learned that the best way of presenting his business to the sovereign was via Thomas Wolsey. We even find Edward Howard, while absent on naval campaign in 1512, writing to thank the Almoner for treating with Henry on his behalf. Less than a year after his appointment Wolsey took his seat on the Council.

Wolsey's rapid promotion was partly due to Henry VIII's love of spectacular generosity and partly to the fact that he had an influential advocate at court in the person of Richard Fox. It may be that the venerable bishop saw in the new chaplain a man after his own heart. Wolsey, like him, had come from humble origins, via Oxford, to a place at the centre of national life. If ecclesiastical dominance in the Council was to be retained and safeguarded against any attempted baronial takeover bright young clerics would have to be found to receive the baton from such as himself and Warham – and they did not come much brighter than Wolsey. A fragmentary correspondence between the two men beginning in September 1511 gives us a picture of an elderly political bishop who had a genuine desire to withdraw himself gradually from affairs of state and who probably felt out of place in the new dispensation, encouraging an energetic priest who was already popular with the King. Yet it would be naïve to impute to Fox (whom several contemporaries regarded as being very aptly named) pure and disinterested motives. Rifts were beginning to open up in the Council and he needed all the allies he could find. It is instructive to refer again to the first extant letter of Wolsey to Fox of 30 September 1511. Having described Surrey's cool reception by the King, the writer continued, 'he departed home again, and yet is not returned to court. With a little help now he might be utterly, as touching lodging in the same, excluded: whereof in my poor judgement no little good should ensue.'[23] Wolsey must have realised that there was no possibility of the Lord Treasurer being deprived of his apartments at court and the privilege of regular attendance on the King but he also knew that his aside would be music to Fox's ears. The royal chaplain begins to emerge from the shadows of distant time as a man well skilled in handling people and playing on rivalries.

Henry regarded himself as being good at everything to which he set his mind, an overestimation encouraged by all members of his entourage. He *was* accomplished in the courtly arts and he liked to think of himself as naturally endowed with all those gifts needful for the more serious aspects of kingship. In his own estimation he fully grasped the intricacies of foreign relations. He was devout and reasonably well read on matters theological and enjoyed discussing religious issues with his clergy. When he was in the mood for it he found intellectual debate stimulating, though he was always convinced that sovereignty endowed his opinions with unassailable truth. If he chose not to immerse himself in the nitty-gritty of government it was not, he believed, because he could not grasp the complexities of administering his realm but because he was a good judge of character and knew how to delegate. When, therefore, he took a liking to Thomas Wolsey, as he obviously did in the early days of the reign, he did not hesitate to repose the royal trust in his chaplain. Fox drew attention to his protégé. All men spoke well of him. In his sermons he said the things the King wanted to hear. Any task assigned to him he executed with despatch. He was an amusing and intelligent companion. He fitted in comfortably with that group of men and women Henry liked to have around him. Wolsey seemed to the young monarch to be exactly the sort of man he needed to construct that resplendent image of Tudor kingship, combining surface brilliance and solid political substance which he wished to project.

At the heart of government there was a vacuum into which a man of Wolsey's talents and inclinations would have been sucked even if he had not jumped feet first. Business was handled by a group of between eight and a dozen councillors, meeting usually in the Star Chamber at Westminster. Not only was the King rarely present, he was frequently miles away on progress or at Greenwich or Richmond. Thus, there existed an executive of which Henry VIII was the head *de jure* but seldom *de facto*. This meant, in the first instance, that someone had to mediate between King and Council; ascertain the royal pleasure; report the result of debates; secure the seal of the royal signet on state documents. Someone as dignified as an Earl of Surrey or an Archbishop of Canterbury could not be expected to go scurrying about the countryside on horseback or be rowed up and down the Thames on such routine matters. Yet the potential power which might be wielded by such a 'messenger' was considerable. More important still was the fact that a headless executive could not frame policy. Without a controlling hand conflicts could not be resolved and debates might degenerate into arguments between factions and individuals. Warham doubtless chaired meetings effectively but even when there was broad agreement the Council could not confidently make policy when it might be altered by the King or his appointed intermediary. The only answer, if the system was to be made to work, was for that intermediary to become the royal deputy. And that is what happened.

CHAPTER 7

Obscure Origins

The tourists who throng Cambridge every year in their hundreds of thousands are, doubtless, impressed above all by its ancientness, its traditions, its permanence. The Perpendicular splendours of King's chapel, the quiet medieval intimacy of closed quadrangles, the student puntloads drifting lazily along the backs, the solemn Senate House ceremonies, the portraits of the long-dead gazing down on the passing generations of the living – all, it seems, have been there from time immemorial in the enclosed, changeless world of town and gown. Anyone who lives there knows better. It is not just that new buildings appear which change the appearance of the city or that the council is constantly driven to creating new strategies to deal with the impossible problem of traffic congestion. Academic life at all levels also mutates: women ensconced in the once all-male colleges; student accommodation hooked up to the Internet; and, in all disciplines, old orthodoxies continuously challenged by fresh research and the latest intellectual fashions. It was ever thus: stability and change have always been the identifying marks in the life of the ancient university city. Certainly, they were very evident in the years around 1509 when John Fisher was Chancellor and Thomas Cranmer was a student, proceeding steadily through the stages of the first-degree course.

It took Cranmer an amazing eight years (1503–11) to gain his BA and we can only speculate upon this unimpressive start to an academic career of one whose later learning would make him a major creative force in the English Church and nation. Did ill health or family difficulties interrupt his studies? Was he an inattentive student or simply a late developer? Any attempt to answer such questions involves a fair degree of clutching at straws but the attempt must be made if we are to gain an understanding of the future archbishop's character development. It seems likely that his commitment to his studies was less than wholehearted. At Aslockton young Thomas had enjoyed the athletic, outdoor pursuits in which Thomas Cranmer senior had trained his sons and had loathed his earliest experiences of book learning. It may have seemed to him profoundly unfair that, while brother John was prepared for the life of a country gentleman, he was packed off to the university and destined for a dull ecclesiastical career. Perhaps it is significant that he was only sent to Cambridge after his father's death, when his mother took sole charge of his education.

Once lodged at Jesus College there were plenty of distractions which made inroads into the time which, in the opinion of his mentors, might have been more profitably spent in scholarly and devotional exercises. The statutes of King's College, which were certainly not unique, by their very prohibitions provide an insight into the pursuits of some members:

> we command, ordain and will that no scholar, fellow, chaplain, clerk, or servant whatsoever to the said King's College, do keep or possess dogs, hunting or fishing nets, ferrets, falcons, or hawks; nor shall they practise hunting or fishing. Nor shall they in any wise have or hold within our royal college, singly or in common, any ape, bear, fox, stag, hind, fawn, or badger, or any other such ravening or unaccustomed or strange beast . . . Furthermore, we forbid and expressly interdict the games of dice, hazard, ball and all noxious inordinate unlawful and unhonest sports, and especially all games which afford a cause or occasion for loss of coin, money, goods or chattels of any kind whatsoever, whether within King's College or elsewhere within the University . . . whereas through incautious and inordinate games in the chapel or hall of our said King's College, which might perchance be practised therein by the wantonness of some students, the said chapel and hall might be harmed and even deformed in its walls, stalls, paintings and glass windows; we therefore, desiring to provide against such harm, do strictly command that no casting of stones or balls or of anything else soever be made in the aforesaid collegiate chapel, cloister, stalls, or hall; and we forbid that dancing or wrestling, or other incautious and inordinate sports whatsoever, be practised any time within the chapel, cloister or hall aforesaid.[24]

Most undergraduates were at Cambridge not to pick up a degree or prepare for a life in the Church, but to obtain a smattering of liberal learning before going on to be merchants, landowners or lawyers. It was these relatively well-to-do and non-academic adolescents who largely set the tone of the student body. They helped to keep alive the ancient traditions of drinking, wenching, gambling and gang warfare versus the young men of the locality. These were among the constants of university life and there is no reason to see Cranmer as a 'swot' immune to such distractions. Indeed, we know that he was prone to some lures of the flesh (see p. 166).

The town would have seemed to Cranmer to be undergoing considerable change. Great St Mary's, the university church, was approaching completion after thirty years. In 1508 masons and carpenters returned to the empty shell of King's College chapel which had been an abandoned building site since the time of Edward IV. The structure that would be

Christ's College was girded with scaffolding throughout most of Cranmer's undergraduate years, and when the workers had finished there many of them moved up the road to ply their saws, chisels, hammers and adzes at St John's. The composition of the student body was changing as an increasing number of wealthy parents sent their sons to Cambridge for a few terms to finish their education. However, the presence of the religious was a constant: orders of monks, friars and secular canons were obliged to send a proportion of their inmates to the university to gain theological qualifications. Theoretically, at least, such students maintained high moral and devotional standards in the midst of their more rumbustious peers. Such was the mixed company of the Nottinghamshire youngster's formative years.

Whether or not his nose had to be kept by his teachers to the academic grindstone, Cranmer did develop a love of books. He bought several during his student days and, unlike many colleagues who sold theirs on again as soon as they were finished with them, he kept his as the foundation volumes of what became a substantial library. Economic conditions had changed since the days of Chaucer's Clerk of Oxenford, when indulging a passion for literature involved stark choices:

> For him was lever have at his beddes heed
> Twenty bokes, clad in blak or reed,
> Of Aristotle and his philosophye,
> Than robes riche, or fiddle, or gay psaltery.

Printing had brought standard works and popular commentaries within the price range of many students and, whether or not Cranmer spent money on fine clothes and musical instruments, he certainly bought books. Some have survived and the copious, careful marginalia in the undergraduate's hand suggest a student who was methodical rather than brilliantly incisive.

Young Cranmer's careful, dispassionate note-taking and the length of time he took to complete his studies suggest that he found the degree course somewhat less than stimulating. The syllabus had been changed in recent years – a nod towards the new educational theories. Students studied more classical authors at first hand rather than through the accumulated glosses of medieval commentators and there was less emphasis on subtle logic-chopping. However, the changes consisted more of rearrangements than of a drastic rethinking of the purpose of a university foundation course. Centuries of deference to the traditional methods and interpretations of the schoolmen had yet to be dislodged. Rational dissection of propositions designed to achieve intellectual conviction had not been superseded by the humanists' preference for that persuasive discourse coloured by rhetoric which met the deeper longings of human personality. In later years Cranmer wrote scathingly of his

Cambridge teachers and an early biographer claimed that the future archbishop was reared 'in the grossest kind of sophistry, logic, philosophy . . . (not in the text of the old philosophers, but chiefly in the dark riddles and quiddities of Duns [Scotus] and other subtle questionists)'.[25]

Yet, complete the BA course Cranmer eventually did – and immediately went on to study for his MA. His timing could not have been more propitious: in 1511 Erasmus was back in town. The Dutch scholar had paid a brief visit to Cambridge in 1506 before he left England, despairing of attracting significant patronage while Henry VII was on the throne. On the change of regime his friends urged him to return for a much more extensive stay and to make his learning available to a new generation of students. He lost no time in responding, leaving Italy immediately and arriving in London sometime in the summer of 1509. He stayed several months with More and it was probably while there that he received the offer of a teaching post. John Fisher invited Erasmus to Cambridge to lecture in Greek and even gave up his chair of Lady Margaret Professor in Divinity to the visitor.

Cambridge was to be the intellectual nursery of the Reformation so it is particularly unfortunate that we have no clear indicators of the interaction of personalities and ideas in the second decade of the century. Several of the men who would uphold and, in some cases, die for evangelical values were studying alongside Cranmer in those years. Many of them will have attended Erasmus's lectures and have been thrilled or challenged by his fresh and outspoken approach to theological study. We know of at least one such young man, Thomas Lupset, because Erasmus wrote to More about him: 'with my help he has been reborn and fully returned from the underworld. But the masters are trying every trick to drag the youth back to their treadmill, for . . . he had sold his books of sophistry and bought Greek ones instead.'[26] It is inconceivable that many in the student body did not warm to this visiting celebrity who was saying something new and who enjoyed cocking a snook at the establishment. Stories of his clashes with pompous reactionaries must have been passed from college to college almost as gleefully as the professor himself recounted his rhetorical triumphs, such as that over a religious 'of some reputation' who pooh-poohed the vocation of schoolteacher:

I replied with a good deal of modesty that this function of bringing up youth in good character and good literature seemed to me one of the more honourable; that Christ did not despise the very young, and that no age of man was a better investment for generous help and nowhere could a richer harvest be anticipated, since the young are the growing crop and material of the commonwealth. I added that all who are truly religious hold the view that no service is more likely to gain merit in God's eyes than the leading of children to Christ. He grimaced and sneered: if anyone wished to serve Christ properly he should enter a monastery and live as a religious. I replied that St Paul defines true religion in terms of works of love; and love consists in helping our neighbours as best we may. He spurned this as a foolish remark. 'Lo,' said he, 'we have left all; there lies perfection.' That man has not left all, said I, who, when he could help very many by his labours, refuses to undertake a duty because it is regarded as humble. And with this I took my leave of the fellow, to avoid starting a quarrel.[27]

It was typical of Erasmus to refute his opponents from the Bible. During his Cambridge years he was saturated in Holy Scripture. He lectured on St Jerome, the creator of the Vulgate and, more importantly, he prepared a purified edition of the Greek New Testament, together with a fresh Latin translation, published in 1516 as the *Novum Instrumentum*. This was a highly controversial undertaking since reactionary scholars held the Vulgate to be inerrant. Erasmus's monumental piece of scholarship and his later commentaries and reflective treatises aimed at nothing less than the reform of the Church from within by recalling it to the uncorrupted text and straightforward understanding of the Bible. Those who sat at his feet in Cambridge between 1511 and 1513 were the first to benefit from his systematic thinking on this great theme.

Against this background Thomas Cranmer pursued his advanced studies in music, geometry, arithmetic and theology. It may be that he was, at last, finding the work stimulating, for he completed the MA course in twelve terms. During those terms, partly as a result of Erasmus's influence and partly of the steady assimilation of the New Learning, the intellectual climate in Cambridge rose. Other teachers were challenging their charges to think new thoughts. William Warner of Corpus Christi was lecturing on Bible texts rather than well-thumbed commentaries. George Stafford of Pembroke took up the teaching of Greek from where Erasmus laid it down. Thomas Benet and Thomas Bilney, both Corpus men, became so committed to unorthodox beliefs that they would become the first of the university's twenty-five Protestant martyrs. And among Cranmer's contemporaries were many who, in those years, began grappling intellectually with the theological issues which would impel them, in little more than a decade, to take up their arguments in a public and more dangerous forum – one where doctrinal niceties would become issues of life and death. The waters of humanism would flow into different channels, sweeping Cambridge friends and fellow students towards government, the episcopal bench, the persecutor's platform or the stake. There is, thus, a poignancy about the very obscurity of these peaceful years when Cranmer, Latimer, Bilney, Gardiner, Shaxton, Crome, Joye, Lambert, Bale, Barnes and Tyndale were learning together at the fenland university.

*

If Thomas Cromwell were alive today he would undoubtedly be a commercial phenomenon, a whizz kid, one of those brilliant and thrusting young men who borrow seed capital, carve out a niche in finance or computers or the travel industry, become millionaires in their twenties and are seldom absent from the columns of the financial press and the social gossip mongers. With nothing to declare but his genius, no prospects of inheritance and, therefore, nothing to restrict his ambition within the land of his birth, he went abroad, literally to seek his fortune. It is no surprise that the earliest fragmentary references to his career place him in Renaissance Italy. It was a place where money and reputations were made.

The vibrant city states attracted adventurous foreigners for a variety of reasons. Erasmus and his English humanist friends were drawn thither by the great ducal and monastic libraries, the cultural and intellectual sparkle of universities and princely courts and by the physical contact with the relics of the classical world. International businessmen regularly travelled to Milan, Florence, Naples and Venice for the highly profitable trade in luxury goods. Such centres dominated commerce with the Levant and the Orient and would continue to do so until Portuguese and Spanish mastery of long-haul routes challenged the traditional supremacy of Mediterranean traffic. A list of exotic perfumes, spices, drugs, medicaments, costly fabrics, rare woods, and foodstuffs made a little later in the century included, in heady profusion: musk, cloves, cinnamon, ginger, pepper, sugar, nutmeg, aloes, dragons' teeth, agaric, ebony, cane (a highly figured hardwood), tutty (zinc oxide), senna, colocynth, scammony (pine resin), theriac (a poison antidote made from vipers' skins), mithridate (another antidote), camlet, an abundance of figured silks and brocades, cloth of gold, grogram, silver and gold thread, rice and Parmesan cheese. The trading centres of north Italy also housed the establishments of the great finance houses whose expertise facilitated continent-wide commerce. It was the wealth of the region coupled with the political instability and vulnerability of the states which attracted the royal dynasts of France and Spain. From 1494 the Habsburgs and Valois contested sporadically the ownership of Naples.

We find the eighteen-year-old Cromwell serving in Louis XII's army in central Italy in December 1503. The rival forces faced each other across the wide River Garigliano and there was stalemate until the Aragonese commander, Gonzalo de Cordoba, secretly constructed a bridge of boats upstream and conveyed his army to the north bank. The French, taken by surprise, fought a fierce but hopeless battle before fleeing to Gaeta, some twenty kilometres up the coast. A few days later they were obliged to surrender this, the last French fortress, and take ship for home. Not so Cromwell. We next find him in Florence.

Here he had first-hand experience of raw politics. The nine-year-old republic was governed by an uneasy alliance of merchant families. In 1494 Florence had chased the ruling Medici out of town and ransacked their palaces only to fall under the holy tyranny of the reforming friar Savonarola. He, too, had been swept aside four years later – excommunicated by the Pope and burned in the Piazza della Signoria by his own people. The ensuing years were years of uninvigorating oligarchic rule and party intrigue. Some Florentines harked back to the days of Lorenzo de Medici – the Magnificent – when their city had attracted the finest artists to design and embellish their great churches and *palazzi* and when scholars had been drawn thither from all over Europe (including Linacre and Grocyn from England) to envy and admire. Other citizens lamented the passing of the Dominican friar whose electrifying oratory had stirred the people to cleanse Florence of corruption and make bonfires of all their 'vanities'. The Medicean party suffered a severe setback in the aftermath of the Battle of Garigliano when their champion, Pierro de Medici, was drowned in the river while hastening to escape with the remnant of the French army, but they continued to plot the return of the ducal house with the aid of Cardinal Giovanni de Medici in Rome.

Meanwhile, the Signoria who ruled Florence were incapacitated by their own internal squabbles, an empty treasury and a long-running disastrous war with Pisa. They tinkered with the constitution, eventually appointing a *gonfaloniere*, a ruler for life. They spent money hand-over-fist on *condottiere* until one of the government secretaries, by name Niccolò Machiavelli,[2] organised a citizens' militia.

Thomas Cromwell entered the service of one of the Signorial families, the Frescobaldi, who had for generations been bankers with interests throughout north Italy. The work involved a great deal of travelling and we glimpse the young apprentice financier operating in Pisa and even Venice over the next couple of years. He had plenty of opportunities to study the realities of international politics, commerce and religion. He would in later years be accused of adopting amoral Machiavellian policies, though it is unlikely that he read *Il Principe* until very late in his career, if at all. But he had witnessed at first hand those very political realities which informed Machiavelli's own thinking (it is not impossible that he may even have met the philosopher-diplomat). For those with eyes to read, the fortunes of the Italian states wrote valuable lessons in bold capitals. The conflict between Savonarola's ardent puritanism and the notorious corruption of Rome (described by Lorenzo de Medici as 'a sink of iniquity') under the Borgia Pope Alexander VI (1492–1503) and Julius II (1503–13) cannot fail to have impressed the young traveller. The necessity for strong government as a guarantee of the security and well-being of subjects was underlined by the weakness of the Signoria. Perhaps the sharpest lesson Cromwell learned was the necessity of financial stability. The once-great mercantile house of Medici had fallen on evil days thanks to the profligacy of *Il Magnifico* and his lack of centralised control. Branch banks in London, Bruges and Milan were closed down and, though still a force to be reckoned with in international finance, the Medici name had lost its Midas magic. Lorenzo and his republican successors lacked the resources either to rule efficiently or to dress government in that splendour and power which command respect. Such events cannot fail to have provided Cromwell with powerful apophthegms.

He was an excellent student. Though denied the opportunity of a formal higher education, Cromwell learned very effectively in the university of life. He picked up languages very easily and seems also to have taught himself Latin. Business skills he mastered without difficulty and potential employers were impressed by his shrewd grasp of clever trade practices, finance and commercial law. It is not surprising that we see him next working as an agent for English merchants in Antwerp, the great northern entrepot, the boom city of early sixteenth-century Europe, fast taking over leadership from silted-up Bruges. By 1514 he was dealing on his own account. It was time, he concluded, to return home as the local boy made good.

PART THREE

1519

But, however he* was born,
Men would have the less scorn
If he could consider
His birth and room† together,
And call to his mind
How noble and kind
To him he hath found
Our sovereign lord, chief ground
Of all this prelacy,
And set him nobly
In great authority
Out from a low degree
           John Skelton, *Why Come Ye Not to Court?*

*Wolsey.
†Present circumstances.

CHAPTER 8

Warrior King

This year also, on the day of the Exaltation of the Cross, *Te Deum* was sung in Paul's Church for the victory of the Scottish field, where King James of Scotland was slain. The King of England that time lying at siege before Tournai in France, and won it and Tourraine also.

Wriothesley's *Chronicle*[1]

Charles Wriothesley, fourth son of Sir Thomas and last member of the family to wear the tabard (he was Windsor Herald 1534–62), kept an account of the major events in England during his lifetime. The earlier years when he was but a child were of necessity covered rather sketchily, being comprised of the reminiscences of older people, but his record does indicate those happenings which were acknowledged in retrospect to be the most significant or, at least, the most memorable. There was no doubt about what people looked back on as the dramatic occurrences of 1513: they were the spectacular feats of arms accomplished by English forces against the French and the Scots. For historians the military and diplomatic importance of these triumphs is a matter of debate but for Henry VIII the capture of two French towns and the victory of Flodden would always be highlights of his reign. They were also vital staging posts in the careers of Thomas Howard and Thomas Wolsey.

The first decade of Henry VIII's reign was one of dynamism and euphoria. The new King, determined to cut a dash in foreign affairs, engendered a spirit of eager nationalism. Devotees of the New Learning were confident that the sun of enlightenment was spreading light and warmth as it climbed higher in the European sky. There was a solid base to the era's sustained optimism. On the land farmers enjoyed an unusually long run of good or, at least, adequate harvests. Trade expansion was constant and the virus of price inflation had yet to be introduced to the body economic. These were years of conspicuous consumption. More wine was being drunk and more food flavoured with imported spices than ever before and the chronicles of the period were aglow with descriptions of the expensive clothes worn by trendsetters at major ceremonial occasions. Hampton Court and York Place, Wolsey's residences, led a fashion in impressive domestic building which was taken up throughout the realm by magnates of Church and State. In such an England able men, ambitious for themselves or their ideals, could work for advancement – men like Wolsey and Howard, More and Cromwell. The King was determined to play a positive role in world politics, to be recognised, not as the young playboy prince of an offshore island, but as a leading sovereign in deciding the destiny of Christendom. His commitment to belligerent statesmanship and his determination to march to war at the head of an English army were not the effluvia of a mind overstuffed with chivalric romance. Henry certainly did long to emulate the feats of arms of Henry V, particularly in renewing his claim to the throne of France, and he certainly dressed up all his warlike preparations in the gaudy panoply of chevachance. His aspirations also had a religious gloss: he indulged the fantasy of joining his brother monarchs in a crusade against the Turk and he 'received' the crown of France at the hands of Pope Julius who bestowed on him the title of 'Most Christian King', recently stripped from Louis XII. But the vision of 'empery' was one that evolved from deep in the royal psyche and one that would take on more shimmering substance as the reign progressed. The prospect of becoming the head of a European empire was more than a passing fancy. In 1512 Maximilian I, the Holy Roman Emperor, offered to nominate Henry as his heir and, the following year, joined the English King on campaign in France. Henry licensed the use of an Imperial crown in the coinage designed for Tournai; he set about providing himself with an impressive navy which would facilitate involvement in the affairs of the Continent and two of the first ships laid down bore the word 'Imperial' in their names. When James IV defiantly indicated his determination to stand by his French ally, Henry instructed the Scottish herald, 'thus say to thy master, that I am the very owner of Scotland, and that he holdeth it of me by homage, and in so much as now contrary to his bounden duty he, being my vassall, doth rebel against me, with God's help I shall at my return expel him his realm'.[2]

All this semi-mystical theory and princely discourse occurred on the high plane occupied by anointed kings. It was for lesser mortals to turn the aspirations and convictions of sovereigns into successful policy. Such was the conviction Henry held and which he was encouraged to hold by his close companions. The early months of the reign witnessed a struggle between the King and those of his councillors who wanted to steer him away from the horrors and expense of war into more irenic courses. What Warham, Surrey and others of the 'peace party' discovered too late was that, by discouraging Henry's involvement in the administrative work of the Council, they had played into the hands of the 'irresponsible' members of the Privy Chamber, such as Charles Brandon and Edward Howard, whose influence vastly outweighed their own. To their number was soon added the awesomely accomplished figure of Thomas Wolsey, who not only encouraged Henry's belligerent foreign policy but possessed the flair and industriousness to make it work. Opposition crumbled under the bulldozer advance of the royal Almoner, and the anxious rump of the Council whose members were slow to swing with self-serving enthusiasm behind the new programme were obliged to recognise that, given Henry's determination to cut a dash in European affairs, war with France had a certain logic. There were three ways kings could influence international power politics – marriage, treaty and conquest. Henry had no children and only one sister to use in matrimonial horse-trading and he had no territory to offer in exchange for favours from brother monarchs. Only the offer of military aid and the successful outcome of belligerent ventures could put him on an equal footing with the lead players in European statesmanship.

Henry's first major foray into European power politics occurred in 1512. It would prove to be a near disaster for Thomas Howard and an opportunity for Thomas Wolsey. The English King was duped by his father-in-law, Ferdinand of Aragon, into undertaking a joint invasion of Gascony. The justification (if Henry needed one) could not have been more impressive. The expedition was dressed up as a Christian crusade against Louis XII, denounced as a 'schismatic' by Julius II because of his Italian pretensions. The Pope drew France's rivals into a Holy League which would launch a series of attacks against the Church's disloyal son. Should religious zeal prove an inadequate spur and Henry be tempted to demand, 'What's in it for me?', a juicy inducement was offered. The Duchy of Guyenne (formerly known as Aquitaine), comprising the greater part of south-west France, had been a bone fought over by England and France since the reign of Henry II and had been eventually conceded by Henry VI at the conclusion of the Hundred Years' War in 1453. Ferdinand proposed that another Henry should take the territory as his prize but this was merely a ploy to lure an English army into the region to act as a decoy while he seized the small but strategically important kingdom of Navarre which straddled the Pyrenees.

Henry VIII entered enthusiastically into the conflict and entrusted its conduct to his closest friends. The first objective was to secure control of the Channel so that an English army could be safely conveyed to the war zone. Sir Edward Howard was appointed Admiral of the Fleet for this undertaking and immediately set out to ravage the coasts of Brittany and Normandy, a task he accomplished with such panache and thoroughness that Louis's royal navy was kept locked up in its ports. This enabled the army to get away in grandiloquent good order. Command was given to the Marquess of Dorset, one of Henry's favourite jousting companions. Thomas Howard was appointed his deputy and the third of Surrey's sons also held a commission. The assemblage of the host in Southampton was a sight to stir the blood of any patriotic Englishman:

To see the lands and gentlemen so well armed and so richly apparelled in cloths of gold and of silver and velvets of sundry colours, pounced and embroidered, and all petty captains in satin and damask of white and green and yeomen in cloth of the same colour, the banners, penons, standards . . . fresh and newly painted with sundry beasts and device, it was a pleasure to behold.[3]

The army went on shipboard, sailed down the Channel without let or hindrance, bounced their way across the Bay of Biscay and landed safely in the region of San Sebastian (south of Biarritz). So far so good.

Delighted with the way things were going, Henry held a joust at Greenwich in June which the royal 'gang' of Edward Howard, Thomas Knyvet, Charles Brandon *et al.* bravely displayed their martial ardour. Eager now for a share of easy glory Howard's friends clamoured to join him in fresh naval exploits. Henry was in the process of laying the foundations of the English navy, rapidly commissioning and buying ships and he determined to follow up Howard's earlier success with a further demonstration of sea power. He ordered the fleet to be assembled at Portsmouth, rode down in person to review it and nominated Thomas Knyvet, Charles Brandon, Henry Guildford and other favourites to serve as captains under Howard's leadership.

The king made a great banquet to all the captains and everyone swore to another ever to defend, aid and comfort one another without failing, and this they promised before the king, who committed them to God, and so with great noise of minstrelsy they took their ships, which were in number twenty-five of great burden and well furnished of all things.[4]

Thus, like a maritime version of the Knights of the Round Table, the band of brothers issued forth. Edward Howard was appointed Lord Admiral of England.

They discovered the French navy (some thirty-nine sail) congregated in the harbour of Brest. At the approach of the English their antagonists sailed out to meet them. On 10 August there was a fierce engagement. Naval warfare at that time was little more than an extension of conflict by land: ships were principally troop carriers which attempted to grapple the enemy as a precursor to hand-to-hand fighting. In the thick of the battle Henry's capital ship, the *Regent*, commanded by Knyvet, was successfully shackled to the French carrack *Marie La Cordelière* and, after a fierce exchange of arrows, her company got on-board the enemy. At this point a death-or-glory French gunner fired the carrack's powder store. Within minutes both vessels were ablaze. No other ship or boat could get close enough to rescue the crews who faced death by fire or water. Knyvet and 700 of his men perished and the shock of this tragedy was, apparently, so great that both fleets called off the action. Howard was devastated and swore that he would not look upon the King's face until he had avenged his brother-in-law's death.

According to Wolsey, Henry was scarcely less affected, though he controlled his grief. On 26 August the Almoner gave a detailed and colourful report of the loss of the *Regent* to Fox and continued,

> And, my lord, at the reverence of God, keep these tidings secret to yourself; for there is no living man knoweth the same here but only the king and I. Your lordship knoweth right well that it is expedient for a while to keep the same secret. To see how the king taketh the matter and behaveth himself, ye would marvel and much allow his wise and constant manner. I have not on my faith seen the like.[5]

This letter gives us a very vivid impression of the intimacy which had rapidly sprung up between King and Almoner. Henry, at this stage of his life a young, inexperienced monarch who was determined to appear strong, decisive and forceful and who lived surrounded by a buzzing swarm of sycophantic mendicants, needed an inner circle of companions who could meet the needs of his kaleidoscopic personality – now game-some, now pious, now intellectually curious, now businesslike. It is significant that those the King admitted to his confidence – his wife and his friends – were all a few years older than himself, who belonged to a generation between his father's and his own. Wolsey had very rapidly joined this select band and other royal servants, like Fox, had recognised that a special relationship existed between him and the King. As the 1512 campaigns continued by land and sea Wolsey was one of the few people with whom the King discussed his reaction to the news coming in from the war zones.

The news was not good. While Edward Howard raged along the coasts of Brittany, Normandy and Picardy in an orgy of revenge, capturing or burning whatever French vessels he came across, his brothers and their companions were watching the disintegration of their army. The five plagues that troubled the host were an untrustworthy ally, inadequate supplies and equipment, indifferent leadership, poor communications and disease. Dorset and his 10,000 men were abandoned in the coastal area around Fuenterrabia (close to St Jean de Luz) for the greater part of five months. The Marquess had been instructed to place his force at Ferdinand's disposal and had been assured that he would receive horses and ordnance from his ally. All he received was empty promises. The King of Navarre was as bemused as the English by all this – which was precisely what Ferdinand intended. His troops made an easy conquest of the kingdom after which he had no further need of his son-in-law's aid.

The English troops became ungovernable and their leaders fell to quarrelling among themselves. Dysentery and inactivity sapped the men's morale. A diet dominated by garlic and 'hot wines', according to one diagnosis, caused the soldiers' blood to 'boil' and 1,800 died of the flux. Discipline rapidly broke down among the survivors, who were soon fighting among themselves, stirring up trouble with the local people and deserting. The officers failed either to provide their followers with military objectives or to devise other work for idle hands to do. No fresh orders arrived from England and they could not agree on-the-spot strategic decisions. Some were for marching into Guyenne but others were paralysed by the fear of what would happen if they disobeyed their original instructions. When they did take initiative and bought hundreds of pack animals locally at exorbitant cost they became the laughing stock of the Basques and of their own men: the beasts were untrained and useless.

In the midst of all this Dorset fell ill and responsibility shifted squarely to Thomas Howard's shoulders. He buckled. Admittedly, he inherited a near-impossible situation but it was one which demanded decisive action and he failed to provide it. When in mid-October the latest Aragonese envoys turned up with a fresh batch of excuses and the suggestion that the English disperse into winter quarters until the next campaigning season, Howard rehearsed his grievances against Ferdinand and then gave voice to his real anxiety: 'What shall the king our master report of our slothfulness, which hath spent innumerable treasure and nothing gained?'[6] However, having made his protest, Howard, in concert with his colleagues, agreed to spend the winter in the villages around San Sebastian. This only served to antagonise the men further. The officers were now between a rock and a hard place – a situation partially of their own making. If they stayed put they ran the risk of being lynched by their own men who were by now on the verge of mutiny. If they trooped home in total humiliation they faced the equally unpleasant prospect of the King's wrath. In the event, the present threat was more persuasive than the future one. At the beginning of November the remnant of the expedition braved the autumn gales and set off into the Atlantic.

Henry was, predictably, furious, especially when Ferdinand castigated Dorset's army as cowards who had struck camp when all was in train for a successful spring invasion of Guyenne. By the time Dorset and Howard returned with their well-prepared story of Aragonese perfidy Ferdinand's ambassadors, aided by his daughter, had persuaded the King into an extension of the existing treaty involving further joint military action against France in 1513 (the scheming politique was also entering negotiations with Louis XII for a truce). Henry talked about stringing his traitorous commanders from the highest gallows. But he was not yet the man it was fatal to disappoint and the black mood passed. Dorset and his colleagues did not, however, get off scot-free. They were brought before the King in full Council with Ferdinand's ambassadors in attendance and there they received a severe dressing down for their misconduct. Henry distanced himself from the failings of his servants – a manoeuvre in which he was to become highly skilled over the years. That done, the sun re-emerged from the clouds. The chronicler observed that the King 'kept a solemn [i.e. sumptuous] Christmas at Greenwich to cheer his nobles'.[7] And soon there would be rewards for those commanders who, in Henry's estimation, had quitted themselves well in the recent conflict. In February Charles Brandon was created Viscount Lisle (Erasmus's caustic comment on Brandon's rapid advancement was that the King had turned him 'from a stable boy into a nobleman')[8] and Henry planned to confer the Garter on Edward Howard when the next vacancy occurred. No new honours were projected for Edward's elder brother. Thomas went home, where his wife lay dying. Anne's passing provided the opportunity for a new dynastic alliance and, as we have seen, the widower was married within weeks to Elizabeth, daughter of Edward Stafford, Duke of Buckingham, England's premier peer and richest subject. Enjoying the dowry and body of his nineteen-year-old bride doubtless went some way towards salving the wounds Thomas's pride had suffered in recent months.

Wolsey may well have been among those who poured oil on the King's anger in November and December 1512, carefully pointing out that many experienced captains would be needed in the next phase of the war against Louis XII. The lesson the royal Almoner took from the Guyenne fiasco was that the logistics of war must be planned with meticulous care. If Henry was to be delivered the impressive victories that he craved, he would have need of a tireless administrator who could oversee every aspect of supplying and provisioning the army and navy. Nothing could be left to chance – ships, timber, sailcloth, munitions, armour, horses, wagons, victuals, tents, everything would need to be organised, checked and double-checked. And Wolsey knew the very man who had the mental and physical stamina to undertake this mammoth task. Even before the last shipload of dispirited men arrived back from Iberia, he and the King were planning an impressive military venture which would erase from memory the recent misfortunes. And just as Henry publicly rewarded those friends who had served him well under arms, so he demonstrated his confidence in Wolsey by beginning that trickle of major preferments which grew rapidly into a flood. In the early months of 1513 the Almoner became Dean of St Stephen's, Westminster and Dean of York. Henry could always afford to be very generous to his leading churchmen: the cost did not come out of his own purse.

If 1512 was a bad year for Thomas Howard, 1513 was his *annus mirabilis*. It was, first of all, the year that removed brother Edward from the scene. The Lord Admiral died in suitably heroic and probably foolhardy fashion. The basics of the new invasion plan were the same as those of the old one; a naval operation to secure command of the sea so that a land force could be safely conveyed to the war zone. The differences were that this time the English attack would be directed at northern France via the English stronghold of Calais and the army would be a much more impressive one led by the King in person. Accordingly, at the end of March, Edward Howard left Portsmouth with forty-two ships.

The French King, well informed of the preparations Henry was making, had assembled the greater part of his navy at Brest. Besides the capital ships that had seen action the previous year, this now included a squadron of galleys brought round from the Mediterranean by Chevalier Prégent de Bidoux, a Knight of St John. These maritime wasps were a real worry; as agile fighting machines not dependent on the wind and potentially deadly in inshore waters they enjoyed a perhaps exaggerated reputation. But they could certainly have posed a threat to Henry's lumbering transports en route for Calais. Howard discovered the greater part of the naval force sheltering in Brest harbour, one of the most secure roadsteads in the world. He brought his own ships to the outer anchorage, Berthaume Bay, and lay there within full view of the enemy. It would have been the easiest and wisest course simply to blockade the French but passive campaigning was not in Sir Edward's nature. Within days he attempted a frontal assault – and immediately discovered why Brest was such a good defensive position. One of his ships struck hidden rocks and rapidly sank. The only result of the attempt was to make the French set out a defensive line of hulks across the entrance to the inner harbour with the intention of firing them if Howard tried another assault.

The Lord Admiral now turned his attention to the galleys moored in Blancs de Sables Bay, another part of the harbour, but these lay in shallow water, which was just as effective a protection as the rocks of the inner haven. From this position Prégent taunted the English by sending some of his smaller vessels ('foists' or 'feluccas') to make lightning attacks and daring the English to pursue them. Howard did manage to capture one of these foists by using boats but his men came under such a murderous fire as they approached the galleys that the experiment was not repeated. Thus there existed a stalemate; the French could not get out and the English could not get in.

According to an early legend, after a couple of frustrating weeks, the Lord Admiral sent an invitation to Henry VIII to come in person to lead his navy to glorious victory – a suggestion which was rebuffed with the order for Howard to proceed without delay to the annihilation of the enemy. If there is any truth in this it seems more likely that Sir Edward wanted the King to come and see for himself just why his instructions could not be carried out. Be that as it may, propelled either by the King's command or his own impetuosity, Howard decided to make another assault on the galleys. In true, heroic style he called a secret meeting of his close friends among the captains, 'and declared to them that the matter was little and the honour great if they alone took upon them that enterprise and let none other know of it. They, like men of high courage and desiring honour, gladly assented.'[9] Thus, on 25 April, Howard, with five boatloads of men, was rowed across the shallow waters to assay what would have been impossible with a larger force. It may be that he was banking on the element of surprise and, although he and his men came under heavy fire, some did reach the galleys. Sir Edward led the assault on Prégent's own ship and began laying about him with his sword. It was magnificent but it was not war. As soon as the Frenchmen recovered from their initial shock they gathered themselves to repel boarders. The Lord Admiral and his companions were forced back over the side and, because their boat had been cut free from the galley, they fell into the water where their heavy part armour dragged them down.

The effect on the English fleet was catastrophic. Sir Edward Howard was such a charismatic leader – a commander in the Drake mould – that his loss totally demoralised his followers. No other captain either would or could step into his shoes and the entire force weighed anchor for England. Prégent grabbed the opportunity to sally forth and raid at will along the Sussex coast.

At last, at the age of forty, Thomas Howard could emerge from the shadow of his popular, dashing and ostentatious younger brother. Henry immediately gave him the opportunity to prove that he was of the same mettlesome blood. Someone had to take charge of the fleet and do the job for which Edward had been sent across the Channel and Henry gave the task to Thomas. He appointed the elder Howard as Lord Admiral and urged him to go and avenge his brother's death.

Howard may well have taken up his new duties with furiously conflicting emotions. On the one hand, he had been brought in from the cold and given a chance to redeem himself. On the other hand, there was a woeful similarity between his new responsibilities and those that had been thrust upon him the previous autumn. Once again he was being asked to rally dispirited men and redeem a desperate situation. His orders were specific: he was to lick his men and ships into shape and bring them from Plymouth to Southampton, where he would take on-board a contingent led by Lord Lisle, who was to lead a diversionary attack on Brest while Henry and the main army crossed the Channel farther east. The King, of course, wanted all this done without delay and Howard found that he could not immediately meet the royal wishes. Under the circumstances he was concerned above all else to watch his own back. In Plymouth he bullied and fussed his men while despatching letter after whingeing letter to Wolsey blaming the delay on everything and everyone but himself. Hundreds of crewmen, he claimed, had deserted; those left were demoralised and would as soon go to purgatory as back into battle; he had conveyed to the captains the King's stern displeasure but instead of putting fresh fire in their bellies this had only further dampened their ardour; as to his ships, they were pitifully short of equipment and provisions and he was unable to make good the deficiencies locally. On top of all his other problems the wind was blowing in the wrong direction so that even if His Majesty insisted on Howard putting to sea with his vessels inadequately manned and supplied he would be unable to do so.

By mid-May, when Howard had been only a week in post, Henry was already growing very restive. His army was assembled. The ships for the main invasion were lying in the Thames, including his new-built pride and joy, the *Henri Grace à Dieu*. The impressive siege weapons known as the *Twelve Apostles* had been delivered from the foundry. Thanks to Wolsey's tireless co-ordination, everything was being brought to a pitch of readiness. But the campaign season was well advanced and everything was waiting on the Lord Admiral. Impatiently, the Almoner wrote to Richard Fox, stationed in Southampton, demanding to know when the fleet would be ready there for his inspection. On 19 May the worried Bishop passed on the information he had received from Howard: 'the Lord Admiral . . . with their whole army and their victuallers lie so far within the haven of Plymouth, that they cannot come out of it without a north-west wind and the wind hath been south-west continually three days past'.[10] The excuse was a weak one: a south-west wind was precisely what Howard needed to bear up the Channel to Southampton. Though this might have made it impossible to sail out of the inner harbour there was nothing to prevent Howard having his ships towed into the Sound.

By the time that Fox wrote to his master the Lord Admiral was no longer with his fleet. Alarmed at how gossiping tongues might be representing his inaction, he had left for London to report in person on the situation, only to discover when he got there that neither the King nor Wolsey would see him. This is both surprising and significant. For Henry to refuse an audience to one of his principal military officers can only indicate just how out of favour Howard was. Of course, with the King's back turned to the Lord Admiral, it was easy for Henry's Almoner to follow suit. He could claim, with a large degree of justification, that he was so immersed in the minutiae of the great adventure that he had no time to spare for Howard's problems. The son and son-in-law of the country's greatest nobles found it hard to take such treatment lying down. To have to go cap in hand to a jumped-up cleric must have been galling enough; to be snubbed by him was salt in the weeping wound of Howard's gashed pride. Wolsey's meteoric rise to power inevitably provoked jealousy in many others vying for royal favour and the fact that the extant correspondence between the nobleman and the priest shows Howard as cringingly respectful to the new kid on the block should not deceive us into thinking that he felt genuine respect and admiration for Wolsey.

The Lord Admiral's persistence and self-abasement paid off; he got his supplies, although he had to provide his own transports to convey them from London to Southampton. By the middle of June he was, at last, able to weigh anchor and convey Lord Lisle's force across to the Brittany coast. They saw little action there largely because Louis XII, knowing where the real conflict was going to be, had marched most of his men to the environs of Calais. However, the Channel was kept sufficiently free of French ships for the main army to cross and to be joined by Henry VIII and his sumptuous retinue on 30 June. Brandon and Howard now hastened to Calais. The English commanders all wanted to be at the centre of the action where they could do and, more importantly, be seen to be doing valorous deeds. Howard's contribution to the campaign was a lightning attack on the little harbour town of Wissant, halfway between Calais and Boulogne.

Meanwhile, Henry, having assembled his host in full battle array, led it in cumbersome progress towards his first objective, the siege of Thérouanne. On 16 July the King was able to claim a 'victory' in the field when his friend the Earl of Essex won a cavalry skirmish known as the 'Battle of the Spurs' on account of the French horsemen's swift flight. There can be no doubt that other captains looked forward to notching up similar personal triumphs as the French campaign proceeded. But it was not to be for Thomas Howard. He was sent away from the gaudy and the razzmatazz to a distant and altogether more drear theatre of war.

Before his departure Henry had taken thought for the security of his realm. He had every reason to suspect that James IV would grasp the opportunity of coming to the aid of his French ally with some diversionary tactic intended to oblige the English King to divide his forces. The man charged with keeping a watch on the border was the Earl of Surrey. He was the obvious choice and an eminently suitable one. No one better understood Anglo-Scottish relations nor the psychology of the forty-year-old Caledonian King. However, Lord Howard was less than delighted with the trust Henry reposed in him. After receiving his instructions

the earl could hardly speak when he took his leave [because he was sent away] from the noble prince his sovereign lord and king and from the flower of all the nobility of this realm, being ready in such an honourable journey. When he had somewhat [recovered his composure] he said to some that were about him, 'Sorry may I see him [i.e. James IV] or die that is [the] cause of my abiding behind, and if ever he and I meet, I shall do [all] that in me lyeth to make him as sorry if I can.[11]

Surrey was Earl Marshal and must have assumed that his place in the French venture would be at the head of the army. To be sidetracked into watching the wild northern border while others were grabbing all the glory in France must have seemed like a return to those years of banishment from the court when he had worked so hard to earn the trust of the King's father.

By the beginning of August, Surrey was back on familiar territory, checking the border defences and sending out reconnaissance parties. His intelligence revealed that the King's suspicions were fully justified: James had mustered his men at Edinburgh and was ready to march south at the head of a truly formidable host. No less than Henry, his brother-in-law was possessed by mingled motives of chivalric honour, personal splendour and political opportunism. He rivalled the Tudor in his determination to establish a scintillating court and an impressive military machine. His 1,000-ton flagship, the *Michael*, was the inspiration for the *Henri Grace à Dieu* and James, too, could boast the most technically advanced field ordnance. Louis had urged him to war with no less a prize than the English crown and the French Queen had stirred the Scot's chivalric soul by nominating him her champion in the coming fray. James had already sent Lyon King of Arms to Henry's camp in France with an ultimatum that he would attack if the English invasion was not immediately called off. It was an empty formality though observed with all the customary ceremonial. Henry entrusted Thomas Wriothesley, the Scottish herald's opposite number, to entertain Lyon lavishly and, on the latter's departure, rewarded him with 100 crowns. But by then James had already crossed the English border. It was at this point that Henry detailed Thomas Howard and his brother, Edmund, to take four shiploads of men and go to their father's aid. Thus the whole Howard clan were detached from the royal venture with all its splendiferous panoply to prosecute a very different, less dressed-up, more utilitarian kind of war that was only expected to amount to a few inglorious border skirmishes. In the event it was the French campaign which resulted in little more than polychromed, belligerent posturing and the conflict with Scotland which climaxed in a major, bloody battle that was destined to have long-term consequences. The English victory which has always been difficult to account for was the outcome of luck, of poor judgement on the part of the Scottish King and of Surrey's intelligent generalship. But, whatever the reasons for English success, one immediate result was the enhancement of Howard prestige and the securing of their position within the scheme of domestic politics.

Surrey's force was heavily outnumbered. He sent messengers scurrying around the northern shires with instructions to the nobility and leading gentry to assemble their levies and hurry to his standard. These, together with his own retinue and the troops spared from France, amounted to some 20,000 men and the speed with which they had been assembled created for the general the problem of extended supply lines. It suited Howard in his report of the campaign to give a vastly inflated estimate of the size of the Scottish army and surviving accounts claim that James brought between 80,000 and 100,000 men into England. The reality is likely to have been closer to 30,000, including a small French contingent. It was, however, still formidable in that it was half as large again as the English host and was equipped with several impressive pieces of field artillery. But James was not without his logistics problems. The further he pressed into enemy territory the more extenuated his communication system became. He also needed to keep his amorphous cohort under as tight control as possible. His ill-disciplined Highlanders might easily be lured away by the chance of plunder while his more faint-hearted followers grew more nervous with every English mile. For these reasons a pitched battle, rather than a series of running engagements, suited both commanders.

James passed over the Tweed on 22 August, overthrew the fortified strongholds of Norham, Etal and Ford and had made his headquarters at the latter by the end of the month. And there he stayed, his main camp established nearby on the heights above Flodden. Surrey, meanwhile, assembled all his contingents at Alnwick, some thirty miles to the south-east and it was there that his sons joined him. The weather was foul; a cold rain sweeping across Lammermuir turned the roads into quagmires as the grumbling soldiers left Alnwick and trudged towards the enemy. More than ever Surrey needed a quick conclusion but the prospect looked far from good. He was marching towards a superior enemy occupying a strong position, for James, having taken the precaution of dismantling the fortifications at Ford, had now joined his army at Flodden.

The Earl Marshal, veteran soldier as he was, knew that to storm Flodden

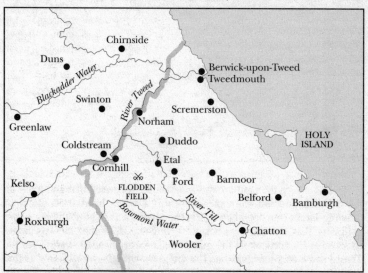

The Scottish border country

Hill would be suicidal. Somehow he had to lure the Scots from their vantage point. To this end he tried to play on James's chivalric nature by sending Rouge Croix pursuivant, the herald accompanying the army, to challenge his adversary to meet him with his host in open field. This received the eminently reasonable reply, 'his grace will take and keep his ground at his own pleasure'.[12] Surrey bypassed the Scottish position on the opposite side of the River Till and set up his sodden camp at Barmoor. On the evening of 8 September the prospects for the English could hardly have looked more bleak: 'there was little or no wine, ale, nor beer for the people to be refreshed with but all the army for the most part were enforced and constrained of necessity to drink water . . . without comfort or trust of any relief in that behalf'[13] and the situation was not improved by the knowledge that the Scottish camp was well provisioned and that James and his nobles slept on feather beds. Many of Surrey's men, some of whom may well have suffered similar privations under Howard's leadership on the Guyenne venture, were close to mutiny. It was at this point that the younger Thomas Howard came up with a plan.

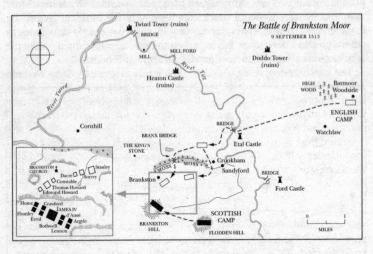

Reconnoitring the land around Flodden, he theorised that an attack on the Scottish position from the *north* might have the desired effect of drawing James into open battle. His suggestion was to bluff the King into believing that his supply lines were threatened or that he was being checked at Flodden while the main English army headed straight for the Tweed and a counter-invasion. The difficulty with this stratagem was that James had chosen his ground well and his rear was protected by a mile-and-a-half stretch of marshy ground known as Brankston Moss. Thomas's investigation, however, revealed some firmer ground and a simple bridge at the centre of this swamp. He persuaded his father to allow him to lead the vanguard via this route in the hope of provoking Scottish retaliation. The plan seems to have been that Surrey with the main army and the artillery would skirt Brankston Moss and join the fray, forcing James to divide his host. It was a hazardous manoeuvre and one which seems out of character with what we know of Thomas Howard. While struggling through the swamp he and his men would be at the mercy of the Scottish guns. If they crossed in fair order they would be obliged to fight with the marsh at their back. It may be that Thomas was intent on proving himself as brave and impulsive as his dead brother. More pragmatically, the tactics may suggest nothing beyond Surrey's need for a quick battle.

The following dawn saw Thomas and Edmund Howard and Sir Marmaduke Constable captaining the three contingents of the vanguard and marching towards the Till. It was afternoon before astonished watchers on Flodden Hill observed the English struggling across the swampy ground. Legends abound about this battle. One has James's master gunner beseeching the King with tears in his eyes to batter the helpless enemy with his artillery only to be informed that this would be dishonourable. What James did do was order the burning of large piles of camp rubbish and, under cover of the smokescreen it provided, move his host to Brankston Hill, thus covering the English line of advance without forsaking the advantage of high ground. His vanguard, led by Lords Hume and Huntley, descended in good order and were upon the Howard contingents before they realised what was happening. In the ensuing hand-to-hand struggle Thomas's men fared well but Edmund's force was routed and the Lord Admiral was obliged to go to his aid.

Seeing the English reverse on his left, the Scottish King now committed the blunder which lost him the day. He couched his lance and led a thunderous downhill charge against Surrey's contingent. This was exactly what the Earl Marshal had hoped for; a pitched battle on level ground, with the enemy spread along a wide front. But the result was still no foregone conclusion. The combat in the centre was violent and fierce with neither side breaking off. Not until Sir Edward Stanley appeared with the remainder of the English army and turned the Scots' right wing was the issue decided. As the evening darkened, King James was struck down in the midst of the fray and the day was lost. The carnage by contemporary standards was truly appalling. The Scots lost perhaps 10,000 fighting men including several nobles. No battle more demoralised a nation than Flodden.

> The flowers of the forest that fought aye the foremost,
> The prime of our land lie cold in the clay.[14]

CHAPTER 9

Friends, Lovers and Creatures

The Howards stayed to see the 1,500 English dead respectfully buried, and the battlefield protected as far as possible from local scavengers whose families had, for generations, profited one way or another from cross-border violence. Surrey dubbed several knights including Edmund Howard whose bravery and effectiveness had certainly not been conspicuous. Then the victors turned south, bearing with them in triumph the embalmed body of James IV of Scotland. The Earl had certainly carried out his threat to make the King 'sorry' for keeping him away from the French war. Left to mount an inglorious rearguard, Surrey had fought the bloodiest and most conclusive battle of the reign and one which made Henry's sieges of Thérouanne and Tournai look very small beer. Now his task was to ensure that the King understood just what had been achieved in the hope that he might recognise Howard services in some tangible form. He lost no time in sending to Queen Catherine, Henry's regent, a detailed report of the campaign accompanied by a powerful visual aid – James IV's slashed and blood-soaked surcoat. He directed his own first-hand account to France to augment the summary Henry's consort provided – together with the gory trophy. Edmund, typically and to excuse his own lacklustre performance, wrote to grumble that some of Stanley's Cheshire levies had deserted him in the thick of the battle – a complaint Henry chose to ignore. The Howards had no opportunity to speak personally to the King for several weeks. Henry was investing Tournai when the first news of Flodden arrived and after it had fallen he devoted three weeks to exuberant festivities. The Howards were not invited to join the jousting, feasting and dancing. Perhaps the presence of the victors of Flodden would have taken the gilt off the royal gingerbread. Some might have identified an unfortunate Old Testament parallel: 'Saul has slain his thousands and David his tens of thousands.' Only at the end of October, when Henry came to Calais to embark for England did he meet up with his Lord Admiral and offer congratulations, and he had been home several days before he wrote 'loving letters' to the other captains. Henry's vanity was heavily invested in the French enterprise and his accomplishments had high diplomatic significance so no one dared say or do anything that might appear to overshadow the humiliation the fledgeling King of England had inflicted upon his wily and experienced brother of France. Catherine was careful to refer to Flodden as her husband's victory won in his name by God's grace, through the bravery of his captains and we may be sure that everyone else was just as circumspect in their references to it.

The prize Surrey coveted was the restoration to his house of the dukedom of Norfolk and he felt that his recent services, including the sacrifice of his second son, must have washed away the last vestiges of the stain of Bosworth. He had his friend Bishop Ruthal plant the idea in Wolsey's mind that Lord Howard might be elevated to the highest rank and the King's acquiescence is likely to have owed something to his Almoner's advocacy. The patent was issued in the following February: Thomas Howard senior became Duke of Norfolk and his heir was nominated Earl of Surrey in his own right.

Yet, the circumstances surrounding these grants suggest that there were still qualifications about Henry's appreciation of the Howards. First of all the family were not allowed to enjoy their promotion in isolation; two earls and two dukes were created on the same day. Charles Brandon, less than nine months after his viscountcy, was made Duke of Suffolk and Charles Somerset, Baron Herbert, was created Earl of Worcester. Both the other men honoured had been with Henry in France and their sharing of centre stage during the impressive ceremonies at Lambeth Palace on Candlemas Day was a pointed visual reminder that Henry would exalt whom he wanted, when he wanted. And there were more signals to be picked up by those who had an eye to the finer nuances of royal favour. Subtle distinctions were made in the letters patent accompanying the new appointments. The Howards were specifically rewarded for Flodden but the King recognised Somerset's long and faithful service and acknowledged that it was the high esteem in which he held Brandon which had unlocked his generous bounty. Heraldic symbols were of the utmost importance to the prestige conscious in Tudor England. The permission granted to Norfolk to add a bend to his arms carrying the Scottish demi-lion pierced with an arrow was a permanent endorsement of Flodden but it did not look very impressive beside the achievement of the new Earl of Worcester which carried, within a border, the quartered arms of England and France.*

The truth underlying all this was that, while the King could not avoid publicly recognising the debt owed by Crown and people to the house of Howard, he had no affection for its members. Others of the royal entourage towered above them in terms of personality and of the trust reposed in them by Henry. It was these men who featured prominently in tournays and court ceremonial and enjoyed high-profile roles when

*The new grant was a revival of the Beaufort arms, Charles being an illegitimate son of Henry Beaufort, Duke of Somerset, who perished in the Lancastrian cause in 1464.

representatives were needed in foreign courts. Somerset was chamberlain of the King's household and Lord Mountjoy occupied the same position in Catherine's entourage. Both men were assigned important tasks in Henry's prized new possession of Tournai: Mountjoy was the King's lieutenant, whom the citizens were instructed to reverence and obey as they would their sovereign, and Somerset was charged with redesigning the fortifications of a city Henry intended, initially at least, to use as a springboard for further conquest. When dignity and grandeur had to be supplied to delicate foreign missions it was men like Suffolk, Worcester, Dorset and Lord Berners who were assigned to lead them. But the two men closest to the King, who were made by him and received a breathtaking outpouring of grants, honours, titles and favours from the royal cornucopia, were Charles Brandon and Thomas Wolsey.

For Surrey there was to be no basking in post-Flodden glory at court. The war rumbled on and he was sent back to sea to harry French shipping and coastal towns. Not being the charismatic leader his brother had been, it took him a while to reassert his authority in the fleet. Where Edward had been an inspirational commander who led from the front, Thomas drove his men into action with cajolery, fits of temper and threats. Nor did he hesitate to use the powers of life and death over his crews that his commission permitted him. Surrey lacked the imagination and the self-confidence amounting to recklessness that had so endeared his brother to those who followed him. His were the solid virtues of the officer who played strictly by the book, anxious to do the right thing and to be seen by his superiors to be doing the right thing.

Once he got his ships across the Channel Howard was in his element. Short forays of destruction against unprotected towns and villages could be accomplished without creating logistical headaches. Having his fleet operating in home waters and only away a few days or weeks at a time reduced to a minimum the problems of supplies and repairs. And the reports he sent the King made impressive reading. For example, in mid-June Surrey exulted that he had devastated a seven-mile swathe of land around Cherbourg (which was too well defended for him to attempt) and left nothing standing but churches and abbeys. His men had burned several gentlemen's houses 'well builded and stuffed with hangings and be[d furnishings?] of silk, of which neither they nor our men have little profitted for all or the more part was burned'.[15] We must take with a pinch of salt the Lord Admiral's claim that his officers and men did not engage in private pillage; this was the chief attraction for his troops. The suggestion that the English marauders were motivated by loyalty to their sovereign, were indifferent to personal gain and were men under strict discipline would, Surrey calculated, play well with the King.

This phase of activity soon came to an abrupt end. About the time that Howard and his men were rampaging through the Normandy countryside news reached London of a secret truce signed by Ferdinand and Louis. Henry was furious at being deserted by his ally and immediately entered into his own peace negotiations with the French King. The centrepiece of the treaty signed in August was a marriage between Louis and Henry's younger sister, Mary. This introduces an intriguing episode involving Henry, Mary, Brandon, Wolsey, the French court and the Howards which, though still clouded with wisps of mystery, does provide fascinating insights into the characters of the leading actors in the drama. Henry had to have about him men and women who were 'strong'. They needed physical stamina to keep pace with the energetic routine of the royal household but more than that they had to be 'good company'; outward-going people who knew what they believed and felt and who expressed themselves vigorously. Severally, they reflected aspects of the King's own personality – companions who could match him in tiltyard exertions, sparkling conversation, bawdy humour or madcap revels. But the young monarch, consciously or unconsciously, also needed them to be people from whom he could learn – whether about seduction, classical scholarship, military strategy or international diplomacy. In the early years of the reign Henry's exuberance covered the insecurity of a young man of little experience and it is no coincidence that his closest confidants were men and women of strong will and character – his first two wives, Wolsey, More, Edward Howard, and Charles Brandon.

Brandon was, in his earlier years, a very forceful presence at the Tudor court. The *arriviste* of whom Erasmus made the snide remark about being turned from a stable boy into a nobleman was the equivalent of a modern sporting celebrity with a macho public image and a dubious private life. Some seven or eight years older than his sovereign, he had been a companion of Henry's for as long as the King could remember. Charles can have had little or no recollection of his father but grew up with proud stories of the national hero who had shared exile with the Earl of Richmond and been cut down defending the red rose standard at Bosworth. The orphan was taken into the royal household and raised with the new King's sons. From being a kind of elder brother to the young Prince Brandon became Henry's alter ego. The two young men were similar in build, in their love of sport and in the roistering escapades that marked the early years of the new reign.

There was a strong animal magnetism about Brandon which many women found difficult to resist. As well as his clandestine amours he had a matrimonial record which was as colourful as it was calculating and amoral. His first marriage, to Anne Browne, probably a love match, was conveniently set aside on the grounds of consanguinity when a rich widow, Margaret Mortimer, became available but she, in turn, was discarded and Brandon returned to Anne, the relationship barrier having been, somehow, cleared away. When Anne died in 1512 he lost no time in contracting marriage with his rich young ward, Elizabeth Grey, a cousin of the Marquess of Dorset. In right of Elizabeth an indulgent King nominated Brandon as Baron Lisle and he continued to enjoy the dignity even after Elizabeth declined the honour of sharing her life with the notorious womaniser.

Unfazed by this rebuff, Brandon and his royal friend were soon plotting a more exalted alliance. During the 1513 campaigning, Charles, aided and abetted by the King, paid court to the thirty-three-year-old Archduchess Margaret, Regent of the Netherlands and daughter of the Emperor Maximilian. Initially the good lady dismissed the approach as a silly flirtation but the following year the ardent suitor, now Duke of Suffolk, reappeared in Lille to press his suit more energetically.

At this point another player entered the game of courtly romance and high politics. Princess Mary, an eighteen-year-old young woman who was, by all accounts, genuinely beautiful and certainly possessed the Tudor trait of stubbornness, set her cap at the attractive Charles Brandon. The friendship they had long shared as members of the royal inner circle blossomed into love – at least on the lady's part. But princesses were not free to follow the dictates of the heart. They were bargaining counters on the exchequer board of international diplomacy and Mary had, in fact, long been betrothed to Prince Charles of Castille, the heir of King Ferdinand and the Emperor Maximilian. This singular political coup had been brought off by Henry VII and he regarded it as one of the major triumphs of his statesmanship. However, years passed and it became clear that the Habsburgs had gone cold on the alliance. When, in 1514, Ferdinand 'treacherously' made peace with France, the common enemy, Henry was furious. Talks were immediately started with French emissaries and young Mary was put forward as a bride for the decrepit, fifty-two-year-old Louis XII.

It is not difficult to envisage Mary's dismay. Having accustomed herself to the idea of marriage with a glittering prince close to her own age (he was three years younger) she now found herself faced with the physical advances of a gouty old man living amongst courtiers who regarded England as their country's natural enemy. She did not hesitate to express her revulsion to her brother and angry scenes ensued. Mary afterwards claimed that they had reached an understanding: she would consent to be Louis's wife but when she became Louis's widow (which could scarcely be very far off) she would be allowed to choose her own husband. Henry's recollection of the conference may well have differed from his sister's.

In mid-September a disconsolate Princess set off for France. There seems to have been some suggestion at one stage that her entourage should have been headed up by Wolsey but in the event the Duke of Norfolk was chosen for this honour and the Howard clan turned out in force to participate in this important diplomatic event. It was, perhaps, some recompense for missing the previous year's martial cavalcade. Exactly why the Duke should have been preferred over the churchman is not wholly clear. Perhaps, Henry felt that the old soldier would have less truck with Mary if she tried any of her tantrums on him. Peace with France having been agreed, the King certainly did not want anything to sour relations between the two courts and Howard will have been instructed to ensure maximum harmony between the Princess's party and their French hosts.

Surrey, as Lord Admiral, was responsible for seeing his father and his father's royal charge safely across the water. What happened over the next three weeks almost turned into the worst disaster of his career. First of all embarkation was delayed for fifteen days while a savage autumn gale lashed the coast. Henry and his queen had come down to Dover to see Mary off and her deferred departure made the leave-taking all the more difficult when it did happen. It was a weeping Princess who took a clinging farewell of her brother on 30 September to go on shipboard. That was when the real trouble started. The convoy had hardly worn out of the harbour before the weather turned again. For four days and nights the ships were thrown to and fro on the heaving waters of the narrows, their elegant passengers prostrate with seasickness and fear. Mary's vessel was separated from the fleet and the Howards must have passed several panic-stricken hours, terrified that she might have come to grief. She almost did. Being, at last, within sight of Boulogne her ship juddered to a halt on a sandbank. The Princess had to be rowed ashore in a small boat before collapsing, soaked and retching on the beach.

She had scarcely recovered from her ordeal when her impatient bridegroom met her at Abbeville two days later, bizarrely affecting the dress style of a younger man. The wedding took place on 9 October but immediately disagreements broke out between the leaders of the French court and Mary's English entourage. Louis ordered his wife's personal servants to be dismissed and replaced by his own people. To the new Queen this was an outrage and one to which, in her opinion, Norfolk had submitted all too easily. She lost no time in complaining to her brother:

> ... on the morning next after the marriage my chamberlain with all other men servants were discharged and likewise my mother Guildford* with other my women and maidens, except such as never had experience nor knowledge how to advertise or give me counsel in any time of need ... as my mother Guildford can more plainly show your Grace than I can write; to whom I beseech you to give credence. And if it may be by any means possible, I humbly require you to cause my said mother

*Joan, widow of Sir Richard Guildford and sister of Sir Nicholas Vaux, Lieutenant of Guisnes, had been Mary's nurse and confidante for years.

Guildford to repair hither once again . . . I marvel much that my Lord of Norfolk would at all times so lightly grant everything at their requests here. I am well assured that when you know the truth of everything as my mother Guildford can show you, you would full little have thought I should have been thus intreated . . . would God my Lord of York had come with me in the room of Norfolk: for then am I sure I should have been left much more at my heart['s ease] than I am now.[16]

Mary wrote in much the same vein to Wolsey, referring to Joan Guildford as someone by whose wisdom 'the king and you bade me in every wise to be counselled'.[17] What she did not say was that Norfolk had taken the opportunity of thinning Mary's entourage to place his own clients among her attendants. This suspicion was noted by Charles Brandon in a letter to the Archbishop. Suffolk had been sent over separately as a witness of the marriage and as a personal emissary to Louis, to urge him to enter an aggressive alliance against Spain. Suffolk knew that the Howards strongly disapproved of the recent volte-face of English policy. They shared the Francophobia indulged by most of Henry's subjects and, in Brandon's submission, since they dared not voice their opinions in Council, they were using every other means at their disposal to sabotage Anglo-French relations, including trying to engineer his own recall. Norfolk 'loves neither you nor me', he told Wolsey, 'wherefore, my Lord, I beseech you hold your hand fast that I be not sent for back; for I am sure that the father and the son would for no good I should [reach agreement] with the French king'.[18] Wolsey noted all these things and he did take action. As soon as the Howards had returned to England he wrote a careful letter to Louis suggesting that he had been ill advised to banish Lady Guildford from Mary's entourage.

Brandon stayed on for the Queen's coronation and took part in the jousts celebrating the event. It must have been heartbreaking for Mary to sit next to her aged husband and watch her dashing young champion displaying his skill and athleticism. He left the French court on 15 December bearing messages for Henry and Wolsey from Their Majesties of France declaring their love for their brother monarch and the complete confidence they reposed in Suffolk. By the end of the month he was back in London. He thus missed by a few days the death of King Louis XII of France (1 January 1515).

Mary should have been delighted that her ordeal had been far shorter than she had dared hope but her husband's death had complicated her life. Clad all in white, she shut herself away for the statutory period of mourning. She longed to be allowed home but for that she was dependent on the favour of the new King, Francis I, Louis's cousin, and he had designs to use the Dowager Queen on the marriage market. Henry wanted his sister back – and for much the same reason. He would have no hesitation about setting aside for *raison d'état* any pledge that he had made to Mary and was already toying once again with a Habsburg marriage alliance. He wrote instructing his sister not to make any promises to Francis – and received a very sharp reply to his letter. The distraught young woman was in a state of despair. Francis's visits, which mingled attempts at seduction with talk of dynastic unions, terrified her. All she could do was hope against hope that somehow her champion would ride to her rescue.

And that is precisely what happened. At the end of January Henry despatched Charles Brandon to express his condolences to Francis I and to arrange for Mary's return. The choice of emissary is extraordinary. Suffolk's ambition and Mary's feelings for him were the subject of court gossip. The King and Wolsey even had a serious talk with the Duke forbidding him to raise the subject of marriage with the Queen Dowager of France. But why send him at all? He was certainly popular at the French court and it was important to entrust a high-ranking representative with such delicate matters. Norfolk was out of the question because of his anti-French sentiments but there were other nobles who could have managed the job. It was almost as though Henry was throwing the young lovers together.

Before Suffolk's arrival Mary, perhaps to keep Francis at bay, had told him that she and Brandon had made a solemn pledge to each other and that she was resolved to marry none other. The French King immediately changed his tune and promised to support the proposed match. It had become clear to him that he could not use the Queen Dowager in his own matrimonial schemes without Henry's agreement. That being so, the next best solution was to see her taken out of the international bride market altogether. What happened when Brandon arrived is best related in the anxious words he wrote Henry:

> . . . when I came to Paris the Queen was in hand with me the first day I [came], and said she must be short with me and [open] to me her pleasure and mind: and so she b[egan] to show how good lady [she] was to me, and if I would be ordered by her she would never have none but me . . .

She feared that if they returned unwed to England they would not be allowed to marry.

> . . . she said that the best in France had [said] unto her that, and she went into England, she should go into Flanders (i.e. to be married to Prince Charles). To the which she said that she had rather to be torn in pieces than ever she should come there, and with that wept. Sir, I never saw woman so weep; and when I saw [that] I showed unto her grace that

there was none such thing [upon] my faith, with the best words I could: but in none ways I could make her to believe it.

Brandon claimed that he told Mary about the promise he had made to the King – a promise he dared not break. The determined young woman was ready for that argument.

. . . Whereunto, in conclusion, she said, 'If the King my brother is content and the French King both, the one by his letters and the other by his words, that I should have [y]ou, I will [choose] the time after my desire, or else I may well think that the [reports] are . . . true and that is that you are come to take me home [to the in]tent that I may be married into Fland[ers], which I will never, to die for it; and so [informed] the French King before you came . . . [if] you will not be content to follow [my] lead, look never after this d[ay to have] the offer again.' . . . and so she and I were married.[19]

At the same time Suffolk wrote to Wolsey, urging him to intercede with the King and describing in more detail Francis's enthusiastic support for the match. The letter, dated 3 February, also hints at the political situation at home, suggesting that in the matter of friendship with France he and Wolsey and the King are standing alone against 'the council as all the other nobles of the realm'.[20]

Five days later he was passing on more specific information about the activities of his enemies' agents. A certain Friar Langley, one of Norfolk's appointees to Mary's household, had been trying to poison her mind, 'advising her to beware of me of all men, for he knew that you and I meddled with [the] devil and by the puissance of the said [devil] we kept our master subject . . . He did not make this overture without a schoolmaster.'[21]

Wolsey's response to the impetuous couple's entreaties was to assure them of his support and his promise to bring the affair to 'a successful conclusion'. He insisted that he was the Duke's 'firm friend' and he shared Brandon's sense of being part of a daring and delicious conspiracy against the jealous and disapproving members of court and Council. Should the King be persuaded by these hostile elements not to allow Charles and Mary to return as husband and wife, 'all men here, except his grace and myself, would be right glad'.[22]

The central enigma in this episode is Henry's real attitude. Was he genuinely taken by surprise and therefore angry with his sister and his friend or had he been, to some degree, an aider and abetter in the escapade, viewing it perhaps as a real-life version of those disguisings and court revels he and his close companions so often indulged in? Mary, who presumably knew her brother better than anyone, believed that he was furious. 'Pleaseth it your Grace,' she wrote sometime in February, 'to my heartiest discomfort, sorrow and disconsolation but lately I have been advertised of the great and high displeasure which your Highness beareth to me and my Lord of Suffolk for the marriage between us . . . I will not in any wise deny but that I have offended your Grace, for the which I do put myself most humbly in your clemency and mercy.'[23] Yet at the same time that he was expressing shocked disbelief at his friend's effrontery, Henry was making him a substantial grant of lands to support his dignity as royal brother-in-law (see below).

Suffolk, somewhat ungallantly, represented himself as having had his arm twisted by Mary, aided by the French King and begged Henry not to allow his enemies to triumph. 'Your Grace knoweth best,' he protested, 'I never sought other remedy against mine enemies but your Grace . . . for it is your Grace that has made me . . . and holden me up hitherto, and if your [pleasure] be so for to do, I care not for all the world.'[24] Despite such protestations, Suffolk and his bride, either through calculation or unbridled passion, proceeded to put matters beyond recall, as the Duke confessed to Wolsey in secret: 'to be plain with you, I have married her heartily and lain with her, insomuch [as] I fear me that she [may] be with child'.[25] Wolsey recognised this crossing of the Rubicon as an act of folly and defiance that Henry might find difficult to forgive. It was a *fait accompli* that had forced him into either rejecting the lovers or welcoming them back and, thereby, seeming to endorse their presumption. The clandestine wedding ceremony could easily have been set aside but now that the scapegraces had had the effrontery to consummate their marriage that option had gone. To Henry their action smacked almost of blackmail – especially as Mary had written hysterically to say that she would enter a nunnery if Henry tried to come between her and her husband.

Wolsey was scarcely less angry than his master. He had been working to create a situation that would have enabled Henry to receive the Brandons back at court in due course with the minimum of adverse comment and diplomatic inconvenience. Now he had been put in the position of breaking the news to Henry (keeping it secret was out of the question, he told the Duke) and withstanding the royal wrath. The King ranted at him: he would have thought that Brandon would have been torn by wild horses rather than break his vow. 'Cursed be the blind affection and counsel that have brought ye to [this],' he scolded. 'Such sudden and ill-advised dealing shall have sudden repentance.'[26] Wolsey knew that he, too, might have been compromised. The Howards and their conciliar allies were producing evidence that Suffolk was in league with Francis and demanding that he be brought back to face treason charges. If they gained the upper hand they would not hesitate to try to implicate the Brandons' confidant.

Fortunately, when Henry calmed down he was more concerned about laying his hands on Mary's dowry and the fabulous jewels that her late husband had bestowed upon her. He decided that his royal honour would be assuaged if Suffolk could extract these from the French King and also make financial restitution on his own behalf. Brandon was far from successful in meeting all Henry's terms but he and his wife were allowed to begin their homeward journey in mid-April. Even then they were kept waiting for several days in Calais for permission to embark. Only then did they realise how unpopular they had become with many of their fellow countrymen, for they had to barricade their lodging against a mob screaming abuse at them. Not until they reached Dover to be greeted by a smiling Wolsey and were conveyed hence to the royal court at Barking where Henry received them with open arms were their anxieties finally assuaged.

This incident demonstrates clearly that with Henry VIII personal considerations always came first. It mattered not how disreputable or unpopular a man was or how many poisonous accusations were made about him by his court rivals: Henry could be almost reckless in the trust he reposed in those who took his fancy. In the early years the King was generous and loyal to a degree towards members of his inner circle. That is why the royal favourites were essential intermediaries for all who aspired to Crown patronage and why there is little evidence of factions at the Tudor court before the 1530s. The Howards loathed Brandon as an upstart and resented his closeness to the King and they had other reasons for heartily desiring his downfall. His elevation to the dukedom of Suffolk gave him administrative significance and a power base in East Anglia where the Howards had become accustomed to holding sway. Worse was to follow. In 1514 the new peer had been granted some of the estates confiscated from Edmund de la Pole the previous Duke of Suffolk but other lands belonging to the attainted Yorkist family were retained by the Crown. Then, a year later, at precisely the time of the marriage scandal, Henry made over to his friend all the remaining de la Pole lands – including one parcel valued at over £700 per annum which had previously been held by the Earl of Surrey. The signal to the Howards could hardly have been stronger: the King would bestow his favour where he chose. Even when Brandon was at his most vulnerable his rivals dared take no concerted action against him.

The same was true in equal measure of Wolsey and there is a real parallel between the Archbishop and the Duke of Suffolk, for both men were literally Henry's 'creatures'. It was inevitable that they should be 'friends' and give each other mutual support. The picture that emerges from their correspondence in the opening weeks of 1515 is of a little caucus – Henry, Wolsey, Brandon – ranged against a disapproving majority of the King's senior advisers who hated the *arrivistes* and their influence but lacked the power and the concerted will to act against them.

Wolsey's advance in the first years of the reign was as remarkable as Brandon's. The royal Almoner's correspondence with his mentor, Richard Fox, provides a running commentary on a rise which might otherwise seem incredible. In September 1511 Wolsey was a useful go-between for the Bishop: 'Yesterday at mass,' he wrote, 'I broke with the King on this matter and showed him how much honour and also furtherance of all his affairs in time to come should ensue to him.'[27] At this point Wolsey was very much his master's eyes and ears at court. Eight months later the Bishop still relied on his protégé for information but acknowledged that Wolsey had grown in importance: 'I require you, though I know well ye have no leisure to write me news yourself, make Bryan Tuke [Clerk of the Signet and Wolsey's secretary] by your information write me soon.'[28] But only a few weeks further on (June 1513) Fox had assumed a deferential, even apologetic tone. Explaining that his slowness in replying to Wolsey's letters was because of delays in the post, he assured the royal Almoner that he had risen from his bed in the middle of the night in order to respond.[29] In April 1514 Fox's wishes had become subservient to those of the younger man. Sending some documents to Wolsey he wrote, 'I pray you look upon them and advise me as ye shall see cause.'[30] By this time Wolsey had become Bishop of Lincoln and Fox no longer addressed him as 'Brother Master Almoner' but as 'My singular good lord'.

It was Wolsey's conviviality, his dedication to an adventurous foreign policy, his assistance in freeing the King from the restraining influence of the Council and his capacity for sheer hard work which commended him to Henry. But the advance of the Ipswich butcher's son to be *de facto* viceroy of England might not have been so easy had it not been for a tragic occurrence in 1512. In that year the palace of Westminster was gutted by fire. The residential apartments were all destroyed. Only Westminster Hall and the adjoining offices, including Star Chamber, where the Council occasionally met, were spared. Thus, while the work of government could continue there was no room for the royal court. Greenwich was the nearest palace with sufficient accommodation for the King's entourage.

Within two years the pattern of government business changed dramatically. The immense amount of work involved in masterminding the war effort increasingly demanded Wolsey's presence, with other leading councillors, at Westminster. This was potentially dangerous for the ambitious Almoner: it meant that others who had the King's ear on a daily basis might upset his plans. It was as a member of the Council with the King that Wolsey had been able to impress Henry with his grasp of national and international affairs. As long as the small group of Henry's personal advisers was able to initiate or change policy they could upset the plans on which he was working throughout laborious days and, often, sleepless nights.

He had two ways of counteracting any such trends. The first was to maintain contact with and impress his personality on the young ruler. The fun-loving, easily distracted Henry of these early years could be 'managed' as long as he could be persuaded that he was the real instigator of the policies pursued in his name. Wolsey convinced the King that he knew better than his unimaginative advisers and that he was fortunate in being served by the cleverest chief minister in Christendom. With amazing rapidity a routine of communication and decision-making fell into place which was to remain operative for many years. Written and oral messages passed back and forth between King and minister every day and both men kept sufficient couriers and horses on hand to maintain an efficient service. When Henry was at Greenwich Wolsey reported to him in person every Sunday, the regular ritual becoming a popular spectacle which children and tourists were taken to see in the same way that, generations later, 'Christopher Robin went down with Alice' to witness the changing of the guard. The Archbishop left his palace in his polychromed and gilded barge attended by a large, liveried retinue and travelled downstream to Paul's Stairs or Queenhithe. Here horses were waiting to convey the party in solemn procession through the City. Below the bridge and its treacherous rapids Wolsey boarded another barge for the final stage of the journey to Greenwich.

Wolsey's other ploy was to keep possible rivals busy at Westminster. He greatly increased the routine work and particularly the judicial activity of the Council (often called 'the whole council' to distinguish it from 'the council attendant upon the king') which met daily in Star Chamber during legal term time. It would, however, be putting the cart before the horse to suggest that the vigorous development of the superior court of law was merely a subtle stratagem by which Wolsey could keep his eyes on potential rivals. The creation of a more just society and the extension of the King's peace to all subjects were issues about which Wolsey cared passionately. The structure of society which enabled the rich and powerful to exploit their inferiors and wage local war on each other with little compunction had not changed in the few years since Henry VII and his unpopular ministers had attempted to make a reality of royal justice. Wolsey set himself to invigorate the courts and establish greater respect for law and order at all levels of society. The strengthening of conciliar justice in Star Chamber was a part of this process. Wolsey was determined to demonstrate publicly that no one, whatever his estate, was exempt and that all would-be malefactors should learn, 'the new law of the Star Chamber which, God willing, they shall have indifferently ministered to them according to their deserts'.[31] Litigants who believed that they had suffered in local courts at the hands of perjured witnesses, intimidated juries and justices who abused the law to maintain their own power were encouraged to bring their complaints into Star Chamber. It still took courage and persistence to stand up to the leaders of shire society and the process of effective reform was inevitably slow. Sir Richard Sacheverell, a Leicestershire landowner who was a not infrequent visitor to the Tudor court and a member of the whole council, was just one shameless offender who was only with difficulty brought to heel. It was said of him in his locality that 'he cometh with such a company that he ruleth the whole [assize] court' and that newly sworn jurors were left in no doubt by Sacheverell agents about where their best interests lay. It took more than a decade for the knight's victims to have him subpoenaed to appear in Star Chamber but subpoenaed he eventually was (sadly, gaps in the records prevent us knowing the outcome).[32]

Wolsey did not wait for complaints to reach Westminster. He was not slow to initiate proceedings on behalf of the Crown. In 1516, when Queen Margaret of Scotland paid a state visit to her brother, some members of the Council attended a reception accompanied by retainers in their own liveries. This display of independence could not be tolerated and Wolsey initiated an in-depth investigation into illegal retaining. Once again, Sir Richard Sacheverell was one of the offenders but several bigger fish were trawled by the Star Chamber net. They included Lords Hastings and Bergavenny and the Marquess of Dorset, all of whom faced the humiliation of answering formal charges before the royal judges.[33]

Three years later the long arm of Star Chamber reached into Surrey to tap the shoulders of other perverters of justice, including the feckless Edmund Howard. It was reported to Wolsey that 'the good rule and execution of justice in the county of Surrey hath been of long time letted and misused by the great maintenance, embracery and bearing* [of parties at law] to the great hurt and damage of the king's subjects'. Of the three local leaders accused, two stoutly rejected the accusations against them and duly suffered close examination in Star Chamber (though, again, the outcome is not known). Lord Edmund, who knew that his stock was already very low in royal circles and that the Howard name would avail him little, made a grovelling confession and pleaded with Wolsey and his colleagues 'to be mediators to the king's highness' for him.[34]

Over the years several members of the royal household and men who were prominent in their own shires felt the hot breath of Wolsey's Star Chamber on their necks. Thus Wolsey continued the policy which had been begun by Henry VII and his ministers of concentrating all power in royal hands. Whether mighty subjects sought to build their power and prestige by attendance on the King or by strengthening their political positions in the provinces, they found it difficult to escape the minister's scrutiny. Moreover, by involving many members of this class in the

---

*Maintenance = wrongfully abetting litigants; embracery = corruptly suborning juries; bearing = putting pressure on witnesses.

judicial activities of the Council Wolsey made it next to impossible for them to reinvigorate old feudal loyalties and alliances against the government. His methods were more subtle than those of Empson and Dudley – the re-introduction of swingeing fines might still have provoked dangerous resentments – but the end result was very much the same; the 'taming' of the nobility. The leaders of those houses which had survived the baronial wars were kept busy supervising the household offices, parading themselves on ceremonial occasions, captaining the King's armies and helping to despatch conciliar business. The one traditional function denied them was the duty and privilege of advising their sovereign on matters of high policy. There were those who resented this change of role but the majority acquiesced and the tiny, proud minority who preferred to stay away from court and give no support to the new *status quo* that attendance implied were closely watched.

By the middle of the decade Wolsey had effectively neutered the conciliar process. In September 1514 he was nominated Archbishop of York and moved into the archiepiscopal residence of York Place, Westminster, which henceforth became the centre of government business. A few months later he obtained a lease on Hampton Court so that he would have a no less impressive residence from which to conduct the nation's affairs when he was away from the capital. All the available evidence points to Henry as a willing collaborator in the system whereby he and his friend dealt with other advisers on a strictly need-to-know basis. In a letter to Wolsey of April 1518 one of the King's secretaries, John Clerk, reported that His Majesty 'was not only well contented with such order as you have taken in all matters, with the advice of his council there [i.e. at Westminster] but gave unto you openly, before all his council [attendant] great lauds, commendations and right hearty thanks for the same, saying these words: "that there is no man living that pondereth more the surety of his person and the commonwealth of this his realm" '. In the same letter the writer refers to certain 'London matters' raised by Wolsey that the King had enjoined Clerk 'in no wise' to mention them before the other council members.[35]

Wolsey enjoyed adorning himself grandiosely and surrounding himself with objects of beauty. He loved impressing people: both York Place and Hampton Court were extended and refurbished to the highest possible contemporary standard; in his various homes Wolsey kept a sumptuous table and his generous patronage filled them with books, paintings, bijouterie and works wrought in gold and silver; every journey he made, no matter how short, was a progress in which the minister, often seated on an ass (as befitted a servant of Christ) was dressed in costly robes and attended by cross-bearers, pikemen and liveried retainers carrying the emblems of his various offices. There is not the slightest evidence that this ostentatious display angered the King. Quite the contrary: Henry regarded it as fitting that his representative should make an impressive show. Since he chose not to go frequently abroad among the people he delighted vicariously in Wolsey's magnificent pomp. Just as Henry appropriated the praise for victories won by his generals and diplomatic triumphs achieved by his emissaries, so he regarded Wolsey's splendour as his own.

The King's support for his right-hand man was unstinting and frequently public. A report sent to Rome in 1515 when Henry was angling for Wolsey to be elevated to the cardinalate scarcely exaggerated when it affirmed 'the king can do nothing of the least importance without him and esteems him among the dearest friends'. George Cavendish, a gentleman usher to Wolsey and his first biographer, emphasised the warmth of that relationship. He recorded that Henry was a frequent and sometimes impromptu visitor and that on such occasions,

> there wanted no preparations of goodly furniture with viands of the finest sort that might be provided for money or friendship. Such pleasures were then devised for the king's comfort and consolation as might be invented or by man's wit imagined. The banquets were set forth with masques and mummeries in so gorgeous a sort and costly manner that it was an heaven to behold. There wanted no dames or damsels meet or apt to dance with the maskers or to garnish the place for the time, with other goodly disports.[36]

There is no doubt that Wolsey equipped and bedecked his palaces so gorgeously precisely so that he could thus pleasure the King and his court whenever he was called upon to do so. He well knew the value of such entertainments in fuelling the warming fire of royal favour. Among Henry's greater subjects Wolsey, alone enjoying as he did the steady flow of enormous ecclesiastical revenues, could hope to match the splendours of Henry's own household. The fact did not endear him to the leading nobles, and the gaudy opulence of his lifestyle drew hostile comment from many of the common sort but none of that mattered as long as he had the friendship of the King.

The honours and appointments continued to flow. In September 1515 Leo X yielded to the pressure of the English King and made Wolsey a cardinal. He was now supreme in the national Church but lacked a major office of State. This was remedied three months later. 'The Archbishop of Canterbury,' Thomas More soon afterwards reported to Erasmus,

> after some years of strenuous effort to secure his liberty, has at last been allowed to resign the office of Chancellor and, having secured the privacy he has so long desired, is now enjoying the delights of leisure among his books and the memories of a most successful administration. His Majesty has appointed the cardinal of York in his place, and he is doing so well

that he goes far beyond universal expectation, although this was very great on account of his other virtues, and (a very difficult achievement) wins golden opinions even after such an admirable predecessor.[37]

Humanist scholars always made a point of extolling each other's intellectual activities and we should not accept completely uncritically this picture of Warham as the aged sage ardent to relinquish all worldly affairs in order to enjoy the blessed seclusion of his library. At sixty-five he may well not have been unwilling to escape affairs of state in order to concentrate on his ecclesiastical duties but it is equally likely that Henry was happy to let him go. There was a generation gap between the King and the Archbishop; Warham's sobriety and stern-faced disapproval of the court's frivolities must have reminded Henry of his father's joyless regime. Certainly, the Chancellor did not approve the drift of foreign policy. But there was much more significance in the transfer to Wolsey of the trappings of authority. Warham had not proved himself a sufficiently pliant ecclesiastic for the King's taste. Church and State issues which had from time to time flared up among the embers ever since the days of Henry II and Becket blazed out again in two high-profile conflicts in 1514–15 (see pp. 152ff) and had ended with Henry angrily reminding his clergy that 'kings of England in time past have never had any superior but God only'.[38] This provided the King with a good reason for elevating Wolsey to a position in the Church superior to Warham. If we may believe Andrew Ammonius there was a story going around London early in 1516 that Warham had even been replaced as primate. Wolsey, 'after urgent entreaty', he confidently informed Erasmus, had been appointed Archbishop of Canterbury.[39]

CHAPTER 10

Eminence

Depriving Warham of the Great Seal may have been an expression of Henry's lack of confidence; it was certainly a further degrading of the relevance of the Council. The Cardinal was now its president and the removal of the Great Seal into Wolsey's safe-keeping deprived it of any influence over major decrees and enactments. When, in April 1516, Fox was induced to render up the Privy Seal Wolsey's control over the mechanism of royal government was complete. Thomas Ruthal, the new guardian of the seal, was the Cardinal's creature; the Venetian ambassador described him as singing treble to Wolsey's bass. Traditionally the chain of authentication and enactment began with orders under the royal signature or signet, which, after any necessary deliberations, were issued under the Privy Seal or, where required, received the endorsement of the Great Seal. After 1516 the Lord Chancellor effectively controlled the whole process. No matters of importance were initiated by the Council with the King and no laws, orders, grants or decrees could be made without the approval of the Cardinal, who, as the ultimate insurance policy, kept the Great Seal with him at all times, even when travelling abroad.

There remained one final step on the Jacob's ladder to Wolsey's personal heaven.* In 1518 Leo X wished to send Cardinal Campeggio to England as legate *a latere* to negotiate Henry's participation on a crusade against the Turk. A legate *a latere* was the top rank of papal emissary, empowered to decide and act on the Pope's behalf. European monarchs were understandably chary about admitting to their territories such officials who might be used as stalking horses for the extension of Rome's control and the King and his minister were united in their concern to limit Campeggio's authority. But Leo's passion for a campaign against the infidel could be used to personal and political advantage and the events of spring and summer 1518 reveal just how adept Wolsey was at diplomatic

*We may discount the suggestion that his ultimate ambition was to become pope. Although he did on a couple of occasions allow his candidacy to be canvassed he understood well enough the politics of the curia which ensured that St Peter's chair was an object of Italian rivalries. He also regarded himself as indispensable to the well-being of King and country, a belief endorsed by Henry.

blackmail. He made two 'requests' to Rome. The first was that in the coming negotiations he should also be appointed a legate *a latere* of equal standing with Campeggio. The second involved the pursuit of a personal vendetta against Cardinal Castellessi, who held the bishopric of Bath and Wells. The two princes of the Church were locked in a long-running dispute and Wolsey now saw his opportunity for victory. He demanded Castellessi's deprivation (on the grounds of the Italian's marginal involvement in a plot against the Pope). Leo dug his heels in. Wolsey reacted by leaving Campeggio stranded in Calais, denied a permit to cross the Channel. Only when the Pope had given way on both points was his representative allowed into England. Wolsey appropriated the temporalities of Bath and Wells to his own use, holding the see in commendam with his archbishopric, and retained his legatine powers to the end of his life.

There now existed two courts, as John Skelton famously pointed out in *Why Come Ye Not to Court?*:

> To which court?
> To the King's court?
> Or to Hampton Court?
> Nay, to the King's court!
> The King's court
> Should have the excellence;
> But Hampton Court
> Hath the pre-eminence!
> And York Place
> With, 'my lord's grace',
> To whose magnificence
> Is all the confluence,
> Suits and supplications,
> Embassies of all nations . . .

Foreign ambassadors certainly did throng Wolsey's 'court' and it is largely on the evidence of their reports that a picture of the Cardinal's supremacy has been built up. Discovering the minister's omnicompetence and the trust Henry reposed in him, the new appointee soon realised that he had to maintain a presence at York Place. The Venetian, Sebastian Giustinian, reported, 'I have informed the Signory at least a thousand times, that . . . were it a question of neglecting his majesty or his right reverend . . . lordship the least injurious course would be to pass over the former'.[40] Those who did not understand the nuances of English political life might have been forgiven for assuming that Wolsey was the real power in front of as well as behind the throne, especially if they received the rough edge of his tongue:

a few days ago the nuncio was sent for by the right reverend cardinal who . . . took him into a chamber, where he laid hands upon him, telling him in fierce and rude language that he chose to know what he had written to the King of France . . . and that he should not quit the spot until he had confessed everything and, unless he told him by fair means, that he would put him to the rack.[41]

Wolsey was a formidable, larger-than-life personality and when angry or feigning anger he could be terrible indeed. He was a consummate actor who could use to good effect not only the theatricality of pomp and ceremony, but also the high drama of well-managed emotion as when he confronted the bemused Imperial ambassadors with a 'deadly pale' countenance and implored them to tell their master 'that I, with a profusion of sighs, and as his good servant, beg him to act sincerely with this king'. When the envoys tried to discover precisely what had provoked this impassioned outburst, Wolsey enigmatically 'changed the subject abruptly and would say nothing further'.[42] Of course, the minister could allow himself to give free reign to a greater repertoire of emotions than would have been appropriate for the sovereign. This had distinct political advantages. For example, Henry and Wolsey between them achieved a considerable PR coup in 1517 when 341 bedraggled men and women guilty of a City riot were brought before the King in Westminster Hall with rope nooses round their necks, clad only in shirts and feverishly telling beads as a symbol of humble petition and submission. Coldly Henry pronounced sentence of death upon them. Wolsey thereupon prostrated himself before the throne and begged mercy on behalf of the miscreants. The King turned a deaf ear and a long-faced Cardinal conveyed the royal diktat to the doomed throng. When they heard it they fell to their knees as one man, crying out for mercy, whereupon,

the cardinal again besought his majesty most earnestly to grant them grace, some of the chief lords also doing the like. So at length the king consented to pardon them, which was announced to these delinquents by the said right reverend cardinal with tears in his eyes, and he made them a long discourse, urging them to lead good lives and comply with the royal will . . .

Giustinian's secretary, who recorded the event, permitted himself the aside, 'it was a very fine spectacle and well arranged'.[43]

Because Wolsey's brief was so wide, because he was a workaholic and because he could not or would not delegate, his antechambers were daily a-throng with suitors. Under these circumstances delay and frustration were inevitable. Giustinian soon tired of waiting upon the Cardinal and sent his secretary instead. The subordinate had to wait even longer for an audience but at least the ambassador was not wasting his time. Other petitioners were less patient and pragmatic. The Earl of Shrewsbury's representative had to follow the Cardinal from pillar to post in 1517 in order to further his master's business:

He commanded me to wait on him to the court. I followed him and there gave attendance and could have no answer. Upon Friday last he came from thence to Hampton Court, where he lieth. The morrow after I besought his grace I might know his pleasure; I could have no answer. Upon Monday last as he walked in the park at Hampton Court, I besought his grace I might know if he would command me any service. He was not content with me that I spoke to him. So that who shall be a suitor to him may have no other business but give attendance upon his pleasure. He that shall so do, it is needful should be a wiser man than I am. I saw no remedy, but came without answer, except I would have done as my Lord Dacre's servant doth, who came with letters for the king's service five months since and yet hath no answer. And another servant of the Deputy of Calais likewise who came before the other to Walsingham, I heard, when he answered them, 'If ye be not content to tary my leisure, depart when ye will.' This is truth, I had rather your Lordship commanded me to Rome than deliver him letters, and bring answers to the same.[44]

We might readily imagine that the great men of the realm who had to suffer such indignities at the hands of butcher's-son-turned-cardinal would bitterly resent not receiving the consideration they felt they deserved. They might protest at Wolsey's autocratic pride and arrogance. When he chose, Wolsey could be an accomplished massager of egos, but he did not very often choose. We might well expect, therefore, an atmosphere of growing resentment among members of the court and Council and the emergence of an anti-Wolsey aristocratic faction. Can we detect any such phenomenon? More specifically is there compelling evidence of Wolsey–Howard animosity?

The earliest chroniclers were in no doubt about the Cardinal's unpopularity. Describing the arrival of Wolsey's coveted red hat from Rome, Hall recorded how it was 'brought to London with such triumph as though the greatest prince of Christendom had come into the realm'. His account of the ceremony at St Paul's when the new Cardinal was invested was contemptuous in its tone. Wolsey was ceremoniously bedecked with all the 'vainglorious trifles' of his office, 'and when he was once a perfect cardinal he looked then above all estates, so that all men almost hated him and disdained him'.[45] Polydore Vergil agreed that Wolsey was universally despised 'not only on account of his arrogance and his low reputation for integrity, but also on account of his recent origins'.[46] However, the writings of both these hostile witnesses reflect the very changed atmosphere prevailing after the 1530s watershed. By then the great Cardinal had died in disgrace and Henry VIII's vindictiveness had been unleashed against the presumption of Rome, the ostentatious wealth of the Church hierarchy and the corruption of the clergy, all of which had been, in the common mind, personified by Wolsey.

John Skelton must be taken more seriously because his verse diatribes were contemporaneous with the personalities and events they described and because he is supposed by some to have been the mouthpiece of the 'Howard circle'. This erstwhile tutor to Prince Henry had, by 1519, become something of a turbulent priest, whose blundering career bounced between the royal court and the London stews, his Norfolk pulpit and a city jail. His personal life was as shameless as it was outrageous. On one occasion when confronted by his parishioners with the charge of openly keeping a mistress, he stood up in church brandishing a newborn baby, the latest result of his irregular lifestyle, and challenged the congregation to make of it what they would. Like many an *enfant terrible* before and since, he was simultaneously fêted and condemned by a fashionable society whose foibles and hypocrisies he constantly exposed. Satire was much in vogue at the time (see pp. 145ff) and Skelton's comments on the mores of the day are in the same vein as Sebastian Brant, Erasmus, Holbein, Alexander Barclay *et al.*, though cruder in both sentiment and execution. His attacks on Wolsey occurred in poems dating from the 1520s – *Speke, Parott; Collyn Clout* and *Why Come Ye Not to Court?*. They were comprehensive in their accusations but they were particularly incensed at the Cardinal's attitude towards his 'betters'.

> Ye are so puffed with pride
> That no man may abide
> Your high and lordly looks.
> Ye cast up then your books
> And virtue is forgotten
> For then you will be wroken [revenged]
> Of every light quarrel
> And call a lord a javel [rascal] . . .
> And if ye may have leisure,
> Ye will bring all to nought.
> And that is all your thought . . .

Collyn Clout

> No man dare come to the speech
> Of this gentle Jack Breach, [i.e. a fellow who upsets the social order]
> Of what estate he be
> Of spiritual dignity;
> Nor duke of high degree,

Nor marquess, earl nor lord;
Which shrewdly doth accord!
Thus he, born so base,
All noblemen should outface,
His countenance like a caesar.
'My lord is not at leisure . . .
And sir, you must dance attendance,
And take a patient sufference,
For my lord's grace,
Hath now no time nor space
To speak with you as yet . . .
But this mad Amalek*
Like to a Mameluke†
He regardeth lords
No more than potsherds

Why Come Ye Not to Court?

Obviously Skelton was voicing what was common currency – at least in and around London – but was he put up to it by aristocratic patrons and, specifically, by the Howards? In fact there is no reliable evidence for any such connection. The material for Skelton's life is sketchy in the extreme and what there is provides no indication of a relationship between the poet and the noble house. Neither Norfolk nor his son was a notable literary patron and, interestingly, one of the writers they did encourage and support, Alexander Barclay, was a sworn enemy of Skelton's. Nowhere does the raucous versifier eulogise members of the Howard clan, not even in three poems he wrote about the victory of Flodden. By contrast when, by 1525, he had actually found favour with Wolsey, he completely changed his tune and the vilified Cardinal became his 'most worthy patron' and the 'most honourable, most mighty, and by far the most reverend father in Christ'.[47] Perhaps Wolsey had decided that the best way to silence this yapping cur was to feed it. Perhaps that had been Skelton's intention all along – if such a wayward and frenetic spirit was capable of calculated forethought.

However, if the Howards were not bold enough to associate themselves with Skelton's sulphurous lines that does not mean that they did not agree with them and hugely enjoy them. Wolsey gave the Howards, their friends and relatives several reasons for resentment. In 1511 Master Almoner had crowed over Norfolk's discomfiture and abrupt departure from court. Three years later the two men were involved in the much more serious

---

*The Amalekites were the perpetual enemies of God and his people in the Old Testament.
†The Mamelukes were a slave caste who seized the throne of Egypt in the thirteenth century.

altercation concerning the Howard family's conduct of Mary Tudor's affairs when conveying her into France. As we have seen, this set the Princess, Wolsey and Brandon firmly against the Duke of Norfolk.

As Wolsey grew in confidence so did his determination to check the 'pretension' of the nobility. He had scarcely had time to warm the woolsack when he began rigidly to employ the laws against livery and maintenance. In May 1516 he delivered an impassioned speech to the King and Council in which he warned his colleagues that His Majesty was minded to administer justice to high and low impartially and would, if necessary, employ 'his most terrible power' against offenders whosoever they might be.[48] The Chancellor was true to his word. Within days the Earl of Northumberland was in the Fleet prison and Dorset, Bergavenny and Sir Edward Guildford were under examination. This led to a major storm in the Council. Some members left in a huff, obtaining leave from the King to return to their estates. Shrewsbury refused to come to court, disdaining to involve himself in what he splendidly referred to as the 'great snerling'. Others, however, were temporarily dismissed. Among them was the Earl of Surrey and this fracas may have been the occasion, recorded by Polydore Vergil but otherwise unsubstantiated, on which the younger Thomas Howard drew his dagger and threatened Wolsey. The mass exodus from Council and court shook Henry, and the Cardinal realised that he had gone too far. In a move not unique among politicians of all times, he passed the buck to a civil servant. The instigator of the trouble, he claimed, was Sir Henry Marney, who had displayed more 'cruelness against the great estates of this realm than any man living'.[49]

Class solidarity and personal animosities certainly existed but the temptation to identify a noble faction working against Wolsey must be resisted, as must the notion of widespread hostility towards the Cardinal's grandiloquent lifestyle. These misunderstandings rest upon a desire to find deep-seated 'causes' for Wolsey's fall. In 1519 he still had a whole decade left to him as cock of the walk. At the end of that time it was the King who, feeling betrayed by a friend who had, uncharacteristically, failed his master over an issue which touched him personally, created the conditions for a noble caucus to emerge and demonstrate their loyalty by putting the boot into the disgraced minister. And it was only in the 1530s that the caricature of Wolsey as the archetypal proud prelate emerged which was, ever afterwards, to be the dominant image of the Cardinal. By then Henry had taken his stand against the Roman hierarchy, and the spread of humanist and proto-Protestant ideas had provoked widespread anti-clericalism. Certainly there were those in the earlier years who resented Wolsey's ostentatious display of wealth and power, just as today there are those who criticise the expensive privileges enjoyed by the royal family, but there were many more who were impressed by the great Cardinal and enjoyed the pomp and circumstance which accompanied his public appearances just as in our own egalitarian age flag-waving crowds turn out to applaud the glittering spectacle of state occasions. As Thomas More observed when rejecting the grey uniformity of life in *Utopia*, it 'utterly overthrows all the nobility, magnificence, splendour and majesty which are, in the estimation of the common people, the true glories and ornaments of the commonwealth'.[50]

The leading magnates certainly had grievances which they discussed when they gathered together in the privacy of their own homes but they were longstanding grievances concerning the relationship between Crown and nobility and were unlikely to be resolved simply by the removal of Wolsey. Henry was maintaining his father's vigilant watch on potentially over-mighty subjects, determined not to permit a return to the tumults which had preceded the Tudor peace. He was also continuing Henry VII's policy of relying more on the spiritual lords than the hereditary peerage. Nobles who thought they were being elbowed aside from their proper places at the King's right hand could not complain that Wolsey's position was unique. Since 1396 only twice had the lord chancellorship not been held by a senior ecclesiastic. The coupling of that office with the archbishopric of Canterbury had become traditional – which probably explains the rumour that Wolsey was going to be translated to Canterbury in 1516. No less than five of Wolsey's predecessors since 1396 had been cardinals. They were all politicians first and spiritual shepherds second. They wielded considerable power and kept impressive households. Cardinal Morton, whom most men still remembered, had been a wealthy pluralist, a great builder and renovator of palaces and, according to a contemporary, 'trained in party intrigue'. Francis Bacon described him as 'a wise man and an eloquent but in his nature harsh and haughty, much accepted by the king but envied by the nobility and hated of the people'.[51] Wolsey, then, was no novelty. Rather was he the latest in a line of powerful ecclesiastics who combined spiritual and viceregal authority and stood between the barons and the throne. The notion that the King should govern solely with the counsel of his great territorial magnates was widely and deeply accepted but it had been in abeyance since 1485 and the Tudors were determined that it should remain so.

There are three compelling reasons why no noble faction appeared. The first is the skill with which Wolsey kept possible rivals otherwise engaged. The second, and related, reason is that no leader emerged capable of challenging the Cardinal. Suffolk, who was not noted for original thought, preferred to court Wolsey's favour. Norfolk was too old to make a bid for independence and, in any case, had spent too long laboriously inching his way along the greasy pole of royal favour to risk everything by a show of disloyalty. Dorset was dismissed from the Council in 1516, probably at Wolsey's suggestion. Surrey was often absent on naval business and was of little account when he did appear in Star Chamber. Shrewsbury preferred to spend as much time as possible on his Midland estates grumbling that the country was going to the dogs. The only man bold enough or rash enough to stand up to Wolsey was Edward Stafford, Duke of Buckingham. England's premier duke, descended from Edward III, related to the Percys, Howards and Nevilles, master of vast estates, Lord High Constable, councillor of long standing, military commander in the 1513 campaign, was a man overwhelmed with self-importance. He was proud of his heredity and his own social standing. In his great houses, Penshurst and Thornbury Castle, he lived in almost kingly splendour and whenever he travelled it was with an impressive retinue. Such a prominent secular lord could not but resent the challenge presented by the upstart churchman. Nor could he prevent himself showing his contempt. He had a quick temper and a tongue ever ready to express his anger. He and Wolsey crossed swords on more than one occasion. The most notable occurred when Henry and the Cardinal were dining together. Buckingham was waiting upon the King and holding a bowl of water for his sovereign to wash his hands in. It was galling enough for the Duke to be standing in attendance while Wolsey was seated at table but when, after Henry had completed his ablution, the butcher's son dipped his fingers in the same basin, Buckingham snapped. He threw the water over Wolsey's shoes. The records do not tell us whether the Duke was punished for creating a scene before the King but on another occasion the Cardinal did send him a message warning him to mind his manners in the royal presence. That must have made Buckingham fume.

These incidents may be connected with an undated enigmatic letter from this period which has survived. Its contents were so confidential that Henry took the almost unprecedented step of writing it himself and not entrusting it to a secretary. 'I would you should make good watch,' the King ordered, 'on the Duke of Suffolk, the Duke of Buckingham, on my lord of Northumberland, on my lord of Derby, on my lord of Wiltshire and on others which you think suspect to see what they do with this news. No more to you at this time but these few discreet words.'[52] It is unlikely that this referred to anything of the nature of a nascent plot but it does indicate that Henry and his chancellor were both aware of ill-feeling among the leading nobles and that the King was fully behind Wolsey in his determination to keep an eye on them. Buckingham was especially a marked man and he would eventually be destroyed by his own intemperance or Wolsey's malice or a combination of the two. But he was no faction leader. He was too much of a hot-headed individual ever to have been adept at intrigue and Wolsey was far from being the only man he turned into an enemy. Among others with whom he was on bad terms was his son-in-law, the Earl of Surrey.

CHAPTER 11

Wisdom and Folly

The third, and most compelling, reason why Wolsey did not have to contend with organised opposition was the character of the King. Factions only flourish in the courts of weak rulers. Schemers play on the vanity and paranoia of insecure monarchs to arouse those suspicions and fears which they can direct against their enemies. Henry VIII was not the sort of man who could be easily manipulated. There were occasions later in life, as we shall see, when pain, self-pity, despair or disillusionment opened up chinks in his colossal self-confidence and will power. Then others were able to use him for their own ends. But in the time of his vigour and high resolve, no one could make Henry do what he did not want to do – not even Wolsey. The King had raised 'his' cardinal to the pinnacle of power. The two understood each other and between them had constructed a system for putting the royal will into operation. Both were convinced that no one could oversee the affairs of the kingdom more effectively than Wolsey – and they were probably right. In 1519 Wolsey's position was secure and all who hoped for Henry's favour had to live with and, if they could, take advantage of that reality. That was certainly true of Thomas More who worked hard for his advancement and saw his labours crowned with success.

The years 1509–19 should have been the happiest in the lawyer's life. As he approached what in the sixteenth century was middle age he was at the height of his intellectual powers; he was a popular and successful advocate; he was well thought of by the City of London's opinion formers; he was surrounded by a growing family he loved dearly; through the humanist network he was well in touch with Christendom affairs; and he began to enjoy a Europe-wide reputation as an observer of the human scene. He should have been more at peace with himself than he had been in the period of intense spiritual turmoil that had preceded his marriage and his settling into a legal career.

Having turned his back on the cloister and the scholar's solitary desk, he applied himself to the vocation that God had called him to follow. In September 1510 he became one of the undersheriffs of London which meant that he acted as a judge in the sheriff's court and as an adviser to the senior justices. This work and his private practice brought him in £400 a year, a very handsome income for a lawyer of his age. He was good at his job, respected by litigants and had a wide circle of friends in the legal and mercantile communities.

Yet always there was the hair shirt. And the daily devotions in his chapel. And the pressure he applied to his wife and his children to achieve virtue and learning. Thomas More was still a driven man – driven by ambitions, spiritual and material, which could never be reconciled. It is significant that the only book he had published by this time, apart from some Latin verses and the translations of Lucian, was an English version of the biography of Pico della Mirandola. The Florentine humanist had found what More earnestly sought, a pattern of lay spirituality. Pico had struggled with issues which also tormented More: the authority of the Church and the challenge of the New Learning; the call of the spiritual life; political involvement; sexuality. In Pico, as in More, the enquiring mind and the temptations of the world and the flesh came into conflict with his devotion to Rome. He fled from the Inquisition, was later imprisoned for heresy but subsequently exonerated and eventually became a disciple of the puritanical Savonarola. His brief life ended as the motley army of Charles VIII rampaged through Italy in 1494. But if More took Pico as a model, there were areas of life into which he could not or would not follow him. The Florentine refused to embroil himself in the sour and noisome politics of the city states and he shunned the concupiscence of matrimony.

More was freed from the slimy coils of sex when Jane died in 1511. Technically the widower could now have embraced celibacy and taken refuge in the cowl with a clear conscience. He did not even contemplate it. His path was set before him and he did not deviate from it. Jane was scarcely laid in the earth before her husband was making new arrangements. Within a month he had married Alice Middleton, a plain matronly widow who was his senior by eight summers and who was approaching or had already reached the end of her fecund years. Financially the marriage was advantageous. Domestically it made sense: Alice was an excellent household manager. Morally it was perfect, for procreation was out of the question and sexual desire not existent – More could live in matrimonial chastity.

As to resisting the lodestone of power and influence under the Crown, he no more countenanced that than abandoning the married state. If he could cohabit with a woman in purity, he could with the grace of God hold high office and remain unspotted by pride, bribery and lies. More constantly drew himself to the attention of men in vogue at the court; old friends like John Colet and Lord Mountjoy, new men such as Richard Pace – humanist, diplomat and, from 1515, the King's Secretary – and Cuthbert Tunstall – advancing rapidly as a member of Warham's entourage. Beyond this he took every opportunity to see and be seen by the nation's leaders. In November 1511, a mutual friend, Andrew Ammonius, reported to Erasmus, 'never a day passes but [More] sees the archbishop or addresses him' and a little over four years later the same correspondent observed, 'he haunts those smoky palace fires in my company. None bids my lord of York good morrow earlier than he.'[53] More allowed Erasmus to believe and Erasmus passed the word on to others that when the London lawyer entered royal service he did so with the utmost reluctance. Nothing could have been further from the truth.[54]

His career through the second decade of the century reveals the steady advancement of one who was determined to reach as high as he could. In 1510 the Mayor and aldermen of the City elected him to be one of their MPs in the first parliament of the new reign – perhaps recalling the impression he had made in the previous session six years earlier. This helped to draw More to the attention of royal business managers and he was soon being employed on government commissions. In 1513 he wrote a Latin eulogy extolling Henry's martial exploits in France, despite the fact that, as a humanist, he deplored war. He was brought in as a consultant to the court of Chancery and, in 1514, he was appointed to the commission of sewers which had the responsibility for maintaining all 'walls, ditches, banks, gutters, sewers, sluices, causeways, bridges, streams and other defences' in the area lying between Greenwich and Lambeth. The following year his patient cultivation of top people bore fruit when he was appointed to a diplomatic and trade mission to the Low Countries. More's legal expertise and his contacts with the London mercantile community made him an obvious choice as negotiator of a treaty absolutely vital to national prosperity. Wool and cloth exports, the bulk of which travelled from London to Antwerp, made up four-fifths of England's outward commerce and duties collected in the capital's customs houses alone contributed £25,000 a year to the royal coffers. The 1515 embassy was, thus, far from being an empty diplomatic formality.

Eighteen months later it was his legal and mercantile connections in the City which brought him into the limelight at a time of crisis. The May Day riots were a manifestation of xenophobic mob rage directed against immigrant traders and artisans in London who were accused of taking bread from the mouths of honest citizens. Among those who deliberately inflamed the more irresponsible elements was William Colt, who may have been a relative of More's first wife and was certainly a fellow member of the Mercers' Company. 'Whoreson Lombards!' he lambasted a group of Italian merchants. 'You rejoice and laugh, by the mass we will one day have a day at you, come when it will.'[55] In the days after Easter (12 April) the mood of the City became progressively more anxious. Everyone sensed impending crisis. Yet, it was not until 30 April that the Mayor and aldermen with other leading citizens, including More, gathered at the Guildhall to discuss the situation. Darkness was already falling when a delegation rode to York House to acquaint Wolsey of the mounting unrest. As More and his companions made their way along West Cheap and Newgate Street they saw the gangs of young apprentices and students gathered round alehouse doorways and the worried householders closing their shutters and barricading their doors. Within the hour they were back with the Cardinal's authority to impose a curfew. It was too late. More was almost certainly among those who toured the streets adding weight to the constables who tried to force drunken and querulous citizens within doors. Soon after eleven he confronted an angry crowd on the corner of Newgate Street and St Martin's Lane. He rode in amongst the people, calling upon them to disperse but they were in no mood to listen. Stones and brickbats were thrown and the officials wheeled around and fled for their own safety. Chaos reigned throughout the hours of darkness as screaming, cudgel-brandishing mobs rampaged through the streets, breaking into houses, smashing and looting at will, their destructive energies not limited to the houses of the accursed foreigners. Did More hurry home to ensure the security of his own household or did he rush back to Westminster to report that the City fathers had lost control of London? It was dawn before Thomas Howard junior and George Talbot, Earl of Shrewsbury, arrived with sufficient armed retainers to reimpose order and arrest 300 curfew-breakers.

For More it had been a nasty experience, not only because of the indignity and potential danger to which he and his colleagues had been subjected, but also because of the ugly spectacle of the breakdown of law and order and the friction this created between the King and the City authorities, whom he judged to have 'failed' to contain the disturbance. More had recently published *Utopia* (see pp. 149f), a fantasy-satire in which he had condemned the greedy and exploitative activities of the rich and powerful and yearned for a society where, because all men were materially equal and voluntarily practised restraint in their common dealings, peace and harmony reigned. Now he was appointed one of the commissioners charged with enquiring into the uprising. What recommendations would he make? Would he plead for the majority, who were simply caught up in the excitement of the moment, intoxicated by the rhetoric of rabble-rousers, or more simply by strong drink? Would he argue that his fellow citizens had genuine grievances which required careful consideration? Or would he show himself as an establishment man sharing the paranoia that always afflicted the ruling class when confronted by common unrest and unwilling to invite royal displeasure by appearing sympathetic towards the disturbers of the King's peace? Sixteen years later, he claimed that he had spent hours interviewing the accused and witnesses and concluded that the trouble had all been started by two malicious apprentices. He excused himself from responsibility for the summary executions of these and a handful of other supposed ringleaders by commenting that they had been condemned under 'an old statute made long before'. But there is no evidence that, at the time, he had urged clemency; that was left for Wolsey's theatrical pleading; and even in retrospect More reserved his most damning censure for the rioters when he observed that they were no better than 'heretics'. The choice of comparison is significant: unorthodox believers and disaffected subjects were alike in their rejection of God-given authority and whenever he was obliged to choose between the rights of the individual and those of the secular or religious authorities More always chose the latter.[56]

More had, once again, served his king conscientiously and not long after the May Day riots his name was added to the list of royal councillors. In the previous year King Henry had offered him a pension which, as he informed Erasmus, he had declined. By the summer of 1517 he had apparently changed his mind. More's reluctance to accept the royal shilling, which is so plainly at odds with his deliberate and dogged courting of influential councillors and courtiers, is only difficult to understand if we swallow the explanation offered by Erasmus and More's early biographers that their modest and high-principled hero shunned the life of the court until overborne by a king who recognised his remarkable qualities. The truth is more prosaic and more revealing: he was holding out for better terms. In the middle of the decade his career was delicately poised. His legal work and his services to the City were providing him with a comfortable income and fresh honours and perquisites undoubtedly awaited him if he restricted his activities to London and occasional circuit work. On the other hand, the government needed a constant supply of accomplished lawyers and the route to high office lay through the chambers of those very friends and acquaintances whom More was careful to cultivate. But that route was not without hazards which had to be negotiated with subtlety and calculation. The royal pension which More was first offered was equivalent to less than a quarter of what he was already earning but it carried with it the obligation when summoned in the King's name to drop all other work. That might be all very well if the remuneration received made up for income lost elsewhere. It did not. The Crown was notoriously bad at paying its debts. Diplomats and commissioners were expected to dig deep into their own pockets when on royal business and frequently had to pester the King's financial officers for their fees and expenses. More than that, becoming a paid employee of the national government would set up potential conflict with the fiercely independent London corporation and More was quite open with Erasmus about the divided loyalties to which he could become a prey. While on the one hand he might be a useful conduit between Guildhall and palace, on the other he would be mistrusted as a man whose first allegiance was to the King. It seems more than likely that the May Day fracas finally forced Thomas More to choose between Crown and

City and his appointment to the great Council followed very soon afterwards. Before the summer was out he was despatched on another diplomatic mission, this time to Calais. It would be inconceivable that the highly intelligent lawyer had not carefully negotiated the terms of his new employment (he certainly campaigned assiduously for payment of arrears arising from the Calais mission).[57]

What then are we to make of Erasmus's interpretation of events and his friend's motivation, an interpretation More seems to have done nothing to discourage? The two humanists most certainly did not see eye to eye on all matters and entering the service of princes was one of them. The Dutchman was scathing of the reasons why rulers surrounded themselves with erudite men of conviction.

> They command over others, but are themselves in servitude to their own violent passions, and think themselves kings precisely in this, that they can with impunity live in bondage to wickedness. Sometimes they summon to themselves men noted for sanctity of life, sometimes they converse with them, and do certain things on their advice: not because they care for true piety, but because by this deceit they gain for themselves the reputation of honesty, and mollify resentment of their evil deeds, so that when they fleece the people, or launch impious wars, or rage against those who wish well to the commonwealth, these things, too, may seem to be done by the advice of the most upright men.[58]

(This passage, coming as it does, from that part of Erasmus's St Luke commentary where he deals with the relationship between Herod and John the Baptist, was cruelly prophetic when applied to More and Henry VIII: the Jewish King and the prophet fell out over Herod's matrimonial situation and John lost his head.)

Erasmus believed in the total independence of the scholar. He spent several years striving to break the shackles imposed on him by his own Augustinian order and he steadfastly refused offers to join the entourages of European princes. He paid a high price for his freedom – years of uncomfortable wandering and constant anxiety about money – but he remained consistently true to his principles. Other humanists either lacked his commitment to intellectual and spiritual purity or saw no reason to depart from the conventions of patronage. Many of Erasmus's close friends had taken a handful of royal silver, not a few of them in England, and, while regretting that they had sold out just for a riband to stick in their coats, he did not hold back from taking advantage of their increased wealth and influence. Nevertheless, it was something of an issue between More and Erasmus and it would not be surprising if More chose to play down his increasing involvement in national politics and his ambition to be so involved.

The changing relationship between the two friends throughout this decade played a significant part in the progress of More's career. It falls very neatly into two phases. In the summer of 1509 Erasmus arrived in England, bursting with hope and creative energy. He stayed exactly five years during which he was a frequent guest at Bucklersbury, and with the More-Colet circle he worked eagerly at fostering in the universities the study of Greek and the new approach to Scripture. After he left, in July 1514, Erasmus paid only three fleeting visits to Henry VIII's kingdom, the last being in April 1517. The Dutch scholar was now the greatest celebrity in Europe, in demand wherever new thinking was fashionable, fêted by radicals, viewed with suspicion and hostility by the traditionally minded. Fissures began to craze the even surface of Christian humanism. Some observers saw Erasmus as the white charger of reform; others as the Trojan horse of heresy. He and More met occasionally on the Continent during these years and corresponded sporadically. Their last encounter was at Calais in June 1520 by which time the Lutheran challenge had moved the conflict of ideas away from the tiltyard of stylised academic disputation and on to the real politico-religious battlefield where the weapons were rebellion, excommunication and the stake. Thereafter it would not be possible for More and Erasmus to tread the same path. There was no falling-out between the two men, simply an acceptance that their friendship worked better at a distance, because this allowed affection and respect to flourish without being strained by disagreement over the best means of changing society.

Both of them were concerned to do precisely that. Both were convinced that Christendom was 'going to the dogs'. Both were reformers committed to spiritual imperatives in private and public life. Both could be called 'evangelical', but only if we use that word in its widest interpretation to imply a concern to bring individuals and society into line with the faith and precepts of the Christian Gospel. As such they were inevitably caught up in the argument about how best to achieve the transformation they desired – an argument which always confronts religious activists. There is a range of options available. There is the ascetic approach: the Christian withdraws from society in order to devote himself to interceding for it. Most of the zealous who remain in the unredeemed world are obliged to adopt the 'one by one and silently' policy of inspiring their neighbours to take up the religion of inwardness. Those for whom this is too slow and undynamic strike the confrontational stance, exhorting and challenging sinners, from pulpit and printed page, to mend their ways. Some espouse the technique of infiltration, seeking through public office to influence religious and secular establishments to conform human polity to that of the Kingdom of God. By contrast there are the extreme radicals who consider existing institutions to be so completely under the sway of Satan that only their demolition will allow a holy commonwealth to be constructed on the site. Finally, there are the rejectionists who, like the ascetics in the first category, feel the need to escape from the contagion of a fallen world and withdraw into the wilderness, not to pray for that world, but to set up alternative communities. The Reformation provided striking examples of all of these.

More and Erasmus worked out those hues of the colour band of reform which suited them in two remarkable books published in this decade: *The Praise of Folly* and *Utopia*. When Erasmus reached London in that roseate dawn of the new reign, eager to return to friends 'as learned as they are beloved', he already had in mind a suitable literary offering for his host at Bucklersbury. The little book would appeal to More's mischievous and barbed sense of humour. It would echo the satires of Lucian in which both scholars delighted. It would take up and carry forward the theme of Sebastian Brant's immensely popular *Ship of Fools*. It would elegantly expose – in a way designed, according to its author, to evoke 'pleasure rather than censure' – the ignorance and corruption humanists identified in the contemporary world. Even its title, by a happy chance, could pay a neat compliment to his friend, for More when latinised becomes *Morus* and *morus* is the ancient word for 'fool'. Thus was born the *Moriae Encomium, The Praise of Folly*.

In it the author mocked all sorts and conditions of men. Folly, in the form of a female preacher, capped and belled, climbed into the pulpit to demonstrate that men and women of every rank and calling were her devotees. Lovers, gamblers, debauchees, libidinous clergy, superstitious worshippers of images – all the obvious targets were mercilessly lampooned with a playful laugh and a dig in the ribs from Folly's elbow. But she became harsher-voiced when her denunciations were directed elsewhere. Within the cloister she discerned those,

> who generally call themselves 'the religious' and 'monks' – utterly false names both, since most of them keep as far away as they can from religion and no people are more in evidence in every sort of place.

Erasmus, who had been put to the monastic life as a child and came to loathe it, scorned the empty precisionism of observing petty regulations:

> What is funnier than to find that they do everything by rule, employing, as it were, the methods of mathematics; and to slip up is a great crime. There must be just so many knots for each shoe and the shoe-string must be of a certain colour; the habit must be decked with just so much trimming; the girdle must be of a certain material and the width of so many straws; the cowl of a certain shape and a certain number of bushels in capacity; the hair so many fingers long; and one must sleep just so many hours.

And what could be more absurd than the rivalry between religious orders?

> . . . nor is it so much their concern to be like Christ as to be unlike each other. Thus a great part of their felicity derives from their various names. Those of one order delight to call themselves Cordeliers, but among them some are Coletes, some Minors, some Minims, some Crutched. Again, there are the Benedictines and the Bernardines; the Bridgetines and the Augustinians; the Williamists and the Jacobines; as if it were not enough to be called Christians.
>
> The greater number of them work so hard at their ceremonies and at maintaining the minutiae of tradition that they deem one heaven hardly a suitable reward for their labours; never recalling that the time will come when, with all these things held of no account, Christ will demand a reckoning of that which He has prescribed, namely, charity.

The ultimate hypocrites were the supreme pontiffs.

> . . . the popes are generous enough with . . . interdictions, excommunications, re-excommunications, anathematisations, pictured damnations, and the terrific lightning-bolt of the bull, which by its mere flicker sinks the souls of men below the floor of hell. And these most holy fathers in Christ, and vicars of Christ, launch it against no one with more spirit than against those who, at the instigation of the devil, try to impair or to subtract from the patrimony of Peter. Although this saying of Peter's stands in the Gospel, 'We have left all and followed Thee,' yet they give the name of his patrimony to lands, towns, tribute, imposts, and moneys. On behalf of these things, inflamed by zeal for Christ, they fight with fire and sword, not without shedding of Christian blood; and then they believe they have defended the bride of Christ in apostolic fashion, having scattered what they are pleased to designate as 'her enemies'. As if the church had any enemies more pestilential than impious pontiffs who by their silence allow Christ to be forgotten, who enchain Him by mercenary rules, adulterate His teaching by forced interpretations, and crucify Him afresh by their scandalous life!

Temporal rulers did not escape Erasmus's scorn:

> Fashion me now a man such as princes commonly are, a man ignorant of the laws, almost an enemy of the public welfare, intent upon private gain, addicted to pleasure, a hater of learning, a hater, too, of liberty and truth, thinking about anything except the safety of the state, and measuring all things by his own desire and profit. Then put on him a golden chain, symbolising the union of all virtues linked together; set on him a crown adorned with gems, which is to remind him that he ought

to surpass others in every heroic quality. In addition, give him a sceptre, emblem of justice and of a heart in no way corrupted, and finally a scarlet robe, badge of a certain eminent love for the realm. If a prince really laid his own life alongside these symbols, I believe he would have the grace to be ashamed of his finery.[59]

Yet Erasmus's catalogue of cynical exposés is not an exercise of despair dressed in fashionable clothes. He was at heart an optimist. He believed that society and individuals could be changed and *The Praise of Folly* was a contribution towards creating a dominant ideology in favour of reform. His rumbustious tour through the varied landscape of human stupidity ends at a wayside shrine dedicated to the *dementia divina*. He urged his readers to seek that holy madness experienced by the mystic, the ecstatic, the truly devout who alone are permitted occasional entry to the heavenlies.

When presently they return to themselves they say that they do not know where they have been, whether in the body or out of it, waking or sleeping; they do not remember what they have heard, seen, spoken, or done; and yet through a cloud, or as in a dream, they know one thing, that they were at their happiest while they were thus out of their wits. So they are sorry to come to themselves again and would prefer, of all good things, nothing but to be mad always with this madness. And this is a tiny little taste of that future happiness.[60]

How did Thomas More react to this satirical masterpiece which would for ever be associated with his name? It was published in 1511 and immediately became a runaway bestseller.

The *Moriae Encomium* took its place as the leader of a growing genre of creative anti-establishment works including books, poems, pamphlets, plays, engravings and paintings. For the time being most of the European intelligentsia were disposed to nod and laugh and say 'how clever' but as the ripples created by the new book spread wider and wider, reaching non-academic readers and, via translated fragments, those who in no sense belonged to the educated élite, anxieties began to be voiced. Jerome de Busleyden was concerned that Erasmus's outspoken strictures might do him harm in those very quarters to which he looked for patronage: 'I have given much thought to what you wrote . . . at some length, and rather freely, about kings . . . I hope you will be discreet enough to moderate them . . . and treat of them (the kings) with caution, lest someday you give the ill-disposed crowd of blackmailers and informers the opportunity to say a word against you in the ear of princes.'[61] Maarten van Dorp of the Louvain theology school informed Erasmus that his book had 'aroused a good deal of feeling' in that very conservative centre of learning. The faculty members were particularly incensed at Erasmus's attack on the traditional teaching of theology and resented his undermining of their authority. 'Astringent pleasantries,' van Dorp warned, 'even when there is much truth mingled with them, leave a bitter taste behind,' and the writer showed how well he understood Erasmus when he pleaded,

> . . . please do not take refuge in asking, 'What business is it of mine what objections are raised by these illiterate and barbarous busybodies. My conscience is clear: enough for me that I and what I write should enjoy the approval of all the best scholars, although they may be fewer than those who condemn me.'[62]

Such voices were few before 1520. The general feeling was that Erasmus had given witty form to 'what oft was thought but ne'er so well expressed'. Yet even among those who applauded, this very fact caused disquiet: if the *Moriae Encomium* had struck such a common chord might it not seem to encourage those irresponsible semi-educated elements who wanted to tear apart the very fabric of Christian society? Anticlericalism and heresy were symbiotic growths; to feed one was to provide sustenance for the other. Moreover, Erasmus was known to be an opponent of overzealous prosecutions for heresy.

More, it is safe to hazard, was among those who were a prey to divided inner counsels. It was flattering to find his name bracketed throughout academe with that of the brilliant, the audacious, the stylistically elegant Erasmus. In the halcyon days when the New Learning was advancing on all fronts, not to be associated with it was to be regarded as unfashionable and obscurantist. And More was genuinely just as scornful as his friend of the weaknesses and foibles of those who were neither teaching nor living by the faith they professed. When writing to Erasmus he could make *en passant* jibes such as, 'priests . . . have no wives and children at home, or find them everywhere'.[63] He proved his overall support for the *Moriae Encomium* in a prodigiously long letter answering Maarten van Dorp's complaints. More joined in the attack on scholastic theology and insisted that only good could come of fresh, no-nonsense readings of Scripture aided by sound linguistic and historical research – *provided that they were interpreted conscientiously and took account of the garnered wisdom of the Christian centuries*, a significant caveat which signposted a fork in the paths followed by More and his radical friends. It is also noteworthy that he did not associate himself with some of Erasmus's other sallies. It is hardly likely that he could have been comfortable with attacks on the religious life *per se* when the holy calm of the cloister still seemed to him so desirable, nor would he want to be seen endorsing the unworldly scorn poured upon the denizens of royal courts when he was seeking the patronage of men in the inner circles round the King.

It was partly to commend himself to such influential figures that More attempted to enhance his literary reputation. Until now his modest output had embraced only a few Latin verses, his English version of Pico della Mirandola's biography and the Lucian translations. Nothing he had yet produced sprang from the head and heart and addressed itself to major social and political issues. The *History of Richard III* and *Utopia* were horses of a very different colour.

More's most famous work was written during 1515 and 1516 and Erasmus assisted in its publication at Louvain at the end of the latter year. In purely commercial terms More probably intended *Utopia* to ride on the back of *The Praise of Folly*. It, too, was a work of fiction, a fantasy, an intellectual diversion and if it proved anything like as popular as Erasmus's book it would contribute to those coffers depleted by the expenses incurred in royal service. Travellers' tales were much in demand in these years when transit of the great western ocean was becoming less of an adventure and more of a routine to service colonies and facilitate the exploitation of new-found lands. The possibility of starting a civilised society from scratch could be imagined without complete absurdity. But how would one go about it? What would be the marks of a well-ordered state? How would it be governed? What values would be enshrined in its constitution and laws? Erasmus might expose everything that was amiss in European kingdoms but what, ideally, should the humanist seek to put in its place? What kind of polity would enshrine the virtues extolled by Plato and all the ancients? And if one could devise such an οὖτοπος, a 'No-place', would it be feasible in this fallen world – or even desirable? Pessimistically, More confesses that 'many things be in the Utopian weal public, which in our cities I may rather wish for, than hope after'.[64] In those very words the author was satirising the Erasmians who did precisely that – they wished for a better world but were not prepared to dirty their hands or bend their backs in the political building site. And, anyway, is this dream world all that attractive? The island state eulogised by the much-travelled humanist, Raphael Hythloday, is a regimented, monochrome, egalitarian nation whose citizens dress (significantly) in uniform grey.

Yet the description of this never-never land is only one part of More's book. Through the artifice of Hythloday's censure of the way public life is conducted in the states of Europe, the author allows himself deprecatory observations which, unlike *Folly*'s nostrums, are not sweetened by light-hearted ridicule. He who had lauded King Henry's victorious 1513 campaign expresses the humanist's abhorrence of war, 'an activity fit only for beasts and yet practised by no kind of beast so constantly as by man'[65] and expresses disgust for the warrior caste headed by kings who 'occupy themselves in the pursuits of war . . . rather than in the honourable activities of peace'.[66] He even dismisses as barbarous such noble and royal pastimes as hunting and hawking. Even when monarchs do seek to settle disputes by treaties rather than by force of arms they reveal themselves to be duplicitous and faithless, or so More asserts in a passage of rather laboured sarcasm:

in those parts where the faith and religion of Christ prevails, the majesty of treaties is everywhere holy and inviolable, partly through the justice and goodness of kings, partly through the reverence and fear of the Sovereign Pontiffs. Just as the latter themselves undertake nothing which they do not most conscientiously perform, so they command all other rulers to abide by their promises in every way and compel the recalcitrant by pastoral censure and severe reproof. Popes are perfectly right, of course, in thinking it a most disgraceful thing that those who are specially called the faithful should not faithfully adhere to their commitments.[67]

Utopia's scorn was not reserved for the upper echelons of society. More the wealthy burgess and property owner castigated a class system based on landed and mercantile wealth:

Is not this an unjust and unkind public weal, which gives great fees and rewards to gentlemen, as they call themselves, and to goldsmiths and to such other . . . idle persons . . . and makes no gentle provision for poor ploughmen, colliers, labourers, carters, ironsmiths and carpenters, without whom no commonwealth can continue? . . . I can perceive nothing but a certain conspiracy of rich men procuring their own commodities under the name and title of the commonwealth.[68]

More the lawyer had little good to say for either the law or its administration. Gleefully he had Hythloday announce that the Utopians 'absolutely banish from their country all lawyers'.[69] Justice was rarely served by clever barristers swapping specious arguments and technical quiddities and the law had largely become a tool wielded by property owners against their less fortunate neighbours:

. . . great and horrible punishments are appointed for thieves, whereas much rather provision should have been made . . . whereby they might get their living, so that no man should be driven to this extreme necessity, first to steal and then to die.[70]

More was fiercely indignant about the injustices in which society abounded; peasants turned off common arable and pasture by enclosing landlords, war-wounded veterans forced into beggary and vagabondage by potential employers who refused to show compassion, householders molested by bands of armed retainers kept by their 'betters'. The root of all these evils was the love of money and More's prose mercilessly flayed those who worshipped Mammon, just as Bosch, in *The Haywain*, a few years earlier had exposed the vices of men and women of every rank who, having decided that dried grass was the world's most valuable commodity, tricked, cheated, belaboured and scrambled over each other to stuff the precious herbage into their scrips and purses.

Significantly, the author's castigation of the abuse of spiritual power and privilege was more muted. He made slantwise allusions to the corruption of the clergy. The Utopians had, according to Hythloday, 'priests of extraordinary holiness, and *therefore very few*'.[71] More deplored the contrast between the exemplary lives of these non-Christian religious experts and their European counterparts who, in so many cases, disgraced their order. Yet he went out of his way to applaud another custom of the Utopians, regarding their priests:

> To no other office in Utopia is more honour given, so much so that, even if they have committed any crime, they are subjected to no tribunal but left only to God and to themselves. They judge it wrong to lay human hands upon one, *however guilty*, who has been consecrated to God in a singular manner as a holy offering.[72]

This was the extent of More's comment on one of the burning issues of the day, the relationship between common law and canon law. In 1512 a worried Archbishop Warham had summoned his clergy together to discuss the problem of mounting anticlericalism. Bravely he appointed John Colet, a radical modernist viewed with suspicion by many of the old guard, to preach the inaugural sermon. The Dean of St Paul's pulled no punches in drawing attention to the various sins to which priests and bishops were prone. 'In these times,' he acknowledged,

> we experience much opposition from the laity but they are not so opposed to us as we are to ourselves. Nor does their opposition do us so much hurt as the opposition of our own wicked lives, which are opposed to God and Christ . . . We are troubled in these days too also by heretics – men mad with strange folly – but this heresy of theirs is not so pestilential and pernicious to us and the people as the vicious and depraved lives of the clergy, which . . . is a species of heresy, and the greatest and most pernicious of all.[73]

CHAPTER 12

Prince, Priests and Philosophers

Within months London gossip was blazing with a scandal which amply demonstrated the reasons for Colet's concern. The Hunne case was debated in every alehouse and marketplace in the City and sharply divided public opinion. Worse than that; feelings over the issues raised did not die down quickly but continued to be felt and loudly expressed for more than three years. In brief, Richard Hunne, a prominent merchant tailor of somewhat choleric disposition and more than a passing acquaintance with suspect religious views, had an altercation with his parish priest, Thomas Dryffeld. In the spring of 1512 Dryffeld hauled his enemy before an archiepiscopal court presided over by More's friend, Cuthbert Tunstall, and received judgement in his favour. From this point on the conflict got increasingly out of hand. Neither side would give in and charge and counter-charge were brought in various courts. Hunne went to King's Bench to accuse his adversaries of *praemunire* (i.e. arrogating to a spiritual court matters properly falling within the competence of royal justices) and the Bishop of London, Richard Fitzjames, a no-nonsense ecclesiastic who had no truck with newfangled ideas and who, the following year, banned Colet from preaching, sent his own officials to arrest the merchant on suspicion of heresy. Now a very sinister element entered the story. After a preliminary hearing in the Bishop's court, Hunne was found hanged in his cell. A coroner's jury found against the Bishop's vicar-general, William Horsey, for murder and he and his accomplices were indicted to stand trial. However, by then (February 1515) Fitzjames had already made matters worse by passing posthumous judgement on Hunne and handing his body over to be burned.

The Hunne case would have remained nothing more than a passing cause célèbre or an incident which lodged itself in anticlerical and Protestant folklore had it not acted as a powerful irritant in the body politic of Church–State relationships. Most people wanted a clerical elite they could respect. When they were confronted with a hierarchy that either would not or could not reform itself, some began to give credence to alternatives: perhaps secular government should bring the clergy into line; perhaps heretics who demanded root and branch reform had a point. The timing of the Hunne case was – for the government and for all men who opted for a quiet life – unfortunate: it coincided with the latest round in a long-running conflict between civil and ecclesiastical lawyers. Equality before the law is always an aspiration rather than a reality but the roots of that aspiration reach down to springs gushing from the very bedrock of the human psyche. The fact that in the early sixteenth century justice frequently had little to do with the outcome of court cases does not mean that practitioners and litigants did not strive ardently for the principles of equity. Much of Wolsey's energy in Chancery and Star Chamber was directed towards defending the rights of the poor and underprivileged against the machinations of the rich and powerful and in the lesser courts the Tudor clean-up campaign still waged war against those who befouled them with bribery and main force. In the same way the generality of common lawyers resented the fact that in civil and criminal cases involving lay and clerical adversaries the scales were weighted in favour of the latter. This was because two mutually exclusive legal systems existed side by side – those presided over by the royal courts and the ecclesiastical courts. Any man who could claim benefit of clergy (and that had come to include those in all the seven minor orders – psalmist, lector, acolyte, exorcist, subdeacon, deacon, priest) was exempt from prosecution in the King's courts for most crimes. Instead, they were examined by their spiritual superiors and this usually entailed them performing an act of penance and continuing to enjoy their freedom, their property and their lives. The justification for this rested on the fiction that those who had received the grace of orders were different from ordinary mortals; they partook of a sacredness which could not be violated by accusation in lay courts. Opponents of this privilege took the common-sense view that those clergy whose alleged behaviour pronounced them to be very un-sacred had no right to a degree of protection greater than that enjoyed by laymen and that the Crown itself was being demeaned. Over the years parliament had launched sporadic attacks on clerical immunity but the barricades had always been fiercely defended and Church authorities had conceded little. The last minor advance had been in 1512 when the Commons had pushed through an act denying benefit of clergy to the lower orders in cases of felony. This act was due for reconsideration when parliament reassembled in February 1515 – the very time that Horsey's fate was on the line.

There was no possibility of the legal considerations being explored in calm debate by Lords and Commons. Public opinion in the City was after the vicar-general's blood. The Church hierarchy, determined to save him, bayed hysterically against the threat of 'heresy' in their desperation to have the 1512 act repealed. The argument thus became a very public row between parliament and the bishops in which the latter did not hesitate to use City pulpits to billboard their case. Now the King, himself, stepped into the highly charged atmosphere. He called for the matter to be debated in his presence and appointed the learned Franciscan Henry Standish to defend the rights of the Crown courts. After an initial debate everything went into abeyance during parliament's summer recess. Then it was that Fitzjames, whose arrogance immunised him against learning from experience, made the mistake of trying to silence Standish, who could not by any stretch of the imagination have been called a theological radical, by citing him for heresy. The Franciscan appealed to the King and Henry, not prepared to have his champion's orthodoxy called into question, summoned all the parties to appear before him again in November. Now the stakes were raised higher still. Against the cry of 'Heresy!' made by the churchmen the parliamentarians screamed '*Praemunire!*', insisting that Fitzjames and his cronies had no right to deploy papal authority against the King's spokesman. Tempers flared and at one point Wolsey went on his knees before his sovereign to beg pardon for his brothers who had not intended to encroach on Henry's prerogative. However, he felt himself obliged to defend the principle for which they were contending, that bringing clergy into temporal courts 'seems contrary to the laws of God and the liberties of the Holy Church, the which he . . . and all the prelates . . . are bound by their oath to maintain'.[74] Eventually compromise and diplomatic fudge triumphed because the parties concerned all realised that it was not in their interests to push for total victory. But the proceedings were not concluded before Henry had clearly stated his own position:

> By the ordinance and sufferance of God, we are king of England, and kings of England in time past have never had any superior but God only. Wherefore know you well that we will maintain the right of our Crown and of our temporal jurisdiction as well in this point as in all others, in as ample a wise as any of our progenitors have done before us. And as to our decrees, we are well informed that you yourselves of the spirituality do expressly contrary to the words of many of them, as has been well shown to you by some of our spiritual Counsel: nevertheless, you interpret your decrees at your pleasure. Wherefore, consent to your desire more than our progenitors have done in time past we will not.[75]

The issues raised by this politico-religious crisis in the capital in the early years of the reign did not hit the headlines again until 1529 when the outcome would be more catastrophic because the strong-minded but circumspect King of 1515 had become an autocrat with a personal agenda to which everything else had to be subordinated. But it would be unrealistic to suppose that passions, beliefs and rivalries had seeped away just because they are less visible to us in the written records. The attitudes we observe in the troubles of 1511–15 were, for contemporaries, part of the continuing procession of life in the ensuing years. There was an entrenched ecclesiastical establishment determined to maintain its privileged position, conscious of clerical shortcomings but not very effective in redressing them and ready to brand as heretics any lay folk who challenged the ancient rights of the clergy. Among the disaffected, little cells of men and women existed who *were* heretics. Richard Hunne, indeed, may have been of their number and was certainly connected by marriage with a Lollard network through which he obtained Bible fragments in English. The general citizenry, though conventional in their religious observances, could easily be stirred to anger by demonstrations of clerical arrogance and were just as outraged at the busybodies who came ferreting out heretics as they were at the existence of those heretics in their midst. In the Inns of Court and those hostelries where men of law customarily met together the rivalry between Church and Crown jurisdictions was often debated and if the conflict of interest between parliament and convocation did not arise it was merely because parliament was only summoned once (1523) between 1515 and 1529. This was an uneasy time for common lawyers. Wolsey's judicial reforms which revised the profile of Chancery and Star Chamber exaggerated a long-running trend of declining business in the courts of King's Bench and Common Pleas so that practitioners were eager to claw back categories of plaint which they believed had been usurped by other courts. Thus '*praemunire*' became a buzzword in the vocabulary of common lawyers.

This was the background to Thomas More's literary endeavours in the middle years of the decade and to his gradual advancement towards royal service. London was not a grumbling volcano of anticlericalism waiting to erupt of its own volition but there were tensions within its bustling life which a man of More's intelligence and widespread connections was fully aware of. Most significant was the King's final response in the Standish affair. Henry's determination to be complete master demonstrated not a contrast with his father's policies but an enhancement of them. The first Tudor had concentrated on overawing the English nobility. His son carried that assertiveness across the Channel in his first campaigns and now, seemingly, he was disposed to regard the Pope as just another foreign monarch with no authority to challenge Henry VIII's imperium within his own dominions. More probably arrived back from his first oversees mission just in time to witness, or at least to hear, the outcome of the Standish affair. Its legal implications were not lost on him any more than the arguments over criminous clerks were lost on him. On the latter issue he declared his position quite clearly over the next few months as he completed *Utopia* – priests, however unworthy, were not subject to laymen's courts.

This defence of ecclesiastical privilege and the mildness of More's censures mark a significant moment in the history of Christian humanism.

It is the point at which, while Erasmus strode purposefully along the rock-strewn path of spiritual freedom, hacking away at the nettles of ecclesiastical intimidation and the tangling briars of doctrinal convolution, More began to hang back, casting thoughtful eyes at the great, wide pilgrim way, worn smooth over centuries by the feet of the traditionally devout. For a few years yet the Englishman would, with faltering steps, follow his friend. He applauded Erasmus's Latin version of the New Testament (1516) and defended it against detractors. He even supported the enthusiastic biblicist's call for sound vernacular translations. Nothing could have been more emphatic than his endorsement of Erasmus's extra-cloistral life a couple of years later when the Dutchman's restless wanderings were criticised by a champion of monasticism: Erasmus 'does more work in one day than you people do in several months . . . He sometimes has done more for the whole Church in one month than you have in several years, unless you suppose that anyone's fastings or pious prayers have as deep and wide an influence as his brilliant works, which are educating the whole world to the meaning of true holiness.'[76] Yet faithfulness to the sweet insistence of an interiorised religion cannot coexist with obedience to the croaking demands of an unyielding institutionalism. Erasmus moved onwards, increasingly misunderstood and despised by the Catholic hierarchy which eventually consigned his writings to the flames. By then Thomas More, convinced that the ancient Church could not be wrong – indeed, that it held out the only hope for social cohesion in this world and eternal bliss in the next – had ceased to travel with him.

For the time being More was silent on the relationship between King and Pope. Henry had indicated that he would not tolerate papal interference and had rejected appeals by Warham and Wolsey to allow the point at issue to be referred to Rome. Was this sheer bravado on the part of the young monarch or should More dampen down the euphoria he had felt at the inauguration of the reign? Such questions must have already begun to concern him.

In *Utopia* he cautiously propounded a view of Christian kingship which no one could find objectionable:

Let him live harmlessly on what is his own. Let him adjust his expenses to his revenues. Let him check mischief and crime and, by training his subjects rightly, let him prevent rather than allow the spread of activities he will have to punish afterwards. Let him not be hasty in enforcing laws fallen into disuse, especially those which, long given up, have never been missed. Let him never take in compensation for violation anything that a private person would be forbidden in court to appropriate for the reason that such would be an act of crooked craftiness.[77]

In Utopia this kind of benign rule was guaranteed by a system of checks and balances which prevented any tyrant from seizing power.

Now, having hinted at the imperfections of real-life monarchs, More could not avoid confronting the humanist dilemma. Since he and his friends aimed at the reformation of society and since this could only be achieved by Europe's rulers how could the wise philosophers of the age best bring their influence to bear? It was an issue he had often debated with Erasmus but now Erasmus had departed and More in the section of the book which he wrote last of all set out the arguments clearly. The Erasmian policy of detachment was predicated on the conviction, now put into Hythloday's mouth, that wise counsel would always be swamped and the wise councillor always corrupted.

> At court there is no room for dissembling, nor may one shut one's eyes to things. One must openly approve the worst counsels and subscribe to the most ruinous decrees. He would be counted a spy and almost a traitor, who gives only faint praise to evil counsels.
>
> Moreover, there is no chance for you to do any good because you are brought among colleagues who would easily corrupt even the best of men before being reformed themselves. By their evil companionship, either you will be seduced yourself or, keeping your own integrity and innocence, you will be made a screen for the wickedness and folly of others.[78]

But More had by now reached the conclusion that the intelligent Christian layman could not opt out of the political process. He should follow 'another philosophy, more practical for statesmen, which knows its stage, adapts itself to the play in hand and performs its role neatly and appropriately'.

> If you cannot pluck up wrongheaded opinions by the root, if you cannot cure according to your heart's desire vices of long standing, yet you must not on that account desert the commonwealth. You must not abandon the ship in a storm because you cannot control the winds.
>
> On the other hand, you must not force upon people new and strange ideas which you realise will carry no weight with persons of opposite conviction. On the contrary, by the indirect approach you must seek and strive to the best of your power to handle matters tactfully. What you cannot turn to good you must make as little bad as you can. For it is impossible that all should be well unless all men were good, a situation which I do not expect for a great many years to come![79]

In this diplomatic, pragmatic assessment of the councillor's role, More was signalling his willingness and his ability to serve his king. He would be, like Pace, Tunstall and other men of the New Learning, an adviser of conviction but no bigot. In personal terms he had now chosen his path. He had decided that to seek a place of honour close to the King was not ambition; it was fulfilling his lay vocation. He had reached this decision after a period or internal warfare, though the conflict may not have been as fierce as he would have had some of his friends believe. When he agreed to join the Council he left behind one struggle with conscience but he cannot have been unaware that fresh contests lay ahead. That would be for him a willing self-mortification, another hair shirt.

About the time that he accepted a royal salary More laid aside *The History of Richard III* that he had been working on for some years. The reason may simply have been that he no longer had the time for literary endeavours or that he no longer needed a book designed to ingratiate himself with the Tudor regime. However, there may be other explanations of why More started and then stopped writing this narrative. In his unpublished manuscript the author grappled with themes of practical and theoretical politics, not as they might be in an ideal society but as they had been in England within living memory and might be again. It was that 'might be again' that was at the centre of More's thinking. He knew from his reading of the classics how easily a state can decline into tyranny and he shared the humanist conviction that, since history repeats itself, the past could be used to demonstrate exemplars to follow and abominations to shun. *Richard III* and the planned sequel on Henry VII which More never got around to must be seen as a contribution to the contemporary debate on the best kind of government for a commonwealth.

The book opened with a description of the last years of Edward IV's reign as a golden age: 'this realm was in quiet and prosperous estate; no fear of outward enemies; no war in hand nor none in [prospect]'. Subjects related to their king, 'not in a constrained fear, but in a willing and loving obedience'.[80] Into this Eden slithered the serpentine Richard of Gloucester, as black of heart as he was vile of appearance. More did not invent the monster later to be given immortality by Shakespeare; oral records, as well as chronicles and histories in print and manuscript had already cast the last Plantagenet in the role of murderer, intriguer, psychopath and usurper. More simply took the available source material and dressed it with theatrical embellishment. *Richard III* was serious history not in the sense of weighing all the available evidence, but only insofar as its author accurately reflected the testimony of the witnesses he chose to examine and those witnesses were ones who were acceptable to the Tudor regime. What the projected work really was was a humanist tract in which Richard is likened to Tiberius, another tyrant during whose reign amorality, dissimulation and sudden death – 'kings' games played on scaffolds', as More stunningly described them – were the order of the day. Alternatively we could view it as a courtroom exercise: More, as council for the prosecution, presented as damning a case as possible, piling Pelion on Ossa to construct an unanswerable indictment. *Richard III* provides us with our first clear sighting of the adversarial More, the advocate who ignored no stratagem and neglected no piece of evidence that might be used, slanted or twisted to service his cause. As political and religious pressures increased in the following years, this unattractive side of his character would come increasingly to the fore.

Why did he embark on this history and why did he abandon it? *Richard III* was designed as a contribution to a popular humanist genre. Rediscovery of great classical historians – Herodotus, Thucydides, Livy, Suetonius, Tacitus – led on to writing which emulated that of the ancients in various ways. There were some, like Jacob Wimpfeling's *Epitome rerum Germanicarum* and Pietro Bembo's *Historia rerum Venotarum* which were expressions of civic or national pride. Those such as Polydore Vergil's *Anglicae Historia*, written at the behest of Henry VII, came into being to provide intellectual buttressing to princely dynasties. Francesco Guicciardini's *Storia d'Italia* was, probably, the best attempt to discern those patterns in human affairs which had gone to the shaping of contemporary events. Several authors quarried the past for examples of successful rulers to present to their living counterparts. Machiavelli's *Il Principe* and Thomas Elyot's *The Boke named the Governour* stand as very different instances of this sub-genre. In addition there were numerous critical essays on the sixteenth-century political scene. Pure objectivity – the setting down of as accurate a record as possible – was a principle no humanist writer would have understood. They all wrote to have an effect on their world. Because many of these works dealt with sensitive issues they existed only in manuscript and were designed to be read only within restricted academic fraternities. *Richard III*, a study of tyranny and the ways that it can grow and flourish in a once-happy state, certainly treated of people and events which could have been embarrassing to men still occupying positions of power and influence. More was very circumspect about what he did and did not say. For example, he was silent about the role of Norfolk's father as one of Richard's staunchest supporters. There is no doubt that More intended his manuscript to be an object lesson. Whether he never intended it for publication or whether changing circumstances persuaded him to leave the work unfinished is something we shall never know.

More was certainly increasingly vulnerable as he ascended the ladder of royal favour. He had to be very careful about anything from his pen which appeared in print and he implored Erasmus and other humanist friends to be discreet when publishing his correspondence or earlier works. He desired the fame but not the jealous gossip which invariably accompanies it and which could well harm his career prospects. This anxiety lay behind the furious storm in an academic teacup which blew up in 1518. Germanus

Brixius (de Brie), a scholar at the French court, had written some verses in praise of the French naval actions of 1512. More responded in a mocking tone and from that point the two writers were at daggers drawn. When, in 1518, some of More's Latin poems appeared in print for the first time, Brixius set his linstock to what he intended as a literary broadside. His *Antimorus* was comprehensive in its attack on both the style and content of the Englishman's oeuvres. The most sensitive issue was the coronation ode More had written in which he had criticised the policies of Henry VII and also brought in a reference to Tiberius, an emperor whose dark deeds More was now paralleling with those of the monster the first Tudor had conquered at Bosworth. Brixius affected surprise that More should have chosen to calumniate the King's father and suggested that Henry VIII might wish to purge his realm of such a disloyal poet. The jibes clearly stung More, who riposted with robust vindictiveness. In his *Ipistola ad Germanum Brixium* he gave a foretaste of the mordant brews he would later concoct against heretics. Affronted in both his personal and national pride, More lashed out with an array of jibes and insults:

> When you described this sea battle in verse, you set out not to combine truth with falsehood but to fabricate practically the whole of your story from out-and-out lies, tailoring new facts according to your personal whim . . . With false maledictions and unsurpassed petulance you assailed all of England as pact-breaking and perjured . . . When . . . I happened to get a copy of your book . . . I observed such portentous monstrosities, such disgraceful, such shameful lies, such absurd fabrications, and those patches of other men's purple you wore stitched all over your ill-woven bardic *surtout* . . .[81]

While rejecting Brixius's accusations, More was careful to soften his criticisms of Henry VII: the King had been wise and prudent and the only ill-advised actions he had authorised had been carried out in the last years of the reign when unscrupulous councillors had taken advantage of their master's ill health. This was untrue and More knew it but saving his reputation was worth a lie.

By this time More was vulnerable because he had reached the unstable centre of the nation's political life. He had bouge of court (dining rights), sometimes joined the royal household on progress and was frequently in the King's company. On his appointment to the Council Wolsey found More useful in two ways: in Star Chamber his legal expertise was valuable in attending to the humdrum business of the hundreds of suits which now came before the conciliar court; in the council attendant More occupied, with Richard Pace, the function of secretary. The Chancellor, who kept a very wary eye on everyone who had access to the King, calculated that he could trust More as a go-between. The London lawyer was a high-principled idealist whose ambition was not of that viperous nature which would strike at anyone who stood in its path. But he was also an acute realist who had no illusions about the inner workings of court politics. He was a man well-suited to a highly confidential bureaucratic role. More, thus, found himself employed in reading Wolsey's despatches to Henry and taking down Henry's dictated responses.

For his part, More must have found his new role congenial. Although it is impossible to reach beyond the formal sycophancy of official correspondence to discover his real feelings about Wolsey there is no reason to suppose that he lacked respect and even admiration for the Cardinal. Wolsey was the King's chief minister, the Pope's representative and had also been more than a little influenced by the New Learning. From the time of More's admission to the Council his patron was working on a grandiose scheme which had the approval of all humanists. The military adventures of the early years had been designed to enhance Henry's prestige throughout Christendom and to contain French expansionism. They had succeeded in the first, failed in the second and proved very expensive. Pacificism and eirenicism had always been important planks in the humanist platform. At the height of war fever in 1513 Colet had been bold enough to preach against armed force as a means of settling international disputes and had been taken to one side by Henry for an explanation (he allowed himself to be overawed by the King). In the winter of 1517–18 Wolsey decided to make his master – and, of course, himself by association – the grand arbiter of universal peace. Over the ensuing months hectic diplomatic toings and froings brought some twenty-five European states into a scheme of mutual defence and amity which was sworn in London and celebrated, in October, with a magnificent high mass in St Paul's, presided over by Wolsey and followed by days of jousting, banqueting and mummery at Greenwich. Henry was even persuaded to part with his prize conquest, Tournai, which was now returned to France. More's participation in these events was minuscule but it must have seemed to him that his decision to enter the service of a Renaissance prince was justified.

William Roper and early biographers who followed his lead painted a picture of More rapidly striking up an intimacy with the King. According to More's son-in-law, Henry often summoned the secretary to his private apartments to debate with him about 'astronomy, geometry, divinity and sometimes of his worldly affairs'. Occasionally the two men would ascend to the palace roof to consider 'the diversities, courses, motions and operations of the stars and planets'. And there were more light-hearted moments when Henry and Catherine would summon More to their supper table 'to be merry with them'.[82] These are pleasant tableaux, easy to imagine, and they have been elaborated on by hagiographers and dramatists eager to highlight More's stark change of fortune. Roper can only have gleaned the details of such intimate moments from More himself and there is no reason to doubt their accuracy. However, we must remember that the writer carefully *selected* the anecdotes he included in his *Life* and also that he assigned no dates to most of them. We obtain a much more accurate impression of More's early position at court from a letter he wrote to Fisher in 1518:

> So far I keep my place there as precariously as an unaccustomed rider in the saddle. But the king (whose intimate favour I am far from enjoying) is so courteous and kindly to all that everyone who is in any way hopeful finds a ground for imagining that he is in the king's good graces, like the London wives who, as they pray before the image of the Virgin Mother of God which stands near the Tower, gaze on it so fixedly that they imagine it smiles upon them. But I am not so fortunate as to perceive such signs of favour, nor so despondent as to imagine them.[83]

More was as yet very far from being an intimate of the King. Wolsey, who was swift to remove overfriendly courtiers from Henry's immediate entourage, would scarcely have permitted it. If More ever did achieve the position, advocated by some modern writers, of 'tame humanist', the scholar to whom Henry turned from his more intellectually challenged companions, that did not happen until sometime in the 1520s, when evidence of royal favour is also provided by a stream of valuable perquisites.

The caution of More's letter to Fisher reflects the realities of court life where always there were currents and cross-currents running beneath the surface. As the first decade of Henry VIII's reign drew to a close Wolsey's grasp on policy and personnel was firm and assured. But it was only maintained by vigilance and it could be loosened by unforeseen events. Although the young King was content to have his Chancellor shoulder the burdens of Church and State government, he was jealous of his own perceived authority. He was always interested in theories of royal power. He had revealed Imperial pretensions over the government of Tournai[84] in 1514 and, eighteen months later, had asserted sovereignty over the English Church during the Standish affair. Another issue that touched his *amour propre* was his lack of councillors. From time to time he grumbled that his prestige demanded that he should always have at his disposal a body of mature advisers. Such complaints never lasted long: Henry's court life had settled into a comfortable and agreeable rut and Wolsey was always able to keep it there. However, the separation of the King from the actual work of government had its dangers. Although Wolsey's potential rivals were quiescent they were still there. The conviction never faded among members of the more ancient families that they were the natural advisers of the sovereign and there was always the possibility that some courtier might jostle his way into Henry's confidence.

Something of this sort seems to have happened in the second half of 1517 and it may explain why More was quickly despatched to wait upon the King. In the summer there was a virulent outbreak of the sweating sickness. It had two important political consequences. The first was that King and court kept well away from the capital. The second was that Wolsey contracted the disease. He withdrew to Hampton Court and was out of action for several months. Gaps appeared in day-to-day administration and into them stepped members of the Privy Chamber, notably Nicholas Carew and his brother-in-law, Francis Bryan, well-connected young men who combined genuine intelligence with a roistering lifestyle. They both appear in the records as cipherers, which must imply that they were already privy to some of Henry's confidential correspondence, and they now began to influence the flow of information to and from the royal office. Something had to be done about this alarming situation and it seems likely that More was detailed to join Pace as part of the King's itinerant bureaucracy as soon as he returned from Calais in November. The ensuing months saw something of a clash between the King's gentlemen and the Cardinal's appointees. Wolsey won, for early in 1518 Carew was exiled from the court. When he was allowed back in March, Pace tartly reported to Wolsey, 'Mr Carew and his wife be returned to the king's grace – too soon after mine opinion'.[85] The courtier seems not to have been chastened because a year later he and some of his friends were again banished for being too 'familiar' with the King.

The bare records do little more than hint at the personality and policy clashes which went on behind the scenes of the royal household. Wolsey, realising perhaps that he had too long ignored the Council Attendant, was attempting to maintain control through his own creatures; the King was restless and wanted his friends in his council; and young bloods, doubtless egged on by some of the greater nobles, tried to muscle into the running of government. By the end of 1519 what seemed to be a compromise had been reached. The Council Attendant had been enlarged to include four senior advisers to be called 'Knights of the body in the Privy Chamber'. However, since the knights were Wolsey's appointees it is clear that the 'accommodation' really marked a victory for the Cardinal.[86]

More's new job, thus, had its share of irritants and anxieties but they were, on the whole, minor ones and his first months as a royal councillor passed quite smoothly. Even the letter he received in mid-March 1518 did not suggest any major disturbance to his life. It was a chatty note from Erasmus enclosing a couple of pamphlets that the sender thought would not yet have reached England. One of them was a document that Richard Pace had asked him to acquire. It was entitled *Conclusions on Papal Indulgences* and it was the work of an obscure professor at an obscure German university – Dr Martin Luther of Wittenberg. The Augustinian monk had become incensed with the spiritual pretensions of the papacy as manifested in a current marketing exercise to raise funds for the building of St Peter's basilica. This energetic sales drive involved Leo X's agents in emotional market-cross appeals to the superstitious and gullible to purchase remission from the pains of purgatory for themselves and their departed loved ones. Luther's resentment at this crass exploitation focused on his rejection of the Pope's authority to levy advance taxes on the future residents of heaven, but his criticisms were more numerous and extended to ninety-five theses which he made available for debate by fellow theologians. Persistent legend insists that he also displayed them publicly on the door of the castle church on (appropriately) Hallowe'en 1517. What happened next was quite unforeseen, certainly by Luther. His theses were copied without his permission, printed, circulated and added to the growing volume of literature critical of the Church establishment. But their impact went far wider and deeper than anything published by Erasmus. They touched several nerves – nationalistic, religious and political – throughout the German states and beyond and were read avidly by all sorts and conditions of men (in April 1518 Luther did produce his own explanatory *Resolutions Concerning the Ninety-Five Theses*). When leaders of the Dominican order, the principal indulgence-hawkers, overreacted, demanding Luther's condemnation as a heretic, a little local difficulty became a Christendom-wide calamity.

In 1519 few would have prophesied this. On 30 May Erasmus informed the German monk that many highly placed persons in England thought well of his writings. He almost certainly included Thomas More in this category. At this point the humanist councillor would have welcomed Luther as another forceful and witty advocate of much-needed Church reform. It was an opinion he was to change rapidly and radically.

CHAPTER 13

In the Thickets of Obscurity

As with most new and fashionable ideas, Luther's onslaught against the practices and underlying rationale of the contemporary Church created most excitement, when it reached England, among the student body. In particular, it attracted many devotees in Cambridge. The university was ready for it. Although it would be an exaggeration to claim that Erasmus primed the Cambridge pump from which Lutheranism later gushed, there are, nevertheless, strong links between the years 1511–14, when the Dutch humanist taught (first as Greek lecturer and later as professor of Theology), and the 1520s, when several of the Church's future leaders were captivated by the works of the Saxon revolutionary.

Thomas Cranmer is one of those links, though, it must be confessed, not a very satisfactory one. In 1511 he began on the MA course and an early biographer described him as delighting in the works of Erasmus and the French biblical scholar Jacques Lefèvre d'Etaples, whose studies on the Psalms and the Pauline epistles were hot off the presses in these years. Cranmer must have been among those who sat at the feet of the great humanist whom Fisher regarded as a major 'catch' and one who added greatly to the prestige of the university. Erasmus thought as well of the Cambridge curricula as the Chancellor thought of him. In 1516 he catalogued the improvements that had been made in recent years:

> . . . literature (bonae literae) was introduced; the study of mathematics was added, and a new or at least a renovated Aristotle. Then came some acquaintance with Greek, and with many authors whose very names were unknown to the best scholars of a former time. Now, I ask, what has been the result to the university? It has become so flourishing that it may vie with the first schools of the age, and possesses men, compared with whom those old teachers appear mere shadows of theologians.[87]

Even when allowance has been made for Erasmian flattery the impression we gain is of an educational centre well and truly baptised into the New Learning.

Yet, the Thomas Cranmer who received his higher degree in 1515 was no effervescent humanist eager to continue the crusade against obscurantism. He was a plodding, cautious scholar of conventional views. He was also a young man and a prey to the normal distractions of youth. Soon after taking his MA he was offered a fellowship by his college and all seemed set fair for him to follow an academic career. Then, suddenly, he threw it all away.

He married a local girl called Joan. This stuffy bookworm fell for the charms of a woman and did the honourable thing – even though, in accordance with the rules of his college, that meant giving up his fellowship. He could, of course, have kept Joan discreetly as his mistress. That would probably have been the normal thing to do. Yet he chose a different course and this – his first important decision of which we are aware – provides the earliest clue to his character. It suggests a straightforward man, a simple man, not given to the complexities of careful calculation; a man who, once he perceived what was the virtuous and honest thing to do, tried to do it. As far as we know, he did not take his bride home to Aslockton, where brother John was well ensconced as head of the family. This may suggest that the match was socially 'unsuitable', involving no considerations of dowry or property. Certainly the couple could not afford to set up house together. While Thomas found digs elsewhere in the town, Joan was lodged with a relative at the Dolphin Inn. This may have been because she was pregnant for within little more than a year of the wedding Mrs Cranmer was brought to childbed. Neither she nor the baby survived.

It is not difficult to imagine the grief and guilt the young man must have felt at losing his chosen partner in adversity. What we less easily appreciate is the context of divine judgement within which Cranmer viewed his double tragedy. The granting or withholding of progeny was a sign of God's favour or disapproval. The loss of his child will have occasioned much conscience-searching for the young scholar. In years to come when Cranmer had to advise and console a king from whom God had taken almost all his children he could speak from shared experience.

In the immediate aftermath of his loss the young scholar picked up the career that had been briefly interrupted. Jesus College reinstated him in his fellowship and soon afterwards he took holy orders. He had spent half his lifetime in Cambridge and showed no desire to be anywhere else. It is interesting to compare Cranmer's life at this stage with that of More. Whereas the London lawyer was a man of intense and competing passions, Cranmer gives the impression of drifting with the tide of events. More went through angst before reconciling himself to marriage and a lay vocation. Cranmer was overtaken by a love that almost cost him his chosen career. More was driven by ambition. Cranmer was content to accept the life of a fenland academic and, incidentally, the priestly vocation that went with it. His regimen now involved teaching undergraduates while studying for his Divinity doctorate. This would be the time when he had to apply himself carefully to the conflicting ideas doing battle in the world of theology and his first biographer tells us that he 'applied his whole study for three years into the . . . scriptures. After this he gave his mind to good writers both new and old . . .'[88] Yet, however open he was to fresh ideas, he was certainly not among the small coterie of daring students receptive to the disturbing ideas from Wittenberg.

It was about the time that Luther's exciting challenge to papal pretensions was first awakening student interest in Cambridge that a teenage Thomas Wriothesley arrived at St John's (or possibly King's Hall which stood next door). As far as his prior London upbringing is concerned, it appears that he, his mother and his three siblings lived together in the fine Garter House built by his uncle adjacent to the Barbican, for their father, William Wriothesley, appears to have died in or about 1513. Substantial though the building was, it was well filled with Wriothesleys for Sir Thomas and his first wife, Joan, had six children. It will have been a lively ménage with all these young cousins around. It was also a well-to-do ménage. The energetic and ambitious elder Thomas continued to be the presiding genius of court ceremonial and to pocket impressive perks. When, for instance, he travelled to the court of Ferdinand, King of the Romans, to confer upon him the Order of the Garter, he received a very impressive silver-gilt cup worth £22 as well as 100 Rhenish guilders. As King's herald it was Sir Thomas who, in 1513, rode up to the walls of Tournai to demand surrender. A few months later he accompanied Princess Mary to Paris for her marriage to King Louis.

As Garter King of Arms, Sir Thomas was busy, important and prominent in the life of the court. He remained a more dynamic personality than his brother. Of William Wriothesley a historian of the College of Arms recorded, 'though he early entered into the College, and was very industrious in his profession, making great collections in matters relating to it . . . yet he never rose higher than York . . .'[89] The older brother was more self-contained and, perhaps, more bookish than his sibling and it was on his thrusting uncle that young Thomas Wriothesley modelled himself. The man who was Garter King of Arms for twenty-nine years did an enormous amount to enhance both the prestige of his office and his own social and economic standing. He was never entrusted by Henry with an important diplomatic post but was left largely unsupervised to develop his heraldic activities. These included deciding issues of precedence between peers, confirming inheritance and introducing them into the House of Lords, conducting visitations of all families bearing arms and, where necessary, removing from churches and private houses any false armorial devices in windows and other memorials, confirming old grants of arms and making new ones, including those to corporations, livery companies and ecclesiastics (he granted arms to Wolsey in 1526-7). All of these activities carried handsome fees and the temptation to accommodate wealthy suitors was considerable and, in 1530, Thomas Wriothesley was accused of abusing his position. The resulting scandal became a major cause célèbre (see pp 408f).

The uncle who was a role model for the younger Thomas Wriothesley was acquisitive, proud, influential, conscious of his social and professional standing and deeply immersed in the dynastic and ceremonial lore which counted for so much in the upper echelons of Tudor society. From childhood Garter's nephew had been accustomed to having easy access to the court. Not only did he enjoy a good vantage point on spectacular ceremonial occasions, he was privy to court gossip and he understood the workings of the royal household. Adolescence brought with it a clearer perception of court politics; he knew who was in favour and who out. He was the complete courtier in embryo, absorbing almost without realising it, the arts of charm, flattery and careful calculation of personal advantage. In a reaction to his father's lack of ambition Thomas Wriothesley determined that he would use his connections to reach the top of the political ladder: he would not be content to be a mere herald. He spent two or three years at Cambridge but did not take a degree. This was long enough to acquire the kind of education which would fit him to enter that growing Tudor bureaucracy staffed by laymen.

*

. . . such was the activity and forward ripeness of nature in him, so pregnant in wit, and so ready he was, in judgement discreet, in tongue eloquent, in service faithful, in stomach courageous, in his pen active, that being conversant in the sight of men, he could not be long unespied . . .[90]

For the Protestant martyrologist, John Foxe, Thomas Cromwell was a great 'valiant soldier and captain of Christ' and one would expect him to wax enthusiastic about his hero's virtues. In fact, there is little exaggeration in the apologist's description. Cromwell was a polymath who, with little formal education, had mastered Latin as well as a handful of continental languages. He was a lateral thinker who followed different careers simultaneously – commerce, law, diplomacy, administration – because his mental energy could not be confined to one vocation. Like most men who set out from unpromising beginnings to achieve success, he developed intellectual and physical stamina, determination and an eye to the main chance. By his mid-twenties his sundry adventures had taught him quick thinking and an ability to handle men which had become intuitive. But the dynamo which generated all this energy was a mind which for clarity and power had few contemporary equals. Moreover, the thought processes of that mind had not become cluttered by any of the established academic disciplines. Cromwell was not inhibited by the theories of the humanists, the dogmas of the churchmen, the methodologies of the scholastics or the inbred prejudices of the nobility. He was a businessman who was never apprenticed, a lawyer who had not studied at the Inns of Court (he did not join Gray's Inn until 1524), a bureaucrat who was a stranger to office routine. He, therefore, possessed that rare intellectual freedom and freshness which 'not only diagnoses the problem but supplies the answers'.* If evidence for all this is required it is to be found in the fact that within three years of his return to England around 1513 Cromwell had come to the attention and entered the service of no less a person than Cardinal Wolsey. One would love to know exactly how the young adventurer achieved the patronage of the most powerful man in England under the King but there can be little doubt that Wolsey instinctively recognised a kindred spirit. The energetic statesman who was rapidly accumulating offices because (whatever his personal ambition) he had creative ideas about the governance of Church and State needed a growing bureaucratic staff. In Cromwell he saw a man whose energy matched his own, a man accustomed to 'getting things done'.

Foxe provided various anecdotes about his subject's early life, the most reliable of which (because it was based upon documents and reminiscences in his own home town of Boston) concerned a mission Cromwell undertook to the papal court in Rome *c.* 1510. In Antwerp he met up with some merchants from the east coast port which was already in decline as a result of silting and changing trade patterns. They were on a civic deputation to obtain renewal of certain papal privileges and indulgences granted to members of the Guild of Our Lady in their magnificent Perpendicular church of St Botolph, of which they were justly proud. To encourage membership of the guild – and, therefore, regular financial support for the maintenance of the church's worship and fabric – previous popes had been prevailed upon to assure guildsmen substantial heavenly rewards. This deal now had to be renegotiated and the unsophisticated Lincolnshire emissaries felt overawed at the prospect of presenting their case before the supreme pontiff in his magnificent Vatican apartments. In Cromwell they recognised a man of the world who had lived in Rome and was not likely to find himself out of his depth there. They pressed him to join the delegation.

Arrived in Rome, Cromwell was anxious to complete his commission as soon and as inexpensively as possible. He was fully aware of the delays and the necessity of palm-greasing that beset all supplicants in the papal court and applied his mind to the problem of gaining an audience. The answer he came up with was – jelly! He reasoned that Julius II's epicurean

*Robert Graves's definition of genius.

169

curiosity might be stirred by this unique English confection and so he had dishes prepared. It now only needed the careful choice of the right moment. Cromwell decided to approach the Pope as he returned, hungry and thirsty, from hunting. As Julius reclined in his tent the Bostonian delegation came towards it, lustily singing an English song so that their approach would reach His Holiness's ears and the guards would not be able to turn them away unheard. It worked. They were summoned into the papal presence, whereupon Cromwell, 'showing his obedience and offering his jolly junkets, "such as kings and princes only," said he, "in the realm of England use to feed upon," desired the same to be accepted in benevolent part . . . as novelties meet for his recreation'.[91] The end of the story was, of course, that the delighted pontiff stamped the necessary documents there and then. It is helpful to remember this example of Cromwell's boldness, ingenuity and understanding of character when considering those revolutionary policies Cromwell was able to persuade Henry VIII to initiate a quarter of a century later.

Cromwell returned to London, a man of no little substance, acquired a house close by the little church of St Gabriel in respectable Fenchurch Street and made a marriage which added to his fortune and contacts. His bride, Elizabeth Wykes, was the daughter of a man who had connections with the royal court and who ran a shearing and wool-dealing business. It seems likely that Cromwell took over the management of his father-in-law's commercial interests while pursuing his own other activities. Like any ambitious man with slight court connections he proceeded to make the most of them. Cromwell was a pleasant companion, witty and attentive, who acquired friends easily and it was not long before he was acting as legal adviser to a number of wealthy and influential clients. Wolsey employed him initially as his lawyer and the first major task he performed for the prelate of which we have record is that of collecting revenues in the archdiocese of York, obviously a responsibility of considerable trust. By the end of the decade he was high in the Cardinal's councils.

This means that he was moving in the same circles as Thomas More. The two men shared friends in common in the City, the legal fraternity, in Wolsey's household and in the royal court. Both were especially intimate with the printer and lawyer John Rastell, who was More's brother-in-law. Despite their different backgrounds the two men had a great deal in common. As well as their legal and official activities they were involved in London business, international affairs and the world of ideas. Cromwell was widely read in the classics and, to some extent, in theology. According to Foxe he was one of the first to be excited by Erasmus's *Novum Instrumentum*, though whether, as the martyrologist insists, he learned it by heart we may doubt; his voluminous correspondence does not reveal a man steeped in Scripture. Sadly nothing has survived which throws light on Cromwell's relations with More in these early years, nor, indeed, on his opinions about the currents of ideas which occasionally stirred the life of the City or the nation, but that this was a formative period both intellectually and socially there can be no doubt.

In January 1519 the Emperor Maximilian died and the electoral princes of the Holy Roman Empire had to give their minds to the choice of a successor. Three names were soon being canvassed: King Charles of Spain, King Francis of France and King Henry of England. The Tudor monarch took very seriously the possibility of such an extension of his prestige and power. In his wildest dreams Henry may well have pictured a Christendom which had himself as emperor and Wolsey as pope. In reality the placing of a non-Habsburg on the throne of Charlemagne was as likely as that of a non-Italian stepping into the fisherman's shoes.

The King's advisers were well aware of this. In 1517, when Maximilian had suggested resigning the Imperial crown in Henry's favour, Cuthbert Tunstall, on embassy in Germany, had to point out, as tactfully as possible, that this really was not on. Having enumerated the constitutional barriers, the envoy suggested that his master had no need to be ambitious for the Imperial title: 'the crown of England is an empire of itself much better than now the empire of Rome, for which cause your Grace weareth a close[d] crown . . . if your Grace should accept the said election thereby you must confess your realm to be under subjection of the empire to the perpetual prejudice of your successor'.[92]

However, such cold considerations were of little account when the royal blood was stirred. When issues of his *potestas* or *imperium* were raised Henry always became politically hyperactive. The French war had been one cause in which he had felt the need to assert himself; the Standish affair had been another. Now, once again, the question of his status in Christendom was raised and Henry bestirred himself. It was not coincidental that, in May, the King authorised another purge of his court. Nicholas Carew and his cronies had once more disgraced themselves and this time not at home. They had been in Paris behaving like the sixteenth-century equivalents of lager louts. They had then, perversely, returned to England as ostentatious Francophiles, 'all French in eating, drinking and apparel, yea, and in French vices and brags, so that all the estates of England were by them laughed at . . . nothing by them was praised but it were after the French turn'.[93] This boisterousness on the part of Henry's household companions did nothing to enhance his electoral chances and the offenders were banished, this time to Calais.

In the aftermath of this upset Henry once again decided to place his hand firmly on the tiller of government and show himself to the world as a caring and involved monarch. He caused Wolsey to draw up reformist documents setting out the mechanics of his personal supervision of the major administrative departments and specifying areas in which His

Majesty 'intendeth in his own person to debate with his Council and to see reformation done therein'.[94] Did Wolsey smile knowingly to himself as he drafted these papers and had them circulated? He may well have reflected that the mood would not last and, indeed, he was right. Henry's candidature was never seriously considered by the German princes. The miscreants were back in court after a few months. And nothing more was heard of the grandiose bid for personal government.

Yet such demonstrations never failed to send tremors through the weights and levers of England's equipoised political life. The twenty-eight-year-old King might be content to be served by a 'medieval' chief administrator who efficiently oversaw the day-to-day running of Church and State and to give him such backing as discouraged the emergence of factions but issues might at any time arise which, Henry considered, touched him personally. Then he could become unpredictable, inflexible and stubborn. It was when he upset the smooth running of the administrative machine by making difficult or unreasonable demands and venting his anger on servants who could not or, in good conscience, would not accede to his wishes that members of his court and Council saw the possibility of personally profiting from instability.

PART FOUR

1529

We Englishmen behold
Our ancient customs bold,
More precious than gold,
Be clean cast away,
And others new be found
The which (ye may understand)
That causeth all your land
So greatly to decay . . .

Great dearth and much idleness,
Little money and much sickness,
Great pride and small riches,
How can these agree?
Great authority and small wisdom,
Simple officers and great extortion,
Light offence and sore correction,
An end of this must be . . .

The farmer [creator] of heaven above all thing,
In the celestial courts sitting,
There in one without beginning,
The Father, Son and Holy Ghost,
Of thy infinite mercy
Send to us some remedy,
Or else I fear shortly
This realm will be lost.
                    Nowe a Days, a popular ballad.[1]

CHAPTER 14

Wolsey – The Peacock Years

By the end of Henry VIII's first decade the honeymoon was long over. The young King welcomed so exuberantly as the one who should end oppression and bring in the Age of Gold had failed to deliver. Expectations had, of course, been unrealistic: the mere change of monarch could not right ancient wrongs, solve the commonwealth's inherent social and economic ills and sustain what we are today obliged to call the 'feel-good factor'. But expectations – or, at least, hopes – there had been, even if they had not reached the level of More's hyperbole, 'the people . . . rejoice, they exult, they leap for joy and celebrate their having such a king'.[2] By 1520 those who found their lot no better or even worse were murmuring agin the government. For most this was nothing more than the Englishman's birthright of grumbling against his betters and convincing himself that the country was going to the dogs but many voiced specific grievances – the cost of foreign wars, trade imbalance, enclosures and rural depopulation, indolent, power-abusing clergy and (age-old cry) the perversion of justice by the wealthy. However, during the 1520s general malaise turned to anxiety, unrest and the threat of rebellion. The perception grew that, not only was the people's material well-being threatened, but that the very national ethos was under attack. This intuitive assessment of the situation was all too accurate. The revolution in English life came in the next decade but the twenties put its major components in place. They were economic dislocation, religious heresy, and the King's resolve to be disencumbered of his wife. These were the issues which affected the lives of many subjects and which sundered court and Council into rival cliques.

Our story is not concerned with such fundamental wealth indicators as grain prices, land usage and trade balances but since they affected the day-to-day well-being of men and women across the social spectrum and, therefore, featured in the political thinking of the great and powerful, we cannot ignore them. The 1520s witnessed the beginnings of that scourge of the Tudor age – price inflation. A disastrous run of harvests (1519–21) ushered in the decade and, although the situation improved throughout the middle years, yields were not plentiful and, in 1527, production plummeted to the worst level in living memory. Market prices fluctuated on a seasonal basis but only around a rising mean. The cost of wheat doubled between 1509 and 1519 and trebled between 1509 and 1527. The fact that the latter was an abnormal year only made the householder's burden weightier. Raw wool exports had largely financed the prosperity of the late fifteenth century and the great Perpendicular churches and half-timbered merchants' houses testify to the surplus wealth of the boom years. By 1520 the economic cycle was on a downturn. Although cloth had replaced wool as the commercial staple, the changes in production and marketing patterns bore heavily upon traditional suppliers and their communities. For example, London now dominated the export market and this had a disastrous impact on east coast ports such as Boston and Ipswich.

Henry and his advisers tried to find simple answers to complex problems. In the summer of 1526 the King informed Wolsey that

> we, after long debating of [currency value variations between England and the Continent] with you and sundry other of our Council, and after remission [i.e. submission] made to outward [i.e. foreign] princes for reformation thereof, and finding finally no matter of remedy to be had at their hands, have by mature deliberation determined, that our coins and monies . . . shall be . . . from henceforth . . . equivalent, corre-spondent and agreeable to the rates . . . in outward parts . . .[3]

The very wording of the royal memo indicates just how seriously the government regarded this decision. And rightly so: it was the worst debasement of the coinage since the Norman conquest. The move, intended to stop the outflow of precious metal in the interests of both the State and the individual, was the first step on a very slippery slope, for, when money is cheapened, goods become more expensive. And, in other ways, too, government policy was adding to the hardships of the people. Henry VII had worked hard to remain at peace with England's neighbours and buttressed international commerce with protective laws. His son's wars and rumours of wars destabilised relations with the realm's trading partners. This made life difficult for the mercantile community and impacted immediately on customs revenue. In 1520 it reached an all-time peak. Within two years it had dropped by two-fifths and it never sub-stantially recovered until the last years of the reign.

People always fear change and at a time when economic life tended to evolve slowly, almost imperceptibly, sudden shifts in relationships or challenges to traditional customs were especially traumatic. Thomas More famously indicted enclosures when he wrote in *Utopia* of sheep who had 'become so great devourers and so wild that they eat up and swallow down the very men themselves'.[4] Wolsey set up a commission to hear com-plaints against landlords who dispossessed tenants in order to hedge their arable fields and turn them over to stock-rearing for the more profitable wool and meat trades. Whether or not, as some historians have argued, the 'enclosure problem' has been exaggerated, there is no doubt about its impact on those families who suffered at the hands of powerful nobles and gentry. Some simply had their land appropriated; others had to cope with large rent rises at the hands of landlords caught up in the fashionable rush to build impressive houses or cut a dash at court. The desperate and distressed not infrequently took the law into their own hands. In 1528 a group of young men in Norfolk were hanged for waylaying wagons to prevent the export of grain. East Anglia was still fizzing with anti-establishmentarianism which, three years earlier, had come close to real rebellion. The occasion was Henry's attempt to raise extra-parliamentary taxation to fund a fresh bout of war against France. The inappropriately named Amicable Grant aroused such widespread opposition that collection had to be called off. This was the first time that Henry had had to bow to the wishes of his subjects and the effect on his psyche was profound.

It was natural that men and women in the grip of anxiety and despair should seek the consolation of religion. Many reposed their trust in the traditional ministrations of the Church, devoting themselves to local shrines and altars, receiving absolution at the hands of their parish priests, trekking to pilgrimage sites to invoke the aid of saints who specialised in assisting with specific problems. But there were those whose faith in ecclesiastical personnel had been shaken and who were sceptical about dogmas they were expected to espouse without question. Human reason identified clerical celibacy as a sham, rejected the spiritual stratagems with which the hierarchy justified their privileges and power claims, resented the prohibition against reading the vernacular Bible and other devotional aids and might even question the 'hocus-pocus' which, at the altar, transmuted bread and wine into 'real' flesh and blood. Both those traditionally and radically inclined were likely to react strongly to Luther's dangerous ideas, and this could only lead to the disruption of the realm. Or so the authorities believed. In January 1521, Cuthbert Tunstall, on a mission to the Emperor, was writing with alarm to all his influential friends to describe the chaos into which Luther had plunged Germany. 'The printers and booksellers,' he urged Wolsey, should be 'given straight charge that they bring none of his books into England, nor that they translate none of them into English, lest thereby might ensue great trouble to the realm and church of England, as is now here.'[5] In May the Cardinal presided in full pomp over a ceremonial burning of the reformer's books. He had already encouraged his royal master to enter the fray and in July the rather bland theological fruit of Henry's uncharacteristically assiduous studies appeared as the *Assertio Septem Sacramentorum*, a sumptuously bound copy of which was immediately carried to the Pope. Leo X was apparently greatly impressed by this defence of the Church's means of sacramental grace from so exalted an author. At home Henry enthusiastically backed the onslaught against peddlers of suspect teaching. In October he issued letters in support of John Longland, one of his more zealous episcopal persecutors:

> Forasmuch as the right revered father in God, our trusty and right well-beloved counsellor the Bishop of Lincoln hath now within his diocese no small number of heretics . . . we therefore . . . do straightly charge and command you, and every of you, as ye tender our high displeasure, to be aiding helping and assisting the said right reverend father in God, and his said officers in the executing of justice . . . not failing to accomplish our commandment and pleasure in the premises, as ye intend to please us, and will answer to the contrary at your uttermost perils.[6]

The result was an immediate purge concentrated in southern Buckinghamshire. The machinery of the ecclesiastical police state was brought to bear – nocturnal visits, the use of paid informers, virulent interrogation, house searches. In the end fifty people were rounded up. Most abjured their opinions but some were burned and, according to Foxe, children were obliged to set the flame to their parents' funeral pyres. Other witch-hunts followed – in Coventry, in London, in southern Essex and other areas where records have not survived.

Was the government, thus, falling into line with Vatican overreaction? Were King and minister exhibiting the triumph of zeal over prudence? Were they making common cause with the alarmist defenders of traditional religion in unleashing fury and hate against an alien culture which they perceived as a major threat? The answer to all these questions is 'No'. Wolsey was too pragmatic a politician to allow himself to be swept along by reactionary ardour and Henry was too independent to become the Pope's tool. England had its own way of dealing with heretics and this did not involve systematic, institutionalised extermination as represented by the Inquisition. Religious deviants were customarily tolerated as long as they did not make too much nuisance of themselves and sporadic persecution by enthusiastic bishops was regarded as sufficient to prevent the development of a heretical movement on the scale of that launched by John Wycliffe, 140 years before. The need to defend the English Church always had to be balanced with the need to defend ordinary subjects from power-crazed ecclesiastics such as those who had disturbed the capital in 1514–15. Neither King nor minister saw himself as deviating from established national policy. Wolsey's attitude towards the upholders of unorthodox belief seems to have been largely in line with that of Erasmus who, in 1524, pleaded with Duke George of Saxony, 'It is not right that an error of any kind be punished by burning unless it is linked with sedition or any other crime which the laws punish by death.'[7]

Wolsey was not by nature a vindictive man and he was too exalted a personage to fear grumbling artisans, over-inquisitive scholars and 'scribblers'. The scurrilous poet John Skelton was silenced, not by a few months in prison but by receiving Wolsey's patronage and when members of the Oxford college the Cardinal was building were apprehended on suspicion of heresy he merely ordered them to be placed in the stocks.

The sudden burst of energy exhibited in 1521 by the King of England and the papal legate had much more to do with international politics and diplomacy than with the preservation of the ancient faith. Leo I chose to make a major issue of the German monk's apostasy. He excommunicated Luther and exhorted all Christian princes to co-operate in suppressing his errors. In May 1521 the Emperor duly placed the condemned heretic under Imperial ban. All across Europe sermons were preached denouncing Luther, and ecclesiastical scavengers sought out his books for burning. This was the bandwagon on to which Wolsey and his master jumped in 1521. Since they were determined to keep England at the centre of Christendom affairs they could not be seen to be standing aloof from the Pope's latest crusade. But they had a more specific reason for joining the lighters of bonfires and the writers of Catholic apologetic. For more than a decade they had been badgering Rome for a title which would put Henry on a par with the Most Christian King of France and the Catholic King of Spain. Their entreaties had hitherto fallen on deaf ears but now the virulent campaign against 'the wild boar in the vineyard' offered a fresh opportunity. It was to this opportunity that Henry spent long hours at his desk and consulted with chaplains and scholars over the production of the *Assertio Septem Sacramentorum*. This, at last, did the trick: a few months later Henry was able to glory in his new title: Defender of the Faith.

But old policing policies soon proved inadequate to cope with new situations. What neither the King nor his advisers foresaw in 1521 was how rapidly and devastatingly the situation would change. So far from being swiftly silenced, Luther became the strident voice of the German 'nation', displaying a genius for turning abstruse theological controversy into the common currency of tavern debate. Hundreds of books and pamphlets poured from his pen and the pens of reformers still more extreme in their criticisms of the Church's practices and personnel. In England the authorities had always been able to keep a close watch on the output of printing houses but now dangerous material from foreign presses was smuggled into east coast ports, creating and nourishing a demand for theological novelty. As ecclesiastical and secular authorities feverishly sought out this propaganda, so students, members of Lollard cells, merchants, civil lawyers and even courtiers tried, with equal ardour, to lay their hands on it. Not only did imported heresy mingle with native strains of Wycliffite teaching, anticlericalism and scepticism, it also spread across all levels of society. It was no longer simply the popular radicalism of the underdogs; it was on the way to becoming a movement with articulate spokesmen, a growing literature and effective means of proselytism. Back across the Channel the march of events gave even further cause for alarm. Years of frustration and resentment exploded in violence against people and objects representative of the old, oppressive religion. In state after state and city after city throughout Germany and Switzerland churches were taken over by the reformers, old rites and ceremonies were abolished, non-co-operative clergy were turned out of office, and in many places the changes were accompanied by the smashing of altars and the burning of mass books and other objects of 'superstition'. Religious houses were closed down and their inmates ordered to fend for themselves as ordinary lay people. Throughout much of central Europe religious change formed an unholy synergy with social revolution: between 1524 and 1526 several areas were convulsed by revolts known collectively as the Peasants' War. Luther roundly denounced the uprisings and was fearful that they would reflect badly on his movement but nothing could halt or divert the Reformation flood. It rushed across Scandinavia and rolled more slowly eastwards. In France and the Low Countries whole areas fell under the sway of different kinds of 'Protestantism', and even where the new churches did not gain control, pockets of reformed faith established themselves.

England was, as always, of Europe but not in Europe. She would go her own way and it is unlikely that she could ever have developed into an outer bulwark of papal Catholicism, Lutheranism, Zwinglianism or Calvinism. The political nation was pulled violently to and fro by the advocates and enemies of change.

We have reached the point where we cannot avoid addressing ourselves, however briefly, to the central issue of the 'Reformation debate': was the convulsion inevitable? Over the centuries partisan historians with axes to grind or reputations to make have enjoyed playing the futile Reformation numbers game, battering each other with statistics, new evidence and fresh interpretations of old evidence designed to prove that the late medieval Church was in a state of holy revival or unholy decadence, that the overthrow of the old religion was or was not popular, that by the mid-century the majority of English men and women thought of themselves as 'Catholic' or 'Protestant'. Reformation England was a crowded and complex landscape and searchlights played upon it from one direction or another merely illuminate different features while casting their own shadows. What occurred throughout the greater part of Henry VIII's reign was a revolution – as opposed to a coup – from which the country emerged both physically and psychologically changed. Since there are certain common features to all revolutions we can make valid comparisons.

Most eastern Europeans in the 1980s were not ideologues who longed for western-style democracy or dreamed of the overthrow of oppressive regimes. They were good communists inured by conviction, custom, fear or preoccupation with daily living to a system that had its drawbacks but which also possessed the advantages of familiarity and stability. That did not prevent huge numbers of them being caught up in the euphoria and the iconoclastic frenzy which followed the toppling of the old regimes. And that, in turn, did not inhibit them from grumbling against their new masters or looking back with wistful nostalgia to the certainties of the 'golden years' when free market economics failed to deliver good times for all. So it was in Tudor England. The majority were willing or complaisant subjects of a pan-European ecclesiastical hierarchy. Those who were spiritually sensitive tended to demonstrate their devotion in traditional ways – funding masses, decking altars and 'goon on pilgrimages'. But a minority of them, precisely because their spiritual antennae were finely tuned, could not be at peace within a Church which seemed to them to be so much at odds with the moral and devotional teachings of its founder. Such people had always existed and the authorities had dealt with them by external or internal exile or, when necessary, by more extreme measures. It was from their ranks that the leaders of the new revolution emerged. When they sensed a 'change in the air' – an unusual willingness of their neighbours to listen, an interest in the ideas blowing across from the Continent – they were ready to force the pace of change and to become allies of a government which had its own reasons for attacking Rome and all its works. Once the 'Berlin wall' was breached there could be no going back (as Mary's disastrous reign made clear). The explosion of the 1520s and 30s had set off a chain reaction which could not be halted. There were some who were unhappy with many of the ecclesiastical novelties but there were others who were equally convinced that reform had not gone far enough. The majority only wanted to settle down to a quiet life under the new order and when the tumultuous years had passed, few of Elizabeth's subjects doubted that their system was superior to those of their Catholic neighbours.

Into this land, feeling the first spasms of economic and religious nervousness, came the third element of disruption – the royal divorce. In real terms it mattered far less to the average subject than the price of food or the destruction of a local shrine, yet it became one of those 'headline-grabbing' issues that aroused passions out of all proportion to its importance. In political terms it was significant because it projected Henry into a long-running battle of wills with Pope Clement VII. However, what the man and woman in the street saw was a wronged royal consort. Catherine of Aragon was an immensely popular Queen, frequently cheered when she appeared in public. The English people have always been easily aroused to sympathy for discarded royal wives. They defied George IV's troops in order to escort Queen Caroline's body through the streets of London. Their mourning at the death of Princess Diana was the most remarkable display of public emotion in recent years. Similar feelings were widely expressed for Henry VIII's discarded queen. They felt that she belonged to the nation as well as her husband and they showed their support in displays of protest and in their sullen resentment of her successor. It was a response that irritated Henry, arguably setting him more firmly on his determined course. Certainly the fate of Catherine became entangled with the progress of the English Reformation to such an extent that its precise contribution has always remained a matter of debate. Was the divorce the *prima causa* or a major contribuent or a mere catalyst in the transition of England from an integral part of Catholic Christendom to an independent Protestant state? As far as our six Thomases are concerned, it would be the divorce and the issues dependent upon it which sealed their destinies.

Within a few months of each other in 1518–19 two children were born to Henry VIII. In November Catherine produced another – a daughter – in a succession of babies who were either stillborn or survived but a few days or hours. Early in the next year the King's mistress, Elizabeth Blount, presented him with a healthy boy. At a court celebration, which was low-key but by no means clandestine, Henry proudly displayed his son, christened Henry Fitzroy. As for the Queen, she had to endure no more pregnancies. Whether this was because of gynaecological complications or because Henry thereafter disdained to play his part in any more experiments is not clear. The fact that doctors were brought from Spain to examine Catherine might suggest medical reasons for her inability to conceive. At thirty-four (in 1519) she was certainly not past child-bearing age. She had, however, lost much of her physical appeal. Six pregnancies and more than one miscarriage in less than a decade had added both years and inches so that she who had once been regarded as a beautiful adornment of the court was now described by a diplomat as 'rather ugly than otherwise'. The difference in age between Catherine and her husband was beginning to tell. Henry was still a youthful twenty-eight, enjoyed vigorous pastimes and, in all likelihood, vigorous bedmates. That he had mistresses is not in the least remarkable; what is worthy of note is that, to the best of our knowledge, he had only two and that these liaisons produced only one surviving child. (The Emperor Maximilian had eleven acknowledged bastards.) This has led some biographers to speculate about Henry's sexual prowess and it may be that he was defective in that department. It is certainly not unusual for men who deliberately project a macho image to be lacking in the skills of lovemaking and his intense sensitivity late in life to the possibility of being cuckolded might suggest that, beneath all the bluster, he lacked confidence with women.

The relationship of husband and wife was certainly changing. They had been close friends, happy partners in revels, dances and a host of court entertainments. Catherine and her ladies had played their parts in the chivalric rituals of the knightly tournament. They rode together in the chase. After 1520 King and Queen increasingly found their pleasures separately. Catherine had to endure her spouse's infidelities but in that she was no different to other women of her station. She remained the dutiful consort presiding with charm and dignity alongside Henry on ceremonial occasions. The public face of this marriage was serene and dignified – all that it should have been. There was no reason why it should not have continued – save that it had failed to provide an heir.

Henry was acutely aware of just how precarious the Tudor dynasty was. He, himself, occupied the throne because his elder brother had died. With only a girl child to succeed him what could prevent England falling back into that chaos which had prevailed throughout much of the previous century? Alternatively the Tudor 'empire' risked being subsumed into another political unit. Already foreign monarchs were speculating on the possibility of taking over the prosperous island kingdom. Having a son and heir was something vital to Henry's manhood and the responsibility he owed his people. The failure (and, of course, that failure was assumed in a male-dominated society to be entirely Catherine's) was a growing anxiety long before the King set eyes upon Anne Boleyn. When he was awaiting the outcome of Catherine's pregnancy in August 1519 he made a most elaborate promise to Pope Leo which reads like a desperate man trying to strike a deal with God. In fulsome words Henry pledged an English contingent for a crusade against the Turk and in the midst of setting out the logistical details – 20,000 foot, 70 ships, carrying 15,000 men, paid for by a tenth raised from the clergy and a fifteenth from the laity, to which royal cohorts would be added contingents from 'those many gentlemen and nobles of England who will hasten to this holy expedition' – he added, 'If our longed-for heir shall have been granted before the expedition sets out to do battle with the Infidel, we will lead our force in person.'[8] The crusade never materialised but within months Henry had immersed himself in that study of the Bible and other holy writings which was to result in the *Assertio*. Can it be that he was trying to buy the divine favour which had so far been withheld?

It was not just that Henry craved a male heir; he had to have one quickly. To leave the throne to a minor would, potentially, be worse than leaving it to a daughter. The glories of Henry V's reign had turned to the dust of baronial conflict because his successor was a nine-month-old child. The pattern was currently being repeated in Scotland. Henry's sister had borne James IV three sons. Two had died in infancy. The present King had been a child of seventeen months when his father fell at Flodden and was now the victim of a tug-o'-war between pro-French and pro-English factions. Henry needed no doom-mongering court preacher to make him aware that death was a frequent visitor and no respecter of kings. The only repository of the Tudor seed might be snatched away at any time and his desire to establish a peaceful succession became stronger with each passing year, creeping like a chilling fog into the once bright and buoyant atmosphere of the court.

Henry did his utmost to keep the grim reaper at bay – although that did not include refraining from exposing himself to danger in the lists. He took a close interest in matters medical; it would be no exaggeration to say that he was a health freak. In a book of recipes for ointments, poultices, lotions, potions and pills published by the royal physicians there appeared scores of concoctions devised by the King himself, including 'a medicine for the pestilence [by] King Henry the Eighth which hath helped divers persons'. Brian Tuke, a royal secretary, reported to Wolsey how the King enquired after an inflammation of the bladder and kidneys that he was suffering, 'and I promise your Grace gave me as direct counsel and showed me the remedies as any cunning physician in England could do'. Henry kept an almost hypochondriacal eye on the health of his household, particularly when any contagion threatened. At the first sign of the sweating sickness he led his court as far from the capital as was practicable and kept on the move, having made a close study 'of the manner of that infection, how folks were taken, how little danger was in it if good order be observed' and what care must be taken to avoid the 'returning in of the sweat before the time'.[9] Yet man's preventative and curative skills were, as Henry and all his contemporaries knew, of little account in the scheme of divine providence. If God withheld his favour then the Tudor succession would be lost and, in all probability, the independent empery of England. It was Henry's attempt to win that favour in the midst of a religious upheaval when it was far from clear who was on the Lord's side that gave its particular colour to the English Reformation.

For Wolsey the decade began with two immensely high-profile events; the Field of Cloth of Gold and the trial of the Duke of Buckingham. Both were expressions of established government policies and attitudes. The costly and elaborate diplomatic pantomime which brought together the courts of England and France in a setting of unparalleled splendour in the Pale of Calais between Ardres and Guines exhibited the continuing determination of King and Cardinal to remain at the centre of Christendom affairs. The indictment of the realm's premier peer for treason declared the implacable Tudor will to brook no aristocratic dissent or displays of independence. That said, it is far from easy to read the detailed significance of these outstanding events. What they immediately demonstrate about Wolsey is that, as he entered his fifties and began to experience bouts of ill health, he had lost little of his industriousness, his administrative skill or his commanding presence.

The series of statesmanly exchanges he brokered between 1520 and

1522 were 'like some colossal anachronistic game which all the monarchs, all their ministers, and all their retinues had decided to play'.[10] Each competitor had his own agenda, his own strategy and his own understanding of the rules. Wolsey had several concerns to balance: maintaining his master's reputation as a European leader, preserving peace (with its attendant economic advantages at home), watching over the integrity of Christendom and bearing in mind the succession and England's long-term security. 'Wolsey's' peace of 1518 was doomed; Francis and Charles were dynasts determined to assert their territorial rights by martial conflict. Yet the Cardinal was disposed to hold on to hope as long as possible. In March 1521 he counselled the King, 'in this controversy between these two princes it shall be a marvellous great praise and honour to your grace so by your high wisdom and authority to pass between and stay them both, that you be not by their contention and variance brought into the war'.[11] Wolsey's instincts were informed by a mix of idealism and pragmatism. He shared the humanist concern for universal Christian brotherhood between the rulers of the nation states, a concern voiced (for several complex reasons) by Leo X. He also knew that war was seldom profitable. The campaigns he had masterminded at the beginning of the reign had brought no fiscal return for the close on a million pounds laid out in equipping and victualling armies in the field and subsidising allies. The money had to be found from taxation and no one ever enjoyed paying taxes. Commissioners always reported back to the Council how difficult their job was and the 1515 levy had been met 'unwillingly with extreme complaint'. Yet, if it came to a choice between angering the King by his desire for continued overseas adventure and upsetting parliament by demanding from them the necessary cash for such belligerence there could be no doubt about whom Wolsey would choose to face.

Nor could there be any doubt about which of the continental rivals would receive his support if he was obliged to take sides. Despite the provocative actions of Nicholas Carew and his clique, the prevailing mood at court and throughout the political nation was as ever anti-French. As for Henry, the fact that the cloudy aspirations of Holy Roman Empery had dissolved in the sunlit air of political reality meant that any territorial designs he had could only be realised at the expense of his Valois rival. Imperialism was an *idée fixe* in the King's mind and one in which he had been tutored since his earliest days. What it actually meant for England was something still being defined by events and theorists but it would be impossible to underestimate its potency. At a pageant staged in June 1522 to welcome Charles V to London several scenes stressed the equality of the two monarchs and at one station an actor representing Charlemagne presented a sword and an imperial crown to *each* of them. Other scenes elaborated Henry's descent, via Arthur, from Constantine and thus implied that he enjoyed a longer and more impressive lineage than his guest.

During the ensuing days Henry made a point of conducting Charles to Winchester Castle to view King Arthur's 'original' round table, upon which the painted visage of the ancient hero bore a remarkable resemblance to the Emperor's host.[12]

Any duel over prestige between Henry and Charles was of quite a different order to the very personal rivalry which existed between Henry and Francis. The French King was closer in age and temperament to Henry and his equal in terms of athleticism, chivalric display and egotistical magnificence. On his first visit to England Charles was a gawky and ill-favoured young man of twenty who made a point of treating Henry with the respect due to his age and wisdom. And he was family. Queen Catherine was eager for good relations with the nephew she had never seen and did all in her limited power to bring about a meeting between him and her husband. She was also keen to un-arrange the betrothal of Princess Mary to the Dauphin so that a marriage alliance could be concocted between her daughter and the royal house of Spain. Initially, Henry was less enthusiastic about showing himself overtly pro-Habsburg. With both continental monarchs contending for his support, he was in no hurry to show his hand – and he still had bitter memories of being cheated and double-crossed by Charles's grandfather, King Ferdinand. However, as the swirling waters of diplomacy throughout the years 1520–2 settled down Henry saw with increasing clarity where his real interests lay and Wolsey, as ever, tuned his fiddle to his master's pitch.

> There hath been much excess
> With banqueting brainless,
> With roistering reckless,
> With jousting thriftless,
> With spend and waste witless,
> Treating of truce restless,
> Prating for peace peaceless,
> The encounters at Calais
> Squeezed us in our purses.

Such was Skelton's sour verdict on the sumptuous toings and froings of these twenty-four months and the wanton extravagance of it all he attributed to Wolsey. He was right in identifying the choreographer of these ornate spectaculars but his mood did not echo that of many of his fellow countrymen. To evaluate the series of meetings attended by Henry, Francis and Charles purely in terms of their political outcome misses the point. Conspicuous display was part and parcel of national and international politics and Wolsey's mastery of the logistics of royal exhibitionism was one of the main reasons for his success. Processions, pageants and the whole panoply of public and semi-public ostentation proclaimed Tudor greatness, not only to foreign potentates and their representatives, but also to the English people at large and especially to those members of the feudal minority who might still be disposed to think of themselves as potential rivals to the Lord's anointed. The great men of the land invited to attend their sovereign were expected to respond enthusiastically to this manifestation of favour and while they and their followers were, at great expense, members of the royal entourage they could not be hatching mischief elsewhere. Gentlemen throughout the land petitioned Wolsey to be included among the ninety-seven shire knights selected for the expedition to the Field of Cloth of Gold and, when they were chosen, mortgaged themselves to the hilt to clothe and equip themselves and their attendants in suitable magnificence. For the majority of the King's subjects – or, at least, those who dwelt in the south-east – there was an element of bread and circuses about the processions of gorgeously dressed celebrities who paraded through their bunting-clad streets and the tableaux and dramatic presentations which proclaimed Tudor propaganda.

The three-week extravaganza outside Guines caught the imagination of a generation of Englishmen and has gone down in history as the biggest party thrown in Europe since the days of Nero. Wolsey helped the King to spend something in the order of £15,000 (a seventh of his annual income) on what was, for sheer theatre, his finest production.

The Field of Cloth of Gold intended as a 'summit conference', turned into many other things. It was an Olympic Games: the jousts, tournaments, archery, wrestling. It was a musical and dramatic festival: the solemn music of royal choirs, the evenings' minstrelsy, the masques. It was an architectural competition: the English raised a large temporary palace, the French a myriad tents and pavilions. It was a wine and food festival: the banquets, with every luxury in food and drink, and free wine for all. It was an international 'concours d'élégance' in dress and costume, in jewellery, and in caparisons for the choicest mounts. Add to this that almost every notable member of the French and English courts strove to be present, and that many succeeded. The numbers, including the large retinues, probably exceeded 6,000.[13]

In the Val d'Orée Henry VIII and Francis I met for the first time but another introduction had already taken place. Charles V, fresh from his election, had hurried to Dover in order to catch his uncle before the rendezvous with his Valois rival. They arranged a more substantial conference and this occurred at Calais and Gravelines straight after the Anglo-French summit. This more hastily arranged gathering was not on the same scale as the recent extravaganza but Wolsey did his best and his army of carpenters, glaziers and painters worked feverishly to produce temporary theatres and banqueting houses worthy of the occasion. It was this that set in train the serious diplomacy which was to create a new pattern of alliance for the 1520s.

The stages by which England moved from arbiter of universal peace to partner in an Anglo-Imperial war council are concealed within the private exchanges between King, Cardinal and diplomats, most of which have not survived in written form. We are obliged to speculate about just how strenuously Wolsey sought to defend the Treaty of London. The high-profile demonstrations of amity and the constant interchange of embassies suggest a concerted effort to prevent Henry being bounced into a belligerent policy and, as we have already seen, Wolsey was, as late as March 1521, strongly urging his master to avoid being caught up in the Habsburg–Valois struggle. However, within weeks Francis I opened hostilities and the role of peace broker became redundant. Tunstall was recalled from the embassy to Charles V that had occupied him inter-mittently since 1515 and it was decided that Wolsey should travel in person to the Imperial court with full powers to conclude a treaty. By then King and minister had agreed the terms to be sought in negotiations with the Emperor.

The tragedy of Wolsey's life – and arguably the life of the nation in the middle decades of the century – was that he accustomed the King to getting what he wanted. It is true that throughout the early years this often amounted to persuading an inexperienced monarch that what he wanted was what his minister had decided he should want. Henry would never be wholly immune to manipulation but, by 1520, he had begun to display that independence, wilfulness and volatility that his advisers came to respect and fear. Increasingly, he looked upon his ministers as political pimps whose duty it was to procure for him those desirables on which he had set his heart. Because Wolsey fulfilled that role with spectacular success the King readily assumed that he only had to will something and his Cardinal would make it a reality. One wonders how often the icy fingers of doubt must have encircled Wolsey's heart as he reflected what might happen if that day ever arrived when he had to disappoint his master. At the very time that King and Cardinal were coming to an accord over the Anglo-Imperial treaty Henry gave his first demonstration that no subject was great enough to be allowed the luxury of independent thought and action.

As soon as the Easter celebrations were over, Henry summoned to court from his Gloucestershire estates England's premier nobleman, Edward Stafford, Duke of Buckingham. Suspicious of no trouble, Surrey's father-in-law arrived in London on 16 April. A month and a day later he was beheaded on Tower Hill. Predictably, Polydore Vergil attributed Buckingham's fall to the machinations of his enemy, the Cardinal. Certainly the two leaders of the temporal and spiritual peers had clashed on more than one occasion and Henry's mysterious warning to Wolsey *et al.* is still on record (see p. 137). In later years the dead man's son blamed Wolsey's vengeful spirit for his family's disgrace and he was voicing what was, by then, a popular story. Nor is there any doubt that the proceedings against the Duke had their beginning in that horticultural interest the Cardinal maintained in those whose power and hauteur needed occasional pruning. But was he responsible for the destruction of Stafford? Does the draconian uprooting of this noble plant hint at the existence of an aristocratic faction?

If anyone was to take a stand on the ancient rights of the feudal nobility against churchmen and upstarts it was Edward Stafford. The forty-four-year-old Duke was directly descended from Edward III and, via his mother, was related to both Edward IV and Henry VII. His father, executed for treason by Richard III in 1483, had reached out his own hand for the crown before deciding to broker Henry Tudor's bid. Buckingham regarded himself as very close to the throne, and the King as being beholden to the house of Stafford. Buckingham stood at the centre of a network of aristocratic marriage alliances embracing Percys, Poles, Howards and Nevilles. His wealth was prodigious and his estates in the Welsh border counties constituted a formidable power base. To crown all he was in the process of building himself at Thornbury, Gloucestershire, the last fortified castle in England. Any monarch would have kept a wary eye on such as Edward Stafford and made sure that he spent much of his time at court. This is precisely what Henry did. And any trusted royal adviser would have kept a sharp ear open for any gossip about so powerful a man. That is precisely what Wolsey did.

Buckingham's worst enemy was not the Cardinal; it was himself. He had a tightly wound ego and a loose tongue. He saw no need for caution in voicing his opinion of Wolsey and Wolsey's policies. He railed against Wolsey as a necromancer and a pimp who had used various evil wiles to obtain and maintain a hold over the King. He was highly critical of the expensive diplomacy of 1520 and loudly voiced his Francophobia. He left no one in any doubt that national affairs would be handled better if he, not the Cardinal, were at the sovereign's right hand. But he went further. In private conversation he flouted the prudent convention of confining his disapprobation to royal advisers. Thus, instead of blaming Empson and Dudley for the governmental misdemeanours of the previous reign, he expressed his contempt for Henry VII in person. From such observations Stafford's confidants might reasonably infer whom he regarded as the source of all contemporary evils. When he also drew attention to his own closeness to the succession he was sailing dangerously close to the rocks of verbal treason.

Towards the end of 1520 Charles Knyvet, a discarded servant of the Duke's, laid information against his ex-master to Wolsey. Wolsey passed on the details to the King. Whether or not this gave him personal pleasure is irrelevant, he had no choice; to conceal possible treason was, in itself, treasonous. Henry now took personal charge of the investigation and there can be little doubt that he was determined to have Buckingham condemned. Two of the Duke's noble relatives spent a brief sojourn in the Tower while Knyvet and two erstwhile colleagues were closely questioned. From their evidence royal agents had little difficulty in making up a ragbag of alleged remarks which proved that Buckingham had imagined the death of the King and envisaged his own succession. For several years he had been encouraged in these fantasies by the 'prophecies' of a disgruntled Carthusian monk who had assured him that Henry would die without a direct male heir and the Duke had from time to time discussed this prognostication with others and how its fulfilment might be hastened. Nothing could have been designed to prey more upon Henry's deepest fears than such threats to the succession. He appointed nineteen peers under the chairmanship of the aged Duke of Norfolk to try Stafford. This court of the High Steward was a judicial process developed by Henry VII for achieving the desired result in state trials; it ensured the Crown a compliant jury and avoided the summoning of the House of Lords, which might not have been so amenable. Buckingham was duly found guilty by a group of his equals, *nem. con.*, and Thomas Howard senior pronounced sentence upon him with tears in his eyes.

Well might Norfolk have been overcome by emotion. The ease with which Buckingham was disposed of, with the contrived concurrence of his peers, vividly demonstrated how the Tudors, father and son, had emasculated the nobility. It may also have come as an unwelcome surprise to Wolsey. He had very successfully used Star Chamber and the common law courts to keep the temporal lords in check and had never attempted to hound any of them to death. Now the King had taken matters out of his hands. The demonstration of Henry's ruthlessness in matters that touched him closely, even though it strengthened Wolsey's position against possible enemies, was a signal that no one was so high that he could not be brought down. It must have weighed with Wolsey in his discussions with the King over foreign policy. Henry had taken up a distinct pro-Imperial, pro-papal stance. From the spring of 1521 Wolsey cast aside thoughts of universal peace and applied his considerable talents to the realignment of English diplomacy.

As the news of Buckingham's condemnation spread through London the common bruit was that this was the Cardinal's doing. This provides us with the first clear glimpse of Wolsey's growing unpopularity but it does not prove his culpability. The prevailing conspiracy theory had Wolsey inducing Knyvet into perjuring himself by giving false testimony against his old master. The subsequent history of the chief prosecution witness casts serious doubt on this interpretation of events. We would expect that Knyvet would have been well rewarded for revealing such dangerous treasons but, so far from seeing his informant all right, the Cardinal turned his back on him. Knyvet pointed out that his loyalty to the King had earned him 'the most extreme slander, hate and disdain'. He had lost not only the remuneration from his service to Buckingham, but also grants and perquisites from others who had employed him. His letters to Wolsey became increasingly desperate but the Cardinal did nothing for him. It fell to Lord Berners, the impecunious Deputy of Calais and a kinsman of Knyvet's, to offer him a place in his own retinue. Thereafter, according to a contemporary moralist, he took service with a ship's captain and eventually met a miserable, lingering death.[14]

If people were ready to believe Wolsey capable of Machiavellian scheming it was because he was the focus for dissatisfaction with the government and the Church. Prudent subjects would not grumble against the King but the man who, beneath the throne, wielded almost regal power – and did so with unstinted ostentation – was the obvious target for discontent. The Cardinal, Archbishop and papal legate was also the epitome for anticlericalists of everything that was wrong with the Catholic hierarchy. He represented a system emanating from a distant place called Rome which filled many benefices and episcopal sees with foreigners and other well-connected 'fat cat' absentees. Many of the King's subjects believed that their ills were largely bound up with the diminishing authority of the great ancient families, feudal magnates, like Buckingham, who were thoroughly English and had a major stake in the country. Such prejudice was irrational but popular politics always owes more to emotion than to logical argument. Wolsey, of course, was far too secure to care what the commonalty thought and, particularly after Stafford's fall, none of the nobles was prepared to play the populist card in mounting a challenge to him. But there was one person who was aware of the Cardinal's bad press and who may, even at this stage, have tucked away at the back of his mind just how widely welcomed the minister's fall would be. Henry had started his reign on a tide of euphoria by throwing his father's most trusted advisers to the wolves. What he had done once he could, if necessary, do again.

Any such prospect would seem firmly in the realm of wishful thinking in the high summer of 1521. On 25 July Wolsey set off with even greater pomp than usual for a series of meetings with the Emperor. Charles fêted his visitor royally, calling him his 'second father' (Henry VIII being his 'true father') and even promising to support Wolsey's candidacy for the next papal vacancy. Politically the end result was the drawing of England into an offensive alliance with the Empire and the papacy against France. Wolsey pledged Henry to providing ships, men and gold for an invasion in 1523 (later postponed to 1524). Perpetual amity between Henry and his nephew was to be secured by the marriage of Princess Mary (when she reached the age of twelve) to Charles. That projected event was still six years off and anything might happen in that time. God might yet bless Henry and Catherine with a son. Catherine might die and open the way for the widower to find a bride whose womb might be more favoured. Yet, if the worst came to the worst, England (to which a considerable part of France would have been added by right of conquest) would be united with the most powerful political force in the world whose territory embraced most of Europe and lands beyond the seas whose potential was yet to be realised. Charles made a point of emphasising the wealth of the Indies in the summer of 1522 when he paid a lengthy state visit to his aunt and uncle. While Henry and Wolsey laid on a series of spectacular entertainments, in an attempt to strike the mood which had prevailed at the Field of Cloth of Gold, Charles displayed for his amazed hosts the stunning treasures of Montezuma recently plundered in Mexico by Hernan Cortes.

Once more Wolsey had given King Henry what he wanted. The Tudor monarch may have sacrificed his role as independent arbiter of Christendom and pledged himself to more costly wars, about both of which Wolsey had misgivings, but he had maintained a centre-stage role in the affairs of Europe. He had shown himself a strong ruler who had dealt firmly with the French King, a German heretic and a troublesome English magnate. His nephew and future son-in-law was a young man who looked upon him as a guide, philosopher and friend and who exhibited none of his grandfather's guile and perfidy. He was Defender of the Faith and a staunch supporter of papal Christianity. As such he may well have felt that God owed it to him to grant him his heart's greatest desire, a healthy son. Still Henry was prepared to share his glory with the great Cardinal. When Wolsey celebrated mass in St Paul's on Whitsunday he was attended by over twenty prelates drawn from both royal entourages and was served at the altar by two dukes, two earls and two barons. The future for both King and minister seemed gilded indeed. And that made the subsequent repeated disillusionments doubly bitter.

The first disappointment had already occurred. Leo X had died the previous December and, instead of fulfilling his pledge to Wolsey, the Emperor had backed Leo's nephew Giulio de Medici. In the event, the conclave surprised everyone by electing Cardinal Adrian Boeyens, who would be the last non-Italian to occupy the throne of St Peter for 456 years. Adrian VI is one of the intriguing might-have-beens of history. He was by no stretch of the imagination an ecclesiastical politician. Rather, he was a devout man of ascetic habits whose great strength lay in teaching. He had been a tutor to both Erasmus and Charles V, and scholar and Emperor now expected a reformist pontificate. Charles told his old friend that he was convinced that God had raised him up 'to set in order the affairs of Christendom'. Erasmus felt able to urge the new Pope to abandon the disruptive policy of denouncing the Lutherans. 'This cancer has gone too far to be curable by the knife or cautery,' he observed, and pressed Adrian, instead, to call together wise and holy men from all parties.[15] The pontiff did set out on a programme of reform, beginning with the curia but, after a reign of a little more than twenty months, he died. This time Giulio de Medici *did* reach the summit of his ambition and he used his position to advance the interests of his family. Christendom affairs were once more in the hands of politicians, businessmen and administrators who lacked spiritual vision. Had the disintegration of the western Church been slowed down in the 1520s and a programme of humanist reform instigated, the history of Europe would have been very different. After Adrian's death a turbulent quarter of a century passed before the Vatican even began to get its act together. Then it was far too late.

The grandiose schema for redrawing the map of Europe was a fantasy concocted by monarchs and diplomats who believed their own rhetoric. As soon as the downpour of cold realism began the colours soon streamed from the sagging bunting of Christian fraternity. Put simply, the alliance disintegrated because its signatories pursued their own interests and because they could not afford the military adventures to which they had pledged themselves. The Emperor's primary concern lay in forcing the French out of northern Italy while Henry's ambition involved striking out from Calais into northern France. Throughout the campaigning seasons of 1522 and 1523 they proved unable or unwilling to co-ordinate their military activities for maximum effect. Ineffective skirmishing across the Channel had already cost the treasury £400,000 for which there was nothing to show and the major invasion plan which was the centrepiece of the great united enterprise had yet to be launched. It never was, though the war still had a few more twists and turns in it.

As soon as Wolsey had found himself committed to belligerence he had set about raising the necessary revenue with his usual energy. He instigated a county by county census to discover the nation's military capacity and the distribution of its wealth. In itself it was a reasonable administrative measure; the taxation-assessment statistics had not been revised for a couple of centuries and a king about to embark on a major war needed a reliable estimate of the nation's fighting potential. But, of course, the probing commissioners were resented and people's suspicions were confirmed when all lay subjects of middle incomes and above were required to make a loan to the King of ten per cent of their wealth. The result was inadequate and the following spring the government was forced to the unwelcome expedient of summoning parliament.

Wolsey knew that the representatives from the shires and boroughs were going to give him a hard time but nevertheless he underestimated their resistance and had to resort to various shades of bullying, cajolery and deceit. Even then he failed to squeeze as much as he had hoped out of the Commons. His first tactic was to appoint Thomas More as Speaker. More was a thoroughly trustworthy King's man but he was popular in the mercantile community and an advocate skilled with honeyed words. If anyone could charm money out of the members' purses it was he. As soon as parliament assembled (18 April) Wolsey personally presented the King's demand for a swingeing £800,000. He hoped, perhaps against hope, that the business would be concluded quickly but even More's advocacy could not secure a majority in favour of the desired taxation. In the event the session became a seventeen-week war of attrition (with a three-week recess). The MPs, outraged at being asked to pay for what many considered a futile foreign adventure, debated the matter back and forth without conclusion. After each day's business they retired to the City's alehouses and went on discussing the issue, their inhibitions doubtless weakened by liquor. Having London abuzz with indignation was certainly not part of Wolsey's plan. Once again he descended on the assembly in all his scarlet magnificence and harangued them for their unwillingness to meet their prince's reasonable demands. The ranks of knights and burgesses listened mute and resentful until Wolsey made the mistake of trying, contrary to the customs of the house, to engage individual members in debate.

. . . seeing the company sitting still silent, and thereunto nothing answering and contrary to his expectation showing in themselves towards his requests no towardness of inclination, [he] said unto them.

'Masters, you have many wise and learned men among you, and since I am from the King's own person sent hither unto you for the preservation of yourselves and all the realm, I think it meet you give me some reasonable answer.'

Whereat every man holding his peace, then began he to speak to one Master Marney, after Lord Marney: 'How say you,' quoth he, 'Master Marney?' Who making him no answer neither, he severally asked the same question of divers others accompted the wisest of the company . . . none of them all would give so much as one word, being before agreed, as the custom was.[16]

Wolsey tried other stratagems, assuring the Commons that the upper house had approved the levy and that part of the money raised would be used to repay the forced loan of the previous year. The first was a lie and the second a promise he had no intention of keeping.

The most telling comment to emerge from all the documents is the one attributed to the Cardinal by Hall when, a few days later, a Commons' deputation called upon him with the offer of a compromise sum. Wolsey replied, 'that he would rather have his tongue plucked out of his head with a pair of pincers than move the King to take any less sum'.[17] To expect Henry to lose face with the Emperor by admitting that his own subjects would not permit him to honour his treaty obligations was quite out of the question. Eventually More came to his patron's rescue by devising a formula which gave Henry most of what he wanted, though spread over a longer period and ensuring that the matter was put to the vote when there was a majority of the King's courtiers and other supporters in the chamber – men who knew what was expected of them. An anonymous member of the parliament reported to the Earl of Surrey how the crisis stood at 15 May:

> There hath been such hold [impasse] that the House was like to have been dissevered [divided]; that is to say, the knights being of the King's Council, the King's servants and gentlemen of the one party, which in so long time were spoken with and made to say 'yea', it may fortune contrary to their heart, will and conscience. Thus hanging the matter, yesterday the more part, being the King's servants, gentlemen, were there assembled; and so they, being the more part, willed and gave to the King 2s. of the £ . . . I have heard no man in my life that can remember that ever there was given to anyone of the King's ancestors half so much at one grant; nor I think there was never such a precedent seen before this time. I beseech Almighty God it may be well and peacably levied and surely paid unto the King's Grace without grudge and specially without losing the goodwills and true hearts of his subjects, which I reckon a far greater treasure for a king than gold or silver.'[18]

A relieved Wolsey was only too happy to reward More by doubling his Speaker's salary.[19] However, any rejoicing was premature: the royal commissioners were able to collect only a quarter of the money agreed by parliament. This assembly, which had its first meetings in the church of the London Blackfriars and subsequently moved to the house of the Black Monks (Benedictines) in Westminster, was commonly known as the Black Parliament, a nickname both its members and Wolsey must have considered particularly appropriate.

Throughout the next few months Wolsey was under the greatest pressure of his career so far. He needed either a peace which would stop the outflow of treasure or a stunning victory that would justify the continuance of the conflict. Meanwhile, his royal master, little interested in pounds, shillings and pence, continued to indulge dreams of conquest and the Church Militant. Inevitably under these conditions, policy became a handmaid of the fortunes of war. At the end of 1523 Wolsey saw an opportunity to end a 'dribbling war' by a direct assault on Paris and persuaded Henry to abandon a more long-term strategy and order Suffolk to strike for the French capital. A few months later, that plan having failed miserably, he was secretly discussing peace with Francis I's envoys. Then, in February 1525, the French were soundly beaten by Imperial forces at Pavia and their king was captured. Suddenly all bets were on again. Henry was delirious with joy at the news of Pavia, likening the messenger who brought it to the angel of the Annunciation. He envisaged himself riding to glory on the back of his ally's success, although that was not, of course, how the matter was presented to Charles. England's ambassadors were instructed to impress upon him that, once Henry had been placed on the throne of France, the Emperor could look forward to enjoying

> the whole monarchy of Christendom. For of his own inheritance he hath the realm of Spain and a great part of Germany, the realms of Sicily and Naples, with Flanders, Holland, Zeeland, Brabant, and Hainault and other his Low Countries; by election he hath the Empire, whereunto apperaineth all the rest of Italy and many towns imperial in Germany and elsewhere; by the possibility apparent to come by my lady Princes[s Mary] he should hereafter have England and Ireland, with the title to the superiority of Scotland, and in this case all France with the dependencies.[20]

Once more the possibility of repeating the exploits of Henry V enlivened his namesake's easily roused imagination. With the recklessness of a gambler staking all on the basis of a hot tip the King instructed Wolsey to make the arrangements for a grand invasion of France.

This was the point at which the objectives of King and minister parted company. Henry was out of touch with the mood of the country and even, to some extent, with the real implications of complex and often contradictory diplomatic exchanges. Wolsey the realist now understood beyond a peradventure that the grand enterprise simply was not on. He had completely lost faith in Charles V and he realised that there was not the remotest chance of raising yet more taxation from a populace that had failed to produce the revenue demanded of it over the previous three years. It was not only the lay representatives who had proved obdurate in 1523. When he had summoned convocation in order to press the clergy for their contribution they had tried to wriggle out through a legal loophole. Their leaders claimed that they could not be made to appear before the Cardinal Legate because the instructions to convene had been issued under the authority of the Archbishop of Canterbury. Wolsey had been forced to acknowledge himself beaten and had been put to the tiresome expedient of sending out a fresh batch of letters to all the parish priests in the realm. The correspondent who reported these events accurately reflected the prevailing anxiety: 'I do tremble to remember the end of all these high and new enterprises, for oftentimes it hath been seen that to a new enterprise there followeth a new manner and strange sequel. God of his mercy send his grace of such fashion that it may be all for the best.'[21] Wolsey understood the mood of the country. He understood the mood of the King. He understood the mood of the Emperor – so much so that he once expostulated that he heartily wished that, on disembarking for his meetings with Charles in 1521, he had fallen, broken both arms and both legs, and so been incapacitated from carrying out his master's instructions. Now, in 1525, he had to juggle three sets of incompatibles and ensure that Henry emerged with his honour and reputation intact. His first response was a very public rejoicing at the overthrow of the King's enemy.

The Archbishop of York, Cardinal and legate a latere, sung mass . . in Paul's church, in his 'pontificalibus', and 11 bishops and abbots, with their mitres, being present, the Duke of Norfolk and the Duke of Suffolk, with all the nobles of the realm. And the said Cardinal granted the same to all manner of persons, being within the precinct of the church in the time of the mass, plenary remission of their sins, a poena et culpa; and, after mass, Te Deum was sung for the said victory, the Mayor, Aldermen, with the head crafts of the City standing in the body of the church in their liveries; and that night great fires were made in divers places of the city, with vessels of wine at every fire for the people to drink.[22]

Less grand celebrations were ordered to be made in every town and village throughout the realm. Wolsey's next move was to send out orders for the collection of a non-parliamentary levy, euphemistically called the Amicable Grant. Instead of appointing the local gentry as commissioners he nominated members of the Council, thus ensuring that they would share the inevitable unpopularity. He appointed Thomas Howard junior, recently become Duke of Norfolk on the death of his father, as commander of a new army to be despatched across the Channel. It was a smokescreen. Wolsey had no intention of sending good troops after bad and certainly no intention of appointing Howard to such an important command. So far from being allowed to get on with the logistics of an invasion force, the Duke was ordered to East Anglia to oversee the collection of the Amicable Grant and his repeated pleas to be allowed back to London were rejected. However, to all observers at home and abroad, and paramountly to King Henry, it appeared that England was, indeed, preparing to invade France. If, now, she failed to do so the reason must appear to be a genuine change of heart and not weakness. Wolsey needed a scapegoat, and one was readily to hand.

Charles V had gained all he wanted from the war and he had no money with which to continue it. With Francis as his prisoner he could enforce peace on his own terms. These included removing the French threat from Italy and the Low Countries and the yielding of Burgundy to Habsburg control. They did not include deposing Francis in favour of Henry VIII or ceding any French territory to England. Charles no longer had any need for little Mary Tudor and could cast around for a more profitable marriage. He found one near at hand in the person of Isabella of Portugal, the twenty-two-year-old daughter of a king grown phenomenally rich on the wealth of the eastern trade routes. Henry had been snubbed. Charles of Habsburg had used him as long as it suited him and then thrown him over. It all seemed humiliatingly familiar.

If Henry was shocked and outraged by this outcome, the same could not be said for Wolsey. He had kept his options open and allowed himself neither to be dazzled by the Emperor nor blinded by Francophobia. The Cardinal had his own channels of communication with Paris and for some months had maintained a highly secret correspondence with the French court to which even Henry was not privy. This very hazardous proceeding shows just how confident Wolsey had become about pursuing independent policies. But, of course, the King had to be persuaded of the need to change those policies. Thus, while Norfolk, Suffolk, Warham and the other commissioners were struggling to extract money from reluctant countrymen and Norfolk was dutifully reporting the suspicious activities of French ships off the East Anglian coast, Wolsey was carefully doctoring ambassadorial reports from the imperial court and commenting, 'I doubt not but your Highness of your profound and great wisdom [will easily deduce] what this manner of proceeding doth imply' and realise that what Charles intends 'will be little or nothing to your Highness's benefit'.[23]

The complaints about the Amicable Grant coming in daily from the shires were, in fact, grist to Wolsey's mill. On 5 April, for example, Warham listed for the Cardinal's 'secret ear' the reactions he was encountering in Kent:

The people speak cursedly, saying they shall never have rest of payments as long as some liveth. 2. That some of the commissioners, through fear of the people, will only announce the King's command without pressing it further, leaving the obnoxious portion to the Archbishop. 3. That complaint is made that the [1522] loan is not repaid, nor will this grant be. 4. They would give, but cannot; and will not at any other than the King's appointment. 5. That too much coin of the realm is exported already into Flanders. 6. That it would be the greatest means of enriching France to have all his money spent there, out of the realm; and if the King win France, he will be obliged to spend his time and revenues there. 7. They are sorry, rather than otherwise, at the captivity of Francis I. 8. That all the sums already spent on the invasion of France have not gained the King a foot more land in it than his father had, 'which lacked no riches or wisdom to win the kingdom of France if he had thought it expedient'.

Warham sourly concluded that the whole exercise would have been easier if it had been left until 'the cuckoo time and the hot weather (at which time mad brains be most busy) had been past'.[24]

The fact that widespread reluctance to comply with the Amicable Grant played into Wolsey's hands does not mean that he was blasé about the disobedience of the King's subjects. Incipient revolt was something sixteenth-century governments always took seriously – and never more so than in 1525. This was a crisis time and had long been prophesied as such. Astrologers pointed out that, in the autumn of 1524, all the planets would be aligned in Pisces and that this could only be a portent of great disaster. Right on cue in the closing weeks of the year the first rumblings of what would become the Peasants' War were heard. Over the coming months Wolsey's diplomatic postbag brought him alarming news of violent clashes between the lower orders and their masters and of a large area of the Continent becoming sundered along confessional lines. A band of Lutherans had plundered abbeys in Burgundy. The princes of Germany were grouping themselves into Catholic and evangelical (the word 'Protestant' would not be coined until 1529) leagues. 100,000 people had supposedly been killed in the war provoked by the 'accursed sect of Luther'. The Cardinal of Salzburg had had to pay off the rebels with two-thirds of his revenues. Bishops had been forced to allow their clergy to marry.[25] It was clear that while Charles, Henry and Francis had been indulging their private war games the united Christendom by which they all, professedly, set so much store was disintegrating. The Emperor certainly wished to be rid of all distractions so that he could respond to the crisis in his German territories. The troubles within England were minuscule in comparison but the authorities could not help casting anxious glances at the ominous glow in the eastern sky. In London Wolsey was resisted to his face by City councillors opposing the Amicable Grant and out in the shires many gentry refused to confront their angry neighbours. Willing subjects in Kent would not pay up for fear of the mob. On the Essex–Suffolk border thousands of artisans, fearing for their jobs, banded together to resist the latest exaction which, they believed, threatened the cloth trade. There were rumours of similar organised unrest throughout neighbouring counties and the University of Cambridge and the Dukes of Norfolk and Suffolk urged Wolsey to keep close watch on the Lords Stafford and Bergavenny and the Buckingham connection lest they take advantage of the prevailing mood.

Wolsey's reactions allowed him to exercise all his thespian and propagandist skills. The cancelling of the invasion had removed the urgency for raising a huge sum of money, so he could afford to be generous. He first of all reduced the demanded levy and then, 'on his knees' as he allowed it to be believed, pleaded with Henry for its total abolition. When 4,000 repentant Suffolk demonstrators pleaded for mercy from Howard and Brandon the Cardinal advised that severe measures should be taken against the ringleaders but subsequently issued the King's pardon. Finally, he allowed himself to absorb all the residual unpopularity arising from the whole pointless exercise. The official line put out was that the Amicable Grant was conjured up by Wolsey and the Council without the King's knowledge.

It remained only to give legal form to the realities of the changed international situation and to save as much face as possible while doing so. In the summer clandestine negotiations with France blossomed into formal discussion of an independent treaty, signed at Wolsey's Hertfordshire retreat, the More, at the end of August. It was not the end of a period of complex European diplomacy; merely another stage in it. Francis was Charles's prisoner and there was still unfinished business between them. The French King's release would make possible a range of new options but for the moment the English actors in the political drama could withdraw to the tiring house and catch their breath.

However, there was to be one novel element in the emerging situation, as yet concealed even from the King's intimates, which would come to dominate everything. Various components went into its construction. The most obvious was Henry's emotional reaction to Habsburg perfidy. The rejection of Mary and with it the prospect of England's entering a new phase as an integral part of a grand Christian empire had been a deeply felt blow to his *amour propre*. The young nephew he had warmly clasped to his bosom and who had promised to be guided by his avuncular wisdom had deserted him as soon as it suited his purpose to do so. It had taken intricate and cynical diplomatic manoeuvrings and a new accord with the untrustworthy Francis to avoid him appearing as a fool throughout Christendom. Henry's anger with Charles spilled over on to his own wife who had constantly championed the imperialist cause. Perhaps it also spilled over on to God. In his self-pity Henry must have asked himself what more the Almighty could demand of him that he had not already given. He had supported the papacy, denounced Lutheranism and striven for the unity of western Christendom. Yet his reward for all this was the prospect of the end of his dynasty and his kingdom being absorbed into the territory of a foreign power.

His first act was one of defiance against the pro-imperialists and that blind fate which seemed to be controlling his family affairs. As soon as he heard that Charles wished to break his engagement to Mary he brought his own illegitimate son out of discreet obscurity. On 15 June 1525 a series of impressive ceremonies took place at Bridewell Palace. From them the six-year-old Henry Fitzroy emerged as Duke of Richmond, Earl of Nottingham, Lord Admiral, Warden-General of the Marches (these two titles taken from Thomas Howard), Knight of the Garter, Keeper of the City and Castle of Carlisle and first peer of England. At the same time Mary was ordered to the border castle of Ludlow to fulfil her responsibilities as Princess of Wales and within days Richmond was despatched northwards as Lord Lieutenant to take up his duties over against Scotland.

The symbolism was obvious: the two royal children were treated equally and were being inducted into the responsibilities of government. It could no longer be assumed that Henry would be succeeded by his daughter. Sending Mary away also satisfied the vindictive streak in Henry: the little girl was to be removed from her mother's pro-Habsburg influence.

After this demonstration the King, it seems, lapsed into a mood of introspection. He and Catherine would have no more children. History showed that succession by daughters and by bastard sons was fraught with perils. If everything was going wrong for himself and the Crown which had been entrusted to his stewardship, could it be that he was in some way to blame? Had he unwittingly offended God? Was the curse on his marriage a divine punishment? It has become customary to refer to Henry VIII's 'convenient' conscience but the fact that he had a keen conscience should not be underestimated. Doubtless, as with most men, it responded to some stimuli more readily than to others but we should not dismiss it with a smirk of post-Christian cynicism. Nor should we undervalue the sixteenth-century belief in divine providence. Henry knew that God was active in human affairs. As a student of the Old Testament (and no mean student, as the *Assertio* demonstrated) he saw clearly the hand of the Lord in raising up and casting down kings, in crowning the righteous with success and punishing those rulers who erred from the divine path. In 1525 and 1526 Henry was desperately seeking an answer to the central problem of his life and, sometime during these months, he came to the conclusion that he had found it in Leviticus 20.21, 'If a man marries his brother's wife, they will die childless. He has done a ritually unclean thing.'

CHAPTER 15

Out in the Cold

One of the few great families not represented at the Field of Cloth of Gold, just as it had not been represented in the martial cavalcade of 1513, was the Howards. It was Buckingham and Suffolk who, in their sumptuous clothes and each attended by five chaplains, ten gentlemen, a hundred and forty retainers, fifty-five servants and a travelling stable of ninety horses, were allowed to flaunt themselves in tiltyard and banqueting hall as the cream of the English nobility. The Duke of Norfolk was left behind as the King's deputy. This was undoubtedly a position of trust but what the elder Thomas Howard really enjoyed was authority without power. Wolsey took with him across the Channel all the paraphernalia of government – secretaries, officials and the seals which authenticated royal decisions. Norfolk was little more than a postmaster, receiving and rerouting messages to and from the court.

His son had been even further distanced from the centre of activity; he had been despatched to Ireland. This territory, theoretically under English rule but in reality dominated by a handful of feuding Irish lordlings, required a massive investment of money, soldiers, administrators and imaginative government if it was ever to be integrated into the Tudor state. The cost was too high. Apart from occasional military forays and displays of enthusiastic intent, Ireland had, since 1485, remained out of sight and out of mind. Effective English rule was confined to the Pale around Dublin and the ports of Cork and Waterford. Henry's representative there was Gerald Fitzgerald, ninth Earl of Kildare, who behaved as a virtually independent magnate, little troubled by directives from London. He was an energetic and intelligent campaigner (aged thirty-three in 1520) whose raids on recalcitrant nobles enriched himself, established a degree of peace and ensured a volume of complaints reaching London. Wolsey had no time to spare for the neighbouring territory but part of Henry's sudden burst of executive energy in 1519 had been a determination to 'do something' about Ireland, and Kildare was, accordingly, summoned to court. Significantly, Wolsey could not find an opportunity to see him for several months. When the two men did meet in the autumn they took a profound dislike to each other. The Cardinal was disposed to believe the version of events presented by Kildare's enemies. He deprived the Earl of his post and ordered him to remain at court. Wolsey had another reason for wanting to keep a careful eye on the headstrong Anglo-Irishman. Kildare's much-loved first wife having died in 1517, he married in the summer of 1520 Elizabeth Grey, the Marquess of Dorset's sister. In so doing he became a first cousin of the King so it is not surprising that Henry and his minister wanted to vet his loyalty and were reluctant to permit him to return to his own country. He was, therefore, detained in England and, the following summer, was obliged to join the royal entourage at the Field of Cloth of Gold, where he acquitted himself with noticeable élan in the tournays.

Someone had to be appointed to fill Kildare's place. On the other side of the Irish Sea many regarded the obvious choice as Piers Butler, eighth Earl of Ormond and the Fitzgeralds' most prominent and bitter rival. However, the Earl's claim to his title was challenged and there was nothing to be gained by appointing Kildare's enemy and fuelling the clan conflict. These were the circumstances under which Surrey was given the job of Lord Lieutenant of Ireland. Was this promotion or exile? Howard was sent with the brief to employ a firm hand in establishing efficient (and profitable) administration. He may have welcomed the opportunity to be energetically employed after years of frustrating inactivity. Peace had kept him away from battle by sea or land and, though he was still Lord Admiral, he was not involved in any of Henry's adventurous plans to build up the navy and improve harbour fortifications. Yet even before he set out, Surrey must have realised that there was little prospect of any glory being gleaned from his new appointment. It must, indeed, have been part of Wolsey's decision-making process that Ireland would not provide the Howards with another Flodden. The Earl had certainly drawn the short straw. He was denied any part in the spectacular and important affairs of state which engrossed his conciliar colleagues in 1520 and 1521. If he had not been given this mission Surrey could hardly have been excluded from the royal entourage. The likeliest answer to the question why he was excluded is that Henry or Wolsey or both wanted him excluded.

Conspiracy theorists from Vergil and Hall onwards have pointed to deeper, darker waters of realpolitik. Surrey's 'banishment' to the Ultima Thule of English domestic affairs was, they claimed, part of Wolsey's plot against Buckingham: the Cardinal deliberately got the doomed Earl's son-in-law out of the way before proceeding against him. This is a theory that tells us more about the gathering ill feeling provoked by Wolsey than it does about the actual relationships between the leading men of the court. After the great minister's fall his critics could talk openly about the 'proud churchman's' crimes. High on the list was his deliberate usurpation of that position which by ancient right belonged to the King's tenants-in-chief. What better proof could there be of Wolsey's hostility to the nobility than his destruction of Buckingham? Every convenient fact became a thread woven into the design of a subtle Machiavellian scheme and Surrey's mission to Ireland was one of them. However, even if we leave aside the fact that no surviving evidence exists which locates the beginning of the case against Buckingham earlier than the autumn of 1520, by which time Surrey had been gone for six months, can we really visualise the Earl as a man who would defy the King in order to come to the aid of his wife's father?

As soon as the question is posed the answer stares one in the face. The old Duke of Norfolk, who still ruled the Howard clan, had gained everything by subservience to the Tudors, and his vapid son had learned the lesson well. The Duke was chosen to preside at Buckingham's trial and, though he may well have delivered judgement with tears streaming down his face, there is not the slightest suggestion that he would have contemplated doing anything other than accommodate Henry's wishes. Surrey, for his part, was very unlikely to have wept for his father-in-law for the very good reason that he disliked – perhaps even hated – the man. There was a twenty-three-year age gap between the Earl and his wife. When Elizabeth Stafford was forced into marriage in 1513 she was, at the age of seventeen, already a self-willed young woman and she loudly voiced her protest at being obliged to abandon her true love for an older man she disliked. Age, Thomas's frequent absences and his infidelities did nothing to sweeten her temper. Surrey, whose emotions also tended to be very black and white, responded with verbal and, perhaps, physical abuse to his wife's tantrums. By 1520 the marriage was, if not on the rocks, sailing perilously close inshore. So far from cementing the relationship between two noble houses, it chipped away at whatever harmony existed. At his trial Buckingham apparently referred in open court to the hostility between himself and Surrey. Howard later recalled the Duke's words: the doomed man had confessed 'that of all men living he hated me most, thinking that I was the man that had hurt him most to the king's majesty'.[26]

The truth about Surrey's Lord Lieutenancy is simple. It was an unpopular job that none of the King's other generals wanted. Henry was not prepared to be deprived of any of the impressive ornaments of his court at the time of his cavalcade into France. The man he could most readily spare was the dullard, Thomas Howard.

Surrey set out for the graveyard of reputations knowing that the government was almost completely preoccupied with other matters and that he could expect no support from the relatives of the deposed Kildare. He may even have learned that the Earl was actively plotting to frustrate his endeavours. It took him only a few weeks to discover that this was, in fact, the case. As soon as Howard's appointment was known Kildare wrote urging several of the Irish lords to create so much havoc that the King's deputy would have to be recalled. Surrey lost no time in reporting his suspicions but Wolsey did nothing about them. This was for the very good reason that, like him or loathe him, Kildare was a political asset. His territorial possessions and his extensive clientage network made him the only person likely to maintain any kind of rule in Ireland and Wolsey's primary concern was to ensure the Earl's genuine loyalty to the Crown. His detention in England, his participation in the Field of Cloth of Gold and the government's acceptance of his marriage into Dorset's family were all designed to bind Fitzgerald more tightly to the house of Tudor. Wolsey, the realist, worked towards Kildare's eventual restitution. It may even have been he who brokered the marriage to Elizabeth Grey, daughter of his old patron and friend. Henry had a different view of the situation, a view as usual coloured by idealism and personal feelings. He neither liked nor trusted Kildare and, now that he had woken up to the Irish situation, he saw it as encumbent upon his Imperial responsibility and dignity to ensure effective and orderly government in the island. This was to be achieved, he instructed Surrey, by 'sober ways, politic drifts and amiable persuasions, founded in law and reason [and not] by rigorous dealing . . . by strength or violence . . . to bring the Irishry in appearance only of obeisance . . . were a thing of little policy, less advantage and no effect'.[27] If Wolsey looked to Surrey for subtle diplomacy, wisdom and the graciousness that wins hearts and minds he sorely misjudged his man. He certainly misjudged the state of affairs over the water.

While Wolsey worked with his patient, practised skill to bring his master round to the acceptance of a policy which stood a remote chance of success, Surrey had the task of trying to carry out the King's orders. He was hampered by his complete ignorance of the complexities of those clan rivalries which formed the basis of Irish politics and, as was usual with Tudor overseas ventures, by the inadequacy of available resources. Henry insisted that his representative carry out the necessary reforms and pay his staff and soldiers out of Irish revenues but Surrey soon discovered that taxes could only be extracted when backed up by force. He thus found himself in a Catch-22 situation: without reinforcements of men and money he could not raise the necessary funds; with adequate means he could raise revenue but it was gobbled up by the costs of military action. Within weeks he was writing to the King for more money and his appeals were repeated several times. Funds did dribble in from a reluctant and increasingly impatient monarch and Howard made a reasonably good fist of putting them to good use. In the 1520 campaigning season he won over Ormond and his influential allies and, with shows of strength to the south-west and the north, he achieved truces with other leading clans. However, it rapidly became clear to him that, so far from being won over to the English cause, the wily lords were using Surrey in their own power games. In December he reported to Wolsey in desperation, 'this land will never be brought to due obedience but only with compulsion and conquest'.[28]

However, he had been working for several months on a political solution which would also enhance the prestige of his own kindred. The dispute over the earldom of Ormond involved his own brother-in-law, Thomas Boleyn, who had a claim on the Butler title and estates via his mother. The legal situation was at an impasse with the Irish family supporting Piers Butler and Boleyn enjoying the favour of the King. Sir Thomas had continued to be a close companion of Henry and had steadily advanced in royal service through several important diplomatic missions. In Ireland Surrey made the close acquaintance of Butler and was sufficiently impressed with what he saw to suggest an arrangement which would satisfactorily tie up several loose ends. Butler's title should be recognised and he should be appointed Henry's deputy in Ireland. At the same time his son and heir, James, should be betrothed to Sir Thomas Boleyn's thirteen-year-old daughter. As well as the long-term advantages for his own kinsfolk and the possibility of establishing a degree of stability in Ireland, this would enable Howard to escape from an extremely uncongenial job. He pushed his plan vigorously over several months and received the backing of both Wolsey and the King. Henry was content to support Piers Butler as a workable alternative to Kildare and Wolsey was prepared to regard Ormond as a back-up candidate if he could not win the King's support for Fitzgerald. James Butler was, in fact, one of his wards and a member of his household. If he were to be married to a daughter of Henry's friend and kept at court the government would have a permanent hold over Ormond. Negotiations stumbled on for several months but eventually came to nothing, perhaps because of a certain reluctance on Ormond's part to have his hands tied. This failed liaison was fraught with significance for it was in anticipation of her marriage that a fifteen-year-old Anne Boleyn was brought home from France and made her appearance at the Tudor court.

Long before he had completed his first year in Ireland, Howard realised that he was wasting his time, his money, his reputation and his health and achieving nothing either for himself or his master. He was approaching his fiftieth year and finding forced marches and life in campaign tents less easy to cope with than when he was younger. He suffered occasional bouts of dysentery as well as perpetual anxiety and depression. He could honestly assert that his failure was not his fault. Caught between Irish lords who made and broke pledges with equal ease and a home government which would not give him the tools to do the job, it was impossible that he should achieve anything. But, of course, he would be blamed for the failure; discredit would be on his head and no one else's.

Above all the Irish fiasco was keeping Howard away from court and that was potentially disastrous. The longer he spent in Ireland the more stories would be told about him, the more jibes made at his expense. Access to the King was vital for any political lead player who wanted to maintain his position and outface rivals. While Henry was always susceptible to the personal approach, to be out of his sight was usually to be out of his mind. That is why royal servants who, for whatever reason, were sent away from the King's presence were always desperate for readmission to the Privy Chamber and why their enemies were equally determined to keep them out. Howard simply had to get back to the centre and away from this godless place. In one of his increasingly urgent appeals he entreated Henry to allow him 'to do your Highness service in such business in your own presence'.[29] As his horse stumbled through mist and rain in uncertain lands beyond the Pale he must have cursed Wolsey, because Wolsey knew how impossible the Irish situation was. Yet, in fact, Wolsey was no more to blame than Surrey for the fiasco. He had had to respond to Henry's sudden enthusiasm for Ireland. Now that that enthusiasm had waned the only thing to do was to extract the King and his deputy from the mess with as little damage as possible.

Still Surrey had to wait a year before the Cardinal could engineer his recall and the summons only came then because the prospect of renewed military action in France meant that his services as Lord Admiral would be required. In March 1522 the retiring Lord Lieutenant handed over to Ormond. The new deputy proved a disaster. The withdrawal of English troops and Butler's determination to operate from his base in the far west of the country created a power vacuum, swiftly filled by rebellious and feuding clansmen. In August 1524 he was removed from office and Kildare was reinstated. It was as though the last four and a half years had not happened.

Surrey, meanwhile, had returned to an activity more to his liking and one to which he was temperamentally better suited – laying waste to farms and homesteads first in France, then in Scotland. He spent June to October 1522 in raiding the Brittany coast in preparation for the projected major invasion of the following year. His only achievement – or, at least, the only one which required any military leadership – was the storming of Morlaix, a rich seaport from which he and his men carried off much plunder. Then he was despatched to the northern border.

The conflict with France followed the traditional pattern, part of which was that the French tried to distract their enemy by fomenting trouble on the Scottish border. Francis I's chosen agent this time was John Stuart, Duke of Albany, uncle and regent of the boy King, James V. A decade after Flodden a rerun of the 1513 campaigns seemed to be taking place. The Duke of Suffolk led an impressive invasion force across the Channel and the Earl of Surrey was sent north to guard England's postern gate. But there was to be no repeat of the triumphs of Tournai or Brankston Hill. Brandon's army, which had set out so bravely, disintegrated and dispersed with the onset of winter. Surrey contented himself with border raids, the most spectacular of which was the sack of Jedburgh. He was soon boasting, 'There is left neither house, fortress, village, tree, castle, corn or other succour for man . . . Such is the punishment of Almighty God for disturbers of the peace.' This solved nothing and Albany and Surrey settled to manoeuvring their forces either side of the border, trying to second-guess each other and eagerly gathering intelligence reports. Howard was anxious to bring matters to a swift conclusion. He had no desire to try to hold his army together through the winter. His health was indifferent – though probably not as bad as he made out in his letters to Wolsey. His father was ill and unlikely to live much longer and Surrey would need to be on hand to assume his new responsibilities and dignities. But above all these considerations was Howard's perpetual desire to be at the centre of affairs, a desire constantly frustrated by the determination of King and Cardinal to keep him occupied elsewhere. The Earl tried every stratagem to persuade Henry and his minister to lend a sympathetic ear to his entreaties. A letter to Wolsey of 23 October, for example, ended with a note in Surrey's own hand exuding self-pity and self-vindication:

> Most humbly beseeching your Grace that [if] I fortune to miscarry in this journey to be good lord to my poor children, assuring your Grace that without the king's gracious favour and your Grace's showed unto them they are undone. For I have spent so much to serve the king's highness, that if God do now his pleasure [upon] me, I shall leave them the poorest nobleman's children that died in this realm these 40 years, having neither goods nor foot of land to put in feofment to do them good after me. And therefore most humbly I beseech your Grace to be good and gracious lord to them for my poor service done in times past. Scribbled the 23rd day of October at 11.0 at night.[30]

Despite all his efforts, Surrey's repeated requests for a recall were met with refusal. This situation persisted even after Albany had obligingly ruined his own cause. At the end of October he crossed the border to invade Wark Castle, only to retreat ignominiously on hearing exaggerated reports of the host with which Surrey was advancing to relieve the garrison. The Earl claimed a significant victory and once more asked to be allowed south to recoup his strength.

This time the King relented and, on 4 December, Surrey left Newcastle and set off down the Great North Road. The next day he was fifty miles south of York and travelling fast when a royal messenger met him with fresh instructions. Henry had changed his mind. Scottish affairs were still complex and required his lieutenant's personal attention. For once Howard disobeyed. He continued his journey, explaining to Wolsey that any more time spent in the North would be the death of him; that his credibility would suffer if he turned back without having reported to the King ; and that he had matters of great importance to discuss with His Majesty.[31] A few days later he had an audience with the King and, apparently, managed to convince him with his own assessment of Anglo-Scottish affairs, for, after an absence of several years, he was able to take his place in the household and the Council. The following spring the old Duke of Norfolk died at the age of eighty-one.

The man who took his place was already well into his fifties. All his adult life he had been dominated by his father, had pursued cautious and watchful policies, suffered in silence when passed over for honours he considered to be rightfully his, had bitten his tongue when confronted by the arrogance of Wolsey or Brandon. Now he was England's premier peer and must have expected that he would step into his father's shoes in the life of the realm. He had already, in December 1522, taken over as Lord Treasurer, a lucrative role worth £365 a year, but much more valuable in terms of patronage. He could look forward to filling other prominent and influential posts, to representing the King on major diplomatic missions and, more importantly, to becoming a permanent member of court and Council. In the event his ambitions were blocked and he was forced to relearn the lesson that claims to privilege based on noble birthright cut little ice with Henry VIII. The first shock was losing the office of Earl Marshal which his father had held since the early days of the reign. While Surrey had been away in the North Charles Brandon had persuaded Henry to grant him the reversion of the prestigious leading military and ceremonial position. In 1525 Norfolk had been obliged to yield to the little Duke of Richmond both the Admiralty and the lieutenancy of the North. The work of both these departments was, of course, carried out by deputies but Howard was not of their number.

Nor did he edge any closer to the policy-making executive. Henry and/or Wolsey decided that the new Duke's limited talents could best be employed, as they had been in the past, on the Scottish border. However, what the King needed now was not a general but a diplomat capable of entering the labyrinth of Scottish clan politics and emerging with a settlement that would pacify that troubled realm and tie it to England's interests. There were three factions vying for power and Wolsey cannot have been best pleased when, asked for his opinion on the relative strength of the parties, Norfolk replied, 'this matter is of so great importance and the persons of so unstable demeanour that be the chief parties that I dare not give my advice to the one or the other'.[32] Nervous about giving the wrong lead, the Duke gave no lead at all and Wolsey was obliged to try manipulating events at a distance. This sometimes led to a situation in which Norfolk demurred at carrying out instructions from London because they took no account of the realities which he could see at close quarters, even though his reports had not clearly represented those realities.

Once again Howard asked for a recall as the northern winter approached. This time a disgruntled Wolsey ordered him to send for his wife and such comforts as he required from home and 'to make your abode there for a season'. However, a month later, he was reprieved. England's bold policy of sending the Earl of Angus, Queen Margaret's estranged husband, back into Scotland to assume control, worked and for a few years there was to be peace on the border. Immediately, and without awaiting permission, Norfolk rode south, ostensibly to take charge of the Anglo-Scottish truce negotiations in London.

He was not long in the capital. Come the spring he and Suffolk were sent into East Anglia to oversee the collection of the Amicable Grant. It was another unenviable task; the nobles were torn between their duty to the Crown and their sympathy with the knights and burgesses upon whom the intolerable tax burden fell. The commissioners appointed by the Dukes to collect the revenue did so grumbling and unwillingly. The substantial merchants and landowners resisted payment as long as possible in the hope that Wolsey would reduce his demands, as he had already done in London. Then came the artisans' rising around Lavenham and disturbing rumours of organised discontent elsewhere. Howard and Brandon were responsible for maintaining peace in their 'country' but with contradictory signals coming from the centre they were hard put to it to know what line to take with troublemakers. Norfolk reported that tough measures had yielded a satisfactory result in Norwich and that he intended to make the whole county an example of what was expected elsewhere. A few days later the commissioner-in-chief informed Wolsey that they had overwhelmed the potential rebels on the Suffolk–Essex border. When the men of Lavenham and Brent Eleigh approached in their shirts, begging on their knees for mercy, the King's representatives had 'aggravated their offence, declaring it to be high treason'. They arrested the ringleaders and ensured that their unyielding treatment was well publicised. However, within days they had been wrong-footed by the Cardinal's change to a policy of leniency and compromise. Wolsey insisted that malefactors should only be charged with unlawful assembly rather than treason and that the people should be pressed to pay no more than they were prepared to offer of their own goodwill.

All was confusion. Those who had already paid the full amount were naturally aggrieved when their neighbours were let off more lightly. The delivery of pardons and light sentences to troublemakers made it seem that Howard and Brandon lacked government backing for their stern words and deeds. Respectfully the Dukes pointed out the need for clear policies and concerted actions and opined that never was a time so needful for the calling of the King's Council. These are the observations which have survived in the state papers. The comments the two peers made to each other as their difficult task was made more difficult by the Cardinal we can readily conjecture. Norfolk and Suffolk were very far from being friends but now, for the first time, they began to make common cause against Wolsey. It is significant that, when urging the King to convene his Council, they asked that they should be allowed to attend together. The experience of the Amicable Grant had caused a groundswell of discontent in the political nation such as had not been seen since the days of Empson and Dudley. Wolsey's opponents were allowing themselves to hope that the fall of Henry VII's grasping ministers might constitute a precedent.[33]

Wolsey was well aware of the danger. There was no question of a Council meeting to deliberate on matters of domestic policy. Moreover the East Anglian dukes were sent to their estates, ostensibly to ensure the pacification of the region. Suffolk's favourite residence was Westhorpe, scarcely a dozen miles from Kenninghall where Howard now embarked on an impressive building programme. Here, he made a deliberate attempt to rival the splendours of Hampton Court and York Place by turning an old hunting lodge into a grand palace in the latest style. For three years he supervised the construction and sumptuous equipping of a house that should declare Howard greatness. Here, at least, he could play the great man without being overshadowed by the butcher's son from nearby Ipswich.

CHAPTER 16

A Man of Property

In the summer of 1521 when Wolsey journeyed to Bruges to hammer out the details of an anti-French treaty with Charles V another meeting took place. Thomas More was a member of the Cardinal's delegation and Erasmus was in attendance on the Emperor. It was to be the last time that the two friends came face to face and because the growing Reformation storm would drive them on to very different shores it is difficult not to read significance and poignancy into the event.

There was a great deal to talk about. Luther had just been condemned by the Imperial Diet at Worms. Henry VIII had completed the *Assertio* and undoubtedly discussed it with More during its composition. The educated world was abuzz with the ideas coming out of Wittenberg and opinions were divided about the degree of scholarly free speech which could be permitted in such dangerous times. More specifically Erasmus was coming under mounting attack as an aider and abetter of heretics. At this stage he enjoyed the full support of Sir Thomas (More had just been knighted), who had, in fact, been waging a written war on his behalf against Edward Lee, an up-and-coming ecclesiastic who would end his days as Archbishop of York. Lee rounded on the Dutch scholar for presuming to produce a fresh translation of the New Testament because, as he not unreasonably pointed out, the doctrinal implications of the Church having for centuries based some of its teaching on mistaken translations of the Greek were very serious. 'You tear up the roots and opinions of our forefathers and do not allow even the decrees of the Church to remain inviolate; you appear . . . to give superficial support to the ravings of heretics,'[34] he fulminated.

More took up the cudgels, during 1519 and 1520, in three letters, intended for publication, as was the custom. He defended Erasmus's character, his scholarship, his devout manner of living and his contributions to theology. He chided Lee for stirring up controversy and suggested that he had misunderstood the writings to which he took exception. He spiced his argument with humour and attempted to keep the debate on a civilised basis. In fact, he did everything except answer the charge. It was the practised defence lawyer using accomplished courtroom technique: befuddle the jury with appealing but irrelevant information about the accused in order to create the impression that he could not possibly be guilty. But the prosecution case had to be faced and More's unwillingness to do so suggests that he, too, was uneasy about it.

As long as Erasmus was holding up an indignant mirror to the vices and hypocrisies of churchmen, ridiculing superstitious practices, working for a better understanding of Scripture and the Fathers, and pleading for holiness of living and the reformation of manners, More was eager to defend him against the enemies of true piety and learning. What he was reluctant to acknowledge was that Erasmus had pointed seekers after truth down a different road to that trodden by conventional churchmen and believed by them to be the only highway. This spiritual alternative was described eloquently by Thomas Bilney, student of Trinity Hall, Cambridge, who, about this time experienced an evangelical conversion:

> But at last I heard speak of Jesus, even then when the New Testament was first set forth by Erasmus; which when I understood to be eloquently done by him, being allured rather by the Latin than by the word of God (for at that time I knew not what it meant), I bought it even by the providence of God, as I do now well understand and perceive: and at the first reading (as I well remember) I chanced upon this sentence of St Paul (O most sweet and comfortable sentence to my soul!) in 1 Tim.i., 'It is a true saying, and worthy of all men to be embraced, that Christ Jesus came into the world to save sinners; of whom I am the chief and principal.' This one sentence, through God's instruction and inward working, which I did not then perceive, did so exhilarate my heart, being before wounded with the guilt of my sins, and being almost in despair, that immediately I felt a marvellous comfort and quietness, insomuch 'that my bruised bones leaped for joy'.
>
> After this, the Scripture began to be more pleasant unto me than the honey or the honey-comb; wherein I learned, that all my travails, all my fasting and watching, all the redemption of masses and pardons, being done without trust in Christ, who only saveth his people from their sins; these, I say, I learned to be nothing else but even (as St Augustine saith) a hasty and swift running out of the right way.[35]

Little Bilney (who went to the stake as a heretic in 1531) was far from alone in being caught up in the evangelical dynamic. All over Europe men were, as Erasmus urged that they should, coming to the Bible to discover what he called the *philosophia Christi*. But, in an inversion of the old adage, the Dutch radical could lead them to the water but could not stop them drinking deeply and intoxicatingly. The reality of their faith made them set the authority of the Bible over against that of the Church hierarchy and made them question the validity of sacramental means of grace. This kind of affective religion was not novel but it was unprecedented on the scale that the Church now encountered it. Small wonder that a growing number of critics were blaming Erasmus for the infestation or that friends were urging him to prove his Catholic *bona fides* by going into print against Luther.

He was uneasy about doing so. He found the growing controversy distasteful and unnecessary, arguing that most of the doctrinal disputes resolved around *adiaphora*, 'things indifferent', and that all Christians should be able to find common ground in the essentials. Looking down from his intellectual eyrie, the leading scholar of the age urged the necessity of understanding the motives of those who differed from tradition. The problem facing the clergy was essentially a pastoral problem. Disruptive spirits, who were always looking to make trouble, should certainly be brought to book but there were others caught up in the Reformation who were deserving of sympathy and gentle guidance: 'those heresies seem least far removed from true religion which, from some excessive zeal for the full vigour of the Gospel, demand of men more than is right'. Name-calling and physical persecution were abhorrent whether the perpetrators were preachers of novelties or defenders of ancient customs. 'The man who makes an honest mistake is deserving of mercy,' Erasmus pleaded.[36]

More found this level of detachment unattainable. He had read *The Babylonian Captivity of the Church*, which in 1520 Luther had addressed, in Latin, to the scholars of Christendom. This was the tract above all others that, in Heinrich Boehmer's words, 'resounded like a tocsin throughout the whole western world [and] produced a benumbing shock or evoked passionate anger'.[37] It certainly undercut Erasmus's hopeful optimism: 'the breach is irreparable,' he observed mournfully on reading the latest example of Wittenberg theology. In it the reformer laid his axe to the Church's sacramental system and, thereby, to the power of the priesthood. He reduced the seven standard means of grace to two – baptism and holy communion, being the only sacraments instituted by Christ. Ordination he described as 'the source of that detestable tyranny over the laity by the clergy who, relying on the external anointing of their hands, the tonsure and the vestments, not only exalt themselves above lay Christians, anointed by the Holy Spirit, but even regard them as dogs, unworthy to be included with them in the Church'.[38] The doctrine of transubstantiation, whereby the mass became an offering validated by the grace of orders rather than a divine blessing apprehended by the faith of the recipient, was absurd and unscriptural, a diabolical con trick. This attack went beyond anticlericalism; it was antisacerdotalism. Instead of merely deploring, with the humanists, the arrogance, immorality and laxness of the clergy the *Babylonian Captivity* took away their *raison d'être*. It offered theological justification to everyone who, for whatever reason, set himself in

214

Solomon and the Queen of Sheba, Hans Holbein the Younger, c.1534.

The ultimate Tudor icon. Henry VIII, likened to King Solomon, is surrounded by servile
and admiring subjects and visitors. Above his head in gold are words from II Chronicles 9:
'Praised be the Lord your God. He has shown his pleasure in you by making you king to rule in
his name.' On either side of the throne runs the legend: 'How fortunate are the men who serve
you, who are always in your presence and are privileged to hear your wise sayings.' 'Fortunate'
was not always the most appropriate description of those dwelling in the Lion's Court.

The Field of Cloth of Gold (at Hampton Court), artist unknown.

The ultimate pageant. This summit meeting between Henry VIII and Francis I in 1520 was a ruinously (literally for some participants) extravagant display of royal splendour and national pride. Wolsey organised it, Howard was excluded. More was present but made no comment on the spectacle. His humanist friend, John Fisher, was less diffident: 'These were assuredly wonderful sights…nevertheless… take away the glistering garment, take away the cloth of gold… And what difference is betwixt an emperor and another poor man?'

Der Künig.

'The King' and 'The Pope' from *The Dance of Death*, Hans Holbein, c.1523–6.

These cynical observations of contemporary life went beyond the moralising of the conventional dance of death theme and remained un-published until 1538. Free thinkers had to tread warily. Erasmus's friends were worried that he might find him-self in trouble for exposing the vanity of royal courts. Not even Erasmus dared depict the pope as inspired and supported by the demons of hell.

Der Bapst.

(*Facing page*)
Henry VIII, c.1537,
after Hans Holbein.

The ultimate propaganda. This is the king as he wished to be seen – strong, immovable, implacable, indomitable, domi-neering. The success of the image is proved by the fact that, after four and a half centuries, it still dominates our understand-ing of Henry. The reality was more complex. The king could be influenced, moved, 'managed', but only with extreme caution.

Thomas Howard, 3rd Duke of Norfolk, 1540, Hans Holbein.

In his mid-sixties Howard chose to be depicted by the royal painter in all his splendour, clad in ducal ermine, wearing the garter chain and carrying his staffs of office as Lord Treasurer and Earl Marshal. By presenting the Duke's features as an expressionless mask the artist, perhaps, suggests that if the trimmings are stripped away all that is left is nonentity.

Thomas Wolsey as founder of Cardinal (later Christ Church) College, Oxford, Sampson Strong.

Wolsey's earliest role model was William Wainfleet (see next illustration), the founder of Magdalen College, Oxford. A passionate lover of learning, the Cardinal determined to leave his mark on his own university. He devoted enormous amounts of time, energy and money to the foundation of Cardinal College and was desperately concerned that his foundation should not share his own fate.

*Christina of Denmark,
Duchess of Milan*, 1538, Hans Holbein.

This portrait of the delectable and witty
niece of Charles V might be labelled
'the one that got away'. Fired up by the
princess's charms and her political possibilities, King Henry sued ardently for her
hand in marriage. Nothing came of it,
partly because Christina was wary of
following in the footsteps of Catherine of
Aragon, Anne Boleyn and Jane Seymour.

opposition to parish priest, bishop or pope.

It offended Thomas More to the very core of his being. The mass was his devotional rock, the mediating priesthood a well-rooted tree to which he clung for support, the Church a high hedge of authority protecting him from the winds of doubt and insecurity. To question the eternal validity of these things was to go far beyond the privileges of scholarly debate. The issues raised by Luther certainly could not be characterised as *adiaphora*. More eagerly supported his royal master in writing his defence of the seven sacraments, perhaps hoping that refutation from a kingly source might stop the German boar in his tracks and, at Bruges, he almost certainly added his voice to those of others who were seeking to draw Erasmus into the fray. The existing one-sided correspondence of the scholar suggests that he was not unmoved by the blandishments of friends in England.

One would love to have been a fly on the wall listening to the conversation of the Rotterdam philosopher and the London lawyer at this crucial moment in the history of western Christendom. It was a turning point for both of them and a turning point of which they were probably well aware. 1521 was the high tide mark of Christian humanism. In subsequent inundations the turbulent waves of Protestantism, gathering impetus from the New Learning, would crash farther up the beach. They would do so without Erasmus and without More. Overtaken by the march of events, each had to find his own response. Erasmus retreated from the 'unseemly' conflict. Within weeks of their meeting he withdrew from the battleground of conservative Louvain to take up residence in Basel, one of the few towns in Europe where there still existed an atmosphere of free debate. More knew that he had to take up the cudgels and go on the offensive for traditional Catholicism.

From this point Sir Thomas divided his energies between serving the King and serving the Church. Initially, the two went hand in glove and involved no deviation from the pursuit of worldly ambition. Henry was Defender of the Faith and working in harmony with Pope and Emperor against those who would disturb the peace of Christendom – notably Francis I and Martin Luther. The German reformer reinforced this interpretation of affairs in 1522 when he published a refutation of the *Assertio* entitled *Against Henry, King of the English*. It was a piece of unwise and vulgar buffoonery in which the writer was more concerned to make his adversary look ridiculous than to answer his arguments. The treatise began 'From Martin Luther, minister at Wittenberg by the grace of God, to Henry, King of England by the disgrace of God' – and it got worse, much worse, as it went on. How much of this crude lampoon Henry read we do not know but he could not but be riled by it. There had to be a reply and, since the King could not be expected to roll about in the sty with his porcine adversary, he needed a champion. More was the obvious choice.

He had probably provided theological advice over the *Assertio* and he was a Latin scholar with a European reputation. It was he, therefore, who penned the *Responsio ad Lutherum*, his first work of theological controversy.

Whether he was instructed by Henry to defend the royal honour or did so of his own volition to gain brownie points, the King's Secretary fell to his task with a will. He had already cut his adversarial teeth on the spat with Brixius but the verve of his invective against the Frenchman was as nothing compared with that which he adopted against Luther. The *Responsio* was totally lacking in wit and elegance. Its theological arguments were so ponderous as to be unreadable. Its only light relief – if so it may be called – lay in the inventiveness of its invective:

> Since he has written that he already has a prior right to bespatter and besmirch the royal crown with shit, will we not have the posterior right to proclaim [his] beshitted tongue . . . most fit to lick . . . the very posterior of a pissing she-mule . . .[39]

Nowhere in this tedious work can one recognise the author of *Utopia* and it is not surprising that More published it under a pseudonym. Even when we allow for the fact that he was in the ring on his master's behalf and wanted to be seen to be bloodying Luther's nose, we must still recognise that the passionate bigotry of the *Responsio* contrasts with the urbane cynicism of the translator of Lucian or the writer of the satirical *Epigrammata* (the collection of Latin poems published in 1520). The correct diagnosis of that apparent schizophrenia is that the detached, scholarly, public More – the More of the Privy Chamber and the law court – was a mask. His cynicism was despair in fashionable clothes – and despair, according to Freud, is frozen anger. That anger blazed through the pained, knowing smile when a Brixius or a Luther touched the inner man where conflicting uncertainties, ambitions and desires were never kept fully under control. Luther's threat was the threat of anarchy, the breakdown of that rigid spiritual discipline which was essential to civilised Christian society and which bolted and riveted More's own life.

Sir Thomas was not as close to the King as Roper and other biographers have tried to make out. This was a state of affairs he actually made a virtue of in some of his satires, like this epigram to a courtier which is clearly about Henry's character:

> You often boast to me that you have the king's ear and often have fun with him, freely and according to your whims. This is like having fun with tamed lions – often it is harmless, but just as often there is the fear of harm. Often he roars in rage for no known reason, and suddenly the fun becomes fatal. The pleasure you get is not safe enough to relieve

you of anxiety. For you it is a great pleasure. As for me, let my pleasure be less great – and safe.[40]

This is not the irascible Henry of 1530 embittered by the failure of his divorce proceedings or the Henry of 1540 rendered unpredictable by spasmodic bouts of excruciating pain. It is the Henry of 1520, across whose life black shadows were yet to fall.

More spent most of his time at court attending this King, reading letters to him, taking down letters at his dictation and generally liaising between Henry and the Cardinal. In July 1521, when Wolsey, with More in tow, was about to embark for his series of meetings with the Emperor's negotiators Henry instructed him to draw Sir Thomas into the inner circle of government:

The king signifieth your Grace that whereas old men do now decay greatly within this realm, his mind is to acquaint other young men with his great affairs, and therefore he desireth your Grace to make Sir William Sandys and Sir Thomas More privy to all such matters as your Grace shall treat at Calais.[41]

The coupling of names is interesting. Sandys had long been a great court favourite, a soldier of panache and distinction and, from 1517, treasurer of Calais. He was, therefore, a very different type of royal servant to More. Perhaps what links the two men most closely is that they were both apolitical. Their task was to carry out orders, not to have opinions or to seek to influence policy.

When he was not with the court at one or other of the royal manors More was occasionally involved with diplomatic business but, much more often, he was employing his judicial skills in Star Chamber or on the legal circuit. John Guy has compiled an itinerary of Sir Thomas's movements in 1525 which provides a factual basis for discussing More's varied activities:

More's Itinerary in 1525

January 3, 7	Royal secretary (Greenwich)
19, 22–23	Royal secretary (Ampthill)
26	Council in Star Chamber
27	Royal secretary (Ampthill)
February 13	Council in Star Chamber
March 18	Royal secretary (London)
24	Royal secretary (Greenwich)

April 8	Diplomatic duties (Greenwich)
14, 29	Royal secretary (Greenwich)
May 8, 17, 24	Royal secretary (Windsor)
June 6	Public orator (Windsor)
18	Public orator (Bridewell)
23	Council in Star Chamber
28	Royal secretary (Greenwich)
July 10	Council in Star Chamber, then royal secretary (Greenwich)
20	Royal secretary (Windsor)
21–25	*Oyer et terminer* commissioner in Berkshire
29	Diplomatic duties (Richmond)
31	Diplomatic duties (Anglo-French negotiations)
August 14	Diplomatic duties (Anglo-French negotiations)
20	Royal secretary (Hunsdon)
23	Royal secretary (Hatfield)
27	Royal secretary (Dunstable)
28–30	Diplomatic duties (Treaty of the More)
September 3, 8, 10, 11, 13	Royal secretary (Stony Stratford)
17	Royal secretary (Olney)
October	
November 1	Royal secretary (Windsor)
8, 19	Royal secretary (Reading)
December 10	Royal secretary (Greenwich)
12	Royal secretary (Windsor)
27	Royal secretary (Eltham)

J.A. Guy, *The Public Career of Sir Thomas More*, 1980, p.19

The gaps in this schedule do not indicate the periods that More had for his own family life, domestic affairs and literary endeavours. The dates given above are those when he was known to have been in specific locations. Many of the intervening days would have been spent at court, travelling to and fro and packing and unpacking the paraphernalia necessary for his different tasks. Among the latter was the under-treasurership of the Exchequer, a perk which came his way in 1521. The duties were not onerous and the rewards – £173.6s.8d – generous but More, being More, would have given scrupulous attention to the accurate recording of government income and expenditure and to the preparation of the annual 'declaration of the state of the treasury' presented to King and Council.

Any attempt to probe the relationships behind the formalities of day-to-day business largely relies on reading the extant correspondence of King, minister and secretary – both on and between the lines. A sequence of letters for September 1523 from More to Wolsey has survived which is illuminating. The first point we might note is the distinction between More the humanist and More the royal servant. The humanist disdained the fawning of courtiers and the mob's adoration of royalty. Among his epigrams is what might be seen as an early version of the tale of the Emperor's new clothes. A naïve peasant comes to town for the first time and encounters a crowd cheering and waving as the King passes by 'resplendent with gold, escorted by a large company and astride a tall horse'. Puzzled, the countryman asked a bystander which one was the King. On His Majesty being pointed out, the yokel grinned. 'You're pulling my leg,' he said. 'That's just a man in fancy dress.' Another drollery debunked an arrogant courtier who dismounted in a street and called out to a passer-by, 'You, whoever you are, hold this horse.' The wily townsman eyed the handsome mount and observed, 'Surely it would take more than one man to hold him.' 'Nonsense,' the popinjay retorted, 'one man can hold him,' to which the pedestrian, strolling away, responded, 'Then, hold him yourself.'[42]

More, the royal servant, was much more circumspect with tongue and pen, employing to the full the customary epistolary flattery. He seldom omitted to aver just how delighted the King was to receive the latest missive from the Cardinal: 'His highness well perceived and marked what labour and pain your Grace had taken' 'His highness . . . commanded me to write unto your Grace his most hearty, and not more hearty than highly well-deserved thanks', etc. etc. Occasionally More added his own approbation: 'as help me God in my poor fantasy . . . it is for quantity one of the best made letters for words, matter [sound judgement] and [sensitive expression] that ever I read in my life'.[43] Years later, when it was safe to do so, More told a story, partly against himself, to show how insatiable was Wolsey's thirst for praise. The great man had given a speech at a dinner and afterwards turned to his table-neighbours to ask their opinions of his eloquence. Those around tumbled over themselves to outdo one another in lavish flattery. When More's turn arrived he pretended to be completely lost. He uttered 'a long sigh with an "Oh" from the bottom of his breast, and held up both of his hands, and lifted up his head, and cast his eyes to the heavens and wept'.[44] Between the self-seeking, but very necessary, flattery and the lampoon there lies a void. Nowhere can we read anything that speaks of real affection from More for the man who was largely responsible for his promotion. Certainly, he was grateful for favours from the Cardinal and expressed his gratitude with conventional effusiveness. In thanking Wolsey for praising him to the King in the spring of 1523 he wrote, 'I were, my good Lord, very blind if I perceived not, very unkind if ever I forgot, of what gracious favour [your kindness] proceedeth, which I can never otherwise repay than with my poor prayer which, during my life, shall never fail to pray to God for the preservation of your Grace in honour and health.'[45] Well might he intercede for his patron: over the years he acquired, via Wolsey, an impressive number of perquisites and sinecures (see pp. 223f). However, when Wolsey needed private orisons to be fronted by public acts of loyalty More would be singularly backward in coming forward. Of the Cardinal's trust in Sir Thomas there is no doubt. The minister who carefully watched those who were close to the King and removed any who might constitute a threat felt, during the early 20s, no anxiety about the Secretary who had access to the King at all hours. John Guy is probably right in concluding that More came near to being Wolsey's 'man at court'.[46] For his part, More was the dutiful Secretary, speaking when spoken to, doing what was expected of him, entertaining his court associates with witty repartee – and keeping his own counsel.

It was as the perfect bureaucrat rather than as an amiable companion that More was most useful to Henry. In a well-known passage of his biography William Roper related how his father-in-law was so popular with the King and Queen that he had to use subtlety in order to have any time to himself.

And because he was of a pleasant disposition, it pleased the King and Queen after the council had supped, at the time of their supper, for their pleasure commonly to call for him to be merry with them. Whom when he perceived so much in his talk to delight that he could not once in a month get leave to go home to his wife and children, whose company he most desired, and to be absent from the court two days together but that he should be thither sent for again – he, much misliking this restraint of his liberty, began thereupon somewhat to dissemble his nature, and so by little and little from his former accustomed mirth to disuse himself, that he was of them from thenceforth at such seasons no more so ordinarily sent for.[47]

Study of the official correspondence suggests some modification of this pleasantly coloured family story. That More was often summoned to the King after supper is confirmed but this was primarily for doing business. After all the posts for the day were in and More had perused them and made a digest of them he would report to his master. Thus, for example, on 22 September 1523 he must have been closeted with the King until well into the night, for he read to him a long letter from Wolsey, four from Queen Margaret of Scotland, copies of two letters from the Cardinal to Margaret and two from the Earl of Surrey. Henry weighed them all carefully, discussed several matters with his Secretary, then dictated his replies. After this More had to write out the King's replies and concoct his own report to Wolsey before he could turn in. Doubtless there were times when Sir Thomas's private conversations with Henry took an informal turn, when the King listened with pleasure to his Secretary's witty observations on life, or talked theology with him or strolled with him on the leads to gaze on the night sky and discuss the stars in their courses, but there can have been few opportunities for such pleasantries in what was essentially a business relationship.

The role of go-between was potentially powerful, as Wolsey had good cause to know but, unlike England's master-ecclesiastic, Thomas More did not use his privileged position to advance himself. However, his efficient secretaryship did have a potent effect on the chemistry between King and Cardinal and one which has gone largely unrecognised. As the 1520s wore on Henry took a closer interest in the details of government. He remained selective about the issues which interested him but no longer could Wolsey get away with providing a vague digest of events, secure in the knowledge that the King would endorse his decisions. Diplomatic exchanges had, now, to be carefully explained and political options clearly set out. More, with his lucid, legal mind, transparent honesty, lack of political agenda and easy manner, was excellently equipped to do this. During those late-night sessions when he and his master pored over the day's foreign and domestic news Henry obtained an ever-improving working knowledge of what his agents were doing. And the more he learned the more he wanted to learn. It cannot have greatly pleased Wolsey to receive, via More, in his letter of 22 September 1523, the following instruction about the conduct of Anglo-Scottish relations:

. . . forasmuch as his Grace much desireth in these things to be advertised of your most politic advice and counsel, which he thinketh your Grace intendeth to declare by way of instructions to be given unto my said Lord of Surrey, his highness, therefore, heartily requireth your Grace that it may like the same to send to him the said instructions, that his Grace may by the same be learned of your Grace's prudent advice and counsel . . .[48]

Henry, now, frequently pressed his chief minister for more detailed information. The debate has long run among historians as to whether Henry VIII or his Cardinal ruled England. Now, it seems that we must allot to Thomas More a role – albeit unconscious – in the process by which the King gradually took more power into his own hands. This may help us the better to understand certain events of 1525–6 to which we must return shortly.

Before we leave the September 1523 correspondence it is worth noting, *en passant,* how well-grounded were the Earl of Surrey's anxieties about the damage that might be done to his reputation when he was far from court and unable to defend himself. We can see from these letters that his activities in Scotland came under very close scrutiny and that reports which reached the King via Wolsey had the Cardinal's gloss on them. The perspectives of politicians notoriously differ from those of their commanders in the field but personality issues are also involved. While Wolsey had no desire to undermine Surrey completely, it was certainly in his interests that Henry should not be completely satisfied with the activities of his general. As summer turned to autumn the Lord Admiral sat at Berwick, exercising caution and garnering his resources. Wolsey chose to interpret Howard's inaction as foot-dragging and told the King so. More dutifully relayed the Cardinal's version and was able to report back,

> . . . his highness is of the mind of your Grace and singularly commendeth your policy in that your Grace determineth [to urge] my Lord Admiral [to] set forth his enterprises without any longer tract of time, not ceasing to press [the Scots] with all the annoyance possible . . . And verily his highness thinketh as your Grace writeth, that [despite] the lack of those things which, as he writeth, are not yet come to him, he should not have [failed to carry out smaller raids in order] at least [to cause] some annoyance in the mean season.[49]

More's judicial activities were largely involved with the rapidly increasing work of Star Chamber. As this court gained a reputation for dealing impartially with cases which in lower courts were subject to all manner of pressure from interested parties, so more and more litigants resorted to it. The volume of both criminal and civil suits grew alarmingly, so much so that many 'poor men's causes' were referred to another body, the Court of Requests, which took on a more sedentary guise and met during legal terms in the White Hall. More was among the councillors who presided in both these courts. Many of the issues on which he and his colleagues were called to give judgement indicate just how lawless parts of the country still were and how vital was the reform which Wolsey was carrying out: 'a cause of misdemeanour . . . for carrying away the prioress of Michell Kynton and taking away the goods of that priory'; John Devereux of Huntingdon stirred a riot to prevent commissioners collecting the Amicable Grant; Sir Robert Constable charged with 'taking away Anne Cresacre, the King's ward, and affiancing her to his son, Thomas, and suffering him before marriage to know her carnally'; two jurymen 'sore menaced because they will not find according to the minds of their suborned colleagues'; Robert Pownall, wanted in Cheshire for brutal murder has been spirited away by accomplices; Thomas Banewell 'with divers other rioters and evil disposed persons' prevented William and Joan Nype from 'entering an inherited property'.[50]

The Thomas More of the mid-1520s was an establishment man through and through. Like many an 'angry young man' before and since, he had slipped from the critical radicalism of his early years into traditionalist, reactionary middle age. It was as the King's man that he was installed as Speaker of the Commons in 1523. Roper made great play of a speech More supposedly made in this capacity in defence of members' freedom of debate:

> It may therefore like your most abundant grace, our most benign and godly King, to give all your Commons here assembled your most gracious license and pardon, freely, without doubt of your dreadful displeasure, every man to discharge his conscience . . . And . . . to take all in good part, interpreting every man's words, how uncunningly soever they be couched, to proceed yet of good zeal towards the profit of your realm and honour of your royal person.[51]

Even if Roper possessed a verbatim account of this address (and it is over a thousand words long) it still would not justify More being labelled as an early champion of parliamentary rights. Freedom from arrest for words spoken in the chamber had long been a privilege claimed by the assembled gentlemen and burgesses. More was simply reiterating this right, though doubtless with great eloquence. When it came to it, he was there to get the government's programme through. He made a speech strongly supporting Wolsey's demand for taxation and, as we have seen, was rewarded for his pains.

Nor was the £100 he received in 1523 the only tangible recognition that came his way. High office was a key that opened all manner of income sources. There were perquisites and sinecures that came from the King and there were gifts and 'considerations' from those who hoped that More would use his influence on their behalf. He was not slow to take advantage of his position. In 1524 the put-upon, rich heiress Anne Cresacre entered More's household, when Wolsey granted him her wardship. This gave Sir Thomas the administration of her considerable estate and, in 1529, she was married to his only son. More also obtained the wardship of Giles Heron (heir to one of the officers of the household), who was married to Cecily More in 1525, and of John Moreton, a lunatic. Among numerous other grants and awards were: the high stewardships of both universities, the joint keepership of the foreign exchanges, lands from the estates of the attainted Sir Francis Lovell and the Duke of Buckingham, a Kentish manor, a retainer from the Earl of Northumberland, a licence to export woollen cloths and a pension from Francis I. More picked up perks as a modern ex-public servant picks up company directorships.

He was not reticent about living up to his enhanced income. He went into the property market in quite a big way. In 1523 he bought a speculative parcel of dwellings in Bishopsgate Street and sold it within the year for a twenty-five per cent profit. In 1525 he acquired impressive building sites in Kensington and Chelsea. It was at Chelsea that he set about constructing a residence suitable to his new station in life. It was nowhere near as grand as the mansion Thomas Howard was erecting in Norfolk but it was impressive enough with its gatehouse, drive, red-brick dwelling presenting to the visitor a frontage of 164 feet, its separate chapel and library building which was the owner's sanctuary-cum-oratory, its twenty-seven acres of gardens, orchard and park and its river frontage allowing Sir Thomas swift access to the court. It was the home of a man of substance, fashionably distanced from the ill-humours of the City yet within a few minutes' rowing of Westminster. It was the home of a man well-favoured by his prince (Henry had lent him £700, presumably for the Chelsea project) and a man who, it must have seemed to the world, had more steps on the ladder yet to climb. He did, indeed, ascend higher but the topmost rungs were wormy and would not for long bear his weight.

This prominent royal servant, this man of consequence now adjudged that the time had come to leave some token to posterity: he decided to have his portrait painted. By one of those happy chances that ensures that some men achieve a fame beyond their deserts, he became the first English patron of the finest 'limner' of the age (and, some would say, of any age). Hans Holbein the Younger was a fellow resident of Basel with Erasmus and travelled to London at the end of 1526 with a letter of introduction from More's old friend. The German artist was given a place in the Chelsea household and Sir Thomas introduced his protégé to other members of the Tudor élite. Holbein rapidly became the latest fashion. In his first couple of years in England he painted Archbishop Warham, Sir Henry Guildford (Controller of the Household) and his wife, Sir Brian Tuke (who had advanced from Wolsey's service to become Henry's French secretary) and other leading figures about the court. More commissioned several portraits of himself as gifts for friends and family. All show him splendidly clad in a fur-collared coat with velvet sleeves, a gold chain round his neck. Yet more remarkable was the group portrait the patron had Holbein make of eleven members of his household. As well as being an artistic *tour de force*, this painting was an extraordinary commission. Representations of Renaissance families were extremely rare. They were occasionally produced to commemorate princely dynasties. Mantegna had painted a fresco for Lodovico Gonzaga in Mantua and Holbein would create a similar Tudor apotheosis for Whitehall. For a member of the royal executive class to order such an ambitious work was a thing unheard of. Together, these works from a great genius have created an enduring public image of More as the gentle humanist and family man. This was how he wished the world to see him – a man of standing in his impressive house, surrounded by his adoring wife, children and wards. The portraits have achieved their propaganda ends far more effectively than Holbein's patron could ever have conceived.

CHAPTER 17

Storms and Storm Damage

Over the next two years there was a seismic shift in the atmosphere of the English court and the epicentre of the disturbance lay deep in the personality of the King. Henry, as More knew well, had always been subject to mood swings – kid gloves were an essential part of any royal servant's wardrobe – but the change that now came over the King was profound and lasting. There were many contributory factors. Perhaps the most fundamental were those intimations of mortality that afflict most people with the onset of middle age. In 1524 and 1525 Henry had two nasty scares. In the spring of the first year he was jousting with Charles Brandon and omitted to close his visor. Suffolk's lance shattered against the King's helm, and spattered his face with vicious, potentially fatal splinters. Months later, while hawking near Hitchin, he fell head first into the thick mud of a waterlogged ditch and was only rescued in time by a quick-thinking attendant. As Henry progressed through his thirties his body began to protest at his earlier over-athleticism and overindulgence. He suffered increasingly from severe headaches (perhaps migraines) and experienced the first twinges of osteomyelitis in his thigh (probably the result of falls in the tiltyard or hunting field). Brushes with sudden death and the evidence that, such risks aside, he was getting older and could no longer expect to enjoy rude health induced, as is common, contradictory reactions. Alongside growing anxiety, particularly about the succession, went a determination to prove his vigour and virility. He refused to abate his sporting activities and he began an affair with Mary Carey, the wife of one of his esquires of the body (and the sister of Anne Boleyn).

The resumed adultery of a king not noted for promiscuity created something of a stir in the court. It certainly laid Henry open to damaging gossip but it also opened up another interesting avenue for families seeking royal favour. Habitués of the household could not fail to notice the growing estrangement between Henry and his queen. Catherine took very badly the sudden advancement of the bastard Duke of Richmond and the exile of her daughter to the Welsh border. She disapproved of moves to marry Mary into the family of the Valois, the enemies of her own relatives. When she made her displeasure known Henry reacted violently and the atmosphere at court became arctic.

As we have already seen, he was experiencing one of his periodic bouts of restlessness about his personal control of state affairs. With the advent of peace in 1525 he turned his mind to a wider range of national business and once more he reached the conclusion that he was bereft of a good council attendant. It may be that after the debacle of the Amicable Grant Norfolk and Suffolk had managed to get to the King and air their concerns. Whatever the catalyst might have been, he instructed Wolsey to rearrange the routine of government so that at all times he had around him a corps of senior advisers with whose aid he could originate policy. This would obviously limit the Cardinal's control over the flow of material to and from the King and was not a change he welcomed. When he cast about in his mind for whoever might be responsible for revival of interest in the nitty-gritty of government his suspicions might well have focused on More. That, at least, is one explanation of what happened next.

Wolsey set in hand a major reshuffle of government and household personnel and one of the first to suffer as a result was Thomas More. In September 1525 the under-treasurership was taken away from him and given to Sir William Compton, a member of the Privy Chamber. By way of recompense More was made Chancellor of the Duchy of Lancaster. What looks at first sight like a sideways move was, in fact, anything but. Sir Thomas was obliged to exchange a remunerative sinecure for a less well-paid job which involved a considerable amount of administrative and legal work. Of greater significance, however, than the loss of income was the fact that More's new duties precluded him from continuing as the King's Secretary. Most of the duchy work was carried out at Westminster which meant that Sir Thomas was kept more closely under Wolsey's eye as well as having little access to the King. More settled to his new tasks with his usual industriousness but he would have been less than human if he had not felt resentment at Wolsey's high-handed treatment.

Without men close to the King who might stimulate his appetite for tedious business detail the Cardinal could now set about dealing with his master as he always had done. He knew well enough that Henry's zeal for administrative involvement would soon fade provided that he believed his instructions for reform had been complied with. Accordingly Wolsey drew up a detailed plan for the restructuring of the household which he presented to the King who was at Eltham, keeping well clear of the plague in January 1526, and which is known as the Eltham Ordinance. It provided a body of twenty worthy councillors to attend Henry, including Suffolk and Norfolk, the Marquesses of Dorset and Exeter, the Earls of Shrewsbury and Worcester and Thomas More. However, the document went on to establish that in the event of the great officers of state being absent about their duties the Council could function as a sub-committee of ten and if that quorum could not be achieved His Majesty should not be served by less than two honourable councillors. In other words the *status quo ante* was to be restored. Wolsey had won again.

The Eltham Ordinance, however, was not a mere exercise in cynical manipulation. It was a comprehensive report intended to deal with every aspect of household administration. Its preamble suggested that the pre-occupation of the principal officers with the wars had 'greatly hindered' the 'accustomed good order' of Henry's court. While that may well have been the case, there was a more pressing need for a thoroughgoing review: the King was broke. Fifteen years of lavish expenditure on royal lifestyle and military posturing had drained the pot which the first Tudor had left well filled. The tales of woe presented by Henry's tax collectors made it clear that the King's needs and wants could not be simply furnished by going to the people and that the dominant mood in the country was for a cessation of war and for less ostentation on the part of the nation's leaders. The English are Janus-faced when it comes to the pomp and ceremony of royalty; they can wallow in its dazzling splendour and enjoy a warm glow of national pride but, when anything happens to estrange prince and people, they can grumble heartily about needless expense. The prevailing tone in the late 1520s was one of resentment:

> Great pride and small riches
> How can these agree?

The populace had tired of the image of the magnificent warrior prince and the lavish spectacle that always accompanied him and his cardinal. They sensed an incongruity about a ruler who called on his subjects for sacrifices while himself indulging in spectacular display. Just how aware Henry was of this we cannot know but it was Wolsey who had the unwelcome task of intimating to his master that the royal coat must be cut according to the available cloth. Stringent economies must be made to ensure that the King could 'live of his own' (i.e. from the revenues from estates and prerogative rights without relying on taxation).

Wolsey's new broom swept away many corrupt practices that had crept in. For example, scores of officers claimed 'bouge of court' which entitled them to eat in the King's hall, but instead of doing so they were taking their food and selling it privately. The reform tightened up the financial administration of every department in order to cut down on wastage. But the most noticeable effect of the radical economies now imposed was the household's reduction in size. Over the years an ever-growing posse of hangers-on had attached themselves to the court. It was not only the great men of the Council and chamber who found places for relatives and clients; the competition for places at court was fierce and courtiers could add substantially to their incomes by using their influence on behalf of petitioners. Now such practices were severely curbed by the simple expedient of trimming the numbers of household personnel. For example the body of 112 gentlemen ushers was cut to twelve. This, of course, changed the whole atmosphere of the court. Something of the earlier youthful boisterousness must have been lost in the sparer, more serious household. These changes in the King's surroundings cannot have improved his humour, particularly when he noticed that his reduced magnificence contrasted with the enhanced splendour attendant upon Wolsey's international showmanship (see p. 239).

The Eltham Ordinance was not devised as an elaborate personal agenda on Wolsey's part but it inevitably carried with it distinct political advantages. The major purge of court personnel was an excellent opportunity to remove those of whom he entertained any suspicions. He deprived the Queen of several ladies suspected of ardent pro-Imperial sympathies and, when she complained to her husband, Wolsey 'regretfully' informed his master that they had been turning Catherine against the little Duke of Richmond. The Cardinal did not hesitate to encourage and play upon the growing estrangement between King and Queen. Henry's aversion to his wife made it easier to pursue the pro-French policy which was anathema to almost all Henry's other advisers. Those contrary voices were effectively stifled by the main provisions of the Eltham Ordinance. The dearth of places to be sued for reduced the power of the Cardinal's opponents at the same time that it enhanced his own as principal patron under the King. One other development which was associated with this move to greater efficiency and the reinforcing of Wolsey's authority was his giving up of Hampton Court. Henry had long envied his minister the ownership of this splendid palace and the Cardinal now made him a present of it as a place close to the capital where the reduced royal household could be accommodated in suitable splendour. What may appear at first sight a mortifying sacrifice was nothing of the kind. In exchange Wolsey received his own permanent (and lavish) quarters at both Hampton Court and Richmond. Now, whenever the King was at one or other of his principal residences the great Cardinal could be at hand, keeping a close eye on the comings and goings in the royal apartments.

Personal and family problems were not the only causes of the malaise which descended upon the King and his entourage. Henry, for so long accustomed to seeing his whims and desires given substance, was experiencing various frustrations in his public life. For the best part of two decades the King of England had played a leading role in the affairs of Christendom, thanks largely to his cardinal's diplomatic mastery. After 1526 he became an impotent bystander who could only watch the game being played by his more powerful rivals. There were two reasons for this: his treasury was empty and European affairs had developed a complexity beyond even Wolsey's power to manipulate to his master's advantage. For a proactive ruler like Henry the change in his international position was intolerable.

The situation on the Continent was not only bewildering, it seemed to be insane. The certainties that had once provided Christian Europe's parameters collapsed. The Peasants' War was appalling, not only for the death and destruction it unleashed or the permanent loosening of feudal bonds it hastened, but also for its smashing of the Christendom myth. Catholic Europe was sundered into different confessional shards and Charles V's attempts to restore religious unity failed. By 1526 the Empire was already moving towards that compromise solution of the conflict within the Emperor's territory whereby each prince decided whether the church in his dominions should be of the old religion or the new (*cuius regio, eius religio*). Nor was the Continent divided merely along Catholic and Lutheran lines: the Protestant camp was already fragmenting into Lutheran, Swiss Reformed and Anabaptist groupings. In the midst of all this, Suleiman the Magnificent won a resounding victory at Mohács (August 1526), added most of Hungary to the Ottoman Empire and went on to besiege Vienna in 1529.

These events were plain to all and, though tragic, readily comprehensible to those given to seeking simple solutions: this was what happened when heretics challenged the authority of the Pope, and territorial rulers, for their own ends, protected them. To most establishment figures it was axiomatic that Luther (though he vehemently condemned the rebels) was the Antichrist responsible for the holocaust. What happened next threw such easy analyses into confusion. The war between Charles V and Francis I was resumed and the French King used every means at his disposal to be revenged on his adversary, including collusion in the Muslim invasion of Hungary. It suited England's book to keep the two great continental monarchs at each other's throats and Wolsey played a prominent part in forging the League of Cognac between France, the papacy and various north Italian states, with England (too impoverished to provide troops or war funds) as 'protector of the league'. Charles was furious and ordered his mercenary army to cross the Alps. His general, the Duke of Bourbon, laid siege to Rome in May 1526, with a horde of violent professionals intent on plunder. The fact that Bourbon himself was struck down by an arquebus ball at the first attack did not deflect the invaders. Driven onwards by dreams of the Eternal City's fabled wealth, they tore savagely at the walls with their bare hands, impervious to the slaughter of their comrades, until all resistance was broken and they could tumble into the deserted streets. What happened next stunned the whole western world. Palaces, churches, monasteries, shops, workshops and humble homes were subjected to pillage and desecration of every description. Drunken soldiers even disentombed the body of Julius II and dragged it through the streets. The eight-day orgy of plunder and wanton destruction was far worse than that perpetrated by French troops in 1494. In fact, nothing like it had been suffered by the city of popes and caesars since

Genseric's Vandals had visited upon it, in Gibbon's words, 'a memorable example of the vicissitudes of human and divine things'. Yet these marauders were no barbarians; they were the forces of His Catholic Majesty, the Holy Roman Emperor, Charles V.

The sack of Rome was one of those rare events that jolt the thinking of a generation. It dislocated conventional values and assumptions. It tore up the rule book by which Christendom politics had been conducted. The dismay of the Catholic world was the vindication of the Protestants. Could anyone doubt that this was God's judgement on the scarlet woman? Even the Emperor, who was personally shocked by the outrages perpetrated in his name, invoked the Almighty when defending himself to Henry VIII. For his own part, he said, he would as soon not have had such a victory but God had decided otherwise and he could only submit himself to the will of Providence. But Charles's reluctance did not extend to any immediate withdrawal from papal territory. Clement VII was left skulking in the Castel Sant' Angelo and Italy remained under Habsburg dominance for three decades.

The latest twists and turns in Europe left English foreign policy in limbo. The Emperor, whom Henry now heartily loathed, had triumphed in the power game. The French King, whom he liked little better, wanted England's support in the continuing struggle but an impoverished Henry could provide little by way of practical aid to a military ally. By the same token, he was in no position to be the broker of Europe. Throughout his reign, in peace and war, his subtle and accomplished minister had kept him at the centre of Christendom affairs. Now he had been sidelined – yet another cause of frustration.

The consensus of opinion among the King's councillors was that England should stay out of a quarrel from which she could expect to gain nothing. This was certainly More's view. He later recalled a debate in which Wolsey had countered the peace argument by quoting an old fable. A group of wise men had learned that anyone caught in the rain would be driven mad, so they sheltered in a cave, believing that when they emerged they would be able to rule a world peopled by fools. Unfortunately, when they did come out they were set upon by maniacs. So much, Wolsey commented, for splendid isolation.

He now pursued the French alliance with a fervour and determination remarkable even for him, driven by the principle that had always inspired his foreign policy: to keep his master at the centre of European affairs. The hand he had been dealt in the latest round of international poker was not impressive but, by 1526, he had become the master of bluffs and he played it with insouciance and panache. His two highest cards were Henry's fury with Charles V and his own reputation throughout Christendom. Wolsey could rely on the King to support any move that would antagonise and incommode his nephew. As for his, Wolsey's, own prestige, it had attained an all-time high by 1526. John Clerk, Bishop of Bath and Wells and Wolsey's principal emissary to the Vatican, reported at the end of the year that, with a Church in turmoil and under the leadership of an ineffective Pope, many people were looking to Cardinal Wolsey and King Henry as the only saviours of united Christendom.[52] Even when we make allowances for the obligatory flattery and hyperbole, Clerk's words ring true. Wolsey was one of Europe's leading statesmen, the most famous prince of the Church outside Italy, and the fact that he *was* outside Italy kept him above local politics and imperial pressures. He and his king had taken a lead in the crusade against Luther and had been seen to labour for the recovery of the Church under papal and Imperial headship.

Wolsey was not given to modest disclaimers. On the contrary, when French ambassadors arrived in February 1527 to discuss arrangements for a marriage and martial alliance, he eagerly received from them the proffered garments of flattery and drew them around his ample form. He assured them that he had laboured long and consistently in French interests. When he had first set eyes on Francis I at the Field of Cloth of Gold, he averred, he had been overwhelmed by the King's nobleness and manifest virtues and no subsequent circumstances had undermined his affection. He had worked hard and long to achieve Francis's release from captivity in Spain and to preserve the security of France during her monarch's absence. This had included even deterring his own master from invading, as certain of his advisers had pressed him to do.[53] Reading these words in cold, unvarnished print brings to mind phrases such as 'bare-faced cheek' and 'brazen effrontery'. Of course, we have to put them in the context of negotiations aimed at setting aside the destruction, pillage and bloodshed of the recent past and constructing a new amity. Yet even when we have done that we detect a degree of hubris and self-aggrandisement that goes beyond anything that England's Cardinal had demonstrated before. Wolsey was projecting himself as a figure of international stature. He had been twice thwarted of the papacy but his ambitions had not abated and within a few months he was claiming the role of Vicar-General of the Church – *de facto* Pope. This was the time that Thomas Wolsey took the first stride towards his own nemesis – he began to overshadow Henry VIII.

It was not only in the political arena that the Cardinal presented himself as a Christian gladiator. He determined to achieve immortality, not merely in the hereafter, but among future generations on the terrestrial globe. Like the great ecclesiastical politician of his own early years, William Wainfleet, Wolsey made a bid for recognition in the educational world by gracing his university and his home town with splendid new foundations. It was in 1524 that he took the first steps in a plan that must have been long maturing in his mind. He obtained two papal bulls permitting him to suppress St Frideswide's monastery in Oxford in order to convert the buildings into a college and to close down other, unspecified, religious houses to endow his new foundation. Cardinal College would be, as its creator assured the King, 'a virtuous foundation for the increase of your Highness's merit, profit of your subjects, the advancement of good learning, and for the wellbeing of my poor soul'.[54] The Cardinal Archbishop who patronised Erasmus and other humanists believed with them in the reform of the Church through purified learning, and his college was designed as a contribution to the much-needed establishment of a revivified Catholicism. Having seen his university graced with a fine, new educational establishment, Wolsey went on, in 1528, to extend and transform the existing grammar school at Ipswich into a complex of chapel, school and almshouses on a scale which would rival Winchester and Eton. More old religious centres had to fall for this second creation. In all, twenty-nine monasteries and nunneries were closed down and their inmates moved to other establishments to provide for Wolsey's educational initiative.

This was fully in keeping with the spirit of the times. The demand for education was rising and was being met by churchmen, nobles, gentlemen and merchants the land over. Humanists kept at the top of their agenda the need for teaching establishments where the new principles would be followed. However, we might note that at Cardinal College study of Scripture did not receive the prominence Erasmus and his friends might have hoped for – presumably because the evangelical explosion had thrown dust over the shining appeal of the open Bible. There was nothing new about diverting the capital and income of religious houses to other uses for the public weal. Patrons, including the traditionalist Fisher, had been doing it for years. Vocations to the withdrawn life were declining and many who might once have embraced the cloister had, like Thomas More, faced up instead to the challenge of living a holy life in the world. Wolsey could reasonably claim that most, at least, of the houses he appropriated were places where the communities had dwindled to only a handful of men or women and where 'neither God is served nor religion kept'.[55]

What was new was the scale and the manner of the closures. Everything Wolsey undertook had to be writ large and he designed his new foundations to be grander than anything that had existed before. That required money and efficient execution of policy: when a religious house had been targeted the Cardinal's agents swooped, expelling, inventorying, and rapidly packing all movables on to carts. It gave onlookers the impression of a brutal mini-movement, and one organised for the greater glory of the 'butcher's cur'. There were local protests. The citizens of Tonbridge petitioned for a stay of execution against their priory and at Bayham in Sussex a group of gentlemen, heavily disguised, reinstalled the Premonstratensian canons in defiance of the commissioners. Hall, who was of course biased, baldly asserted that the Cardinal's men 'entered into the said houses, put out the religious and took all their goods, movables and scarcely gave to the poor wretches anything'.[56] Whatever the facts, the chronicler accurately recorded the common perception of what Wolsey was about. Complaints reached the court in an intermittent stream. In August 1527 William Knight, recently appointed royal Secretary, wrote in some alarm to Wolsey, 'I have heard the King and noblemen speak things incredible of the acts of Dr Aleyn and Cromwell.'[57] Only eighteen months earlier the Cardinal had been driven to the unusual expedient of having to defend himself against attacks by enemies at court, dutifully relayed to him by More. Writing with his own hand, Wolsey was careful to remind the King that the acts of suppression were carried out 'with your gracious aid and assistance' in order to annex them unto '*your* intended college of Oxford, for the increase of good letters and virtue' (my emphasis).

The founder had invested much emotional capital in his Oxford college and criticism stung him sharply. 'Some folks,' he commented sourly,

which be always prone to speak evil and report the worst without knowledge of the truth, have perchance informed your Highness of some disorder that should be used by my commissaries in suppressing of the said monasteries, yet most humbly I shall beseech your Highness, after your noble and accustomed manner, to give no credence unto them unto such time as your Grace may hear my declaration in that behalf. For Sire, Almighty God I take to my record, I have not meant, intended, or gone about, nor also have willed mine officers, to do any thing concerning the said suppressions, but under such form and manner, as is and hath largely been to the full satisfaction, recompense, and joyous contentment of any person which hath had, or could pretend to have right or interest in the same . . . Verily Sire I would be loath to be noted, that I should intend such a virtuous foundation for the increase of your Highness's merit, profit of your subjects, the advancement of good learning, and for the wellbeing of my poor soul, to be established or acquired *ex rapinis*.[58]

Wolsey was now more sensitive to criticism than in bygone years. There had always been those who sneered at his humble origins, mocked his ostentation, resented his influence with the King, opposed his policies, or fathered upon him all the nation's ills. But when a John Skelton lampooned him or an ex-Speaker of the House of Commons insisted that if only the temporal lords had acted in consort then 'my lord Cardinal's head should have been as red as his coat',[59] the King's favourite could shrug them off. However, by the 1520s he was looking about him for potential enemies and responding sharply to any slights, whether real or imaginary. When the students of Gray's Inn revived for Christmas 1526 an old play by one their sergeants, John Rowe, some were apprehensive lest certain material in it might seem rather pointed. The partisan John Foxe put his gloss on the events which followed:

> The authority of the bishop of Rome, and the glory of his cardinals, were not so high, but such as had fresh wits, sparkled with God's grace, began to espy Christ from Antichrist; that is, true sincerity from counterfeit religion: in the number of whom was . . . Master Simon Fish, a gentleman of Gray's Inn. It happened the first year that this gentleman came to London to dwell, that there was a certain play or interlude made by one Master Rowe, of the same inn, gentleman, in which play partly was matter against the cardinal Wolsey; and when none durst take upon them to play that part which touched the said cardinal, this aforesaid Master Fish took upon him to do it. Hereupon great displeasure ensued against him upon the cardinal's part, insomuch that he, being pursued by the said cardinal the same night that this tragedy was played, was compelled by force to void his own house, and so fled over the sea.[60]

It was the little people who began to rock Wolsey's pedestal, not his potential political rivals. More and Howard were among several habitués of court and Council who had cause to wish the Cardinal's downfall. They disagreed with his policies and they had been personally slighted by him. Even his erstwhile friend, Charles Brandon, had turned against him. In Suffolk's case the motivation seems to have been anticlericalism. He, above all men, resented the power of the clergy over the temporal nobility and Wolsey represented that power in full, assertive measure. Yet, there is no evidence of any organised faction or any concerted action to topple the great man. On one occasion in the early spring of 1527 Norfolk's never very elastic temper snapped and he exchanged angry words with Wolsey over the pro-French policy in the King's presence but there is no evidence that anyone else backed him up nor that Henry was influenced by the Duke's outburst. On the contrary, we only know about the incident because the Cardinal himself mentioned it to the French emissaries and he would scarcely have done that had he felt unsettled by concerted opposition. No, Howard, More, *et al.* were little men who would never by themselves have had the courage to attack. Like jackals they would wait until their quarry was weakened. What first rendered vulnerable the butcher's son-turned-arbiter of Christendom was public opinion and the disquiet of a king who saw his trusted servant shining forth in ever more effulgent glory while he was being obliged to restrict his own expenditure.

CHAPTER 18

The Fatal Failure

We have reached the fulcrum moment in the lives of the six Thomases, and of King Henry, and of his dynasty, and of his people. We can actually narrow down to one month – May 1527 – the time during which all their lives were dislocated. A cluster of events spread over four weeks made it, without exaggeration, a month of destiny. On Saturday 4 May, Greenwich was en fête to receive the French ambassadors who had been involved, since the end of February, in labyrinthine negotiations with Wolsey and his team. Those, in turn, had been the culmination of eighteen months of heart-searching diplomacy, during which each party had had to set aside its natural feelings, reverse its recent public stance, and, in the face of hostile criticism at home, learn to embrace a traditional enemy and protest undying love.

Sunday began with a solemn mass, followed by the signing of the treaty pledging joint military action against Charles and agreeing the marriage of Mary Tudor to either Francis or his second son, the Duc d'Orléans. The solemnities accomplished, the celebrations began. Henry was determined to prove that he could still put on a good show and for three months ironworkers, carpenters, gilders, painters, embroiderers, pageant-masters, playwrights and set-designers had been hard at work to create a sumptuous and well-rehearsed series of spectacles. Prominent among their number was Hans Holbein, whose long enjoyment of court patronage began with this Greenwich celebration. Over a triumphal arch at one end of the banqueting hall he painted *The Siege of Thérouanne* (not, one would have thought, the most tactful subject for the occasion) and he decorated the ceiling of the theatre with a breathtaking cosmography displaying the planets and the signs of the zodiac. This May Day was a red-letter day in Holbein's calendar. It marked his stunning arrival at Henry VIII's court.[61] The afternoon of 5 May was devoted to an elaborate tourney, presided over by Garter King of Arms, at the conclusion of which Henry and his guests retired to a specially constructed pavilion for a banquet followed by plays, 'combats', music and dancing. The whole event was the icing on the cake of Thomas Wolsey's latest triumph and for men like the Duke of Norfolk, who resented it but were obliged to witness the elaborate symbolism of

Anglo-French entente and listen to the crude satirising of the Emperor, it must have seemed that the Cardinal was more unassailable than ever.

Yet, there was something else that Howard observed on this occasion, something which set many court tongues wagging: the King spent much time dancing with Norfolk's niece, Anne Boleyn. We know nothing of the early stages of the love affair between Henry and Anne and so cannot specify what stage of the relationship this represents but 5 May is the first occasion on which their names were linked together and it seems almost like a very public declaration of the King's interest in his ex-mistress's sister. Sir Thomas Boleyn had achieved for Anne a place in Queen Catherine's household in the early weeks of 1527 and it may be that Wosley had approved this placement as part of his campaign to increase Francophile influence at court and especially on the Queen's side. Henry was vulnerable. He had, by now, determined to end his marriage and had confided as much to Wolsey. This meant that he could lift his own spirits and prove his manhood by contemplating fresh, novel amours and seeking a wife to bear him sons. When a new face appeared among his queen's maids of honour and one whose charms he had reason to believe might equal those of her sister, Henry was more than ready to be hooked. In the spring of 1527 he probably cast Anne in the role of lover rather than bride.

Marriage for kings was a matter of politics and Wolsey would have certainly begun contemplating the negotiating advantage of an unwed monarch. Whether or not his feelings for Mistress Boleyn, which he now knew to be reciprocated, thrust Henry into positive action, within a week he took the first fateful step towards the annulment of his marriage: he ordered Wolsey to determine in his legatine court the validity or otherwise of his marriage to Catherine. He was, in a very real sense, taking Wolsey at the latter's own valuation: if England's leading churchman possessed almost papal prestige and authority, it should be a small matter for him to sort out his King's matrimonial problems.

One other event occurred in May 1527 which had an emotional impact on Henry, although he did not hear of it until the middle of the following month. On the 21st, Charles V sent couriers speeding through his dominions with the happy news that he had become a father. His empress, the Portuguese princess for whom he had spurned Mary Tudor, had presented him with a healthy son and heir. How that news must have twisted the knife in the entrails of Henry's disappointed hopes and reinforced his determination to rescue his own dynastic fortunes!

On 17 May Wolsey convened, in secret, a legatine court, comprising himself, William Warham, his fellow archbishop, and a small company of other divines and canon law experts. They summoned Henry before them (having first obtained his permission so to do) to answer a charge of living in sin with his dead brother's widow. The court held four sessions during May before deciding, on the last day of the month, to abandon their proceedings. This was not because they had concluded that they could not deliver the verdict the King required – though their discussions will have revealed that the issue was fraught with legal and theological complexities – but because news had arrived of such shattering import that it forced Wolsey to review all his political options. The papacy had been reduced to impotence by the onslaught of the Emperor's marauders and as, over the ensuing days, further details of Clement's immurement in Castel Sant'Angelo were brought in by messengers, merchants and travellers, the Pope's English representative bethought himself how to turn the unique situation to his advantage.

The first impression made by the news from Rome was that it was a remarkable piece of good luck for Wolsey and Henry. The abomination of desolation carried out in the name of Charles V totally vindicated the government's pro-French policy and discommoded all those who still favoured an imperial alliance. Good, indignant Catholics could scarcely deny the imperative of freeing the head of the Church and, as Wolsey prepared a major diplomatic excursion to France in July, he could do so in the knowledge that criticism at home had been effectively stifled. He had also worked out new tactics for dealing with the King's secret matter. There had always been the possibility that Catherine might challenge the findings of the legatine court and appeal directly to the Pope. After 6 May, there was no Pope – or so it could be argued. When Charles V's blood was up, he could, like his English uncle, be stubborn to the point almost of lunacy and he was determined to make Clement pay for intriguing with his enemies. He forced the Pope and his allies to yield into his hands the ports of Ostia and Civitavecchia and the northern strongholds of Parma, Piacenza and Modena, imposed a swingeing 400,000 ducats' ransom for the release of Clement and his besieged cardinals and decreed that even after its payment the Pope was to be lodged in Gaeta or Naples under the firm control of Imperial agents. With the Pope effectively reduced to the status of Imperial chaplain there was clearly a vacancy in the leadership of the Church and Wolsey decided to fill it *de facto* and *de jure*.

What he had in mind presents one of history's intriguing 'ifs'. He proposed to call a meeting of free cardinals under his chairmanship at Avignon – a significant choice of location since popes and antipopes under French control had ruled from the Rhone valley city between 1309 and 1449. They would, presumably through secret messengers, obtain a papal commission conferring full powers on Wolsey until such time as Clement was able to resume 'normal service'. Their eminences would then settle the main items of European business, including the annulment of Henry's marriage and lay plans for a general council of the Church to deal with the urgent issues of reform and the combating of heresy. The plan was bold; it was presumptuous; but, given Wolsey's actual international status, and no serious shifts in the political situation, it could have worked. The subsequent history of England would have been very different if it had – the swift marriage of Henry and Anne, perhaps the birth of an heir, no break with Rome, a Crown unable to refloat its finances on the plunder of the monasteries and obliged to watch its powers progressively whittled away; 'much virtue in an "if" '.

On 3 July the would-be arbiter of Christendom set out in inordinate pomp on his holy mission to Francis I and the princes of the Church. He ordered that his endeavours should be supported in every English parish by three days of fasting and prayer for the release of His Holiness (though he may well have added in his own intercessions that the Almighty need not hurry to grant this petition). Accompanied by 900 gentlemen, he made his way to the coast and thence to Calais. As he journeyed through French territory he was everywhere greeted with official pageants and crowds ordered out to cheer. When the cavalcade reached Amiens for the ratification of the treaty Francis received the Cardinal with all the formalised affection usually reserved for the visits of brother monarchs. In the elaborate court decorations and masques Wolsey was, for the first time, represented as the equal to, if not the superior of, his royal master. The Cardinal-Legate enjoyed messianic acclaim: *he* would heal the centuries-old wounds caused by Anglo-French hostility; *he* would forge the politico-military weapon which should humble the Emperor, *he* would rescue the Pope; *he* would bring peace to the Church. Wolsey lived up to the image with his customary aplomb. The banquet he laid on for Francis on 19 August surpassed anything that the French King had been able to provide. The food was more varied, the gold and silver on display more spectacular and, whereas those who waited on Francis at his court did so with a degree of informality, Wolsey was served by those who proffered dishes to him kneeling and bare-headed.

One witness of all this exaggerated mutual admiration was Thomas More, who attended as a member of the Cardinal's suite, and one wonders what he made of it all. The man who wore a hair shirt beneath the velvet gown to remind himself of the vanity of outward show and scoffed at 'light-minded' men who were 'lifted to the stars by the fickle wind of opinion'[62] must have looked upon the apotheosis of the butcher's son with disdain, if not genuine dismay. Another question which suggests itself is why More was selected to accompany Henry's plenipotentiary on this mission. He had never been sent on a French embassy (apart from his attendance at the Field of Cloth of Gold) and had taken no pains to conceal his dislike of England's closest neighbour and oftenest enemy. In lampooning a courtier who aped French fashion he had written:

> . . . he pays [his] servant nothing like a Frenchman; he clothes him in wornout rags in the French manner; he feeds him little and that little poor, as the French do; he works him hard like the French; he strikes

him often like a Frenchman; at social gatherings and on the street and in the market place and in public he quarrels with him and abuses him always in the French fashion . . .[63]

In Thomas More's xenophobic mind nothing good could come out of France – hardly a suitable attitude for a diplomat working to achieve eternal peace between the two nations. Was he, perhaps, appointed by the King to keep an eye on Wolsey and report back any evidence that the Cardinal was exceeding his authority? Certainly Henry had planted spies within his own emissary's entourage. Over the next few weeks secret communications flew frenziedly between the two travelling courts. Suspicion and mistrust were, it seems, mutual and the boot may, indeed, have been on the other foot. Wolsey, knowing full well More's prejudices, might have made sure that he was kept well away from the King during his own absence.

Despite the pomp of his progress and the adulation of his hosts, Wolsey was anxious, and with good reason. Cavendish, writing thirty years later, claimed that 'the great lords of the Council, bearing a secret grudge against the cardinal because they could not rule in the commonwealth because of him as they would' arranged for him to be sent to France so that 'they might have convenient leisure and opportunity to adventure their long-desired enterprise; and by the aid of their chief mistress (my lady Anne) to vilify him unto the King in his absence'.[64] This is a conflation of events viewed in retrospect and it attributes to Wolsey's enemies more cunning and organisational skill than they possessed. Thomas Howard and his associates were mere opportunists but fate had presented them with an opening that even the most incompetent of conspirators would have found difficult to make a mess of exploiting. Not only was the butcher's cur out of the country on a mission that would occupy several weeks – perhaps even months – not only were his efficient communication lines greatly extended, but for the first time in years there was someone constantly at the King's side whose influence rivalled the Cardinal's. More important still, Henry, always impulsive and suggestible, was now at a peak of emotional volatility because he was in love. If there was one thing that Wolsey had taught his opponents it was that influence rested on giving the King whatever it was that, at any particular moment, he desired. Anne Boleyn's uncle and her father and their supporters set out to ease the way to the divorce. As we shall see, their bungling interference made a difficult business more complex and destroyed any chance of bringing the matter to a swift conclusion.

What emerged in Wolsey's absence was not a faction with its own political agenda. There was no attempt to sabotage the French treaty or realign England with the Empire. Certainly Anne's family had no intention of coming to the aid of Queen Catherine. The Howard–Boleyn caucus was a power clique, trading on the King's love for Anne, favouring the divorce, aligning themselves with Henry's desire to marry their kinswoman and hoping for manifold benefits as Henry's in-laws. They envisaged themselves, like the Woodvilles in Edward IV's reign, as a 'royalised' family guarding the door to patronage and influence. Others, like Suffolk and the Marquess of Exeter, who associated themselves with Norfolk's party, did not share the Howards' aspirations. The Brandons, husband and wife, for example, were opposed to the idea of Henry marrying Anne. However, all were united in their desire to remove Wolsey from the seat of power. The mechanism for doing so lay ready to hand in the Eltham Ordinance, which had provided, in theory, for a twenty-strong council attendant. As soon as the Cardinal was not around to deflect his conciliar colleagues into other activities, they clustered around the King as, seldom far from his lady love's side, he embarked on a summer progress that, for the size and gaiety of the court, recalled the earlier, carefree years of the reign.

As he travelled around France, an increasingly agitated Wolsey sent and received a flurry of messages commending his own activities and bringing intelligence about who was at court and what they were doing. The most unnerving information he received was that Henry had determined on marriage with Anne. At what point suspicion turned to knowledge we do not know. Anne's refusal to be anything less than the King's wife certainly sprang from her own will. She was, no less than Catherine, a devout, intelligent and determined woman – qualities that Henry obviously admired. But her resolve was stiffened by her clan. Her uncle and her father, who could not resist the prospect of seeing their family become the second in the realm, will have impressed upon her her duty to her kindred. As their plans developed they made every effort to keep them secret from the Cardinal, a plot in which Henry colluded. But Wolsey was much too old a hand at intrigue to be long deceived. He could read the signs better than most.

In May he had despatched Thomas Boleyn (Viscount Rochford since June 1525) on a separate mission to France but just as Wolsey, in late June, was preparing to set out for the Continent he learned that Anne's father had been recalled, ahead of his fellow envoys. As soon as the Cardinal reached France he sent to his protégé Sir William Fitzwilliam, Treasurer of the Household, to know who was keeping company with the King and received the disquieting news that mostly 'he suppeth in his privy chamber ... with ... the Dukes of Norfolk and Suffolk, the Marquess of Exeter and the Lord of Rochford'.[65] It became very clear from other intelligence that while this caucus was keeping secrets from him, his confidential reports to the King were being freely shared and discussed with the King's new group of intimates. Wolsey countered by sending his most trusted emissaries and by couching his letters to Henry in the most fawning and obsequious terms that he could devise. The kind of poison he had to try to neutralise is clear from these epistles:

> God I take to be my judge that whatsoever opinion . . . your grace hath or might conceive, I never intended to set forth the expedition of the said commission [i.e. the proposed Avignon meeting] for any authority, ambition, commodity, private profit or lucre, but only for the advancement of your grace's secret affair . . . Assuring your highness that I shall never be found but as your most humble, loyal and faithful, obedient servant . . . enduring the travails and pains which I daily and hourly sustain without any regard to the continuance of my life or health, which is only preserved by the assured trust of your gracious love and favour.[66]

As soon as he could, in mid-September, Wolsey scurried homeward. But by then irreparable damage had been done to the divorce, to Wolsey's subtle schemes and to Henry's hopes and dreams.

The successful partnership between King and Cardinal had been based on the latter's subtlety and understanding of diplomatic intricacies, which had enabled him either to achieve what Henry wanted or to persuade Henry that what he wanted was what was, in reality, achievable. The royal divorce and remarriage could not be handled in the same way. Henry would not budge and the international situation seemed equally intractable. Left to his own devices, might Wolsey have found a way to square the circle? Probably not. His initial scheme – the Avignon summit – came to nothing because Clement, determined not to have his authority any further undermined, forbade his cardinals to attend and only a handful were prepared to defy the ban. However, one thing is clear, the actions Henry took in Wolsey's absence, egged on by Anne and her intellectually challenged uncle, threw away whatever diplomatic advantages he had.

Henry VIII's intention to rid himself of his first wife and to marry his young paramour must go down as one of the worst-kept secrets in history. While Wolsey was urging the King to keep the annulment issue under wraps Henry had confronted Catherine with his doubts about the validity of their union and informed her that they must live apart until the issue was resolved. She lost no time in sending the news to the head of her family, the Holy Roman Emperor. Henry got wind of this secret message but completely bungled an attempt to apprehend the carrier. By the beginning of August a shocked Charles had issued instructions to the Pope to cancel Wolsey's legatine powers and personally to pronounce that Henry and his aunt were lawfully husband and wife. Meanwhile Norfolk and the Boleyns had persuaded Henry to go over Wolsey's head. The Cardinal, they suggested, had no intention of furthering the 'great matter' and, in any case, an issue which touched the King so personally should not be entrusted to a creature of His Majesty's own raising.

The result was that William Knight, a seasoned diplomatist 'of the old school which regarded dissimulation as one of the requisites of success'[67] was despatched, against his will, on an embassy to Rome which had all the elements of farce. He was to call at Compiègne and pay his respects to Wolsey without revealing the nature of his business in Rome, which was to secure a dispensation for nothing less than bigamy! Clement, it was suggested, should permit Henry to marry while the 'mere formalities' of the annulment took their course. Wolsey's espionage system proved too efficient for this stratagem to succeed; by the time of Knight's arrival he knew all and halted the emissary in his tracks. But Henry now knew that Wolsey knew and he hastened to reassure the Cardinal that he trusted him implicitly to handle the negotiations. However, he had 'another matter' for Knight to attend to in Rome and the envoy should, therefore, be allowed to continue his journey. Knight's new instructions were to deliver another hair-brained request to the Pope. In the event of his marriage being annulled Henry should be granted a dispensation to marry a woman consanguineous with another he had known carnally (i.e. he could marry Anne despite having had sexual congress with her sister). The contents of the letter Knight was to deliver were such that 'no man doth know but they which I am sure will never disclose it to man living for any craft the Cardinal or any other can find'.[68]

What this cloak-and-dagger correspondence reveals is a king desperate to wed his lover, determined to cover all his bases so that the marriage could never be challenged, and hopelessly badly advised as to how to go about it. 'I am King of England; when I pray, God listens!' The line is from an old film about the romance of Henry VIII and Anne Boleyn and the real Henry would never have gone quite so far as to declare that he had the Almighty in his pocket but he did expect the Lord's human representatives to do his bidding. Pronouncing a royal marriage void was a matter of ecclesiastical law and it certainly had moral and theological ramifications. But it was primarily an issue of politics. The granting of dispensation from vows and obligations and even the occasional reversing of dispensations formed a major part of curial business and a significant source of income and Henry initially regarded his divorce as a routine matter. He who was not accustomed to being denied what he wanted felt aggrieved when his marital dilemma turned into such a cause célèbre. In his more self-pitying moments he may well have looked around him and considered how hard done by he was. In the autumn of 1527 his sister, Margaret, obtained from Pope Clement a divorce from her second husband. His other sister, Mary, had, perhaps, with his own connivance, married for love, and as for her second spouse, his old friend Charles Brandon, what a chequered marital career he had had! Nor had Wolsey denied himself connubial bliss: he had kept a mistress for several years and had children by her. When it came to Clement VII, all the world knew that he only occupied St Peter's chair because his cousin, Leo X, had obligingly declared that his uncle's illegitimate son, had, in fact, been born in wedlock, thus removing the barrier that would have prevented his advancement to senior Church appointments. All in all, it must have seemed to Henry grossly unfair that everything was conspiring to prevent him marrying the woman he loved and siring a legitimate heir for the dynasty. Even if he had come to acknowledge (as he never did) that his case was morally, legally and theologically weak (as it was), he still would have been infuriated that no one could find a political means of inducing Rome to find in his favour. He saw himself as being thwarted by a wife who was a vindictive shrew, a pope who was as weak as he was corrupt and an emperor who was the last word in perfidy. Historians have often written about Henry VIII's 'convenient' conscience but it needs more than that to explain his limpet-like determination for six years to have his way, whatever the cost. He certainly persuaded himself of the righteousness of his cause and it followed that those who opposed him could only be acting out of warped and debased motives. Instead of questioning these convictions he listened only to those advisers who supported him. They, whatever their own opinions, turned this way and that to find some mechanism which would, with a reasonable semblance of respectability, deliver the King from his dilemma. Time and again they failed until a man emerged of a sufficiently radical and innovative cast of mind to be able to sever the Gordian knot.

For the moment, Henry realised, his only hope lay in his cardinal. Divorce was an ecclesiastical matter and he needed his senior churchman to help him secure it. This explains why the conspiracy against Wolsey evaporated as soon as he returned. His first priority on landing in England was to report to his master and, on 30 September, he presented himself at Greenwich for one of his accustomed private audiences with the King. It was a meeting he approached with considerable apprehension. He would have to put a bold front on his failure to achieve a conclave and wax enthusiastic about the new strategy he had developed for obtaining the divorce. He would need to deprecate, implicitly or explicitly, initiatives taken without his approval – but could not appear to criticise the King. And he expected to have to outface his rivals who might be expected to be waiting at court to enjoy his discomfiture.

The reception he received seemed to confirm his fears. On entering the Privy Chamber he found Henry and Anne together and waited patiently for the King to dismiss his lover in order to talk business with his minister. But the King did no such thing and Wolsey was faced with the embarrassment of having to report on his dealings in France under the cool eye of Mistress Boleyn. It says much for his political acumen that after such an unpromising start he was swiftly able to reassert his supremacy. Although, as we have already said, there was an inevitability about this, the Cardinal showed his mastery of court politics by the energy with which he made himself agreeable to Henry's woman. During the following weeks and months, according to Cavendish, he put on a very good act: '[disguising] the matter that lay hid in his breast, [he] prepared great banquets and solemn feasts to entertain [Henry and Anne] at his own house'.[69] By associating himself thus publicly with an alliance which was already scandalising and angering most people Wolsey continued to enjoy the support of the only people who mattered.

Wolsey's open advocacy of the King's divorce and remarriage was the final straw which broke his reputation. Many disapproved of his ostentation. There was widespread resentment at his usurpation of the influence that people believed should be wielded by his 'betters'. He was the focus of increasingly vocal anticlericalism. But what damned him in the eyes of the majority was his attempt to drag down Queen Catherine. Charles V, informed of public opinion in England by his ambassador, opined (of the man he had but a few years before called his 'second father'), 'now that [Wolsey] has . . . persuaded the King of England to leave his queen, so beloved by all, no doubt the people will rise against the cardinal and bring him to his well-deserved end, the scaffold'.[70] The irony, of course, was that, of all the decisions for which the Cardinal might have reasonably been blamed, this was not one. His heart was not in the King's matrimonial adventuring: Cavendish recorded that his master had tried, on bended knees, to dissuade Henry from marrying Anne Boleyn. But he not only accepted the inevitable, he embraced it ostentatiously and, therefore, in the eyes of the world he took the blame for it.

He did so in order to regain his position and, in this, he succeeded completely. Anne's immediate family continued to be at the centre of court life but Norfolk's brief ascendancy ended abruptly. He was ordered back to East Anglia to supervise surveys of such matters as grain production and North Sea trade, which could certainly have been done by local gentry. The old pattern reasserted itself: the frustrated and resentful Duke chaffing at his rustication and his frequent requests to be allowed to return to court being refused. Even when he fell ill in the spring of 1528 he was denied leave to come to London to consult leading physicians. In July he found another reason which rendered his recall imperative: the King would need to consult him on the Irish situation.

Affairs in Ireland had sunk back into the usual chaos of squabbles between the leading clans. Kildare proved either unable or unwilling to restore order on behalf of the Crown and, in 1526, he was summoned back to England and immediately locked up in the Tower. Norfolk took an interest in his plight and stood bail for the Earl's release. For the best part of two years he was the guest of Howard, who made available to him his house at Newington, some three miles north of London, and it is reasonable to suppose that the exile met often with his host to discuss Irish affairs. But Fitzgerald was soon up to his old tricks. Wolsey's agents were watching him carefully and in July 1528, when they caught him sending letters to his allies to foment war against the Pale, the Earl was sent back to the Tower. There was no question of Norfolk's complicity in Kildare's seditious activities but he certainly suffered by association and was blamed for not having exercised more control over his charge. Small wonder that Howard wanted to come to court in July 1528 to discuss 'Irish matters'. Anxious to demonstrate his loyalty and desperate to be entrusted with a real job, he wrote to Wolsey and dropped a broad hint that he might be sent back across the sea, since there were those in the Pale who regarded him as their only hope for peace and security. Yet again, all the Duke received for his pains was a snub. When Kildare was stripped of his post the Duke of Richmond was given the honorary title of Lord Lieutenant of Ireland and the man chosen as his deputy was not even a nobleman. The task of pacifying the country was given to Sir William Skeffington, Master of the Ordnance, the first middle-ranking official ever to have been entrusted with such a prominent position.

Something else which embarrassed Norfolk and may have rendered him *persona non grata* at court was the behaviour of his wife. Howard, no less than the King, had tired of his spouse. He had been married to Elizabeth (daughter of the hapless Buckingham) for thirteen years when, in 1526, he took up with one of his own servant girls, Bess Holland. He consorted with her openly in contempt of his wife, who, unsurprisingly, was furious. Elizabeth later claimed that she suffered physical abuse at her husband's hands and that he set the servants to pin her to the floor until her fingers bled with scratching at the boards. However, it would seem that the put-upon Duchess was capable of giving as good as she got and was widely known for a shrew. The Howards became a byword for marital dysfunction. They could scarcely see each other without each flying into a violent rage. It is no wonder that Henry found it difficult to endure having the couple at court. However, there was one other reason why Elizabeth was not popular. She had, understandably, a great deal of sympathy with that other discarded wife, Queen Catherine, and she was not the sort of woman to keep her opinions to herself. Henry would not want in his company anyone who gave the Queen such open succour and may have in exasperation banished her to Kenninghall with orders to her husband to go also and keep her in order.

Norfolk only became once again a regular at court at the end of 1528 after a year of mounting tension. It began the previous December when the Emperor aided Clement's 'escape' from Rome to Orvieto. He thus dispersed much of the odium that had gathered around him for imprisoning the Pope while effectively still being able to threaten the pontiff's freedom of action. At Orvieto Clement cowered in the bishop's 'ruinous and decayed old palace [with] roofs fallen down and thirty persons, riff-raff and others, standing in the chambers for a garnishment'. Days later

Thomas Wriothesley together with his French heraldic counterpart presented themselves before the Emperor at Burgos to deliver an ultimatum of war if the Pope was not released and certain other extreme conditions complied with. They were put out of countenance by news of Clement's enlargement but stuck to their guns and, on 21 January 1528, announced that England and France were at war with the Empire (later, when things turned out badly, Henry and Wolsey claimed that the heralds had exceeded their commission). When English envoys arrived in Orvieto to present the case for Henry's divorce, a tremulous, bankrupt and dishevelled Pope could do nothing but prevaricate. He was anxiously watching the military situation, as, indeed, were the English King and Cardinal. If the Imperial forces in Italy were defeated Charles could be brought to the negotiating table. In the spring of 1528 this seemed possible, so much so that Wolsey actually envisaged the Pope dethroning the Emperor. A French army and a Genoese fleet had Charles's soldiers hopelessly penned up in Naples. In April Clement felt confident enough to make a cautious move on Henry's great matter. He empowered two Cardinals, Wolsey and Lorenzo Campeggio, a seasoned and much-respected Vatican diplomat, to decide the issue in England. So far so good. But weeks passed, then months and there was no sign of Wolsey's fellow commissioner. The truth was that, though he was genuinely incapacitated with gout, Campeggio was under orders to *festina lente*. Henry fumed at the delay, blaming Wolsey and everyone else involved for not trying hard enough. In August the Italian Cardinal eventually set out – slowly. He reached England on 29 September, to be eagerly received by Wolsey and his master. But almost simultaneously messengers arrived with less welcome news of events in Naples. Charles V had bought off the Genoese. Without naval support and with his force ravaged by plague the French commander had been forced to withdraw. Hostilities between France and Spain rumbled on but in reality the battle for Italy was over and Charles V had emerged as the victor and peacemaker of Europe. It needed only a bad outbreak of the sweat which claimed several members of Henry's entourage and sent him fleeing from royal manor to royal manor to fill up his bitter cup.

Such, in brief outline, are the main strands of a very complex set of interwoven events running through 1528. It was a year of almost unbearable tensions for those at the centre of English life. Wolsey was stretched to his uttermost, on the one hand keeping alive the hopes of Henry and Anne, on the other urging on Campeggio and his own agents the dangers of failure. Anne, writing in August to thank the Cardinal for a 'rich and goodly present', acknowledged the 'great pains' he was taking and promised to recompense him when she came to her crown.[71] Cavendish and historians who have followed him insisted that the King's mistress was Wolsey's implacable enemy and that her enmity sprang from the

Cardinal's nipping in the bud an earlier love match with Henry Algernon Percy but there is no evidence that she nursed a grudge, and if the Cardinal's intervention prevented her marrying the heir to the Earldom of Northumberland it also made her available to marry the King, so she can have had no cause for complaint on that score. There is no doubt that as month followed sterile month of negotiation her patience grew very thin and, like Henry, she was ready to vent her anger on Wolsey. For the moment she kept up at least an outward show of friendship. She had no choice.

The Cardinal, for his part, stunned Campeggio with the urgency of his entreaties. Failure, he warned, would mean not only his own personal ruin but might also lead to Henry throwing off his allegiance to the Pope. This may have been no more than a scare tactic but it indicates that the possibility of a very drastic solution was in the air five years before it became a reality. In November Thomas Howard made his contribution to the solution of the King's intractable problem. It took the form of a kind of petition to be presented to Campeggio demonstrating that the divorce had the overwhelming support of the people of England. This document received three signatures – those of the Duke of Norfolk, Viscount Rochford and George Boleyn (Anne's brother) – and then disappeared into limbo.

That absurdity shows that, though the members of the Howard–Boleyn clique were anxious to play their part in hastening the divorce, they did not have a constructive, positive idea between them. In the early weeks of the new year that clique coalesced again, determined on nothing but the removal of the butcher's cur and the restoration of conciliar government which they would dominate. Foreign ambassadors watched closely the barometer of royal favour. Henry, understanding full well what was going on, was not ready to abandon Wolsey who, though a blunted sword, was the only weapon he had. And, as the French envoy observed, the Cardinal was certainly not to be written off: 'the Duke of Norfolk and his party already begin to talk big but certainly they have to do with one more subtle than themselves'[72] and Iñigo de Mendoza, Charles's ambassador, concurred. Rochford, Norfolk and Suffolk, he stated, 'have combined to overthrow the cardinal but as yet they have made no impression on the king, except that he shows him in court not quite so good countenances as he did and . . . he [has] said some disagreeable words to him'.[73] However, the longer Campeggio managed to find technical problems and create diversions, the bolder the opposition became and Wolsey was immensely relieved to be able to open the extraordinary legatine court on 31 May in the magnificent church of the Dominican friars (Blackfriars) at the western extremity of the old city, even though the building may have recalled unwelcome memories of the Black Parliament. That assembly had prefaced his first major failure as the King's servant and he had good reason to fear that he was on the brink of another.

The events of the next two months were a PR disaster for the King and his cause. What Henry wanted, and what an ecclesiastical court by its very nature was unable to give him, was a state trial moving inexorably to a pre-ordained verdict. For a Christian tribunal to maintain any credibility it had at least to *consider* the evidence on both sides. Therein lay Henry's problem. If a deal could have been privately struck with the Vatican all would have been well for the King but when the issue came into open court the balance of advantage shifted in the Queen's favour. Henry's lawyers were outmanoeuvred because their case was weak. Even that might not have mattered had not Catherine and her champions put on excellent public performances in what was far and away the biggest show in town. Those who were present at the trial would long remember its two most dramatic incidents. The first was the Queen of England publicly prostrating herself before her husband and tearfully beseeching him for the sake of her honour and their daughter's to abandon the proceedings. The audience watched stunned as Catherine then swept out of the church deaf to the shouts of officials ordering her to return. The second high point occurred a week later. The much revered Bishop Fisher, now in his seventieth year, came forward to give his considered opinion on the validity of the royal marriage. Speaking with the quiet authority of a scholar and an ascetic he must have drawn gasps from his hearers when he offered a biblical parallel. As John the Baptist had been prepared to lay down his life to defend the sanctity of marriage and condemn adultery, so, Fisher said, was he. The Bishop fully intended to shock and to dare the coadjudicators to risk divine wrath by finding for the King. He was openly comparing Henry VIII to one of the most depraved tyrants of the New Testament, Herod Antipas, who had disembarrassed himself of his wife in order to take his brother's, and, at her instigation, had then executed John the Baptist for daring to criticise the royal couple. Fisher was only voicing more eloquently the hostility to Henry and Anne that was finding more bawdy expression on the streets of London but it is not difficult to imagine the fury the King now conceived for a man he had never liked and who had always been free with his criticisms of Wolsey and the court. In fact we do not need to speculate for when the King's new secretary, Stephen Gardiner, showed him a transcript of Fisher's speech Henry scrawled abusive comments in the margins.

While the legal process was making its ponderous, jolting progress, suspicion, doubt and mistrust were much more effectively at work. Every intelligence Henry received from Rome indicated that the duplicitous Clement would never accede to his wishes and that the Pope's secret instructions to Campeggio were to concede nothing. Malicious pens suggested that Wolsey knew the situation well and was keeping it from his master. The King was now driven to the brink of paranoia, casting around desperately for confirmation or otherwise of this information and not knowing whom, if anyone, he could trust. At the end of May he sent Suffolk on an embassy to the Duke's old friend Francis I with orders to sound out the French King about what he had heard about the ecclesiastical 'conspirators'. Francis admitted that he had always regarded Campeggio as tricky and devious, then pressed by Brandon for his opinion of Wolsey he added words to the effect that churchmen always stuck together and that his advice to Henry would be not to 'put so much trust in [any] man, whereby he may be deceived as nigh as he can' but rather 'to look substantially upon his matters himself'.[74] How much of a personal, anticlerical gloss Suffolk put on these words in his report to the King we cannot know. Certainly by setting the Duke to spy on the Cardinal Henry was playing into the hands of Wolsey's enemies. He was also creating the conditions which made it impossible for him to reach rational decisions, by deliberately canvassing information, rumours and prejudices from all and sundry.

Everyone on the King's side knew that things were going badly at Blackfriars, though whether anyone had the courage to point this out to their master is problematical. The chances are that they were all relieved when Campeggio, on 23 July, found a way of proroguing the court. It was his most transparent piece of time-wasting yet: he decreed that since ecclesiastical proceedings always took a three-month break during the Mediterranean high summer the London trial should do the same! This was too much for the bluff Brandon, who banged his fist on the table and shouted out, 'It was never merry in England when we had cardinals among us!' Wolsey was not to be browbeaten. 'Sir,' he retorted,

of all men within this realm ye have least cause to dispraise or be offended with cardinals; for if I, a simple cardinal, had not been, ye should have had at this present no head upon your shoulders wherein ye should have a tongue to make any such report in despite of us who intended you no manner of displeasure, nor we have given you any occasion with such despite to be revenged with your [haughty] words. I would ye knew it, my lord, that I and my brother here intended the King and his realm as much honour, wealth, and quietness as ye or any other, of what estate or degree so ever he be within this realm, and would as gladly accomplish his lawful desire as the poorest subject he hath . . . Wherefore, my lord, hold your peace, and pacify yourself, and frame your tongue like a man of honour and of wisdom, and not to speak so quickly or so reproachfully [of] your friends; for ye know best what friendship ye have received at my hands, the which yet I never revealed to no person alive before now, neither to my glory nor to your dishonour.[75]

Unfortunately for Wolsey, the court of Henry VIII was no place in which to call in debts of gratitude or look for loyalty in return for acts of kindness. It was an unstable microcosm, losing the cohesion it had enjoyed for twenty years, in which jealousies and ambitions long held in check now escaped from restraint.

CHAPTER 19

Hopes and Fears

In fact the legal delay mattered not a jot; events elsewhere had decided the issue. On 29 June Clement VII and Charles V had settled all their differences in the Treaty of Barcelona. On 5 August French and Imperial negotiators meeting at Cambrai made peace between their two countries. Wolsey, preoccupied with the divorce, had very nearly been caught on the hop by the latest round of diplomacy. Tricked by Charles and Francis, both of whom wanted to see England sidelined, he had attached little importance to the Cambrai talks. Only at the last moment did he send envoys thither and manage to have English interests included in the final draft of the treaty.

The mission which hastened to the northern French textile town, the home of cambric, was led by Thomas More and Cuthbert Tunstall. They set out on 30 June and reached their destination a little over a week later. By the time they arrived there was little they could contribute to the headline clauses of what came to be called the Ladies' Peace, because the principal negotiators were Louise of Savoy (Francis I's mother) and Margaret of Austria (Charles V's aunt). Wolsey had hoped to keep the two main rivals at loggerheads over their rival claims in Italy, Flanders and Burgundy but the exhausted combatants had already come to terms. The more 'important' delegates deliberately kept King Henry's representatives out of any substantive discussions and the Englishmen were only able to enter into separate peripheral negotiations with the major parties. More and Tunstall concentrated on securing a return to mutually beneficial trade relations between England and the Low Countries and obtaining guarantees regarding certain longstanding payments owing to Henry by the Emperor. Despite their limited success More always felt proud of the Cambrai mission. It was the most important diplomatic errand on which he was ever sent but, more than that, its objectives and results were ones with which he was fully in sympathy. It brought a general peace to Europe, something he and his fellow humanists had always urged. It re-established the friendship between Henry VIII and Charles V. It appeared to restore the traditional image of Christendom, headed by Emperor and Pope and supported by Christian princes. It created the conditions for concentration on combating the real enemies of the faith – heretics and Muslims. And it produced a situation which would make it impossible for Henry VIII to have his marriage annulled. More, though he studiously avoided advertising his opinions, had moved into a position of clear opposition to the Cardinal on the two most important items on his policy agenda – opposition to the Emperor and the King's great matter. He returned, well pleased with himself, when all the negotiating was done in the third week of August.

It would be naïve to suppose that because More had been out of the country he had been unaware of the rapid developments at home but, nevertheless, he must have found them confusing. The King had gone on progress, leaving his cardinal in London, and refused him permission to come to court. The Norfolk–Boleyn clique and their friends constituted the council attendant and were involved in all government business. However, Henry was still in correspondence with the Cardinal, via Stephen Gardiner, and asking his opinion on matters of importance. Writs had gone out for a parliament to be summoned and Wolsey was denied the chance to secure Commons places for his own supporters. It was all very ominous but no one knew exactly what Henry had in mind for his Chancellor or how or when he would show his hand. More, apparently, had no hesitation about what he should do. He made his report to Wolsey on 23 August before joining the court on progress. It was 19 September before Wolsey was allowed to come to the King and then only to accompany Campeggio who was taking his formal farewell. The court was at Grafton, beyond Oxford, and the Lord Chancellor and Cardinal Archbishop discovered that no accommodation had been reserved for him. Wolsey was obliged to accept the cramped quarters proffered by a loyal ex-protégé in which to tidy himself up before venturing into the royal presence.

The élite of the court watched to see how he would be greeted, some hoping to see the self-important churchman snubbed, others not believing that Henry would really turn against his cardinal after all those years. And here we come to a conflict in the evidence. According to Cavendish the events of the twenty-four hours went as follows: Wolsey knelt to the King, who smiled at him, raised him up and drew him over to a window where the two men had a long, private talk. For the most part it seemed very amicable though Henry did sometimes raise his voice and, at one moment, brandished a letter or paper, as though accusing the Cardinal of some written offence. They parted seemingly on good terms and, after dinner they had another long session together. It all looked like old times. However, everything changed drastically the following morning. Anne had been working on her royal lover and when Wolsey turned up to continue his discussion with the King he found Henry and Mistress Boleyn about to go riding. The Cardinal was brusquely dismissed and ordered back to London. Thus Cavendish, committed to his view of Anne as the manipulator of events, remembered those September days years later. However, a contemporary letter puts a very different gloss on the comings and goings at Grafton. Thomas Alward, a member of Wolsey's entourage, wrote to Thomas Cromwell to scotch certain 'vain bruits which goeth against my lord . . . [which] be marvellous false'. Alward's account of the first day broadly agrees with Cavendish's but he knows nothing of any sudden change of mood on the King's part.

> On Monday in the morning my Lord . . . went again unto the king's grace, and after long talking in his privy chamber together, the king, my lord, and all the whole council sat together all that forenoon about the king's matters and affairs. In the afternoon, my lord's grace having then with him the legate Campeggio went to the king's grace, and after talking and communication . . . a long while with the legate apart they both took their leave of the king's highness in as good fashion and manner, and with as much gentleness, as ever I saw before. This done, the king's grace went hunting . . . My lord's grace tarried there in council till it was dark night. Furthermore my lord of Suffolk, my lord of Rochford, master Tuke, and master Stevyns [Stephen Gardiner] did as gently [comport] themselves, with as much observance and humility to my lord's grace as ever I saw them do at any time heretofore. What they bare in their hearts I know not.[76]

However, King and Cardinal never met again and within days Henry was authorising the various stages of his minister's downfall. As always, what mattered was access to Henry. When Wolsey was with him he could effectively employ the mixture of charm and deference which had always worked. His enemies were as determined to keep the Cardinal away from court as he had been to isolate Henry from them over the years. The point was well made by Cavendish in his version of the Grafton events. When the company went in for dinner on the Sunday Wolsey was seated next to Thomas Howard and they fell to discussing arrangements for the parliament. Norfolk suggested that it might be advisable for the Archbishop of York to oversee personally the selection of candidates in his province. For Norfolk, who had so often been despatched northwards far from the centre of power, this must have been a delicious moment.

So, are we forced to the conclusion that Henry VIII was putty in the hands of his close attendants, and particularly of Anne Boleyn? Were his changes of mood and policy the result of listening to whoever happened to have his ear on a day-to-day basis? If, on the contrary, we agree with Wolsey's latest biographer that Henry had decided months before on the Cardinal's destruction, we have to ask why he hesitated and why he sent out contradictory signals. Were his changes of mood simulated to keep people guessing as one who had learned to 'smile and smile and be a villain'? Was this just a different aspect of Henry's old love of 'dis-guisings' and practical jokes? Perhaps we should not seek such clear-cut solutions to the enigmas of Henry's character. It may be that he underwent a long inner debate between various emotions and rational reflections.

One fact is obvious: Henry did not ruin Wolsey in a fit of anger. That might have been the action of a conventional tyrant. Certainly, Henry was prone to mood swings and was perfectly capable of doing things in a bad temper which he regretted afterwards, but this was not one of them. He had had months to brood on the failure and incompetence of his cardinal. He had pondered Wolsey's loyalty and questioned other people about it. To the very end he hesitated about just how severely to punish his failed servant. He obviously considered his course of action carefully, apparently changing his mind often during the process, and eventually acted with calm purposefulness. The two history-changing decisions he reached were to strip Wolsey of his power and to summon what came to be known as the Reformation Parliament.

If we are to reach a satisfactory interpretation of the conflicting events of the late summer and autumn of 1529 we must not fall into the trap of forcing them into a mould of tidy consistency. Rather we must grasp the nettle of seeking to identify the heterogeneous components of the King's character. In doing so we run the risk of being accused by purists of dabbling in pop psychology but since Henry VIII's persona was the maypole around which so many people and events were obliged to dance it would be very odd to evade such an analysis. The King was egotistical, hypochondriacal and proactive. In modern parlance he was a control freak, a man who sought to govern events rather than wait upon them. The fact that he resigned much day-to-day government into Wolsey's hands does not contradict this assertion. Having originated or approved policy, he expected others to carry it into effect but it was still *his* policy. He was an enthusiast whether thundering, lance-couched, along the tiltyard barrier, planning impromptu disguisings, indulging his passion for showmanship in diplomatic ceremonial, or defending the Church against Luther. Henry was not a man for half-measures or subtle-minded caution. He committed himself wholeheartedly and, usually, publicly. Therefore, when things went wrong he was vulnerable to frustration and humiliation. And in the 1520s several things went wrong. He was outwitted by rival monarchs. His military adventures had led to no permanent territorial gains. He was defied by his own people over taxation. He was thwarted in his desires to arrange his own marital and dynastic affairs. The combined effects of all these was that, by 1529, he had little say in the affairs of Europe, had limited control over a contrary people who were hostile to war against the Empire and refused to finance war against France, had to endure economies in the life of the court and was saddled with a wife he could not get rid of. In short, Henry VIII was being prevented from being the kind of king – *rex et imperator* - that he wanted to be, which seems to have consisted of an idealised feudal monarchy (enriched by Arthurian legend and the heraldic propaganda inherent in chivalric display), overlaid by a hankering after French-style absolutism and an, as yet undefined, caesaropapism, which would give him spiritual as well as temporal authority. Wolsey, who not only advocated Tudor splendour but in his own person embodied it, had striven manfully to give substance to the Henrician vision, only to be defeated by the realities of a populace who could not or would not fund it, foreign rulers who had the resources and acumen to resist it and a papacy powerless to support it.

Henry had two ways of reacting when events conspired against him. One was to blame other people – as he blamed Wolsey for inaugurating the Amicable Grant. The other was to dig his heels in – his foreign policy consisted largely of a series of impracticable martial adventures, pursued regardless of failure and cost. Both of these came into play in 1529. Wolsey was made the scapegoat for the King's failure to achieve a divorce. Throwing the Cardinal to his many enemies would be popular, it would send a dramatic signal to Rome and it would draw a line in the sand between past discord and failure and a new era of politics. What the King probably had in mind for his former minister was progressive stages of disgrace which could be halted, or even reversed, when they had achieved their objective. Henry was not so foolish as to deprive himself utterly of a servant who had been immensely useful and might still have more to give. After September 1529 Wolsey's court enemies knew full well that they had not completely won the King over and they remained nervous of the tables being turned again. The French ambassador reported that Anne worked hard to prevent Henry granting the disgraced minister an audience for fear that he should take pity on the old man.

At the same time the King persisted in his determination to obtain his divorce. This stubbornness sprang from the very centre of Henry's being and not from his love for Anne Boleyn. Wolsey, himself, testified to this trait in the King when speaking to the soldier-courtier, Sir William Kingston.

He is a prince of a royal [disposition], and hath a princely heart; and rather than he will either miss or want any part of his will or appetite, he will put the loss of one half of his realm in danger. For I assure you I have often kneeled before him in his privy chamber on my knees the space of an hour or two to persuade him from his will and appetite; but I could never bring to pass to dissuade him therefrom. Therefore, Master Kingston, if it chance hereafter you to be one of his privy council (as for your wisdom and other qualities ye be meet so to be) I warn you to be well advised and assured what matter you put in his head; for ye shall never pull it out again.[77]

The suggestion that if Henry's *princesse lointaine* had agreed to go to bed with him the entire history of England would have pursued a different course cannot be sustained. Had it been a simple matter of lust, the King had at his disposal a host of bribes and threats he could have employed with Anne and her family which would have delivered her into his arms. Rochford and Norfolk would have settled for titles, lands and influence and instructed their kinswoman accordingly. Anne, for her part, was no liberated modern woman in full command of her own body and her own destiny. No, the decision to marry was Henry's and he took it in order to enjoy the happiness he believed that Anne would bring him as queen and that, together, they might make sons.

So, we conclude that there *was* an aristocratic coup but only in the sense that a recognisable group of conspirators existed who took every opportunity to undermine Wolsey's power. They lacked any consistent plan for achieving the Chancellor's downfall and the courage to implement such a plan had it existed. Meanwhile, the King *did* determine on Wolsey's disgrace but only as one option for achieving his personal and dynastic objectives. It is the intermittent engaging and disengaging of the gears of royal and Howard–Boleyn ambition that account for the jerky progress of the political vehicle during the eighteen months beginning in the summer of 1529.

In the closing months of 1529 Henry could still only see one way of achieving his desired objective and that was by increasing pressure on the Pope. Various threats had been made to Rome concerning England's possible alienation. The time had come to act upon them. One impression Henry wished to give because, in an era of spreading heresy and anticlericalism, it might – and certainly should – worry the head of the Church, was that he had the nation behind him in the matter of the divorce and in a more generalised disillusionment with Rome. Perhaps the idea had its origin in Norfolk's aborted petition of the previous November, which as matters had developed might have seemed not quite so foolish after all. A simple – and obviously contrived – document would not serve but a highly vocal parliament clamouring for redress of a whole raft of clerical abuses? That was a horse of quite a different colour. After the trouble he had had with the House of Commons in 1523 Henry felt little affection for that assembly but when he thought back to the angry diatribes members had directed against the ecclesiastical hierarchy in 1515 he realised that it might serve his purpose to bring together the leaders of the political nation for a few weeks and allow them to express their grievances.

Just how strong feelings were had recently come home to him very forcefully – if we are to trust a story told by Foxe. It concerns Simon Fish, the lawyer chased into exile by an irate Wolsey for lampooning him at the Inns of Court Christmas celebrations of 1525. This outspoken and ill-spoken campaigner angered Church leaders more than once and seems to have yo-yoed between London and the Low Countries. While there, in 1528, he wrote a rumbustious diatribe against the clergy in the form of an appeal to Henry VIII to redress abuses, entitled *A Supplication for the Beggars*. A copy came into Anne Boleyn's hands and she, at the instigation of her brother, showed it to the King. George must have guessed that Fish's complaints would chime with Henry's present mood and so it proved, for the King 'kept the book in his bosom three or four days' and subsequently sent for the author, welcomed him warmly and assured him of royal protection. The following extract gives a flavour of those opinions and feelings Henry felt he could harness for his own purposes:

. . . the bishops, abbots, priors, deacons, archdeacons, suffragans, priests, monks, canons, friars, pardoners, and summoners . . . have gotten into their hands more than the third part of all your realm. The goodliest lordships, manors, lands and territories are theirs. Besides this they have the tenth part of all the corn, meadow, pasture, grass, wool, colts, calves, lambs, pigs, geese and chickens. Over and besides, the tenth part of every servant's wages, the tenth part of the wool, milk, honey, wax, cheese and butter . . . What money pull they in by probates of testaments, privy tithes, and by men's offerings to their pilgrimages and at their first masses? . . . What money get they by mortuaries, by hearing confessions . . . by hallowing of churches, altars, superaltars, chapels and bells, by cursing of men and absolving them again for money? . . . Is it any marvel that the taxes, fifteenths and subsidies that your Grace most tenderly of great compassion hath taken among your people to defend them from the threatened ruin of their commonwealth have been so slothfully, yea, painfully levied, seeing that almost the utmost penny that might have been levied hath been gathered before yearly by this ravenous, cruel and insatiable generation? . . . And what do all these greedy sort of sturdy, idle, holy thieves with these yearly exactions that they take of the people? Truly nothing but exempt themselves from the obedience of your Grace. Nothing but translate all rule, power, lordship, authority, obedience and dignity from your Grace unto them. Nothing but that all your subjects should fall into disobedience and rebellion against your Grace, and be under them . . . For the which matter your most noble realm wrongfully (alas, for shame!) hath stood tributary, not unto any kind temporal prince but unto a cruel, devilish bloodsupper, drunken in the blood of the saints and martyrs of Christ . . .[78]

We might be inclined to dismiss the story of King Henry spending time on such a rant and showing favour to its author were it not for the fact that no less a Catholic champion than Thomas More took the *Supplication* so seriously that he wrote a long answer to it (see p. 283). Whatever the King thought about it, hundreds of copies of Fish's pamphlet were fluttering around London as the nation's knights and burgesses assembled there in November.

By then the hottest news was of Wolsey's fall from grace. Members who knew their law were discussing the means that had been taken for disposing of the Cardinal. Many must have assumed and some hoped that parliament had been summoned to pass an act of attainder against him which would have led to his imprisonment and, possibly, to his death. However, the King had chosen a different route. As soon as the new law term had opened Wolsey had been indicted into King's Bench to face a charge of *praemunire*, for which the only punishment was forfeiture of goods. It was urged (and the original indictment was subsequently enlarged) that in accepting and deploying legatine authority he had, to the detriment of the King, acted as the agent of a foreign government. It was a vivid signal to the Pope and the entire ecclesiastical world of where real power lay in Henry's England. On 17 October the Dukes of Norfolk and Suffolk arrived at York House and demanded that Wolsey deliver the Great Seal into their hands. The Cardinal, preserving his dignity to the last, asked to see their warrant from the King. They blustered but were unable to produce any such document. Wolsey declined to comply without it and their lordships were obliged to ride back to Windsor empty-handed. It could be no more than a gesture and the following day Howard and Brandon were back with the necessary authorisation. They declared to the ex-Chancellor that it was the King's pleasure that he should retire to his manor at Esher, one of the few possessions left to him. The *praemunire* charge having been proved, Wolsey had been stripped of everything, save for certain properties and chattels which the King in his mercy had restored to him.

Within days the ruined man left for his rural retreat. Yet uncertainty about his fate stalked him still and disturbed his enemies. Rumour, of course, had spread, and as he descended the privy stairs it became obvious that he was going to have to run the gauntlet of the London citizenry.

> . . . at the taking of barge there was no less than a thousand boats full of men and women of the city of London [sailing] up and down in Thames, expecting my lord's departing, supposing that he should have gone directly to the Tower; whereat they rejoiced.[79]

The day's dramas were not over when the Cardinal reached the far bank and escaped the jeering crowd to mount his mule for the ride to Esher, as Cavendish's vivid narrative declares. A hurrying horseman was espied cantering down Putney Hill and hailing the party. It was Sir Henry Norris, one of the King's most intimate friends, and he had come post-haste from the court with comforting tidings:

> . . . although the King hath dealt with you unkindly as ye suppose, he saith that it is for no displeasure that he beareth you, but only to satisfy more the minds of some (which he knoweth be not your friends) than for any indignation. And also ye know right well that he is able to recompense you with twice as much as your goods amounteth unto. And all this he bade me that I should show you. Therefore, sir, take patience. And for my part I trust to see you in better estate than ever ye were.[80]

What makes this incident so difficult to interpret (and perhaps to accept) is that Norris was hand-in-glove with the Boleyn clique and devoted to Anne (too devoted as it later transpired). Was this a cruel jest, designed to rub salt into Wolsey's wounds or was Henry genuinely keeping his options open?

Meanwhile, there was a vacancy to be filled in the country's top judicial position. Wolsey's sacking as Lord Chancellor marked the end of an era. He was the last great ecclesiastic to combine leading positions in Church and State. The next holder of the office was a layman, a lawyer, with none of the wealth or pretension of the Ipswich butcher's son. His name was Thomas More.

On 23 October Henry met with his leading councillors to decide on Wolsey's successor. There was some suggestion of reinstating Warham as chancellor, perhaps as an interim measure, but he declined and the King was not disposed to press him – the Archbishop was, after all, almost eighty! The aristocrat-dominated Council was in favour of a lay appointment because only this could prevent the possible emergence of another Wolsey, grown so rich on ecclesiastical revenues that he could overawe his fellow advisers and even appear more splendid than the King. It was this that ruled out the choice of Cuthbert Tunstall. The Duke of Suffolk canvassed hard for the job but Henry recognised that his brother-in-law was totally lacking in the necessary qualities and Norfolk would have blocked any move which would have bolstered Brandon's authority. It took two days of discussion before the majority agreed on a compromise candidate. Thomas More, they decided, would provide a safe pair of hands. Manifestly, he possessed the judicial qualifications necessary for the job and he was known to entertain no ambition for personal power. There was the problem of his known opposition to the divorce. More had not concealed his unease about the great matter but, on the other hand, he had not paraded his views and no one could question his obedience to the King. There was probably no one around the Council table, including Henry, who doubted that, when push came to shove, Thomas More would fall into line. The new Chancellor, himself, went almost this far when he wrote to Erasmus a few days later to justify his acceptance of the post: 'I am loyal to my king, as loyal to him as anyone on earth can be. My inability to approve of his divorce and to argue for it in public in no way detracts from the essential loyalty I feel for him, a loyalty that will keep me from ever saying a public word in opposition to him.'[81]

Sir Thomas received the Great Seal from Henry's hand on the afternoon of 25 October and the next morning he was escorted by fellow councillors to the Chancery bench. Norfolk then took the unprecedented step of making a speech to commend the new incumbent. This served to make a double impression on the surprised and curious listeners in Westminster Hall: it explained how so relatively obscure a figure had come to take the place of the great Cardinal and it also made clear that if the mantle of *real* power had fallen upon anyone it was not on the judge, but the Duke.

CHAPTER 20

The Rise of the New Men

Sometime in November 1529 Wolsey wrote to the man he had come to rely on above all others.

> My own eternally beloved Cromwell, I beseech you, as ye love me and will ever do any thing for me, repair hither this day as soon as the Parliament is broken up, leaving apart all things for that time; for I would not only communicate things unto you wherein for my comfort and relief I would have your good, sad, discreet advice and counsel, but also upon the same commit certain things requiring expedition to you, on my behalf to be solicited: this, I pray you therefore, to haste your coming hither as aforesaid, without omitting so to do as ye tender my succour, relief and comfort, and quietness of mind. And thus fare ye well: from Esher, in haste, this Saturday, in the morning, with the rude hand and sorrowful heart of your assured lover
>
> T. CAR^{LIS} EBOR

> I have also certain things concerning yourself which I am sure ye will be glad to hear and know: fail not therefore to be here this night, ye may return early in the morning again if need shall so require. *Et iterum value* [So, farewell again].
>
> M. Agostini showed me how ye had written unto me a letter wherein ye should advertise me of the coming hither of the Duke of Norfolk: I assure you there came to my hands no such letter.[82]

In this instance the flattery and hyperbole were more than mere convention. Thomas Cromwell was one who ever loved and would do anything for his master. It was loyalty as well as energy and professional expertise that raised him during the 1520s from being one among hundreds in the Cardinal's employ to the position of right-hand man.

The same qualities caused him to emerge as a well-known figure in the City. His private legal practice and his commercial interests brought him into contact with the leaders of the merchant community and, as always, he made an impression on those who had any dealings with him. The fact that he was a protégé of the great Cardinal was obviously an important business asset and one he exploited to the full. He was, in his mid-thirties, a self-made man and a man of the world. His experience of foreign parts and his command of languages gave him a broad view of contemporary affairs and marked him out as a well-informed councillor and a fascinating conversationalist. He moved easily among the growing foreign population of the capital and had clients in the wealthy Hanse community. These German merchants were the main conduits for the flow of Lutheran ideas and literature into England. This was so worrying to the government that they carried out several raids on the Steelyard, the Hanseatic merchants' headquarters fronting the river in Dowgate ward, in the middle of the decade to confiscate books and arrest suspected heretics (see pp. 281f). It is inconceivable that an intelligent, well-read man like Cromwell had no interest in the raging religious debates of the day and quite probable that, like other members of the Inns of Court (he was admitted to Gray's Inn in 1524) he had actually tasted the forbidden fruit of banned books. Among the London smart set, dabbling in dangerous ideas was as fashionable in the 1520s as experimenting with hard and soft drugs was among their successors in the 1970s and 1980s. Cromwell's thinking is likely to have started out on a radical course in these years.

The next step on Cromwell's emergence into public life came in 1523 when he was nominated for a seat in the House of Commons. It would be helpful to know which of his clients or patrons was responsible for securing his election. The balance of probability is that he was one of Wolsey's place men, insinuated into a parliament that was going to be difficult, in order to help get through the vote on taxes. The maiden member may have sat for Taunton, a borough controlled by Wolsey. This was the constituency he represented in 1529. However, there is no evidence for such a supposition. What appears to argue against it is the draft of a speech Cromwell prepared and, presumably, delivered on the subject of Henry's proposed war. It has been characterised as an opposition address because in it the speaker argued against the sending of a large invasion force into France. However, that misconstrues the nature of debate at this early stage of the development of the House of Commons. Speeches were less overtly confrontational than they became in later centuries when the assembly had become polarised into pro- and anti-court lobbies or parties based on sectional interests. Despite the existence of rudimentary parliamentary privilege, discreet speakers were cautious about being recognised as 'agin the government' (Roper's account of More's supposed opposition to Henry VII in 1504 was cited as an example of unusual courage and one which brought dire consequences). Cromwell's draft is a very rare survival and an accomplished piece of oratory but it may not be atypical of the techniques used by effective parliamentarians in the early Tudor age. It was couched in highly respectful tones. It castigated the King's foes. It was supportive of the King's general aims and objectives, while suggesting other methods for achieving them. What it did *not* do was incite the House to reject Henry's demands for war finance. It is worth quoting some passages from this speech because they demonstrate both the subtlety of his mind and his brilliant grasp of a wide range of material.

He began with high flattery and acknowledgement of the justness of Henry's cause:

> To recover again by the sword the realm of France, belonging to our most redoubted Sovereign by good and just title, and to [transform] the sums of money which we have in sundry years received from thence into the whole and just revenues that might there from year to year be levied if we did peaceably enjoy the same, who is here present that would not gladly expend not only all his goods but also his life if every of us had ten thousand lives to help to obtain unto our most benign sovereign and his most noble succession, besides the high honour and wide spreading of his most glorious fame, which while this world endured should ever be had in memory, such yearly revenues and upwelling springs of treasure as should by this means continually be brought into this realm?

Cromwell was careful to embrace within his praises Wolsey – 'my lord legate's good grace' – and More – 'the right merciful, best assured and discreet Speaker'.

He expressed abhorrence at the prospect of war, 'of which slaughter must needs ensue the most lamentable cries and ringing of hands that hath happened in Christendom many years', but acknowledged in words of trenchant Francophobia, that now was not the time to speak of peace because

> want of truth is so deeply [ensconced] in the French nation, and their insatiable appetite to extend their borders and to [encroach] from other their dominions and possessions to the great molesting and troubling of all the nations about them, is so manifest and notorious to all the world, without any regard having either to God or justice, that though we had for our own particular causes no manner [of] quarrels [with] them, yet could we not but have in detestation their false and flighty dealing wherewith other Christian princes be by them so sore molested.

Cromwell praised the 'well fortunate and sage Earl of Surrey' for his depredations in Normandy 'where all the power of France durst not give him battle, which said valiant captain, I trust, by God's help, shall overthrow and subdue also the Scots'.

In a purple passage of shock horror he sought to dissuade the King from any suggestion that he might personally lead his army into a foreign field. Henry's safety was so vital to the well-being of the realm, 'that I am sure there is no good Englishman which can be merry the day when he happeneth to think that his grace might perchance be distempered'.

Having cleverly raised in his hearers' minds the appalling prospect of misadventure befalling the King in battle, Cromwell moved to the substance of his speech, a carefully considered account of the logistical problems attendant upon a major invasion. It would be difficult to victual a large army over an extended period of time. The outflow of bullion might be so severe that the government might have recourse to minting leather money. And just think – horror of horrors – what might happen if their sovereign lord were taken prisoner and they were unable to meet the ransom! Without adequate coastal bases beyond the Channel it would be nigh impossible to supply the army and maintain control of conquered territory.

Cromwell now turned to political realities. How would France respond to a war she could not win militarily? By doing what she always did – make trouble elsewhere for England and her allies. She would employ her gold and her diplomats in Scotland and Spain. And thus he moved smoothly to the logical conclusion of his argument. He was, he declared, 'as desirous that all [the King's] most noble enterprises should prosperously go forward as any simple creature that ever was born under his obeisance' but he advised that the royal objectives would be most likely to succeed if pursued little by little. Let the King first direct

his whole intent and purpose not only to the over-running and subduing of Scotland but also to join the same realm unto his, so that both they and we might live under one . . . law and policy for war. He should thereby win the highest honour that ever did any noble progenitors since this island was first inhabited to join unto his noble realm so populous a country whereby his strength should be of no small part increased and of this act should follow the higher [dismay] to the said French that ever happened to him or any of his progenitors before.[83]

It was not an original argument. The adage had long run,

> Whosoever France would win
> Let him with Scotland first begin.

What it was was a logical argument, couched in eloquent terms well judged for the intended audience. Coming, as it did, from a self-educated man of humble origins it was in its own way remarkable.

Cromwell was living proof that, in early Tudor England, it was possible, without noble ancestry and without ecclesiastical preferment, for a man of talent to get to the top. Had he confined himself to the commercial world he would probably have ended his days as a leading London merchant with a country estate, who had served at least one term as Lord Mayor. Instead he espoused the law in order to become a gentleman, to extend his acquaintance, to become the friend of scholars like Sir Thomas Elyot, poets like Sir Thomas Wyatt, courtiers, noblemen and diplomats. But he was no dour, self-obsessed social climber. He was erudite and genuinely good company. He collected books and curious old manuscripts. As his means increased, so he became a keen patron of writers and men of learning. That he had a sense of humour and a skilled way with words is indicated by an oft-quoted letter he wrote to John Croke, a fellow lawyer and a clerk in Chancery, soon after the end of the 1523 parliament.

I amongst others have endured a parliament which continued by the space of sixteen whole weeks, where we communed of war, peace, strife, contention, debate, murmur, grudge, riches, poverty, truth, falsehood, justice, equity, deceit, oppression, magnanimity, activity, force, [compromise], treason, murder, felony, conciliation, and also how a commonwealth might be edified and also contained within our realm. Howbeit, in conclusion we have done as our predecessors have been wont to do, that is to say, as well as we might and left as we began.[84]

It is not surprising that Cromwell's circle of friends overlapped considerably with that of Thomas More.

As a lawyer/secretary/agent working ever more closely with Wolsey he observed and ruminated upon the Cardinal's working methods. He saw an administrator of prodigious energy who took on more than he could possibly accomplish. Immersed as Wolsey was in matters of foreign policy and the law courts the attention he was able to devote to other affairs was at best sporadic and at worst scanty. National finance was one area which suffered from the Lord Chancellor's inattention. Another was the state of the Church. He had reformist ideas, perhaps even vision but, obliged as he was to put secular affairs first, he neglected his specifically legatine duties. His attacks on heresy were inconsistent and he never really appreciated the growing power of religious radicalism. By contrast, Cromwell was not blinkered by ecclesiastical office. He had seen at first hand the corruption of Rome and had talked with men full of the new ideas. In his legal practice he had been at the conflict point of common and canon law. During these years of tutelage his logical mind was shaping theoretical policies and drastic solutions which would restore health and vigour to State and Church.

The area of Wolsey's activities that he was increasingly concerned with after 1524 was the Cardinal's great educational enterprises. Cromwell was in charge of the group of agents who travelled around the monastic houses marked for closure. The procedure was that the legate's representatives presented to each of the religious who were to be dispossessed a form setting out the inadequacies of their house and the reasons for its dissolution. They signed it and were then given the option of being transferred to a sister establishment or going into secular life. As soon as the buildings were empty Cromwell and his colleagues went round inventorying the contents and packing all movables on to carts for subsequent disposal – either to be sold or to be used in the new foundations at Oxford and Ipswich. As we have seen, complaints were made by or on behalf of the monks, nuns, friars and canons who were turned out of their homes. Wolsey was obliged to protest to the King,

> I have not meant, intended, or gone about, nor also have willed mine officers, to do anything concerning the said suppressions, but under such form and manner as is and hath largely been to the full satisfaction, recompense and joyous contentation of any person which hath had, or could pretend to have right or interest in the same, in such wise that many of them, giving thanks and laud to God, for the good chance [offered] unto them would for nothing, if they might, return or be restored and put again into their former state.[85]

We cannot possibly form a judgement about how sensitively or insensitively the agents went about their business. The modern historian of the monastic movement has dubbed Cromwell and his colleagues as 'able, overbearing and unscrupulous'[86] and so they must certainly have appeared to those who had no desire to leave the hallowed security of their cloisters. But most of the houses which were closed were only served by a handful of inmates who had difficulty maintaining the rituals to which they were dedicated and were enjoying endowments which could be put to better use. Cromwell's tidy mind rebelled against the waste and shared his master's enthusiasm for diverting the resources into religious/educational/social enterprises which would make better use of them.

The transfer of the property of twenty-nine small religious houses to the colleges at Oxford and Ipswich was only a small part of an organisational shake-up Wolsey planned for the English Church. He proposed to change the balance of monastic and secular religious life by carving out several more dioceses each with its own cathedral resources and staffed from dissolved abbeys. As with many of his other reformist ideas he never got around to it but the vision was not lost on Cromwell. It became increasingly obvious to him that much of the malaise in the Church sprang from clinging to old institutions which had become corrupted or simply outlived their usefulness. Just as the humanists were taking scholastic theology apart in order to refresh or reject parts of it and build a new system for the education of the clergy, so Cromwell saw that the same methods could be applied to the material and human resources of the Church.

Right up to the last days of Wolsey's power Cromwell was immensely busy with the complex business of the closures. It was not simply a question of seeing the religious relocated and their goods inventoried. All the legal work had to be attended to – conveyances, new tenancy agreements, land transfers, compensation agreements and the like. Furniture had to be allocated to the new foundations. Building materials had to be acquired and transported. Foundation deeds for Cardinal's College and Ipswich College had to be agreed in detail and drawn up. And, towards the end, this activity had to be carried out against a background of increasing uncertainty. Those around Wolsey began to be anxious about the future and Wolsey himself worried above all else about his foundations. He had invested so much of himself in his colleges, designed to preserve his fame for posterity, that he did not want them to fall with him. He wrote to the King desperately pleading for His Majesty to be 'good lord' to them. And he besought Cromwell to do all in his power to care for the foundations.

In the very month that Wolsey and his king met for the last time, September 1529, Ipswich College was formally opened and Thomas Cromwell was there casting an efficient overseer's eye on the comings and goings of clergy, workmen, VIPs and members of the public, preparing for or enjoying the celebrations. William Capon, until recently Master of Jesus (Cranmer's college) at Cambridge and now dean of the new foundation wrote to commend his energy:

> Sunday the sixth day of September, master [Stephen Gardiner], Doctor Lee, with Mr Cromwell, repaired to Ipswich and came to your Grace's college there, and brought with them copes, vestments, altar cloths, plate, and other things, the particulars whereof have been comprised in a pair of indentures made between me and the said Mr Cromwell . . . the said Mr Stephens, Mr Lee, and Mr Cromwell tarried in your grace's college the space of four days, in which time Mr Cromwell did take much pain and labour not only in surveying your grace's stuff hither carried safely, but also in preparing and ordering of hangings, benches, with all other necessaries to the furniture of our hall which is now well trimmed and ordered through his good diligence and help.

Gardiner, the King's secretary, headed up the official delegation but it is clear who was doing the bulk of the work. On 8 September there was a mass and a great procession in the church at which 'were eleven of your copes worn there, and as much people as could stand in the church and in the church yard'. Other business to which Cromwell and Co. attended were the appointment of an assistant verger, the provision of cloth for making altars and the distribution of food, drink and money for the townspeople to be able to share in the celebrations. It is interesting to note that Brandon and Howard were among the contributors to the festivities, each providing two bucks.[87]

Stephen Gardiner, who here appears so attentive to his first patron's interests, was but one of the many who hastened to desert the Cardinal's sinking ship. He owed his elevation as much to Norfolk as to Wolsey, having been a tutor to one of the Duke's sons, and his adherence to the Howard cause grew stronger over the years. If his loyalty was divided in 1529 that certainly did not show in his actions. He replied brusquely to Wolsey's pleas to be allowed to come to the King and when his old master begged him to intercede for his colleges, Gardiner did nothing lest he should appear to be a supporter of the fallen minister. Gardiner, who soon received the lucrative bishopric of Winchester, after it was removed from Wolsey, had, of course, a lot to lose. He had just gained his perch in the court and did not want to be toppled. Cromwell was not so fortunate. He had not obtained that preferment to royal service for which he hoped. In one sense that made his situation more precarious: he was unavoidably tarred with Wolsey's brush. On the other hand he had less temptation to disloyalty.

The vivid picture given of him by Cavendish in the dark autumn days of 1529 shows him caught very much in a cleft stick. He describes coming across the disconsolate lawyer on 1 November lounging against a window jamb at Esher, uncharacteristically reading matins with tears streaming down his face. When asked the cause of his dismay Cromwell self-pityingly muttered that he did not know what would become of him. He had spent himself in the Cardinal's service, he insisted, and unlike His Grace's clerical servants all of whom had been provided with benefices, he had nothing to show for his years of devotion. Now he feared that he would lose what little property he had because of his involvement with the Cardinal. However, the gloom soon dispersed or, perhaps, turned into anger, for in the next affecting scene related by Cavendish we find Cromwell rounding on the priests of Wolsey's establishment and shaming them into coming to the aid of their less fortunate colleagues. He pulled out £5 from his purse and brandished it before Wolsey's assembled household, saying that it was to be distributed among his fellows. 'And now let us see what your chaplains will do,' he called out. 'I think they will proffer much more than I have done who be more able to give you a pound than I one penny.' One by one the shamefaced clerics coughed up.[88]

This did not solve Cromwell's own problems and he now decided, although it was almost too late, to try for a seat in the new parliament. He rode to court and sent, via the Duke of Norfolk, to know whether the King might be glad of his services in the Commons. The reply came back that, providing he did as he was told, he might try for a place. Now Cromwell had to rush around looking for a constituency that was not already bespoken. With parliament due to meet in two days (and with Wolsey having been deprived of all his patronage) this was far from easy. However, there was one last avenue to try. Sir William Paulet, Master of the Wards, had charge of the lands of the diocese of Winchester during the vacancy in see and there might be a town for which he had not yet appointed a member. At the last moment Cromwell's name was inserted on the return slip for Taunton. Membership of the House of Commons was not a major step forward. In a sense he was back where he had been six years before. But it was an opportunity. If he could prove himself useful to the King other possibilities might open up.

Exactly what was Cromwell's motive in supplicating Wolsey's enemies? Had the adventurer changed his allegiance? Was he, by contrast, trying to ensure that his old master would have at least one person to speak up for him in parliament? Or was he playing both sides against the middle? Personal ambition must have been his dominant motive and we need not doubt Cavendish's picture of the lachrymose servant fearing that he was doomed to go down with Wolsey's sinking fortunes. The depressing atmosphere at Esher can only have convinced Cromwell that the Wolseyan bandwagon had ground to a permanent halt and, not being a man to wait on events, he took his destiny firmly in his own hands. However, he seems to have departed with the Cardinal's blessing for the two men had a long, secret conversation before Cromwell left for court and certainly he did not cease in his efforts to be of service to his patron. One wonders, therefore, how he can have commended himself to the Norfolk clique. Did he present himself as a turncoat and did he have his fingers firmly crossed when he accepted the Howard shilling? It is difficult to see how the Duke could have given his backing to Wolsey's right-hand man without some assurance that the clever lawyer had not reassessed on what side his bread was best buttered. It seems clear that, in this first recorded encounter between Howard and Cromwell, the latter showed himself the more skilful politician. Norfolk must frequently have kicked himself in later years for being hoodwinked into giving a leg-up to the man who was to become his bitterest rival. But if Cromwell was subtle and duplicitous he was not disloyal. He did not forget his other master. If he could still be of service to Cardinal Wolsey he would – discreetly, of course. As for the exile at Esher, he had few other people apart from Cromwell to whom he could turn. He was desperate:

If ye love my life, break away this evening and come hither . . . At the reverence of God, take some pains now for me and forsake me not in this mine extreme need, and whereas I cannot, God shall reward you. Now is the time to show whether you love me or not . . .[89]

*

At about the same time that the disgraced Cardinal was bewailing his lot, the man destined to be the age's greatest preacher was delivering his first recorded sermon from the pulpit of St Edward's church in Cambridge:

> Who are thou? The answer to this question is . . . I am a Christian man . . . the child of everlasting joy, through the merits of the bitter passion of Christ. This is a joyful answer. Here may we see how much we be bound and in danger unto God, that hath revived us from death to life and saved us that were damned: which great benefit we cannot well consider, unless we do remember what we were of ourselves . . . and the more we know our feeble nature and set less by it, the more we shall conceive and know in our hearts what God hath done for us . . . and the more we shall love and please God . . .[90]

Those words from one of Hugh Latimer's 'Sermons on the Card' contain the essence of the evangelical dynamic which excited the younger generation of students in the 1520s. They speak of a personal relationship with God, through Christ, not dependent on the performance of traditional acts of devotion or the mediation of a sacerdotal priesthood. Such teaching – fresh, liberating, anti-establishment and potentially dangerous – thrilled the hearers who flocked to hear it. 'I was present,' wrote a young St John's man, Thomas Becon,

> when with manifest authorities of God's word and arguments invincible . . . he proved in his sermons that the holy Scriptures ought to be read in the English tongue of all Christian people, whether they were priests or laymen . . . he inveighed against temple works, good intentions, blind zeal, superstitious devotion [such] as the painting of tabernacles, gilding of images, setting up of candles, running on pilgrimages and such other idle inventions of men . . .[91]

Latimer was not of the student body; by 1529 he was a senior member of the university in his fortieth year; but he had earlier been converted through the ministrations of the young zealot, Thomas Bilney, from whom, he admitted, he had learned more than in twenty years of theological study, and had become one of the gurus of the new movement. It was hard for men like Latimer and his contemporaries to change. It was as true of the sixteenth century as the twenty-first that today's radicals are tomorrow's establishment men and reactionaries. Most of those who had been students of the New Learning were, like Erasmus and More, disinclined to follow Luther down the path of further reform and many became fervent opponents of religious novelties, even to the extent of repenting of their earlier admiration of the Dutch scholar. Of the

Cambridge fraternity Edward Lee, as we have seen, entered into acrimonious public debate with Erasmus. When Latimer was hauled before Wolsey sometime in 1524 or 1525 for preaching a sermon that had angered the Bishop of Ely, one of his examiners was William Capon, Master of Jesus. Stephen Gardiner, who was on his way to becoming the arch-conservative of Henry's reign, was Master of Trinity Hall, as well as being the King's secretary. Prominent, respectable academics in full pursuit of their careers were very unlikely to associate with the latest fashionable protest movement encouraged by irresponsible 'crowd-pleasing' hotheads like Latimer.

The attitude of university seniors towards undergraduate radicalism probably changed little over the centuries before the late 1900s. Discipline was not too heavy-handed and divergent opinions were tolerated but the authorities were nervous about protests that might turn into riots and movements that might discredit the university in the eyes of the higher powers. In 1520 there was a ceremonial burning of Luther's books in front of Great St Mary's church, opposite the newly completed chapel of King's, and thereafter occasional sweeps were made through student rooms by officers looking for illegally smuggled literature. In the lecture halls and chapels the new doctrines were frequently and fiercely denounced. Such activities, of course, only provided an added frisson to those bent on intellectual rebellion. Some of them met clandestinely in the White Horse Inn, between King's and St Catherine's, dubbed 'Little Germany' by their opponents, to study the Bible, discuss the latest ideas from Wittenberg and to encourage one another in the faith. However, devotees and sympathisers did not always keep their heads down. When Robert Barnes was arrested and examined by the Vice-Chancellor in 1525 the proceedings were interrupted by noisy student demonstrations.

Barnes, prior of the local Augustinian friars, was the second evangelical hero in 1520s Cambridge. In lectures and sermons he upheld Luther's teaching and, on at least one occasion, launched a blistering attack on Wolsey. His subsequent arrest set the whole town by the ears and it became clear to the authorities that trouble could only be averted by removing the popular friar, whom Gardiner described as 'of a merry, scoffing wit . . . a good fellow in company and well beloved of many',[92] and making an example of him. He was taken to Westminster and there interrogated by Wolsey, assisted by Gardiner and Edward Foxe, another Cambridge academic prospering under the Cardinal's patronage. Thus cowed, Barnes confessed his error and, so that his humiliation should be public, he was obliged to take part in a spectacular display of awesome Catholic power and the futility of 'foreign' heresy. Before a crowd of Londoners in St Paul's yard, Wolsey, attended by thirty-six mitred abbots, priors and bishops, presided over a public burning of Lutheran books and a grovelling submission by Barnes and four Hanse merchants, while

Bishop Fisher preached against them, trying vainly to make himself heard above the hubbub and the crackling flames.

However, the Cambridge man who most alarmed the Church fathers was William Tyndale. This young priest completed his studies in 1521 and moved to Gloucestershire to work as a tutor and preacher. A fervent admirer of Erasmus, Tyndale essentially bridges the gap between him and Luther. He yearned to make the great scholar's wisdom available to ordinary people and, to this end, he translated Erasmus's *Enchiridion Militis Christiani* (*The Manual or Dagger – enchiridion* had a double meaning in Greek and Erasmus's choice of it demonstrates his love of word play – *of the Militant Christian*). The book, published as long ago as 1503, was a practical, devotional guide to the inner life but it did include some of the author's barbed attacks on superstitious practices and mechanistic ceremonial which was not in itself edifying. Its translation out of scholar's Latin was exactly what Erasmus's critics had feared. It was all very well for academics to question the teachings and practices of the Church but to encourage unlearned men – and even women – to do so could only have disastrous consequences. Working-class heresy could be kept under control if it was distanced from permissible intellectual speculation; under no circumstances should it be given the apparent seal of approval of Europe's leading scholar. Local clergy scotched any possibility of Tyndale's *Manual* getting into print. Undaunted, the young enthusiast naïvely pursued his vision, asking Erasmus's friend, Cuthbert Tunstall, Bishop of London and Lord Privy Seal since 1523, to back a vernacular rendition of Erasmus's purified Greek New Testament. The discouraging response he received persuaded him that neither in the Bishop's household nor in England would such a project be countenanced. He travelled to the Low Countries where, with the backing of merchants who saw both spiritual value and material profit in an English Bible, he began the work which was to make him famous.

The demand was enormous; the reaction hysterical; and the combined effect of both ensured that Tyndale's New Testament would go into other, more contentious, editions and become the handbook of the English Reformation. Colporteurs found scores of ingenious methods of conveying the slim volumes into and around the country. From 1526 preachers, teachers and leaders of small conventicles were able to lay their hands on a book that 'proved' what they had long believed and passed on to others. Individuals – students, merchants, lawyers, gentlemen, courtiers, parish priests, yeoman farmers and their wives – could now nourish their souls – in private – with divine truth, without relying on official interpretations of it. As fast as the bishops' agents made search for concealed copies, bought up consignments themselves, organised bonfires and hauled people before the courts for possession or dealing, users found new suppliers and better ways of avoiding detection. As for Tyndale, the reports which reached him

in Cologne, Worms, Wittenberg, Antwerp or wherever else his pere-
grinations took him as he kept ahead of agents bent on his destruction,
confirmed his conviction that the Roman Church was at enmity with the
Word of God. That being so, he urged in *The Obedience of a Christian
Man* (1528) that godly princes must rise up to reform the Church, as they
had done in Germany, for, in his own realm, 'the king is . . . without law .
. . and shall give account to God alone'. Such extreme Erastianism would
be music to Henry VIII's ears when the Pope's enemies whispered it to
him. Meanwhile, in the enclosed world of the fenland university
radicalism and reaction split into different streams which ran in several
directions as men of learning and academic compulsion pondered in their
studies what they believed, what it was politic to believe and what it was
politic to admit they believed.

Where did Thomas Cranmer stand in all this? The answer seems to be:
cautiously apart. No records survive which suggest that he might have
been even an occasional member of the White Horse Inn holy club.
Equally he did not feature prominently in any disciplinary action taken
against heretical students. Confronted by such unhelpful negative
evidence, Diarmaid MacCulloch comes to our aid in his excellent
biography of the future archbishop by analysing the marginalia in a couple
of books which formed part of Cranmer's library. The volumes were
written in the 1520s by controversialists who had entered the lists against
Luther and the fact that Cranmer acquired them soon after publication
shows that he was keeping up with the debate. They also reveal that he was
not convinced by the German's arguments. Cranmer read with obvious
approval John Fisher's retort to Luther's trenchant defence of all the
articles condemned by Leo X in the bull *Exsurge Domine (Assertion of All
the Articles Wrongly Condemned in the Papal Bull)* (1520). In 1523
Fisher's *Confutation of Luther's Assertion* made a point-by-point answer
to the reformer's tract. Like the Bishop, Cranmer was obviously appalled
by both the content and the tone of the diatribe. Luther denounced the Pope
as 'impious and diabolical' and one of the ecumenical councils as 'the
synagogue of Satan'. Approving of Fisher's ripostes, Cranmer scrawled in
the margin of the *Confutation* as he read, Luther 'accuses a whole council
of madness; it is he who is insane!' and 'Oh the arrogance of a most
wicked man!'.

In 1524 Erasmus was, after years of evading controversy, nudged into
theological conflict with Luther by publishing *The Freedom of the Will*.
Cranmer rapidly acquired a copy and, once again, it is clear from his
annotations that he fully supported the author, particularly in his insistence
that it was wrong to dogmatise about the divine plan where Scripture left
a mystery.[93] Clearly we seek in vain for Cranmer the reformer in the
1520s.

What we find is Cranmer the conventional university don accepting advancement. Prominent academics might enter royal service in a variety of ways – as chaplains, secretaries, administrators, tutors, diplomats – and several of Cranmer's friends had already begun to travel these roads. He was drawn into the flurry of activity following the capture of Francis I at the Battle of Pavia in 1525. Sir Francis Poyntz and Dr Edward Lee were despatched to the Emperor's court in Spain in an attempt to assert an English influence in peace negotiations. Cranmer was selected to take part in this mission, perhaps drawn to Wolsey's attention through the good offices of Lee or Capon. He seems to have enjoyed being transferred from the quiet world of Cambridge to the exciting one of international diplomacy, even though his return journey involved a thirteen-day transit of the Bay of Biscay and the English Channel in atrocious conditions. Landed safely in June 1526, he sped to Greenwich where he had the thrill of being warmly received by Henry in person and granted a half-hour audience. It seems to have been an example of love at first sight – at least on Cranmer's part. The overawed scholar-diplomat found the King to be 'the kindest of princes', an opinion from which he never deviated.[94]

However, the experiences of 1525–6 do not seem to have given him a taste for the higher life. Cranmer was a self-deprecatory intellectual and not a thrusting politique. He accepted, often with a genuine air of surprise, such advancement as came his way but he manifestly had little ambition and certainly no game plan. He settled back into his Cambridge routine and showed no interest in pursuing any other way of life. A few months after his return from Spain Wolsey was recruiting staff for his new Oxford college. Several of Cranmer's friends and colleagues made the move to the other university which was obviously a good way of incurring the Cardinal's favour. But when the call came to Cranmer, he politely declined.

Cambridge, of course, was not insulated from the burning issues of the day and the King's great matter was much discussed among the university's theologians and canon lawyers. Cranmer had, probably, already reached the conclusion that the Levitical prohibition was conclusive. What is certain is that he believed, good academic that he was, that the thorny issue was capable of rational solution. One explored Scripture and the Fathers and one arrived at a conclusion. Any political considerations which might militate against the implementation of that conclusion were of no consequence; man's futile manoeuvrings should not go about to frustrate God's law. Cranmer was, at heart, a very simple man.

His propulsion into a central place in English government and, indeed, a central place in English history, was not of his designing. We might attribute it to chance. He saw in it the working of a higher power. In the summer of 1529 the plague was rife in Cambridge and to avoid it Cranmer rode into the country. He went to stay at the house of a kinsman, a Mr Cressey, close to the great Augustinian abbey of Waltham Holy Cross in Essex, and to see safely delivered home his host's two sons, who were his pupils. It so happened that the royal court arrived there at the same time (the first days of August) because Henry's progress brought him as a guest to the abbey. As it also happened Stephen Gardiner and Edward Foxe, now advanced from Wolsey's service to become Henry's Almoner, were billeted on the Cresseys. Over supper the old university friends inevitably fell to discussing the impasse over the divorce. Gardiner and Foxe had recently returned from a mission to Rome and knew better than most just how impossible it would be to obtain a favourable decision from the Pope. Cranmer responded:

> I do think that you go not the [most convenient] way to work, to bring the matter unto a perfect conclusion and end, especially for the satisfaction of the troubled conscience of the king's highness. For in observing the common process and frustrating delays of this your courts the matter will linger long enough, and peradventure in the end come unto small effect. And this is most certain, that there is but one truth in it, which no men ought or better can discuss than the divines. Whose sentence may be soon known and brought so to pass with little industry and charges, that the king's conscience thereby may be quieted and pacified.[95]

It was obvious to Cranmer that by simply canvassing the theological specialists of Europe the 'truth' could be ascertained. Perhaps we should not regard this as unduly simplistic; we are, after all, accustomed to seeing academic experts wheeled out on television news programmes to pontificate on all manner of contemporary events. Whether Gardiner and Foxe considered their fellow guest's observation as a breakthrough or as the only available straw at which to clutch, they reported their conversation to the King. Cranmer thought no more about the conversation and so it was with genuine surprise that he found himself summoned to London a few weeks later. More than that, he was lodged in some splendour at Durham House (on the sight of the modern Adelphi) in the entourage of Viscount Rochford. His brief: to organise the polling of Europe's theology faculties and obtain from them a verdict favourable to the King.

Thus in the last days of 1529, while Thomas Howard was assuming what he considered his proper place at the King's right hand and Thomas Wolsey was wondering just how complete his fall was destined to be and Thomas More was feeling his way into the position of England's leading judicial officer, Thomas Cromwell and Thomas Cranmer had both been removed from their accustomed habitats and were, with mingled hope and confusion, contemplating how they might best serve their king. What neither can have contemplated was that Thomas Wolsey's mantle was about to descend across them both, making one, under the Crown, the leader of the English Church and the other the most powerful man in the state, and making them jointly architects of a revolution.

PART FIVE:

1539

. . . by divers sundry old authentic histories and chronicles it is manifestly declared and expressed that this realm of England is an empire, and so hath been accepted in the world, governed by one supreme head and king having the dignity and royal estate of the imperial crown of the same, unto whom a body politic, compact of all sorts and degrees of people divided in terms and by names of spirituality and temporalty, be bounden and owe to bear next to God a natural and humble obedience; he being also institute and furnished by the goodness and sufferance of Almighty God with plenary, whole and entire power, preeminence, authority, prerogative and jurisdiction to render and yield justice and final determination to all manner of folk resiants [i.e. residents] or subjects within this realm, in all causes, matters, debates and contentions happening to occur, insurge or begin within the limits thereof, without restraint or provocation to any foreign princes or potentates of the world.

Act in Restraint of Appeals, 1533[1]

CHAPTER 21

New Brooms

The 1530s were exciting years. England came perilously close to civil war. The institution of monasticism was swept from the land. The King exiled the Pope and the Pope excommunicated the King. Vast tracts of ecclesiastical property changed hands, leading to new social and political relationships in the shires. Thinkers pedalled novel and challenging ideas about what they called the 'Commonwealth' in books which were increasingly written in the vernacular. And ideas broke into the lives of the unlearned when, by government order, long-venerated objects of 'superstition' were removed from and English Bibles set up in parish churches. The King's matrimonial life lurched from crisis to crisis and became a standing joke throughout Europe. Yet, disturbing as were the changes and chances of this hectic decade, there were compensating stabilities. England was not embroiled in continental war. The people did not suffer exorbitant demands for taxation. Parliament met more frequently than ever before and gave its attention to a wide range of issues. After a run of bad harvests, of which that of 1527 was particularly disastrous, the nation's economic life took a decided turn for the better. Even religious conflict had settled to a kind of stalemate with the formulation of the Confession of Augsburg defining Lutheran belief and the uniting of Germany's 'Protestant' princes in the Schmalkaldic League (1530).

It is not fanciful to suggest that more people now had both the stimulus and the opportunity to contemplate the 'Great Question of Life, the Universe and Everything'. There was, as Diarmaid MacCulloch suggests, 'a sense of a new world of possibilities'.[2] Heresy was no longer an underground movement (except in its more extreme forms). Catholics and evangelicals inveighed against each other from pulpit and printed page. People could take sides. Indeed, it was increasingly impossible not to do so. When, for example, Tyndale asserted, in *The Obedience of a Christian Man*, Christ 'is a priest for ever; and all we priests through him, and need no more of any such priest on earth, to be a mean for us unto God',[3] that was a take-it-or-leave-it declaration. One either believed it and exulted in a new-found freedom from old ecclesiastical tyranny or rejected it as totally subversive of all Church (and potentially all civil) order.

Thomas More was one of the first prominent Englishmen to perceive that the cracks appearing in the nation's religious life would, beyond a peradventure, widen into fissures and chasms, unless something was done to stop them. This explains the utter ferocity of his attack on heresy from the late 1520s. As he explained to Erasmus, the world had changed so much that tolerance of extremism (such as his friend still advocated), fearless attacks on acknowledged clerical abuses, and encouragement of the theologically naïve to seek the truth in Scripture could only do irreparably more harm than good:

> I am keenly aware of the risk involved in an open-door policy towards these newfangled, erroneous sects . . . some people like to give an approving eye to novel ideas, out of superficial curiosity, and to dangerous ideas, out of devilry; and in so doing they assent to what they read, not because they believe it is true, but because they want it to be true . . . All my efforts are directed toward the protection of those men who do not deliberately desert the truth, but are seduced by the enticements of clever fellows.[4]

More became the arch-priest of reaction. All his satirical scorn, courtroom rhetoric, special pleading, bitter invective and penchant for vulgarity, fed by the insecurity and tensions concealed by worldly success, were now focused upon one target.

Why did Hans Holbein execute no commissions for members of the Steelyard between 1526 and 1529? The question may seem irrelevant to our subject. It is not. The artist's English career spanned the years 1526 to 1543 and during that time he only spent one prolonged period out of his adopted country – August 1529–April 1532. He was, as we have seen, an immediate success, securing employment at court and gaining enough private commissions to keep him gainfully occupied. From 1532 he painted several portraits of German Hanse merchants and undertook important murals for the Steelyard banqueting hall. Yet, during his first stay in London he appears to have had little or no contact with them. It has to be regarded as odd that this Augsburg-born artist, living in a strange land and struggling to master a foreign tongue, should not have resorted to and formed friendships among London's German community, settled in and around Dowgate ward.

The answer is that as long as Holbein was enjoying More's patronage and living under his roof it was professionally unwise and even potentially dangerous for him to be seen to be associating with men suspected of bringing into England books by Luther, Tyndale and other heretics. More's attitude towards the denizens of the Steelyard was bitter and personal. In 1521 William Roper had married Sir Thomas's favourite daughter, Margaret, and the couple lived together in the More home.

Before or shortly after the wedding, Roper became one of the earliest English converts to Lutheranism. With all the zeal of the new believer the young man gossiped his faith wherever he went and contemplated becoming a preacher. Naturally, Sir Thomas was alarmed and made frequent attempts to talk his son-in-law out of such erroneous and dangerous opinions but, eventually, he confessed himself beaten and told Margaret that he could now do no more than pray for her husband. Meanwhile, Roper had begun consorting with fellow believers in the Steelyard. The young rebel obtained his own copies of Luther's Bible and some of the reformer's inflammatory tracts. By 1526 the German community had gone so far as discontinuing the celebration of mass at their parish church, Allhallows the Greater in Thames Street. Although the government strove to maintain good relations with the wealthy foreigners and permitted them considerable freedom of action, such an open rejection of the host country's official religion could not be tolerated and it was probably this step which prompted Wolsey to authorise a raid on the Hanse headquarters in February 1526. As we have seen, a cache of books was confiscated and subsequently burned, and four merchants were forced to make public recantations, alongside Robert Barnes. Roper was also caught up in this investigation. He was hauled before the Cardinal and given a vigorous dressing down. There the matter rested. No further action was taken against the young zealot, who, it seems, had had a sufficiently bad scare to convince him of the error of his ways. Certainly it was about this time that Roper returned to the Catholic fold and would, thereafter, be as stalwart a reactionary as he had hitherto been a radical. Wolsey's leniency was out of respect to More and his family but it also reflects the embarrassment upper-class heresy always caused the government. The leaders of Church and State had little compunction about publicly humiliating, and even executing, peasants, artisans, lowly clerics and foreigners but when members of the ruling élite and their families fell into heresy they became a serious embarrassment. To parade such people before the populace was not only detrimental to public order, it also revealed the unpalatable fact that dangerous beliefs had taken root in high places.

Be that as it may, when Holbein arrived in the More household a few months later the Steelyard was scarcely a welcome topic of conversation, though the artist may well have heard about recent events from servants and, perhaps, even from Roper, who certainly spoke German. The news might have come as a real shock: when the artist had first decided to try his luck in England there was a strong rumour circulating the Continent that Henry VIII was contemplating throwing in his lot with the evangelical cause. Sir Thomas, whose religious conviction must have been sharpened by outrage at what had happened to his own family, scotched any such stories by writing for Henry a letter to Luther which reasserted the King's orthodoxy and took the opportunity to lambaste the reformer afresh. At the same time he hit out at London's German Lutherans. Convinced that the Hanse community had not yet yielded up all their guilty secrets, he ordered, on his own authority, two further attacks on their headquarters in 1527. Under these circumstances Holbein deemed it wise to keep quiet about his personal religious sympathies which had been vividly demonstrated in his illustrations for Luther's New Testament, propaganda engravings for evangelical tracts and, most personally, in the magnificent set of *Dance of Death* engravings, recently completed but as yet unpublished. It is significant that in this satirical series exposing the vices and follies of all sorts and conditions of men, Holbein only suggested that two of his subjects were in league with the devil. One of them was the Pope, whom he depicted with a demon whispering in his ear and another brandishing a papal bull (perhaps the one against Luther, *Exsurge Domine*). Old assumptions about Holbein being a detached observer of the religious scene and enjoying a warm relationship with the 'More circle' of liberal-minded humanists simply disintegrate when hit by the facts that the artist was already committed to the reformist cause and that More was, at this very time, embarking on his ardent anti-evangelical crusade. The relationship between the two men was kept on a purely professional basis and, on Holbein's side at least, was fraught with tension. In 1529, when More took up in earnest his campaign of literary polemic, Holbein abandoned his lucrative prospects in England and went home to Basel.[5]

Sir Thomas never devoted himself to anything with more energy and conviction than he did to his personal campaign against the 'new false sect'. His polemical books were negative, unlovely and, for the most part, tedious. His treatment of suspected heretics was inquisitorial. No amount of hagiography concentrating on More's urbanity, humour, humanism, sanctity and martyrdom should conceal from us the man who coveted for himself the role of defender of Catholic truth and was prepared to sacrifice all finer human feelings to that ambition. He believed, and said as much to Erasmus, that the post of Lord Chancellor was his platform from which to contend for 'the interests of Christendom'.[6]

'The difficulty for the leaders of conservative opinion in resisting the evangelical message was to present a coherent and exciting alternative.'[7] More epitomised this truth. The eight polemical works to which he devoted much of his leisure time between 1526 and 1533 were based upon the assumptions of the university disputation or the courtroom submission, that an argument could be won or a case proved. Over and again he piled Pelion on Ossa, erecting what he considered to be unassailable walls of proof to withstand the battering of Lutheran apologists. Either he could not grasp or did not agree with the point Erasmus frequently made that the tree of religious controversy yielded abundant thorns but little fruit. While the Englishman was busy denouncing every single article in the Lutheran canon his friend was writing letters of encouragement and counsel to the German theologians gathered at Augsburg, helping them to find ways of coming to agreement and preserving peace. He could even speculate that Luther might be God's instrument for punishing the sins into which the Church had fallen – a concept totally anathematical to his erstwhile fellow traveller. More's frustrating discussions with young Roper might have indicated to him that it was the heart, not the mind, that must be converted, but he continued his bulldozing way, publicly lambasting the enemies of Catholicism just as privately he thrashed any servant caught expressing Lutheran ideas.

He and Cuthbert Tunstall had been ardent opponents of the Wittenberg monk ever since the one assisted Henry with the *Assertio* and the other had been at the Diet of Worms where all the talk was of Luther's forthcoming examination before the Emperor. Both men had been frustrated by Erasmus's disinclination to trounce the reformer in print and with what they considered as Wolsey's relaxed attitude towards the spread of heretical literature. More had seen in his own family how the new ideas could take hold of individuals and the Peasants' Wars in Germany indicated to him their devastating powers *en masse*. He was in no doubt that the storms and devastated harvests of 1527 were God's punishment on his Church for failing to root out heresy. The phenomenal spread of vernacular Scripture was, for him, the last straw. He who had been lavish in his praise of Erasmus's Greek New Testament was appalled at its translation into English. The Bible was a book for scholars to understand and interpret and for priests to convey to the people. Nothing but disaster could follow.

> When an hatter will go smatter
> In philosophy,
> Or a pedlar wax a meddler
> In theology.[8]

There could never be a conflict between Church and Scripture because the clergy existed to mediate divine truth and not to be judged by it as mediated by the laity.

Tunstall and More concluded that if no one else was going to launch a determined offensive they must do so. The Bishop drew up a list of undesirable books and received royal sanction to have them banned. By 1529 this *index librorum prohibitorum* included over a hundred titles. The one person who was allowed to read them, by episcopal licence, was Thomas More and his task, of course, was to refute them. Thus, in June 1529, he published his *Dialogue Concerning Heresies*, the opening bombardment of his literary siege. Weeks later Holbein said goodbye to his promising English career and returned to Basel, a city which, in his absence, had fallen hook, line and sinker for an even more radical version of reformed faith than Luther's. By one of those ironies to which the confused situation of those years gave rise, only four months before Holbein took refuge in Basel from Catholic extremism in London, Erasmus had departed, fleeing from the city's Protestant extremism.

As More took his place, theoretically at least, among the nation's leaders he found the political weather at the centre changeable and unpredictable in the extreme. Norfolk and his allies had two prime objectives: to prevent Wolsey regaining power and to accomplish successfully those policies which the Cardinal had failed to achieve. As we have seen, Wolsey's complete destruction was by no means a foregone conclusion in the closing weeks of 1529 and the occasional favours Henry persisted in showing to his fallen minister were alarming to those who aspired to take his place and who knew how terrible Wolsey's vengeance would be should he ever clamber back into the King's undivided favour. For more than half his lifetime Henry had liked and admired his chief executive and been genuinely grateful for his cunning and industry. Of those men pushing and shoving their way into the Cardinal's vacated room only Suffolk was an equal to Wolsey in terms of enjoying the King's long-term friendship and none possessed a fraction of the ex-Chancellor's political acumen. Each had a different agenda: Suffolk sought an official position in government and intended to use it to break the power of the Church hierarchy; More, as we have seen, craved power to undergird the ecclesiastical structure and exterminate the heretical termites eating away at it; Rochford was desperate to become the King's father-in-law; Howard was the typical unthinking reactionary whose gut instincts were for the preservation of a strong monarchy, buttressed by the aristocracy and the Church and dealing firmly with any dissent which threatened the combined supremacy of crown, coronet and mitre. As the leader of this disparate alliance, and as a man who had never been a recipient of the King's confidence or friendship, Norfolk found himself in a precarious position. His first objective and the only one that could be easily achieved was to unite his colleagues in opposition to the common enemy – Wolsey.

Though Howard was nervous about anticlericalism, he knew that the hostility of parliament towards ecclesiastical abuses could be used as a weapon against Wolsey. The King was persuaded to hand over the writs of summons for shires where Wolsey was the dominant political force and the Duke personally made the nominations. Having seen the Cardinal stripped of the power to muster his own supporters in the Commons, Norfolk and his associates used their influence to ensure that counties and boroughs, wherever possible, returned members likely to serve the Council's purpose. More co-operated fully with these manoeuvres. With Howard's support, he obtained the elections of William Roper and Roper's friend Henry See, as the two members for Bramber, Sussex. Sir

Giles Alington, the husband of More's stepdaughter Alice Middleton, sat
for Cambridgeshire and something of a Chelsea 'circle' has been identified
in the make-up of the 1529 House of Commons. Most intriguing of all is
the case of Thetford, where William Dauntsey and Giles Heron, More's
sons-in-law, were duly elected to represent a town which had never before
sent burgesses to parliament and which did not do so for some years
afterwards. Thetford belonged to the Duchy of Lancaster and was,
therefore, under Sir Thomas's influence and was, of course, in the middle
of Howard country.[9] Thomas Cromwell's nomination should probably be
seen against the background of Norfolk's eagerness to gain as much
support as possible in the lower house. It would be a minor coup if such a
prominent servant of Wolsey's were to add his voice to the rising murmur
of discontent against the Cardinal. Nor in the current situation can this
have seemed unlikely, for almost everyone else whose career had been
advanced by the great man was now eager to stab him in the back.

Among their number was Thomas More. On 3 November 1529, having
processed with the King and the great and the good of the realm from
Bridewell stairs to Blackfriars church for a solemn mass and thence to
Bridewell palace, the new Lord Chancellor positioned himself beside
Henry's chair of state, then rose in his scarlet robes trimmed with miniver
to proclaim for the assembled Lords and Commons the opening of their
parliament. During the course of his oration he made the required attack
on his predecessor:

> Amongst a great flock of sheep some be rotten and faulty, which the
> good shepherd sendeth from the good sheep, so the great wether [ram]
> which is of late fallen as you all know, so craftily, so scabbily [as of a
> sheep afflicted with scab], yea and so untruly juggled with the king, that
> all men must needs guess and think that he thought in himself, that he
> had no wit to perceive his crafty doing, or else that he presumed that the
> king would not see nor know his fraudulent juggling and attempts; but
> he was deceived, for his Grace's sight was so quick and penetrable, that
> he saw him, yea and saw through him, both within and without, so that
> all things to him was open, and according to his deserts he hath had a
> gentle correction, which small punishment the king wills not to be an
> example to other offenders but clearly declareth that whosoever
> hereafter shall make like attempt or commit like offence, shall not
> escape with like punishment.[10]

What is most interesting about this denigration of Wolsey is its muted
nature. The speech, if not actually vetted by the King, was certainly written
with the King in mind. It was not the Cardinal's vanity and ostentation, or
his failed policies, or his personal ambition, or his domination over the
aristocracy, or any of the other sins commonly laid to his charge, that More

chose to highlight, but his relationship with his sovereign. Even here the new Chancellor's message was kept deliberately vague. Wolsey had tried to deceive his royal master – but in ways unspecified – and Henry had reacted by showing clemency and not dealing with the false minister according to his deserts – again unspecified. Any leaders of the political nation hoping to hear a thoroughgoing denunciation of the fallen Cardinal-Legate must have been disappointed in the words chosen and delivered with all the skill of a clever barrister. More could not tell his hearers the real reason for Wolsey's fall – his inability to secure a royal divorce – because it was a highly sensitive issue and one which found many members of Lords and Commons (including More himself) on Catherine's side. He could not declare the royal intent to destroy the disgraced ex-Chancellor totally because such was not Henry's will and he had, in fact, given express command that parliament was not to debate Wolsey's failings in detail.

However, any suggestion that More might have been, out of lingering loyalty, praising his predecessor with faint damnation, must be rejected in the light of what happened less than a month later. In mid-November Henry's ambiguous attitude towards Wolsey took a step towards greater clarity; he lifted some of the penalties incurred by the Cardinal's *praemunire*. This rattled his court opponents so much that they drew up an extraordinary forty-four-article petition for presentation to the King which accused Wolsey of a Pandora's box of heinous offences from perverting justice in the courts, despoiling the Church, and indulging insatiable vanity to approaching the King while suffering from 'the foul and contagious disease of the great pox' and 'whispering in your ear and blowing on your most noble grace with his perilous and infected breath' (an accusation designed to stir Henry's hypochondria).[11] The supplicants revealed the root cause of their anxiety when they asked His Majesty to confirm that never again would the Cardinal exercise 'power, jurisdiction or authority . . . to trouble, vex and impoverish this your realm'. The authors of this exercise in overkill were Howard and his aristocratic colleagues but the name that headed the list of signatories was 'Thomas More'.

Sir Thomas, who had once addressed his patron as a man 'whose honours, despite the respect and esteem of the people, fall far short of your worth', had apparently moved to the position of regarding Wolsey as so overweening in his pride as not to be worthy of high office. It is unlikely that this volte-face was motivated by naked opportunism or that More had his arm twisted by the Norfolk–Suffolk clique. We can detect items on the *index maleficiorum* that are much more likely to have been contributed by More than by his noble co-signatories. Neither Brandon nor Howard would have been incensed by Wolsey's alleged fiddling of the books of religious houses marked for confiscation, or overruling the jurisdiction of bishops and archdeacons, or 'slandering' parish priests. And who but

More would have insisted on the including of an article concerning the spread of heresy at Cambridge? According to his charge two bishops had declared their intention of going to the university to put a stop to errors which 'were reported to reign amongst the students and scholars' but the Lord Cardinal 'expressly inhibited and commanded them in no wise so to do'. The result was that 'the same errors crept more abroad and took greater place'. From incidents it was alleged, 'that the said lord cardinal, besides all other his heinous offences, hath been the impeacher and disturber of due and direct correction of heresies; being highly to the danger and peril of the whole body and good Christian people of this your realm'.[12] In these and several other charges relating to matters ecclesiastical More was acting as the defender of Church liberties and privileges. He saw the chancellorship above all as a means of guarding 'the interests of Christendom' and that meant not only bearing down hard on heretics, but also preserving the material well-being of the clergy so that they could effectively fulfil their role. His predecessor had done none of these things. On the contrary, More had watched him weaken the English Church in many ways: he had not given a strong enough lead against false teaching; he had created a dangerous precedent in the scale of his plundering of religious houses for educational purposes; by his own ostentation and power lust he had provided a focus for the diffuse rays of anticlericalism; and he had encouraged Henry to flout canon law and papal authority over the divorce. Thus, Thomas More had his own quite distinct reasons for wanting to prevent Wolsey's political resurrection and for joining the loose, temporary alliance headed by Norfolk.

Uniting opposition to the fallen Cardinal was, thus, the easier part of Norfolk's programme. His other priority was to provide Henry with an effective alternative to Wolsey and that meant delivering to the King the results that he wanted in those matters that touched him most closely. Success in those matters was the Duke's only guarantee of keeping the 'great wether' permanently exiled from the flock. By the same token, his failure would almost inevitably be the signal for Wolsey's recall by a monarch making a display of forgiveness and magnanimity. The outlaw knew this, knew also how devoid his opponents were of political solutions, and was busy scheming with allies at home and abroad in the hope of recovering his position.

Norfolk and Co. were desperate to find pathways through the two enormous problems facing them. One was the divorce and it is always this that has dominated debate about these crucial years but the other difficulty – money – was equally pressing. Despite enforced economies the Crown was heavily in debt. Technically Henry owed his subjects over £350,000, being the amount collected in forced loans in 1522 and 1523. His new chief advisers cast about wildly for any ideas which might serve them. A hotch-potch agenda of radical measures was drawn up by Thomas Darcy in the summer of 1529. Lord Darcy, an aged courtier-warrior and one-time comrade-in-arms of Norfolk's on the border, was a considerable land-owner in the Midlands and the North. Originally a supporter of Wolsey, he now threw in his lot with the Howard–Brandon group, probably in the interests of baronial solidarity. Darcy's proposals did not constitute a blueprint for radical reform but they did affirm the right of the King to bring both Church and State firmly under his personal control and to curb the power of the clergy:

> Item that all knights' fees, baronies and earldoms be viewed, and how many of them be in spiritual hands.
> Item to view what of all temporal lands the spiritual men hath, and by what titles . . .
> Item better and much more merit, honour and virtue is it for the king's grace to proceed and determine all reformations of spiritual and temporal [matters] within this realm . . .
> Item that never legate nor cardinal be in England.
> Item their legacies and faculties clearly annulled and made frustrate.
> Item that sure search and inquiries be made what hath been levied thereby.
> Item that it be tried whether the putting down of all the abbeys be lawful and good or no, for great things hang thereupon . . .[13]

There was nothing new about royal councillors contrasting the straightened circumstances of the Crown with the wealth of the Church or advocating that clergy should not enjoy exemptions from laws and imposts endured by their lay neighbours. What was new was the convergence of the King's needs and a growing discontent, particularly prominent in the eastern and southern parts of the country more easily accessible to radical ideas from the Continent, with the ecclesiastical infrastructure (anti-clericalism is too precise a term) coupled with a belief, supported by events in both Catholic and Protestant lands, that the King should exercise greater control over the clergy.

The unstable atmosphere in England of the 1530s and 40s may, as we suggested earlier, be reasonably compared with that of an era closer to our own time. Among the citizenry of eastern Europe in the 1980s there was unrest bordering on ferment directed against communist power élites who told people what to believe, punished dissidents and exploited the system for their own advantage. The majority raised no protest because they feared the authorities, or mistrusted change, or disliked troublemakers, or had a Panglossian belief in Marxist-Leninism as the best of all possible political systems. But the intoxicant of freedom emboldened minorities throughout the Eastern Bloc and gave them a mass identity which climaxed in the last heady weeks of the penultimate decade when totalitarian regimes crumbled, the 'people' took over in capital after capital, Berlin's citizens attacked the city's dividing wall with hand tools and mobs of delirious men and women went on an iconoclastic rampage, defacing government buildings, toppling statues of their former oppressors, burning police files and removing all hated symbols of the past. Only when the dust had settled did it become possible to see how much – or how little – had changed. Some of the old bosses had managed to reinvent themselves in order to keep their places at the top table. Some new democrats turned out to be but old tyrants writ large. Even socialist parties had not been swept into the garbage can of history. Continuity and contrast were mingled in the political make-up of the new Europe.

Life moved more slowly in the sixteenth century. England was well into the reign of Elizabeth before the shake-out of the Reformation years could be evaluated. Yet the comparison with the last days of monolithic European communism will stand. Rome-centred Catholicism was smashed in England, as it was in other northern-European countries. A new State–Church political machine was established. The revolution was carried through by a minority, as revolutions always are. It succeeded, as revolutions only can, because it attracted the willing support of significant numbers of the populace drawn from the influential classes and because, beyond them, it struck chords of discontent in the populace as a whole. Most English people resented change or were apathetic towards it. Old devotional practices survived. Clergy – high and low – who certainly would have rejected the label 'Protestant', accomplished the necessary juggling with conscience to keep their jobs. Many older worshippers looked back nostalgically to the 'good old days', while Elizabethan zealots complained that the transformation had not been radical enough. Yet to claim, as partisan historians have, that the engine of traditional belief continued to throb beneath the newly applied, tawdry, Protestant bodywork put in place by the government is special pleading of a monumental order. The Church of the 1570s had no pope, no mass, no sacerdotal priesthood, no Latin liturgy, no organised asceticism and no elaborately decked altars. It did have new pulpits for preaching, new pews for listening to preaching, new vernacular Bibles which were actually read by an increasing number of people and congregations which included both devout and nominal believers, but who were united in their hatred of Spain because it was seen and wished to be seen as the champion of a revived, militant Catholicism.

The transition from 1530 to 1570 could not have taken the form that it did without the existence of deep resentments, without a commonly held gut feeling that reform was not only desirable but possible, or without an exciting evangelical dynamic which provided the impetus for change, not only in the Church, but in the 'Commonwealth'. The Reformation was a movement of hope and moral fervour, capable of generating a mood of intense excitement . . . This was a time of apparently infinite possibilities, when ordinary people believed that they could themselves influence the future, and when the government appeared to agree.[14]

In 1530 those responsible for government policy perceived only dimly the aspirations and determination of the nation's religious and social radicals. Brandon looked to the newly summoned parliament to carry through a series of reforms which would reduce the influence and independence of Church leaders. Norfolk wanted the assembly, as well as coming to the King's aid financially, to complete Wolsey's ruin and to declare its support for the divorce. Any anticlerical sentiment would be a valuable ally in achieving these ends. Only More was apprehensive about what the leaders of the Commons might wish to discuss. He hoped for parliament's backing in the fight against heresy and intended to head it off if it turned on the clergy. His speech on 3 November took 'reform' as its keynote. His Majesty, England's good shepherd, had observed several ancient laws which were in need of revision and had become aware of 'divers new enormities . . . sprung amongst the people' which called out for redress. The words are those recorded by the Protestant Hall. Interestingly, other contemporary accounts spoke not of 'enormities' but of 'new errors and heresies',[15] which is likely to be closer to what More actually said.

Sir Thomas, who, six years earlier, when Speaker of the Commons, had made eloquent plea for freedom to debate, now found that liberty irritating. Edward Hall detected a new boldness in the assembly. Whereas members had before been reluctant to discuss Church matters for fear of being dubbed heretic and dragged off to the ecclesiastical courts, now, 'when God illumined the eyes of the king and . . . [the clergy's] subtle doings were once espied . . . men began charitably to desire a reformation, and so at this parliament time men began to show their grudges'.[16] Within days the members had fallen to discussing clerical abuses under six headings. And they did not mince their words: in a bill about clerical fees sent up to the Lords, the clergy were denounced as 'vicious', 'ravenous' and 'insatiable'. The bishops responded in kind and a battle royal between the two houses ensued. It was More's friend Bishop Fisher who took the lead. Adopting a forthright ecclesiastical arrogance which did his cause no good whatsoever but which had become customary for reactionary bishops when their profession was under attack, he compared the Commons complainers to Lutherans and Hussites. Their presumption sprang from a lack of faith in Holy Church; they were seditious; if the lay lords did not 'resist manfully . . . this violent heap of mischief' they would 'shortly see all obedience withdrawn, first from the clergy, and after from yourselves, whereupon will ensue the utter ruin . . . of the Christian faith and in place of it . . . the most wicked and tyrannical government of the Turk'.[17] Norfolk was among the members of the upper house who listened with some alarm to this tirade. Bellicose bishops of Fisher's stamp were precisely the kind of allies he did not need and he took Rochester aside to tell him that his speech was decidedly OTT. But the damage had been done. The Commons made a formal complaint to Henry and the King summoned Fisher, whom he had never much liked, to receive a royal reprimand. Parliament was to be the scene of further clashes between clergy and laity before the session came to an end.

This interference of parliament in Church affairs alarmed More greatly but worse was to follow from a different quarter. His old literary adversary Simon Fish had recently returned from abroad and the King had asked to see him. Henry, so the story goes, 'embraced him with loving countenance', took him out hunting and discussed theology with him as they rode. When Fish explained that he feared the Lord Chancellor's malice, the King gave him a ring in token of royal protection and told him to confront More and to advise him not to molest the heretical author. Sir Thomas duly received Master Fish and his message. Chagrined at being balked, the clever lawyer was unable to let matters rest there; he found another means of hitting at the writer of a banned book. He pointed out that the King's protection did not extend to Fish's wife and that he had every intention of investigating her conduct the very next day. Apparently the only thing that saved Mistress Fish was the fact that she was tending her daughter who was sick with the plague, so that More, fearing contagion, declined to press the matter.[18]

From the very beginning of his term of office as England's chief legal officer More was increasingly kept out of political life. He was the first Chancellor not to be *de facto* leader of the Council and his own appearances on that body were very irregular. There were several reasons for this. He had no ambition to be among the arbiters of England's destiny except insofar as he could combat heresy and support the Church hierarchy, and this made it easier for politically motivated rivals to elbow him aside. The large and growing volume of work in Chancery and Star Chamber kept him busy. The situation had come full circle since Wolsey had emasculated the Council by ensuring that his colleagues danced attendance on him at Westminster. Now the leading political figures were back at court and it was the Chancellor who was isolated. Though he introduced no innovations to the working of the courts, he continued Wolsey's reformist activity, seeking to render the administration of justice as efficient and equitable as was humanly possible. He took great care to be a good judge weighing carefully the cases brought before him and adjudicating by precedent tempered by conscience and common sense. He believed that justice resided not in applying the rigour of the law as a cold abstraction, but in considering cases on their merits and regarding every plaintiff and defendant as an individual. The point is worth emphasising because More's humane attitude in the courtroom contrasts markedly with his behaviour towards those suspected of heresy. For him there were no special cases or mitigating circumstances in matters of belief. A man either believed everything laid down by Holy Church or he was a heretic, and if the latter persisted in his error More was his implacable enemy, as he boasted to Erasmus: 'I find that breed of men absolutely loathesome, so much so that, unless they regain their senses, I want to be as hateful to them as anyone can possibly be.'[19] More gave up much of his own time to the pursuit and examination of suspected heretics and this also prevented him filling an active political role.

But his separation from the Council was also engineered by those in power. In these tense and vicissitudinous times Howard needed allies who had more of the willow than the oak about them; men who could respond to changing situations and royal moods without being too much troubled by conscience. The King was set upon the divorce and was currently prepared to allow considerable latitude to criticism of the Church. More's attitude on both was straightforward: the integrity of Christ's body on earth under the headship of his vicar, the Pope, must be preserved at all costs and for any monarch to defy the Holy Father would not only imperil his own immortal soul but would damage the fabric of Christendom. Henry had, on more than one occasion, discussed the divorce privately with Sir Thomas and had come to realise that he could look for no support in that quarter. The two men had reached an agreement that More would remain silent on the great matter and that the King would not press him for public support. However, the Lord Chancellor's presence in Council when sensitive matters were discussed could only be an embarrassment and Howard excluded him from the board on several occasions. In February 1530 More was deprived of one of his closest friends and supporters: Cuthbert Tunstall was translated to the see of Durham and provided with plenty of work to keep him busy in the border regions. His place at London was taken by John Stokesley, a contemporary of Wolsey's at Magdalen, an active agent in securing the divorce and pliant on many aspects of Church reform.

CHAPTER 22

Out of Control

Life at the political centre was entering a new and distinctive phase. The high tension at court, the fluctuations of policy, the feverish activity and the making and breaking of reputations that marked the years 1530–33 were the results of two new phenomena: royal initiative and court rivalries. The quest for some means of extricating Henry from one marriage and projecting him into another dominated all policy-making. The more the ardent wooer was frustrated in his dynastic and carnal desires by a helpless Pope, 'intransigent' ecclesiastics, 'incompetent' councillors, scheming supporters of Catherine, and a hostile public opinion, the more stubborn and irascible he became, the more he intervened in the work of government generally, the more susceptible he was to the ideas of new men who offered innovative or radical solutions. As Henry became increasingly desperate individuals in court and Council vied earnestly and frenetically with each other to win favour or avoid the sovereign's wrath. They thrust their way into the large void left by the departure of the Cardinal's bulky figure. They coagulated into groups and dispersed to form other combinations.

Historians intent on tracing a pattern in the events which led to the political Reformation have tended to portray Henry as either at the mercy of his advisers and willing to do anything to secure the divorce or ruthlessly controlling people and events so that they delivered the results he demanded. Reality requires that we shun the temptation to systematise and to provide neat answers. The King's will certainly brooded over all. It always had done but now the psychological power surging from the nation's political centre was more puissant. Henry was less susceptible to the distractions of his younger days – sport, courtly festivities and games of international prestige. The hypochondriac monarch was beginning to feel and to fear the pain of the vein inflammation (cellulitis) which presaged his later, more severe condition. Above all, he was emotionally involved. This undoubtedly led to his constant interference in those affairs of state he had previously left to others but it did not result in consistency or a clearly conceived political strategy. Henry's Janus attitude towards Wolsey well illustrates the dilemma into which he was driven. His degrading of the Cardinal was an attack not on the minister who had managed his affairs for two decades; still less on an old, much-loved companion; it was an assault on the Pope's representative. The voltage of royal wrath was intended to run along the cables connecting the English Church to Rome. It was simply unfortunate that Wolsey took the full force of the shock and the King went out of his way on several occasions to assure the fallen servant that there was 'nothing personal' in his actions.

Of course, there was very much that was personal in the actions of Wolsey's court and conciliar foes. Among them there was unity only on one issue: the Cardinal, objectionable in himself and representative of an ecclesiastical hierarchy too powerful in the state, had to be forced out and, more problematically, kept out of power. Anne, Norfolk, Suffolk and their associates, for varied individual reasons, did all in their power to poison Henry's mind against the Cardinal. Given the King's ambiguous attitude this was not easy, particularly when it became painfully clear that they were no more successful than their rival in resolving the King's great matter. When central policy issues led on to attacks on the clergy, encouragement of radical/heretical thinkers, the threat of real severance from Rome, and the promotion of humble unknowns to the inner sanctum of government any agreement as to objectives and means evaporated. Thus arose the confusion, the tension, the mutual recriminations, the suspicion and the occasional panic which marked the period between the fall of Wolsey and the rise of Cromwell.

Now, for the first time in the reign, we can use the word 'faction' in relation to the political life of the court. Henry made it known that 'he had determined to take the management of his own affairs and had appointed several councillors'.[20] To assert his presence, the King requisitioned Wolsey's residence of York Place and, within a few years, began to extend and embellish it to form the palace of Whitehall. The Cardinal protested strongly that the house belonged to the Archdiocese of York but such arguments cut little ice with his sovereign. Henry now had the permanent body of personal advisers he had so long desired. To give it greater dignity and coherence he revised the old office of President of the Council and, in February 1530, the Duke of Suffolk assumed this position. Interestingly, Brandon was only expected to chair meetings when the Treasurer and the Chancellor were absent from court. This arrangement confirms Norfolk's supremacy. He had succeeded in outranking Brandon and, as we have noted, he excluded More from meetings, even though the Lord Chancellor was the *de jure* leader of the Council. As for Brandon, his attendances were so irregular that the office of President of the Council lapsed after a few months. Henry, totally absorbed by the divorce issue, summoned to attend him and displayed favour towards men who were sympathetic to his cause; men like Robert Ratcliffe, created Earl of Sussex at the end of 1529, Edmund Bray (cousin of Lord Chamberlain Sandys) raised to the peerage at the same time, and Anne Boleyn's father who now became Earl of Wiltshire and Ormond.

Howard set about creating a conciliar inner core, an aristocratic faction such as he had always believed should exercise power under and on behalf of the Crown. His principal supporters were the Marquess of Exeter, the Earls of Wiltshire and Sussex, Lords Darcy, Hussey and Sandys, Sir William Fitzwilliam (who had taken over from More as Chancellor of the Duchy of Lancaster and was one of those who owed his rise to Wolsey) and Stephen Gardiner, soon to be Bishop of Winchester. Suffolk was excluded as much by his own indolence and his distaste for the divorce as by Norfolk's animosity. Among those who did not enjoy Howard's confidence were the Earl of Oxford who, perhaps, inclined too much to religious novelties, Lord Mountjoy, More's old friend and, as Queen Catherine's Chancellor not dependable, and the Earls of Northumberland and Shrewsbury who were probably happy to be preoccupied with their northern estates in these troubled times. Yet even within Howard's caucus there was little personal unity and even less agreement over policy. There were those, notably Henry Courtenay whose wife was a close friend of the Queen, who were less emotionally committed to the annulment of the royal marriage. But the main problem was that noblemen who had effectively been kept out of the nation's affairs for twenty years had no training in and little stomach for the hard work of government. And these were the men who were faced with a conundrum well beyond the wit of men of mediocre political talent.

They certainly did not enjoy the unqualified confidence of the King. Holbein's image of the bull-like Henry – four square, dominant, aggressive (itself, of course, a work of propaganda) – all too easily dominates our assessment of his character. That character changed with age, declining health, emotional pressures and external circumstances. In 1530 what was important about England's sovereign was that he was a middle-aged man in love with a young woman in her prime. He was experiencing all the silliness, frustration, joy, pain, hope, anxiety and need to prove himself that accompany that situation. Eagerly he grabbed at every way out of his religious and moral stalemate. Impatiently he pressured his Council to come up with new ideas and urged his ambassadors in Rome to threaten, cajole and promise whatever was necessary to free him from Catherine. Petulantly he harangued his advisers when their barren deliberations failed to offer any real solution to his problem. Norfolk's only playable card at the moment was Cranmer, masterminding the consultation process with English and foreign universities and also researching ancient documents dealing with royal-papal relations. While encouraging this activity with displays of kingly generosity towards Cranmer, Henry kept other options open. Certainly he was not ready to discard Wolsey. The wily and industrious Cardinal had extricated him from difficult situations in the past and might still have some shots in his locker.

The 'geographical' tussle between Wolsey and Norfolk continued unabated with their relative positions reversed. Now it was the ex-Chancellor who was moving heaven and earth to get back to court and the Duke who was equally determined to exile his rival to the North. After the first shock of his disgrace and despite the anxiety he still felt for his colleges, Wolsey's confidence gradually returned. He knew how tense the atmosphere was at court and knew that he enjoyed a rapport with Henry that Howard lacked. Personal relationships counted for a great deal with the lyricist of 'Pastance with Good Company' and the Cardinal was much more concerned about Anne's influence than her uncle's. Mistress Boleyn's antipathy towards the Cardinal has almost certainly been exaggerated but he urged Cromwell (and probably other allies) to ascertain her true feelings and he was delighted when, in January 1530, he received, as well as a token of the King's regard, a remembrance from the Lady Anne.[21]

In early February Wolsey scored an important victory. Without consulting the Council Henry gave him permission to move from Esher to Richmond, where he took up residence, not in the old palace, but a small house called the Lodge. The importance lay not in the fact that this brought the exile ten miles closer to the court, but that it located him on the Thames, whence a royal barge could, at any time, convey him to Westminster or Greenwich. Little more than a month later he removed to a more commodious residence which John Colet had built for himself adjacent to the Charterhouse at Sheen, where, according to Cavendish, he daily sat in holy discourse with the monks. The second triumph took the form of a complete pardon granted by the King on 12 February. This galvanised Norfolk into more urgent importunity. He petitioned the King and persuaded him to order the Archbishop of York to visit his province. Before Henry had a chance to change his mind, he sent a directive to Wolsey ordering his immediate departure. The Cardinal tried bargaining: if the Duke was concerned about his servant's proximity to the court he would willingly remove himself to Winchester. Norfolk was obdurate: the Archbishop must go north. Wolsey procrastinated. Only on 28 March, when Henry sent some of his own people to help the Cardinal pack and wrote letters to the leaders of the northern society to prepare them for his coming, did Wolsey accept that he must move. Another week passed and still the cavalcade had not set out. This sent Norfolk into one of his rages. He despatched a messenger with these words: 'Show him that if he go not away shortly, I will, rather [than that] he should tarry still, tear him with my teeth!'[22]

The man selected as the go-between for these sensitive exchanges was Thomas Cromwell. The forty-four-year-old lawyer was in the process of successfully making the transition from Cardinal's court to King's court and it took courage and genuine loyalty to be known in royal circles as the representative of the fallen minister. To say that it also took careful calculation is not to detract form the protégé's sincerity. Had Wolsey's fall been total no friend, however devoted, would have dared to defend him before the House of Commons, before Norfolk and before the King. But, as we have seen, Wolsey's fall was not total and the shrewd Cromwell realised that he might even gain favour by appealing to the affection Henry still felt for his master. He 'willily defended' the Cardinal in parliament. When Wolsey fell ill in January he moved the King to send the royal physicians and further tokens of friendship. How much access Cromwell actually had to the King in these months we cannot know but it is clear that, as Wolsey's representative, Henry insisted that he be treated honourably. Thus, while others furthered their careers by hastening to abandon the Cardinal, Cromwell achieved the same end by the opposite means.

Thomas Cromwell's rapid metamorphosis from legal adviser to a minister who died beneath the shadow of the axe into the most powerful man in England under the Crown has puzzled historians as much as it did contemporaries. With no powerful patronage and no personal following, with neither a university education nor the accomplishments of a courtier, without noble birth or family connections, he penetrated the closed ranks of Norfolk's aristocratic faction and grasped the standard of 'chief minister' which Howard believed himself to have appropriated. Foes and admirers in the sixteenth century both fell to the temptation to seek simple answers which would explain the phenomenon. In 1535 Chapuys told his master what a surprise Cromwell's emergence had been and asserted that it had been the result of a sudden royal whim. Towards the end of 1530, he explained, Cromwell, having a dispute with Sir John Wallop, a royal ambassador and a gentleman of the Privy Chamber, 'asked and obtained an audience from King Henry, whom he addressed in such flattering terms and eloquent language – promising to make him the richest king in the world – that the king at once took him into his service and made him councillor, though his appointment was kept secret for four months'.[23]

Chapuys's hostile explanation is no less unreliable than Foxe's partisan explanation of the rise of this 'champion of the Gospel'. According to the martyrologist, Cromwell gathered important information against the bishops which would prove that their allegiance to the King was sub-ordinated to that that they pledged to the Pope. But Henry was reluctant to give the lawyer audience because he had been defamed 'by certain in authority about the king, for his rude manner and homely [i.e. unpleasant] dealing in defacing the monks' houses and in handling of their altars'. Only when he was brought into Henry's presence by Lord Russell (whose life Cromwell had, supposedly, saved several years before) was he able to make his revelations. On hearing them, the King immediately despatched him to the convocation house, armed with the royal signet, to confront the spiritual peers face-to-face.[24]

The real explanation, as is usual in such cases, is more prosaic: Cromwell got where he did by virtue of his own talents and the King's recognition of those talents. The same Chapuys who sneered at the minister's cynical exploitation of the King had, at an earlier stage in their relationship when he thought it prudent to butter up the new prodigy, praised Cromwell to his face in words which were probably more than empty flattery:

> I said I had often regretted he did not come under his master's knowledge and favour at the same time as the cardinal, for being as he was a more able and talented man than the latter and there being now so many opportunities to gain credit and power, he might undoubtedly have become a greater man than the cardinal, whilst the king's affairs would have gone on much better.[25]

Intellectually Cromwell outshone most of the established members of the Council. The leaders of the aristocratic establishment were place-seekers who attempted to rank themselves among the King's advisers as of right. Cromwell achieved his supremacy, like Wolsey and More, by virtue of his own qualities. If he was more dynamic than the Cardinal and the Lord Chancellor it was in large measure because he had had to propel his career without the advantages they had enjoyed. His adolescent feet had not been set on an academic/ecclesiastical ladder or a judicial/legal stairway. Yet he had missed out on little that a university or Inns of Court training would have provided. His agile and voracious mind explored the writings of ancient and contemporary masters and he possessed a sizeable library. In the summer of 1530 we find Edmund Bonner (currently Wolsey's chaplain, he would follow a well-signposted career path culminating in the bishopric of London) seeking to borrow from him Italian books by Petrarch and Castiglione. He easily outshone the courtiers and most of the scholars of the royal household and he carried off his erudition with the wit and good humour that always appealed to the King.

Mere cleverness and companionability would not have won him a seat at the Council board. What Cromwell did was catch the attention of a king grappling with seemingly intractable problems by bringing a new imagination to those problems. Like Cranmer, he entered the circles of power as a fresh breeze blowing into rooms stuffy with the stale odour of tired minds, frustrated desires and failed remedies. Cromwell's reading encompassed the wisdom and speculations of Aristotle, the political thinkers of the Italian Renaissance, and the contemporary humanist and Lutheran apologists. He had arrived at a rationalistic view of the separation of Church and State which owed much to the fourteenth-century Marsiglio of Padua who, in his *Defensor Pacis*, had bidden the clergy to stick to the exercise of their spiritual office, abandon the distractions attendant upon ownership of property and enforcement of law and to submit themselves in all things lawful to the princes to whom God had entrusted temporal power. To one not trained to give awesome respect to fifteen centuries of Church tradition it became self-evident that many of the world's current ills (including Henry's quarrel with the Pope) derived from the usurped temporal power of the ecclesiastical hierarchy.

Such were the complaints being taken up, with varying degrees of ferocity, by humanists and reformers – and being listened to, with varying degrees of attention, by rulers. Simon Fish had pointed out that the clergy 'exempt themselves from the obedience of your grace and translate all rule, power, lordship, authority, obedience and dignity from your grace unto them'. He singled out the monasteries as houses of idle 'loobies', sitting on great wealth which might be better applied.[26] As we have seen, the possibility of appropriating monastic wealth was an idea the Council had already toyed with, perhaps because the King had shown favour to Fish. Another book Henry had read was Tyndale's *Obedience of a Christian Man*. It seems likely that Cromwell noted the King's approval. A few months later his Netherlands' agent, Stephen Vaughan, tried to press Tyndale into becoming an apologist for the King's great matter. Anne Boleyn had introduced her royal lover to the *Obedience* and, as with the *Supplication*, Henry had found much in it to support his own prejudices. Tyndale pointed out all that the King of England had been inveigled into doing for the papacy – and for what? Like other monarchs throughout Christendom he had become a mere shadow 'having nothing to do in the world but when our holy father needeth help'.

The king ought to count what he hath spent in the pope's quarrel, since he was king. The first voyage cost upon fourteen hundred thousand pounds. Reckon since what hath been spent by sea and land between us and Frenchmen and Scots, and then in triumphs, and in embassies, and what hath been sent out of the realm secretly, and all to maintain our holy father; and I doubt not but that will surmount the sum of forty or fifty hundred thousand pounds: for we had no cause to spend one penny, but for our holy father. The king therefore ought to make them pay this money every farthing, and fetch it out of their mitres, crosses, shrines, and all manner treasure of the church, and pay it to his commons again: not that only which the cardinal and his bishops compelled the commons to lend, and made them swear, with such an ensample of tyranny as we never before thought on; but also all that he hath gathered of them: or else by the consent of the commons to keep it in store for the defence of the realm. Yea, the king ought to look in the chronicles, what the popes have done to kings in time past, and make them restore it also; and ought to take away from them their lands which they have gotten with their false prayers, and restore it unto the right heirs again; or with consent and advisement turn them unto the maintaining of the poor, and bringing up of youth virtuously, and to maintain necessary officers and ministers for to defend the commonwealth.[27]

Cromwell will have been very circumspect about expressing at court views which were already creating divisions within the household but he appeared to the King (or perhaps to Norfolk) as a man who had ideas and contacts which might prove useful, in solving His Majesty's matrimonial and financial problems.

He was also already recognised as a workaholic with considerable legal talents. In 1527 when he and Gardiner had both been working for Wolsey, he wrote to the Secretary excusing his tardiness in returning from Ipswich post-haste. With a slight touch of asperity he enumerated the documents he was working on in connection with the new college:

That is to say, a deed of gift from his Grace to his said College of the late monasteries of Felixstowe, Rumburgh, and Bromehill; the King's letters patents of assent to the suppression of the same late monasteries; the King's letters patents of assent to the Pope; his bull of exemption of the said College; the King's letters patents of licence for the appro- priation of the benefices belonging to the said late monasteries; a deed of gift from the Duke of Norfolk to my lord's Grace of the said late monastery of Felixstowe; a release from the Prior and Convent of Rochester of all their right, title, and patronage of, in, or to the same late prior of Felixstowe; a release from the Abbot and Convent of Saint Mary's in York of all their right and title in or to the late Priory of Rumburgh; a release from my Lord of Oxford of all his right and title in the late Priory of Bromehill; and a release from the French Queen and the Duke of Suffolk of all their right and title in the Manors of Sayes court and Bickling, and in the late Priory of Snape: all which [documents] be not yet in a readiness nor perfected.[28]

Nor was it only in his service to Wolsey that Cromwell had given evidence of his tidy mind. Within days of joining the 1529 parliament he was being called upon to draft bills which cut out excess verbiage and were models of legal precision.

For the moment, however, his preoccupation lay in helping his master back into favour. That sometimes entailed some straight speaking. Wolsey, making a very slow progress towards his archdiocese, could not refrain from the habits of twenty years in power. He was determined to impress his splendour and importance on the towns and villages through which he passed. Not only did he travel with a sizeable entourage, but a veritable army of carpenters, stonemasons, glaziers, locksmiths, painters, plasterers and furnishers had to go on ahead to ensure that all his residences were of a sufficiently high standard of comfort and splendour to receive him. The impression given to the Cardinal's enemies was that he was not a whit chastened and that he intended to demonstrate in the North that he was still a prince of the Church, due almost equal respect to the King. Cromwell sought to impress on him the need for discretion:

> Sir, some there be that doth allege ye doth keep too great a house and family, and that ye are continually building. For the love of God, therefore, I yet again, as I often times have done, most heartily beseech your Grace to have respect to everything, and considering the time, to refrain yourself for a season from all manner of buildings more than mere necessity requireth; which I assure your Grace shall cease and put to silence some persons that much [prate] of the same.[29]

The semi-royal progress which had set out at the beginning of April had only reached Peterborough by the 14th, where, in the abbey, he performed the Maundy Thursday ritual of washing the feet of fifty-nine poor men.* It was another two weeks before he arrived at Southwell. The palace was still in the process of being vastly and hastily refurbished for his coming and it was a further six weeks before he could take up residence. Once installed, he sumptuously played the role of lord of the manor, feasting the local gentry, distributing alms to the needy, hearing civil cases, handing down judgements and 'not sparing for any costs where he might make peace and amity, which purchased him much love and friendship in the country'.[30] He also paid scrupulous attention to his archiepiscopal duties; visiting churches, saying mass, examining fabric, talking with priests and laity.

Much of this very public display of conscientious pastoral care might be explained as the attention given by a father in God belatedly making up for years of neglect. There would have been nothing unusual about that. Fox and Warham were among statesmen-bishops who had sought release from secular politics in order to devote the last years to their ecclesiastical duties. The difference between such bishops and Wolsey was that Wolsey did not go willingly. Not only did he dawdle his way northwards, but having reached Southwell, just inside the boundary of his province, he settled there for the summer and the elaborate building works set in train there indicate that this had always been his intention. Daily he awaited his recall and it was not until mid-September that he resumed his journey towards York.

---

*The figure is recorded by Cavendish and is probably incorrect. The number of paupers to whom the Cardinal ministered would, by custom, have corresponded to his own age and it is very unlikely that Wolsey was born in 1471.

Nor was he politically idle during these months. In fact, he was engaged in vigorous intrigue. So were his enemies and the problem of determining just what Wolsey was up to arises from the fact that most of the information available was gathered, interpreted and, where necessary, manufactured by his foes. The charge levelled against the Cardinal was that, while pretending to continue in support of the King's proceedings regarding the divorce, he had secretly thrown in his lot with Catherine's supporters at home and abroad in a cynical attempt to propel the government into such confusion that Henry would be forced to summon him to resume his former position to sort out the mess.

He was certainly far from dispensable to the new regime, as was demonstrated in mid-June. Late one night after the household had all retired two mounted messengers came clattering into the courtyard having ridden hard from London. They carried with them a document urgently requiring Wolsey's signature and seal and they demanded an immediate audience. As he pored over the paper in his night attire the Cardinal may well have been alarmed, not so much by its content, as by its tone and nature. It bore his own name at the very top (before even those of Norfolk and Suffolk) and it was followed by the cognomens and titles of eighty leading churchmen, noblemen and parliamentarians. The King had summoned several of these notables to court a few days before to authorise a virtual ultimatum to Clement VII. Some of them were so disturbed by what they were being asked to assent to that the document had to be redrafted. However, Henry was too impatient to have the papal legate's signature and it was the letter in its original form with which Wolsey was now confronted. He complied and within hours the messengers were hurrying on their way to collect other autographs. This forthright letter was the last attempt to persuade Clement to give judgement in Henry's favour. It stated (in its final form):

> We now have a king most eminent for his virtues, seated upon the throne of his ancestors by right undoubted and unquestionable, who would entail lasting peace and uninterrupted tranquillity on his realms if he leaves a son to succeed him from lawful and true marriage; nor will that be possible unless your holiness will by your authority, pronounce the same sentence concerning his former marriage, which so many learned men have also delivered. But if your holiness, whom we justly call our father, shall, by refusing to comply herein, esteem us as castaways, and resolve to leave us orphans; we can make no other construction of it but that the care of ourselves is committed to our own hands, and that we are left to seek our remedy elsewhere . . .[31]

The declaration was deliberately vague about the 'desperate remedies' Henry and his advisers might apply and doubtless there was an element of bluff in the threat of some severing of relations with Rome but the fact that the Cardinal-Legate associated himself with it shows that he was – to all outward appearances – setting his loyalty to the King above that which he owed to the Pope.

The two young men entrusted with this sensitive mission were William Brereton, a groom of the chamber, and Thomas Wriothesley, the one chosen for his closeness to the King, the other for his familiarity with Wolsey. Wriothesley's family connections had gained him early placement in the Cardinal's household. He was no more than eighteen (possibly younger) when he was placed under Cromwell's tutelage. Occupied at first in menial tasks (a sort of Tudor office junior), he gradually worked his way up. In terms of industry and ambition he could not have had better role models than his master and his master's master. He showed himself to be a quick learner. As a clerk he worked with speed and accuracy – vital qualifications when we consider the sheer volume of paper that must have flowed daily from the desks of Wolsey and Cromwell. By 1525 (when he was twenty) he was acting as a secretary to the Cardinal and was writing letters to the King and the leading men of the realm. This brought him into close contact with Stephen Gardiner and it may have been through him that Wriothesley gained his first position in the Tudor administrative machine.

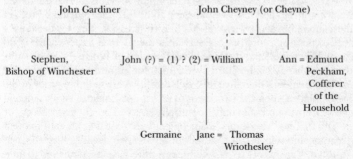

Kinship connections counted for everything in the inner circles of society and sometime in the late 1520s Wriothesley made a useful marriage. Stephen Gardiner had a nephew, Germaine, who also acted as his personal secretary. Thomas worked closely with Germaine and knew him well. He also knew Germaine's half-sister Jane Cheyney who was related to Edmund Peckham, Cofferer of the Royal Household. In this senior position, answerable directly to the Comptroller of the Household, Peckham had the appointment of several court positions. A marriage was arranged between Thomas Wriothesley and Jane Cheyney and soon afterwards (May 1530), appropriate strings were pulled to obtain for him a position as Clerk of the Signet, one of the junior members of the King's office. It is probable that Sir Thomas Cheyney, a long-serving courtier-diplomat and close companion of the King, was Wriothesley's new brother-in-law. He had thus successfully made the transition from Wolsey's entourage to the King's and was well placed to draw himself to Henry's attention. He was an obvious person to choose when a vigorous young man was needed to ride hard to Southwell to obtain the Cardinal's endorsement of the King's hard-line policy.

But was Wolsey sincerely committed to that policy or was he covertly working against it? His enemies were eager to prove the latter. But did they discover evidence, or manufacture it or employ agents to entrap their quarry? These are the questions that hang over the last months of Wolsey's life and his final disgrace and they have been answered differently by historians and biographers over the years.

Two facts are beyond dispute. The first is that, following his pardon, the Cardinal maintained a vigorous correspondence with anyone at home and abroad who he thought might aid his restoration and that he was certainly indiscreet in some of his dealings. The second is that, having recovered his almost boundless egotism, Wolsey believed that his recall was inevitable. He made no show of humility and, so far from donning the sackcloth and ashes of repentance, he paraded himself before the world in all his accustomed finery – to the frustration of Cromwell and other friends who were trying to engineer his rehabilitation. Wolsey trusted in the King's friendship and his own indispensability. To that extent he brought nemesis upon himself by making his foes' task easier. Yet it was Henry's indecisiveness as much as his servant's hubris that hastened the final tragedy. When the King restored a large portion of Wolsey's possessions and topped this by lending him over £1,000 for his northward progress he made him wealthier than the Duke of Norfolk – very tangible proof of the value he placed upon the two rivals. The Cardinal, whose eager demand for news from court could only be partially satisfied, might be forgiven for believing that his 'temporary' banishment was almost at an end and that the relationship which had endured for almost two decades was about to be restored. Various of Henry's comments must have been relayed to him, such as the angry outburst that all his councillors put together did not have the brains of Wolsey.

He maintained his diplomatic contacts as though he were still at the helm of national affairs. While he was at Richmond he held meetings with the French and Imperial ambassadors and thereafter he kept up his correspondence with them. The principal object of these exchanges was to persuade the foreign sovereigns that he could be of service to them if they would assist him back into his king's good graces.

In all this he could scarcely avoid treating of the annulment issue. His own feeling, as he confessed during his last days, was that Henry's position was impossible and that he should not have got himself into it in the first place. Wolsey's dreams of restitution rested upon the failure of the King's trusted advisers to deliver an understanding with Rome which would permit him to swap wives, after which the Cardinal would be called upon to untangle the complications of royal affairs as he had done in the past. He could not, of course, express such hopes and opinions. Any intervention had to be by winks and nudges. In June Eustace Chapuys, the Imperial ambassador, was the recipient of one of these innuendoes:

> While writing the above I have received a letter from the cardinal's physician in which he tells me in rather obscure terms that his master, not knowing exactly the state of the queen's affairs, cannot give any special advice upon them; that if he could get the fuller information he would give counsel and directions . . . and that it seemed to him that now was the time to take stronger measures and call in the assistance of the secular arm . . . The physician did not further explain the cardinal's meaning, and therefore I am at a loss to interpret his message and wishes.[32]

No one knew better than Wolsey the need for circumspection. Over the years he had employed scores of agents and informers to intercept correspondence, spy on suspicious characters and extract information by bribery or threats. Now that Cromwell was no longer at his right hand he relied upon his physician (referred to by Chapuys) as amanuensis and chief intelligence gatherer. It was this man, Agostino Agostini, who was to prove his Achilles heel.

Agostini was a Venetian who was well-travelled, well-connected, had settled in London some eight years previously, numbered several leaders of English society among his patients and, soon after his arrival, had entered Wolsey's employ. There was nothing unusual about the Cardinal employing him in matters extra-medical and Agostini's command of language and easy access to the sickrooms of the great and powerful made him an excellent intelligence officer. In January 1530, for example, he was sent to tend a French emissary, Jean Joaquim de Passano, Sieur de Vaux, who was ill in London. Wolsey reposed high hopes in his French connections as he hoped that Joaquim had been sent over to intercede for him with Henry. It seems more likely that the Sieur de Vaux had arrived to assess the situation and to calculate whether Francis would gain any advantage from coming to Wolsey's aid.

When hinting to foreign diplomats that the time was ripe for a vigorous prosecution of Catherine's cause, because the opposition to it was in disarray, he was stating no more than the truth. The Council was divided and cracks were even appearing within Norfolk's own following. Over and again the recall of parliament was postponed because the government had no clearly defined borders in which to engage it. Anne, despairing of ever being lawfully united with her royal lover, rounded on Howard for his incompetence and the first signs of estrangement between uncle and niece can now be discerned. It would be difficult to overemphasise the panic and confusion at court in the middle months of 1530. Chapuys recorded a conversation with Norfolk in April. The Duke asked anxiously how interested the Emperor really was in his aunt's matrimonial problems. If Henry went ahead and married Anne in defiance of Rome what would Charles V do? Might he invade England? If we can believe that Norfolk really did entertain the possibility of such a catastrophe we can understand what a turbulent state his thoughts and emotions were in. The ambassador's reply was scarcely reassuring. His master, he said, would have no need to take such direct action because Henry's own subjects would rise up against him. Howard knew that there was an element of truth in this chilling observation. The heads of the houses of Tudor and Howard were united in pursuing a dynastic policy which was as unpopular as it was, seemingly, incapable of achievement.

The difficulty historians have in trying to sort out the complex interaction of personalities is probably an accurate reflection of what those personalities were themselves experiencing at the time. Norfolk needed all-round vision if he was to maintain his precarious supremacy. He certainly kept a close watch on all Wolsey's machinations and it may well have been in response to the Cardinal's claim that his party was at sixes and sevens that he reverted to his old idea of the ultimatum to Rome signed by as many of the nation's leaders as could be quickly found.

As far as it was in his power to do so, Wolsey laboured to destabilise the Howard regime. In May Cromwell warned him that the King knew of his attempts 'to make sedition between him and my lord of Norfolk'.[33] Such activity will not have worried Henry, who had his own reservations about the way the Duke was running the show. What would have angered him was any suggestion that the Cardinal was trying to undermine Anne and sabotage the divorce campaign. Had Wolsey unequivocally changed sides, or let it be known that he considered the King's liaison with Anne to be sinful or even merely politically undesirable, that would have destroyed any possibility of his rehabilitation. Can we really believe that the man whose phenomenal reign as royal deputy had rested on giving Henry what he wanted had now so far taken leave of his senses as to intrigue with Catherine's supporters in order to frustrate the King's passionate desire?

The fact that he signed the June letter – even if he had, as it were, a pistol held to his head – indicates that he wanted Henry to believe that he still enjoyed his cardinal's support over the annulment. Yet, at the same time, he was, according to Chapuys, sending daily messages 'to inquire how the queen's cause is progressing and why it is not more energetically pushed'. The Imperial ambassador opined that Wolsey saw the swift burial of the divorce issue as his best means of regaining power.[34] As papal legate and ex-'foreign minister' no one knew better than Wolsey how hopeless the King's cause was. He had long believed that the divorce plot was a bridge too far and may well have thought, as Chapuys suggested, that the sooner Henry could be brought back to political reality the sooner the affairs of the state could be restored to an even keel (i.e. returned to his care). Furthermore, if Wolsey entertained any doubt whatsoever about Anne's unpopularity this will have been dispersed during his slow journey through Middle England, when he talked with all sorts and conditions of men. Sympathy and support for Catherine were almost universal. From his point of view – and from the point of view of most observers in the summer of 1530 – all the cards were stacked against the King and the Howard–Boleyn faction.

However, the Cardinal could not afford to give his enemies any ammunition they could use against him. He never provided Catherine's faction with any guidance about how best to conduct their campaign – or if he did, it was never produced in evidence against him, which is unlikely. His urgent entreaties to Chapuys were almost certainly delivered orally by messengers and not committed to writing. At the same time the Archbishop was in direct contact with the men in power. He fawned on Norfolk, seeking his good offices with the King, and ensuring him of his lack of interest in regaining power. In October one of the Cardinal's gentlemen attendants, Thomas Arundel (who would later show himself a feverish political intriguer), reported back that he had been rebuffed by the Duke who was convinced from approaches his adversary had made directly to the King that he 'desired as much authority as ever'.[35] Moreover, Wolsey was not lacking in that oil necessary to lubricate the wheels of faction: he made, through Cromwell, several land grants to prominent courtiers. Wolsey was playing a double game and it had one objective: to bring down his rivals. If the imperialist party kept up their pressure they would either succeed in removing Anne from the equation or they would expose the inability of the Howard–Boleyn faction to satisfy their royal master. One way or the other Henry would move against Anne's relatives and would have nowhere else to turn but to his faithful old minister.

Norfolk's main reaction was to suborn Wolsey's servants. The Cardinal kept the providers of post horses extremely busy and his messengers passed in a never-ending stream between his archbishopric and the royal court. This, ironically, may well have made it easier for his enemies. Constant contact with those far better able than Wolsey to offer patronage and financial inducements may well have loosened the loyalty of some of the Cardinal's men. In July Norfolk claimed to have 'turned' three of his rival's agents. He volunteered no names. Could one of them have been Thomas Cromwell?

CHAPTER 23

End of an Era

There is evidence of some slight cooling of the relationship between Wolsey and his former right-hand man. The Cardinal was annoyed that Cromwell did not travel north to report in person and he suspected that his agent was not doing everything in his power to save the colleges at Ipswich and Oxford from confiscation. Cromwell denied any derogation of duty although he was unable to save Ipswich from the royal plunderer. Until the very end he attended closely to the business affairs of Wolsey's foundations. A sad letter of 22 November 1529 from Dr Capon to Cromwell describes the arrival of a posse of commissioners sent to Ipswich by the King to parcel up and pack on to carts all the plate, vestments and jewels which the Cardinal had appropriated for the use of the college. Pathetically, Capon passed on the assurances he had been given about this rich booty: 'they say how the king desireth but to have the sight of the foresaid parcels and, that done, they suppose the king will return all the same again to the college'.[36] In fact, the sight of all those silver-gilt chalices, ewers and pyxes, gem-studded monstrances and costly embroidered altar coverings stirred quite different intentions in the mind of the cash-starved King. For the first time he set eyes on the crated-up wealth of a tiny part of the English church and could envisage in imagination what an Aladdin's cave of treasure was represented by the wealth of all those abbeys, priories, friaries and nunneries as yet unmolested. The following summer Cromwell had to pass on the sad news about Wolsey's educational establishments:

> . . . the king is determined to dissolve them and that new offices shall be found of all the land belonging to them . . . but whether his highness, after the dissolution of them, means to revive them again and found them in his own name I know not. Wherefore, I entreat your Grace to be content and let your prince execute his pleasure.[37]

For his part, Cromwell was busy cementing his position at court. The formalities of patronage were very clearly delineated. Any ambitious man had to attach himself to a master. Once a relationship had been entered into, usually by the swearing of an oath, the obligations of service and protection were accepted by both parties. Cromwell seems to have formally entered the King's service early in 1530. It is reasonable to assume that Henry appreciated the lawyer's gifts and the training he had received in Wolsey's household and was persuaded that Cromwell deserved something better than to be dragged out of the public arena in the train of his fallen patron. The new relationship did not imply frequent attendance at court. Henry VIII had hundreds of 'servants', some of whom seldom, if ever, came near Greenwich or Westminster. Cromwell's status meant that the King could call on him at any time to perform tasks quite unspecified in any pre-contract. However, it must have been Cromwell's legal skills that commended him to Henry. From time to time sovereign and subject will have had business to discuss together relating to the transference of Ipswich College to the Crown and to various other administrative matters which the King had previously negotiated directly with the Cardinal. Cromwell was obviously anxious to build on these occasional meetings but, for the time being, his visits to court were punctuation marks in the narrative of a busy legal and commercial life.

The tone of his letters to Wolsey suggests that Cromwell was beginning to find his old master an embarrassment. Trying to help someone who would not help himself or listen to sound advice was not only frustrating; it could hamper his own career prospects. The Cardinal frequently demanded Cromwell's personal attendance but the lawyer had his own affairs to attend to and also knew that it was vital to maintain his presence on the fringe of the court. One could never know when an unexpected conversation or chance encounter might prove profitable, when a valuable snippet of information might come one's way, when an opportunity might present itself to be seen by the King, or when a few days' absence might set one at a disadvantage. So he made his excuses to the Cardinal and wrapped them up in flowery phrases:

> I trust, verily, that your Grace doth perfectly think that I would be glad to see you and unfeignedly I would have seen your Grace long ere this, if I had not been [prevented] by importunate business; wherefore I [yet again] most humbly beseech your Grace of pardon, and though I am not with you in person, yet be ye assured I am, and during my life shall be, with your Grace in heart, spirit, prayer and service to the uttermost of my poor and simple power . . .[38]

There was a more fundamental difference between the descending churchman and the rising lawyer. In order to maximise his opportunities Cromwell had to show himself in favour of the divorce. He could have no part in any intrigues with Catherine of Aragon's supporters and this must have limited his usefulness to Wolsey. There was undoubtedly an element of cool calculation on Cromwell's part in determining just how much he could afford to be associated with his master's tactics and ambitions. Yet we cannot charge him with unadulterated opportunism: he stood by the Cardinal longer than most of Wolsey's other servants. He was constantly busy about the Cardinal's affairs; making arrangements for Wolsey's library, paying some of his bills, representing him in land disputes and looking after a variety of other legal and financial matters. These services often went unremunerated. At one point, in July 1530, Cromwell could claim, 'I am £1000 worse than I was when your troubles began.'[39] If that was not a wild exaggeration, Cromwell's devotion to his former patron was sacrificial indeed. How hurtful, therefore, must have been the niggling complaints he received and even more so the rumours that Wolsey had come to doubt him. In October he challenged the Cardinal directly:

I am informed your Grace hath in me some diffidence as if I did dissemble with you or procure anything contrary to your profit and honour. I much muse that your Grace should so think or report it secretly, considering the pains I have taken.[40]

Cromwell had a difficult tightrope to walk; impressing the men in power around the King with his legislative abilities and ideas while representing the interests of the man who was trying to topple them. Throughout these months during which the record is silent about his career we have to imagine this clever and amiable politique with an immense capacity for absorbing information, keeping himself informed of what was happening among the vying groups at court, in the Cardinal's household, in London's legal and mercantile fraternities, in various foreign capitals, and within the councils of the Lutherans and the secret gatherings of their English admirers. The Putney brewer's son turned adventurer, merchant and lawyer had developed a remarkable ability to be all things to all men. This is not to say that he was a shallow, unprincipled opportunist; rather that he had a disarming penchant for getting on well with almost everyone he met. It was the skill of the diplomat rather than the rogue and one which he certainly employed to personal advantage. As to his true relationship with the disgraced Cardinal, the final word came from the Imperial ambassador, Eustace Chapuys. Describing Cromwell's rise five years later, he noted, 'At his master's fall he behaved very well towards him.'[41]

One group with which Cromwell had established close links was a fellowship of evangelical intellectuals who had by now emerged, drawn largely from the fenland university which, according to his enemies, Wolsey had refused to purge. The new Lord Chancellor and his supporters among the conservative bishops made good the deficiency and the result was England's first religious exodus. Robert Barnes had theatrically made his escape, leaving a suicide note and a pile of clothes on the seashore before taking ship for the Low Countries. Others – Tyndale, George Joye, William Roye – were established in Lutheran centres from where they bombarded the home market with vernacular Scriptures and treatises. Some had already gone beyond the German reformer's position. Miles Coverdale, as well as preaching against penance and the worship of images, insisted (with Zwingli and the Swiss heretics) that the Holy Communion service was an act of memorial and not a repetition of Christ's sacrifice performed by the priest. Cromwell was in touch with these fugitives through the mediation of his friend and agent Stephen Vaughan, a zealous and headstrong evangelical, whom the more circum-spect Cromwell had to restrain from time to time. Hugh Latimer also enjoyed the lawyer's sympathetic encouragement if not his active patronage. This turbulent priest led a charmed life at this period of his career. Hounded by ecclesiastical enemies because of his unorthodox preaching, he was yet supported by several prominent courtiers who brought him to the King's attention as one who was in favour of the divorce. In March 1530 he was invited to preach at court and, to Henry's delight, offended at least one ecclesiastic who was opposed to the King's matrimonial proceedings. Henry's dealings with the likes of Latimer, Fish and Tyndale were always dictated by his personal interests. If a preacher or polemicist supported him over against the Pope, he was prepared to turn a blind eye to whatever outrageous heresies the man might espouse. Thus, he attempted to recruit Tyndale to the ranks of royal propagandists even though More was locked in fierce conflict with him. Only when the Bible translator came out firmly against the divorce did Henry fiercely turn against him.

It was not so with Anne Boleyn. Early in the next century a descendant of Sir Thomas Wyatt described Henry's break with Rome and the evangelical reformation thus:

> . . . it was the pleasure of God [that] this noble prince should . . . shake off that most unworthy yoke that long had been thrust upon us, contrary to the laws of God and those very ancient [laws] of our country [so that, together] with the Gospel, they both by him recovered their former force and vigour . . . this excellent lady [i.e. Anne Boleyn] showing him the way . . . both of them having the thread of the Gospel [as] their guide, by God put into their hands through her means who ever watched every opportunity for the same . . .[42]

In recent years the Lady Anne's role in supporting the cause of reform has been reassessed and now it is clear that to her must be given the credit for fostering that grouping of court evangelicals which would grow into a faction, surviving numerous vicissitudes, over the next twenty years until it was able to take power in the reign of Henry's son.[43] Anne not only read banned literature and commended it to her lover, she had the English New Testament read to her ladies, she was well versed in the works of French reformers, she protected the importers of Lutheran books, she patronised clergy and scholars of advanced views and encouraged within her entourage open theological debate.

The freedom enjoyed by Anne and her friends frustrated the enemies of radical religion and encouraged them to hope that she would never become queen, even if they dared not openly oppose the divorce. All the Boleyns were suspected of being unsound in matters of faith. George, Anne's brother, was an open advocate of reform. Chapuys later complained that whenever he dined with Lord Rochford his host tried to strike up a religious argument. Their father, Thomas, Earl of Wiltshire, was an eager patron of Erasmus who wrote for him a commentary on Psalm 23 in 1530. But Boleyn protégés of evangelical persuasion had to play carefully the game of courtly snakes and ladders. Take, for instance, the Barlows. William and John were both clerics who benefited handsomely from their Boleyn connection as Thomas rose in royal favour. In 1528 we find Anne writing to Wolsey and to the King in support of William Barlow, now her father's chaplain, for the living of Sundridge, Kent. The following year Henry issued a proclamation against Lutheran literature and among the polemical works specifically condemned was *The Burying of the Mass*, a virulent attack on Wolsey penned by one Jerome Barlow. This Barlow was a friend and colleague of Simon Fish (who, as we have already seen, was defended by Anne) and produced his tracts from the safety of foreign havens (Strasbourg and Antwerp). We do not know what the connection, if any, was between Jerome, William and John but it may be no coincidence that in 1531 William thought it advisable to publish an anti-Lutheran tirade, *A Dialogue Describing the Original Ground of These Lutheran Factions*. That this did not represent his sincere opinions emerged clearly as soon as a more tolerant official attitude emerged in the mid-30s, when, as Prior of Haverfordwest and successively Bishop of St Asaph and Bishop of St David's, he zealously enforced reform measures (supported by his brother, who was now Dean of Westbury). Throughout the troubled years ahead William became very adept at coat-turning, though he did eventually go into exile during the reign of Mary.

Even more significant was the extension of Anne's protection over a notorious nest of London heretics. In the same letter in which she approved William Barlow's preferment she asked relief for 'the parson of Honey Lane' who was in trouble for reading heretical books. All Hallows, Honey Lane, in the very heart of the City, was appropriately named at this time, for it was a veritable honeypot for people of unorthodox views. It was currently under investigation by Tunstall and More as a place for 'the secret sowing and setting forth of Lutheran heresies'. The 'parson' for whom Anne pleaded may have been the rector, Forman, who, while

Master of Queens', Cambridge, had been a member of the clandestine evangelical brotherhood, or his curate Thomas Garrett, similarly connected at Oxford. More identified these two clergy as the very hub of a trade in illicit books. Forman, he claimed, secretly imported and stored the volumes and Garrett was the leading colporteur who disseminated them among impressionable university students. Much to the Bishop's chagrin Forman's illicit activities were all carried out in the 'back of the shop'. When he sent agents to listen to the rector's sermons they could find no fault with them. More sourly observed that Forman had 'two faces in one hood'. However, the upholders of orthodoxy were determined to persevere until they could find evidence. It was this 'troubling' which encouraged the Honey Lane clergy to appeal to their friends at court. Little wonder that More should be horrified at the prospect of Anne Boleyn becoming queen.[44] Those with careers to make and reputations to protect had reason to be circumspect. The enemies of heresy were, at last, getting themselves organised. Charles Wriothesley, whose Chronicle entries were still very brief, had only these incidents of note to record for the years 1531–2:

HENRICI VIII. Anno 22.
This year was one burned at Maidstone for heresy and one Bilney, a priest, degraded and burned at Norwich for heresy.

HENRICI VIII. Anno 23.
This year, in November, on St Edmond's day, there was one convict of heresy which was some time a monk in St Edmondsbury, and was degraded in Paul's by the Bishop of London of the orders of priesthood, and so delivered to the Sheriffs of London; and the 4th day of December following he was burnt in Smithfield.

This year Mr Rees was beheaded at Tower Hill, and one that was his servant was drawn from the Tower of London to Tyburn, where he was hanged, his bowels burned, and his body quartered.

This year was a purser of London burnt in Smithfield for heresy, who bare a fagot at Paul's Cross the year afore.

The last day of April, 1532, one Bainham, a gentleman, was burnt in Smithfield for heresy.[45]

Foxe recorded a dozen Protestant martyrdoms during these opening months of the Reformation conflict and there were many more suspects who were examined and abjured their errors.

This increased vigilance by the ecclesiastical authorities provoked immediate reaction from those who complained against 'excessive' prosecutions for heresy. Scarcely a month now passed without some incident provoking the ire of the clergy and the indignation of their critics. One such, which began late in 1530 and rumbled on for eighteen months, became a cause célèbre scarcely less sensational than the Hunne case. William Tracy, a prominent member of the Gloucestershire gentry, made a will shortly before his death which unequivocally proclaimed his Lutheran convictions:

In the name of God, Amen. I William Tracy of Toddington in the county of Gloucester, esquire, make my testament and last will as hereafter followeth: First and before all other things, I commit myself to God and to his mercy, believing, without any doubt or mistrust, that by his grace, and the merits of Jesus Christ, and by the virtue of his passion and of his resurrection, I have and shall have remission of all my sins, and resurrection of body and soul, according as it is written, I believe that my Redeemer liveth, and that in the last day I shall rise out of the earth, and in my flesh shall see my Saviour: this my hope is laid up in my bosom.

And touching the wealth of my soul, the faith that I have taken and rehearsed is sufficient (as I suppose) without any other man's works or merits. My ground and belief is, that there is but one God and one mediator between God and man, which is Jesus Christ; so that I accept none in heaven or in earth to be mediator between me and God, but only Jesus Christ: all others to be but as petitioners in receiving of grace, but none able to give influence of grace: and therefore will I bestow no part of my goods for that intent that any man should say or do to help my soul; for therein I trust only to the promises of Christ: 'He that believeth and is baptized shall be saved, and he that believeth not, shall be damned.'[46]

Copies of the will were soon circulating in the radical underworld and, in 1531, William's son, Richard Tracy, a lawyer, a member of parliament and a friend or acquaintance of Thomas Cromwell, was summoned before convocation. The upshot of the examination was that Warham pronounced William a heretic and ordered him to be dug up. The chancellor of the diocese exceeded his instructions and had the corpse burned at the stake. This highly distressing event for the Tracy family was, as far as the ecclesiastical authorities were concerned, as stupid as it was insensitive. The fuel it added to the anticlerical flames kept them burning brightly for years.

The privileged denizens of the royal court were free from the prying eyes of the bishops and the prattling tongues of informers. Close attendants on the King like Anthony Denny, a gentleman of the Privy Chamber, and William Butts, the royal physician, could espouse radical views and even extend their protection to lesser men who shared their beliefs. It was unthinkable for those in the upper reaches of society to be proceeded against for heresy; only artisans and errant clergy went to the stake. That said, the growing sense of social instability could only add to the tensions and uncertainties which had marked the life of Henry's household since the end of the Wolsey era.

Thomas Cromwell could only be encouraged by the presence at court of people who shared his own attitudes towards the great issues of the day but his place in the household was not yet so invulnerable that he could afford to express his opinions freely, especially since those opinions were extremely radical. Cromwell was essentially a rationalist and this was why he sympathised with the challenge emanating from Germany and the centres of humanist thought. He was not impressed by arguments based on tradition or dogmatic assertion. As a man of affairs whose mind was not cluttered with academic baggage, he thought issues through from first principles. He saw clearly what all anticlericalists saw, that claims to privileged status unsupported by godly living were untenable. He understood that the ecclesiastical establishment was totally incapable of reforming itself. He knew that the conflict between temporal and spiritual authorities was one of power. He realised that society was in need of fundamental renewal and what excited him about Luther, as it excited many free-thinking intellectuals, was that the Wittenberg monk had established a theological schema which destroyed the basis of Rome's temporal power and had used that schema as the foundation of a practical programme of religious, political and social improvement.

The English Reformation has, not unreasonably, been described as 'the triumph of the laity'. A major strand in the new thinking was spun by Luther in 1520 in his *Address to the Christian Nobility of the German Nation*. It was his concept of the 'priesthood of all believers' which insisted that the distinction between clergy and laity was one of function and not status.

As many of us as have been baptized are all priests . . . without distinction for thus it is written in 1 Peter 2, 'Ye are a royal priesthood and a priestly kingdom' . . . We are priests, which is a far greater thing than being kings, for priesthood makes us worthy to stand before God and pray for others. For to stand before God's face is the prerogative of none except priests.[47]

This set a debate raging of which Cromwell will not have been ignorant. Luther's outraged opponents leaped into the arena to defend the traditional evaluation of the sacerdotal caste:

As the soul excels the body, so does the priesthood excel the lay estate. The priest has no equal on earth, for he who brings salvation to princes is greater than princes. The role of the laity is entirely subordinate: to provide for the physical needs of priests, and to defend and protect them. Indeed, priests are superior even to heavenly powers, for unto which angel or archangel did God ever promise that whatsoever they bound or loosed on earth would be bound or loosed in heaven? And Scripture refers to priests not as men but as angels (Malachi 2 v.7) or even gods (Psalm 82 vv.1,6). In short . . . the superiority of priests to people is not just permitted by Christianity, it is its very 'soul and foundation'.[48]

The explosion resulting from this head-on collision of irreconcilable doctrines threw up several issues of interest to legislators and theologians: whether clergy and laity are equal under the law; whether masses for the dead have any efficacy; whether the miracle of the altar is a fraud designed to enhance the power of the priesthood; whether secular governments have the right and duty to reform the Church; whether ecclesiastical bodies might own property in perpetuity; whether Church courts could maintain a separate existence independent of common law. Such were the topics of literary polemic and also of everyday debate among the intelligentsia.

In the autumn of 1530 the case for the common lawyers was trenchantly made by one of the pillars of the London bar. Christopher St German, who was approaching his three score years and ten, had long been a campaigner for restricting the competence of Church courts but had restricted his activities to the legal world. Now, he expanded on earlier Latin textbooks for law students into an exploration, *in English*, of the relationship between Church and State. *Doctor and Student* was immediately popular and was reprinted again and again, sometimes with additional material, over the next few years.

Cromwell and all the lawyers of his generation looked up with great respect to old St German and it was the veteran lawyer who, with careful logic and stunning directness, exposed the pretensions of the clergy. First of all he untangled the confusion of common and canon law: Church courts should only have competence in spiritual matters; ordination conferred no exemption from royal justice; issues concerning ecclesiastical property, criminal cases and civil suits involving clergy and laity should all be tried before the King's judges and, where appropriate, lay juries. The principle underlying this was that all temporal authority belonged to the Crown. If the clergy had usurped some of this authority or if earlier Kings had granted away some of their rights, the sovereign might – and should – resume such powers into his own hands. St German knew that if this thinking was followed to its logical conclusion the end results would be tyranny and the separation of Church and State. He avoided such *reductio ad absurdum* by insisting first on the sovereignty of statute law: it was, as later thinkers would more precisely define, the King in parliament who was supreme. Secondly, St German was not prepared to ditch the concept of the Christian commonwealth. The nation church and the nation state were synonymous; the former no less than the latter comprised all Henry's subjects because all were assumed to be Christians. It followed that 'Church' did not mean the clergy, who were only part of the company of believers. That led to the inevitable conclusion that the head of state must also be head of the church and, therefore, invested with spiritual oversight. And that meant issues of faith and order were subject to statute law. The impact of all this on the personnel and possessions of the English ecclesiastical establishment and upon the unity of Christendom was revolutionary. Small wonder that, between 1532 and 1534, St German was locked in public controversy with Thomas More. Small wonder, too, that Cromwell, seeking apologists for his reform programme, should enlist the old lawyer as a government propagandist.

Cromwell was at one with this daring ideology which interlocked with the theological innovations approved by members of Anne Boleyn's circle. Like More, he had a vision of a new society. Unlike More, he believed that it could be realised or, at least, that it was the responsibility of government to work towards it. Acting for Wolsey in the suppression of ailing religious houses and the transference of their assets to vigorous educational establishments had given him an insight into just how much wealth was unproductively tied up in Church foundations. A thousand years of lay devotion had endowed the English Church with millions of pounds' worth of land, buildings, jewelled shrines and altars and rich vestments. As we have seen, the theoretical possibility of appropriating some of this for the Crown had already been considered in government circles – considered and, presumably, rejected as impracticable and, probably, sacrilegious. But once think the unthinkable, and the way lay open to a course of action which would enable the King to pursue whatever internal and external policies took his fancy. It would put him on a par with the rulers of Spain and Portugal, whose treasuries were enjoying a steady inflow of funds from long-distance trade and colonisation. To do this would involve a new relationship with the Pope and his English representatives, as St German had indicated. To suggest that such ideas were already formulating in Cromwell's mind in 1530 is not to imply that he entered government circles with a ready-made scheme of reform. The Thomas Cromwell who touched the hem of power's robe in 1530 was too pragmatic to believe that he could manipulate royal policy in line with some detailed programme. What he was was a man imbued with humanist thought who had a passion for getting things done.

Throughout 1530 Cromwell had business to do with the King and his secretariat. Henry appreciated his legal abilities, was pleased by his manner and, perhaps, impressed by some of his audacious ideas. By the end of the year Cromwell had been admitted to the Council in a junior capacity as legal adviser. The common elements that emerge from the two accounts quoted above is that the rise of this parvenu took people by surprise and created resentment. From Henry's point of view there was a degree of obviousness about raising Cromwell, gradually and cautiously, to the position of most trusted adviser that the Cardinal had held. The two men were alike in personality, in industry and in intelligence. It may have seemed that Elijah's cloak had fallen on Elisha. To Norfolk and his aristocratic and conservative associates there was nothing at all inevitable about the emergence of a commoner who did not belong to their élite and who might fill the King's head with dangerous ideas. If, in 1529–30, they did not realise that Cromwell posed a threat it was because they were too concerned about Wolsey to notice anyone else. Cromwell was just Wolsey's man and he did not seem to be engaged in any questionable activities.

In any case, there was quite enough going on throughout the summer and autumn of 1530 to keep the Council fully occupied. We can discern three centres of activity operating throughout these months, like three cogs in some ponderous machine, each working to its own rhythm and responding to its own pressures; all interconnecting to move England towards an unseen destiny. Government was bringing increasing pressure on the Pope over the divorce. Wolsey, in the North, continued to behave with incautious bravado. And a group of outraged conservative ecclesiastics tried to regain the ground the English Church had lost in its trial of strength with parliament the previous winter.

The bishops concerned were Fisher, West (Ely) and Clerk (Bath and Wells), all of whom were attached to Queen Catherine's household. They reported to Rome about the issues on which the episcopal bench had been made to yield. Fisher, despite having been forced to apologise for his outspokenness in the House of Lords, led the way in seeking to obtain papal support against parliament's usurpation of powers in matters ecclesiastical. The government responded in July by indicting the three Bishops and a dozen of their more intransigent colleagues into King's Bench for *praemunire*. The absurd reaction was justified by the legal fiction that the offenders had paid Wolsey for certain of their rights and privileges, thus acquiescing in his legatine authority and trespassing on Crown prerogative (in October the charge was dropped). The *praemunire* accusation was followed up at the end of July by a royal proclamation ordering the ports to be closed to prevent further unauthorised communication with Rome. One result of this was that in September Wolsey's chaplain was apprehended trying to leave the country with messages from his master to the Pope. They contained nothing incriminating and it was perfectly reasonable that the legate should communicate with his superior but Wolsey's enemies could, and did, make the activity appear suspicious.

By now, Wolsey had resumed his leisurely progress towards York and, despite the warnings and hints of his friends, he had abated nothing of his customary pomp and circumstance. The renovations and refurbishments continued; the wagonloads of furniture, hangings and tableware still preceded him, so that at every halt on the way the Cardinal could dwell and entertain in splendour. Meanwhile, an increasingly paranoid Henry was convinced that the hierarchy of the Church were determined to defy him and force him to climb down. When a special nuncio, Antonio de Pulleo, Baron de Burgo, arrived from Rome at the beginning of September bringing no constructive proposals for resolving the conflict, Henry was incensed to such an extent that on at least three occasions he lambasted the envoy so fiercely with invective that Norfolk had to intervene to soothe ruffled feathers.

The King was finding himself increasingly isolated. At one Council meeting he put the question what would happen if he went ahead and married Anne in defiance of the Pope. Only Norfolk and Wiltshire supported such a move. He sounded out other groups of prominent citizens, always with the same negative result. After one of these meetings, according to Chapuys:

> The king was very angry, and adopted the expedient of proroguing parliament till the month of February in the hope, as may be supposed, that in the meanwhile he may hit upon some means of bringing over to his opinion the said lawyers as well as some members of his parliament, with whose power he is continually threatening the pope, and see whether by compulsion or persuasion he can ultimately gain his end.[49]

Parliament was emerging as the vital component in any resolution of the situation which might prove favourable to the King. The fact that it was not dissolved but repeatedly prorogued indicates that King and Council intended to make use of it but only when they could be sure of its compliance. The calculation Henry and his supporters had to make was that, however much MPs disliked the divorce, they disliked the pretension of the clergy even more. Henry told de Burgo that he was being hard-pressed to summon parliament.

> For the punishment of the clergy who were indeed so hated throughout his kingdom, both by the nobles and the people, that but for his protection they would be utterly destroyed.[50]

The King hinted that he could not keep his people on a lead much longer if the Holy Father continued to refuse his reasonable request. This was not entirely bluff, as we have seen. Was Cromwell among those urging Henry to wield the parliamentary cudgel? In that the King was asking the opinions of all and sundry it seems not at all unlikely that he would have sounded out the Member for Taunton.

The game of Anglo-papal poker went on. On 21 October Cromwell reported to Wolsey that the court action against the fifteen was to be dropped but that in its place a more devastating legislative process was to be set in motion. This (as later transpired) was nothing less than a process against the entire body of English clergy for *praemunire*. Two days later Henry was shaken by the playing of Clement's latest card. It effectively answered the King's hints of withdrawing England from papal allegiance: His Majesty was forbidden to remarry without papal permission *on pain of excommunication*. News reached London at about the same time that Wolsey had summoned the northern convocation to meet on 7 November for his enthronement (a mere fifteen years after his appointment). The Archbishop had every right to do this but his unilateral action flew in the face of custom, as Tunstall tactfully tried to point out. It was usual for the northern province to follow the lead of Canterbury in such matters and the two convocations by tradition met at the same time as parliament. In all probability Wolsey intended no defiance, having been caught out by the repeated deferring of parliament. However, he did refuse to change the arrangements and this was a display of independence Henry, in his present mood, could not tolerate. He entertained a genuine concern that the Cardinal might become a popular figurehead in the North, where he could never be certain of the loyalty of the great nobles, and that his dealings with Rome and other foreign courts had been designed to bring about just such a state of affairs.

Thomas Howard played on the King's insecurity and uncertainty in his bid to complete Wolsey's destruction. He found the means to accomplish this in Dr Agostini. He had intercepted letters sent by the physician to the Sieur de Vaux. Whether in these Wolsey had raised the portcullis of his habitual caution or whether the Duke was able to put his own sinister gloss on their content we do not know. What is clear is that this opportunity presented itself at a time when the King was incensed by the excommunication threat. Norfolk was able to plant in Henry's mind the suspicion that the Cardinal was behind this latest papal manoeuvre and that the captured letters contained 'presumptuous sinister practices made to the court of Rome for restoring him to his former estate and dignity'.[51] These 'sinister practices' subsequently elaborated into a Byzantine plot to lure Henry into war against the Emperor and the Pope, which would cause such widespread unrest that the nation would become ungovernable. On the basis of these suspicions a gentleman of the Privy Chamber was despatched with orders to the Earl of Northumberland to bring Wolsey to London to face a charge of high treason. At Cawood on 4 November both Wolsey and Agostini were arrested.

If the proceedings against the Cardinal had been open and transparent he would now have been hustled to the Tower and disposed of in short order but nothing in the long saga of Wolsey's downfall was straightforward. Agostini was certainly handled roughly – clapped on a horse, his legs tied together under the animal's belly and taken away under escort. Wolsey, by contrast, was allowed to make a leisurely journey southwards, even staying for two weeks as guest of the Earl of Shrewsbury at Sheffield Park. Agostini was taken straight to the Tower and the normal routine would have been for him to be rigorously examined with the aid of such instruments of torture as were necessary to elicit all he knew. Yet the next time he appears is as a guest enjoying the comforts of Norfolk's hospitality. 'Ever since the second day of his coming here, [Agostini] has been, and still is, treated as a prince in the house of the Duke of Norfolk, which clearly shows that he has been singing to the right tune.'[52] So Chapuys reported and it is difficult to dissent from the ambassador's cynical interpretation of events. Suspicion is strengthened by a curious undertaking to which the Italian doctor signed his name on 22 December. This was never, on pain of a £100 fine, to disclose the contents of a paper 'written with his own hand concerning the late cardinal of York'.[53] It seems that Agostini had been bribed or threatened into providing 'proof' of Wolsey's treasonable activities. Such written testimony would, inevitably, have implicated others (including, presumably, the representatives of foreign governments). As events turned out the evidence was never required in court. But it still existed and could prove an embarrassment to those who had helped fabricate it. The doctor, therefore, had to be pledged to silence.

It is not difficult to understand Agostini's 'treachery'. Only months before he had taken out English nationality believing that his best prospects were to be found in the Tudor kingdom. As the Cardinal's doctor he was perfectly placed to know the real state of his patient's mental and physical well-being. The strain of recent events had taken an enormous toll of Wolsey's robust constitution. He alternated between moods of defiant euphoria and trembling despair and this instability had undermined his health. Whenever he reflected rationally on his situation he may well have realised – what More in a similar situation did not grasp – that a prominent, discarded minister would always be seen as a threat. If he failed to regain his place in government, being allowed to live out his days in peaceful obscurity was an unlikely option. Cavendish told a story which, if not too highly coloured by the wisdom of hindsight, might support this view: Wolsey was entertaining Edmund Bonner to supper when Agostini accidentally knocked over a large silver cross which struck the guest and drew blood. Wolsey immediately regarded it as a bad omen and later interpreted the sign as an indication that he would be cast down and that Agostini would be the agent of his destruction. When Norfolk set certain stark choices before him the physician was very vulnerable. One way or another, it would soon be all up with his master, and Agostini had his own future to think of.[54]

Some historians have suggested that the apparent spontaneity of these events is an illusion; that Norfolk was working to a long-maturing plan; that he even may have 'turned' Agostini and been using him as a mole. This must be rejected if for no other reason than that Howard lacked the wit for it. Chapuys, who lived and breathed intrigue, dismissed the Duke as 'a bad dissembler'[55] and everything we know about this arrogant aristo who was always anxious and unsure about the impression he was making, confirms the ambassador's judgement. There is no evidence of any relationship between Agostini and Norfolk before November 1530. When the physician needed help in securing his naturalisation papers it was to Cromwell that he turned, not Howard. In the aftermath of the Cardinal's death, when Norfolk might have been expected to make good use of Agostini's espionage skills, he quickly abandoned the Venetian doctor. There were, clearly, no clientage bonds between the two men. Back in the summer of 1530, Howard had boasted to Chapuys that he knew, from some of Wolsey's own servants, what plots were being hatched in the Cardinal's household but he mentioned no names. If this was more than braggadocio or wishful thinking, why did Norfolk not strike earlier and why, when he did strike, did he permit the arrested traitor to make a dignified progress southwards, instead of reinforcing Wolsey's humiliation by displaying him to the world as a prisoner in chains? A demonstration of royal power against the Pope's representative would, surely, have appealed to a king who had just been threatened with excommunication. The truth is that Norfolk had not skilfully built up a cast-iron case against his rival with the aid of a 'turned' intelligence agent. He could only grasp opportunities as they appeared. There was nothing proactive about Thomas Howard.[56]

Making sense of the odd features of Wolsey's arrest has to take account of the delicate political situation and Henry's ambivalent attitude towards his former minister. Relations with Rome had to be very carefully calculated. Open defiance was not (yet) on the cards, as every opinion poll the King took indicated. Clement's co-operation was still needed, either in deciding in Henry's favour or allowing the divorce issue to be tried in England. The trumped-up treason charge against Wolsey was just the latest in a series of demonstrations of royal power. Alongside it went a demonstration of royal clemency: the Cardinal would be shown every courtesy while in captivity and would be accorded what passed in the sixteenth century for a fair trial. If it ever came to that. It is far from clear that the government would have brought the treason case into court any more than they did the *praemunire* case against the fifteen churchmen.

But what would they have done with him? The anxiety of Norfolk and his friends increased with every mile of Wolsey's journey. They had successfully engineered their enemy's exile and that plan had backfired on them when he attracted support in the North and refused to slink into quiet retirement. Now, he was being brought back to the capital. Conviction as a traitor would surely finish him – the headsman or the damp quarters of the Tower would ensure that. But supposing there was no trial, or it did not go according to plan, or the King weakened and issued a pardon? Howard needed the extermination of Wolsey. Henry did not; it was sufficient for him to have the Pope's representative demonstrably at his mercy.

In all probability everything would hinge on whether the Cardinal gained an audience with the King. In July Norfolk had sworn to Chapuys that Wolsey would never be permitted to see his old master. Yet, right to the end, the prisoner hoped and begged to be able to put his case to His Majesty in person, knowing from long experience that Henry found it difficult to resist personal appeals to his clemency. Discussing his fate with Shrewsbury, he pleaded,

> I desire you and most heartily require your good lordship to be a mean for me that I may answer unto my accusers before the King's majesty. The case is his. And if their accusations should be true, then should it touch no man but him most earnestly; wherefore it were most convenient that he should hear it himself in proper person.
>
> But I fear me that they do intend rather to dispatch me than [that] I should come before him in his presence; for they be well assured and very certain that my truth should vanquish their untruth and surmised accusations, which is the special cause that moveth me so earnestly to desire to make my answer before the King's majesty.[57]

In response to entreaties made on Wolsey's behalf, Henry sent to assure the Cardinal of his continued favour, expressed confidence that the accused would be able to clear his name, agreed that he would preside over the trial in person and sent one of his most trusted servants, Sir William Kingston, to escort the prisoner on the last stage of his journey. It all seemed very reassuring but Wolsey was less than one hundred per cent delighted at the King's response. Among Kingston's many offices was the constableship of the Tower of London. Moreover, the royal messenger seemed more concerned about his charge's assets than his security. There was a strong strain of cupidity in Henry VIII. He had been quick to take possession of Wolsey's houses and their contents in and around the capital. He had appropriated the goods of Ipswich College to his own use and would have done the same with Cardinal College had he not been persuaded that it would be in his greater interest to re-establish it as a royal foundation (Christchurch College). The first task of the officers sent to arrest Wolsey at Cawood was to make an inventory of all his goods. And now, notwithstanding the fact that the Cardinal had taken to his sickbed, Kingston pestered him as to the whereabouts of £1,500 that could not be accounted for.

However, this was to be one of the last irritations Thomas Wolsey had to endure. His catalogue of trials and triumphs was about to be closed up. Death proved to be an attentive friend to Thomas Howard. It removed the brother who overshadowed him; it now removed his hated rival; years later it would perform an even more timely service. At Sheffield Park Wolsey was struck down by an enteric disorder, probably typhoid or dysentery, and subsequent days spent jogging about in the saddle hastened his deterioration. By the time he arrived at the Augustinian abbey at Leicester the massive constitution, for years tried to the uttermost by unremitting labour and constant overindulgence, could take no more.

Cavendish made the most of the death scene in the biography which later inspired Shakespeare. He described the aged churchman's remorse – 'if I had served God as diligently as I have done the king, he would not have given me over in my grey hairs'. There followed a long speech in which Wolsey deplored the divorce proceedings and warned that if this 'new perverse sect of the Lutherans' was not crushed swiftly England would be convulsed in civil turmoil. On 29 November, at eight o'clock in the morning, the very hour that, days before, he had prophesied for his departure, the great Cardinal died.

The manner of his departing was in arid contrast to the way he had lived throughout his years of greatness. His body was put on display for the rest of the day to local notables so that there should be no possible doubt about his demise. That night the monks of Leicester performed his obsequies and during the hours of darkness the Cardinal Archbishop was interred, simply, efficiently and without undue pomp.

His passing was little mourned. One might have expected a sour observation from the Catholic Chapuys. Hearing that Wolsey was buried within yards of Richard III, he noted that people were already beginning to refer to the abbey church at Leicester as 'the sepulchre of tyrants'.[58] Protestant commentators, with equal relish, reported common gossip and drew their own moral.

It is testified by one, yet being alive, in whose arms the said Cardinal died, that his body, being dead, was black as pitch; also was so heavy, that six could scarce bear it. Furthermore, it did so stink above the ground, that they were constrained to hasten the burial thereof in the night season, before it was day. At that burial, such a tempest with such a stench there arose, that all the torches went out; and so he was thrown into the tomb, and there was laid.

By the ambitious pride and excessive worldly wealth of this one cardinal, all men may easily understand and judge what the state and condition of all the rest of the same order (whom we call spiritual men) was in those days.[59]

The common opinion at the time seems to have been much in agreement with Foxe's analysis. Wolsey's fate indicated the truth of the biblical apophthegm, 'pride goeth before destruction, and an haughty spirit before a fall'.

In the Norfolk–Boleyn camp there was joy unconfined. Anne, her father and her uncle had achieved their objective – or, rather, Providence had achieved it for them. Their immediate reaction was to make Wolsey the scapegoat for all the nation's ills and to drive him into the wilderness of the forgotten with every conceivable sin piled upon his back. George Boleyn commissioned a masque entitled 'Of the Cardinal's Going into Hell' and it was performed at Greenwich for the delectation of the court. With it they thought to have closed a disagreeable chapter in the political life of the nation. Now, matters had been set to rights. There would be no more upstarts in the Council, no more overweening ecclesiastics. Thomas Howard had assumed his rightful place as the King's undisputed principal adviser. A woman of the Howard blood would soon be queen. And it was rumoured that the alliance with the house of Tudor would shortly be strengthened by the marriage of Norfolk's eldest son to Princess Mary. But all this euphoria rested on a worm-ridden platform. Wolsey was not and, for several years, had not been the barrier between the Howards and greatness. It was the King's will that stood in their way. All that Wolsey's fall demonstrated was that Henry could raise up and cast down whomsoever he chose. It was a lesson they would all do well to ponder as they laughed – with Henry – at the grotesque stage demons dragging a screaming, scarlet-clad figure towards the vividly painted canvas jaws of a pretend abyss.

CHAPTER 24

Under New Management

By 1530 all the moral, political, legal and doctrinal arguments for and against the royal divorce had been rehearsed *ad nauseam*. The irresistible force of Henry's will was set against the immovable object of Clement's intransigence and the latter was prevailing. All the King's advisers could think to do was continue with the threefold strategy which had so far proved unavailing: to harass the Pope's English subordinates; to produce evidence that Albion's rulers were from time immemorial independent of curial restraints (so that the annulment issue could be settled in England); and to gather support for the King's cause in the academic centres of Europe. The last two were essentially intellectual exercises and the main burden was thrust upon the shoulders of Henry's new-found theological champion, Thomas Cranmer. In the tidy reckoning of history the two 'TCs' have become 'the architects of the English Reformation'; Cromwell providing the legal and administrative framework for the refashioned Tudor Church/State and Cranmer giving it its ideological *raison d'être*. In that the Reformation had not run its course by 1540, when Cromwell died or 1556, the date of Cranmer's martyrdom, that judgement can only be partially true. The Tudor revolution had several more twists and turns in it after the two TCs had left the stage. However, the course they set in the 1530s was locked into the English Reformation and, despite violent deviations in the years ahead, the movement was not permanently deflected from those co-ordinates. What Cranmer and Cromwell attempted, what they achieved and what their motives were are vital components to an understanding of the movement.

The forty-year-old ponderous academic who was plucked from fenland seclusion in 1529 underwent a complete life transformation. It was not just that he found himself at the centre of national and international affairs, living amidst unaccustomed glamour and luxury; he also came under new intellectual influences which gave a new direction to his cast of thought. Essentially an uncomplicated man who had never set his sights on the prizes of fame, luxury and power, he was overawed by his changed circumstances and to a large extent the sense of inhabiting an unreal world never left him. A telling letter written at Christmastide 1532 throws a brief beam of light on Cranmer's lifestyle. It was written from Bologna by Nicholas Hawkins who had just taken over from Cranmer as ambassador at the Imperial court. He had been shocked to make a surprising discovery: whereas the tables of all the other diplomats were furnished with silver vessels, his predecessor had, for the best part of a year, contented himself with pewter. Hawkins immediately sought permission to have some of the King's plate recast for his personal use, commenting, 'Judge you how they are content to be served in tin or pewter, who are accustomed to dine at home off silver.'[60] Cranmer, it seems, had been perfectly content. His was not the self-denial of the ascetic; rather was it the frugality of the man whose tastes were simple and wants few.

This straightforward, retiring, rather dull scholar found himself placed not just at the royal court, one among several Crown servants, nor merely the latest intellectual novelty taken up and made much of by the powerful Boleyns. He became, in a short space of time, an intimate of the King, rapidly surpassing men like Gardiner, who had trodden a long, obstacle-strewn path to the heights of kingly favour. As early as the summer of 1531 a continental reformer, Simon Grynaeus, visiting the court, could describe Cranmer as a close companion of the King, 'sufficiently of our school' with whom Henry was accustomed to discussing important matters before going public on them.[61]

From their early encounters a special relationship developed between Cranmer and the King. After his first meeting with his sovereign Thomas wrote gushingly to a friend about 'the kindest of princes' who had showered him with gifts and granted him a long audience.[62] It is unlikely that the interview impacted equally forcibly on Henry but when the cleric entered royal service the King rapidly acquired a respect and affection for him quite unlike anything he felt for any of his other principal servants. By the mid-1530s Cromwell could comment enviously, 'You were born in a happy hour, for, do or say what you will, the king will always take it at your hand.'[63] This bond can partly be explained as the attraction of opposites: sophistication and simplicity; proud assertiveness and honest humility; *raison d'état* and disinterested kindness. It owed a great deal to Cranmer's convinced Erastianism. He held a high view of kings as divine appointees with authority in all areas of life, both secular and spiritual. The King also appreciated his new chaplain's clarity of mind. Cranmer had a gift, well developed in the Jesus years, for summarising complex arguments and exposing logical flaws in propositions, and Henry approved of councillors who could pre-digest information and regurgitate it with economy of words.

But what first made Cranmer and Henry soulmates was their shared attitude to the divorce. The King was certain to the point of obsession that the papal dispensation sanctioning his marriage to Catherine had been flawed because it flew in the face of scriptural prohibition. Cranmer sincerely believed the same. Henry was surrounded by men who would do his bidding in the annulment proceedings, who would produce arguments in support of the royal position and devise stratagems for political warfare. Only Cranmer, he came to believe, really *understood* him, sympathised with his predicament, and interpreted as he did the signs of divine disapprobation. Henry VIII certainly did not lack for spiritual advisers but in Cranmer he found a man to whom he could, in complete confidentiality, unburden himself. This gave a unique quality to the relationship and one which Wolsey, Brandon, More and others close to the King never shared.

Another characteristic of Cranmer's that may have attracted Henry was that he had no private agenda. His service to the King was not distorted by the dynastic ambition of a Howard, the hubris of a Wolsey or the anti-heretical vendetta of a More. Throughout his first three years at court the ex-Cambridge don was fully engaged in the royal matrimonial issue and nothing distracted him. However, by a supreme irony, it was those very researches that he undertook on the King's behalf and the radical, anti-papal theologians whose support he sought for the divorce which moved him away from the theological conservatism to which the King clung. Thereafter, Cranmer *did* have his own agenda: to hasten the English Church along the path of evangelical reformation. When the conversion occurred it was not of the Damascus road variety but it was, in terms of the thought processes of a cautious scholar, rapid. Grinaeus certainly could not have described the Cranmer of 1529 as 'sufficiently of our school'. By mid-1531 the royal chaplain had left traditional Catholicism behind. However, the qualifying adjective, 'sufficiently' suggests that he had some distance still to travel – certainly in the eyes of Europe's more radical Protestant thinkers.

Simon Grynaeus was based in Basel, a friend of Erasmus and a colleague of the city's religious leader, Johannes Oecolampadius. The reformers of Basel favoured a broadly Zwinglian religious settlement and laboured to restrain the wilder elements. Their failure in February 1529 led to a brief but thorough orgy of iconoclasm, as Erasmus reported to his old friend Willibald Pirckheimer:

There was no one who did not fear for himself when those dregs of the people covered the whole market place with arms and cannons. Such a mockery was made of the images of the saints, and even of the crucifixion, that one would have thought that some miracle must have happened. Nothing was left of the sculptures, either in the churches or in the cloisters, in the portals or in the monasteries. Whatever painted pictures remained were daubed over with whitewash, whatever was inflammable was thrown upon the pile, whatever was not was broken to pieces.[64]

This was too much for Erasmus, who, within weeks, left the Swiss haven where for seven and a half years he had sought sanctuary from traditionalist bigots. After the disturbances a thoroughgoing *Reformationsordnung* established a new Church–State polity, whose architects saw it as a model Christian commonwealth suitable for transplanting to other states which had thrown off the papal yoke. Such were the type of men with whom Thomas Cranmer found himself consorting as his master's cause sent him in ever-widening circles to canvas Christian opinion. However, these were not the only influences he came under. He had the excitement of witnessing at first hand several Protestant experiments and of discussing revolutionary ideas with theologians of many different hues. It was all very challenging and invigorating after the learned debates and empty-headed undergraduate protest of Cambridge.

In 1530 and again in 1532 Cranmer was sent on foreign embassies to the Imperial court at a time when Henry was desperately bombarding European governments and universities. Cranmer's presence was partly to give academic weight to the arguments being put forward in support of the annulment and partly to continue the task of gathering scholarly opinions favourable to the King. It was the 1532 mission that wrought the most dramatic changes in Cranmer's life. First of all it marked a significant promotion. Various ecclesiastical preferments had come his way (thus augmenting his income out of Church funds), the latest being the archdeaconry of Taunton, but now he achieved a major diplomatic post as ambassador to the court of Charles V (in earlier missions his had been merely a support role). Cranmer's appointment in January was as a replacement for Sir Thomas Elyot who had only been in post a few months and who was very bitter about being deposed. Like his friend Thomas More, Elyot struggled to harmonise personal ambition, royal service and disapproval of the drift of policy. He had been advanced by Wolsey, transferred allegiance, in the nick of time, to Anne Boleyn and gained the post of clerk to the Council, only to be dismissed in June 1530, presumably on suspicion of being pro-Catherine (as he certainly was). Elyot clawed his way back into favour with the publication of the *Boke named the Governour*, a humanist treatise on the education of statesmen. On the strength of this and, according to Chapuys, with the support of the Boleyns, he obtained his ambassadorial appointment. However, within three or four months his patrons had obviously changed their minds and Elyot, who had not travelled farther than the Low Countries, had the humiliation of having to accompany the new ambassador up the Rhine and thence, via Frankfurt and Nürnberg, to the Imperial court at Regensburg.

In Nürnberg the travellers encountered the full force of Lutheranism and their reactions are significant. This city was the first major urban centre to espouse the new order and among its supporters were such diverse citizens as Albrecht Dürer and Hans Sachs (the cobbler-poet later immortalised by

Wagner in *Die Meistersinger von Nürnberg*). Elyot reported back to the Duke of Norfolk. He acknowledged his grudging admiration for the good order and evident prosperity of the Nürnbergers before going on to discuss the religious situation. He explained that he had been forbidden to have his chaplain say a private mass and been obliged to attend public service. This was conducted partly in Latin and partly in German, the epistle and Gospel being clearly read in the vernacular. Elyot was scandalised: 'I, lest I should be partner of [i.e. party to] their communion, departed then and the ambassador of France fo[llowed], which caused all the people in the church to wonder at us [as though] we had been greater heretics than they.'[65] Cranmer stayed and followed the service with great interest.

Surprisingly, one custom which received Elyot's blessing was that the clergy were married. This certainly would not have pleased More but many humanists regarded wedlock as a more honourable course for priests than the alternatives which gave rise to ribald comment and scandalised denunciation. As for Cranmer, he not only approved, he hastened to follow suit. For the second time in his life he put his career in jeopardy by plunging into matrimony. His bride was Katharina Preu, a niece by marriage of Andreas Osiander, one of the leading theologians.

Clearly, Thomas Cranmer was 'the marrying kind'. Clearly, he believed that compulsory clerical celibacy had no scriptural sanction. Clearly, he saw marriage as a means of escape from temptation. But what possessed him to make, at this particular moment, a gesture which could scarcely improve his standing at Henry's court and which would be interpreted by his enemies as making common cause with heretics? From a career point of view it might not have been quite as foolhardy as at first sight it appears. Cranmer had every reason to believe that his future lay in diplomacy and that much of his time would be spent outside England. To accede to the customs of a host country might almost be regarded as a courtesy. He may have reflected that, in the event of his marriage creating real problems, he could resign his orders and, God willing, continue to serve the King. Whatever rationalisation Cranmer may have indulged is likely to have been only the jam spread upon the bread of what was, essentially, an emotional response. Seduced by Katharina's charms or her uncle's persuasion, or both, Cranmer gave way to the intellectual impetuosity to which he was sometimes prone. Once convinced that something was right – and that might take years – he had a tendency to embrace it whole-heartedly without giving an eye to the consequences.

Impulsive or not, Cranmer might have hesitated had he received earlier the totally unexpected news that reached him, at the very latest, around the end of October 1532. In July, the octogenarian William Warham died, his end perhaps hastened by his ineffective efforts to ward off the hammer blows aimed at the independence of the English Church by the Reformation Parliament. Stephen Gardiner might well have entertained the hope that he might step into Warham's shoes but he had blown his chances of promotion by staunchly defending the privileges of the clergy. However, it was not only the Bishop of Winchester who was surprised and aggrieved by Henry's next action. The King bypassed the entire episcopal bench and nominated as the sixty-seventh Archbishop of Canterbury the current Archdeacon of Taunton, Thomas Cranmer. Henry signalled yet again that neither birth nor position counted for much beside the royal will when he was selecting men for positions of leadership.

Was the man who returned to take up the primacy of the English Church at the beginning of 1533 a Lutheran? If he was, he concealed the fact for over four years. It would scarcely have been safe to do anything else while Henry was spurning the Pope with his left hand and brandishing the banner of orthodoxy with his right. Trying to keep pace with the King's religious opinions was a nightmare not only for progressives: everyone aspiring to hold on to office (and even life) was hard put to it to know what views they could safely express and what they should keep to themselves. Thomas More gave up the struggle in May 1532 when he resigned as Lord Chancellor (see pp. 343–4) but even then he maintained a judicious silence on the great matter. Elyot told a friend that his earnest prayer was that 'truth may be freely and thankfully heard' and insisted, 'I am determined to live and die therein.' The example of Cranmer's promotion, he insisted, would not tempt him to change his convictions but nor would he ever 'abuse my sovereign lord to whom I am sworn'.[66] In a bitter satire, *Pasquil the Plain*, of 1533 he launched an attack on the man who had elbowed him out of office. Significantly his – thinly veiled – complaint against Cranmer was not that he was pouring heresies into the King's ear, but that his silence was preventing error from being answered. At the same time Elyot was careful to distance himself from More and to shore up his friendship with Cromwell.

Elyot was well placed to know the extent of Cranmer's infection with Lutheranism. We can only draw inferences but it is safe to assume that he had, by 1533, become committed to some fundamental evangelical tenets. He approved the availability of vernacular Scripture and the use in public worship of a language 'understanded of the people'. We know that he already set more store by the Bible than by canon law, papal bull or Church tradition. It was but a short step from there to the endorsement of Luther's central doctrine of justification by faith and not works, and, what followed, the rejection of any idea that sacraments convey grace automatically.

On matters ecclesiological his position was already clear and needed no support from Wittenberg. Later in life he recalled telling Henry that he scrupled about becoming Archbishop of Canterbury, because

if he accepted the office, then he must receive it at the pope's hand; which he neither would nor could do, for that his highness was only the supreme governor of this church of England, as well in causes ecclesiastical as temporal, and that the full right and donation of all manner of bishoprics and benefices . . . appertained to his grace, and not to any other foreign authority . . . Whereat the King, said he [Cranmer], staying a while and musing asked me, how I was able to prove it. At which time I alleged many texts out of the scriptures, and the fathers also approving the supreme and highest authority of kings in their realms and dominions, disclosing therewithal the intolerable usurpation of the people of Rome.[67]

In between his diplomatic excursions Cranmer had been busy in Henry's PR department. This had largely involved researching and editing three books designed to convince people of the justness of the King's position. Henry had persuaded himself and wished to persuade others that he was not an innovator. He had behind him not only the weight of Scripture, but also of history and unbiased scholarly opinion. The *Collectanea Satis Copiosa* was an anthology of texts drawn from ancient documents 'proving' that the English Church had always possessed a large degree of independence and that English kings enjoyed complete sovereignty over it. *The Determinations of the most famous and most excellent Universities of Italy and France that it is unlawful for a man to marry his brother's wife; that the Pope hath no power to dispense therewith* was, as the title suggests, the verdicts provided in Henry's favour by eight foreign seats of learning plus a lengthy disquisition on the central issue based on Scripture and tradition. *The Glass of Truth* was primarily an abbreviated version of the *Determinations* for popular consumption. Through such documents the government hoped to whip up English nationalism against the monolithic ecclesiastical state ruled from Rome.

But the propaganda battle was far from one-sided. Opponents of the annulment produced a snowstorm of papers and part of Cranmer's job was to read, evaluate and refute them. This was how he became involved in a sad family conflict in the summer of 1531. Reginald Pole was a kinsman of the King on his mother's side, a sprig of the lush Yorkist tree which abounded in potential claimants to the throne and contrasted so sharply with the fragile Tudor stock. Reginald, a clever and personable young man in the early years of the reign, was a great favourite with the King and Queen who helped to finance his studies. At Wolsey's old college of Magdalen Pole received a thoroughgoing humanist education under the tutorship of Linacre and William Latimer, and subsequently went on to visit the great Italian centres of learning. Partly out of political calculation and partly out of genuine affection, Henry intended to keep him close to the throne and give him every opportunity to display his loyalty to the Tudor regime. After Wolsey's death the King virtually ordered his relative to accept either the archbishopric of York or the bishopric of Winchester. But Pole, who had early come under the influence of the Carthusians, was opposed to the government's attitude towards the English Church and, in particular, to the campaign for the divorce. Desperately the young scholar tried to keep his distance from the political scene but Henry was persistent and Reginald refused to compromise his conscience. One interview at York Place ended with the King drawing his dagger in a rage and Pole rushing, tearful, from the chamber. Henry refused to let the matter rest there. He demanded from the distraught young man a complete statement of his opinion on the great matter. When it arrived the King handed it to Cranmer to digest.

The chaplain's analysis demonstrates both the strength of the arguments ranged against Henry's position and Cranmer's skill in the art of précis. For these reasons it is worth quoting at some length from a report he made to his patron, the Earl of Wiltshire, on 13 June. Cranmer admits that Pole's 'book' is so well written that 'if it were known to the common people I suppose they could not be persuaded to the contrary'. He applauds Pole's reluctance to enter the debate, fearing that it might revive the Yorkist/Tudor conflict always rumbling subterraneously beneath the surface of English political life. Pole opines that for Henry to persist in shaking off the Aragon marriage would be disastrous.

> The people think the king has an heir already, and they would be sorry to have any other. The emperor would support the queen, his aunt. It is alleged for the king that he was moved by God's law, that the people's judgment has nothing to do with it, and that if the emperor will maintain an unjust cause we shall have the aid of the French king by the league he has made with us, and out of his old grudge to the emperor.

Pole responds that if the King's cause could be shown to be just then he and Catherine would be exposed as having lived more than twenty years in a matrimony 'shameful and against nature'. The impact on the King's subjects would be appalling for 'what loyal person would gladly hear that their prince had lived so long in matrimony so abominable?'. Pole dismisses the support the annulment has received from some universities by pointing out how difficult the King's agents found it to obtain favourable decisions. Politically, Pole insists, persistence with the annulment can only lead to England's isolation.

> . . . as to the pope, the emperor, and the French king, the pope is naturally opposed to the king's purpose, else he would discredit his predecessors, restrain his own power, and sow sedition in many realms . . . He then extols the power of the emperor, and diminishes the aid of the French king towards us, saying that the emperor may injure us

without drawing a sword, by merely forbidding traffic in Flanders and Spain. And what if he drew his sword, seeing that, when of much less power than he is now, he subdued the pope and the French king? As for the French, they never keep league with us, except for their own advantage, and our nation will think themselves in miserable condition if compelled to trust them.

In conclusion, Pole suggests that Henry 'stands on the brink of the water and yet he may have all; but one step further, and all his honour is drowned'.[68]

What is most striking about this letter is its honesty. Cranmer outlines Pole's main points and admits that he finds some of them compelling, although he rejects the conclusion that Henry should submit his cause to the Pope: 'me he persuadeth in that point nothing at all'. Here we see the trained academic rationally evaluating arguments. This is a far cry from Thomas More the lawyer deliberately rubbishing and distorting the opposition's case or Thomas More the polemicist heaping vulgar abuse on his enemies.

Cromwell's rise was coterminous with Cranmer's and based upon the same essential character trait: conscientious attention to his master's interests. Like the faithful stewards in the Gospel parable they each received the accolade, 'Well done, good and faithful servant, you have shown yourself faithful in small things, so I will give you charge over greater things.'

It was on 20 October 1532 that Thomas Winter, Wolsey's illegitimate son, wrote a begging letter to his old friend Thomas Cromwell: 'All my hope is in you. You are now placed in that position which I and all your friends have long wished for and you have attained that dignity that you can serve them as you please.'[69] This is the earliest clear documentary evidence we have that Cromwell had achieved a position of major influence. His rise could scarcely be described as meteoric. He had been a member of parliament for almost three years and a councillor for nearly two. The only household offices he had acquired – and only recently acquired – were the minor ones of Master of the King's Jewels and Keeper of the Hanaper of Chancery. These paid modest stipends in return for careful bookkeeping of Chancery funds and vigilant custody of the King's plate and jewels. But Cromwell's personality and talents had ensured that the King noticed him and reposed increasing trust in him. Just as Wolsey had used his position as Almoner to impress Henry with his usefulness, so Cromwell by similar diligence and careful attention to the King's wishes raised himself from an administrative to an executive position.

His correspondence with other councillors gives us glimpses of his changing position in the hierarchy. Early in 1532 he exchanged letters with Stephen Gardiner who was absent on foreign embassy and longing for a recall. In responding to a plea for news from his old Wolsey household colleague Cromwell permitted himself a hint of impatience: 'all that there is is known to you, who are far more secret than I'. When he went on to explain that he had discussed with the King the possibility of Gardiner being summoned home, he acknowledged the Bishop's ongoing importance to their master. 'He answered that you were not so weary of being there, but he was as sorry, saying by these words expressly, "His absence is the lack of my right hand, for I am now so much pestered with business and have nobody to rid nor despatch the same"'.[70] Cromwell did not enjoy the same frank camaraderie with Norfolk. In August the Duke addressed a peremptory note to his social inferior relating to arrangements for the forthcoming ennoblement of Anne Boleyn: 'I wrote to you that you should provide crimson velvet for three countesses. The king's pleasure now is that no robes of estate shall be now made but only for my wife. I send you the pattern.'[71] However, in October when Norfolk was in Calais with the King it was not to him that Sir Thomas Audley, Keeper of the Great Seal and leader of the Council in London, wrote for advice, but to Cromwell. Was it in order, Audley wanted to know, for him and his colleagues to open letters from Scotland?[72] This is particularly significant bearing in mind Howard's special interest in Scottish affairs. By the autumn of 1532 even Charles Brandon was suing for Cromwell's favours.

As we have seen, Cromwell's quiet emergence as the *de facto* successor to Wolsey took observers like the Imperial ambassador by surprise and made them search around for dramatic explanations. It is not difficult to understand why this should have been the case. In the autumn of 1531, the retiring Venetian ambassador had numbered Cromwell among the eight leading councillors, by which he can have meant only that Cromwell was more frequently in attendance than most of the others. In fact, some of his colleagues had a much higher profile. Norfolk and Gardiner were frequently employed in diplomatic affairs and Anne's close relatives were at the centre of court life. But Henry had never warmed to Howard and, early in 1532, the Bishop blotted his copybook in a way that Henry never quite forgave (see p. 341). There is, therefore, a real sense in which the competition was not as formidable as it might at first sight appear.

By the autumn of 1532 Wolsey's old office manager was recognised as the organiser of Council business. From being brought on to the body as a legal specialist he had, by industry and efficiency, made himself master of all its activity and the man to whom colleagues turned for information and advice. But Cromwell had also emerged as more than just a senior councillor. When, in May 1532, Chapuys took the papal nuncio to court, urging him to seek an audience with the King, de Burgo had to present himself to Norfolk and, only after the Duke had attempted, unsuccessfully, to discover what the nuncio wanted did he admit him to the royal presence. By the following April Chapuys realised that the swings and roundabouts of personal power in the royal household had changed. Norfolk was no longer the one who must be flattered, wheedled, bribed and placated, as he reported to his master: 'Cromwell informs me now of all court affairs and is the man who enjoys most credit with the king.'[73]

There must have come a time, amidst the bewildering, fast-moving events of the next few months, when Norfolk and Gardiner, the leading lay and spiritual princes of the royal entourage, woke up to the fact that they had been sidelined; that the private and clandestine activities involving Henry, Anne, Cranmer and Cromwell were more important than their own tireless political and diplomatic endeavours to achieve the annulment. Enlightenment is likely to have occurred before the shock revelation in January 1533 of Anne and Henry's clandestine wedding. But even that event cannot have prepared them for what was to come, for what rapidly became obvious in the following weeks was that the 'great matter' had ceased to be the central issue. They had assumed that the King was only interested in achieving the dissolution of his marriage and that the bullying of the clergy was merely a means to that end. They would soon realise that a revolution was under way which threatened to destroy much of what they held dear.

In reflective moments they can scarcely have avoided looking back over the events of recent turbulent months and asking themselves, 'How did the devil come; when first attack?' What could possibly explain the 'Cromwell phenomenon'? How had the man they had employed as a Council and Commons go-between insinuated himself 'twixt them and their sovereign, there to advance the causes of social revolution and heresy? How could it be explained other than as part of a Satanic plot against King, Church and people? That was the basis of Reginald Pole's rationale only a few years later when he accused Cromwell of deliberately persuading Henry to establish himself as an amoral ruler modelled upon Machiavelli's *Il Principe*. Pole had left England at the beginning of 1532 and remained in voluntary exile for more than twenty years. His ideas must, therefore, have originated among his Catholic contacts in his homeland and represented the kind of propaganda circulating in conservative circles by the middle of the decade – circles within which Norfolk and Winchester were prominent. According to them everything could be blamed on the object of their hatred. Not only had Cromwell achieved a position of power equalling if not exceeding that of the Cardinal; not only had he pushed through breathtaking changes in Church and State; but also a marked deterioration was apparent in the character of the King. All these things must be connected and must have had their origin in Cromwell's evil and well-matured scheming. It suited the 'upstart's' enemies – as it later suited Henry – to portray the King as a ruler who had come under malign influence but Henry never had been, and was not in the 1530s, a pipe upon which someone else played tunes. He performed a leading role in the unfolding tragedy and, if Cromwell was an important actor in the drama, a yet more effective one was Fate.

In 1530 it had been the Commons who had provoked conflict with convocation. Cromwell had, in fact, toned down the language of their supplication to the King and been active in drafting compromise legislation to which Henry would be able to assent. The following year it was the King who turned up the heat under the convocation by demanding from the clergy's representatives £100,000 in compensation for the charges he had incurred prosecuting his annulment case in Rome, plus their acknowledgement that Henry was 'sole protector and supreme head of the Anglican church and clergy'. This initiative was bred of the King's anger at the Pope's henchmen, his desperate need for cash and his conviction about Christian sovereignty based on the ancient documents he had set his scholars to scour. The bishops squirmed and stormed. Among Fisher's arguments about the royal headship was the question 'What would happen if a woman came to the throne?' and one wonders whether Henry was subtle enough to have foreseen this objection and to realise that it could be used as an argument for barring Mary from the succession. Once again, it seems to have been Cromwell who provided the convocation with a legal loophole that the sovereign's power in the Church might be recognised 'insofar as the word of God allows'.

There was a headline-grabbing sequel to this latest row between King and clergy. Days later nearly all Bishop Fisher's servants fell violently ill and one died. It transpired that a cauldron of porridge had been poisoned and that only Rochester's frugal habits had saved him from the noxious concoction. As a wave of shock horror swept across London and Westminster, a certain Richard Roose was identified as the murderer and duly arrested. Naturally, rumours concerning Roose's motivation abounded and the most obvious – as also the most deliciously outrageous – was that Henry had tried to get rid of his old *bête noire*. So seriously did the King take this slander that he went into the Lords' chamber and there delivered himself of an hour-and-a-half speech on the barbarity of poisoning. The immediate outcome was a new act labelling convicted poisoners as guilty of high treason, to be punished by being boiled alive. Poor Roose was the first to suffer under this statute.

We have to take such incidents of passing moment into account alongside major political events because they indicate what people were thinking and feeling. In February 1531 Henry, though determined to bring the clergy to heel, did not want to be seen as their implacable enemy. A few months later it was Cromwell's turn to ward off any suggestion that he was tainted with Lutheranism. He had commended his friend and agent, Stephen Vaughan, to the King (and secured a place for Vaughan's wife in Anne Boleyn's suite). Initially impressed by Tyndale's work, Henry had instructed Vaughan to persuade the translator to return home. The zealous agent threw himself into this agreeable task, reporting back progress to His Majesty and sending further examples of Tyndale's work. Henry read them and was appalled. Realising that the exile was an out-and-out Lutheran, he summoned Cromwell and gave him a roasting. The lawyer lost no time in writing Vaughan a long letter instructing him in the plainest possible terms to distance himself (and his patron) from the heretic whose works were 'replete with lies and most abominable slanders imagined and feigned to infect and intoxicate the people'. In any future correspondence Vaughan was to 'utterly condemn and abhor the same'. Failure to do so would 'compel your good friends which have been ever glad, prone and ready to advance you unto the favours of your prince to lament and sorrow that their suit in that behalf should not take effect according to their good intent'.[74]

For those in and around the court the most dramatic event of the summer was the final estrangement of Henry and Catherine. At about the time that Cromwell was writing to Vaughan, Norfolk had been despatched on a painful and humiliating errand. He led an impressive delegation of thirty councillors to the Queen's chambers in an attempt to persuade her to abandon her appeal to Rome. Before this impressive company of nobles, churchmen, lawyers and scholars, most of whom were more competent than he, Howard cut a sorry figure. He muddled his arguments and was completely outfaced by a serene Catherine who was crystal clear in her traditionalist faith and had no need to enmesh herself in tongue-tying subtleties. When it came to reporting back to Henry Norfolk was more than happy to let Brandon summarise the result of the mission. The Queen was ready to obey her husband in all matters except those in which to do so would conflict with her allegiance to two higher powers, he suggested. Henry pounced on this wisp of treason. 'What two powers,' he demanded, 'the pope and the emperor?' 'No, Sire,' Suffolk replied, 'God and her conscience.'[75] Six weeks later, on 11 July, Henry VIII literally rode out of his wife's life. He left her at Windsor when he and the court moved on to another royal manor and sent word that on his return he did not expect to find her still there. She was to select a place for her retirement from public life and keep well away from him. Husband and wife never met thereafter. Public support for the discarded Queen reached a new pitch of fervour, but any increase in opposition was more than matched by Henry's stubborn determination.

He openly kept Anne beside him as his consort and he maintained pressure on his advisers to 'do something'. But what? Everyone was devoid of ideas. Cromwell had by now emerged as the controller of parliamentary business and he had laid a legislative programme before the King but the assembly's recall was put off over and again until January 1532 and then it proved troublesome. The body that was supposed to side with the King against the clergy suddenly showed no inclination to do anything of the sort. First of all King and Commons fell out over financial matters. There was nothing unusual in that. What was noteworthy was that both houses had set themselves against the latest big stick Henry wielded against Rome. The Bill in Restraint of Annates had been devised to prevent certain routine ecclesiastical payments being made to the Pope. It was no surprise that the measure had a rough ride in the upper house, where the spiritual peers turned out in force to block it, but the King and Cromwell might have hoped for better things from the Commons. They failed to take account of two factors: payment of annates was not an issue likely to reinvigorate anticlerical feeling and most MPs recognised the bill for what it was; a financial crowbar to prise apart the Pope and the Queen. Henry was driven to remarkable lengths to get this legislation through. Not only did he intervene in the Lords' debate, he also, according to Chapuys, approved into the Commons and ordered a division of the house. Those who supported his bill were to stand on one side and those who opposed it on the other.

Support was leaching away alarmingly. Howard felt more and more exposed by the day. Anne was making life hell for him. The King's patience was almost at snapping point. The Duchess of Norfolk's support for Catherine was an embarrassment. And his own allies were deserting. In February 1532 he summoned them to a meeting for the purpose of endorsing the assertion that matrimonial cases lay in the domain of the temporal rather than the spiritual courts. The suggestion was angrily rebuffed and Norfolk's erstwhile backer, Thomas Lord Darcy, spoke for the majority when he dismissed the proposition as absurd: of course, the Church was the only possible arbiter in cases of matrimonial dispute and it was not for the temporal power to bring pressure to bear upon it.

Easter came and with it a challenge to the King in his own chapel. William Peto, provincial of the Observant Franciscans, confessor to Princess Mary and close friend of Thomas More, preached the court sermon at Greenwich in his capacity as ruler of the attached Observant house. He used the occasion to make a no-holds-barred attack on the divorce and those who were promoting it. He went so far as to compare Henry to Ahab, the weak King of Israel who had fallen under the spell of Jezebel, his heretical queen (no one present would have missed the allusion), and evil advisers who had persuaded him that he was above the law of God. Coming to his peroration, the ardent friar declaimed, 'I beseech your Grace to take good heed, lest if you will need follow Ahab in his doing, you will surely incur his unhappy end also, and that the dogs lick your blood as they licked Ahab's, which God avert and forbid!'[76] Henry took the rebuke on the chin but afterwards, in a private audience, tried unsuccessfully to move Peto from his ground. The following Sunday the King put up Hugh Curwen, one of his chaplains and one of the century's most shameless trimmers, to reply to the friar. Curwen had scarcely got into his stride before he was interrupted from the rood loft by Henry Elstow, Warden of the Greenwich Observants. The sermon turned into a slanging match between preacher and heckler which soon drew in other vocal participants. Henry was furious. He had Peto and Elstow thrown into jail and then sent to Rome for permission to put them on trial (he later relented and allowed the offenders to go into exile).

A few weeks later court tensions again led to an outbreak of violence, this time physical not verbal, in a way that brought home to all concerned what a corrosive influence the divorce issue had become. A mob of Norfolk's retainers, including the courtier brothers Richard, Robert and Anthony Southwell, had chased William Pennington, a member of Charles Brandon's suite, into the sanctuary of Westminster Abbey and there stabbed him to death. When the news reached the Duke of Suffolk he had immediately set off with some of his own men to 'sort out' the culprits. Fortunately a message from the King stopped him before a bloodbath ensued. Brandon's men were sworn to keep the peace but one of them vowed that he would be even with the Southwells, 'although it were in the king's chamber or at the high altar'. The thugs were subsequently pardoned upon forfeit to the King of a couple of Essex manors. The Southwells continued at court, accruing honours and wealth (how fortunate that they chose to run Pennington through rather than poison him!). The case never came to trial, so all we know about the cause of the violent dispute is the theories blabbed by wagging tongues at Westminster. The fracas, they said, was the result of the Brandon–Howard feud and, particularly, of Suffolk's opposition to the annulment.

This was the background against which Cromwell dramatically and, apparently on his own initiative, broke the deadlock, in effect, plucking victory from the jaws of defeat. He deliberately stirred up the one issue which he knew still smarted with the common lawyers and their parliamentary friends: the activities of the Church courts. The result was a petition from the Commons, similar to that which they had presented in 1529, called the Supplication Against the Ordinaries, which asked the King to legislate against a list of offences perpetrated by a priestly cast backed by canon law. Henry handed the document to convocation for their response and the clergy played straight into their enemies' hands. Gardiner himself penned a trenchant rebuttal of the parliamentary accusations, insisting that Church courts came under direct divine authority and should not be interfered with by temporal powers. That was not a wise thing to say to Henry VIII and Gardiner realised too late that he had blundered in setting loyalty to the Church before loyalty to the King. Henry relayed the reply to the Commons with a broad hint: 'We think their answer will smally please you, for it seemeth to us very slender. You be a great sort of wise men; I doubt not but you will look circumspectly on the matter, and we will be indifferent between you.'[77] But it was not only the clergy who had struck a raw nerve. From parliament's lower chamber had come an unwelcome warning about any attempt to extract more taxes and a call for Henry to take Catherine and her daughter back into favour. The King, although he 'marvelled not a little' that matters pertaining to his own soul should have been raised in the parliament chamber, did deign to explain to the Commons' representatives why his conscience was troubled and reject any suggestion that he was motivated by carnal desire ('I am forty-one years old, at which age the lust of man is not so quick as in lusty youth').[78]

That was how matters stood on 30 April 1532 and for a week nothing happened – in public. A kind of mental paralysis seems to have gripped most of the lead players. Norfolk was under a cloud because of his involvement in the recent affray. Council meetings were dominated by personality and policy clashes. Gardiner, so recently regarded as the King's right hand, was suddenly excluded from his master's intimate concerns. Parliament and convocation were poised like armies confronting each other across a potential battlefield, each waiting for the other to make a move. Only Cromwell's mind was whirring with the efficiency of well-oiled clockwork. He analysed the situation succinctly and clearly for the King and outlined a course of action which, if carried through boldly, would deliver all that he desired. For Henry it must have seemed like a return to the good old days when Wolsey had briefed him on current events and guaranteed the careful execution of well-conceived plans.

CHAPTER 25

The End of the Affair

The new, fresh, stratagem was to be a frontal assault on the legislative powers of the clergy. On 10 May Henry presented an ultimatum to convocation. He demanded a complete review of canon law by a mixed lay and clerical commission of his selection. Any item which failed the test was to be abolished and all future canons were to be submitted for the approval of the Crown in parliament. While Warham and the bishops were juggling with this hot potato the King pulled another from the embers. The very next day he invited the Commons to express their views on the status of the clergy's relationship to the monarchy:

> The 11th day of May, the king sent for the Speaker again, and 12 of the Commons house, having with him eight Lords, and said to them, wellbeloved subjects, we thought that the clergy of our realm, had been our subjects wholly, but now we have well perceived, that they be but half our subjects, yea, and scarce our subjects: for all the prelates at their consecration, make an oath to the Pope, clean contrary to the oath that they make to us, so that they seem to be his subjects, and not ours, the copy of both the oaths, I deliver here to you, requiring you to invent some order, that we be not thus deluded, of our spiritual subjects.[79]

Convocation, meanwhile, discussed the King's ultimatum with the threat of more extreme demands from parliament hanging over them and considered the offer of a compromise. But Henry allowed them no leisure. He demanded a speedy answer and the immediate prorogation of the assembly. To demonstrate to the clergy that he meant business he sent Norfolk and groups of councillors to hurry them up. Thus bullied, badgered and hassled, the two houses of convocation voted (probably by narrow majorities; the details are unknown) to accept the royal edict on 15 May and the following day the Submission of the Clergy received legal formulation.

The pulpit battle was still going on. On Sunday 13 May in the midst of Henry's showdown with convocation the preacher at court upset Chapuys by calling the Pope a heretic. The ambassador and the papal nuncio complained to Norfolk who evinced no surprise, saying that the man

> was more of a Lutheran than Martin himself and that, had it not been for
> the Earl of Wiltshire and another personage whom he could not name
> (meaning, no doubt the Lady Anne herself), he would have had the said
> preacher and another doctor, his colleague, burned alive; and ended by
> begging the nuncio not to mention such bagatelles when he wrote to
> Rome, as he would in future surely prevent the recurrence of such
> offences.[80]

This is the first real hint that survives which suggests that court factions were beginning to take on a religious character.

If Howard really thought that radical preaching at court was a 'bagatelle' to which he could easily put a stop he vastly underestimated the problem and overestimated his own influence. Heresy had taken root in the royal household and would prove impossible to eradicate. If he had had the wit to interpret certain other events occurring during these troubled weeks he would not have spoken with such self-assurance.

The most striking was the fate of Thomas More. His stance as public scourge of heretics and private opponent of the divorce was well known. The painful impossibility of his position had driven him to ask Norfolk to intercede with the King to release him from office but Henry was not prepared to take a step which would, in effect, announce to the world that his chief lay officer of state rejected the central plank of government policy. However, the events of mid-May caused the King to change his mind. Now, according to Chapuys, the Commons had brought in a bill to prevent ecclesiastical authorities incarcerating in their own prisons laymen accused of heresy. The ambassador may well have been right (though one must always be cautious about relying on the evidence of this highly partisan witness, there is no reason to doubt the accuracy of his intelligence on this matter) since, only a few days before (30 April), several members had witnessed the burning in Smithfield of a prominent London lawyer, James Bainham, who, it was widely believed, had been abominably treated by More and the Bishop's officers while in custody. Chapuys reported that the spiritual peers were opposing the bill and that they were being supported by the Lord Chancellor.[81] It was out of the question for Henry to countenance More's support of ecclesiastical powers he was in the process of curtailing. If matters were coming to a head in parliament this would explain why the attack on canon law and the prorogation of parliament (14 May) were precipitated *and* why Norfolk was despatched to bring More into the garden of York Place on the afternoon of 16 May to hand over the Great Seal – His Majesty having graciously consented to allow Sir Thomas to spend more time with his family. More insisted to Erasmus, a few weeks later, that he had resigned on health grounds and that this had been explained to parliament by Norfolk and Sir Thomas Audley. We can take the first assertion with a pinch of salt and, since the members of Lords and Commons had already gone home, we must reject the second also.

Howard had never been close to More but he might well have been worried by the wild rejoicing with which the Lord Chancellor's downfall was greeted in the streets of London. Something else which might have sounded warnings bells in the Duke's head was the latest episode in the career of Hugh Latimer. The radical Cambridge preacher enjoyed the support of Cromwell, William Butts and members of Anne's group and had been appointed to a valuable Wiltshire living. However, as a result of remarks made in a sermon in London, he was cited to appear before convocation in March 1532. Latimer submitted to the judgement of his fellow clergy but then annoyed them by writing a letter (soon intercepted) to a friend denying that he had recanted of any substantive heresy. Summoned back into convocation, Latimer now appealed to Henry. His court friends secured him an audience and, though Latimer was instructed to make his peace with the Church leaders, they were ordered, via Gardiner, to receive him back into favour. Unbowed, the reformer returned to his cure where he soon became the centre of fresh controversy. However, his enemies were henceforth cautious about proceeding against him. A year later he was one of Queen Anne's chaplains.

The summer saw some respite of political activity but all the signs were ominous for those who secretly or openly opposed the casting off of Catherine and Mary. Norfolk had no particular affection for the Queen and the Princess but he was pulled in different directions by his loyalty to the King and to the Church. Fortunately for him, choices were made easier by his commitment to a higher loyalty – that to the house of Howard. In order to keep his position, he swallowed his indignation at the continued rise of Cromwell. At last he had learned to control the temper that in earlier years had led to his temporary banishment from court on more than one occasion. But the provocations were many and grievous. Cromwell now had easier access than himself to the King. They discussed policy issues together before they were considered in the Council and sometimes decisions were taken on Cromwell's advice without being approved by Norfolk and his colleagues. What must have been perplexing for Howard was the fact that, unlike Wolsey, Cromwell made no attempt to distance Henry from his advisers. He did not control government business from his own house or deliberately exclude the household officers. Yet he seemed to be achieving the same kind of independent control that the Cardinal had enjoyed. He had begun to receive court positions and other perks and was introducing his own cronies to the life of the court. The Duke was still consulted, particularly on foreign policy, and was normally Henry's chosen representative to other courts but ambassadors' reports make it quite clear that Cromwell was the man to see if one really wanted to know what the King of England was thinking on a given issue.

If the new minister was beginning to be an irritant, Anne had become quite insufferable. She behaved as though she were already queen, wearing jewels that Henry had taken from his wife and ruling the court with an arrogance that seemed boundless. 'The Lady commands absolutely and her will is done in all things,' Chapuys reported, and we gain an impression of her 'high stomach' in a taunt the ambassador relayed to his master. Informed by a flatterer that the Emperor would soon be reconciled to the idea of her becoming queen, she replied, 'that she was nowise anxious for the crown or for her own happiness if they were to come from [the Emperor's] hands'.[82] By this time Norfolk had reached the point of loathing his niece and resenting the fact that his position rested largely on his involvement with the Boleyn faction. His mood cannot have been improved when, in late August, old Warham, finally worn down by his futile attempts to preserve the independence and integrity of the clergy, died and the news spread that he was to be replaced, not by some seasoned ecclesiastic but by the Boleyns' 'creature', Thomas Cranmer.

The Duke, who could not allow his own feelings to become obvious, was involved in the diplomacy and ceremonial which marked the next stage of Anne's aggrandisement. The great matter had forced England into the arms of France and arrangements were being made for a meeting between Henry and Francis. It was hoped that combined pressure might be able to prise Pope and Emperor apart and create the circumstances that would enable Clement to decide the matrimonial issue once and for all in Henry's favour. It was a forlorn hope but all those involved went through the motions, no one more eagerly than Howard. He was in receipt of a healthy pension from the French Crown and this was increased during the autumn as an added incentive. But Norfolk had a personal reason for wanting to bring off what would have been a remarkable coup. The political scene in England was developing into a tussle between those who opposed the annulment and wished to maintain friendship with the Emperor* and those determined, by hook or by crook, to achieve the King's policy objectives. Increasingly the latter were becoming identified with religious radicalism and the former with a determined traditionalism. Norfolk's gut instincts were aligned with the conservatives and he feared what might happen if the Boleyn and Cromwell caucuses actually managed to deliver the divorce. Norfolk knew full well that the

---

*This is referred to by some historians, I believe unhelpfully, as the 'Aragonese faction'. Despite the activities of Chapuys in trying to weld together a party comprising Catherine's household and sympathisers at court, and the tentacles which spread out from this centre to allies at home and abroad, the grouping never possessed the cohesion or clear policy objectives that would justify the use of the word 'faction'. Had such a political force existed, Henry would have acted swiftly to crush it.

nomination of Cranmer as Archbishop was a major step towards having the validity of the royal marriage tried in England and decided in Henry's favour. However, if that objective could, after all, be obtained by agreement with Rome, then the sting of the extremists would have been drawn, there would be no need for further shows of strength against the clergy and Norfolk would be able to regain the ascendancy.

That meant attending Anne Boleyn, with a fixed smile on his face, on 1 September when she was elevated to the peerage in her own right as Marchioness of Pembroke. The ceremony, simple by contemporary standards, took place at Windsor.

> The lady was conveyed by noblemen and the officers of arms at Windsor Castle to the king, who was accompanied by the dukes of Norfolk and Suffolk and other noblemen, and the ambassador of France. Mr Garter bore her patent of creation; and lady Mary, daughter to the duke of Norfolk, her mantle of crimson velvet, furred with ermines, and a coronet. The lady Marquess, who was 'in her hair', and dressed in a surcoat of crimson velvet, furred with ermines, with straight sleeves, was led by Elizabeth countess of Rutland, and Dorothy countess of Sussex. While she kneeled before the king, Garter delivered her patent, which was read by the bishop of Winchester. The king invested her with the mantle and coronet, and gave her two patents – one of her creation, and other of £1,000 a year. She thanked the king, and returned to her chamber.[83]

As well as being a further demonstration of Henry's feelings for his mistress the ennoblement was a necessary preparation for a French visit during which Anne accompanied him as consort.

All the leading members of the court attended the King to Calais on 11 October and took part in the ritual splendours attendant upon a sixteenth-century summit meeting, which lasted from 20 October to the end of the month. After the banqueting, dancing, masquerading, hunting, hawking and 'great shot of artillery' in which Norfolk played his part by feasting the French nobility in Calais Castle 'with many goodly sports and pastimes'[84] the English were delayed by storms from returning until 13 November. Thereafter, the entourage made a very leisurely progress through Kent, not reaching Eltham until the 24th.

These were crucial weeks. The relaxed atmosphere of festivity and holiday turned them, for Henry and Anne, into a prenuptial honeymoon for it was now that they became lovers in the full sense of the word. And, in the intensifying of their relationship there was an element of calculation. Two plans for solving the divorce/marriage crisis were being pursued simultaneously. Beneath the showy diplomacy Norfolk was conducting with his French counterparts, Cromwell was developing his strategy for a purely English solution. With a pliant archbishop in post the way was open for making Anne legitimately Queen of England. However, it was obvious that Catherine would immediately appeal to the Pope against such uncanonical proceedings and that, therefore, some means must be found of preventing such a reaction. Cromwell and the King discussed the legislative means by which this might be achieved. Whether or not Henry committed himself to this course during the French visit is not clear but other events soon made up his mind for him. While he and the court were still at Dover on their way home the latest ultimatum arrived from Rome: the lovers were to separate immediately on pain of excommunication and Henry was to abandon any arrangements he might be contemplating to have the annulment issue decided in England. If that did not break the last strand of the King's reluctance to defy the papacy what Anne told him within the month did – she was pregnant.

Anne's condition now dominated the pace of events. Marriage was essential to legitimise the male heir Henry had no doubt she was carrying. At the same time plans had to be made for Cranmer to dissolve the union with Catherine. Before that could be done Cromwell's new measure – the Act in Restraint of Appeals – had to be on the statute book. And all this must be accomplished before Anne's pregnancy became obvious and set ribald and malicious tongues wagging.

Parliament assembled on 26 January and on 25 January Henry and Anne were married in the west turret of York Place in the presence of three witnesses, sworn to secrecy. The officiant was Rowland Lee, a royal chaplain since the previous August. Lee had been a member of Wolsey's household and had entered royal service at the same time as his close colleague, Thomas Cromwell. In the preliminary formalities for the opening of parliament Thomas Audley, designated Keeper of the Great Seal since the previous May, was now given the full dignity of Lord Chancellor, in order to preside over the upper chamber. Audley was widely recognised as a Cromwell dependant. His place as Speaker of the Commons was taken by Humphry Wingfield and he, too, had advanced with Cromwell through service to Wolsey and been closely involved with his colleague in setting up and then dismantling the Ipswich and Oxford colleges. There can be no doubt about who was at the King's right hand amidst the intrigue and clandestine activities of January–May 1533.

Cromwell had already been working hard on the Bill for restraining appeals to Rome. It passed through as many as eight drafts before reaching the form in which it was presented to parliament. Everything depended on its successful passage and Cromwell was taking no chances. He even had to tone down some of the inflammatory language the King suggested for earlier versions. There was nothing counterfeit about Henry's anger towards Rome by this time. In March 1533 Chapuys relayed to his master the gist of a conversation he had had with the King in the garden at York Place:

... he began to say a thousand things in disparagement of the Pope, and among the rest how vainglorious he was to have his feet kissed [by princes] and what authority and power he unduly assumed over the empire and also over the rest of Christendom, creating and deposing Emperors at will . . . As to himself, he was about to apply a remedy to the Pope's inordinate ambition and repair the errors of King Henry II and King John, who in a moment of need had been tricked into making England and Ireland tributaries to the Holy See. He was also thinking of uniting to the Crown the lands which the clergy of his dominions held thereof, which lands and property his predecessors on the throne could not alienate to his prejudice. This he was bound to do by the very oath he had sworn at his coronation.[85]

Cromwell made sure that such complaints which might have aroused opposition only appeared in general terms in the bill. He submitted it in draft to other lawyers, to churchmen and canonists. In no other matter did this most careful of men take greater care.

The most important change that came over the measure was the widening of its scope. What began as a piece of projected legislation designed to facilitate the King's divorce ended up as a means of cutting the Pope off entirely from any say in disputes involving Henry's subjects.

All causes testamentary, causes of matrimony and divorces, rights of tithes, oblations and obventions (the knowledge whereof by the goodness of princes of this realm and by the laws and customs of the same apperteineth to the spiritual jurisdiction of this realm) already commenced, moved, depending, being, happening, or hereafter coming in contention, debate or question within this realm or within any the King's dominions or marches of the same or elsewhere . . . shall be from henceforth heard, examined, discussed, clearly finally and definitely adjudged and determined, within the King's jurisdiction and authority and not elsewhere . . . without having any respect to any custom, use or sufferance in hindrance, let or prejudice of the same or to any other thing used or suffered to the contrary thereof by any other manner person or persons in any manner of wise; any foreign inhibitions, appeals, sentences, summons, citations, suspensions, interdictions, excommunications, restraints, judgments, or any other process or impediments of what natures, names, qualities or conditions soever they be, from the see of Rome or any other foreign courts or potentates of the world, or from and out of this realm or any other the King's dominions or marches of the same to the see of Rome or to any other foreign courts or potentates, to the let or impediment thereof in any wise notwithstanding.[86]

The bill did not have an easy passage, scraping through just before prorogation on 7 April, but once on the statute book the Act in Restraint of Appeals marked a constitutional turning point as dramatic as the Reform Act of 1832 or the Parliament Act of 1911.

Thomas Cranmer arrived home in the early days of the new year to take up his part in the outworking of the royal triumph. He was immediately in cahoots with Cromwell and became a lead member of the tiny consortium controlling the main business of Church and State. However, he could not act in his archiepiscopal capacity until the necessary confirmatory documents had arrived from Rome. Bearing in mind the effective intelligence service operated by Chapuys and Catherine's supporters and also the curia's infinite capacity for delay, it is surprising that the opposition did not make good use of this opportunity to throw an effective spanner in the works of Henry's plans. As it was, everyone concerned was frustrated at not being able to proceed with delivering the last rites to the twenty-four-year-old royal marriage. The necessary bulls arrived about 26 March and Cranmer's was consecrated on the 30th. In the prevailing circumstances his installation by papal permission was somewhat anomalous and the ceremonies at Westminster were designed to assuage his own conscience and the King's sensibilities. Having sworn an oath of obedience to the Pope, the new Archbishop declared that this would not take priority over his allegiance to God and to the King or to his commitment to 'reformation of the Christian religion, the government of the English church, or the prerogative of the Crown, as the wellbeing of the commonwealth'. Indeed he pledged himself 'to prosecute and reform matters wheresoever they seem to me to be for the reform of the English church'[87] – ominous words for the likes of those who hoped for a period of peace and quiet once the King had finally got his own way over the divorce.

Easter now interposed itself and it was not until the beginning of May that all the formalities had been concluded which would enable Cranmer to call Henry's marital status into court. The trickiest problem to be overcome was how to indict before an ecclesiastical tribunal someone who had thrown off papal supremacy and claimed headship of the English Church. Cranmer agonised over the precise wording of the letter by which he called the King to answer the charge of living in sin for a quarter of a century and Henry had no less difficulty in the reply by which he graciously submitted his cause to God and the judgement of the Archbishop. On 10 May the trial opened at Dunstable Priory, well away from the London rabble, and Cranmer summoned King and Queen to appear before him. Catherine, of course, refused and a couple of days elapsed before the president could pronounce her contumacious and get on with things. With each passing day the needs of haste and decency came more into conflict. Cromwell pestered his colleague for a speedy conclusion and a harassed Cranmer replied that he was moving things as fast as he could. By 17 May he had reached his decision but he could not

formally declare it until the next session of the court. There were, as he
pointed out to Cromwell, other reasons for caution, even clandestinity:

> I pray you to make no relation thereof, as I know w[ell you] will not, for
> if the noble lady Catherine should, by th[e bruit of] this matter in the
> mouths of the inhabitants of the [country, or] by her friends or council
> hearing of this bruit, be [moved, stirred,] counselled or persuaded to
> appear afore me in the ti[me or afore] the time of sentence, I should be
> thereby greatly stai[d and let] in the process, and the King's grace's
> council here pre[sent shall be] much uncertain what shall be then further
> done the[rein. For a] great bruit and voice of the people in this behalf
> [might] move her to do that thing herein which peradventure [she
> would] not do if she shall hear little of it; and therefore I [desire you] to
> speak as little of this matter as ye may, and t[o beseech the] King's
> highness in likewise so to do for the consyd[erations afore] recited.[88]

There was something anticlimactic about the final outcome of the
King's great matter. In the early afternoon of 23 May a hard-pressed
messenger clattered into the inner courtyard at Whitehall bearing a
scribbled note, hastily despatched from Dunstable, by John Tregonwell,
the King's proctor and yet another of the Cromwellian new men recently
brought on to the Council. It informed Cromwell that 'my lord of
Canterbury, this day at 10 of the clock before noon, hath given a sentence
in this great cause of matrimony, whereby he hath declared the same
matrimony to be against the law of God and hath, therefore, divorced the
King's highness from the noble Lady Catherine'.[89]

There was little time to spare. The five days of festivity accompanying
Anne's coronation had been planned to begin on 29 May. Henry had
decreed that it should be a spectacular event, an opportunity for London's
citizenry to demonstrate to the new Queen their loyalty and affection. The
City's notables came in their bravely decked barges to join with nobles and
courtiers to acclaim Anne and then to form a gay flotilla, escorting her to
the Tower, 'where were shot . . . above a thousand guns'. On the last day
of the month the Queen made a triumphal progress through the capital to
be welcomed with pageants and tableaux organised by the guilds and
corporation and hailed by crowds who were supposed to be cheering,
although Chapuys sourly reported that the Londoners were sullen and the
atmosphere was more like a funeral than a celebration.[90] Sunday 1 June
was the day of the actual coronation in Westminster Abbey, followed by
an impressive banquet in the great Norman hall. Everything wound up on
Monday with a tourney and more eating.

The man most notable for his absence from all the celebrations and
solemnities was the Duke of Norfolk. As recently as mid-April he had
sued for the recovery of the office of Earl Marshal which his father had

enjoyed but which had been granted to Suffolk in 1524. The King agreed, offering Brandon as a recompense the wardenship of royal forests south of the Trent, a much less prestigious office and Cromwell was instructed to write to Brandon to that effect. It has been assumed that Norfolk requested this favour with an eye to his niece's coronation and his desire to take a prominent part therein. However, Cromwell's letter conveying the unwelcome news also urged Suffolk to return to the court from East Anglia 'with reasonable speed' because Howard was about to depart on embassy to France.[91] Norfolk duly set off across the Channel in May and it was the other Duke who presided over the coronation as High Steward and Constable for the day. Norfolk's motivation had more to do with the prestige of his house and Anne's great day provided an opportunity rather than the reason for his regaining a hereditary office that he had always bitterly resented losing. It was the frosty relationship between Henry and his sister which made this possible. Mary's loathing for Anne was so intense that she had refused to accompany her brother and his paramour to France the previous autumn. She had pointedly absented herself from court ever since Henry had established Anne as consort and she made it clear that she would not be gracing the coronation. The King's annoyance gave Norfolk his chance to score over his ducal rival and he took it.

As to his own absence from Anne's day of triumph, that will not have dismayed him one iota, any more than it will have troubled Anne (indeed, it may have been the new Queen who barred her uncle from her great day). He was now wholly at odds with the Boleyns and their secretive activities. He had not been privy to the clandestine wedding in January or to the intimate discussion between the King, Anne's family, Cromwell and Cranmer. By the spring of 1533, Norfolk was so bitter about the rise of his niece, from which he had gained nothing, that he actually persuaded Chapuys that he had all along opposed the remarriage and had tried to dissuade Henry from it. The ambassador, always eager for evidence of Anne's unpopularity, actually believed him!

Howard's disillusionment sprang from his own disappointed ambition and a growing awareness that the divorce issue had broadened out into something far more disturbing. He was now being marginalised at court not just, as in the old days, by one overmighty cleric, but by a breed of royal councillors he little understood and trusted less. Like Tennyson's Bedevere he was aware of bewildering and unwelcome change:

> . . . the days darken round me, and the years,
> Among new men, strange faces, other minds.

His springtime embassade was his very last, desperate attempt to secure French help in bringing about an understanding with Rome. He returned, a failure, to find several disturbing events in train.

Clement VII pronounced a provisional excommunication against the King and his Council if he did not put Anne away before the end of September. Whatever Norfolk's concern about his own immortal soul might have been, he knew that this threatened the integrity of the English Church and the stability of the nation. Alarming signs of disintegration were all around.

Trouble had flared up again between the King and the Greenwich Observants. After the previous fracas Henry had obtained the removal of William Peto and his replacement by John Forest, a member of the order he knew well and trusted. Forest had promised to support the divorce proceedings but, once in post, he not only preached himself on Catherine's behalf, but inhibited his brothers from taking any other line. The Greenwich house was split and one of their number appealed to Anne and to Cromwell:

> Truly, good Master Cromwell, it grieveth my heart very sore, to see, persever, and know the unkindness and duplicity of Father Forest against the King's Grace; considering as I know how good and beneficial his Grace hath been both to him and to his poor friends, and that of long time.[92]

Doubtless, this was, in origin at least, an issue of personality clashes not infrequent in the claustrophobic world of the cloister, but the appeals bore fruit within the new regime at court. Henry was informed and, always sensitive to personal betrayal, he had Forest removed and despatched to a community in the far north.*

Hugh Latimer's fate was far different. He could not and would not keep silent and, in the early months of 1533, his preaching was at the centre of serious disturbances in Bristol. He inveighed so powerfully and persuasively against pilgrimages, worship of saints and other aspects of popular superstition that, 'he hath very sore infected the said town of Bristol'.[93] His enemies complained to convocation but that was now a very different body than it had been the year before. Its powers were curtailed and it was under the leadership of Thomas Cranmer. Nothing effective was done and the conflict grew into a test case between evangelicals and conservatives. In July Cromwell intervened. He took depositions from several witnesses and discussed them in Council. As a result it was not Latimer who was discomfited. Quite the contrary; the preacher's enemies had gone too far. They had, in conversations and sermons, criticised the royal divorce and maintained papal authority. They

---

*This was not the end of Forest's troubles. The King's opposition served to strengthen his resolve. A year later he was imprisoned in Newgate charged with opposing the royal supremacy. Ultimately, he died a violent and barbarous death in the fires of Smithfield.

were reprimanded; some were thrown in jail; and as for Latimer, the new Archbishop gave him a licence to preach anywhere in his province.

Norfolk could not but find the new policy trends alarming, particularly when they extended to foreign affairs. Cromwell was now bringing known Lutherans into the King's service. Christopher Mont, a native of Cologne, had been for some time a member of the minister's household. In July the King despatched him to the Protestant princes of Germany to foster good relations between England and the heretical states. The Queen also had overseas connections with religious radicals. Her contacts were among the advanced humanists of the French court, as Howard had good reason to know. Francis I's sister, Marguerite d'Angoulême, extended her patronage to a miscellany of reformists centred at Meaux, to the east of Paris, and used her influence, much as Anne did, to promote churchmen of advanced opinions. Most of her group were disciples of France's leading humanist, Jacques Lefèvre d'Etaples, who had been suspected of heresy and latterly removed himself to Nérac, far to the south (still under Marguerite's protection). When one member of her salon, the poet Nicholas Bourbon, overstepped the mark in 1523 with a swingeing attack on Parisian reactionaries, and found himself in jail, he managed to get an appeal to Anne Boleyn. As a result of her intercession Bourbon was freed and came to England to render his thanks is person and meet members of her circle.

From his letters and the flattering verses Bourbon wrote we can build up a picture of the evangelical 'caucus' in and around the court. The Frenchman mentioned Cranmer, Cromwell, Sir William Butts, Cornelius Heyss (the King's goldsmith), Nicholas Kratzer (the King's astronomer), Hans Holbein and Hugh Latimer. Cromwell he apostrophied as 'aflame with the love of Christ'. Cranmer was 'a gift from God'. Latimer he called 'the best of preachers'. And of Anne he wrote 'the spirit of Jesus inflames you wholly with his fire'.[94] There were others Bourbon might have mentioned, for to Howard's jaundiced eye, the court must have seemed to be awash with dangerous progressives, bent on influencing the King to force England down the road of international evangelical heresy. Men like Nicholas Shaxton, in trouble at Cambridge for possessing banned books and forced to abjure the heresies of Wycliffe, Hun and Luther, and now Queen Anne's Almoner.

Catholic, conservative and Imperial enthusiasts (tending more and more to coalesce) were not prepared to accept the Henrician *fait accompli* and many of them looked to Norfolk as the obvious bridgehead into the English court. A memorandum penned in Rome in the summer of 1533 by a former papal emissary to England who claimed to be a friend of the Duke, suggested a truly Machiavellian piece of deception. Its author opined that Henry was already growing tired of Anne and that after the birth of their child he might be prevailed upon to return to his first wife, as long as the baby was legitimised. Henry could be 'sold' this as the best of all possible worlds – a secure succession, restored friendship with Charles and the opportunity to undo the recent anti-papal legislation. There was only one person, the writer believed, capable of putting this schema to King Henry.

> Only the duke of Norfolk can persuade him to do this by his influence, and relationship to the new queen, pointing out that the peace of the Kingdom and the settlement of the king's son weighs more with him than the good of his own niece, and that if the king were to die before the son became a man, the next heirs might trouble the succession – ie the king of Scotland and the sons of the other sister and of the duke of Suffolk.

However, the real object of this manoeuvring was not to place Anne's as yet unborn child on the throne, but to secure the succession for Mary. The writer, Uberto de Gambara, proposed to open the plot to Norfolk in the greatest secrecy.

> I think I could point out to him that this course would so endear him to the emperor and the pope that they would enable him to have the princess for his son; whose right would not really be put aside, and they would afterwards help to maintain him by force.

The legitimising of the new child would carry no weight and, in any case, it was likely to be still a minor when Henry died. Thus there could be little doubt that the political nation would rally round Mary and her husband.[95]

Had this scheme ever been put to Thomas Howard he would have been scared out of his wits lest news of it should reach the King's ears. It would have been quite sufficient to ensure that he shared Buckingham's fate. What is interesting about it is what Gambara thought about Norfolk. He believed the Duke could be bribed by the chance to unite his family with the Tudors. Howard's ambition had long leaned in that direction, as Gambara knew. It irked him that his rival, Charles Brandon, was married to the King's sister and that they had sons who were, therefore, potential claimants to the crown. Norfolk *had*, indeed, hoped to arrange a union between Princess Mary and his elder son, the Earl of Surrey. However, Henry would not countenance it and, in April 1532, he settled for a union with the house of De Vere and contracted Surrey to the Earl of Oxford's daughter. This presented no real obstacle to Gambara's Byzantine schemes. The bride and groom were too young to be living together and, therefore, the marriage could easily be set aside. This royal avenue having been closed, Norfolk turned to another. At the end of 1533 he married his daughter to the King's illegitimate son, the Duke of Richmond. By this time, Queen Anne had been delivered of her child – and it was a girl, christened Elizabeth. This news, which was as unwelcome to Henry as a biblical plague, was manna in the wilderness to Thomas Howard. Providence might yet deny the King the male heir he craved and, in that case, he might well seek to divert the succession to his only son. Upstarts, lawyers and priests might come and go. Religious novelties might fall in and out of fashion. But the Howards would always be close to the throne. They were part of the fabric of the kingdom and they would not be ousted from their rightful place in it.

CHAPTER 26

The Unholy Maid

Everybody who was anybody and anybody who aspired to be somebody was conspicuously present at Queen Anne's coronation. But there were those who chose to absent themselves and by doing so make a statement about the 'true' Queen and her usurper. One was Henry's sister. There had been a growing estrangement between the royal siblings ever since the King had openly taken up with the Lady Anne. The Princess appeared seldom at court and at the end of May she pointedly remained in Suffolk. Had she wished to do so she could have honestly pleaded ill health for she was, in fact, dying and breathed her last before June was out. Legend has it that she was reconciled to her brother before the end. Another notable absentee had no excuse and did not deign to offer one. Despite the pleading of his friends, Thomas More spent the days of celebration quietly at his Chelsea home. The King said and did nothing but he registered the ex-Chancellor's display of disrespect. More said and did nothing, hoping that circumspection would win him peaceful retirement from public life. But the time for neutrality had passed. The settlement of the divorce issue had been not the beginning of the end but the end of the beginning. England had entered on a new age of clashing convictions about eternal truth and it was impossible for men in the public eye to avoid taking sides. Within a year Thomas More was a prisoner in the Tower of London.

What ultimately destroyed him were those internal forces which had always pulled him in different directions. His psychological complexities interacted with the convolution of events in the outside world. Those events, like the current of a river gradually accelerating towards the thunderous cataract, bore him along and there was no escape to be found at the stream's calmer margins. It was clashing principles, clashing personalities and clashing propagandas that made up the intricacies of More's last years.

Thirty-one months in office was not very long to complete the reform of the legal system which Wolsey had been engaged in, intermittently, for fourteen years, but More did apply himself to the task of simplifying procedures and cutting out those delays which always worked in favour of wealthier and more powerful litigants. Easier access to the courts, a measure of control over corruption and the establishment of Star Chamber as the ultimate tribunal had gone some way towards the provision of truly impartial justice but these measures had also encouraged plaintiffs and defendants, who might not otherwise have done so, to try litigation and, when dissatisfied with the result, to move their actions from court to court.

In endeavouring to improve the situation the Lord Chancellor found himself on the horns of a dilemma; the need to serve both equity and efficiency. Equity demanded that judges in directing juries and in handing down their own decisions sought to interpret the spirit of the law rather than encouraging quibbles over legal niceties. That meant ensuring that all evidence with a reasonable bearing on a case should be presented. Efficiency was all about cutting out time-wasters and concluding hearings with the greatest possible despatch. A judge needed sterling qualities; not only must he be impartial and honest, he must also marry sympathy and severity. He tried, himself, to live up to this combination of virtues and, in the opinion of William Roper, succeeded to perfection.

A case which, in Roper's opinion, proved the wisdom and integrity of his father-in-law was that involving Giles Heron, husband of Cecily More. In a Chancery suit More adjudged his son-in-law guilty of contempt. Heron had, perhaps, presumed on family influence. More refused to proceed with the case and bound young Giles in the sum of 1,000 marks, to present himself in Star Chamber or face a spell in the Tower.

In his attitude towards the administration of the law More displayed that mix of idealism and pragmatism that he expressed in *Utopia*. Judges were to be chosen for their sterling worth and were then to act with unflinching firmness. More once joked that he would rather trust one judge than two juries. At root he was an authoritarian with a vision of society regulated by virtuous men according to incontrovertible laws. *Utopia* was a police state because, when all temptation to disharmony (such as inequalities of wealth) were removed, citizens still had to be dragooned into uniformity.

When it came to religion More's rigorism was undiluted by any faith equivalent of equity. There was no question of a suspected heretic making a case for his beliefs; no room for what Erasmus charitably called *adiaphora*; no necessity for impartial adjudication; and certainly no assumption that a defendant was innocent until proved guilty (More believed that it did a suspect no harm to be subjected to imprisonment and interrogation and required to abjure unorthodox opinions even if he could not be shown ever to have held such opinions). Thomas More was a persecutor of heretics and he gloried in the work. 'The clergy doth denounce them . . . the temporalty doth burn them. And after the fire of Smithfield, hell doth receive them where the wretches burn forever'[96] – so he vindictively exulted.

In the battle against heresy More used to the full his position as principal law officer. He issued, on his own authority, a list of banned books. He devised an oath to be taken alike by senior judges, local JPs and all 'having governance of the people'. It committed them, *as their first priority*, to seek out and apprehend any persons suspected of erroneous beliefs or who criticised the practices and personnel of the Church. He maintained his own army of agents and informers, at home and abroad, to sniff out the supply routes of banned books. More was a man obsessed. The new Lord Chancellor certainly made good the shortcomings of his predecessor: during his two and a half years in office eight men were burned at the stake, more than had perished in the whole of the preceding decade. In any consideration of More as a martyr to conscience these other deaths must be taken into account.

He played his own part in the examination of suspected heretics. Foxe recorded the names of four men who were imprisoned and interrogated at Chelsea. According to the martyrologist, More had George Bainham tied to a tree and flogged and, subsequently, watched him being racked in the Tower. A Cambridge bookseller was tortured with cords tightened round his head. More rejected these and other charges and since the claim and the rebuttal were both the results of prejudice it is impossible to say which was true. What is clear is that, in a capital city very sensitive to wrongful arrests and vexatious heresy hunts, Sir Thomas had a black reputation. Nor was it only Protestant apologists of a later generation who accused him; More had to defend himself against Christopher St German, who charged him in print with excessive persecutory zeal. Even when he was out of office More was seen as the leading champion of orthodoxy. When the sacramentary John Frith was in the Tower of London at the end of 1532 a certain tailor, William Holt (one of More's agents?) tricked the reformer into writing down his doctrine of the mass, and it was to More that the *agent provocateur* rushed hotfoot with the damning evidence.

In the midst of his official duties and his inquisitorial crusade More found time for a prodigious programme of controversial writing. Tyndale had responded to his *Dialogue Concerning Heresies* and Sir Thomas immediately came back at him. The mammoth *Confutation of Tyndale's Answer* appeared in two volumes in 1532 and 1533. As well as the comprehensive doctrinal arguments set forth in the book, Sir Thomas delighted to reveal how much he had unearthed about the clandestine English evangelical cells on the Continent. Nor could he prevent himself dwelling on his favourite sins:

> Then have we from George Joye otherwise called Clark, a goodly godly epistle wherein he teacheth diverse other heresies, but specially that men's vows and promises made of chastity, be not lawful nor can bind no man in conscience, but he may wed when he will.
> And this man . . . determined therefore with himself that he would of his preaching, shew himself an example. And therefore being [a priest];

Thomas More, 1527, Hans Holbein.

This is More the upwardly-mobile royal servant, richly attired and proud to wear the Tudor rose. It is also More the Christian humanist, acutely aware of the vanity of worldly pomp, as signified by the seemingly incongruous rope (Latin *funis* = rope; *funus* = of death). Does the artist suggest that the two Mores are an uncomfortable match – the wary eyes, the restless hands, the skewed rose, the wisp of hair protruding from the cap?

Henry VIII, Mary Tudor and Will Somers, artist unknown.

This crude composite picture is based on images created by Holbein and Antonis Mor. It is a grim portrait, perhaps intended to underline both the dynastic and personality connections between father and daughter. They had little love for each other, but shared a stubborn determination, and the sire's ruthlessness was mirrored in the child. The reason for the inclusion of Henry's jester in the group is not clear.

Anne of Cleves, 1539, Hans Holbein.

Cromwell worked assiduously to achieve a marriage alliance with the house of Cleves as a means of freeing English diplomacy from the see-saw of Habsburg–Valois relations. Henry's aversion to Anne closed this diplomatic avenue and gave Cromwell's enemies the opportunity they had long sought to bring about his downfall.

A Lady: Portrait of an Unknown Lady (inscribed Anna Bollein Queen), c.1530,
Hans Holbein.

Experts disagree about authenticating portraits of Henry's second queen.
This representation from a collection of court drawings made by Holbein was
inscribed 'Anna Bollein Queen' soon after the artist's death (1543).

The Light of the World, Hans Holbein.

Woodcuts and engravings were powerful media for expressing and disseminating religious ideas in an age when few people were literate. Holbein served Cromwell and the evangelical cause with many images like this one which depicts Christ drawing ordinary people to the true light of Scripture, while the pope, and theologians, blindly following Aristotle, fall into the pit.

German woodcut of the deluge, 1524.

Apocalyptic was a common theme of religious imagery. In this picture, widespread destruction is prophesied when the planets came together in the zodiacal sign of *pisces*, the fish.

Thomas Cromwell, 1st Earl of Essex,
c.1530, after Hans Holbein.

The only authenticated representation of
Cromwell depicts him in what might be a frozen
moment in his busy day. He listens warily to some
unseen suitor while holding in his podgy hand the
next piece of business he must get on with. Beside
him are the scattered accoutrements of a royal
administrator – a letter from the king, a handsomely bound book (Cromwell was an eager
bibliophile), purse, pen and scissors.

Cranmer plucked from the pulpit, 1569.

This dramatic, though inaccurate representation of Cranmer being manhandled out of the university church towards the waiting fire appeared in a book by Stephen Bateman (sometimes spelled Batman!) during Elizabeth's reign, by which time the Archbishop's reputation had been reinstated.

Thomas Wriothesley, c.1535, Hans Holbein.

Holbein shows us an intelligent face and this facet of the courtier's personality is reinforced by his letters. Wriothesley wrote with a lively and astute observation of the political scene and it is not difficult to understand how he commended himself to Cromwell and to the King.

Thomas Cranmer, c.1550, artist unknown.

Cranmer vowed never to cut his beard after Henry's death (1547). This may be a testimonial to his genuine affection for the late king, but it is also possible that it demonstrated his identification with continental reformers, among whom beards were in fashion.

(*Overleaf*) Title page of Coverdale's Bible, 1535, Hans Holbein.

The publication of an English text of the Bible was a major triumph for the reformers and one for which both Cromwell and Cranmer had worked assiduously. In the title page of Miles Coverdale's version Holbein crammed several vital images. The quotations in the centre testify to the vital importance of reading Scripture. At the sides are depicted scenes from the Old and New Testaments, while below Henry VIII is shown as the wise sovereign bestowing this boon while bishops and nobles kneel in humble gratitude.

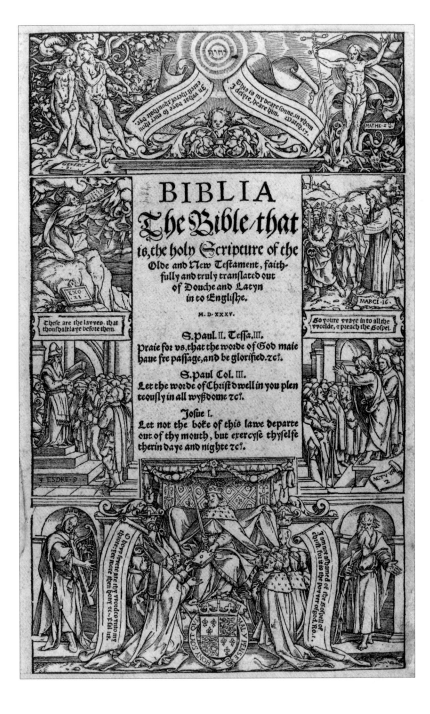

BIBLIA
The Bible/that
is, the holy Scripture of the
Olde and New Testament, faithfully and truly translated out
of Douche and Latyn
in to Englishe.

M. D. XXXV.

S. paul. II. Tessa. III.
Praie for vs, that the worde of God maie
haue fre passage, and be glorified. &c.

S. paul Col. III.
Let the worde of Christ dwell in you plen-
teously in all wyßdome &c.

Josue I.
Let not the boke of this lawe departe
out of thy mouth, but exercyse thy selfe
therin daye and nighte &c.

GENESIS 2.

MATHE. 2 &

These are the lavves. that
thou shalt laye before them.

3 ESDRE 9.

MARCI 16.

Go youre wraye in to all the
worlde, & preach the Gospel.

ACTV VIII.

HONY SOIT QVI MAL Y PENSE

he hath beguiled a woman and wedded her, the poor woman I ween unaware that he is [a] priest.[97]

In the same book the author made fun of Robert Barnes, thus putting a bold face on an episode that was an acute embarrassment to the conservative cause. Barnes, the colourful Cambridge friar who had faked his suicide and escaped abroad where he moved freely among various Lutheran communities, was brought back to England at the end of 1531 on Cromwell's instigation with a safe conduct from the King. This was in line with the prevailing policy of making contact with influential foreign groups who might support the divorce. The Lord Chancellor was powerless to do anything except have Barnes watched and minimise the propaganda advantage the evangelicals had gained by his winning of royal favour. More explained that the King was being graciously lenient to the ex-friar and wished to give him opportunity for repentance. More detailed Barnes's movements and habits: his favourite haunt was the Sign of the Bottle conveniently near the Steelyard and he wore a red beret! More hinted that Henry's name was being linked with that of a notorious heretic but, let the King once give the word, and the renegade could be pulled in within hours.

This was sailing dangerously close to the wind and More made his position still more precarious by an attempted attack on Cromwell. The relationship between the two men had not been good from the start, probably because they were too similar. Both were clever lawyers. Both were well versed in humanist thought. Both were well acquainted with the writings of the Lutherans. Both saw contemporary issues very clearly. Intellectually they were head and shoulders above their conciliar colleagues (and the King). They, therefore, understood each other very well and knew that they represented opposite ideological poles. The words which Roper attributed to his hero and which were reputedly spoken during the early days of the relationship have a decidedly 'wise after the event' feel about them but they do represent More's acute perception of Henry's character and his very real fear of how a clever adviser who also read that character well might try to direct it:

> Master Cromwell . . . you are now entered into the service of a most noble, wise and liberal prince. If you will follow my poor advice, you shall, in your counsel giving unto his grace, ever tell him what he ought to do, but never what he is able to do. So shall you show yourself a true faithful servant and a right worthy councillor. For if a lion knew his own strength, hard were it for any man to rule him.[98]

It was not Cromwell who elbowed More aside. The secret to his exclusion lay in those debates with Erasmus which had surfaced in *Utopia* about whether a philosopher could enter the counsels of his prince without being corrupted. More had, he believed, achieved a pact with Henry, absolving him from public involvement in the major policy issue of the day but his was always an untenable position and it was not necessary for Cromwell to weaken it.

It was probably in March 1531 that More was first pushed farther than he wanted to go. When the King decided to make his position over the divorce clear to parliament it was More who had to make a speech to the Commons:

> You of this worshipful House, I am sure, be not so ignorant but you know well that the king our sovereign lord hath married his brother's wife, for she was both wedded and bedded with his brother Prince Arthur, and therefore you may surely say that he hath married his brother's wife. If this marriage be good or no, many clerks do doubt. Wherefore the king, like a virtuous prince, willing to be satisfied in his conscience, and also for the surety of his realm hath with great deliberation consulted with great clerks, and hath sent my lord of London here present to the chief universities of all Christendom to know their opinion and judgment in that behalf.[99]

The favourable reports extracted from some of Europe's centres of learning were then read before More brought the matter to a close by entreating members to return to their towns and shires to convince their neighbours that 'the king hath not attempted this matter of will or pleasure, as some strangers report, but only for the discharge of his conscience and surety of the succession of his realm.'[100] It was soon after this that More asked, via Norfolk, permission to resign.

But the Lord Chancellor was far from being depressed and despondent – or, at least, that was not his permanent state of mind. The direction in which King and country were now being led was so perilous that it was his responsibility to resist it by all means possible that were compatible with his loyalty to Henry. This drew More into the dangerous coils of intrigue and involved him in making, almost on a daily basis, very fine calculations regarding his honesty and his safety. He kept Catherine's supporters apprised of the latest political and diplomatic developments. One problem the government created for itself by keeping the Reformation Parliament in being for session after session was that opponents of the divorce were able to meet frequently to encourage one another, pass on information and organise their resistance. Some of them congregated (appropriately) at the Queen's Head in Cripplegate. One of them was Sir George Throckmorton, a Warwickshire gentleman who early developed an antipathy for Cromwell. He was later interrogated about his behaviour in these crucial years and reported an interview with

More. The Lord Chancellor summoned him to the parliament chamber and said:

> 'I am very glad to hear the good report that goeth of you and that ye be so good a Catholic man as ye be; and if ye do continue in the same way that ye began and be not afraid to say your conscience, ye shall deserve great reward of God and thanks of the king's grace at length and much worship to yourself,' or words much like to these. Whereupon I took so much pride of this that shortly after I went to the bishop of Rochester, with whom I was divers times, and had much communication.[101]

This was scandalously improper behaviour for an officer of the Crown and it also breached the guidelines he had given in *Utopia* for the conduct of a philosopher/councillor. It was one thing to use tact to make 'what you cannot turn to good . . . as little bad as you can'. It was another to encourage opposition to the policies which, as a councillor, you were pledged to support. More had been corrupted as his own creation, Hythloday, had insisted he would be.

More could not converse openly with dissidents because his movements were watched. If not by Cromwell's appointed agents, certainly by those who would rush to tell tales in order to ingratiate themselves with the man in power. There was no question of More attending the Queen's Head gatherings and he even had to be careful about visitors he received at his house. When Chapuys wanted to travel up to Chelsea with a letter from the Emperor Sir Thomas was alarmed.

> He begged me for the honour of God to forbear, for although he had given already sufficient proof of his loyalty that he ought to incur no suspicion, whoever came to visit him, yet, considering the time, he ought to abstain from everything which might provoke suspicion; and if there were no other reason, such a visitation might deprive him of the liberty which he had always used in speaking boldly in those matters which concerned your Majesty and the queen. He said he would not hold them in less regard than his life, not only out of the respect which is due to your Majesty and the queen, but also for the welfare, honour, and conscience of his master, and the repose of his kingdom. With regard to the letter he begged me earnestly that I would keep it as it is till some other time, for if he received it he must communicate it, and he hoped a more propitious time would come for its acceptance, begging me to assure you of his most affectionate service.[102]

However, no one could object to More's ongoing purge of heretics and it was this that provided him, at the latter end of 1531, with an opportunity to strike at Cromwell through his accomplices. Among the heretics who fell into the Lord Chancellor's clutches was George Constantine, a longtime collaborator with the Tyndale group in the Netherlands and a colporteur of banned books. Constantine was not made of very stern stuff and after a few days' confinement at Chelsea he was ready to do a deal with his captor. More offered lenient treatment of the prisoner in return for information about those in England who were funding the writers of seditious books. Among those named by Constantine was Stephen Vaughan. When Cromwell heard of Constantine's arrest he was worried, and an anxious flurry of letters passed between him and his overzealous friends in Antwerp.

Had More been skilled in intrigue he would have calculated how best to use his information to advantage. The situation was delicately balanced. Henry was a sworn enemy of heresy but he was always ready to set his scruples aside if it was to his advantage to do so. Cromwell was currently riding high in the King's esteem, not least because he was in contact with German courts who might give support to the English King in his battle with the Pope. Vaughan, also, had been employed by Henry. It would be very difficult for More, who no longer enjoyed the King's confidence, to turn the tables on those in favour. While he was still contemplating how best to proceed Constantine broke free from his shackles, clambered over the wall at Chelsea and scuttled back overseas. From the safety of a foreign shore he distributed accusations against More as a vicious persecutor and torturer.

The moment of opportunity had passed but it had signalled clearly to Cromwell and his associates that Thomas More could be a danger. Anne, also, had turned decisively against him. Now that Wolsey was gone, she regarded his successor on the woolsack as the chief opponent of her marriage. She was very close to being right, though she cannot have understood how deeply More felt on the matter. Many people loved Catherine. Many loathed Anne and their hatred intensified the more overbearing the royal mistress became. Those committed to the authority of Rome resented Henry's attempts to set aside that authority. All these attitudes More shared but there were other reactions that sprang from the very foundation of his being. For him it was deeply offensive to see the King and his lover together. To be the servant of a prince living defiantly in sexual sin and contemplating making the relationship permanent was highly embarrassing – because of his own inability to come to terms with sexuality. In *Utopia* adultery was one of the few capital offences and divorce only permissible by mutual consent and the approval of the authorities. When More claimed poor health as his reason for wishing to relinquish the Great Seal he may not have been completely dishonest. He was under considerable mental pressure and this could well have produced the physical symptoms of what we now call 'stress'.

When he did achieve his release in May 1532 the humanist world was shocked and heretics rejoiced, as Erasmus, with his usual hyperbole, indicated:

> With what speed the rumour has flown all the way to your country that the distinguished Sir Thomas More has been removed from the office of chancellor and succeeded by another nobleman, who immediately released those who had been imprisoned by More for their contentious teachings . . . any speed possessed by a winged creature seems to be slow and sluggish compared with the swiftness with which this rumour has quickly spread over all the world. It was almost like the speed of lightning when it flashes into every quarter of the globe . . . He entered upon his office with the warmest congratulations of all the realm, such as no man had ever received before him; and when he resigned, it was with the deep sorrow of all wise and good men. For he resigned after earning the most wonderful praise: that no predecessor had administered that office with more skill or with greater justice.[103]

Probably the most significant words in that letter are those relating to the release of suspected heretics. They indicate that More's reputation as an enemy of religious radicals extended far beyond England and, if Audley really did enlarge some of his predecessor's prisoners (which would certainly have been seen as a popular gesture in London), this is further confirmation that leniency towards dissent was, for the time being at least, an aspect of government policy.

The ex-Chancellor has often been represented by biographers as living in seclusion at Chelsea and wishing only to lead a quiet life far from the dangers of the lion's court. In fact, he was unable to keep away from controversy. Had he confined himself to the theological debate with Tyndale, which few contemporaries took the trouble to follow, he would have been less of a thorn in the flesh of the prevailing regime but within months of his retirement he was engaged in a propaganda war with Cromwell's agents. Around the end of 1532 there emerged from Cromwell's circle an anonymous tract entitled *A Treatise concerning the Division between the Spiritualty and Temporalty*. It was probably by the veteran lawyer Christopher St German and, though couched in seemingly even-handed legal-speak, it was a robust indictment of clerical heresy hunters and was an immediate best-seller, going through at least five printings in as many years. The book was designed to support Cromwell's designs to subordinate the clergy and their courts to the civil law. Was it also issued in the hope of drawing the principal defender of the clergy into open opposition to royal policy? Whether or not that was in Cromwell's mind, the *Treatise* struck More on a raw nerve and he rushed into print without any delay. His *Apology* defended the severe persecution of heretics and also his own actions as Lord Chancellor. He went on the attack, accusing the writer of seeking to encourage heresy. At last More came, unrepentantly, into the open on the difference between human and divine law. Equity, fairness, even-handedness were appropriate in the civil courts but God's decrees, enshrined in canon law, were proscriptive. Those who flouted them were rightly cowed into obedience and the techniques we have come to associate with police states – arrest without cause shown, admission of hearsay evidence, denial of the defendant's right to confront his accusers – were wholly appropriate.

St German riposted with a book in dialogue form, *Salem and Bizance*, published under his own name. More came back with *The Debellation* [Overthrow] *of Salem and Bizance*, to which St German responded with *The Additions of Salem and Bizance*. This literary confrontation, avidly followed by lawmen, parliamentarians and courtiers, occupied no more than eighteen months and identified Thomas More before the world as the epitome of the most reactionary element in the Catholic Church. Most members of the English ecclesiastical establishment he believed himself to be defending took a less extreme view on several of the major issues of the day. This became clear at the time of the coronation. Three of More's old friends, Tunstall, Gardiner and John Clerk (Bishop of Bath and Wells), conservatives to a man, tried to persuade him to attend. Wishing to forestall any claim that More had not a thing to wear, they clubbed together and sent him £20 – sufficient for a suitably luxurious gown. More bought the garment but did not attend the coronation and when his friends called to remonstrate with him, he treated them to a moral lecture. They reminded him, he said, of a story Tacitus told about Tiberius. The Emperor had made a certain crime punishable by death, only exempting virgins from the extreme penalty. When the first convicted offender turned out to be a virgin and Tiberius wanted her executed he was prevented by his own decree – until one of his cynical advisers resolved the dilemma: deflower the girl first and kill her afterwards. More proceeded to underscore the lesson: those who compromised over the matrimonial issue were in the process of having their integrity raped and what flowed from that compromise would destroy them. The biographer does not tell us what mood the bishops were in when they left Chelsea.

Sir Thomas was both open and cautious in what he wrote. He was careful always to speak well of the King, to commend his upholding of Catholic truth and to revile only heretics and those who sought to seduce Henry from the paths of righteousness. Other champions of the faith displayed less integrity and more foolhardiness. When highly religious people find themselves under pressure they tend to seek divine vindication, supernatural signs and wonders that will uphold their own faith and either convince or confound their enemies. This was certainly true in the mid-sixteenth century, an age when simple piety reposed considerable trust in the power of images, relics, talismans, the consecrated Host – and in holy people touched by God with visions or the gift of prophetic utterance. Church leaders were always wary of such phenomena and there existed official procedures for testing supposed miracles and miracle workers. Inevitably, such safeguards were not always rigidly applied. If examiners were gullible or had their own reasons for wanting to be convinced then, of course, they were. In the 1530s many traditionalists desperately wanted to be convinced. They saw the Church under attack as never before from enemies without and within and desperately sought from the Almighty confirmation of ancient beliefs and customs. That is the background to the sad story of the Holy Maid of Kent.

Elizabeth Barton, a serving girl in her teens at Aldington, was spectacularly healed of some internal complaint and in the process she appeared to enter a trance-like state during which she spoke of heavenly things and made prophetic utterances. She rapidly became something of a celebrity in her little corner of south-west Kent. Men and women resorted to her for her blessing or her prayers or her predictions about their future. The more attention Elizabeth attracted the more difficult it was for her to extricate herself from what she later confessed was an increasingly tangled skein of deceit. When even the aged Archbishop Warham took her seriously enough to have her examined, she must have known that there was no going back. One of the commissioners was Edward Bocking, cellarer of the Benedictine monastery at Canterbury. He was convinced by her, entered her at the nearby convent of St Sepulchre and became her spiritual director.

Bocking's instruction centred on the teachings and devotional practices associated with traditional Church discipline and his abhorrence of heresy. Thus conditioned the Holy Maid, or the Nun of Kent as she became known, grew increasingly bold in her pronouncements on the religious issues of the day. Like a latterday Catherine of Siena, she encouraged, exhorted, reproved and anathematised all sorts and conditions of men, regardless of rank, the simplicity and apparent sincerity of her life lending credence to her inspired pronouncements. She travelled widely with Bocking and a small entourage and was, over a period of some eight years, widely accepted as a mystic. It was inevitable that many supporters of Queen Catherine should look to Elizabeth for some divine revelation regarding the divorce and it was equally inevitable that the Nun should declare against it. She went further, prophesying that if Henry proceeded with his plans he would, soon after, die a horrible death, and Bocking had her pronouncements printed and widely circulated. The Maid had become, wittingly or unwittingly, an instrument of anti-government propaganda. Yet no action was taken against her, even when, in November 1532, she thrust herself into Henry's presence and proceeded to harangue him. Not everyone took her seriously. Sceptics tended to agree with Cromwell: 'If credence should be given to every such lewd person as would affirm himself to have revelations from God, what readier way were there to subvert all commonwealths and good order in the world?'[104]

More was certainly circumspect about the Maid and her utterances, but then he had good reason to be so. Over the years devout and enthusiastic friends had pressed Sir Thomas to bestow on Elizabeth his imprimatur but, by his own later testimony, he refused to do so and specifically declined to discuss her statements about the King's affairs. He claimed to have kept an open mind. As long as he was a member of the government More could not afford to become involved with someone who was being used to inspire opposition to the regime.

However, after his retirement he did satisfy his curiosity. On a couple of occasions he talked with the Maid at Syon Abbey and exchanged letters with her. They met on the basis of Christian brother and sister. They prayed for each other and More advised the prophetess to be cautious when dealing with the affairs of her social superiors. Few things touched him more deeply than the affair of this bizarre woman. He admired her sanctity and he believed that God had done remarkable things through her. He set great store by those of his friends who were her devoted followers. Among these were Bishop Fisher and leading members of the Carthusian and Observant communities. He realised her propaganda value for the beleaguered Catholic cause. Here was a holy servant of God to be set against those evangelical martyrs whose faithfulness unto death was being trumpeted by the enemies of the Church. He acknowledged that the Lord of the Church might have raised up this young innocent to be, like Joan of Arc, the standard-bearer of his cause. He wanted to believe and there can be no doubt that, had matters turned out differently, he would have joined her crusade. At the same time, he was aware that the fate which had overtaken the Maid of Orléans might easily destroy the Maid of Kent, and those closely associated with her. Holiness and politics were as compatible as fire and water, as he had good cause to know. If the Nun became a real inconvenience to the King and his ministers they would seek to expose her as a fraud and use her to extract information against dissidents. So he continued to be careful, even to the point of keeping notes of his conversations with the prophetess and a copy of his correspondence with her.

After the events of April–June 1533 the Maid's adherents looked for the visitation of divine wrath on their stubbornly sinful monarch. But Henry and his pregnant wife remained in excellent health and the Barton circus had to come up with dramatic new revelations if their support was not to dwindle. The Maid now 'deposed' Henry VIII. She declared that he was no longer king in the eyes of God. This claim was made at the same time that the Pope's provisional excommunication became known in England and was presumably made to endorse the judgement of the Holy Father. It was now impossible for government not to act. Henry, via Cromwell, ordered Cranmer to examine Elizabeth. The Archbishop had several talks with the woman over two weeks in July and August but, according to one of Cromwell's emissaries, he was but 'dallying' with her. Only when a list of very pointed questions arrived from Whitehall did the interrogation become tougher.

Cranmer was working to a different agenda from that of the King and Cromwell. They wanted evidence which would scotch the Holy Maid movement and incriminate influential people who could embarrass the government. The Archbishop set out simply to make trial of Elizabeth's sincerity and her divine calling. He was a man who looked for the best in people and it may well be that he was moved by the Maid's demeanour and apparent holiness. There is a strange ambiguity about the letter he wrote detailing the whole affair to a colleague at the end of the year. He related her wonderful cure and detailed a 'miracle' in which, while in a trance, a strange voice 'speaking within her belly' told of the 'joys of heaven' and 'spoke so sweetly and so heavenly that every man was ravished with the hearing thereof'. He went on to tell, in almost awed tones, of her 'visions and raptures'. But when Cranmer came to write of his examination of the Maid his tone changed noticeably. The woman, he reported,

> confessed all, and uttered the very truth, which is this, that she never had vision in all her life, but all that ever she said was feigned of her own imagination, only to satisfy the minds of them which resorted unto her, and to obtain worldly praise.

The Maid's 'mischievous and feigned visions . . . contained much perilous sedition and also treason', for, he concluded in horrified vein,

> she said that the king should not continue king a month after that he were married, and within six months after, God would strike the realm with such a plague as never was seen. And then the king should be destroyed.[105]

Elizabeth was subjected to various interrogations, at one of which, interestingly, Hugh Latimer was among her judges. He must have enjoyed the reversal of roles. Now it was he who was grilling a Catholic heretic instead of being himself in the firing line. It is hardly surprising that the poor woman should have disintegrated under pressure and readily named names. She was not of the stuff of which saints and martyrs are made. In September and October her associates were rounded up and found themselves alongside her in the Tower.

The government's first objective was to heap ridicule on Elizabeth Barton, her cause and all the gullible people who had been taken in by her. First of all the entire Council was convened to see her exposed, then, on

20 November, she and her abettors were paraded before a special gathering of leading notables from all over the county. Several of those who had previously been the Maid's supporters fell over themselves to express horror at her crimes and to join in the universal cry of 'To the stake with her!'. A few days later the fraudsters were exposed to the public in St Paul's Yard and at Canterbury, while witty preachers kept the crowds entertained with ribald exposés of Elizabeth's more extreme behaviour.

So much for propaganda. Cromwell and his men had extracted the maximum advantage from the Holy Maid's downfall. There remained the political advantage that might be wrung from the affair. The Council was inundated with letters from worried people who feared that some of the King's anger might rub off on them. More was among the first to write to Cromwell explaining that his association with the Maid had been devoid of any political content. He attended her humiliation at St Paul's Cross and declared his pleasure that her crimes had been exposed. Henry had been badly shaken by the whole affair and was determined to use it to maximum effect in stifling once and for all the rumbling discontent about his divorce and remarriage. He ordered Cromwell to get Elizabeth and her accomplices indicted for treason and to associate with them certain others, notably Fisher and More, who had given credence to her false prophecies. But, after consulting with senior judges, Cromwell had to report that, as the law stood, subjects could not be tried in the courts for verbal treason. However, a simpler, if, from the point of view of transparent justice, less satisfactory alternative was available: parliamentary attainder.

Cromwell drew up a bill for presentation in the Lords against those who 'shall be attainted of high treason and suffer death except the king's majesty do pardon [them]' and also against other named individuals who, 'shall be attainted of misprision and have imprisonment at the king's will and lose all their goods'.[106] By Henry's specific urging Thomas More's name appeared on the latter list. He had finally lost patience with the sullen silence of his ex-Chancellor and the encouragement that silence gave to opponents of his proceedings. Whatever affection the King had once entertained for More had turned to the hatred he reserved for those who resisted his will. But on this occasion he was balked of his prey. The ex-Chancellor announced his willingness to defend himself in parliament and Cromwell knew that the case against him was too slender. Still Henry was adamant. He appointed a special commission of Norfolk, Audley, Cromwell and Cranmer to interrogate More. Even when they reported that Sir Thomas would almost certainly wriggle out of any indictment and, thus, score a propaganda victory, Henry refused to yield. It was not until a later stage of the bill's passage through the two houses that More's name was eventually dropped from it. By then Cromwell had devised another way of giving Henry what he wanted.

The conservative and pro-Catherine groupings were seriously

demoralised by recent events and some were driven to dangerous plotting. Chapuys expressed their feelings with only slight exaggeration when he wrote in December 1533:

> You cannot imagine the grief of all the people at this abominable government. They are so transported with indignation at what passes, that they complain that your Majesty takes no steps in it; and I am told by many respectable people that they would be glad to see a fleet come hither in your name to raise the people; and if they had any chief among themselves who dared raise his head, they would require no more.[107]

It seemed that the King was winning handsomely on all fronts. Catherine had been despatched to Buckden on the edge of the Cambridgeshire fens and would, the following May, be transferred to nearby Kimbolton. Out of sight, if not out of mind, she seldom ventured outside her palace/prison where she was, attended by a much-reduced staff, reminded every waking hour of her reduced status. Cromwell was preparing new legislation which would dot the Is and cross the Ts of the breach with Rome and the subjugation of the clergy. The government was on the watch against any organised dissent. Religious communities were the main focus of attention because their members moved from house to house and pulpit to pulpit stiffening resistance. Cromwell's spies were currently stalking various members of the Observant fraternity and he informed Henry 'it is undoubted that they have intended and would confess some great matter if they might be examined as they ought to be, that is to say by pains [i.e. torture]'.[108] Within a year the entire order had been dissolved and several friars were in prison. At the centre of national life Cromwell was about to achieve the pivotal position. While Gardiner was absent on foreign mission in the closing months of 1533, Cromwell deputised as royal secretary. He proceeded to make that clerical post the most important one in the government. As Wolsey used the office of Almoner to achieve that closeness to the King upon which power depended, so Cromwell now utilised the secretaryship to the same end. Gardiner had failed to regain Henry's good graces and, although he returned to court in the new year, he was unable to reclaim his old office and, in April, he was ordered to his diocese. Norfolk also found himself, though not disgraced, certainly underemployed and his attendance in court and parliament became more sporadic than it had been since 1530.

Cromwell did not deliberately try to destroy men he regarded as rivals or inimical to his interests and in this regard he was unlike the King. Personal friendships and animosities dominated Henry's relationships and influenced his decision on policy issues. That was why any courtier or councillor under threat always tried to gain access to the King. More, in the Maid of Kent crisis, tried to obtain an audience but had to content himself with prostrating himself at the King's feet by letter and beseeching Henry, 'to relieve the torment of my present heaviness'.[109] Cromwell, by contrast, always concentrated on the big picture. Personality clashes were a distraction he tried to avoid and he usually appeared, on the surface at least, to be on good terms with everyone. As soon as he heard that More's name had been dropped from the attainder bill he hastened to seek out William Roper in the parliament house so that the good news could be conveyed to Chelsea as quickly as possible. Writing to Gardiner in the immediate aftermath of ousting him as Secretary he signed himself 'Your Lordship's assured friend'. Cromwell made a great show of cordiality towards Chapuys, assuring him that no member of the Council had the Emperor's interests more at heart than he. Doubtless this was partly playing the diplomatic game but it is also true that friendship was part of his style.

It is important to realise that, although Cromwell devised the legislation that ultimately brought More to the block, he had no animosity towards the semi-recluse at Chelsea and certainly did not plot his destruction. The bill 'ratifying the King's marriage with the Lady Anne' was brought to parliament on 20 March 1534. It was intended to do away with all ambiguities regarding inheritance to the throne by nominating the children born of Queen Anne the first rightful heirs, and declaring it to be treason for anyone, by writing or action, to oppose such inheritance (and misprision of treason to speak against it). To remove all possible doubts the King's subjects were to swear on oath to obey this Act of Succession.

But there was more to this statute than protecting the nation from a recurrence of 'the great divisions which in time past hath been in this realm by reason of several titles pretended to the imperial crown of the same'. The studiously worded preamble succinctly reiterated the issues for which the reforming legislation of the past two years had been contending. He stated,

> The bishop of Rome and See Apostolic, contrary to the great and inviolable grants of jurisdictions given by God immediately to emperors, kings and princes in succession to their heirs, hath presumed in times past to invest who should please them to inherit in other men's kingdoms and dominions, which thing we your most humble subjects both spiritual and temporal do most abhor and detest.

It declared, by the authority of parliament, that the King's former marriage was against the laws of Almighty God. It asserted the legality of the existing marriage as confirmed by the Archbishop of Canterbury, the 'whole clergy of this realm', sundry universities, etc. etc.[110] The Act of Succession was a rod with which to beat all members of the political nation. It prevented neutrality. It forced all those to whom the oath was administered to come into line behind the government. On 13 April several higher clergy were summoned to Lambeth Palace to take the oath. One layman was also sent for. Thomas More. As he awaited his turn in a small chamber overlooking the garden, he watched the clerics gather and noted sardonically that when Latimer arrived he greeted colleagues with such effusive affection that one might have thought they were all women.

When he had carefully read the whole Act, More explained that he was quite prepared to swear allegiance to the King and Queen and their heirs but he could not set his signature to the preamble. Cranmer suggested to Cromwell that subscription to the substance of the Act might be acceptable in the case of More and Fisher. Cromwell took this eirenical compromise to Henry. And Henry turned it down flat. It was all or nothing. He would have Thomas More's openly declared obedience or he would lock him up so that he could ponder the error of his ways. On 17 April 1534 Thomas More was taken by river to the Tower of London.

CHAPTER 27

Morus Contra Mundum

. . . one Dolfin's wife said about midsummer last past in the xxvth year of the reign of our sovereign lord, the king's grace (1534) that it was never merry in England since there were iii queens in it [i.e. the Virgin Mary, Catherine and Anne]. And then the said John Hammulden said there would be fewer shortly . . .

14 June 1535, Oxfordshire.

. . . I received letters of certain words spoken by a priest of Holderness sounding towards the advancement of the Bishop of Rome, which words were these, 'They say there is no pope. I know well there is a pope.'

9 July 1535, Yorkshire.

. . . for divers treacherous and seditious words that [John Heseham] hath spoken, which was 'That if the spiritual men had held together the king could not have been Head of the Church; and also that the Bishop of Rochester and Sir Thomas More died martyrs in the quarrel aforesaid', I have taken him and committed him to the Castle of Chester.

23 September 1535, Cheshire.[111]

The King and his ministers had carried through enormous changes. What had begun as a simple attempt to secure the dynasty had become immeasurably more complicated. Cromwell and his associates, for reasons both ideological and pragmatic, were determined to press on with reform. Henry, for reasons largely personal and acquisitive, was prepared to support them. However, what neither King nor Mr Secretary had succeeded in doing was selling socio-religious revolution to the people. From all over the country came reports from officials, informers and trouble-making neighbours of men and women giving voice to their disaffection. The fact that so many of these reports have survived indicates how numerous they were and how seriously the government took them. All princes feared rebellion and all wise princes took note of public opinion.

Henry, for all his leonine defiance of opposition, did care about what his subjects thought. He demonstrated that when he caved in over the Amicable Grant and every time that he pushed the blame for unpopular policies on to his ministers. The thought must frequently have occurred to him that it would be ironical if his efforts to save England from the anarchy of a disputed succession plunged England into the anarchy of religious war. These were some of the considerations which prompted Henry's fluctuating attitudes and his bewildering ambiguity towards ongoing reform throughout the rest of his reign.

For the moment he refused to be deterred by what he considered as personal defiance of his authority. Having obtained a wife who, in God's good time, would give him a son, and having established that that son should enjoy absolute dominion in Church and State, he set about forcing his people into a united observance of the new pattern of royal authority (or, the old pattern restored, as he now firmly believed it to be). This involved, in the parliamentary session of November–December 1534, the concocting of a new treason law and an Act of Supremacy which established Henry VIII as Supreme Head in *Ecclesia Anglicana*, without any qualifying quibbles about 'insofar as the Word of God allows'. Magistrates, judges and bishops were to enforce all the Reformation measures; clergy were to preach in support of them; authors and pamphleteers were to write enthusiastically about them; spies and *agents provocateurs* were to be assiduous in locating and reporting opposition; and leading dissidents were to be forced into line. Above all, that meant Fisher and More.

The two prisoners were accommodated in the Bell Tower of the Tower of London, adjacent to the Lieutenant's Lodging. There was no question of these important men being thrust into dank dungeons. Their quarters – More's on the ground floor, the Bishop's immediately above – were roomy, light and airy and though there were better chambers within the fortress, there were certainly others far worse. More's confinement was, for several months, quite tolerable. He was attended by his own servant, John a Wood. He had as reasonable a diet as his wife could afford to pay for and he took exercise in the Lieutenant's garden. He received visits from his family. He had books, ink and paper and was free to write to friends (though his letters were, of course, read by his captors). For seven months More was unmolested by the government, except insofar as they encouraged the prisoner's wife, daughters and friends to implore him to swear the oath and thus regain his liberty. Over and again and with as much subtlety as Council members could devise Sir Thomas was made aware of the very simple truth that only his refusal to utter a few words stood between him and freedom.

Throughout this period (which we might call phase one of More's persecution) Cromwell acted as a barrier between the prisoner and the

King. At the outset of Sir Thomas's incarceration the Secretary had told him that he would rather yield his own son to the headsman than see a man who had once enjoyed royal favour now deliberately provoke Henry's hostility. The letter to Margaret Roper in which this revelation was made would, of course, have been brought to Cromwell's attention but More would not have fabricated the incident and it is unlikely that Cromwell had been indulging in specious flattery. Neither the Secretary nor his conciliar colleagues had any reason to wish More harm. They had a genuine respect and affection for the little lawyer whose wit had often enlivened tedious hours at the Council table. In political terms More was yesterday's man, offering no personal rivalry and posing no threat. Cromwell, the political realist, appreciated full well that there was nothing to be gained and much to be lost from turning the ex-Chancellor's defiance into a cause célèbre. Better by far to leave the prisoner to contemplate in isolation the fate of himself and his family. If he stubbornly persisted in his refusal to take the oath then the summer fevers and winter riverain mists that infiltrated the Tower could be trusted to terminate his obstinacy. Furthermore, Cromwell was at one with More's family and conservative friends in being totally mystified at his stance. It could change nothing. Hundreds of men who advocated papal supremacy and thought that Catherine had been vilely used had accepted the *fait accompli*. Failure to do so and refusal to give his reasons (he claimed that if he set out his case in detail he would burden other men's consciences since they, too, would have to face the danger of present persecutions or future damnation) looked like churlishness and More's acquaintances knew that he was not churlish. Even Erasmus in distant Basel (to which, now peaceful, he had returned in 1535) disapproved of his old friend's foolishness: 'Would that he had never embroiled himself in this perilous business and had left the theological cause to the theologians,' he wrote.[112]

It was the King, undoubtedly egged on by his wife, who was intent on turning the issues into a conflict of wills and he who initiated phase two of More's troubles. When parliament reassembled in November 1534 he had Cromwell draft an Act of Attainder against More and the royal bitterness was expressed in the wording of the statute which accused the offender of having 'unkindly and ingrately served our sovereign lord by divers and sundry ways'.[113] Henry pressured the Council and the assembly into granting him what they had denied him in the spring. The result was to make More's imprisonment permanent and to confiscate his goods. The King wasted little time in distributing several of Sir Thomas's lands and perquisites to others, thus reducing Lady Alice to penury and obliging her to write begging letters to Cromwell. Her husband now really did begin to feel the bite of Henry's wrath. He was denied adequate heating and clothing and put on short commons. As he told Cromwell a few months later, 'I . . . have since I came here been divers times in the case that I thought to die within one hour.'[114] As winter turned to spring other privileges were withdrawn – books, paper, ink, recreation in the Lieutenant's garden.

Now, also, the threat of a traitor's death hung over him. The new Treasons Act, which came into effect on 1 February 1535, made it a capital offence to

> maliciously wish, will or desire by words or writing, or by craft imagine, invent, practise or attempt any bodily harm to be done or committed to the king's most royal person, the queen's or their heir's apparent, or to deprive them or any of them of the dignity, title or name of their royal estates, or slanderously and maliciously publish and pronounce, by express writing or words, that the king our sovereign lord should be heretic, schismatic, tyrant, infidel or usurper of the crown.[115]

The comprehensive nature of this measure caused the government a great deal of trouble when Audley attempted to steer it through parliament. Members objected to what appeared to be handing Henry and any future ruler an effective instrument of tyranny and the Lord Chancellor eventually had to bow to the inclusion of the qualifying adjective 'maliciously'. More had his own way of frustrating the legislators: he said nothing and, since silence was still not a punishable offence, Henry had to goad his councillors into putting phase three into operation.

Even then, he might not have intervened so decisively had it not been for the latest irritation from Rome. On 25 September 1534 Henry's *bête noire*, Clement VII, at last died. He was replaced by the sixty-six-year-old Alessandro Farnese, who assumed the title Paul III. The new Pope was a reformist and immediately declared himself in favour of the summoning of an ecumenical council, which Henry and other monarchs had long been calling for (it still took ten years for the Council of Trent actually to get under way, in 1545). The King hoped that the change of regime might lead to greater understanding. Such hopes were dashed when Paul unwittingly blundered. Wishing to elevate men of holy living to major positions in the Church, he included the name of Bishop Fisher in a list of new cardinals. When the news reached England at the end of May Henry was beside himself with rage. He regarded the action as a gratuitous insult and an indication that Rome was permanently set against him. One way and another, he had had quite enough of cardinals and he determined on Fisher's execution. Now, as Cromwell minuted to himself, 'When Master Fisher shall go to execution . . . What shall be done further touching Master More?'[116] The King's response was a determination to press matters to a conclusion.

Only it was not that simple. While Rochester had provided his enemies with plenty of verbal evidence of treason, More had always been circumspect and now remained so. He and the King had now manoeuvred themselves into the corner of the chessboard and there were few moves left for either of them. On 7 May (before news of Fisher's cardinalate arrived) Cromwell visited the Tower with a group of senior lawyers to ask for a clear expression of More's opinion on the Succession and Supremacy Acts. He urged the prisoner to try to see the situation from the King's point of view. More's obduracy was encouraging others to oppose the royal will. Since Henry could not allow this More must surely see that if he persisted the law must take its course. The prisoner refused to give Cromwell any satisfaction but the two men parted on good terms. The Secretary even advised against a compromise More had suggested whereby he would tell the investigators what they wanted to know if the King would guarantee exemption from the penalties laid down in the new statutes. Instead of jumping at this chance to trap the interviewee, Cromwell pointed out that, as the King was not above the law, he could not provide the necessary safeguard. 'In this good warning he showed himself my special, tender friend,' More observed.[117]

For almost four weeks the government dithered but when Cromwell returned on 3 June, having had experience of Henry's anger, his mood was very different. He demanded a plain 'yes' or 'no' on the supremacy. When More declined to oblige, Cromwell left in a huff, saying that he was now convinced of the prisoner's ill intent and could no longer regard himself as More's friend. The Secretary was now between a rock and a hard place. It was impossible to deliver what the King wanted *within the law*, and that was vital to the government's credibility.

Help came unexpectedly from one of his agents, Richard Rich. He was sent two days later to put increased pressure on More by depriving him of his books and papers. While Rich's assistants packed a chest with the prisoner's belongings the two men talked, as lawyers often will, of hypothetical cases.

'If it were enacted by parliament that I should be king, and whoever say nay it should be treason, would it be an offence to say "Rich is king"?'

'No,' replied More, 'but let me put a higher case. If it were enacted by parliament that God were not God and if any repugned at the same Act it should be treason, would it be proper for you, Master Rich, to deny that God is God?'

'Nay, but that is not a true case, for parliament hath no competence to decide on the existence of God. But now I will put you a middle case. Our king has been made Supreme Head by parliament. Will you not take him as such as you would take me for king?'

'A king may be made by parliament and a king deprived by parliament and to such an Act a subject must give his consent. But on the matter of the supremacy a subject is not free to consent to the Act of parliament.'[118]

When Rich reported back to his master, Cromwell detected a chink in More's armour of silence. The prisoner might insist that his words did not apply specifically to the recent legislation but Mr Secretary could see how they might be presented to a jury in such a way as to appear treasonable. This proved to be the case. It was on Rich's evidence that More was condemned in his trial at Westminster Hall on 1 July.

Martyrs are seldom made by events. There has to be something deep within a man's soul to prepare him for, or impel him towards, the ultimate sacrifice. Thomas More claimed that he died for conscience's sake, a dignity he had always denied to those evangelicals who suffered at the hands of himself and his colleagues, but his conscience had been shaped over the years by several forces. Most powerful of those forces was the asceticism in which More had been steeped ever since adolescence. It was written of one of the desert fathers, 'He seemed to live as if he was incorporeal, freed from the flesh and possessing nothing but skin and bone' and it was this path to holiness, the path of self-denial, pain and suffering, that had always appealed strongly to More's imagination, especially so because, *malgré* the hair shirt, it was a path he could not walk. And yet there was a kind of inversion about his following of a lay vocation instead of joining the Carthusians whom he so much admired; entering royal service was, in itself, a spiritual bed of nails, as he had pointed out in *Utopia*. The court of Henry VIII, he more than once intimated, was a lion's cage where the Christian humanist risked being mauled. Despite his public asseverations of loyalty and devotion to the King, he had come to regard Henry as a tyrant in the same vein as his father, famously acknowledging, on one occasion, that if his head could win the King a castle in France it would, without hesitation, be struck off. More was never at home in the political marketplace where men bartered ideas and principles and he derived deep satisfaction from the very fact of his discomfort. In his early writings and his discussions with humanist friends he had passionately adumbrated theories of governance but by the time he achieved high office and had the opportunity to make a difference in human affairs his vision had narrowed to the point where he could see little beyond the defence of the clergy and the crushing of heretics. When the tide of official policy began to run strongly in the opposite direction he found himself swimming against the current which, like Athanasius *contra mundum*, could only convince him that he was in the right. His ideality was at once greater and smaller than that of Wolsey or Cromwell. He saw all human affairs *sub specie aeternitatis* but that effectively prevented him from conceiving and pursuing a wide range of reforms on the merely terrestrial stage.

Flesh and spirit, temporal and eternal interests, human desire and holy passion were, for More, ever in conflict. The human endured the fray but longed for the consummation of being delivered from it. Death held an attraction for him. He told Cromwell that since relinquishing public office, 'I had fully determined with myself neither to study nor meddle with any matters of this world, that my whole study should be upon the passion of Christ and mine own passage out of this world.'[119] In his last months the Tower prisoner fixed his eye on death and what lay beyond. This is the subject he explored from a variety of angles in the devotional writings with which he occupied himself in the Bell Tower. His deepest prayer was

> To have the last things in remembrance,
> To have ever before mine eyes my death that is ever at hand;
> To make death no stranger to me,
> To foresee and consider the everlasting fire of hell.[120]

To welcome death in a righteous cause was the surest way to avoid the everlasting torments prepared for the worldly. There is always an element of selfishness about the martyr's preoccupation with his own eternal well-being.

Was he conscious that by his determination to stay in prison and, if necessary, to die he was hoisting a banner for papal Catholicism and, if he was aware, did he derive satisfaction from the thought? The answer to the first question must be that he was just as aware as Cromwell of the fertilising properties of martyr blood. Knowing this, was his silence a refusal to burden other men's consciences, as he claimed, or a demonstration of loyalty to his king whom he would not publicly contradict, or simply a desire to avoid unnecessary trouble? All these elements may have formed part of his reasoning. But there could well have been another. Thomas More was a trained and matured controversialist. He had laboured day in and day out in courtroom and study to present case-winning submissions. He knew, therefore, that argument begets counter-argument. To have blazoned forth the case against the supremacy would have obliged government propagandists to reply. The whole issue would then have been reduced to the level of rational disputation. But every life laid down for the cause was worth a thousand arguments. Was that not why he left his apologia until the last possible moment, when, in Westminster Hall, the dye of his condemnation already having been cast, he could proclaim to the assembled crowd, in that very place where he had so often presided:

> Seeing that I see ye are determined to condemn me (God knoweth how) I will now in discharge of my conscience speak my mind plainly and freely touching my indictment and your statute withal. Forasmuch as, my lord, this indictment is grounded upon an Act of parliament

directly repugnant to the laws of God and his holy church, the supreme government of which, or of any part whereof, may no temporal prince presume by any law to take upon him, as rightfully belonging to the See of Rome, a spiritual pre-eminence by the mouth of our Saviour himself, personally present upon the earth, only to St Peter and his successors, bishops of the same See, by special prerogative granted; it is therefore in law amongst Christian men insufficient to charge any Christian man. This realm, being but one member and small part of the Church, might not make a particular law disagreeable with the general law of Christ's universal Catholic Church. No more than the city of London, being but one poor member in respect of the whole realm, might make a law against an act of parliament to bind the whole realm. No more might this realm of England refuse obedience to the See of Rome than might a child refuse obedience to his own natural father.[121]

The very human in Thomas More must have mounted the scaffold on 6 July well content.

The manner of More's death and the events leading up to it are lodged deep in the national mythology because later Catholic apologists scripted it so emotively. At the time, it made less of an impact on spectators than had Fisher's execution two weeks earlier. As for those at the centre of affairs, they had other more important concerns. These were uncomfortable months for Thomas Howard. Increasingly marginalised, he vacillated between ill-tempered outbursts against his rivals and shaking the dust of the court off his shoes. Conflict surfaced, first of all, in the strange affair of Lord Dacre of the North. In April 1534, about the time that More was sent to the Tower and the Nun and her associates suffered at Tyburn the fate appointed for traitors, an accusation was laid secretly against William Dacre, Warden of the West Marches. It seems that the person ultimately responsible for the indictment was Queen Anne, who hated Dacre because of his sympathy for Catherine. He was accused of collusion with the Scots, and Cromwell covertly appointed commissioners to make search of the suspect's house at Naworth for incriminating evidence. Despite the fact that two of the agents were members of the Clifford family, who were bitter rivals of the Dacres and who had, in fact, made the original charges, nothing of substance was found. This was the government's first blunder and from then on matters grew progressively worse. Henry decided that Dacre must be brought to trial, and Cromwell appointed Sir William Musgrave to put together a cast-iron case. Musgrave assured him that everything would be set forth 'in so plain a wise and with so substantial witnesses . . . that it shall be undeniable anything that I have alleged'.

The trial was set for 9 July and the Duke of Norfolk was appointed High Steward to preside over what should have been a tribunal loyally performing its duty to the Crown against an over-mighty subject. The scene in Westminster Hall was impressive. Howard took his place on a raised chair of state flanked by twenty peers and an array of judges. The prosecution case was presented, alleging an arrangement of mutual convenience between Dacre and various Scottish lords and for plotting a rebellion in the name of Princess Mary. The prisoner then presented an exhaustive defence which went on for seven hours. The peers retired to consider their verdict and it was then that Norfolk realised matters were not going according to plan. The jury raised various legal quibbles and the judges had to be called in to give advice. When Norfolk reconvened the court to hear the verdict, the peers returned a unanimous answer of 'not guilty'. It was the only state trial of the reign in which judgement was given for the defendant and the King was furious. He was not used to losing and he was not prepared to lose on this occasion. He had Dacre returned to the Tower and consulted with his Council about how the situation was to be redeemed. On 25 July a commission made up of Norfolk, Exeter, Cromwell, Audley, Rich, and the Lieutenant of the Tower confronted the prisoner who 'without any manner of coercion' confessed to misprision of treason. A royal pardon cost him a staggering £10,000 and when Dacre was eventually allowed to return home it was as a ruined man.[122]

The personal and factional sub-plots of this episode are far from clear. Chapuys espied collusion on the part of Howard and his fellow peers. He believed the aristocracy had closed ranks against the upstart, determined that they were not going to suffer the depredations of a second Wolsey. It is, however, very doubtful that Howard would have deliberately dared to engineer his master's disappointment. If the peers did act in concert to preserve the interests of their clan it was probably without Norfolk's foreknowledge. Whatever the truth of the matter, neither the Duke nor Mr Secretary emerged well from it.

But it was Norfolk who was eclipsed by Anne, Cromwell, Cranmer and their supporters. Howard doggedly attended Council meetings only to discover to his chagrin that no one took much notice of him. In September his seasoned advice on Irish affairs was rejected and he hesitated to remonstrate for fear that Cromwell would pack him off to Dublin as his predecessor had done. He confided to Chapuys that he would never return to the troublesome province until the King built a bridge across the sea so that he could come and go at will.

However, if he was not prepared to be exiled from court, he was equally distressed at the prospect of remaining there. Another report from the Imperial ambassador painted the picture of Howard storming out of the Queen's chamber in a rage, bellowing that his niece was a whore because she had treated him worse than he treated his own dogs. As well as the personal affronts he received, Howard was more and more estranged by every lurch of government policy towards religious radicalism. Nor was it a case of simply grinning and bearing the 'trendy' fashion for evangelicalism; he was obliged to put on a show of supporting it. When there were enemies of the Succession or Supremacy Acts to be tried by the Council or conciliar commission, he had to display an outrage which he certainly did not feel. He played his part – though a marginal one – in the harrying of Thomas More and we only know of his involvement because of the put-downs he received at the hands of the witty lawyer. When, airing his limited Latin, he pointed out to Sir Thomas, *indignatio principis mors est* (it is fatal to incur the king's anger), the lawyer replied laconically, 'Then the only difference between your Grace and me is that I shall die today, and you tomorrow.'

By February 1535 he could stand no more and betook himself to Kenninghall. In May he was recalled for another diplomatic mission to France. His temper seems to have cooled over the winter, for he realised that there was no alternative to coming to terms with the new cock of the walk. Just as he had swallowed his pride and worked with Wolsey, so he must, with good grace, accept a subordinate position to Cromwell. He wrote assuring Mr Secretary of his friendship. The French embassy was not to prove a means of regaining Henry's confidence; it was a diplomatic non-starter. Francis, as usual, wanted to draw England into an offensive alliance against the Empire. Henry was, by now, far too experienced to be trapped in the Habsburg–Valois power struggle and saddled his representatives with demands the French King would be quite unable to accept. Cromwell was behind this diplomatic fiasco because he was pursuing his own policy of friendship with the Lutheran German states. The outcome of several wasted weeks was that Norfolk departed the French court in mid-June leaving a trail of ill will behind him. No one could have done any better under the circumstances but another ambassador might have failed with a better grace. Rather than endure further humiliation, Howard once more withdrew to his country estates. He was, by now, convinced that Anne and Cromwell were working together to bring about his downfall. He could not have guessed at the dramatic reversal of fortune that 1536 was to bring.

CHAPTER 28

Annus Horribilis

1536 started badly for Henry and worsened by the month. The first item of major news to reach the court was actually very welcome: on 7 January Catherine of Aragon had died of cancer among the fenland miasmas. This removed the irritant in Anglo–Habsburg relations and restored to English diplomats a range of options they had not enjoyed for almost a decade. Within the country the passing of Henry's discarded wife removed, theoretically at least, the prime cause for his widespread unpopularity. However, Catherine's demise had other repercussions which were not immediately obvious to courtiers and court watchers.

Seventeen days later, while running at the ring at Greenwich, the King fell heavily from his horse. Charles Wriothesley, who, as Windsor Herald, was probably present, insisted in his *Chronicle* that Henry 'took no hurt' from the accident but rumours humming along the diplomatic grapevine told a different story, some suggesting that he was unconscious for two hours. Wriothesley only mentioned the tiltyard incident as a possible explanation for another event in this eventful month: 'Queen Anne was brought abed and delivered of a man child, as it was said, afore her time . . . it was said she took a fright, for the King ran that time at the ring and had a fall . . .'[123]

The problems of understanding, interrelating and interpreting these three incidents and, specifically, of connecting them to the extraordinary crisis which flared up with seeming suddenness a couple of months later, have troubled historians for years. In mid-March investigations began into Queen Anne's conduct and on 19 May she was beheaded within the precincts of the Tower. Various theories have been put forward to explain Henry's sudden and brutal discarding of wife number two. They only really impinge upon this study insofar as they throw light on the behaviour of Thomas Cromwell and his relationship with the King. The central question to be answered is, was the minister acting entirely at Henry's behest in finding a way to disembarrass him of Anne or did he concoct a deep plot to get rid of the Queen because she stood in the way of his accomplishing his own designs?

The answer turns on an understanding of Henry's relationship with

Mistress Boleyn. He fell in love with her when he was in his mid-thirties and she was still a teenager. Throughout the early years of their relationship his passion was unabated but it was gradually joined by another emotion – pride. The more opposition he incurred towards his planned divorce and remarriage, the more determined he became to proceed with them. By the time he had achieved his objectives Henry was into his forties and his bride was no longer a slip of a girl. Moreover, Anne's character had changed as a result of her exalted status. She had always been strong-minded; she became imperious. There is every indication that Henry liked this aspect of her personality. He needed at his side a woman possessed of queenly dignity, who could exercise the control over her side of the household that he displayed over the whole court. However, the relationship changed, as such relationships always do and the King became increasingly irritated by his wife's overbearing behaviour. By the autumn of 1535 Henry and Anne were married and their estate heavily buttressed by statute. Having won his long and arduous battle, the King's pride was satisfied. That left, emotionally speaking, only love to bind husband and wife together. On the level of *raison d'état* two other considerations applied – Henry's desire for an heir and his determination not to go back to Catherine; for if anything had happened to Anne the clamour for a reconciliation with the 'dowager princess' would have been raucous and loud. Hence the importance of the events of January 1536.

Catherine, the hated and despised 'other woman', had become an important guarantee of Anne's security. Her death left the Queen vulnerable. But much more dangerous was her apparent inability to conceive and bring forth a healthy son. The sad end to the latest pregnancy in January was her third natal misfortune. She had successfully given birth to a daughter and had then had two miscarriages. Each mishap increased Henry's disappointment and displeasure. One court gossip claimed that the King's response to the latest disaster was to mutter angrily that his marriage was cursed and that he would never have an heir by Anne.

Is this sufficient to explain why Henry's affection for his wife suddenly turned to hatred; a hatred so intense that he not only had Anne killed but others with her, including old friends? We have seen that personal relationships often dominated Henry's decision-making. What made him turn against Anne and others associated with her with a venom he had never displayed against Catherine? Why did he not contemplate a less drastic method of terminating his second marriage? He now had the English Church under his thumb as well as a corps of propagandists well versed in producing legal and moral justifications for annulment. Even the argument chosen – divorce on the grounds of adultery – did not, of itself, imply treason and call for the wanton slaughter of innocent men and women.

The shocking haste of the events of the spring of 1536 should not confuse us. The marriage had been ailing for some time. There had often been rumours that all was not well between the royal couple and these were reported back to the courts of Europe by gossip-gathering diplomats but they were based for the most part on wishful thinking. Occasionally, however, hints were dropped by people in the know. On the death of Clement VII Norfolk proposed to his master that now would be a good time to seek a rapprochement with Rome, which could not be achieved without removing the obstacle of Anne. The Duke received a hearty rebuff but one feels that even he could not have been so presumptuous if he knew that Henry's feelings for his wife were as strong as ever.

Early in 1535 a French envoy had an interview with the Queen. Negotiations for a marriage between Princess Elizabeth and one of Francis I's young sons were going badly and Anne interpreted French hesitation as a vote of no confidence in the position of herself and her daughter. While Henry and others watched them from a little distance, the Queen confided her anxiety. Francis must be persuaded, she insisted, 'so that she may not be ruined and lost, for she sees herself very near that and in more grief and trouble than before her marriage'. Casting a glance at her husband, she told the Frenchman 'that she could not speak more fully and that she did not dare express her fears in writing'.[124]

Most intriguing of all is a conversation that took place the following June between Cromwell and Chapuys and which left the ambassador bewildered. The minister confided that he and the Queen had fallen out. Only three days previously she had told him she would like to see his head off his shoulders. However, Cromwell claimed that this did not worry him: 'I trust so much on my master that I fancy she cannot do me any harm.' What, Chapuys mused, was he to make of this revelation? Was it an invention of Cromwell's to keep him guessing about the real state of affairs in the English court? 'All I can say,' the ambassador reported,

is that everyone here considers him Anne's right hand . . . Indeed, I hear from a reliable source that day and night is the Lady working to bring about the Duke of Norfolk's disgrace with the king; whether it be owing to his having spoken too freely about her, or because Cromwell wishes to bring down the aristocracy of this kingdom [the Dacre trial was still a vivid memory] and is about to begin with him, I cannot say.[125]

At the very least we can deduce two facts from this interview: Cromwell was distancing himself from Anne and everything at court was not *couleur de rose*.

Henry was certainly having extramarital affairs. The self-imposed restraints (or, perhaps, genuine lack of desire) of earlier years had been discarded by a king who, surrounded by attractive and available women, became a middle-aged roué. For most of their married life Anne was pregnant and court etiquette would have seen nothing wrong in his obtaining sexual satisfaction elsewhere. The Queen could not take such a relaxed view. Every liaison of her husband's was a potential threat to her. Being of a forthright nature, Anne indicated her sadness and anger to Henry. This, of course, was no way to make her spouse honour his marriage vows. Quite the reverse, few things were more calculated to annoy him than complaints about his behaviour. The Venetian ambassador, reading the royal body language and listening to backstairs tales of angry scenes, reported confidently that Henry had grown tired of his queen.

By the turn of the year 1536 the latest young woman to take Henry's fancy was Jane Seymour, daughter of Sir John Seymour of Wolf Hall, Wiltshire, a faithful servant of the Tudors, who managed to place his eldest surviving son, Edward, in the King's household and Jane among the Queen's attendants. The first thing of importance to note about the Seymours is that they represented the new generation of courtiers. Henry liked to surround himself with bright young things, delighting in their antics and unconsciously sucking new life from their physical and mental vigour. They fed his aggressive athleticism, his love of partying and his newly asserted sex drive. Henry was in his mid-forties, feeling his age and doing his damnedest to deny it. His thrombosed legs were carrying a greatly inflated bulk. When he was measured for a suit of armour in 1535 his waist size was set down at fifty-four inches. He was as obsessed as ever with health, on the one hand constantly 'taking his own temperature' while, on the other, insisting that he was fit and more than a match for the young blades of the court.

I suspect that this is how we should understand the message put out about his accident in January. A heavy fall, even if for running at the ring he was not in complete armour, would have been a serious shock to his system. Anxious and chattering spectators will have watched, aghast, as Henry was carried from the tiltyard. The question 'What if?' must have occurred to everyone – including the King. As soon as possible, and however bruised or shaken he actually felt, he insisted on having the message circulated that he had 'taken no hurt'. Some biographers have traced a pronounced deterioration in Henry's character directly from the January 1536 mishap. In itself, the explanation is too simplistic. But the assertion that he 'was not notably more cruel afterwards than he had been before'[126] must also be rejected. Most of the reign's acts of sanguinary statecraft occurred during the last decade. Henry had never shrunk from sanctioning beheadings, burnings and disembowellings at several removes from his own person. Heretics, papist sympathisers and enemies of the supremacy had paid for their 'crimes' and Henry had never forfeited a moment's sleep in regretting their fate but personal vendettas against those he knew and had once liked were very few: He had dithered over Wolsey. He had given More plenty of rope with which to hang himself.

Buckingham had deserved his fate. It was in 1536 that bloodletting of those close to the Crown became frequent. The roll-call includes the names of two Queens and their unfortunate friends, one minister, three prominent Yorkists, several royal representatives scapegoated for not dealing effectively enough with rebellion in the North, and two presumptuous Howards. In his later years the lion's claws were out more often. His temper was shorter and his decision-making erratic. In 1538 Reginald Pole could refer to the King's growing irascibility as if it were common knowledge. In my view these traits can be explained by bouts of mental and physical anguish and by that concern which pressed more heavily as he grew older – the need to sire an heir and then to secure that the dynasty survived the succession of a minor. This was a gradual process but if one looks for milestones the fall of January 1536 may well have been important in that it reminded Henry of his mortality and the possible collapse of the house of Tudor.

Be that as it may, Henry was surrounding himself with a new breed of men. He enjoyed the company of courtiers such as Edward Seymour, John Dudley, Thomas Wriothesley and Ralph Sadler. Vigorous activists in their prime (they were all born between 1504 and 1507), they were very different from their fathers; we might reasonably regard them as the 'yuppies' of their age. They had come to maturity at a time of peace and at a time of new ideas. They lacked respect for old institutions and were naturally drawn to men like Cromwell and his staff who were setting out to fashion a new society. Above all they were thrusting, acquisitive and ambitious. Thomas Wriothesley, for example, was building for himself a territorial power base in Hampshire (see pp. 411f) and Edward Seymour was buying up property in Somerset as fast as he could. From 1533 Seymour (then an esquire of the body) and Dudley (a leading star of the tiltyard and Master of the Tower Armoury) were locked in a long-running land dispute with Arthur Plantagenet, Governor of Calais, and at one stage during the legal proceedings Cromwell castigated Seymour for acting 'very craftily'.

This scheming young courtier provides the last piece of evidence for the disintegration of the royal marriage. He must have been among the first to know of the King's interest in his sister. Equally obviously, Jane would have turned to her brother for advice. That advice was to take a leaf out of Anne Boleyn's book and intimate to the King that it was marriage or nothing. There was a story current in the early weeks of the year that Henry had sent Jane a purse of gold together with a letter indicating how she might earn it. The virtuous twenty-six-year-old maid returned it, modestly observing that she could not offer her sovereign what only a husband had the right to claim. It is inconceivable that the Seymours would have brazenly aimed at a crown if they had no reason to suppose that it did not sit securely on the head of its current owner.

By March 1536, if not before, Henry had decided to detach himself from wife number two in order to marry Jane Seymour. Anne had been foolish enough to alienate many men and women of the court. The King was, of course, fully aware of this and knew that he could take advantage of the prevailing hostility towards his wife. The propaganda portraits of Henry representing him as truculent, defiant and immovable have worked too well over the centuries. There was another side to his character, a side that was very attentive to public opinion and able to respond to it without giving the impression of actually yielding to it. Henry was an accomplished actor and always aware of what his audience wanted. He had abandoned both Wolsey and More, not only because of his own anger at their behaviour, but because they were widely unpopular and because no one of any consequence was likely to come to their aid. The same was true of Queen Anne. She could thus be removed without provoking a reaction. Naturally the King looked to Thomas Cromwell to achieve this for him. And Cromwell knew full well what happened to ministers who disappointed the King in matters matrimonial.

It was probably in February that Henry definitely decided to extricate himself from his second marriage in order to wed Jane Seymour. No decision could have been more popular in the court. Anne's overbearing arrogance had made her so many enemies that there was no lack of men and women ready to tell or invent stories that would aid in her downfall. The person called upon to orchestrate the plot against her was, of course, Thomas Cromwell. For a subtle-minded lawyer versed in manipulating evidence and conducting interrogations the task presented no great problems and he set about it with his usual methodicalness.

But is that all there was to it – a faithful official efficiently carrying out his master's will? The simple plot line does not do justice to the complexity of the central characters or the situation they found themselves in. It leaves unresolved two major issues: Why did Anne have to die? If the Queen and Mr Secretary were the twin leaders of an evangelical movement why did Cromwell have no qualms about a course of action which might have seemed to be playing into the hands of the enemies of reform? The leading theories advanced to fit most of the facts neatly together both involve detailed and subtle plots involving misinformation and the faultless manipulation of people and events. One presupposes that in January 1536 Anne was delivered not only of a dead but a deformed foetus which would be regarded by those who knew of it as proof of witchcraft. Henry was genuinely terrified and had to have an elaborate fiction concocted to distance himself from the mother and her deformed by-product. Anne was therefore accused of adultery and she and her lovers were executed to prevent the truth ever coming out. Events, according to this hypothesis, were completely driven forward by a panic-stricken king. The rival explanation puts Cromwell firmly in the driving seat: The two reformist allies had fallen out to such an extent that the Secretary was forced to launch a pre-emptive strike and he did so ruthlessly and cynically – making a temporary pact with his pro-imperialist opponents.[127] Human affairs seldom consist of parts that can be, like clocks, carefully taken apart and reassembled. If we follow the main events we shall not reconcile them all but we may come closer to the truth.

On 24 February Chapuys reported a conversation in which Cromwell had declared his support for a pro-Habsburg policy. He had dismissed futile attempts to side England with France as fostered by Anne's concern for her own position. Since Cromwell's own preferred policy was to ally England with the Protestant states of north Europe and to escape from decades of frustrating diplomacy which had made England a ball bounced back and forth in a Habsburg–Valois tennis match and since the Secretary only told Chapuys what he wanted him to know we need not take his words at face value. However, the death of Catherine had given a considerable boost to those on the Council who favoured a rapprochement with Charles V and with a papacy under new management. Cromwell could not afford to be seen as out on a limb. Shortly after this conversation the falling-out between Queen and Secretary which Cromwell had hinted at the previous summer became a bitter reality. Probably this indicates nothing more than that Cromwell was doing what most of the others in the royal entourage were doing: distancing himself from a doomed consort. There were many at court who must have been hoping that Anne's fall would drag down her evangelical ally. Fortunately for Cromwell he was able to go on to the offensive with the King's backing for Henry had instructed him to find a way out of the Boleyn marriage.

His first move was to explore the possibility of nullity on the basis of Anne's precontract with Henry Percy, now Earl of Northumberland, but this avenue closed when the unhappy young man, whose short life was a catalogue of misfortunes, denied on oath that he had ever entered upon any contract with Mistress Boleyn. At about the same time, Edward Seymour was appointed a gentleman of the Privy Chamber and he and his sister were lodged in quarters at Greenwich which connected with the King's room by a private corridor and which Cromwell vacated for them. The 'sacrifice' was made willingly and indicates the minister's complicity in the royal 'goings-on'. On 2 April the Queen hit out at the whispering campaign through her Almoner, John Skip. In a sermon on the text, 'Which among you accuses me of sin', he lambasted Cromwell, whom he likened to Haman in the Old Testament book of Esther. Haman was a devious councillor to the Persian King Ahasuerus who tried to encompass the downfall of Queen Esther and ended up being hanged on the gallows that he had constructed for the Queen's protector, Mordecai. This barbed warning, which caused a considerable stir at court, made it quite clear that Anne and Cromwell were now poised like duellists – 'pistols for two, breakfast for one'.[128]

On 18 April there occurred a strange incident – a public argument between Cromwell and the King. It took place in front of Chapuys and other ambassadors and, though no one could overhear the details, it concerned Henry's refusal to make any concessions of substance in the interests of normalising relations with Emperor or Pope. Was this a genuine falling-out or was it staged for effect? Either way it signalled that rejection of Anne did not imply acceptance of the pro-imperialist programme. Henry – and probably Cromwell – was signalling that there was no connection between the King's matrimonial affairs and national policy. Significantly it was from this point that Cromwell was set to gather information about the Queen's infidelities. He and Norfolk were constituted a commission of oyer and terminer and began examining witnesses among the King's and Queen's attendants. This inaugurated an orgy of jealousies, hatreds and rivalries which netted a strange assortment of the Queen's supposed lovers from a humble musician to Anne's own brother. Five men were eventually charged with having carnal knowledge of the Queen and plotting the King's death. All of them denied the indictment except Mark Smeaton, the organist, from whom Cromwell extracted a confession by torture in his own home.

The trials, on 12 and 15 May, had nothing whatsoever to do with truth or justice. They were only tangentially connected with politics. What they had everything to do with was the seamy realities of court intrigue. The royal entourage was a vicious, squirming world of competing ambitions and petty feuds, guilty secrets and salacious scandal-mongering, illicit relationships and hypocritical prudery. Courtiers, vulnerable to threats and bribes, could be induced to perjure themselves, to exaggerate amorous incidents which were innocent in the context of stylised chivalric convention, to indulge personal vendettas. Henry adopted his usual stance of telling his ministers what he expected and then retiring into the shadows, so that he could express horrified astonishment when presented with evidence of his wife's infidelities. Cromwell and Norfolk bullied and cajoled until they had cobbled together some sort of case that could be made to stand up in court. Smeaton, a mere underling and probably homosexual, was easy meat. William Brereton and Thomas Wyatt (later released) were womanisers of whom any scandal would be readily believed. Rochford was hated for his closeness to the throne, his rabid evangelicalism and, perhaps, his homosexuality. Henry Norris perished because he was an honourable man. When the King tried to draw him into the conspiracy, he refused, thereby signing his own death warrant.

No one comes out well from this sordid business, certainly not the King who was far from showing the slightest twinge of remorse at authorising the death of the woman for love of whom he had risked so much, and who willingly sacrificed former friends and loyal servants. In fact, he exulted in the exposure of Anne's enormities, telling any who would listen that she had had a hundred paramours. Norfolk had no qualms about presiding over the destruction of his relatives. His crocodile tears deceived no one. Anne's ascendancy had not advantaged the Howards one iota and he did not regret her passing. As for Cromwell, does he emerge now as a dissembling Iago, pursuing his schemes with efficient ruthlessness and, like Shakespeare's villain, cynically disregarding all moral values?

> Virtue? A fig! 'Tis in ourselves that we are thus or thus. Our bodies are our gardens to the which our wills are gardeners; so that if we will plant nettles or sow lettuce, set hyssop and weed up thyme . . . the power and corrigible authority of this lies in our wills.[129]

Cromwell very readily took full credit for Anne's condemnation, telling Chapuys, who he knew would wholeheartedly approve, that, having received full authority from the King to discover the affairs of 'the concubine' he had taken a great deal of trouble in 'fabricating and plotting' the whole business.[130]

In the years of violent upheaval that the realm now entered upon very many men and women suffered injustice at the hands of powerful central government. Until 1540 there were two strong wills behind this regimen. Henry's was governed by emotions increasingly out of control. Cromwell's was the servant of a clear mind and consistent policies. At the end of his life, he claimed:

> As to the commonwealth, I have after my wit, power and knowledge travailed therein, having had no respect to persons (your Majesty only excepted and my duty to the same), but that I have done any injustice or wrong wilfully I trust God shall bear me witness and the world not able justly to accuse me.[131]

It was not strictly true but nor was it a hypocritical claim. When Thomas Cromwell broke eggs it was with the intention of making omelettes. Henry Tudor sometimes did so for the sheer hell of it.

Did they go too far in the spring of 1536? Was Henry too concerned with the achievement of his immediate objective to care about ways and means? Was Cromwell too aware of the price he would pay if, like Wolsey, he disappointed the King? Did he justify his actions by the knowledge (probably accurate) that Anne had become an embarrassment to the cause of reform? Did the genie of intrigue, once out of the bottle, pursue a murderous programme of its own? These questions will, in all likelihood, ever remain unanswered.

The man who emerged least besmirched by the blood of Anne Boleyn and her unfortunate scaffold companions was Thomas Cranmer. A well-known letter he wrote to Henry in early May reveals his bewilderment, his naïvety and his struggle to be loyal to both King and Queen:

> I am in such a perplexity, that my mind is clearly amazed; for I never had better opinion in woman, than I had in her; which maketh me to think, that she should not be culpable. And again, I think your Highness would not have gone so far, except she had surely been culpable. Now I think that your Grace best knoweth, that next unto your Grace I was most bound unto her of all creatures living . . . And if she be found culpable, considering your Grace's goodness towards her, and what condition your Grace of your only mere goodness took her and set the Crown upon her head; I repute him not your Grace's faithful servant and subject, nor true unto the realm, that would not desire the offence without mercy to be punished to the example of all other. And as I loved her not a little for the love which I judged her to bear toward God and his Gospel; so, if she be proved culpable, there is not one that loveth God and his Gospel that ever will favour her, but must hate her above all other; and the more they favour the Gospel, the more they will hate her.

'God and his Gospel', that was now his overriding concern. He confided to Cromwell at about the same time that he was now 'in a heat with the cause of religion'. He feared that Anne's downfall would set back the progress of evangelical reform which had only just got under way and he begged the King,

> Almighty God hath manifoldly declared his goodness towards your Grace, and never offended you . . . Wherefore I trust that your Grace will bear no less entire favour unto the truth of the Gospel, than you did before; forsomuch as your Grace's favour to the Gospel was not led by affection unto her, but by zeal unto the truth.[132]

He need have had no concern and his enemies had no cause for triumphalism. Any who hoped that Anne's death on 19 May would put an end to dangerous reformist policies were swiftly disappointed. Cromwell immediately picked up the reins of Anne's patronage and, now that he was the sole directing force behind the political Reformation, the pace of change speeded up. On 20 May Henry VIII and Jane Seymour were betrothed. On 18 June Cromwell became Lord Privy Seal. On 8 July he was raised to the peerage as Baron Cromwell of Wimbledon. A year later he married his son, Gregory, to Elizabeth Seymour, the new Queen's sister. How these developments must have rankled with Norfolk.

His cup of bitterness was filled to overflowing by other events in the summer of this fateful year. His dynastic ambitions suffered two sledgehammer blows. One of the beauties of the court was the Lady

Margaret Douglas, daughter of Henry's elder sister by her second husband, the Earl of Angus. She was, therefore, the King of England's niece and the King of Scotland's half-sister. This made her a very important card in the game of royal matchmaking. Margaret was, moreover, a personal favourite of Henry's. He kept her at court as the chief lady of Princess Elizabeth's household and treated her with considerable affection. After Anne's death, Margaret became, at the age of twenty, the highest-ranking lady in England. She was, thus, a magnet for Howard ambitions and covertly Thomas, Lord Howard (Norfolk's thirty-year-old half-brother) paid court to her. In the spring of 1536 the couple were secretly betrothed. Whether this was an impetuous act or a calculated one designed to compensate somewhat for the severance of Howard–Tudor links on Anne's death in not clear. Either way it was ill-advised. When the truth came out in the first week of June the miscreants were hustled off to the Tower and, a month later, Norfolk was obliged to signify his assent when an Act of Attainder was passed against Lord Thomas in the House of Lords. Margaret fell ill and was removed to Syon Abbey, from where she wrote an urgent entreaty to Cromwell on Lord Thomas's behalf, assuring Mr Secretary that she no longer held passionate feelings for the prisoner but Henry was not to be assuaged. Howard remained in the Tower until his death in October 1537. Only then was Margaret released.

On 22 July 1536, about the same time as Lord Thomas's attainder, another Howard–Tudor link snapped. The whole succession issue was thrown up in the air by Anne's downfall. Fresh legislation was necessary to bastardise Elizabeth and proclaim his own heir. Attention focused afresh on the children of Henry's sisters – and on the seventeen-year-old Henry Fitzroy, Duke of Richmond (Norfolk's son-in-law). Any hopes that might have lain in that direction were now dashed. Fitzroy, never a well boy, died at St James's Palace. So embarrassed was the King at what might well have been taken as another omen of divine displeasure that he had his son's body removed secretly from London and instructed Norfolk to arrange for its disposal. Encased in lead, and concealed under a load of hay, the cadaver was trundled away to Thetford for quiet burial.

Even this attempt to meet Henry's wishes in a delicate situation turned sour on the unfortunate Duke. While he was absent performing his solemn duty the King had second thoughts about the obsequies appropriate for his dear son. He wrote angrily to Norfolk, blaming him for not according Richmond the funereal honours due to a prince of the blood royal. Observers pointed to Cromwell as the instigator of this volte-face but Henry's basic dislike of Norfolk and the dark cloud currently stationed over the Howard clan were probably sufficient to earn the Duke another bout of exile from court.

His East Anglian isolation ended in dramatic fashion. On 5 October he was back in London, happier than Chapuys had ever seen him, 'which I attribute either to his reconciliation with the king, or to the pleasure this report has given him, thinking it will be the ruin of his rival Cromwell, to whom the blame of everything is attached'.[133] The 'report' which had so pleased Norfolk was that the flame of rebellion was crackling across the fenland of Lincolnshire.

A vital plank of Cromwell's policy platform for the establishment of a reformed Christian commonwealth under a politically and economically secure government had been the enriching of the Crown out of the vast capital resources held by the Church. This entailed confiscating the property of some or all of the religious houses, an idea which, as we have seen, was neither new nor original to Cromwell. If he had, from the outset, promised to make Henry the richest prince in Christendom (as Chapuys suggested) an impatient king would have soon been looking for results. But, as he would have acknowledged, the timing of such a profoundly disturbing event was crucial. King and minister made their preparations carefully. In January 1535 Henry appointed his secretary to be his deputy in ecclesiastical affairs with the sumptuous titles of Viceregent, Vicar General and Special Commissary to exercise all jurisdictions inherent in the Supreme Head of the Church in England – a species of lay cardinal-legate; a secularised version of Thomas Wolsey, but without his fatally divided loyalties. Cromwell spent much of the ensuing months on a thoroughgoing bureaucratic exercise to determine the financial and spiritual standing of *Ecclesia Anglicana*. No one likes government snoopers and the agents Cromwell sent around the dioceses did little to commend themselves to the clergy, monks and nuns whom they grilled. Suspicion and discontent, therefore, trembled in many areas as the nation waited for the results of the surveys.

The government unveiled its manifesto in the final session of the Reformation Parliament which assembled on 4 February 1536. It was accompanied by a flurry of evangelical propaganda. Books and pamphlets were issued attacking images, pilgrimages, purgatory and other super-stitious elements of popular religion. For the illiterate there were satirical prints to be bought from peddlars and fiery sermons to be heard. Cranmer himself preached for two hours at St Paul's Cross on 6 February. Most revolutionary of all was the first English Bible to be freely on sale. Miles Coverdale had produced a translation (heavily reliant on Tyndale's) and offered it to Cromwell. Cautiously advocating it to the King, the Vicegerent obtained permission for its distribution, though not under royal licence. All these prepared the way for Cromwell's first major act of social revolution, that for the suppression of smaller monasteries. Its preamble was a hyperbolic attack on a decaying system.

Forasmuch as manifest sin, vicious, carnal and abominable living, is daily used and committed amongst the little and small abbeys, priories and other religious houses of monks, canons and nuns, where the congregation of such religious persons is under the number of 12 persons, whereby the governors of such religious houses and their convent spoil, destroy, consume and utterly waste as well their churches, monasteries, priories, principal houses, farms, granges, lands, tenements and hereditaments, as the ornaments of their churches and their goods and chattels to the high displeasure of Almighty God, slander of good religion, and to the great infamy of the King's Highness and the realm if redress should not be had thereof; and albeit that many continual visitations hath been heretofore had by the space of two hundred years and more for an honest and charitable reformation of such unthrifty, carnal and abominable living, yet nevertheless little or none amendment is hitherto had, but their vicious living shamelessly increaseth and augmenteth . . .[134]

Given the trend of Cromwellian policy and its declared principles, the dissolution of the monasteries was essential. Quite apart from the national resources locked up in ecclesiastical ownership and the Crown's manifest need of those resources, was the government's determination to continue its attack on all opponents of the supremacy. The religious orders were potential, and in many cases actual, centres of disaffection. They were international, owing primary allegiance to foreign superiors and ultimately to the Pope, and were not subject to control by Henry's bishops. Cromwell and his propagandists envisaged using the wealth of the monasteries in two ways. Vastly increasing the Crown estates would enable the King to live off his own and render him less dependent on parliamentary taxation. It would also provide the financial backing for the Reformation. The English Church would be reorganised by the creation of more bishoprics, which would make for more efficient administration and the carrying into effect of policies dictated from the centre. Since education was obviously the key to the long-term establishment of religious and social change the public was promised more schools, more colleges and more university courses dedicated to the New Learning. In the event these desirable objectives were only pursued in a piecemeal fashion and, particularly after Cromwell's fall, Crown lands were alienated at an alarming rate to meet short-term needs and to buy the loyalty of avaricious magnates. However, it does not follow from this that the Vicegerent's declared intentions were nothing more than a cynical sales gimmick.

The bill proposed the confiscation by the Crown of all religious houses with less than twelve inmates and incomes of less than £200 per annum. The measure bristled with sticks and carrots. As well as lambasting the wasted lives of the religious and their resistance to reform it provided that those who wished to maintain their vocation could move to larger houses. These major abbeys and priories, which accounted for the greater part of monastic wealth, were untouched – for the time being. And the bill made clear what many of the knights, burgesses and lords will already have calculated – that a lot of valuable property would soon be flooding on to the market. The bill had an easy passage through the Lords, helped by the six reformist bishops recently appointed (including Latimer) but it was apparently eased through the Commons by the King's appearance there.

As soon as the act was on the statute book Cromwell's agents were out and about, taking possession of confiscated buildings, stripping out objects of value, sending the inmates on their way. Nor were these the only disturbances in the ponderous pace of provincial life. Subsidy commissioners were making their rounds. Preachers were ranting their attack and defence of old practices and dogmas. Recalcitrant priests were being interrogated or despatched to London for examination by the Council. There were occasional executions of men and women who fell foul of the supremacy or treason laws. Country people saw their objects of traditional devotion destroyed or exposed to ridicule:

> . . . upon the defacing of the late monastery of Boxley, and plucking down of the images of the same, I found in the image of the rood called the Rood of Grace, the which heretofore hath been had in great veneration of people, certain engines and old wire, with old rotten sticks in the back of the same, that did cause the eyes of the same to move and stare in the head thereof like unto a lively thing; and also the nether lip in like wise to move as though it should speak . . . and considering that the inhabitants of the County of Kent had in time past a great devotion to the same, and to use continual pilgrimage thither, by the advise of other that were here with me [I] did convey the said Image unto Maidstone this present Thursday, then being the market day, and in the chief [i.e. busiest part] of the market time did show it openly unto all the people there being present, to see the false, crafty, and subtle handling thereof, to the dishonour of God, and illusion of the said people . . .[135]

To the actual upheavals of daily life imagination added more: the King was planning fresh taxes; he was going to strip items of value out of parish churches; the new landlords of ex-monastic property would increase rents, enclose commons, etc. etc. etc.

As well as provoking a general, vague conservative backlash the government's programme offended specific groups of people who were better organised, had more power and effective lines of communication. There were the traditionalist clergy who saw their position in society under attack. There were the semi-independent nobility and their gentry clients in the remoter corners of the land for whom dynastic rivalries and resistance to control from London were entrenched character traits. Finally, there were the court Catholics and their extensive networks of kith and kin. Since Catherine's death they had transferred their allegiance to Mary, wanting her to be named as Henry's heir, seeking closer relations with the Emperor and a rapprochement with Rome. Chapuys had long ago convinced himself and attempted to convince his master that the King and his evil ministers were at odds with the bulk of the English people, that a demonstration of military support by the Emperor would be a catalyst that would set off revolt and that sundry great lords would readily enter the fray with sizeable armies at their backs. In the autumn of 1536 this theory was put to the test.

The government was far from unaware of the rising discontent. With letters pouring in to Cromwell daily from his agents round the country it could hardly be so. The Vicegerent's official line was uncompromising:

> Set forth the king's authority as Supreme Head by all possible means. There can be no better way to beat the king's authority into the heads of the rude people in the North than to show them that the king intends reformation and correction of religion. They are more superstitious than virtuous, long accustomed to frantic fantasies and ceremonies, which they regard more than either God or their prince. They are completely alienated from true religion.[136]

But at the same time he took measures, admittedly heavy-handed, designed to quiet the situation. On 11 July Cranmer emerged from convocation brandishing a piece of paper designed to impose on the Church 'peace for our time'. It was the first statement of distinctively Anglican doctrine. The ten *Articles of Faith to Establish Christian Quietness* had a generally evangelical flavour while yet seeking to offend Catholic feeling as little as possible. In fact, by a mixture of ambiguity and silence they sought to appeal to all. To make sure that they did not become ammunition for rival sermonisers, on the very next day the King forbade all preaching in England (with minor exceptions) until Michaelmas (29 September) and even thereafter all preachers were to shun interpretation of the Articles 'after their fantastical appetites'. Royal injunctions to the parish clergy ordered them to preach four times a year against the usurped authority and false claims of the Bishop of Rome and to teach their congregations to recite the Ten Commandments, the Lord's Prayer and the Creed *in English*. If the Supreme Head of the Church and his Vicegerent in Spirituals thought that these measures would quiet the consciences of all English Christians and stay any rebellious spirits, they underestimated the strength of traditional beliefs and customs in many parts of the realm.

Between October and March a total of 40,000 of the King's subjects in the northern and midland shires took up arms at one time or another in what was a type of political agitation such as had never been seen before. It was neither a baronial challenge to the Crown nor a spontaneous peasant uprising, although it combined elements of both. In the affected areas all sections of society were involved. The rebels covered their insurgency with a mantle of holiness: those beyond the Trent marched under a banner depicting the five wounds of Christ and called their movement the Pilgrimage of Grace. Although, to a man, the participants protested their loyalty to the Crown and complained only against Henry's base-born advisers and their heresies (religious and political), this movement shook the Tudor state to its very foundations. That state survived because Henry showed that, when it came to deviousness and ruthlessness, he had nothing to learn from a book which had appeared in print four years earlier – *The Prince* by Niccolò Machiavelli.

The trouble began at Louth in Lincolnshire at Michaelmas, the day the preaching ban was lifted, where the usual crowd of pious citizens had turned out to gaze with mingled devotion and civic pride on the jewel-decked images, reliquaries, banners and silver crosses paraded through the town on the feast day. The atmosphere was more than usually emotional and it needed only someone to shout out 'Follow the crosses! God knoweth whether we shall ever follow them again!'[137] to turn bemused anxiety into frenetic action. Within days church bells all over the fenland were summoning men to gather with such arms as they could lay hands on, oaths were being sworn, local gentry coerced into leadership and demands had been prepared. The principal ones were:

1. The King might enjoy the title of Supreme Head of the English Church and that Church should remain severed from the Church of Rome *but* the King must promise to suppress no more religious houses.
2. The King might have the subsidy voted in 1534 and might collect the ecclesiastical revenues of first fruits and tenths *but* he must not take any more money from the people.
3. The King must yield up to the commons his evil and heretical advisers, namely Cromwell, Cranmer, Longland, Hilsey (Bishop of Rochester), Goodrich (Bishop of Ely), Latimer (Bishop of Worcester) and Browne (Bishop of Dublin).

When the news reached London Henry ordered military preparations and it was this which led to Norfolk's recall. Howard had three reasons for intense satisfaction: he was fully in sympathy with the conservative backlash; Cromwell had brought down a storm on his own head and was unlikely to survive; the King's need for military leaders would give him an opportunity to regain favour. The fact that two of these were in conflict – that he could only prove his worth to the King by taking arms against a movement of which he approved – did not trouble him at all. After an interview with the King, he was back in his county on 7 October mustering his forces.

The very next day he was thunderstruck to receive new orders. Henry had decided to lead the army himself or to send 'some great and notable personage' to encounter with the rebels. That personage was not to be the Duke of Norfolk, Earl Marshal of England. He was instructed to stay at home and keep his own shire quiet. Was this an expression of Henry's mistrust, stirred up by Cromwell, or simply evidence that, in a crisis situation, the King was thinking on his feet, making up his tactics by the hour? Whatever the motivation, the letter sent Howard into one of his rages. He immediately penned an indignant reply, anger lending him uncharacteristic eloquence: 'Alas, Sir, shall every nobleman save I only either come to your person or else go towards your enemies? Shall I now sit still like a man of law? Alas, Sir, my heart is near dead, as would to God it were.' He informed the King that, unless he received by return specific orders to stay put, he would ride northwards, rather than sit at home nursing his shame. He wrote in a similar vein to Cromwell. By evening he had sufficiently calmed down to regret his petulance. He wrote again rescinding his threat to march to Lincolnshire come what may. He would obey the order to stay put – but he was still unhappy. By the next morning the kaleidoscopic military situation had changed again. As responses were received to the King's urgent messages to all the leading men of the realm he was better able to make his plans. He appointed the Duke of Suffolk (enjoying a return to favour now that Mary no longer came between her brother and her husband) as his lieutenant. Swallowing his pride, Howard begged to be allowed to serve under his old rival.[138]

Henry's next moves demonstrate that there were those he feared more than a rabble of Lincolnshire priests, gentlemen and peasants armed with scythes and pitchforks: there were great men in the realm who nursed grievances. He ordered Brandon to set out immediately, without waiting for troops, and stall the rebel leaders while the Earl of Shrewsbury marched towards him from Nottingham and Newark with his own contingent. Meanwhile the King mustered his main army at Ampthill, Bedfordshire, from where they could be advanced northwards or brought back to defend the capital as the situation developed. Henry dared not leave himself exposed. Sparks from the fenland were settling elsewhere and he feared fresh serious outbreaks. Above all he realised the inadvisability of despatching a large body of troops into Lincolnshire, under the leadership of commanders whose personal loyalty might diminish with each mile of their journey. It took him several more days to authorise Norfolk to join other peers at Ampthill and to take command of the reserve army. Even then, he was cautious: he demanded that the Duke's sons should remain at home to guarantee that their father used his best endeavours on the King's behalf.

All was at sixes and sevens. Frenzied instructions regarding the movement of men, money and material passed back and forth between the court at Windsor, the commanders in the field and Cromwell's staff in London. Their letters crossed. They contradicted each other. They encouraged rivalry among the generals. The result was confusion, at times approaching panic. For example, artillery was rushed to Ampthill. Then, when intelligence suggested that the rebels were marching southwards, the order went out to send it to Windsor and London for the defence of court and capital. As soon as better information was available the instructions were countermanded. Some ordnance was to be forwarded to Brandon; the rest kept at Ampthill. Then Norfolk took matters into his own hands, commandeering all the artillery left at Ampthill for his own northbound force.

In fact, by this time the crisis in Lincolnshire was virtually over. Fatally for their cause, the insurgents hesitated. In Lincoln the gentlemen who, with varying degrees of enthusiasm or reluctance, had accepted leadership of the protest movement argued among themselves. On 10 October the King's uncompromising reply was read to the rebel host. Calculating that he was only dealing with a mob of semi-literate artisans and renegade priests, Henry harangued them: 'How presumptuous . . . are ye, the rude commons of one shire, and that one of the most brute and beastly of the whole realm, and of least experience, to find fault with your prince . . .'[139] In the light of the King's intransigence and the approach of royal troops the rebels' courage failed them. The insurrection collapsed without a shot being fired. But the county was far from pacified and reports of more serious disaffection farther north meant that Suffolk had to spend several weeks arresting and examining suspects. He called for reinforcements and Norfolk grudgingly supplied them, remarking on more than one occasion, 'I can do no less than judge that some be desirous to have a greater company more for glory than for necessity.'[140] Brandon conducted himself with wisdom, leniency and moderation, sometimes braving the King's anger for not exacting vengeance and it was largely due to his efforts that the fenlanders remained passive when Yorkshire and adjacent counties launched their challenge.

The Pilgrimage of Grace seemed likely to end in a similar, bloodless way, not because the rebels were weak and disorganised, but because Norfolk, heading a vastly outnumbered royal army, was forced to negotiate. The Duke knew, as he entered territory won by the resistance movement with about 8,000 men, that the military situation was impossible. York and Pontefract Castle were in enemy hands and their 40,000-strong army was waiting for him near Doncaster. In the country beyond, several of the great marcher lords had signed up to the rebellion. He might well have been tempted to throw in his lot with the King's good Catholic subjects who sought only the overthrow of Cromwell and the halting of the Reformation. But loyalty to the Crown had become an ingrained habit and the sheer power of Henry's will impelled him forward even from a distance of 160 miles. And then, of course, there was the question of his sons, vulnerable to the royal wrath at Kenninghall. Knowing that he would have to parley and knowing that the King expected nothing less than military victory, Norfolk anxiously reported the situation and assured His Majesty, 'none oath nor promise made for policy to serve you, *mine only master and sovereign* [my emphasis] can distain [i.e. corrupt] me, who shall rather be torn in a million pieces than to show one point of cowardice or untruth to your majesty'.[141]

At a meeting on 27 October Norfolk listened to the complaints of the pilgrims and represented to them the King's displeasure – though in terms more of sorrow than anger:

> Alas, ye unhappy men! What fancy, what folly, hath led and seduced you to make this most shameful rebellion against our most noble and righteous King and sovereign? . . . Fye for shame! How can ye thus do, and over and besides for offences to your natural sovereign lord, give us too, that have loved you better than any part of the realm, occasion to fight with you, that we have taken for our best friends?[142]

Norfolk offered a truce promising a royal pardon and serious consideration of their grievances, if the protestors would break up their camp and go home while he consulted with the King. It worked. The more moderate insurgents had only intended to stage a demonstration and many of their followers had no stomach for a winter campaign. Howard watched the rebels disperse, then returned to London. But not with a light heart as one who had achieved a famous victory. He knew all too well what enemies at court would be saying in his absence and he was fearful that Henry would accuse him of being too gentle with enemies of the state. He wrote to the Council in great anguish of mind – as usual raking together every possible excuse, magnifying his difficulties and laying blame on others.

> . . . alas my good lords I have served his highness many times without reproach and now [that I am] forced to [negotiate] with the rebels my heart is near broken. And notwithstanding that in every man's mouth it is said in our army that I never served his grace so well as now as in dissolving the army of the enemy without loss of ours yet fearing how his majesty shall take the dispeaching of our band I am the most unquiet man of mind living. All others here [are] joyful and I only sorrowful . . .
>
> Good my lords it was not the fear of the enemy [that] hath caused us to [negotiate], but three other sore points. Foul weather and no housing for horse nor man at the most not for the third part of the army and no wood to make fires withall, hunger both for men and horses of such sort that of truth I think never English man saw the

like. Pestilence in the town marvellous fervent . . .

. . . and if there were left in the town or within five miles one load of hay or one load of oats, peas or beans all the purveyors say untruly. Which three points these are for an army I report me to your wisdoms and to have advanced to the enemy [with] no victuals for man nor horse but all devastated by the enemy and not possible to have even battle but upon apparent loss thereof. And if we should have retired in mighty assured ruin of our company. Having no horsemen and they all the flower of the north and how at every street they should at their will have set on the foremost part or the hindermost your wisdoms can well consider . . .[143]

Two weeks later he was back at Doncaster for more detailed talks. His instructions were to play for time, yielding whatever was necessary to lull the rebels into a false sense of security and asking for leisure to consult with King and Council over the more sensitive issues. Norfolk managed to drag the fresh talks well on into December by which time the northern winter had eaten into the pilgrims' numbers and their resolve. Henry, of course, had no intention of paying the slightest regard to the rebels' demands. Whether or not he was determined to be revenged on his troublesome subjects is not clear but, in the event, they made the decision easy for him. As the realisation spread through the North that the pilgrims had been duped, extremist elements once more began stirring up trouble. In the new year Norfolk was once again sent beyond Trent with explicit instructions to enforce the King's will.

The Duke saw this as his opportunity to scotch all rumours about his lack of loyal zeal. He would prove his worth in the way that came easiest to him – killing people. He spent the early months of 1537 ferreting out the instigators of the rebellion, administering an oath of fealty to all the leaders of northern society and ensuring that monks and nuns who had resisted the suppression of their houses were duly expelled. As far as executions were concerned, Howard's instructions were to be as ferocious as he could without running the risk of backlash. If he encountered the possibility of resistance when making example of offenders he was to 'look through his fingers at their offences and free them . . . till the king's majesty's arrival in these parts'.[144] Along with this licence for pragmatism went taunts from Cromwell, accusing the Duke of too great partiality towards recalcitrant monks and other upholders of the old religion. Week followed week, filled with interrogations, quick trials under the simple, harsh rules of martial law, and summary executions. As Norfolk rode to and fro about this tedious business he longed for some dramatic opportunity to show his military mettle. His chance seemed to have arrived on 14 February.

That was the day that he heard that 6,000 men had laid siege to Carlisle. Before he set out to cross the Pennines from Richmond he paused to dash off a note to Cromwell: 'Now shall appear whether for favour of these countrymen I forbore to fight with them at Doncaster.'[145] Unfortunately for his martial reputation he arrived too late. Sir Christopher Dacre had arrived at Carlisle with 500 spearmen and put the ill-armed commoners totally to rout, cutting down hundreds of peasants as they fled across the fields and taking at least 300 prisoners. When the news reached court it was hailed as a great victory. Dacre was the hero of the hour and Cromwell commented that he ought to be made an earl. Back at Carlisle Norfolk could do nothing but bite his lip and set about the process of administering law. Law not justice. The pathetic skirmish at Carlisle had nothing to do with the Pilgrimage of Grace; it was provoked by the harsh agrarian policies of the Earl of Cumberland. But such nice distinctions were lost on the denizens of the royal court. They were not lost on Howard as, watched by sullen-faced northerners, he condemned seventy-four men to be hanged – so many that the local chain-makers could not keep up with demand and several bodies had to be gibbeted with rope.

Norfolk acknowledged that these wretched people were more sinned against than sinning. He wrote to Cromwell:

What with the spoiling of them now and the [trans]gressing of them so marvellously sore in time past and with increasing of lords' rents by enclosing, and for lack of the persons of such as shall suffer, this border is sore weakened and especially Westmorland; the more pity they should so deserve, and also that they have been so sore handled in times past, which, as I and all other here think, was the only cause of the rebellion.[146]

But if Norfolk felt any compassion it did not prevent him giving the King the victims he expected nor from taking pride in having put to death many more than, in his opinion, deserved to die. As for the King, his vengeance pursued the 'rebels' even after death. When news reached him that the wives and mothers of the executed had taken down their bodies to give them some semblance of decent burial, he was incensed. He accused his lieutenant of dereliction of duty and insisted on the offenders being punished. Mercifully, the records are silent on the fate of the poor widows of Cumberland.[147]

The grisly work in the North finished, Norfolk had good reason to hope for a recall and for some sign of his master's gratitude. Yet again he was disappointed. As in years past, his earnest pleas to be allowed to return to court were denied. Commentators were in no doubt about who was behind the Duke's continued exclusion. Not until October was he replaced by Cuthbert Tunstall as the King's regent beyond Trent.

If Howard was in a state of perpetual unease about how the King was interpreting his actions, his rival was in no position to gloat. Henry angrily rejected any suggestion that he should dismiss Cromwell but that was not out of any sense of loyalty towards a faithful servant. Indeed, Mr Secretary was frequently first in line to face Henry's wrath during these trying months. As he had done with Wolsey and Anne, the King was capable of listening to the hostile clamour against those close to him and, while publicly defying it, echoing it in private. A newcomer to the court was bold enough to boast about his inside knowledge (his loose tongue later got him into trouble):

> As for my Lord Privy Seal, I would not be in his case for all that ever he hath, for the King beknaveth him twice a week and sometime knocketh him well about the pate; and yet when he hath been well pommelled about the head and shaken up, as it were a dog, he will come out into the great chamber, shaking of the bush, with as merry a countenance as though he might rule all the roost.

The young spectator averred that Cromwell had come close to being destroyed by the Pilgrimage of Grace and that others about the court (including Norfolk!) had had to intercede for him.[148] There are elements of this story that we cannot take at face value because the writer was not au fait with the subtleties of personal relationships at the centre of political power. To an outsider it seemed obvious that Henry was casting around for someone else to blame and that Cromwell was laughing off embarrassing brushes with the angry monarch. The King was certainly given increasingly to outbursts of temper expressed in physical violence and all those who attended him had no alternative but to grin and bear such abuse. However, bully though he was, Henry expected his advisers to stand up to him and argue their case when they had strong convictions about issues. Cromwell was not a rubber stamp for the royal will. Had he been content to be so, he might well have outlived his master, as did Norfolk. But, whereas the Duke was ever all a-tremble about rightly gauging and responding to the King's desires, Cromwell had his own ideas about political strategy and diplomatic tactics. Henry would listen to them and discuss them. Sometimes he would casually approve, sometimes firmly reject them. And sometimes he would fly into a petulant rage. His moods and attitudes were always difficult to read and that explains why councillors were frequently caught off guard; sometimes fatally. It also explains why observers often misjudged the significance of Henry's volcanic rumblings and eruptions. Only rarely did they indicate dramatic changes of policy or the imminent downfall of ministers. That said, Mr Secretary may well have been pleased that during the worst weeks of the crisis the supervision of government business kept him at Westminster and that he could maintain contact with the Windsor court through a trusted representative, Thomas Wriothesley. (As we shall see, it was

Wriothesley's proximity to the King at this troubled time that set his feet firmly on the higher rungs of the preferment ladder.) But there could be no question of Henry disowning Cromwell and his policies as long as the assault on Church property – no matter how unpopular – was pouring money and negotiable assets into the royal Treasury.

Norfolk arrived at Hampton Court in time for the rejoicing accompanying the birth of Henry VIII's long-awaited legitimate male heir and the grief attending the death of Henry's third queen. On 12 October Jane Seymour gave birth to a son by Caesarian section. On the 15th the child was christened Edward, Norfolk standing as godfather, along with Suffolk and Cranmer. Three days later Edward Seymour was elevated to the earldom of Hertford. On 24 October Queen Jane died of the post-natal complications Tudor medicine was not equipped to deal with. Norfolk presided over her elaborate funeral. Henry was so distressed at Jane's passing that he was already looking for another bride. These solemn duties completed, Norfolk retired once more to Kenninghall. There was no place for him in the Reformation court.

No place, either, for the only other effective conservative champion. Stephen Gardiner had been despatched to France on a mission in October 1535 and did not return until July 1538. Cromwell, though still openly friendly towards the Bishop, was pleased to have him out of the way. Henry still did not trust the man who, he knew, opposed at heart the religious changes the government had sponsored. In the summer of 1536 the King personally instituted an examination of Gardiner's activities at the convent of Syon. The Bishop had been chosen the previous year to persuade the nuns to swear the Succession oath. The effort had not been very successful and Henry was not satisfied that Gardiner had tried very hard. At the same time the prickly prelate was arguing needlessly with Henry over a minor financial matter. When Cromwell attempted to pour oil on troubled waters, Gardiner sharply accused him of duplicity. This provoked a sarcastic response from Mr Secretary:

> . . . though my talent be not so precious as yours, yet I trust with his help that gave me it, to use it so as it shall do his office without gathering such suspicions upon friendship. I repeat that word again because I meant friendly in the writing of it . . . I wrote unto you friendly advising you rather frankly and with an appearance of a good will to satisfy his grace than so to contend in it, as he might take it unkindly. And now for that advice which I took to be friendly ye take great pain to make me believe that I have neither friendship in me nor honesty, wherein how friendly ye proceed with me.

Cromwell's advancement at Winchester's expense and Henry's promoting of Cranmer over his head to Canterbury still rankled with the Bishop. He found it virtually impossible to accord to either of his rivals the honour new status demanded. He still behaved imperiously towards the Secretary, as this same letter from Cromwell suggests. A peremptory demand from Gardiner for more information about the trial of Anne and her accomplices drew forth the response:

> Touching your great desire of news in good faith I wrote as much and as plainly of the matters that chanced here as I could devise unless I should have sent you the very confessions, which were so abominable that a great part of them were never given in evidence but clearly kept secret.[149]

Gardiner, angry and frustrated at being marginalised, was determined to keep himself as fully informed as possible about events in England. And when he was informed he could scarcely refrain from commenting. In June 1536 he complained bitterly about a sermon Latimer had preached before convocation. And, responding to news of the northern rising the following January, he ventured to give the King advice which Henry regarded as tantamount to surrendering to the rebels. More seriously, Gardiner used his diplomatic position to undermine Cromwell's efforts to make common cause with the Protestant German states. In his reports to the King he pointed out the dangers of this novel shift in policy and attempted to keep diplomacy in the old rut of playing off Habsburg and Valois against each other. Gardiner was so much out of sympathy with the drift of English affairs and so unable to prevent himself airing his views that it was not difficult for Cromwell to veto the Bishop's requests for recall. With little effective criticism at the centre the Reformation rolled on apace.

'Religion is making favourable progress among us. By the order of the king, persons are sent to preach the truth in all parts of England. You have, I suppose, heard long since respecting the lady of Walsingham, and the breaking of other idols.'[150] So wrote an English friend to the Swiss reformer Heinrich Bullinger in September 1538, and he had good cause to be elated. Conservative opinion had made its bid to halt the evangelical advance and it had failed. The Vicegerent now pushed on with mounting confidence. He gathered around him a veritable salon of writers, artists, preachers and lawyers to produce propaganda and to take the argument to the enemy. He encouraged the voluntary liquidation of more monastic houses. Many abbots and priors could read the writing on the wall and hastened to pre-empt government action in order to obtain better terms. He was sympathetic when local zealots took the law into their own hands by destroying objects of superstition. And he was well aware of the value of public entertainment. In June 1539 he organised a riverain pageant. A 'royal' barge and a 'papal' barge 'rowed up and down the Thames from Westminster Bridge to the King's bridge; and the Pope [and his cardinals] made their defiance against England and shot their ordnance one at another . . . but at last the Pope and his cardinals were overcome and all his men cast overboard into the Thames'.[151] The less amusing aspect of the programme was the continuing ruthless persecution of men and women who opposed the supremacy. Cromwell made the new movement a reality in every parish church. New injunctions in 1538 instructed clergy

> that such feigned images as ye know of in any of your cures to be so abused with pilgrimages or offerings of anything made thereunto, ye shall, for avoiding that most detestable sin of idolatry, forthwith take down and delay, and shall suffer from henceforth no candles, tapers, or images of wax to be set afore any image or picture.[152]

His crowning achievement, the one Erasmus, Tyndale, several exiles and martyrs and even, at one time, Thomas More had dreamed of, was the Great Bible. At last, Cromwell persuaded Henry to sponsor an English version of the Scriptures. The new version was printed abroad and ran into production problems when Catholic censors held up the work but Cromwell made it his priority and gave his agents maximum encouragement. In 1538 every parish church was instructed to acquire and prominently display a copy of the Great Bible and the clergy were to

> expressly provoke, stir and exhort every person to read the same, as that which is the very lively word of God, that every Christian person is bound to embrace, believe and follow if they look to be saved, admonishing them nevertheless to avoid all contention and altercation therein, but to use an honest sobriety in the inquisition of the true sense of the same, and to refer the explication of obscure places to men of higher judgement in scripture.[153]

Now the genie really was out of the bottle and there was no telling what it might do.

CHAPTER 29

New Men, New Ideas, Old Anxieties

> . . . your lordship should send some loving letter unto Mr
> Wriothesley, giving him thanks and desiring him of continuance of
> his good mind toward you. And if your lordship did send him some
> gentle remembrance . . . it should be well bestowed. The truth is the
> man standeth in place where he may please and displease. It shall,
> therefore, be good to entertain him amongst the number of your
> friends . . .[154]

Thus Arthur Plantagenet, Deputy of Calais, was advised in August 1537
by his agent, John Hussee. Like all royal servants, especially those who
lived and worked at a distance from the court, Plantagenet (who, as an
illegitimate son of Edward IV, had additional reason to maintain good
relations with the King) needed well-placed friends and advisers to look
after his interests and now the thirty-one-year-old Wriothesley joined their
number.

He had first been identified by Hussee as a useful ally the previous
February and the timing is significant. Throughout the months when
northern rebellion threatened the stability of the Tudor state Thomas
Wriothesley was at the King's side as his chief amanuensis and as Mr
Secretary's trusted representative at court. Cromwell and Cranmer, the
principal targets for conservative arrows of hatred, remained in the
shadows, perhaps by royal command. The Archbishop spent several
months on his properties in Kent, while the Vicegerent, though at the
centre of the government's policy-making and information-gathering
activities in London and Westminster, operated, as it were, from behind
shuttered windows.

The capital had become a dangerously divided city: those who, for
whatever reasons, detested the drift towards reformation were emboldened
by news and rumours from Lincolnshire and Yorkshire. Those who
recognised in civil unrest proof that overt and covert papalists were the
enemies of God, King and country were quick to denounce the rebels and
their sympathisers. Latimer and Barnes attracted crowds to their
denunciatory sermons. Roisterers egged on by disaffected clergy hung

bundles of hay outside Cranmer's house – reference to the scurrilous rumour that the Archbishop was the son of a mere ostler. More seriously, on a raw November morning an assassin lay in wait for Robert Packington – mercer, MP, friend of Cromwell and outspoken advocate of reform – and gunned his victim down as he was on the way to mass.

The government's immediate response was to defuse the situation by every possible means. Barnes and other headstrong preachers were arrested, as much for their own protection as offering a sop to the conservatives. Official rumours were spread asserting the King's orthodoxy and his determination not to tolerate extremists. Cromwell instructed Latimer to preach a conciliatory sermon at St Paul's Cross, which, perhaps reluctantly, he did, 'according to your discreet monition and charitable advertisement, so moving to unity without any special note of any man's folly'. 'All my lords there present seemed to be content with me,' the Bishop reported of his unaccustomed role as peacemaker.[155] In late December a declaration of the King's intention to pass in procession through London threw the security-conscious Mayor and aldermen into a positive frenzy of anxiety. From his central position Cromwell was busy operating the government's propaganda and censorship systems, limiting, as far as possible, any damaging news that might leave the country.

The King, from his virtually impregnable fortress at Windsor, masterminded the war effort and the link between him and his minister was Thomas Wriothesley. An old pattern was repeating itself. Just as Fox had used Wolsey as an intermediary when he was unable to wait upon His Majesty and Wolsey had relied on Cromwell's presence at court, so Cromwell now placed his most trusted apprentice at Henry's side.

Those who have chosen to regard Cromwell as an unprincipled schemer have recognised Wriothesley as his most apt pupil. One biographer stated baldly, 'It is difficult to trace in [Wriothesley's] career any motive beyond that of self-aggrandisement. Trained in the Machiavellian school of Cromwell, he was without the definite aims and resolute will that to some extent redeemed his master's lack of principle.'[156] This does not fit glovelike with contemporary assessments. The evangelical scholar John Ponet called him 'the subtle and ambitious Alcibiades of England' after the Athenian general notorious for coat-turning.[157] And Richard Morison, a fellow client of Cromwell who knew Wriothesley well, commented: 'I was afraid of a tempest all the while Wriothesley was ever able to raise any. I knew he was an earnest follower of whatsoever he took in hand, and very seldom did miss where either wit or travail were able to bring his purpose to pass.'[158]

Ambitious and acquisitive Wriothesley certainly was but these were not traits learned from Cromwell. His uncle and namesake was his earliest mentor in the arts of self-aggrandisement. Garter King of Arms ended his days under a cloud for, in 1530, his bitter rival, Thomas Benolt,

Clarenceux King of Arms, accused him before the King of 'great misgovernance and also misordering that [he] used and did in the same office of arms, the which was against the honour of noble men and of all gentlemen of arms [in granting arms] to bound men, to vile persons, not able to uphold the honour of noblesse'.[159] The elder Wriothesley was accused of making grants on his own authority and without royal warrants. These were years during which society was changing more rapidly than ever before. Education, trade, new patterns of land tenure, career opportunities for laymen – all these made for a more fluid and versatile national life. Men of modest means could aspire to greater wealth and standing so that those, like the heralds, in a position to sell valued status symbols were well placed to profit from such ambitions. At length the whistle was blown on this profitable trade and, though Garter King defended himself against Benolt's charges, the unpleasantness rumbled on until his death in 1534 by which time the proceedings of the College of Arms had been considerably tightened up.

Young Thomas Wriothesley's family background introduced him to the ethos of self-improvement by any and every means which came to hand. It also provided the initial court contacts necessary to facilitate the rise of an eager and able young man. By 1530 he had moved from Wolsey's entourage to Cromwell's and in that year he became a clerk of the signet which brought him within Stephen Gardiner's ambit as royal secretary. Thus, while still in his mid-twenties, he had become acquainted with all the leaders of court and Council and worked closely with some of them. He knew the people. He knew the system. It only remained for him to exploit that knowledge.

Cromwell's rise provided the circumstances for him to do just that. By the time that Cromwell took over the secretaryship Wriothesley was already his most trusted assistant. He was in his master's confidence, he drafted and wrote most of his letters and, by 1537, he was being referred to as 'the principal clerk of the signet under my Lord Privy Seal'. He was the best route to Cromwell and was the recipient of so many appeals for the Secretary's aid that he had his own confidential clerk. He had already been on two foreign missions and the King obviously liked him. He possessed qualities which commended him to the monarch, as to others who worked closely with him. It is clear from his extant correspondence what some of those qualities were: Wriothesley was industrious, enthusiastic, witty and a shrewd judge of character. He was also, and increasingly as the years passed, outspoken, even with the King. He had learned well from Cromwell the techniques required for handling their irascible master.

Wriothesley was a careerist. He avidly garnered the harvest of fees, perks, bribes, titles, sinecures and power that successful progress through the ranks of patronage and royal service brought him. In this he was doing no more than following accepted social convention. For example, there was a clearly defined business arrangement between Cromwell and his protégé whereby Wriothesley paid him a percentage of his profits as Clerk of the Signet. What was different in Wriothesley's case was the rapidity with which he amassed a vast fortune. He was able to do so because he was in the right place at the right time. The 1530s, like the Thatcherite 1980s, were years of sanctified greed. When Cromwell flooded the property market with confiscated Church lands, buildings, furnishings and building materials he gave government encouragement to speculation, profiteering and personal empire-building on a massive scale. The sixteenth-century equivalent of yuppies and fat cats besieged his office and the Court of Augmentations, clamouring to buy or rent. As John Hussee reported to his master on more than one occasion, 'Here is nothing but every man for himself.'[160] Making ex-monastic property available to a wide range of potential customers was a masterstroke of Cromwell's Reformation. Whatever noblemen, burgesses and gentlemen thought about the religious issues, they could scarcely avoid becoming involved in the once-in-a-millennium opportunity to consolidate their estates or buy and sell for profit, and in so doing they gave their support to the permanent alienation of Church property – and the power that went with it. The Dissolution of the Monasteries channelled between a third and a fifth of the landed wealth of England and Wales into the King's hands and, through Crown agencies, much of it ended up in the ownership of Henry's lay subjects.

Some of the plums, of course, went to Cromwell and his close associates. The Vicegerent concentrated his building activities in and around London. In 1538 he acquired the enormous site of the Austin Friar's priory in Broad Street ward close by the City's northern wall. He had already bought up several adjoining properties and now he set about erecting a town house of impressive size and splendour. According to the chronicler John Stowe, Cromwell was not satisfied with what he had come by legally:

This house being finished, and having some reasonable plot of ground left for a garden, he caused the pales of the gardens adjoining to the north part thereof on a sudden to be taken down, 22 ft to be measured forth right into the north of every man's ground, a line there to be drawn, a trench to be cast, a foundation laid, and a high brick wall to be builded. My father had a garden there, and an house standing close to his south pale. This house they loosed from the ground, and bare upon rollers into my father's garden 22 ft, ere my father heard thereof. No warning was given him, nor other answer, when he spake to the surveyors of that work, but that their master, Sir Thomas, commanded them so to do. No man durst go to argue the matter, but each man lost his land, and my father paid his whole rent, which was 5s.8d. the year, for that half which was left. Thus much of mine own knowledge have I thought good to note, that the sudden rising of some men, causeth them to forget themselves.[161]

Cromwell also owned property in Chancery Lane and in the nearby villages of Hackney, Canonbury, Stepney and Mortlake. At Ewhurst, in Surrey, he had a country mansion built which, to judge from the account of his steward, Thomas Thacker, was more than substantial.

On Sunday last past I went to Ewhurst, and there viewed your goodly frames [i.e. framework]. The double floors of your hall and solar under it be finished, and also the two sides of your hall, and part of the same carried from the frame to the waterside, and more daily shall come by the grace of God. They have much business to get carriage because of hay time and harvest; but the parson of Ewhurst which is good and diligent in your business there, saith we shall have carts this next week. Your frame is the goodliest and mightiest that I in my life have seen: but your foundations thereof, with God's grace, is substantial and mighty enough to bear it. And now they be in hand with the roof of your said hall, they have received 600 load of timber of Dandy . . .[162]

The man who ordered all this activity and paid the wages of workmen as well as the staff of the properties he owned was inordinately wealthy. His building works in and around London, the centre of his power, were only the more obvious signs of his increasing splendour. Throughout the length and breadth of the land he carved new estates out of the lands which had belonged to the monasteries of Lewes, Colchester, St Osith, Launde and other houses. Thomas Cromwell was *the* man of the 1530s. That meant that money poured into his coffers from literally hundreds of sources. Threatened monasteries were a major source of income. After the dissolution of smaller houses in 1536 the writing was on the wall for the rest and their superiors bombarded the Vicegerent with appeals for him to be 'good lord' to them – either to stay his hand or to provide generously for them and their dispossessed brethren. Such requests never failed to be accompanied by douceurs. But Cromwell did not need this extra income source. Men and women of all degrees were eager to buy his friendship and harness his influence with the King. He received hundreds of retainers: £40 per annum from Cranmer, £10 from the Duke of Norfolk, £2 from George Rolle, a clerk in the court of Common Pleas, £5 from the Abbot of Glastonbury (previously paid to Thomas More), £20 from Queen Jane Seymour, etc. etc. etc.

Wriothesley early began to share in this largesse and he was not slow to set about some very clear-sighted empire-building. The rapidity of his rise was astounding. He made his first acquisitions in Hampshire in 1534 and by the end of the decade he was the biggest landowner in the county and also its member of parliament. The process began when he received a 'consideration' from John Capon, Abbot of Hyde, near Winchester. Capon, brother of the master of Jesus, Cambridge, and erstwhile chaplain to Wolsey, was one of the clerics who had harnessed his wagon firmly to Cromwell's star and as a reward he was appointed to the bishopric of Bangor in 1533. When the Pope refused the necessary bull, Wriothesley, whom Capon referred to as his 'friend', was despatched to Rome to obtain the necessary sanction. He failed in this but, the following year, Capon was instituted on royal authority. In gratitude for Wriothesley's assistance, the new Bishop granted him a sixty-one-year lease on the parsonage at Micheldever, just north of Winchester. Wriothesley built himself a house there and was soon negotiating to buy other lands in the area. The attack on the monasteries put him in a prime position to build on this modest foundation. In 1537 he acquired Quarr Abbey on the Solent coast of the Isle of Wight. His sights were already set on two more splendid quarries. The Cistercian abbey at Beaulieu was surrendered in April 1538 and there were several would-be purchasers who coveted it. Arthur Plantagenet was one of them but the redoubtable John Hussee warned his master that it was 'out of his star'. So, indeed, it proved. In July Thomas Wriothesley paid £1,350.6s.8d. for the site.

The story of how the Premonstratensian abbey of Titchfield came into his hands provides an excellent example of how he and Cromwell managed the undermining of the monastic system. John Salisbury was a Benedictine monk in his mid-thirties who had become embroiled in heresy during his time at Oxford and spent a year in prison on Wolsey's personal instructions. With the change of regime he was appointed prior of the small house of St Faith's, Horsham, presumably on the understanding that he would surrender it to the King. This he did in August 1534, long before the passing of the first dissolution act. Salisbury was well rewarded. Now that Henry was Head of the English Church he had many cheap ways of recognising faithful service. The ex-prior became suffragen Bishop of Thetford, Archdeacon of Anglesea and received several profitable benefices. He was also made commendatory abbot of Titchfield. This impressive house on the Hampshire coast was one Wriothesley knew well because his sister's home was at nearby Hook. Negotiations for the abbey's dissolution must have begun straight away and, at an early stage, Wriothesley put in his bid for the site. Titchfield was duly surrendered in November 1537 and, within days, Wriothesley had an army of masons, carpenters and labourers transforming the ecclesiastical buildings into an impressive mansion. Down came the church to make way for a great gatehouse. The cloister garth became the courtyard and the conventual buildings were converted into Wriothesley's dwelling. In his haste to make Titchfield a suitably magnificent residence the new owner spared no expense. Within nine months the work was done and Wriothesley could boast 'a right stately house, embattled and having a goodly gate and an enclosed conduit in the middle of the court of it'.[163] In 1539 the Benedictine abbey of Hyde, near Winchester, came Wriothesley's way. This is hardly surprising since his old friend, John Capon, was still abbot (he held the bishopric of Bangor in commendam). Contemporaries noted with amazement the rapidity with which the new owner tore down the buildings and sold off stone, lead, glass, furniture, hangings and everything else that had market value.

Wriothesley demonstrated the same industry and determination in whatever he undertook. He greatly impressed the King with his calm attention to detail during the troubled autumn of 1536. For a few weeks his relationship with Cromwell underwent a subtle change. He was now at the King's beck and call and this not infrequently entailed relaying orders to his superior:

> ... you shall go to the jewel house in the Tower, and there take as much plate as you shall think his grace shall not necessarily occupy and put it straight to coining. His majesty appeareth to fear much this matter, specially if he should want money ... And his grace would have this matter for money well followed, for there resteth with you all our hope ...[164]

One activity for which Wriothesley early demonstrated a penchant was interrogation. This was an essential function of all sixteenth-century government but was especially so for a regime pressing ahead with policies which were unpopular with large sections of the nation and seeking to avoid the kind of tumult which broke out in October 1536. Senior members of the establishment needed to display their ability and willingness to investigate dissidents, to extort confessions and to extract information. Thus, for example, we find Thomas Howard, in August 1538, writing one of his long, self-justificatory letters to Cromwell about the examination of one Anthony Browne, former friar Observant at Greenwich. Browne had been condemned under the Supremacy Act by the assize judges at Bury St Edmunds but Norfolk realised that he might go to his death without having been 'thoroughly examined with whom he hath had communication, aid or comfort in his opinions'. The Duke makes it clear in his letter that he discussed the situation with other local notables before deciding to summon Browne to Kenninghall. Howard and his assistants spent several hours badgering their prisoner but were quite unable to 'get out of him any detection of any person to be of counsel with him or of like opinion as he is of' and so, delivered him to the sheriff for execution. Still Norfolk, knowing the virulence of Henry's feelings about the Greenwich friars, was worried that he might not be perceived to have done enough, thus his letter to Cromwell: 'My Lord, the cause of the sending of this man in so great haste unto you is because . . . the king's majesty and you [may] think it convenient to have [Browne] to be brought to the Tower, there to be more straightly examined and to be put to torture.'[165]

Wriothesley had no hesitation whatsoever about this aspect of his apprenticeship and, as early as August 1536, he was being employed in the interrogation of an important political prisoner. John, Lord Hussey of Seaford, Lincolnshire, was, to all appearances, a loyal servant of the Crown, a member of the Council who had proved himself in war and who held several important offices. However, he was among those whose sympathies lay with Catherine of Aragon and her daughter and who was regarded by Chapuys as one who, given the opportunity, might demonstrate hostility towards the prevailing royal policy. In 1533 Hussey was appointed as Mary's chamberlain and he and his wife, Anne, became very popular with Henry's bastardised daughter. The Husseys were among the many who rejoiced at Anne Boleyn's fall but something about their demeanour, or their associates, or their unwise words aroused suspicion and they were watched. It was reported back to Cromwell that, during a visit to her former mistress, Anne Hussey had referred to her not as the 'Lady Mary' but as 'Princess'. So angry was Henry about any resistance to his will that this was sufficient to get her hauled off to the Tower of London. The men appointed to examine the prisoner were William Petre, Cromwell's deputy as Vicegerent, and Thomas Wriothesley, with the Lieutenant of the Tower, Edmund Walsingham, in attendance. (Edmund's nephew, Sir Francis Walsingham, would be the century's most celebrated interrogator and spymaster.)

Incarceration in the Tower was a terrifying experience and the government deliberately used it to 'soften up' Lady Hussey. She was left to languish there throughout the steaming weeks of high summer, her physical and mental well-being both deteriorating. Her treatment was just part of an attack on Mary and her supporters which was being launched in these weeks. What Henry required of his daughter was that she would accept the Act of Succession and all that it implied about her recently deceased mother and herself. The way that she was handled bears considerable resemblance to the 'Mr Nice and Mr Nasty' tactics of modern interrogation methods, although it is unlikely that they were so skilfully co-ordinated. Cromwell presented himself to Mary as her friend, advising her, showing concern for her comfort and offering to mediate between her and her father. When Norfolk was sent to her it was as a bully, shouting, threatening and demanding total submission. Cromwell drew up for Mary a letter overflowing with self-abasement and protestations of filial devotion and obedience; just the kind of approach which he knew Henry enjoyed. The King's twenty-one-year-old daughter was to represent herself as 'most humbly prostrate before your noble feet' and 'your most obedient subject and humble child'.[166] She was to present herself as content to be guided in all things by her father's wisdom. Mary copied the epistle in her own hand and hoped that her general submission would be sufficient. It was not. Days later Henry sent Norfolk and other councillors with uncompromising instructions to obtain Mary's specific consent to those laws against which her conscience rebelled. They were also to discover who was stiffening her resistance. For resistance she most assuredly displayed, even when Howard screamed violent imprecations at her, assuring her that if she was his daughter he would smash her head against the wall until it was as soft as a boiled apple.

This was the background to the interrogation of Anne Hussey. When Wriothesley and Petre were sent to the Tower on 3 August, they were under orders to discover evidence of a conspiracy against Henry centred on his daughter. It should have been easy to browbeat the weakened prisoner who was anxious on her husband's account as well as her own. As the French ambassador observed about those conveyed to the royal fortress, 'there is no one living that dare intermeddle in his affairs, nor dare ope his mouth save to speak ill of him, for dread that he himself may come under suspicion'.[167] In fact, the King's agents failed in their mission because Lady Hussey was resolute and because there was no plot she could reveal as, perhaps rather abjectly, they were obliged to report:

Item, examined what mo[ved her at divers] times to call her by the [name of princess], she taketh God to rec[ord, and will go to] her death upon the same that . . she named her, so only . . . by the custom of [the time] . . . when she was servant . . .

Item, interrogated whether she at any [other time] before or after the said feast of Whit[suntide], heard any other person call the sai[d lady] Mary princess, since that time she w[as by the] laws deprived that title, answere[th that] she never to her remembrance heard [any person] so name her.

Item, further demanded what she hath heard anybody say of the King's ma[jesty], she sai[th that] she never heard any man say th[at the ma]rriage betwixt the King's highn[ess and the Dowager] was good and lawful, since [the time that the] same was otherwise declar[ed by the laws o]f this realm.

[Item], examined whether she . . . heard th[em speak of bona f]ides parentum, or that the [Lady Mary] was the King's lawful [daughter, she] answereth and saith th[at she never] heard any person so say [or use any] such term . . .

Item, examined whether she thinketh [the marriage] betwixt the King's highness and the [princess Dowager] good and lawful or unjust, unlawfu[l, and] against the laws of God, she an[swereth th]at before the contrary was by [the laws declar]ed she thought the said m[arriage lawful]; but since that time she . . . assure]dly thought and so doth now [think the same] to have been unlawful an[d contrary to the la]ws of God.[168]

Henry was furious that his servants could not discover or invent a conspiracy. There is no doubt that Mary's obduracy threw him into such a rage that he would not have hesitated to send her to the block. Norfolk's tirade about dashing the woman's brains out faithfully replicated the sentiments expressed by his master. The man who took the full force of the royal wrath was Cromwell, so much so that Chapuys insisted that the minister went in fear of his life for several days. The King doubtless reasoned that he who had encompassed the death of a queen should have no difficulty in destroying a queen's daughter. Yet, so far from proceeding with vigour against Mary, as eager tongues would have been quick to relate, Cromwell had actually tried to reconcile her to her father by a clever lawyer's manipulation of words.

Why did Cromwell take the immense risk of declining to give the King what, in his high passion, he wanted? We can best answer the question by envisaging the state of affairs which would have arisen had Henry had his way. All Christendom would have been presented with the spectacle of a tyrant who, in the space of a few months, had exulted in the painful death of his first wife, murdered his second and then gone on to murder his daughter. Henry's reputation at home and abroad already combined elements of the vicious and the absurd. A princess to whom he paid court through diplomatic channels in 1538 observed that if she had two heads she would be delighted to put one of them at the King of England's disposal. At home Mary Tudor was even more popular than her mother had been. Even Jane Seymour pleaded with Henry to welcome her back to court. To loyal advisers with any political acumen it was obvious that Mary's execution would be a death too far. If it did not goad the Emperor into action, it would so far destabilise an already unquiet situation within the realm as to occasion considerable concern among political leaders. Could any hard evidence have been found linking Mary with men of treasonable intent that would have been a different matter but Wriothesley and other agents had discovered little that Cromwell could use. If Mary had been unpopular or had powerful enemies, as Anne had had, that, again, would have changed the situation but Catherine's daughter was the object of near-universal pity and affection. Thus, by stalling, Cromwell probably believed, with justification, that he was saving Henry from himself.

Within weeks Mary's fate was of merely academic interest. Whatever fears and suspicions Henry and his councillors may have entertained gave way to very real concern when the northern rebellions broke out and these, as we have seen, did nothing to improve Cromwell's standing at court. As for Wriothesley, he witnessed his most dramatic example to date of the insecurity of high office under the Crown. However, he also saw how rapidly and completely situations could change in the service of the quicksilver King. His mentor had been appointed Lord Privy Seal in June, created Baron Cromwell of Oakham in July, was under a heavy cloud in August, was at risk of being thrown to his enemies in October and had been fully restored to favour by the early weeks of 1537. The collapse of the insurrection did not vindicate Cromwell but it made it psychologically impossible for Henry to discard him. The fact that the rebels had demanded the minister's dismissal meant that, in victory, the King could not dismiss him. To have done so would have been seen as a weak act of appeasement. If at any time during the momentous year which began with Anne Boleyn's arrest it had occurred to Wriothesley that he might one day replace Cromwell at the King's right hand, just as Cromwell had replaced Wolsey, such thoughts will have been swiftly dispelled as his master, firmly back in the saddle once more, took advantage of the rout of conservatism to accelerate the pace of change.

Government propaganda had once sought to assuage widespread anxiety by insisting that the complete abolition of monasticism was not intended. Now there was no need to keep up the pretence. Several heads of houses were indicted for treason in connection with the events of 1536–7 and still more had been induced to surrender their responsibilities voluntarily. In April 1539 a new parliament assembled and one of its main tasks was to pass the second Dissolution Act which not only ratified the confiscation of all property not covered by the 1536 statute but permitted the Crown to acquire the lands, buildings and contents of all such religious establishments 'which hereafter shall happen to be dissolved, suppressed [etc.]'. A year later the doors closed behind the residents of the last of England's 800 monastic institutions and Henry VIII was richer by some £100,000 a year. Whether or not Cromwell had originally vowed to make Henry 'the richest prince in Christendom', he certainly achieved that and his position was secure while he was in the process of achieving it.

Wriothesley remained Cromwell's man. He entered with a will into the iconoclastic campaign which resulted from his master's proclamation against objects of superstition. He led commissions throughout Hampshire and the Isle of Wight, pulling down statues, dismantling shrines and stripping altars of any valuable adornments that might be sent to swell the royal coffers. He could not avoid being aware of the criticisms such activities provoked and it is significant that when he and his colleagues came to tackle the impressive shrine of St Swithun at Winchester Cathedral they began their task at three o'clock in the morning to avoid attracting a surly audience. Having finished their work there, the commissioners moved on to the nearby abbeys of Hyde and St Mary's, resolved to disarm unfavourable comment by sweeping away 'all the rotten bones that be called relics, which we may not omit lest it should be thought that we came more for the treasure than for the avoiding of the abomination of idolatry'. This indifference to booty hardly squares with the commissioners' precise stocktaking at the cathedral where they valued the plate at £1,500, itemised such specific items as an emerald cross, recommended the dismantling and shipping of the high altar and grumbled that the adornments of the saint's shrine were of poor quality – 'no gold, nor ring, nor true stone in it but all great counterfeits'.[169]

This activity should have brought Wriothesley into conflict with his relative and former boss, Stephen Gardiner, but 'Wily Winchester', as his enemies called him, was careful not to be wrong-footed. After many requests for a recall the Bishop was at last allowed home in July 1538. He came cautiously, fearfully, to a land that had changed much during his absence and which was now being driven headlong along the road to evangelical reform by his arch-foe. In his absence he had been spied on (and Wriothesley had been among the principal information-gatherers) and his credibility had been undermined at court. Well might he be anxious of his reception. Thus, when Wriothesley met him 'by chance' at Dover Gardiner was careful to show him every courtesy. The younger man reported back the encounter with some amusement to Cromwell. It was, he wrote, 'strange' to see the Bishop removing his hat 'as soon as mine or before'. Gardiner's entourage made a brave show with five mules and two carts, all especially tricked out for the occasion with covering cloths emblazoned with Gardiner's arms, and gentlemen attendants 'in gay apparel of velvet chains, capes turned down with capes of velvet very large', as well as yeomen, servants and other officers. Cromwell must have smiled to read this description, knowing the anxious calculation that must have gone into the planning of Gardiner's little cavalcade – splendid enough to honour the King whose representative Gardiner was but not so ostentatious as to suggest undue personal display. When the Bishop fell to discussing politics with Wriothesley he swallowed his pride even more emphatically. The ardent defender of traditional beliefs and practices solemnly announced himself in favour of the removal of objects of superstition. What a good idea it would be, he opined, to make a thorough purge of his own cathedral! He must have known that the man he was talking to had already accomplished this ecclesiological spring clean.[170]

Gardiner was not summoned to court and was obliged for several months to confine his activities to his diocese. He could do nothing to prevent the execution of Cromwellian injunctions but he did exercise his episcopal authority in inhibiting the activities of preachers licensed by Cranmer and supporting those more in keeping with his own theological positions. However, the return of England's most truculent scholar-bishop did put some heart into dispirited traditionalists and the summoning of a parliament in spring 1539 brought him once more to the centre of national affairs. His first clashes with Cromwell were over the election of members to the lower house. The minister promised Henry that he would ensure a 'tractable' assembly and he made concerted efforts to ensure that his nominees would be successful. Gardiner was equally active throughout his diocese and in other places where the Bishop of Winchester traditionally had influence. Both contestants notched up gains and losses in the ensuing contest but the most significant victory was Wriothesley's election by the county constituents of Hampshire. The new MP was not slow to point out that his success was a triumph for the Gospel and a challenge to the Bishop's agents who were guilty of 'dark setting forth of God's word and giving slanders to them that plainly and truly did set it forth'.[171]

Now there came one of those apparently sudden political events that punctuated the reign of Henry VIII and which have led analytical historians to produce explanations based on the covert activities of factions or the enigmatic whims of the King. The Act of Six Articles rocked Cromwell, Cranmer and their colleagues badly but it did not result from the alarm of a King who had decided to stop the Reformation dead nor from the machinations of a 'conservative party' which had achieved sudden coherence. The dramatic events of May 1539 were energised by the current flowing along religious cables already laid and the power surges provided by often unpredictable, day-to-day events.

The Act, which identified six key doctrines to be believed by English Christians on pain of dire penalties, was passed by parliament at a particular time and in response to a particular set of circumstances. If an underlying cause must be identified, it is not the weakness of the reform movement, but its success. The power to deal summarily with suspected heretics had been taken away from bishops and ecclesiastical courts and vested in the Vicegerent and his agents. Cromwell had reasons both political and religious for allowing maximum freedom to radical preachers and writers who would maintain the momentum of change. The impact was exciting and galvanic, transforming lives and relationships for good or ill and provoking thousands of arguments and local riots. When to this was added official vandalism in the form of the purification of churches and cathedrals and the tearing down of abbeys, national adrenalin began pumping at a hectic rate and Cromwell could not control the results. Clergy were attacked, unauthorised iconoclasm was unleashed, rabble-rousers, cranks and extremists whom any educated reformer would have dubbed heretics, loosed their bizarre notions on unsuspecting congregations.

In his record of these years Charles Wriothesley highlighted the 'headline' events which most captured public attention. They included the well-advertised burning of objects of superstition, execution of 'papists' and 'heretics', priests resigning their livings to get married, clergy beginning to celebrate mass in English, the banishment of Anabaptists from the realm and a spate of unauthorised preaching:

This year [1538], in June and July, a bricklayer, called Henry Daunce (in Whitechapel parish without Aldgate in London), used to preach the word of God in his own house in his garden, where he set a tub to a tree, and therein he preached divers Sundays, and other days early in the morning, and at 6 of the clock at night, and had great audience of people both spiritual and temporal, which said person had no learning of his book, neither in English nor other tongue, and yet he declared Scripture as well as he had studied at the universities; but at the last the bishops had such indignation at him, by reason the people followed him, that they sent for him to my Lord of Canterbury, where he was demanded many questions, but they could lay nothing to his charge, but did inhibit him [from] preaching, because of the great resort of people that drew to his sermons.*[172]

The situation was disturbing for everyone concerned with the governance of the realm and it was embarrassing for the evangelical leaders. Their adversaries could, and increasingly did, insist that Cromwell and his 'cronies' were aiding and abetting heretics and creating the circumstances favouring civil unrest.

The King was genuinely agitated by the results of religious discord, and the preamble to the Six Article Act accurately represented this when it described him as calling to mind the blessings of harmony and also 'the manifold, perils, dangers and inconveniences which have heretofore in many places and regions grown, sprung and arisen of the diversities of minds and opinions, especially of matters of Christian religion'.[173] To Henry, in all his monolithic, megalomaniac naïvety the solution was simple: he would consult with his experts, decree what his subjects should believe and they would believe it. Kings were entitled to defy public opinion in obedience to conscience. Subjects did not enjoy a similar liberty if it entailed disobeying royal decrees. Henry was determined to demonstrate that he was still an orthodox believer. In November 1538 he presided in person over the show trial of the sacramentary John Lambert, who was burned for denying the real presence of Christ in the consecrated elements at Communion and, probably, for espousing a ragbag of other unconventional doctrines. As the time for the 1539 parliament approached the King instructed Cromwell to prepare legislation for the unifying of religion. As for the Vicegerent, he had in the forefront of his mind the need to ensure maximum support for his policies by manipulating elections to the lower house.

Yet, it all went wrong. The Act 'abolishing diversity of opinions', to give it its correct title, was a statement of traditionalist beliefs on transubstantiation, Communion in one kind, clerical celibacy, vows of chastity,

*Later in the year Henry Daunce did public penance for heresy at St Paul's Cross.

private masses and auricular confession. Cromwell's adversaries, until recently in such disarray, were able to turn the tables on him. This was the first major public rift between King and minister and it permitted some people to hope that the new decade might witness a return to old and trusted policies.

PART SIX:

1549

. . . I saw a royal throne
Where justice should have sit,
But in her stead was one
Of moody, cruel wit.

Absorbed was righteousness
As of the raging flood;
Satan in his excess
Sucked up the guiltless blood.

Then thought I, Jesus Lord,
When thou shalt judge us all,
Hard is it to record
On these men what will fall . . .

A ballad which Anne Askew Made and
Sang when She was in Newgate, 1546

CHAPTER 30

The Scaffold at the Centre of the Labyrinth

From the point of view of personality politics there was nothing new about the reversal of 1539 and its aftermath. In many ways what happened was a rerun of the events that had ensnared Wolsey exactly a decade earlier. Basically Cromwell was not as secure as his successful run of policies might suggest. Not since the high days of the great Cardinal had any minister been able to be confident of Henry's support. Now that the King was entering his pain-haunted latter years he could certainly not be taken for granted. The French ambassador, listing Henry's vices, described him as one who would 'fain keep in favour with everybody but does not trust a single man'.[1] Ever since the arrest of Empson and Dudley in the very first hours of the reign it had been potentially fatal for a minister to be widely unpopular and Cromwell had now replaced his old patron as the most hated man in England. His downfall would be very well received – as Henry knew. There was, of course, an important contrast between the two great ministers: Cromwell was never admitted to that level of intimacy with the King that Wolsey had enjoyed. The different relationship was entirely a matter of personalities. It had virtually nothing to do with policy. If it had, Cromwell would have deserved the King's unalloyed loyalty. He had untangled his master from two unwanted marriages, preserved peace, broken the power of the Pope and his minions, made the Crown absolute and enriched it beyond anything anyone could have conceived possible a few years before. It all counted for nothing in the lion's court. This was obvious to Cromwell's adversaries. Even when Norfolk and Gardiner were kept well away from the royal presence and the 'upstart' stood high on his pedestal they could console themselves with the knowledge that that pedestal could be shaken and that dizzy heights were dangerous places to fall from. They had witnessed Cromwell's vulnerability in 1536–7 and the lesson had not been lost on them.

However, there were differences between the situations of 1529–30 and 1539–40. The northern revolt had brought about a permanent change in the executive structure of government. Henry had emerged with what he had always wanted, a council attendant or privy council. During the crisis the King was accompanied at Windsor by a group of advisers who made corporate decisions and issued instructions over their joint signatures, since Henry was determined to demonstrate to the rebels that government decisions proceeded from a properly constituted body of nobles and gentlemen. This council operated independently of Cromwell who, as we have seen, was largely absent from court. Its membership was fixed, although it was still subject to fluctuation at Henry's whim. Norfolk, for example, was named as privy councillor but, as we have seen, was either away on campaign or detained in the North. After the suppression of the revolt Cromwell returned to court and to all appearances took up again the role of sole executive but the inner core of advisers continued to meet, sometimes with the King in attendance. Several of its members were opposed to the Vicegerent's policies so that, as well as pushing ahead with a prodigious reform programme, Cromwell also had to manage this body which had now had a taste of power.

He was under enormous pressure and the strain was beginning to tell. As well as the religious revolution he was sponsoring, the Vicegerent was reorganising the Church and setting up agencies to deal with the confiscated monastic lands. At the same time he was putting the royal household on a new bureaucratic footing and making the financial administration more efficient. As if all that were not enough, his 'commonwealth' vision was expressed in plans (not destined to be implemented) for reform of the legal system, education, agriculture and industry. To take just one example, Cromwell used his executive power to carry into effect some of those reforms in university life for which humanists had long called. New professorships were established in Greek, Hebrew, Medicine, Law and Theology. He ordained that every Oxford and Cambridge college should maintain two daily public lectures in Latin and Greek, that scholastic exegesis should be banished in favour of teaching the Scriptures 'according to the true sense thereof' and that all students should be encouraged to read the Bible in their own private studies and devotions. One set of instructions issued in 1536 must have disturbed the well-heeled comfort of many an older academic: all beneficed residents over forty were to remove to their parishes and begin earning their stipends. All this creative activity took its toll and one gets the impression that, towards the end of this extraordinary decade, Cromwell was becoming weary. It seems to be the case that illness kept him away from part of the parliament of 1539.

The next ingredient to consider is the Gardiner factor. If there was to be a concerted attack on the Vicegerent and his policies it had to have brains and vindictiveness behind it. Norfolk possessed only one of these qualifications. Gardiner, on the other hand, was highly educated, very shrewd and possessed that brand of hubris which is unique to ecclesiastical politicians. He believed that any action which preserved the religious establishment and its personnel was not only justified but sanctified. As a politician his major defect was that lack of intelligence which sometimes besets academics and reveals itself in the conviction that whatever can be logically demonstrated to be right must be rigorously pursued. His humourless tenacity won him many enemies and on several occasions infuriated the King. His hatred for Cromwell was total. He believed, probably with justification, that the minister had plotted his disgrace and even his death. He resented having to take orders in ecclesiastical matters from a mere layman. Old grievances continued to rankle and new ones manifested themselves as Cromwell kept him away from the King and 'interfered' with his episcopal parliamentary patronage. By spring 1539 the two men were not on speaking terms. The Bishop's most recent biographer dismisses the notion that Gardiner was behind the Six Articles campaign and the subsequent attack on Cromwell which followed, preferring to regard Henry as the sole villain of the piece,[2] but contemporaries, at home and abroad – and especially in France where the Bishop had been poisoning minds against Cromwell during his years as ambassador – were less inclined to exonerate Winchester. Commentators considered it worthy of note that the Bishop was excluded from the Council but this was precisely because they understood well his hostility to Cromwell and the influence he wielded behind the scenes.

The man who held the key to Cromwell's fate was Thomas Wriothesley. The Lord Privy Seal had taught his protégé all he knew and made him privy to most of his secrets and, in so doing, he had unwittingly placed himself in the younger man's power. Wriothesley's ambition was open-ended. He had ingratiated himself with the King and one reason for the hastily completed splendours of Titchfield was his hope to receive the royal court there when Henry visited Southampton to view his fleet and inspect coastal defences. The agent who oversaw the building works assured his employer, 'you may have with reasonable charge an house for the King's grace to bate [i.e. take up residence] and for any baron to keep his hospitality in'.[3] Increasing royal favour, a peerage – if Wriothesley's servants understood these objectives there was evidently nothing secret about them. His acquisitions in Hampshire had made him the greatest man in the county, a position previously occupied by Lord Lisle and the transfer of power was poignantly underscored when the Deputy of Calais was obliged to remove the remains of his first wife from her tomb in Titchfield Abbey to make way for Wriothesley's new residence. But the rising star of court and county was not content to become *a* great man. He aspired to the place occupied by Wolsey and Cromwell. It was clear from the King's personality and from the various constitutional experiments that had been tried that Henry needed a right-hand man. Wriothesley intended to be that man. In 1540 he was crucially placed. He was Cromwell's man and well known to be so but should the pendulum swing towards his master's enemies he had contacts with Gardiner which could be reactivated and there could be no doubt that the Bishop would welcome his defection.

As ever, foreign affairs provided the ground-bass on which the melodies of day-to-day policy were superimposed. The fundamental issue for Tudor European diplomacy was whether to continue the traditional strategy of being a third, destabilising, force in Habsburg–Valois territorial competitiveness or to bring into being a new political, military and economic force by uniting England with the Protestant states of Germany and the Baltic and, in fullness of time, the prosperous Netherlands, squirming under the yoke of Habsburg domination. The Protestant alliance, like most of Cromwell's proposals, glowed in his mind with an effulgent logic but others could only see it as a puzzling and risky innovation. The King refused to be dazzled by it, and his conservative councillors were appalled at the prospect of England taking sides with the heretics of the Schmalkaldic League.

As long as Francis and Charles were at each other's throats the choice between old-style and new-style diplomacy was less than urgent. Henry continued to hope that the death of Catherine of Aragon would remove the Emperor's excuse for hostility and restore to him real neutrality and freedom of action. But, in June 1538, Pope Paul III brokered a truce between the two great continental rivals and tried to point their swords in the direction of heretical England. At the same time James V of Scotland married a daughter of the Duc de Guise, one of Francis's close companions, thus strengthening the 'auld alliance' and the threat against England's northern regions, so recently in tumult. Over the following months Pope Paul employed Reginald Pole, for whom Henry now entertained a passionate hatred, as the co-ordinator of the English crusade. Cromwell's response was the simple one of despatching an assassin to seek out and strike down the Cardinal. Meanwhile, at home, rumour spread that Pole's relatives and friends were preparing a West Country rising to coincide with the feared invasion.

However, the hand Fate had dealt Henry did contain one ace. The death of his third wife had freed him to rejoin the marriage market.

The Duchess of Milan . . . is of the age of 16 years, very high of stature for that age . . . a goodly personage of body, and competent of beauty, of favour excellent, soft of speech, and very gentle in countenance . . . She resembleth much one Mistress Shelton, that sometime waited in the court upon Queen Anne.
                                    John Hutton to Lord Cromwell, December 1537

The election lieth betwixt Mrs Mary Shelton and Mrs Mary Skipwith. I pray Jesu send such one as may be for his Highness' comfort and the wealth of the realm. Herein I doubt not but your lordship will keep silence till the matter be surely known.

John Hussee to Lord Lisle, 3 January 1538

if I can hear anything of the lady your lordship doth write of, you shall have knowledge. Some thinketh she shall come out of Flanders, the Dowager of Milan, and some say both heirs of Denmark and Milan.

John Hussee to Lord Lisle, 23 February 1538

to write of any queen, there is small speaking of any, but that there is a voice that it should be the Duchess of Milan. But ye shall take it as a wind. But yet I think it shall be an outlandish [i.e. foreign] woman, whensoever it shall happen, which I think shall be about the spring of the leaf.

Robert Warner to Lord Fitzwalter, 21 November 1538[4]

Almost from the moment of Jane Seymour's death the main subject of court gossip and speculation was the identity of the King's next bride. Henry, who now had the son he had wanted for almost thirty years, was in no hurry to marry again but the vacancy for the post of queen was of immense and urgent concern to those about him who had personal, dynastic and political interests at stake. Those who hoped to lock the King into an alliance, which all must have hoped and assumed would be permanent, had to balance two factors; the diplomatic opportunities presented by a royal match and Henry's preference for vivacious, nubile young bedfellows. Mary ('Madge') Shelton, whom Hussee referred to in January 1538, had been Henry's favourite mistress during the last months of Anne's reign and it is very likely that Mary (actually Margaret) Skipwith had also enjoyed the King's nocturnal favour. Madge was a niece of Thomas Boleyn who doubtless hoped to use her to regain something of his former position.

However, Cromwell and Howard were more concerned about the wider implications of the bride quest. The opportunity existed to further their own versions of foreign policy by tying the house of Tudor to one of the continental dynasties. Cromwell hoped to sponsor a marriage with some Protestant princess and John Hutton, his Brussels agent, who, towards the end of 1537, canvassed the charms of the Duchess of Milan, also made tentative mention of a daughter of the Duke of Cleves, cautiously adding, 'I hear no great praise either of her personage or beauty.' The Duke of Norfolk, though seldom at court and not able to press his views vigorously in person, favoured a French alliance, which would have the double advantage of driving a wedge between Francis and Charles and providing Henry with a Catholic consort. The dominant preference among councillors, however, was for an Imperial alliance. Henry went along with this – particularly after he saw a portrait of the Duchess of Milan, Charles V's niece.

Everything that could be learned about her marked her out as favourite in the royal marriage stakes and Cromwell backed her heavily. She was an almost perfect choice from a diplomatic point of view and it seemed that she would also appeal to Henry's libido. His agents wrote in glowing terms of the Duchess and answered his queries with unstinted enthusiasm. In a reply addressed to Wriothesley, Hutton raved:

> There is no one in these parts of personage, beauty and birth like unto the Duchess of Milan. She is not so pure white as was the late queen ... but she hath a singular good acquaintance and when she chanceth to smile there appeareth two pits in her cheeks and one in her chin, the which becometh her right exceeding well.[5]

Young Christina had recently arrived at the court of her aunt, Mary of Hungary, Regent of the Netherlands, and had turned all heads. She was the daughter of Christian II of Denmark, Norway and Sweden, currently a prisoner in his own country after emerging on the wrong side in a civil war. That war had placed a rival, Lutheran, branch of the dynasty on the throne which was now firmly allied with the Protestant German princes and the towns of the Hanseatic League. In the midst of all the troubles Christina and her sister had been taken under the wing of their mother's family and, at the age of twelve, Christina had been married to Francesco, the last Sforza Duke of Milan. After a year her husband died and Christina once more came back on to the marriage market. It was well known that Charles V wanted to restore Christian II's daughter to their father's Scandinavian thrones. Marriage between Henry and Christina would, thus, cement friendship with the Empire while also holding out the hope of England's eventual integration with the states of the Lutheran North.

Henry would never marry a woman completely sight unseen so, at the beginning of March 1538, Cromwell despatched across the Narrow Seas two of his most trusted agents on an urgent and sensitive mission. One was Sir Philip Hoby, an ardent evangelical, advanced by Mr Secretary to the Privy Chamber and groomed by him for a diplomatic career. The other was the artist who had risen under Cromwell's patronage to be royal painter – Hans Holbein. Their task was to bring back both visual and verbal portraits of the Princess. Holbein was granted a three-hour sitting with Christina on 12 March and such was the impatience of Henry and Cromwell that the two envoys were on the way home that very same evening. On the 18th they were back at Greenwich and the King was gazing on one of Holbein's most masterly portraits. It can only have been a worked-up drawing, for Holbein would not have been able to complete an oil painting during the hectic rush back to court. We are fortunate in being able to see the finished work and can easily appreciate why the prospect of marriage to the young Duchess should have set Henry's middle-aged pulse racing. With deceptive simplicity Holbein captured the charm of a pretty, intelligent girl blossoming into womanhood. The visual image was augmented by Hoby's report of a lively princess, well versed in French, Italian and High German and trained in all the courtly arts.

Chapuys reported to Mary of Hungary the King's excitement at the prospect of being coupled with this highly desirable girl: 'Since he saw [the portrait] he has been in much better mood than ever he was, making musicians play on their instruments all day long.' Within days Henry set off on progress, visiting first the site of Nonsuch Palace, a phantasmagorical self-indulgence upon which he had just begun to lavish his new-found wealth and which was designed to outshine all the royal residences of Europe. At every stage of the royal peregrination, the ambassador exclaimed, the King 'cannot be one single moment without masques, which is a sign he purposes to marry again'.[6] Henry was rejuvenated and looking forward with optimistic euphoria to golden years ahead with a full treasury, a settled foreign policy, a healthy son to succeed him, a beautiful young wife and the prospect of yet more Tudor princes to come.

But whatever enthusiasm might be shown for the match by the English King and his minister there was a deal of hard bargaining to be done and this involved months of diplomatic toing and froing. This provided the opportunity for other alliances to be canvassed. In June Thomas Howard returned to court and added his weight to those pressing for a French marriage. He met frequently with Francis I's ambassador, Gaspard de Coligny, Sieur de Castillon, to discuss the merits of French royal ladies likely to attract Henry's fancy and the ambassador was soon able to report policy successes: the King had publicly rebuked Cromwell for being more concerned to please the Emperor than achieve the happiness of his own master. Duly chastened, Cromwell had been manoeuvred into obtaining intimate information about Louise of Guise. In June Hoby and Holbein were back on the bridal trail, this time to Le Havre. Two months later the diplomatic duo were despatched again, this time to Nancy to bring back verbal and pictorial depictions of Anne of Lorraine.

These were only some of the potential wives being examined on Henry's behalf in 1538. The English King enjoyed the situation, as he chose to interpret it, of having brother monarchs competing to throw their female relatives in his path. This was not how Francis and Charles viewed events. The French King was scandalised by Henry's calm suggestion that the candidates should be brought to Calais for his selection, like so many fillies at a horse fair. The territorial, financial and political aspects of the negotiations similarly dragged on with little goodwill on either side.

The failure to advance his Francophile cause was not Norfolk's only problem. Members of his own family were, once again, making life difficult for him. The sixty-five-year-old Duke was, at last, beginning to mellow. Pragmatism was prevailing over family pride and he decided to take a leaf from Cromwell's book and forge an alliance with the powerful Seymour clan. He proposed to offer his daughter Mary, Henry Fitzroy's widow, to Thomas Seymour, the Earl of Hertford's younger brother. All seemed set fair for the wedding and the King's blessing was obtained. But if Norfolk's jack-in-the-box hubris was securely latched down, the same could not be said for his children. His heir, Henry, Earl of Surrey, was as hot-headed as his father had been in earlier years. He loathed the upstart Seymours and, the previous year, had come to blows with Hertford when the latter had accused the Howards of being in sympathy with the northern rebels. That earned him several months' banishment from court. Now he stiffened his sister's resolve to resist the proposed match. Plagued by his dysfunctional family and his inability to influence policy, Norfolk headed off once more to Kenninghall in August.

Now Cromwell decided that the timing was auspicious to take up the Imperial match with renewed vigour and he sent his most trusted aide, Thomas Wriothesley, to Brussels to bring matters to a successful conclusion. But this was only part of the envoy's task. The politico-religious situation was becoming so tense, and confusing information and wild rumours were pouring so unremittingly into his office, that the minister needed someone who had his implicit trust to gather reliable intelligence about the machinations of Cardinal Pole and his associates, about Lutheran activists, and about the real intentions of the French and Imperial governments.

There was a sense, as autumn transmuted into winter, that a real crisis was drifting closer and closer with the destructive inevitability of an ice floe. To obtain a focus on this confused and dramatic situation we can peer closely at events in Calais, which Henry was wont to refer to as the most troublesome part of his dominions. Religious discord had been bubbling there since at least the previous spring and Lord Lisle, twitchy about the approved way to respond to extremists at both ends of the spectrum, frequently wrote to Cromwell for guidance. By July, the preaching of Adam Damplip, alias George Bowker, a former priest who had changed his spots as a result of witnessing at first hand the corruption in Rome, was having a devastating effect and Lord Lisle was concerned about its political and diplomatic implications.

> divers people say they care not for the mass and wish they had never heard mass in their lives, which is a great disturbance and unsurety to this the king's town . . . And further, my Lord, I assure your lordship that both in France and Flanders they do repute us but as heretics, and that we be out of league with the emperor and the French king, and that they trust to have war with us.

A fortnight later Thomas Palmer, Knight Porter of Calais, pointed out other problems which he attributed directly to the dislocation brought about by unconventional preaching:

> here be divers people which do much slander the mass, saying it was ordained to sing for dogs' souls and for hogs' souls, and some say for ducks' souls; insomuch it is blown abroad in France and Flanders, and taken very evil of many persons; whereupon it cannot choose but inconvenience come of the same, unless remedy be had. For where we were wont to have every market day 20 butchers of Picardy come to our market with 20 muttons apiece, some more, some less; this last market day there came not 6: assuring your Lordship, if they come not it will turn this town to great dearth of victual . . .[7]

The Deputy was anxious to show himself as fully in harmony with the King's religious policy. So was Cromwell. The problem was that Henry's chameleon beliefs responded rapidly to his moods, his personal relationships and the vagaries of the international situation. The Vicegerent's responses breathed a lawyer's caution. Lisle was exhorted to punish alike those who maintained the authority of the Bishop of Rome and those who set forth heretical opinions, but at no time did Cromwell define what such opinions might be. When Lisle complained about the destruction of a statue of the Virgin, Cromwell stopped short of condemning unauthorised iconoclasm:

> As concerning the pulling down of the image, though it be thought that many abuses and fond superstitions were maintained by the same, yet if it were taken down after such sort as implied a contempt of common authority or might have made any tumult in the people . . . suchlike order shall be taken therein as shall be thought most expedient . . .[8]

This swift passing back and forth of the buck indicates just how aware Cromwell was that the ground he was treading was unfirm. He was ideologically and diplomatically committed to reform but could only proceed if he carried Henry with him. When it came to religious opinion, he guarded his tongue and his pen with care. Pressed by Lutheran envoys to confess his own faith unequivocally, he admitted that he inclined towards their credo but that 'as the world stood [he] would believe even as his master the King believed'.[9] It was the only realistic attitude he could possibly take, although it frustrates the tidy schematics of modern historians. We are left to pick up hints and innuendoes in our search for Thomas Cromwell's private thoughts. This well-read, highly rational sophisticate had little leisure for theological speculation. Whereas

Cranmer had, by this time, developed an interest in the wide spectrum of reformed thought and engaged in dialogue with reformers such as Grynaeus, with Martin Bucer at Strasbourg and others of the religious avant-garde as far afield as Poland, Cromwell's connections seem to have been restricted to the Lutheran and humanist worlds. His dislike of monasticism, his commitment to the vernacular Scriptures, to the eradication of superstition, the furthering of education, and the raising of clerical standards were all fully in line with Erasmian reform programmes. So was Cromwell's reluctance to be seen as a persecutor. Writing to defuse the situation in Calais, he urged moderation:

> I think that like as the king's majesty cannot better or more highly advance the honour of God nor more prudently provide for his own surety and the tranquillity of his realm, dominions and subjects than in the discreet and charitable punishment of such as do by any mean labour and purpose to sow sedition, division and contention, in opinion among his people contrary to the truth of God's word and his grace's most Christian ordinances. So I think again, on the other side, that he or they whatsoever they be, that would without great and substantial ground be authors or setters forth of any such rumours may appear rather desirous of sedition than of quiet and unity, and may therein show themselves rather devisers how to put men in trouble and despair that be peaceable, quiet, and faithful, than how to reform that is amiss.[10]

Throughout his years in office Cromwell maintained strong links with the German Lutheran states through diplomatic channels and also through the Hanseatic community in London. His principal agent all this time was the highly cultured Christopher Mont (humanist pseudonym, Montaborinus), a citizen of Cologne, whom the minister advanced to royal service in which he continued until his death in 1572. Cromwell's preference seems to have been for the more scholarly and humanistically inclined of Luther's apostles. On his patron's behalf Mont strove long and hard – but in vain – to persuade Philipp Melanchthon, the great reformer's second in command, to come to England. He was more successful in luring to London another of Luther's humanist friends, Georg Burckhardt Spalatinus (or Spalatin). Spalatin appealed greatly to Cromwell as both a theologian and a politician. It was he, as a member of the Elector of Saxony's household, who helped to draw up the Augsburg Confession (the Lutheran statement of faith) and also assisted in cementing the Schmalkaldic League. On more than one occasion the minister had Spalatin's books brought to him by Holbein, by Nicholas Kratzer, Henry's astronomer, and other agents. In February 1539 he presented Henry with a copy of the German's *Solace and Consolation of Princes*. All in all, it seems that Cromwell was most comfortable ideologically in the thought world of humanistic Lutheranism.

Since this was not a world in which the King was likely to take up intellectual residence, Cromwell was obliged to keep his beliefs to himself. If he wanted to nudge Henry further along the Reformation path there were three techniques at his disposal: he could give maximum publicity to Rome-inspired plots and the 'treasons' of disaffected conservatives; he could play down complaints against radical extremists; and he could convince the King that a pro-Lutheran diplomacy was viable.

From the point of view of Cromwellian policy the events of 1538–9 had a distinctly 'swings and roundabouts' air. Throughout the summer Cranmer presided over discussions with a distinguished delegation of Lutheran theologians. The Archbishop and his supporters were anxious to arrive at doctrinal agreement on a wide range of topics but this proved difficult from the outset because the King insisted on his church being represented by bishops of varying persuasions. The situation was made worse by Henry's insistence on being kept informed of progress. This inevitably slowed down the deliberations but what was worse from Cranmer's point of view was that the King kept Cuthbert Tunstall on his side as he went on progress, as his theological adviser, and no one was a more determined opponent of Lutheranism than the Bishop of Durham. The increasingly frustrated Germans eventually (5 August) wrote to Henry expressing their concerns on three unresolved issues – clerical celibacy, Communion in one kind and requiem masses. The King replied with a robust defence of traditional practices and that was virtually the end of the colloquium. Cromwell and Cranmer urged the delegates to stay but by the end of September all the visitors had returned home.

However, this disappointment was more than compensated for by Cardinal Pole's activities and Henry's furious reaction to them. The King decided to strike at Pole's relatives and friends, particularly the Marquess of Exeter who, as well as being an influential member of the Council, had a strong power base in the West Country. The 'Exeter Conspiracy' which royal agents uncovered in the autumn was little more than a loose alliance of disgruntled traditionalists and Yorkist sympathisers who longed for better days, were in touch with Chapuys and papal emissaries at home and abroad, and who spoke a little too freely. Yet, florid tumults were well able to grow from just such seeds and the King was within the bounds of political prudence in ordering an investigation. Cromwell carried it out with enthusiasm. It was a means of disposing of personal enemies. Exeter made no secret of his loathing of those who now had Henry's favour. 'Knaves rule about the King,' he declared, 'I trust to give them a buffet one day.'[11] He and certain members of the Privy Chamber were among the remnant of those who still openly cherished the memory of Queen Catherine and deplored the changes in court and government personnel.

While it is extremely unlikely that the Poles and Courtenays were plotting active treason, it may well be that they discussed ways and means of bringing down the Lord Privy Seal.

Sir Geoffrey Pole, the Cardinal's hapless younger brother, was thrown into the Tower at the end of August and was allowed to languish for almost two months in fear and ignorance. When his spirit was so broken that he attempted to commit suicide he was subjected to a series of interrogations. Assured of the King's favour if he revealed all he knew, Pole poured out information against those the King was most interested in. The end result was the arrest and trial of Exeter (a regular member of the Council), Henry Pole, Lord Montagu, Sir Edward Neville, Exeter's wife and twelve year-old son and another dozen of their associates most of whom were condemned on the basis of spoken words and secret correspondence, subsequently burned. There is no evidence that Cromwell took part personally in the investigation of the accused but he was certainly in charge of the machinery which ground them into oblivion. The fall of the nobles and of the courtiers Sir Nicholas Carew and Sir Edward Neville, who had appeared to be riding high in the King's favour, seemed to add substance to the often-voiced rumour that Cromwell was determined to bring down the old families which were opposed to his progressive policies.

The drama of November and December played differently on the international stage. Pope Paul issued against Henry VIII the bull of excommunication which had been drawn up long since but kept in the locker to be used when all else had failed. The English King was declared a heretic and solemnly deposed. His subjects were discharged from their oath of loyalty and brother monarchs were extolled to combine against him, return England to papal allegiance and see that Thomas Cromwell, that limb of Satan, was cast into the consuming fire. Once more Cardinal Pole, now thoroughly embittered, was employed as the Pope's stooge to hawk this message around the courts of Christendom. There was no question of Charles and Francis combining their forces and their treasure to launch a crusade against the Protestant island or even maintaining their own amity for very long but Henry's government could not afford to sit back complacently and wait for habitual continental rivalries to reassert themselves. These were tense months and, while there was nothing approaching panic, there was certainly a flurry of activity – protest, negotiation, covert diplomacy, and overt attitude-striking. Henry put his realm in a posture of defence and spent weeks surveying his navy and the new coastal fortifications while Cromwell undertook an overhaul of the system for mustering the shire levies. All this activity culminated in a lavish military display put on in London by the Lord Privy Seal to stir the national pride of the King's subjects and to warn any foreign observers against assuming that England was a realm riven by religious dissent and, therefore, a soft military target.

they gathered and assembled together at Mile End and Stepney, and so there were set in array in three battalions, and so went in array in at Aldgate and through Cornhill and Cheap to Westminster, and round about the King's park at St James's, and so over the fields into Holborn and in at Newgate, and there brake off every man to his house. The battalions were thus ordered: first gunners and 4 great guns drawn amongst them in carts; then morris pikes; then bowmen; and then bill men . . .

. . . My Lord Cromwell had among them 1000 men of gunners, morris pikes, and bowmen, going in jerkins after the socagers' [armed tenants] fashion, and his gentlemen going by, to set them in array, in jerkins of buff leather, doublets and hose of white satin and taffeta sarsenet, which he did for the honour of the city; and Mr Gregory Cromwell, and Mr Richard Cromwell, with Sir Christopher Norris, Master of the Ordinance, and other of the King's servants, followed the end of the last battalion, riding on goodly horses and well apparelled. The King's grace stood in the gatehouse of his palace of Westminster to see them as they passed by, with the lords and family of his household; and the Lord Chancellor, Duke of Norfolk, Duke of Suffolk, with other lords of the King's household, stood at the Duke of Suffolk's place by Charing Cross to see them as they passed by. They were numbered by my Lord Chancellor to the number of 16 thousand and a half and more, howbeit, a man would have thought they had been above 30 thousand, they were so long passing by . . .[12]

There was no doubting, now, who was London's leading citizen. The people of the capital had not seen such an impressive display since the days of the great Cardinal.

This brave show by Cromwell, his family and his retainers covered the Lord Privy Seal's mounting anxiety. Things were definitely not going according to plan. Early in the new year diplomatic relations became seriously unstitched. Negotiations for Henry's marriage to Christina dragged on unproductively. Cromwell explained to Mont that he perceived, 'by the proceeding of the affairs in Flanders, after long protraction of time, their disposition to wax every day colder and colder; insomuch that, whereas they would make no plain refusal, yet they make such answers as import impossibility'.[13] The technicality being employed by Mary of Hungary was the issue of consanguinity. Christina was the great niece of Catherine of Aragon. A papal dispensation was therefore required before the girl could marry Catherine's widower – and that was as likely to be forthcoming as an outbreak of chastity in the Vatican. Even if this obstacle could have been brushed aside, Henry's hopes would have foundered on the rock of Christina's unwillingness. The Duchess regarded her proposed spouse as a man who had brutally disposed of two wives and encompassed the death of the third by denying her proper medical care.

Moreover, Francis and Charles reached an accord in January, one of the terms of which was that neither would treat with England without the agreement of the other. This finally scotched any prospect of a French marriage alliance. Following this both monarchs ordered the withdrawal of their ambassadors from London. Castillon departed precipitately in February. Chapuys's recall threw Wriothesley into a panic. If diplomacy broke down he and his suite in the Netherlands might find themselves in real danger. These were desperate times for Englishmen in Catholic countries abroad. Merchants were being arrested in Imperial territory and their goods impounded. In Spain the Inquisition was sending Henry's subjects to the stake. When Henry's ambassador protested to the Emperor he was informed that the Holy Father had set up the Inquisition for a good purpose and it was not for him to impede its work. The Pope's instructions were clear: all English traders were to be assumed to be heretics and treated accordingly. Any good Catholic who killed one of them would be assured of remission of all his sins. At all levels pressure was being increased upon Englishmen going about their lawful occasions, thus, for example, when royal agents engaged in formal business they were likely to have any documents returned to them unread if they included Henry's title of Head of the Church in England. It is small wonder that Wriothesley should have been anxious about what would happen if his diplomatic immunity was withdrawn.

A flurry of letters passed back and forth between Cromwell and his protégé and between Henry and the Imperial Regent. The King 'much marvelled' that the amity between himself and Charles should be put in jeopardy and insisted that it was vital that they maintained a diplomatic presence in each other's courts. Wriothesley was urged to try to dissuade the Regent from recalling Chapuys. One stratagem Cromwell suggested to Wriothesley in February reveals clearly the workings of the political mind. The ambassador was to 'reveal' to Mary of Hungary 'secret intelligence' which had reached him with the knowledge and consent of his royal master. Two of the King's councillors had tried to poison his mind against the Emperor by suggesting that Chapuys's recall was for the purpose of putting improper pressure on Wriothesley. Henry had, of course, refused to entertain such suspicion against his 'ancient friend' and had bidden the cynics to believe that Charles would never countenance such an 'unreasonable, shameful and dishonourable prank'.[14] This oblique approach would warn the Regent that her plans were known and hopefully dissuade her from pursuing them. If she persisted the ambassador was to request immediate leave for departure. Cromwell even wrote to Lisle instructing him to delay the Imperial ambassador in Calais until Wriothesley was safely back in English territory (Lisle circumspectly demanded confirmation of this order under the King's hand!).

Wriothesley, at the centre of this diplomatic storm, was extremely vulnerable and very worried. Cromwell did his best to calm the ambassador's fears and assure him of strong support from home:

> We perceive the state of things . . . and how, after fair weather, there is succeeded beyond all men's expectation a weather very cloudy – good words, good countenance be turned, as we perceive, to a wonderful strangeness. But let that pass. We trust to God. He is our hope. What should we fear; he will defend his own cause, how and after what fashion we leave it to his divine providence. Be ye always of good comfort. We lack nor heart nor courage.[15]

How reassured Wriothesley was by these sentiments we may conjecture, particularly when the letter went on to instruct him to take a polite but firm line with the Regent and demand, in the King's name, his own release. Wriothesley would certainly have been alarmed if he had known that at the same time Cromwell was writing a memorandum for Henry in which he backtracked on the advice given earlier about the withdrawal of the ambassadors. In order not to exacerbate Anglo-Imperial relations, he advised Chapuys should be allowed to return to the Netherlands 'whether . . . Mr Wriothesley be arrived or no'.[16] In the last analysis the royal servant was expendable. When Wriothesley came to hear of this the lesson will not have been lost on him.

He made his escape in mid-March, leaving Stephen Vaughan to continue as head of the embassy. This was a moment when tension had temporarily eased. A replacement for Castillon had been appointed and the recall of Wriothesley's opposite number was not made permanent. International affairs were kaleidoscopic and the patterns were constantly changing. The uncertainties of these months profoundly affected the four Thomases who were stationed in the inner courtyard of national affairs.

The conventional understanding of Cromwell's last eighteen months is that he was intent on pushing Henry into an evangelical alliance and allowed his religious zeal to overrule his political realism. This is to undervalue Cromwell's essential pragmatism. His principal concerns were: to maintain peace, and, thereby, a full treasury; to complete his programme of administrative reform and, particularly, the diversion of the proceeds of ecclesiastical spoliation into educational and social improvements; to create a third force in European politics which would free England from being dragged to and fro by Habsburg–Valois feuding; to stabilise relations with England's primary trading partners; and to achieve for his king a marriage which would further rather than balk these objectives. Since all his policies could not be pursued simultaneously in a situation which was so *movementé* he was constantly adjusting his priorities. With enemies at home and abroad seeking to undermine him

and with overzealous evangelical supporters causing daily fresh
embarrassments, his very survival was problematic (though it may be that,
to the very end, he overestimated his standing with the King).

Cromwell juggled several diplomatic balls during these months.
Although convinced that the Imperial match was running into the sand, he
kept negotiations alive as long as he could. At the same time he revived the
possibility of a marriage alliance with Cleves. William V, Duke of Cleves-
Mark-Jülich-Berg was a serious-minded young man, Erasmian rather than
Lutheran, who commanded a small but strategically important state on the
middle Rhine. Like Henry, he had established control of the church in his
territory and, though not a member of the Schmalkaldic League, was
linked by marriage with its leader, the powerful Duke John Frederick of
Saxony. He seemed to Cromwell to be in every way an ideal brother-in-
law for Henry. In January the minister instructed Christopher Mont to
'diligently but secretly inquire of the beauty and qualities' of the Duke's
elder sister, 'as well what shape, stature, proportion and complexion she
is, as of her learning, activity and behaviour and honest qualities'.[17] The
agent responded enthusiastically that the lady's beauty was universally
praised.

In March Cromwell despatched two seasoned diplomatists, Nicholas
Wotton and Edward Carne, to carry negotiations further. The choice of
emissaries is interesting. They were not Cromwellian protégés and they
were both Catholic by inclination (Carne ultimately opted to die in Rome,
where he was on embassy, rather than return to Elizabeth's heretical
England and Wotton consistently refused to accept episcopal office in
Henry's church). It seems likely that Henry was determined to have an
unbiased report on the attractions of his proposed bride, from men whose
experience and judgement he trusted, rather than from one of his
secretary's German agents. There is no evidence that Cromwell pressed
the royal agents to colour their accounts. To do so would have been
foolish, and Cromwell was no fool. This is not to say that the men sent to
appraise Anne of Cleves did not have a difficult task. They knew that the
King's minister was earnest for the match and they knew that the King
considered himself a connoisseur of feminine charm. Wotton's summary
of Anne's qualities was circumspection itself:

All report her to be of very lowly and gentle conditions, by the which
she hath so much won her mother's favour that she is very loth to
suffer her to depart . . . She occupieth her time most with the needle
. . . She can read and write [her own language but of] French, Latin
or other language she [hath none], nor yet she cannot sing, nor play
any instrument, for they take it here in Germany for a rebuke and an
occasion of lightness that great ladies should be learned or have any
knowledge of music . . . I could never hear that she is inclined to the

good cheer of this country and marvel it were if she should, seeing that her brother . . . doth so well abstain from it.[18]

It was left to Henry to conclude from this whether Anne was a dreary, funless, drab or a modest and virtuous maiden who would make a quiet, dutiful wife and mother. The next obligatory step was the taking of the girl's portrait and for this purpose Hans Holbein was sent to Düren in July. He, too, had a problem. He found a talentless, unsophisticated, naïve, lumpy young woman, whose features might be described as 'homely' rather than pretty and he had to present her in the best possible light without actually exaggerating her attractions. His solution was to paint her honestly, full frontal, so that there could be no question of misrepresenting her features, while at the same time going to town on her elaborate court dress and jewellery (which might arouse Henry's cupidity). The contrast with the portrait of Christina of Denmark could scarcely be more striking. The sixteen-year-old's lively fingers and mischievous smile suggest a vivaciousness undimmed by her widow's black. Anne's face is almost iconic in its expressionless repose.[19] The painting did not fire Henry's ardour but neither did it repel him. He did not appreciate being a widower. The bargaining between London and Düren continued. This was far from being the only shot in Cromwell's diplomatic locker. He took every opportunity to convince the German princes that Pope and Emperor were full of hostile intent towards them and were committed to maintaining divisions within the Protestant world on the principle of divide and rule. Nor was he attempting his own disruptions within the enemy camp. He sent detailed instructions to his agent in Urbino for drawing various North Italian states into an anti-papal alliance.

He also urged Thomas Wyatt, England's ambassador at the Imperial court, to take every opportunity to undermine the traitor, Reginald Pole. To emphasise his lack of religious partisanship he passed on to his German friends Henry's sense of outrage at the usurpation of King Christian's throne by his Lutheran rival. He arranged to hire in Germany 200 bombardiers 'for great guns and ordnance' and 1,500 arquebusiers.[20] At the same time he reported to the King that there was very little to worry about: his own intelligence-gathering about England's potential enemies' preparations for war indicated that stories of naval and military concentrations were nothing but 'bruits, rumours and reports' based on 'suspicions and light conjectures' and 'inconstant and fickle babbling'.[21] This letter is worth quoting at some length because, as well as demonstrating the cringing deference Henry expected from all his servants, it makes clear that Cromwell was not trying to manipulate the King into support for his policies. If he wanted to stir up royal wrath against Francis and Charles he would scarcely have minimised the Franco–Imperial threat. Instead, he hints that a wise ruler, while taking prudent precautions, will not pay serious attention to alarmist talk about invasions:

> I can not but (like as your grace of a marvellous high wisdom for more assurance in all chances and occurrents maketh provision in time for defence) so think that your grace will not be further moved or pricked by such reports or letters upon such unknown reports, suspicions and tales . . .
>
> Like as it is good to be wary and circumspect, so no less is to be avoided overmuch suspicion, to the which, if any man be once given, he shall never be quiet in mind. This I do not write as thinking your grace needeth any warning thereof, being of so high and excellent wit, prudence and long experience, but that I would declare unto your majesty how I do for my part take the things and as I think other men should take them . . .
>
> For undoubtedly I take God to be not only your grace's protector but also a marvellous favourer, so that in my heart I hold me assured, although all the rest should have conspired against your grace, yet ye shall prevail through his grace.[22]

Cromwell's legerdemain in turning potential crisis to his own advantage and obtaining virtually complete mastery of all aspects of policy was alarming to his enemies. If he succeeded in locking the King irrevocably into an alliance of minor Protestant states England would be driven harder and faster along the evangelical path and any chance of rapprochement with the major powers of Christendom would be lost. The Vicegerent brought over a second delegation of Lutheran theologians early in the year and the drift into deeper heretical waters that had seemed to be checked with the departure of their predecessors and the royal denunciation of Lambert now seemed to be in full motion once more. The alarums and excursions of January and February provided another excuse for packing Norfolk off to the North, whither he travelled in the depth of winter to check on border defences. With Gardiner still excluded from regular Council attendance and Exeter's friends cowed by the savage reprisals at the previous year's end the conservative cause was languishing – it must have seemed – hopelessly.

Its salvation lay, not in the subtle machinations of the Gardiner–Norfolk clique, which scarcely yet existed, but in the King's *amour propre*. Henry's monolithic self-regard made him unquiet about some of the things that were happening in his realm and beyond the sea. There was something infra dig about the prospect of forming a political alliance with princelings. He was ruler of the 'empire' of England. He had a just claim to the throne of France. He was in every sense an equal member of Christendom's 'premier league' of monarchs along with Francis I and

Charles V. These were the men he was accustomed to doing business with. Though he had his differences with them he shared certain basic assumptions and faced some of the same problems. The most pressing difficulty was dealing with religious minorities. Henry had a genuine and deeply felt concern about the theological discord which was splitting his people into rival camps. He felt that it reflected on him as Head of the Church and he was determined to make that title a reality by imposing unity of belief. The summoning of parliament in April 1539 was chiefly necessitated by the costs of putting the realm in a state of defence but Henry had other uses for it. He instructed Cromwell to prepare legislation to define where his church stood on certain disputed articles of faith. What stung him most painfully was being branded 'heretic'. He might shrug off being excommunicated by the Bishop of Rome but he was determined to demonstrate to the world that he remained fully orthodox. At Eastertide Henry, never lacking a sense of theatre, personally demonstrated his pious veneration for traditional practices in ways that he knew would be noted and reported:

the Holy Thursday eve, the King's grace took his barge at Whitehall, and so rowed up to Lambeth, and had his drums and fifes playing; and so rowed up and down the Thames an hour in the evening after evensong. And on Holy Thursday his Grace went a procession about the Court at Westminster . . . And the high altar in the chapel was garnished with all the apostles upon the altar, and mass by note, and the organs playing, with as much honour to God as might be devised to be done. And they that be in the King's chapel shewed me, and so did Killigrew also, that upon Good Friday last past the King's grace crept to the cross from the chapel door upward, devoutly, and so served the priest to mass that same day, his own person, kneeling on his grace his knees . . .

And his grace every Sunday doth receive holy bread and holy water, and doth daily use all other laudable ceremonies, and in all London no man upon pain of death to speak against them.[23]

The parliament which convened on 28 April rapidly became an arena for a conflict between the forces of reform and reaction and the star gladiators were brought publicly face to face. Norfolk was back from the North in good time to take his seat and also to influence elections in places where he held substantial property. Gardiner and the conservative bishops were present, as were their supporters in the lower house. Both the traditionalist leaders honed their hatred of Cromwell to razor sharpness and had personal as well as ideological reasons for having their weapons in readiness.

Only a few days before, the Lord Privy Seal had tried to humiliate Gardiner before the King and the court over the issue of royal proclamations. Cromwell proposed to introduce a bill that would regularise and clarify the authority enjoyed by the King's extra-parliamentary legislation and the Bishop was trapped into appearing to oppose it. Gardiner, recalling the event years later, inevitably put his gloss on it, making it appear that he had outfaced Cromwell. The minister, believing he had Gardiner at a disadvantage, crowed,

'Come on, my lord of Winchester . . . answer the King here but speak plainly and directly, and shrink not, man! Is not that,' quoth he, 'that pleaseth the King a law?' . . . I stood still and wondered in my mind to what conclusion this should tend. The king saw me musing, and with earnest gentleness said, 'Answer him whether it be so or no.' I would not answer my Lord Cromwell, but delivered my speech to the king, and told him I had read indeed of kings that had their will always received for a law, but, I told him, the form of his reign, to make the laws his will, was more sure and quiet. 'And by this form of government ye be established,' quoth I, 'and it is agreeable with the nature of your people. If ye begin a new manner of policy, how it will frame no man can tell . . . and I would never advise your grace to leave a certainty for an uncertainty.' The king turned his back and left the matter after, till the Lord Cromwell turned the cat in the pan afore company . . .

It then became apparent, Gardiner insisted, that his adversary was put quite out of countenance.[24]

Cromwell had also recently rubbed Thomas Howard up the wrong way. Anthony Rouse, a gentleman of the Duke's household, and Robert Holdiche, Norfolk's steward, both had designs on a daughter of the late Sir Edward Ichingham who was possessed of a good inheritance. Holdiche abducted the girl, intending to marry her to his son. Mistress Ichingham was one of Henry's wards and the steward must have banked on Norfolk squaring everything with the King. But Norfolk was away in the North and Rouse appealed directly to Cromwell, who awarded the prize to him and ordered Holdiche to hand the girl over. As soon as the Duke returned and heard how Cromwell had 'interfered' in his absence he fired off a series of furious letters, as was his wont. The minister then gleefully passed them on to Henry, coyly observing that he was sorry Lord Howard 'taketh the matter so much to heart', referring the contretemps to His Majesty's judgement and patronisingly requesting the King in forming his judgement to weigh 'my said lord, the Duke of Norfolk's, good merits'.[25]

When parliament assembled a few days later Howard must have been still smarting at this affront from the upstart Lord Privy Seal. Worse was to follow. As a very junior baron Cromwell would have been assigned a lowly place in the House of Lords. Since he was not prepared to lose prestige he arranged parliamentary business so that the upper house could not sit until an act had been passed granting the King's Vicegerent in spirituals the first place among the peers – above Norfolk.

Yet, when it came to managing parliament, Cromwell completely lost the initiative. Suddenly, it was Howard who was speaking for the government and steering the assembly in the direction the King desired. The new Speaker of the Commons was one of Norfolk's protégés, Sir Nicholas Hare. And the Duke played the leading role in manoeuvring the Six Articles through both houses. This complete reversal in the roles of the two rivals can only have been brought about by the King. Cromwell was, apparently, too ill to attend the opening of parliament on 28 April and was absent for some days thereafter. Was this indisposition physical or diplomatic? The Lord Privy Seal was well enough to attend parliament a week later and on 8 May he played a prominent part in the military cavalcade that passed through the City and Westminster (see pp. 436–7). When one of Lord Lisle's associates wrote to inform him of the King's public performance of Catholic observances he recorded, *en passant*, 'the Bishop of Exeter came to London upon Saturday with four score horse in a livery and lighted at my Lord Privy Seal's gate . . . and spoke with my lord'.[26] The incident must have had some significance that we can now only guess at. John Vesey, now well into his seventies, was a bishop of the old school, a senior ecclesiastic well liked and respected by the King. Had he been sent by Henry or come on his own initiative to try to break the deadlock in the theological discussions currently taking place?

Parliament had appointed a committee of eight bishops under the Vicegerent's chairmanship to draft a statement of faith. Since it was composed equally of evangelicals and traditionalists it made very little progress. That might not have mattered if Henry had been prepared to allow his religious experts the leisure to concoct finely balanced formulae backed by volumes of biblical and patristic argument. He was not. He needed, for diplomatic reasons, a speedy demonstration of his realm's orthodoxy and unity. With invasion scares still rumbling around the shires and the international situation as fluid as ever religious concord and national security were two sides of the same coin.

Cromwell knew the outcome Henry desired and that must have been why he kept a low profile. He realised that the episcopal conference was so much window dressing and that the important decisions were being taken at court. It is significant that Gardiner was excluded from the theological committee. The King had found a temporary use for the irascible Winchester. While Cromwell and Cranmer were preoccupied with fruitless debate, Henry laid his plans with Gardiner and Norfolk. On 16 May the Duke presented his fellow peers with six doctrinal issues for discussion, since the bishops had been unable to reach agreement. The evangelicals and their sympathisers in both houses did not go down without a fight. The session had to be extended and Henry had to preside in person on more than one occasion before the Act Abolishing Diversity of Opinions achieved its final form.

Conservatives were cock-a-hoop and evangelicals plunged into despair. The Lutheran theologians left the country disillusioned. Cranmer sent his wife back to her German relatives since clerical celibacy was now enjoined by the law of England. Latimer and Shaxton resigned their sees and were, for several months, placed under house arrest. England witnessed its first religious migration, as men and women who had the means to do so fled the expected wrath of reactionary bishops and made their homes in German and Swiss reform centres. Appalled foreign observers wrote to Cranmer and his friends to register their sense of outrage and the Elector of Saxony expressed his astonishment to King Henry that he had allowed himself to be taken in 'by the conspiracy and craftiness of certain bishops, in whose mind the veneration and worshipping of Roman ungodliness is rooted'.[27]

It was all overreaction. Henry had made his point and that was what concerned him most. A sad event in Castille provided a golden opportunity for him to underline the message. On 1 May the Empress Isabella died following childbirth complications. Henry ordered two days of the most elaborate mourning at St Paul's. All the leading men of Church and State, together with ambassadors, members of parliament and London civic dignitaries, took part in a memorial service and a requiem mass. There was a sumptuous hearse fashioned in the form of an Imperial crown, studded with tapers and festooned with heraldic devices,

> and all the body of the church of Paul's in the middle aisle, from the west door to the high altar, was hanged with black cloth and escutcheons of the Emperor's and Empress's arms; also there was in every parish church within London a hearse made with a coffin and tapers burning, and a dirge sung by the priests in every parish, with an afternoon knell, and the bells ringing at the said dirge till 6 of the clock at night, and a mass of requiem kept in every church the morrow after, with all the bells ringing till noon in every parish church.[28]

Soon after this Henry's zeal for Catholic dogma and ceremonial waned. He was content to allow Cromwell to resume control of government business and Cromwell did his best to ensure that the 'bloody whip with six strings' was not wielded with anything like the ferocity its manufacturers had intended. On the day after the Act received the royal assent the King joined Norfolk, Suffolk and Cromwell 'and all the lords of parliament' at a dinner hosted by Cranmer. It was presumably intended as a reconciliation but, if so, it failed spectacularly. Cromwell, in a mocking courtroom tone halfway between jest and earnestness, suggested that, back in the days when Wolsey was bidding for the papal tiara, Norfolk had secured a promise that if the Cardinal was successful he would employ Howard as his lord admiral. The Duke did not see the joke. He flew into one of his customary rages and refused to be pacified by the host. It is not recorded whether or not Henry enjoyed Howard's discomfiture.

Gardiner had, by now, exhausted his usefulness and ceased to appear in court and Council. Negotiations for the Cleves match continued. During the summer parish church after parish church dutifully bought the new English Bible and set it up where people could have easy access to it. However, it was made clear that this gracious royal gift could be taken away if it was misused and a second edition of the Bible, issued in 1540, carried a new preface by Cranmer which included the words,

> I would advise you all, that cometh to the reading or hearing of this book, which is the word of God, the most precious jewel, and most holy relic that remaineth upon earth, that ye bring with you the fear of God, and that ye do it with all due reverence, and use your knowledge thereof, not to vainglory or frivolous disputation, but to the honour of God, increase of virtue, and edification both of yourselves and other.

With the death of Bishop Stokesley of London, an arch-persecutor who boasted that he had sent thirty heretics to their doom, the Catholic summer came to an end.

But there was one place where the conflict was kept alive. Religious discord made more impact in Calais because it was a small, self-conscious English enclave, closely watched by French and Imperial opinion leaders and vulnerable to attack in a war situation. Lord Lisle was worried about the activities of 'sacramentaries' – a term he used indiscriminately and with no theological precision – and reported several offenders to Cromwell and to Cranmer. They gave him no satisfaction, preferring to be sympathetic towards Calais evangelicals who wrote complaining of persecution. The Vicegerent, for the most part, ignored his letters or lectured him about being over-diligent. The Archbishop had offenders brought into his presence, found them in no way heretical and sent them back with mild injunctions not to disturb the peace. One of Lisle's thorns in the flesh was Cranmer's own representative, the Commissary John Butler.

From May onwards the Deputy began to play the dangerous game of court politics. Emboldened by the Six Articles, news of which, he said, 'made me more glad than any news that I had many a day', he bypassed Cromwell and wrote to friends in high places complaining about the Vicegerent and urging them to present his grievances to the King. He assured Sir Antony Browne, Master of the Horse and one of the King's intimates, that ministerial inaction was making his job impossible and concluded his letter, 'I beseech you, keep this matter close, for if it should come to my Lord Privy Seal's knowledge or ear, I were half undone.'[29]

It was vital that Lisle's intrigue should be cloaked for he had no friends of sufficient weight to prevail against Cromwell and the King was in no witch-hunting mood. By prevarication and empty promises the Vicegerent drew the sting of the anti-heretical legislation and in so doing he had his master's support. There was no question of Cromwell pulling the wool over the King's eyes, nor would he have dared to do so. If he had ever doubted the necessity of trimming his sails to the prevailing royal wind the changeable airs of the last few months would have dispelled any such uncertainty. Henry was content with the *status quo*. The Six Articles had established his doctrinal *bona fides*, and occasional punishment of 'papists' and 'sacramentaries' proclaimed to critics at home and abroad that he was in control. To have thrown his weight behind a purge led by Catholic zealots would have destabilised English society without bringing him any advantages. He was certainly not prepared to see his principal servants come under attack. When Sir John Gostwick rose in the Commons to denounce Cranmer for preaching contrary to the Six Articles, Henry sent for him and angrily ordered him to apologise to the Archbishop. Cromwell knew that his own standing with the King was less secure than his friend's and it was at this time that he made his well-known remark to Cranmer, 'You were born in a happy hour . . . for do or say what you will, the king will always well take it at your hand . . . he will never give credit against you, whatever is laid to your charge; but let me or any other of the Council be complained of, his grace will most seriously chide and fall out with us.'[30] It is inconceivable that, as some historians have suggested, he now tried to hustle Henry into an anti-Catholic marriage alliance against his will. It is also certain that intelligent conservative councillors would not be so foolish as to try to manipulate the King. He made policy on an almost daily basis and mistrusted those who would use it to wage ideological warfare. Wise attendants resisted any pressure to coagulate into factions. When Antony Browne urged Cuthbert Tunstall to head up an opposition party to Cromwell, the Bishop replied with world-weary realism, 'the most highly prized quality in the presence of princes is fluidity'.

Lisle seems not to have understood this. Terrier-like he refused to abandon his cause. Perhaps he was emboldened by correspondents who urged him onwards in his prosecution of heretics. Perhaps he was conscious of being in a state of constant confrontation with the Catholic champions of France and the Empire. Whatever his motivation, he kept up his flow of complaints by letter and, in September when he visited the court, in person.

Cromwell was too preoccupied to pay much attention to Lisle's snapping round his heels. He had the Cleves match to arrange. Henry was now enthusiastic for this. The diplomatic situation had taken another of its intriguing turns. Charles V had a rebellion to put down in Ghent and Francis invited him to travel through France from Spain. The prospect of the Emperor entrusting himself to the hospitality of his rival and being honourably escorted by members of the French King's family was not one which Henry welcomed. It suggested that the amity between the two great continental powers might, at long last, be put on a permanent basis. Once more it seemed prudent to provide himself with allies. Whatever he might later claim, Henry VIII went into his fourth marriage with his eyes wide open.

It was Thomas Cranmer, who by now knew his master very well, who seems to have been the first to have cold feet. Sometime in the autumn he suggested to Cromwell that perhaps a political marriage was not the kind that would most suit their master. He thought it might be better for the King to marry 'where that he had his fantasy and love, for that would be most comfort for his grace'. When his friend sharply retorted that there was no suitable English bride available, the Archbishop calmly observed 'it would be very strange to be married with her that he could not talk withal' and, as Cranmer's biographer observes, 'A man with a German wife should know!'[31] 'Fantasy and love' – how neatly the apolitical churchman summed up Henry's attitude towards women. The King still saw himself as the lusty, bull-like figure with the thrusting codpiece, represented only two years before in the life-size wall painting made by Holbein for Whitehall Palace. Cranmer's was a realism Cromwell did not dare acknowledge. To see Henry married within the realm would be to disturb the balance of court politics. Edward and Thomas Seymour, as the young Prince's uncles, were already exercising some influence over policy-making. The last thing the nation needed was more royal in-laws. All the formalities for the Cleves match were completed by early October and, on 27 December, Cranmer met Anne of Cleves at Dover when she disembarked with her suite of 263 attendants and 228 horses.

Henry's well-known reaction on his first sighting of the his new bride needs no repetition. It occurred at Rochester on 1 January 1540 and he immediately demanded that Cranmer should explore ways of liberating him from his contractual obligations. But Cromwell had done his work too well. The political situation was too finely balanced for the King to extricate himself from the marriage. Immediate rejection of Anne would have made him a Europe-wide laughing stock. Henry and Anne were married by Cranmer on 6 April and the wedding night was a disaster. The Archbishop had been right. Other monarchs married unbecoming women out of political necessity and were content to solace themselves with mistresses. This was far from being Henry Tudor's style. It was not simply that with Anne of Cleves he was unable to close his legs and think of England; marriage to a plain, dull woman undermined his self-image. Within the cumbersome, middle-aged hulk there was a young, athletic, virile, gamesome young prince determined to preside over a cultured and lively court. A suitably vivacious consort was vital to the projection of this myth. Cromwell's enemies were not slow in finding one.

The first quarter of 1540 was a disquieting period of cold war. While Henry brooded on his misfortune and the foreign situation continued to justify England's friendship with the German states, Cromwell's enemies, very aware of the widening personal gulf between King and minister, strengthened their own positions in court and Council and plotted how best to undermine the hated Vicegerent. Cromwell's agents kept his foes under surveillance and watched for ways to discredit them. He managed to maintain Gardiner's exclusion from the Council because Henry simply did not like the Bishop who, despite frequent protestations to the contrary, at heart resented the total subservience of the spiritualty to the Crown. Winchester was, thus, obliged to confine his scheming to the religious sphere by attacking Cromwellian protégés and exposing the Vicegerent's support for 'heretics'. Norfolk, by contrast, had managed to work his way back into regular attendance at the Council board. The committee of royal advisers had, by now, established itself as a permanent instrument of government and was developing its own routines and procedures. No longer could a powerful minister or favourite bypass it or reduce it to impotency. Nor could Cromwell overawe it. Despite recent purges, the Council by January 1540 was divided more or less equally between his supporters and his adversaries, and this was probably an arrangement contrived by the King in order that the body should provide him with balanced advice. All the Lord Privy Seal's political skills were called into play in order to maintain his position and the progress of his policies.

Norfolk notched up a major success in February when he persuaded Henry to open up secret negotiations with the French. Around midnight on the 13th the Duke rode out of London with a small train to lead the first embassy with which he had been entrusted since Cromwell's rise to power. The objective was the old one of prising Charles and Francis apart and Howard, with what little political skill he possessed, played on the divisions within the French court, finding an ally in Francis's sister, Marguerite of Navarre. He returned on 1 March having nothing to show for his subversive diplomacy, since the French King had not hesitated to reveal to the Emperor all that Henry's envoy had said. However, there were aspects of Norfolk's brief trans-Channel foray which were significant in the political situation at home. He was able to report, doubtless with glee, that Francis had pointed out how much Anglo-French relations would be improved if Cromwell were removed from office. The Duke also returned with news of the situation in Calais. Lisle had taken advantage of the visit of a sympathetic and powerful courtier to point out how the town was still vexed by 'sacramentaries' whose activities went largely unchecked by Cromwell and Cranmer.

The Lord Privy Seal was caught off guard. He was obliged to appoint a commissioner to enquire into Lisle's grievances and to acquiesce in the appointment of Sir John Wallop, an ally of Norfolk's and a prominent conservative, as the new resident ambassador to the French court. In his instructions to Wallop, the day following Howard's return, Cromwell paid polite tribute to what the Duke had achieved and instructed the ambassador to continue the lines of policy promoted by him – assurances of friendship and fostering of suspicion regarding the Emperor's intentions. Not only was this contrary to the diplomacy Cromwell wished to pursue, Norfolk's intervention prevented him from having sole direction of the ambassador, for Howard maintained his own correspondence with Wallop. The Duke had, in fact, established a little Catholic network as is indicated by the enclosure of a letter from Norfolk in a message from Wallop to Lisle at the end of March:

> Finally ye shall understand that never prince with more affection and with more charitable dexterity hath and daily doth persecute such ungracious persons as do preach and teach ill learnings or against any of the old ceremonies of the Church than the king doth. Barnes the friar, Garrard, parson of Honey Lane, Jerome, vicar of Stepney, hath recanted from their lewd opinions. And to be plain, his highness is of such sort that I think all Christendom shall shortly say, the King of England is the only perfect of good faith, God save him! This present hour Wriothesley showed me that yesterday my Lord of Winchester dined at London with my Lord Privy Seal, and were more that 4 hours, and opened their hearts, and so concluded that, and there be truth or honesty in them, not only all displeasures be forgotten, but also in their hearts be now perfect entire friends, and in likewise the said Wriothesley with the said bishop.[32]

Cromwell was definitely hurt by Norfolk's return to the political centre and the aggressive tactics the old man was employing. He did his best in time-honoured ways to minimise the threat posed by the Duke. In mid-March he despatched Howard northwards to oversee the dismantling of a surrendered abbey. A few weeks later, when parliament was assembling, he tried to keep Norfolk away from the capital by ordering him to stay at Kenninghall because one of his servants was reported to be suffering from an infectious disease. Norfolk cheerfully replied that since the man had recovered there was nothing to prevent him fulfilling his duty of being at his sovereign's side.

Meanwhile, wily Winchester was making his contribution towards the discomfiture of the Lord Privy Seal. The persecution of the Lutheran ex-friar Robert Barnes and his associates was the outcome of a deliberate campaign by Gardiner. He preached a vitriolic Lenten sermon against key evangelical doctrines hoping to draw Barnes into public refutations. Cromwell warned his friend to be 'circumspect' but Barnes was not much given to caution, particularly when he believed the word of God to be under attack. On 29 February he responded to the Bishop, adopting the same vehement tone that Winchester had taken. Gardiner could not wait to report back to the King and Henry summoned Barnes to Hampton Court for a thorough dressing down. He ordered the preacher to make a public recantation, along with William Jerome and Thomas Garrett, who had expressed similar opinions in recent sermons. In Easter week (Easter Sunday was 28 March), the three men complied but their recantations were considered inadequate and they were conveyed to the Tower. Wily Winchester had achieved two things; he had revived Henry's indignation at the existence of heresy in his church, and he had struck down a man who was known to be close to Cromwell – Barnes had, in fact, been one of the commissioners sent to Cleves to arrange the King's marriage.

As Norfolk exultantly reported to friends abroad, the King's chief minister had been obliged by these events to be reconciled to Gardiner. Notwithstanding their mutual enmity, it may not have been all that difficult for Cromwell to offer the olive branch. He had done so before and it had always been the haughty bishop who had resisted any rapprochement. Also the Vicegerent's position was not as precarious as his recent reverses might suggest. The foreign situation, upon which so much else depended, had not substantially changed. He was in the midst of preparing an important body of legislation for the new session of parliament which was to assemble on 12 April. Among the measures to be put before Lords and Commons were bills which would further order the doctrine and liturgy of the English Church. The Vicegerent did not accept the Six Articles as the last word in such matters and he planned fresh definitions which would provide for a middle way that would be inclusive, rather than providing excuse for more persecution.

He was also preparing some master strokes which would further enhance his position in both court and Council. In mid-March the sudden deaths of the Earls of Oxford and Essex provided opportunities for significant promotions. The King was induced to bestow the earldom of Essex on Cromwell together with the office of Lord Chamberlain of the Household, which had been held by Oxford. At the same time he proposed to resign the secretaryship to his protégés, Thomas Wriothesley and Ralph Sadler, to hold jointly. In terms of increasing Cromwell's power and prestige these moves were immensely significant. The only members of the Council who resided regularly at court were the senior noble great officers, the household officers, the Secretary and one bishop. At a stroke, Cromwell had increased his support on this 'inner ring' by, in effect, exchanging the secretaryship for the Lord Chamberlain's office and by bringing Wriothesley and Sadler on to the body. But there was more to these changes, as those at the centre of affairs knew full well. There were social divisions within the Council which were most pointed at mealtimes. In the Council chamber two tables were set: the Lord President's table was reserved for advisers of the rank of earl and above; everyone else dined at the Lord Privy Seal's table. Just as the year before Cromwell had not been prepared to accept a lowly seat in the House of Lords, so now he intended that his superior status should be recognised formally in the Council. It requires no imagination to realise how these developments must have appeared to Norfolk. The parvenu had worked his way almost to the very top of the ladder and his pre-eminence threatened to be permanent. All that he lacked to complete Howard's humiliation was a dukedom.

Cromwell had one more reason to feel secure in the spring of 1540. Lisle and his associates were about to be hoisted on their own petard. The commission sent to Calais to investigate the radicals had come up with damning evidence but they had also unearthed some unpleasant activity of a different kind. One Gregory Botolf, a former chaplain of the Deputy, had defected to Rome and developed a hair-brained conspiracy to betray Calais into the hands of Cardinal Pole's agents. With this information in his hands Cromwell could counteract whatever potentially damaging information came from across the Channel. He could also use it to strike at the troublesome Lisle and men in higher places whom it might be possible to implicate. The memory of the Exeter Conspiracy and its bloody outcome was still vivid and it would not be difficult to persuade the King that some of his most trusted servants were involved in yet another plot to prepare the way for a Catholic invasion.

Thus were the forces poised in April and May 1540 but there was one more item in the balance sheet of intrigue which was to prove decisive. In December 1539 a daughter of the feckless, recently deceased Sir Edmund Howard arrived at court to take her place among the new Queen's ladies. Catherine Howard had inherited her father's irresponsibility. She was about nineteen, pretty, giddy, vain and her moral upbringing had been, to say the least, skimpy. It did not take long for the King to notice her or for her Uncle Thomas to notice that the King had noticed her. Could it be that an old royal play was about to be revived? Norfolk and his associates lost no time in taking out and rereading the scripts of the dramas that had been performed with Anne Boleyn and Jane Seymour in the lead roles. Those earlier misadventures had proved the power of Henry's lust, particularly when he was seeking to escape from a wife of whom he had tired. Protestant propaganda later suggested that Norfolk and Gardiner actively conspired to further the romance, providing venues for Henry's clandestine trysts with Catherine. There is no need to accept such stories in order to cast Howard in the role of Svengali. He had everything to gain and very little to lose in propelling his niece towards Henry's bed. The more infatuated the King became with Catherine, the more determined he would be to secure a divorce from Anne – with all the implications that would flow from that in terms of foreign and religious policy. This would make life very difficult for Cromwell. If he secured another divorce for Henry, then Norfolk would gain that dynastic link to the Crown that would secure his supremacy. If Cromwell failed then Wolsey's fate beckoned.

By the second half of May Henry and Catherine were, to use the modern jargon, an 'item'. The pace of events was hotting up and those events were as bewildering to observers as they have been to historians. The French ambassador reported by turns that Cromwell was on the brink of the abyss and soaring to new heights of royal favour. Perhaps we should resist attempts to impose order on the seeming chaos. Cromwell was certainly preoccupied with a multitude of affairs. In parliament, he was busy with a profusion of bills covering issues as diverse as the medical profession, land law and overseas trade. He set up two episcopal committees on doctrine and liturgy, only to see them become bogged down in arguments between rival camps, as had been the case the previous year. As if that were not frustrating enough, the behaviour of his German allies was now causing anxiety. A conflict had broken out between Charles V and the Duke of Cleves, Henry's brother-in-law. Briefly this threatened to involve England in unwanted and unprofitable war. Then, the princes of the Schmalkaldic League presented themselves as mediators between the estranged parties. Charles thus achieved a measure of peaceful co-existence with his heretical subjects and talks began on the religious issues between them. At the same time substantive negotiations for a permanent accord with France came to nothing. Within weeks England's alliance with Cleves ceased to have much diplomatic value. Henry now began clamouring for a divorce and, in truth, it would not have been difficult to organise, but Cromwell fatally prevaricated.

He was busy, he was tired, he was angry. He was conscious of enemies on every hand and it was in a mood of desperation that he lashed out in a series of pre-emptive strikes. Lord Lisle was the first to fall. He was summoned to London under false pretences and, on 19 May, clapped in the Tower on a treason charge. A few days later Cromwell arrested two conservative clerics who had resisted in parliament the settlement the Vicegerent wished to enforce. Bishop Sampson of Chichester was charged with treasonous communication with Reginald Pole but the ecclesiastical historian John Strype was probably correct when he ascribed the Bishop's apprehension as due to his combining with others 'to do all their utmost endeavours to preserve the old religion, and the usages and traditions thereof'.[33] Dr Nicholas Wilson, a royal chaplain, was imprisoned supposedly for 'relieving certain traitorous persons which denied the royal supremacy'.[34] The real objective of putting these men in the Tower was to interrogate them and discover evidence that would enable Cromwell to move against his real enemies. The French ambassador astutely assessed the situation when he reported on 1 June:

> By one worthy of credit I am informed that he had heard the Lord Cromwell say that there are still five other bishops who ought to be dealt with in the same fashion . . . [They may be] those who of late have so shook the credit of Master Cromwell that he came very near to the overthrow . . . things are at such a pass that either the party of the said Cromwell must succumb or that of the Bishop of Winchester with his adherents . . .[35]

By early June it was obvious that one or more of the great men of the realm would be plucked down within days. Who would it be – Cromwell? Norfolk? Gardiner? The Lord Privy Seal was now very worried. He confessed to Wriothesley that he was concerned about Henry's matrimonial problem. 'For God's sake,' Wriothesley responded, 'devise for the release of the king; for, if he remains in this grief and trouble, we shall all one day smart for it.'[36]

That day came sooner than either of them can have predicted. Someone else got to the King first. On 10 June Cromwell entered the Council chamber for a meeting. Almost immediately, the Captain of the Guard, a client of Howard's, appeared with a warrant for the arrest of the Earl of Essex on charges of high treason. Cromwell swore and raged. This was fine repayment for his years of service! Unmoved, his former colleagues gathered round to strip him of his Garter insignia. Norfolk watched with satisfaction as his enemy was marched off to the Tower. He had not enjoyed himself so much since the downfall of Wolsey.

CHAPTER 31

Faith and Faction

[The Earl of Essex] hath not only, of his sensual appetite, wrought clean contrary to . . . his grace's most godly intent, secretly and indirectly advancing the one of the extremes and leaving the mean, indifferent, true and virtuous way, which his majesty sought and so entirely desired; but also hath shewed himself so fervently bent to the maintenance of that his outrage, that he hath not spared most privily, most traitorously, to devise how to continue the same and plainly in terms to say, as it hath been justified to his face by good witnesses, that if the king and all his realm would turn and vary from his opinions, he would fight in the field in his own person, with his sword in his hand against him and all other; adding that if he lived a year or two, he trusted to bring things to that frame, that it would not lie in the king's power to resist or let it, if he would.[37]

Whoever it was who finally persuaded the King to turn against his minister, the event had to be justified to parliament, to English and foreign ambassadors and to the wider public. The words above form part of the official statement rushed out on the day of Cromwell's arrest. It was cobbled together in haste and, after much correction in committee, written in its final form by Thomas Wriothesley, the man who had been elevated to the Council expressly to support his patron. What it indicates is that the fury of religious reactionaries was the destructive force unleashed against the Earl, that unsubstantiated accusations (against which he never had an opportunity to defend himself) were the means of encompassing his destruction, and that at his moment of direst need no one cared or dared to stand beside him.

Thomas Cromwell was brought down by the flailing tail of a severely wounded Catholic establishment. Its papal head had been lopped off. Its monastic limbs had been severed. The blood of its ancient dogmas was seeping from a hundred cuts. But it fought blindly on, its clerical and lay leaders furious at their loss of power. They accused the fallen minister of aiding and abetting heretics and seeking to force radical religion on a king and a realm pledged to the middle way. But a heresy trial would not have served their purpose. Henry would never have countenanced the bringing of his closest adviser to the stake. Thus, the fiction of verbal treason had to be added to the indictment as an uncomfortable codicil. Then, the victim could be proceeded against by Act of Attainder and, if his enemies' nerve held and if Henry could be kept on side long enough, the hated enemy of the old religion could be destroyed.

Of course, this was not what Gardiner, Norfolk and their associates at the Council board and on the episcopal bench claimed to be doing. They represented themselves as the holders of the centre ground, the champions of 'Middle England', the true interpreters of the royal desire to eschew all extremes. But the claim to be the representatives of the silent majority, extolling the *media via* that some later historians dubbed 'Henrician Catholicism', was as ingenuous as that of modern politicians who insist that their particular extremism has the backing of the majority. No less unconvincing was Cromwell's assertion of 'my goodwill and continual desire to the repression of errors and to the establishment of one perfect unity in opinion amongst us all' (Cromwell to Lisle 6 May 1539)[38] and his protestation in parliament a year later that he condemned equally the 'inveterate corruption and superstitious obstinacy' of the papists and the 'temerity and carnal liberty' of the radicals and that he 'professed the true faith of Christ' as providentially revealed to the King of England. In fact, the Vicegerent was, of course, partial. He favoured evangelicals and was prone to wink at the antics of some of the wilder spirits on the theological left wing. 'Unity' was the buzzword of the hour, especially since Henry had expressed his desire for it in the 1539 parliament, and it was used alike by both conservatives and radicals. That fact should not confuse us. There was no prospect of the breach being closed which had opened up in the English Church. Those involved at the heart of the conflict were passionately committed to dragging the realm back to a discredited past or hustling it into an unknown, turbulent future. Both parties were trying to lock the English people into their own very distinct systems; one dominated by a sacrificing priesthood holding the laity in thrall by their authority in this world and the next; the other trumpeting the 'freedom' of the open Bible as interpreted by preachers and zealots who applied moral and spiritual suasion in establishing their own dominance.

There was no *media via* because the combatants located the centre line between the goalposts of the sacramentaries and the papalists to suit their own purposes. 'Catholics' and 'evangelicals' have always signposted separate paths to heaven. At the heart of their theologies lie irreconcilables – rival authorities, different understandings of the Church, ideological conflicts over the sacraments, over Scripture, over grace and – ultimately – over redemption. A priest either 'makes God' on the altar or he does not. A believer may either contribute something to his own salvation or be accounted righteous *sola fidei*. The last word in doctrinal dispute rests either with the garnered wisdom of the Christian centuries or with the 'plain, unvarnished' word of God, as accessible to the literate thinker as to the doctor of theology. Cromwell was acutely aware of this. Only a month before his arrest he told Richard Pate, English ambassador at the Imperial court, 'the whole world of Christendom hangeth yet in balance'.[39] A wedge had been driven into the heartwood of medieval Catholicism within which differing pieties had for three or more centuries co-existed awkwardly and been policed with difficulty. Now they were riven asunder. Moreover, on both sides of the Catholic-evangelical divide theology was in flux. Ideas changed. Convictions developed. Thus, for example, in 1540 Thomas Cranmer believed in transubstantiation. Ten years later he emphatically did not.

Nor did there exist a core of faith defined and affirmed by the King to which his subjects could be persuaded or impelled to subscribe. No less than any other believer, Henry's religious opinions fluctuated and were influenced as much by his passions and policy imperatives as by scholarly debate. As Professor MacCulloch has pointed out,

> he had lost his hold on the central organizing principle of traditional theologies of salvation – the doctrine of purgatory – without finding his way to a coherent replacement in the mould of Martin Luther. Given this void at the heart of his religious opinions, it was hardly surprising that the structure of ideas which he gathered for himself had the quality of a theological jackdaw's nest . . . To describe this religious mixture as theologically ambiguous is to indulge in courtier-like understatement. The spiritual portrait of Henry VIII would have been a mask of Janus.[40]

Doubtless the King convinced himself – as he has convinced some historians – that his religion was 'Catholicism without the Pope' but 'it ain't necessarily so'.

So far the word 'faction' has been used cautiously and sparingly in this narrative. That is because the concept can be a deceptively simple way of explaining complex events. If we accept the definition of the word as 'a group organized for political ends, which defines itself at least partly by its opposition to some rival groups',[41] then we can see it applying only sporadically between 1509 and 1539. As long as there was a despotic king on the throne who chose to entrust the day-to-day work of government to an individual minister there was little scope for struggles between organised bands of partisans. Seldom did personal rivalries rise (if that is the appropriate word) to the level of faction feuds. When disaffected councillors and courtiers combined their efforts to bring down Wolsey or Cromwell they did so amateurishly, tentatively, fearfully, always looking over their shoulders to see how Henry was reacting.

Clashes of sectional interests certainly had a greater degree of permanence: nobles versus ecclesiastics competing for supremacy in the Council; clerical and anticlerical interests vying for influence through print and pulpit. There was one great issue – the divorce – which cut across all professional and class bearers and united activists (the so-called 'Aragonese faction') behind something which had the semblance of a 'programme' but, for all that Queen Catherine's supporters claimed to be pitting themselves against 'evil councillors', they were, in fact, opposing the King and that imposed severe limits on how far they could take their protest. In order to lock horns over important issues of policy combatants need an arena. For most of Henry VIII's first three decades as king the Council was not an effective debating chamber. Parliament was, in many ways, a better theatre for the exchange – sometimes the violent exchange – of views and from the mid-30s political leaders were using their patronage to build 'power blocs' in the lower chamber. But parliament was, of course, only summoned at the King's pleasure. Furthermore, however committed members were on particular issues, by the end of a session they were usually more keen to get home than to continue campaigning or combining in pursuit of their ends. So, if we consider a degree of organisation to be essential to the maintenance of a faction, it is clear that circumstances did not favour this kind of activity.

Finally, there is the matter of ideology. A true faction is more than a cynical combination of ambitious politiques for their personal advantage; it is a coming together of people who care – and usually care passionately – about something. That something must be important enough to link together individuals who without it might not make natural allies. The cause of Catherine and Mary was certainly one such issue. Anticlericalism was another. By 1540 the progress of the Reformation had become the citadel to which traditionalists in court and Council laid furious siege and which some of their colleagues doggedly defended. The tone of the bickering in the royal household is captured in a conversation between a group of underlings in September. John Lascelles, one of the King's sewers (i.e. a senior attendant at the King's table) entered the outer chamber at Greenwich and asked his colleagues, Messrs Johnson, Moxey and Smythwick, 'What news is there pertaining God's holy word, seeing we have lost so noble a man [i.e. Cromwell] which did love and favour it so well? I know my lords of Winchester and Norfolk are no lovers of the Bible.'

'No,' replied Moxey, 'I heard my lord of Norfolk declare that he had never read the Scriptures in English and never will. Only yesterday I overheard him say, "It was merry in England before this New Learning came up."'

All present agreed how intolerable the new 'cocks of the walk' had become. Smythwick urged that, notwithstanding the undoubted power of their adversaries, faithful men about the court should stand firm as true soldiers of Christ against the agents of the papal Antichrist.

'Not so,' replied Lascelles. 'Let us not be too rash or quick in maintaining the Scriptures. If we wait quietly and do not oppose Norfolk and Winchester, but rather suffer a while in silence, they will overthrow *themselves*. For they stand so obviously against God and their prince that they cannot long survive.'

Smythwick's zeal could not be so easily compromised. 'The duke has spoken openly against the king's religious policy,' he said. 'Surely we can bring him to justice for that.' He described various occasions on which Norfolk had openly shown his contempt for the religious changes of recent years, opinions far from being reserved for private gatherings. Norfolk had spoken boldly in the King's great chamber, and but recently in the court of Exchequer had 'rebuked a man for marrying a nun. "Marry," says the man, "I know no nuns nor religious folk, nor no such bondage, seeing God and the king have made them free." At this the duke waxes angry. "By God's body sacred," he swears, "that may be, but it will never be out of my heart as long as I live."'

They went on to debate whether or not Howard's words could be construed as verbal treason and eventually decided to report the matter to the Council.[42] Needless to say, nothing came of their protest but the fact that they took the risk of informing on one of the great men of the realm is testimony to their zeal and also to the very real religious divisions opening up in the court.

The Lascelles and Moxeys of the royal entourage took their lead from their superiors. It is extremely unlikely that they would have exposed themselves at the least to dismissal and at the worst to investigation for heresy if they had not known that men close to the King such as Cranmer, Hertford and Sir William Butts, the royal physician, shared their views. Political assassinations seldom achieve the purpose designated by their perpetrators and that was certainly the case with the downfall of Cromwell. As the conversation quoted above indicates, within weeks he was being revered as a martyr to the evangelical cause. Nor was it long before the King repented of his acquiescence in the minister's death, claiming angrily that he had been duped into sacrificing the most loyal servant he had ever had. Under these circumstances the Archbishop was emboldened to continue his work of refashioning the Church and he enjoyed the support of conciliar allies. For their part, Norfolk, Gardiner and their friends strove just as energetically to put the clock back. Some, admittedly, wanted to rewind the hands farther than others, but all shared the same impulse.

Thus we can now speak without reservation of faction conflict in Tudor government. It dominated the remaining six and a half years of Henry's reign. No single individual emerged to direct the formation and execution of policy. The country was controlled by an executive council on which the King rarely sat and, like most committees, it was vulnerable to bifurcation. Given the ideological division now rifting society it was inevitable that, notwithstanding mixed motives, ambitions and personality clashes, the factions in court and Council should assume religious hues.[43] Of course, the alliances were fuzzy at the edges. All moves and counter-moves were not inspired by communal piety and we must respond with caution when we find adversaries claiming to be motivated only by the promptings of true religion. But the political groupings which dominated the years 1540 to 1547 had a new cohesion which can only be described as a gut instinct either to press ahead with or resist the process of socio-religious change.

The triumph of the conservatives in June 1540 was a close-run thing and while those distanced from the centre of power rejoiced in what they expected would herald a major reversal of policy, the leaders of reaction were aware that, as long as Cromwell lived, their position was fragile. Henry's unpredictable changes of mood and commitment to personalities over principles could, at a moment's notice, have reversed the fortunes of the Earl of Essex and his accusers. Their insecurity is suggested by the variety of the charges they adduced against the fallen minister and the witnesses they relied on to support these charges. Take, for example, the two men who accused Cromwell of treasonable utterances. One was Sir George Throckmorton, inveterate opponent of the new religion and a landholder who had a current dispute with the minister over property in Warwickshire. He had opposed the anti-papal legislation in parliament, been in cahoots with More and Fisher, had done a spell in the Tower for suspected sympathy with the rebels in 1536–7 and was the brother of Michael Throckmorton, personal secretary to Cardinal Pole. His partner in perjury was Sir Richard Rich, 'a lawyer of great ability and skill, with considerable ambitions and no scruples at all'[44] who had been made by Cromwell and now saw that it would be to his advantage to turn against his patron. Henry, apparently, saw through Rich's obsequiousness and protestations of disinterested loyalty, for Cromwell, writing to the King from prison about his accuser, observed, 'would to Christ I had obeyed your often most gracious grave counsels and advertisements; then it had not been with me as now it is'.[45]

The ragbag of offences urged against Cromwell included encouraging 'combinations' and 'conventicles', presuming, despite his humble origins, to boast of his influence with the King, illegal retaining, urging the Queen to conduct herself in ways likely to win her husband's affection, and revealing to a third party intimate secrets about the relationship between Henry and Anne. It was these last two charges that most angered the King. He probably saw through the treason and heresy accusations, and had certainly forgiven worse crimes in other intimate attendants, but if he came to believe that Cromwell's behaviour was somehow calling into question his sexual adequacy or widely revealing confidences about activities in the royal bedchamber he would have been embarrassed and furious. If we can read between the lines of Essex's correspondence with Henry what seems to have happened was something like this: in a private conversation the King revealed some of his sexual preferences. The vivacious Catherine Howard was, as later revelations proved, well versed in these skills. Cromwell, desperate to make a success of the royal marriage and wean his master away from the Howard girl's charms, made a clumsy effort to tutor the chaste and innocent Anne in the arts of seduction, urging the Queen's chamberlain 'to find some means that the queen might be induced to order your grace pleasantly in her behaviour towards you, thinking thereby to have some faults amended to your Majesty's comfort'.[46] But Henry did not want these faults amended. On the contrary, he desired his revulsion at Anne's body to be one of the reasons used for annulling the marriage.

The vital service Cromwell could still perform was in providing evidence to the commission set up by Cranmer to enquire into the validity of the Cleves match. No one knew better than him the political, diplomatic and personal details and the Earl of Southampton called on the Tower prisoner, accompanied by a gloating Thomas Howard, to obtain a written deposition concerning Anne's pre-contract with the Duke of Lorraine and the non-consummation of her union with Henry. It has been suggested that this constituted the only reason for keeping Cromwell alive for seven weeks but this is to oversimplify. Those summer days were tense, not only for the prisoner, but also for his adversaries. As with Wolsey, the permanence of Cromwell's fall was far from being a foregone conclusion. Soon after the minister's arrest Henry sent one of his closest friends, and no party man, Lord Russell, to discuss his predicament with him and to reveal just what was being said about him. Cromwell, though denied the King's presence, was given the opportunity to make a private defence in writing. It is true that this availed him nothing. His enemies proceeded against him by Act of Attainder, a legal process that ensured that he was condemned unheard, but it did mean that the conservatives could not let up in their efforts to lop off the head of the evangelical faction. The wording of the act was a vague hodgepodge referring anonymously to a body of witnesses as 'personages of great honour, worship and discretion' who had charged the accused of a catalogue of misdeeds 'overlong here to be rehearsed'. The parliamentary business was all done and dusted by 19 June but ten days later the legislation was superseded by a second attainder bill containing fresh allegations. As late as 24 July Cromwell was having to respond to yet another charge, that of having intervened to his own financial advantage, in a case in the Court of Admiralty concerning the confiscation of a French merchant vessel. The diplomatic kaleidoscope having been jolted yet again, the Council were seeking to cement friendship with France and it suited them to blame the ex-minister for causes of friction between the two countries.

On 28 July two executions took place on Tower Hill. After Cromwell had been gruesomely despatched by a headsman who bungled the job badly, Walter, Baron Hungerford, bared his neck to the axe. The juxtaposition is significant. Whereas the minister had been charged with Lutheran heresies, Hungerford was attainted for employing a chaplain who was known to have sympathised with the Pilgrimage of Grace (accusations of buggery and necromancy were thrown in for good measure). The hauling out of relative obscurity of this singularly unpleasant (and possibly mentally unhinged) baron provided John Foxe with the opportunity for a moralising anecdote: Cromwell

> passing out of his prison down the hill within the Tower, and meeting there by the way the lord Hungerford, going likewise to his execution . . . and perceiving him to be all heavy and doleful, with cheerful countenance and comfortable words, asking why he was so heavy, he willed him to pluck up his heart, and to be of good comfort; 'for,' said he, 'there is no cause for you to fear; for if you repent, and be heartily sorry for that you have done, there is for you mercy enough with the Lord, who, for Christ's sake, will forgive you; and therefore be not dismayed. And though the breakfast which we are going to, be sharp, yet, trusting to the mercy of the Lord, we shall have a joyful dinner.' And so went they together to the place of execution, and took their death patiently.[47]

This shared execution was a signal that Cromwell's death was not to be seen as the start of a Catholic revival. The lesson was underlined two days later when Robert Barnes and two other prominent evangelicals were burned for heresy. They were drawn on hurdles to Smithfield in company with three other condemned men. Edward Powell, Richard Fetherston and Thomas Abell had sojourned in the Tower for several years in connection with their support for Catherine of Aragon and denial of the supremacy. Some historians have doubted whether this should be seen as a demonstration of the King's even-handedness but it is difficult to see what other interpretation can be put on the timing and the choreography of the event. Contemporaries puzzled over the deaths of Barnes, Jerome and Garrett, who suffered by attainder rather than under the Act of Six Articles, and were thereby prevented from defending themselves against heresy charges. As for the papists why, after so long in prison, were they brought forth to die as traitors at the very moment of apparent Catholic triumph? The whole episode smacks of that kind of theatrical display Henry loved and used so effectively.

It must be seen against the background of what was happening in London at the same time. The City jails were at bursting point with prisoners apprehended under the Act of Six Articles. Fresh persecution had broken out the previous October with the election of a reactionary Lord Mayor. Clergy whose power had been progressively undermined over the previous decade were determined to grasp the opportunity to be revenged on their presumptuous parishioners who not only

> denied the sacrament to be Christ's very natural body, but who also held not up their hands at sacring time, and knocked not on their breasts. And they not only inquired who offended in the Six Articles but also who came seldom to the church, or in communication [showed contempt for] priests or images.[48]

The persecution reached its height in the summer of 1540 when, encouraged by the downfall of Cromwell, the officers of the Bishop and the corporation arrested about 500 citizens in the space of two weeks. Their incarceration was particularly uncomfortable because that summer was one of the hottest in living memory, with no rainfall from June till October. All manner of pestilence and disease was rife and the King ordered prayers for deliverance to be said throughout the realm. Evangelical partisans (or possibly it was simply those who were appalled at the threat to public order) brought the state of affairs to Henry's attention and he put a stop to the witch-hunt. Again, the timing is significant: the royal order went out on 1 August, two days after the executions of Barnes and Co. The King had demonstrated his rejection of all forms of extremism and that was where the matter would stop. Although the 500 accused were indicted to appear in Star Chamber three months later the charges against them were quietly dropped.

At the centre, however, the struggle continued. The atmosphere at court now became permanently poisoned because, with no chief minister to give cohesion to royal policy or act as mediator between King and Council, decisions were more frequently referred to Henry and Henry's moods were becoming more and more impossible to predict. It was not just that he was frequently in pain from his ulcerated leg or bitter about his continuing marital misfortunes. What more than anything contributed to instability on a day-to-day basis was the very existence of a new executive situation which neither the King nor the ministerial body was equipped to handle. Ironically, the development which Henry and his nobles had always wanted carried with it weaknesses they had never anticipated. The council attendant, or Privy Council, had a defined composition, and its own officers and procedures. What it lacked was leadership. The members would not permit one of their own number to become *primus inter pares* and the King was not prepared to be his own chief executive with all the sheer hard work and mental agility that that involved. Henry did not attend meetings regularly. He did not automatically accept Council decisions. He consulted individuals and pressure groups. The results were policy and personality clashes, behind-the-arras manoeuvrings, bickerings, manipulation and power plays. Councillors lurched in and out of influence and policy oscillated. This was why Henry soon came to repent the loss of 'the most faithful servant he had ever had'.[49]

Following Cromwell's fall those who had been closest to him were the more vulnerable. Cranmer lost little time distancing himself from the imprisoned minister. He immediately wrote to Henry a letter balancing, as only a theologian could, contrasting thoughts and emotions: Lord Cromwell

> was such a servant, in my judgement, in wisdom, diligence, faithfulness, and experience, as no prince in this realm ever had . . . I loved him as my friend, for so I took him to be; but I chiefly loved him for the love which I thought I saw him bear ever towards your grace, singularly above all other. But now, if he be a traitor, I am sorry that ever I loved him or trusted him, and I am very glad that his treason is discovered in time; but again I am very sorrowful; for who shall your grace trust hereafter, if you might not trust him? . . . [50]

The best way the Archbishop could commend himself to his master was by giving him what Cromwell had been reluctant to supply. A convocation committee under his chairmanship squirmed its way between all the niceties of canon law and within a few days neatly proved that the marriage of Henry and Anne had never happened because of the German Princess's previous contract with the Duke of Lorraine and that no impediment existed to the marriage of Henry and Mistress Howard. Just how jittery Cranmer was at this time is revealed by what might normally have been considered to be a minor incident but which he was very quick to deal with. Some of the clerics who met to draft the necessary documents not unnaturally fell to gossiping about the relationship between Henry and Catherine and the rivalry between Cromwell and Gardiner. They agreed that the Earl and the Bishop were at loggerheads, not over matters of heresy or treason but over the annulment issue. This was no more than was being discussed in every alehouse between Tower Reach and Westminster Abbey but Cranmer felt so compromised by it that he personally reported his loose-tongued colleagues to the Council and paraded them before that body to make grovelling apology.

Cranmer's motivation was a mixture of fear, honesty and profound respect for the Crown. Self-preservation was a strong instinct. Yet it was not an entirely egocentric one. He was passionately concerned for the continuing reformation of the English Church. His own theological journey was still in progress and he would end up espousing doctrines to which Henry could never have subscribed. But for the moment he was the

King's man and this was the King who had freed English Christianity from the strangling coils of Rome. The progress towards evangelical teaching and liturgy had begun. As long as he could remain primate Cranmer could stand guard over the achievements already made and work towards further reform. He was unique among our six Thomases in that he succeeded where Wolsey, More and Cromwell failed: he pursued a policy agenda of his own and managed to pursue it while retaining Henry's trust and support. That he did so is entirely down to the personal chemistry that existed between him and his monarch. Contemporaries observed the relationship and wondered at it. Historians have sometimes dismissed it as time-serving. We do best to accept it at face value as Cromwell did when he observed, 'do or say what you will, the king will always take it at your hand'.

No such complexity can be discerned in Wriothesley's reaction to the crisis of the spring and summer of 1540. This was, for him, the crunch time, the moment when clear-cut, ruthless decisions had to be made if his own ambitions were not to be derailed. He had to calculate coolly who was likely to emerge victorious from the power struggle and make sure that he was on the winning side. His first initiative may have been to try to prevent confrontation and it is likely that it was he who brokered the attempted rapprochement between Cromwell and Gardiner in March. When it became obvious that the two rivals were locked in a life and death struggle he transferred his allegiance to his former master. However, it appears that he remained loyal to Cromwell until the last moment and that Winchester applied not inconsiderable arm-twisting. Wriothesley, with his intimate knowledge of Essex's affairs, was vital to the Bishop's plans and Gardiner was not above using whatever methods came to hand to achieve his objectives. In May the Secretary came under investigation by the Council over alleged fraud relating to some of his Winchester properties. Was this Gardiner's way of bringing pressure to bear upon him? At the end of June, precisely the time when Gardiner became once more a regular member of the Council, the charges were dropped. Perhaps they had served their purpose. And there were carrots as well as sticks. Impressive rewards for Wriothesley's change of allegiance materialised in very short order. Two days before Cromwell's execution he moved into the splendid town mansion at the Austin Friars on which the fallen minister had lavished so much money and creative energy. It was the most tangible of signs yet that he was destined to replace the great minister.

Norfolk had even more spectacularly reached the pinnacle of his wealth and ambition. The marriage of a second niece to the King brought the head of the Howard clan more marks of royal favour. Henry was besotted with his new queen and persuaded himself that he was young again. Once more he rose early to spend hours in the hunting field, before returning for lavish court entertainments and another night spent in dalliance with his nineteen-year-old bride. He could not keep up this regimen and the Catherine Howard tonic provided him with only a few months' remission from the creeping illness of sick old age but those months were happy ones and marked with generosity towards his current favourites. Norfolk enriched himself further with grants of monastic land which he sold at a profit. He became a steward of Cambridge University along with his son, the Earl of Surrey, who was also admitted to the Order of the Garter. More importantly he was able to advance two of his own adherents to the Council. The Duke now became the dominant member of that body and even when he was absent from court he was kept fully informed of its deliberations. Meanwhile, Catherine's patronage filled the royal household with Howard protégés. Now that the Crown was once more ring-fenced with the affiliates of his dynasty Norfolk could feel that he had lived to see the triumph of the old order against social upstarts and the advocates of New Learning.

But any surface calm only concealed vigorous currents of intrigue inspired by personal jealousies, running feuds and ideological confrontations. In October a certain George Wheplay laid information against the Duke concerning corruption in the collection of East Anglian customs. Howard was, significantly, absent from the Council and his rivals – Hertford, Ralph Sadler and Lord Russell – encouraged Wheplay to spill the beans. Norfolk could not be seriously discomfited by such pinpricks but Wriothesley was more vulnerable and he found himself under examination again for financial peculation. All the great men of the realm who had been pocketing profits from the Dissolution were open to charges of malfeasance, and the complexities of land transfer were a gilded maze for lawyers. Sir Thomas escaped scot-free but may have had to buy the support of his new allies by giving evidence against his colleague, Sir Ralph Sadler. Norfolk and his friends took every opportunity to make life difficult for members of the Council's Cromwellian rump and, in January, they were able to have Sadler conveyed to the Tower. Wriothesley was also targeted in this attempted coup but by now he was sufficiently well in with the conservative leaders to avoid serious trouble. Once again, it was a storm in a teacup – but none the less messy for that.

The tremors that shook the King's inner circle of advisers agitated more violently those in less privileged positions. Sir Thomas Wyatt, the ambassador, was arrested at the same time as Sadler. Edmund Bonner had long been seeking his destruction but had always been foiled by Cromwell. Now the Bishop saw his chance to have the diplomat interrogated, believing that the prisoner would provide leads to other progressives. Wyatt was so roughly handled – being conveyed to the Tower bound and handcuffed – that observers assumed that it was all up with him. It was only the intercession of the Queen that achieved Wyatt's release after three months. At the same time Bonner's net caught men who were closely involved with Cranmer. Richard Grafton was the publisher of the Great Bible and his father-in-law, John Blagge, was the Archbishop's business agent. Both were evangelical activists and both spent an uncomfortable few weeks during a fresh outbreak of Six Articles persecution.

These aggravations were far from being one-sided. Sir John Wallop, the ambassador in France who had helped to exacerbate the Calais situation against Cromwell, was brought back in January and joined other occupants in the Tower on suspicion of treason. Examined before the Council in March, Wallop confessed that he had 'meddled above his capacity' in affairs of state and obtained his release once more, it seems, at the urging of Catherine Howard. Not long afterwards Cranmer had the satisfaction of examining one of Bonner's chaplains, reported to him for preaching sedition. All these examples of what seem like petty trouble-making are just the visible upwellings of tortuous underground systems of fast-flowing intrigue and conviction, the activities of partisans who hoped to set in motion trains of events which would topple men and women close to the throne and influence the direction of policy. But Henry had no intention of allowing his government to be destabilised and, therefore, these stratagems were largely ineffective. That was not true of the geyser which was about to gush forth.

In June 1541 Henry and his court made a long-promised progress into the northern parts of the realm. Norfolk, Wriothesley and the other in-favour conservative councillors accompanied the King, leaving Cranmer, Hertford and Lord Chancellor Audley to hold the fort at Whitehall. (Gardiner was, once again, absent on foreign embassy.) There, in October, the courtier John Lascelles sought an interview with the Archbishop and laid before him information he had recently obtained from his sister, Mary Hall. Mistress Hall had been a servant in the dowager Duchess of Norfolk's household when Catherine Howard had been one of the young relatives placed in the care of her step-grandmother and she had many tales to tell of the Queen's early amorous adventures. At the age of fourteen she had held evening assignations in the Duchess's chamber with Henry Manox, her music teacher. This first sally into the excitements of love-play had not gone beyond intimate caresses. Of a different nature was the affair with Francis Dereham. Dereham, a gentleman attendant upon the Duke of Norfolk, took to visiting the girls' dormitory at night in company with other young gallants. They would bring with them 'wine, strawberries, apples and other things to make good cheer' – prepared for nocturnal entertainment and the satisfying of more than one kind of appetite. The relationship between Catherine and Dereham soon developed into something more than amorous dalliance – certainly as far as the gentleman was concerned and he repeatedly asked his mistress to marry him. Mary's assessment of the Queen's character was that she was 'light in both living and conditions' and likely to bring about her own destruction.

There can be no doubting Lascelles's partisan motivation. We have already encountered him as one who lamented the downfall of Cromwell and he had recently been concerned when conservative probes had reached his courtier friend Sir George Blagge, who had been reprimanded for absenting himself from mass. The Howard coterie had become altogether too powerful and Lascelles must have been proud to think his was the hand chosen to pluck them down.

The revelation placed Cranmer in a difficult position. He discussed it with his colleagues who agreed that the King must be told and that Cranmer was the only man from whom he would accept such dire tidings. On 29 October the court returned from its northern tour and took up residence at Hampton Court. Cranmer joined the royal party there and waited, with extreme nervousness, for a suitable opportunity to confront his master. It was not until 2 November that the Archbishop could bring himself to approach Henry. Even then he dared not speak damning words against the Queen. Instead he drew the King on one side as he was leaving a mass celebrated by Bishop Longland and handed him a letter containing a full account of Lascelles's confession. He urged the King to read it privately and then hurried away before the storm broke.

Henry's first reaction was total disbelief and he ordered Southampton to extract confessions of mischief-making from Lascelles *frère et soeur*. Only when they stuck to their story did the King sanction further investigation. Wriothesley was then appointed to interrogate Dereham and Manox. It was an activity he had mastered under Cromwell's tutorship and he did not fail on this occasion. There can be little doubt that he used torture for within hours he had extracted detailed confessions from the two Lotharios. A secret Council meeting was summoned late on 6 November at the Southwark house of Bishop Gardiner (recently returned from Germany). Norfolk had previously been summoned to Hampton Court from the country and the King acquainted him there with the scandal surrounding his niece. It was a shocked and subdued Thomas Howard who accompanied his sovereign downriver. At the forefront of his mind must have been the fate of the last man who had encouraged Henry into a marriage of which he had subsequently repented. At the meeting the incontrovertible evidence of the Queen's premarital affairs was set out and the Council members had the embarrassing experience of watching their master, totally deflated, his monolithic self-belief drained away, weeping tears of bitter self-pity. Eventually Henry left, to be rowed across to Westminster, while others were ordered to confront Catherine and obtain the truth from her own lips.

Those chosen for the task were Cranmer and Norfolk (or perhaps the Duke volunteered in his frantic eagerness to disassociate himself from Catherine's folly). Whatever the faction outfall of the death of Henry's fifth marriage it was essentially a personal tragedy and that is how it struck the two councillors when they went to Hampton Court the next day. Howard was contemplating the loss of all that he had striven for and had seemed to have grasped. The Archbishop was genuinely moved by the sight of his broken-hearted king. How this ill-matched couple of news-breakers comported themselves we do not know. We can imagine Norfolk raging and Cranmer sympathetically cajoling (he had known once, long ago, what it was to lose everything for love). Whatever they said and however they said it, Catherine went to pieces. They could get nothing from her but a frenzy of hysterical denial. Only when Cranmer returned – alone – next day did the Queen's story come tumbling out between sobs.

Over the next few days everyone connected with Catherine's love life was sought out and questioned. At stake was the need to achieve something which was becoming almost commonplace – to extract the King from an unwanted marriage. Annulment on the basis of pre-contract with Dereham seemed the most likely option. But then Wriothesley – and it is no surprise that it should have been he – stumbled upon the name of Thomas Culpeper, a gentleman of the Privy Chamber with whom the Queen had been carrying on a rash and stupid liaison since her marriage. Wriothesley now went to Hampton Court to harangue Catherine into further confessions. His bullying produced an acknowledgement of an intimate friendship with Culpeper which fell short of actual adultery. This did not satisfy Henry who was now determined to extract vengeance on all those who had 'conspired' to humiliate him, and the Secretary was sent back again the next day, this time with Cranmer to try what a gentler approach might achieve.

Now the Council had enough information to proceed against the Queen and her associates, not for a dissolution of the marriage, but for treason. Under the terms of the 1534 Act it was sufficient to show that the accused had maliciously wished or by craft imagined the King's death or harm. On 13 November

Sir Thomas Wriothesley, knight, and secretary to the king, came to Hampton Court to the queen, and called all the ladies and gentlewomen and her servants into the great chamber, and there openly afore them declared certain offences that she had done in misusing her body with certain persons afore the king's time, wherefore he there discharged all her household; and the morrow after she was had to Sion, and my Lady Bainton and 2 other gentlewomen, with certain of her servants to wait on her there till the king's further pleasure: and divers persons were had to the Tower of London, as my Lady Rochford, Mr Culpeper, one of the king's privy chamber, with other.[51]

Norfolk was as assiduous as his conciliar colleagues in carrying out inter-rogations and he was present at the trials of the Queen's lovers on 1

December. He was terrified for his own safety as he watched the Howard clan decimated. So many of Catherine's relatives, friends and servants were arrested that the Tower could not accommodate them all. Dereham and Culpeper were executed at Tyburn on 10 December. Norfolk made his tremulous way back to Kenninghall from where he wrote to the King five days later, in tones of mingled self-justification and remorse. He deplored the actions of his 'lewd' sister, 'ungracious' stepmother and 'unhappy' brother but denied any involvement in 'their false and traitorous proceedings against your royal Majesty'. He had, he assured Henry, been the most assiduous investigator of Catherine and her paramours and he begged the King to relieve his anxiety about where he stood in royal favour:

> Prostrate at your royal feet, most humbly I beseech your Majesty, that by such, as it shall please you to command, I may be advertised plainly, how your Highness doth weigh your favour towards me; assuring your Highness that unless I may know your Majesty to continue my good and gracious Lord, as ye were before their offences committed, I shall never desire to live in this world any longer, but shortly to finish this transitory life as God knoweth, who send your Majesty the accomplishments of your most noble heart's desires.[52]

It scarcely needs mentioning that no one stood up for the Queen or supported her Howard relatives. All the men the Duke had advanced to court places distanced themselves from him and, if any of the progressives had whispered in the King's ear at this stage, the friendless Norfolk might well have been discarded, but none of the Duke's opponents had the necessary inclination or weight. Cranmer and Russell were closest to Henry but it was not in their nature to be vindictive. Hertford and Sadler were still up-and-coming men. Charles Brandon was not the force he had once been and, anyway, devoted most of his time to his Lincolnshire estates. After the rebellions of 1536–7 Suffolk had married a Midlands heiress and had also been obliged to exchange some of his East Anglian estates for land in Lincolnshire in order to pacify the region. This removed the basic cause of friction between him and Howard. Without anyone to urge him on, Henry, who still regretted having thrown Cromwell over, was not inclined to be deprived of another longstanding royal servant. He also needed Norfolk in the House of Lords to take a lead in voting for Catherine Howard's attainder. Parliament assembled on 16 January and by 11 February the legal process had been completed. The Queen had already been brought by water to the Tower and on the morning of the 13th she was beheaded within the precincts in front of a small crowd assembled to witness her end. Her uncle was not present.

The focus of attention now moves, briefly, away from the court. The disgrace of their lay champion and the check placed on conservative initiatives in the Council had no restraining influence on the ecclesiastical reactionaries among the senior clergy. Gardiner, Bonner and their associates were in the majority in the upper house of convocation and they consistently balked Cranmer's attempts to continue the work of reform. Not content with legitimate protest in their assembly, they intrigued for the destruction of their leader who as well as being primate of all England, was, in their view, the nation's arch-heretic. The Catholic ecclesiastical establishment had learned nothing. They still thought they could bounce the King into returning their powers to them. Though they would never risk saying so, many bishops hankered after a restoration of the link with Rome. Preaching at St Paul's Cross in 1555 Gardiner reminisced that

> when the tumult was in the North, in the time of Henry VIII, I am sure the king was determined to have given over the supremacy again to the pope . . . After this in 1540 Master Knyvet and I were sent ambassadors unto the emperor, to desire him that he would be a mean between the pope's holiness and the king, to bring the king to the obedience of the see of Rome.[53]

Nothing could have been further from Henry's thoughts on either occasion; Winchester was flattering the King's memory by attributing to him sentiments that he (Winchester) believed to be wholly good. What England's spiritual fathers *were* aware of and concerned about was the phenomenon of evangelicalism going upmarket. Heresy was no longer the preserve of huddled artisans, rebellious students, and renegade priests. It was becoming fashionable. A new generation of educated men – and women – was growing up, who were well-versed in the Bible, articulate, in touch with the latest international trends in theological thinking and taking over leadership roles in the professions, in trade and at the royal court. One such young rebel was Norfolk's heir, the Earl of Surrey.

In 1543, the conservative leaders struck – repeatedly and hard. A move in foreign policy created a favourable atmosphere for fresh anti-progressive activity. On 11 February Henry ratified a treaty with Catholic Spain. The alliance which Gardiner had advocated for so long had thus come into being. Its effects in England were felt almost immediately. Gardiner's faction now made an all-out attack on influential evangelicals. In this work the Bishop used the services of a very able spy – Dr John London, a born intriguer who had started his persecuting career weeding out Oxford evangelicals in the 1520s but subsequently found agreeable employment driving the dispossessed religious from their abbeys and friaries. In 1543 the inquisitor found himself hot on the scent of a group of heretics in Windsor. The central figure in the group was Anthony Parsons, an active preacher and dispenser of banned books. Other local men such as Henry Filmer were implicated in his heresy but London (and his master) was much more interested in the more important figures who had encouraged and supported the priest. These included Robert Testwood and John Marbeck, singing-men from the Chapel Royal, and a number of courtiers: Sir Thomas Caradine, Sir Thomas Weldon and Edmund Harman. But the most important members of the 'catch' were Sir Philip Hoby, one of the King's gentlemen ushers, and Dr Simon Heynes, Dean of Exeter, a leading ecclesiastic and staunch supporter of Archbishop Cranmer. Armed with all London's evidence, Gardiner unburdened himself to the King at the beginning of March about his concern at the spread of heresy at all levels of society. Henry agreed that it was very disturbing and gave the Bishop licence to take action against the offenders.

Gardiner went straight for the most prominent members of the sect. Hoby and Heynes were arrested and examined by the Council on 18 March. They failed to satisfy their examiners and were sent to the Fleet prison. Gardiner would doubtless have liked the affair to go further, but Henry was not disposed to allow prominent members of the establishment to be put on public trial as heretics. The two men were allowed to cool their heels in prison for six weeks and were then released. Meanwhile Parsons, Filmer, Testwood and Marbeck were also imprisoned. While in custody they were examined by the Council and Marbeck particularly was interrogated repeatedly by Winchester and his agents in an attempt to get him to implicate his superiors.

But while all this was taking place another net was being cast to trap the biggest fish of all, Archbishop Cranmer. Many of his prebendaries at Canterbury had long resented Cranmer's reforming activities. In April, with Winchester's encouragement, some of them, led by Germaine Gardiner (Stephen's nephew and secretary) and the ubiquitous Dr London, formally protested to the King, presenting him with a list of Cranmer's heresies. Henry received the complaints without comment, and after a few days licensed the Council to take proceedings against the Archbishop. But he had no intention of allowing himself to be robbed of a faithful and pliant servant. On the same day that he received the prebendaries' accusations, Henry took the opportunity of a chance meeting with his archbishop to warn him of what was afoot. Summoning Cranmer aboard the royal barge in the damp April evening the King is reported to have greeted him jovially: 'Ah, my chaplain, I have news for you. I know now who is the greatest heretic in Kent,' and he held out the prebendaries' articles. The crestfallen Archbishop had no alternative but to submit himself humbly to the King's justice but Henry was having none of that. He declared that these were serious charges brought by the prebendaries. They must therefore be examined by a wise and experienced commissioner. Who better for the task, he suggested, than Cranmer himself?[54]

Cranmer was thus left to deal with affairs at Canterbury in his own way but the threat of action by the Council remained. Henry had not mentioned this to Bishop Gardiner and he now consented to Cranmer's arrest during a meeting of the Council. Gardiner and Norfolk were convinced that they had triumphed. They envisaged a repeat performance of Cromwell's denunciation and arrest. With both the architects of the Reformation out of the way, there would be no one of any consequence left to uphold their policies.

On the night before the Council chamber drama was scheduled to take place, Henry sent one of his court favourites, Sir Anthony Denny, to fetch Cranmer across the river to Westminster. The Archbishop arose from his bed and hurried to obey the summons. In a quiet corner of the gallery at Whitehall, the King told Cranmer of the Council's complaint and concluded 'Therefore, I have granted their request. But whether I have done well or no, what say you?'

What could poor Thomas Cranmer say, but thank the King for this forewarning and declare himself content to be subject to the royal justice. Such naïve other-worldliness was too much for Henry, the realist.

'Oh Lord God!' he cried out. 'What fond simplicity you have, to let yourself be imprisoned, so that every enemy of yours may take advantage against you. Do you not know, that when they have you once in prison, three or four false knaves will soon be procured to witness against you, and condemn you, which otherwise, you being at liberty, dare not once open their lips or appear before your face. No, not so, my Lord, I have better regard unto you, than to permit your enemies so to overthrow you.' He took one of the many rings from his fingers. 'I will have you come to the council tomorrow. And when they break this matter unto you, require of them that you may have your accusers brought before you. And if they will, under no circumstances, condescend unto your request, but are determined to send you to the Tower, then appeal from them to our Person, and give them this my ring, by which they will understand that I have taken your cause into my hand and away from them.'

Henry was thinking, perhaps, of other occasions when his ministers had overreached themselves. 'They well know this ring, and that I use it for no other purpose but to call matters from the Council into my own hands, to be ordered and determined.'

And that was exactly how it fell out. Cranmer's accusers read the indictment to him: 'That he, and others by his permission, had infected the whole realm with heresy.' They refused to allow him to argue his case before them but ordered him to prepare himself for instant removal to the Tower.

The Archbishop replied calmly, 'I am sorry, my Lords, that you would drive me unto this exigent, to appeal from you to the king's majesty.' He produced the ring as he continued: 'Who, by this token hath resumed this matter into his own hand, and dischargeth you thereof.'

Consternation all round. Gardiner and his supporters had blundered and they knew it. The only thing to be done now was to repair to the King with all haste and hope to salvage something from the wreck of their fortunes. The whole Council, therefore, went straight away to the royal apartments, for all the world like a band of dejected schoolboy offenders on their way to the headmaster's study.

And, in fact, Henry's handling of the matter smacks somewhat of the Victorian public-school pedagogue.

'Ah, my lords, I thought that I had a discreet and wise Council, but now I perceive that I am deceived. How have ye handled here my Lord of Canterbury? What make ye of him? A slave? Shutting him out of the council chamber among serving men?' And he proceeded in this vein for several minutes before ordering them all to shake hands with the Archbishop and to avoid all malice in future. Then he instructed Cranmer to entertain each of the councillors to dinner in the near future as a sign that they were all friends again.[55]

But the bishops saw no need to scale down their campaign against less prominent radicals. Throughout the spring and early summer, the Windsor heretics had remained in prison. The end of their ordeal was now at hand. On 20 July they were returned to Windsor for trial by the local Six Articles commissioners. Their examination and condemnation occurred on 25 July. The result of the trial was immediately communicated to Gardiner, who was with the court at Woking. The Bishop appealed to the King for Marbeck's pardon. The request was granted and when, two days later (Saturday, 27 July), the three remaining heretics (Parsons, Testwood and Filmer) were burned at Windsor, Marbeck remained in prison.

The reason for Winchester's clemency towards Marbeck was that he hoped to get more information out of him. The Bishop had not relinquished his hopes of dragging down prominent men and women of the court. Dr London and his colleagues were still hard at work gathering evidence, but this time they were to be thwarted. On 29 July word reached some of the gentlemen of the Privy Chamber that Gardiner's bloodhounds were on to their scent and accumulating information which their master hoped to use to persuade the King into a full-scale purge of heretics at court. They went on to the offensive, complained to the Council of harassment and instigated their own inquiry into their persecutors. They discovered papers

among the which they found certain of the privy chamber indicted, with other the king's officers, with their wives; that is to say, Sir Thomas Caradine, Sir Philip Hoby, with both their ladies, Master Edmund Harman, Master Thomas Weldon, with Snowball and his wife. All these they had indicted by the force of the Six Articles . . . And besides them, they had indicted for heresy (some for one thing and some for another) a great number more of the king's true and faithful subjects.[56]

The end of the affair was that the witchfinders ended up in jail on charges of perjury. Dr London died in the Fleet and Germaine Gardiner was executed for treason because of his clandestine contact with Cardinal Pole.

This was exactly the kind of religious purge that Cromwell had so much objected to and had tried to forestall in Calais. He understood, and Henry was now coming to understand, that once an inquisition is set in motion there is no stopping it. It is as disruptive of social order as the unchecked spread of heresy – and in most cases more so. When the hounds of Catholic truth came sniffing through his own household Henry knew that the time had come to call a halt.

A few months later, parliament (always antipathetic to clerical heresy hunts) was easily induced to pass an Act to prevent 'secret and untrue accusations and presentments . . . maliciously conspired against the king's subjects'. The new legislation imposed strict limitations on the operation of the Act of Six Articles.

And Henry had no need of distractions. More important matters were on his mind. He had married again and he was planning his first continental war in twenty years.

CHAPTER 32

A Lion in the Daniels' Den

There was not a dry eye in the house. It was Christmas Eve 1545 and the King had come, in person, to deliver the closing speech to parliament. He moved with difficulty, leaning on his attendants, a hugely overweight hulk, now and then wincing involuntarily at the pain in his leg. Many of the Lords and Commons there assembled must have wondered whether they were looking at their sovereign for the last time. The sight of this huge, fearful personality caged within an ailing body was affecting and it added poignancy to the message Henry Tudor had come to deliver, for he was there not to roar imperious commands but to plead, with tears in his eyes.

My loving subjects, study and take pains to amend one thing which surely is amiss and far out of order, to the which I most heartily require you, which is that charity and concord is not amongst you, but discord and dissensions beareth rule in every place . . . what love and charity is amongst you when the one calleth the other heretic and anabaptist, and he calleth him again papist, hypocrite and pharisee? Be these tokens of charity amongst you? Are these the signs of fraternal love between you? . . . I see and hear daily of you of the clergy who preach one against another, teach one contrary to another, inveigh one against another without charity or discretion . . . all men almost be in variety and discord and few or more preach truly and sincerely the word of God, according as they ought to do. How can poor souls live in concord when you preachers sow amongst them in your sermons debate and discord? To you they look for light, and you bring them darkness. Amend these crimes I exhort you and set forth God's word both by true preaching and good example-giving, or else I, whom God hath appointed his Vicar and high minister here, will see those divisions removed and those enormities corrected, according to my very duty, or else I shall be accounted an unprofitable servant and untrue officer . . . you of the temporality be not clean and unspotted of malice and envy, for you rail on bishops, speak slanderously of priests, and rebuke and taunt preachers, both contrary to good order and Christian fraternity. If you know surely that a bishop or preacher careth or teacheth perverse doctrine, come and declare it to some of our Council, or to us, to whom is committed by God the high authority to reform and order such causes and behaviour, and be not judges of your own fantastical opinions and vain expositions, for in such high cases you may lightly err. And although you be permitted to read Holy Scripture, and to have the word of God in your mother tongue, you must understand that you have this licence only to inform your own conscience, and to instruct your children and family, and not to dispute and make Scripture a railing and a taunting stock against priests and preachers as many light persons do. I am very sorry to know and hear how unreverently that most precious jewel, the word of God, is disputed, rhymed, sung and jangled in every alehouse and tavern, contrary to the true meaning and doctrine of the same. And yet I am ever as much sorry that the readers of the same follow it doing so faintly and coldly. For of this I am sure: that charity was never so faint amongst you and virtuous and godly living was never less used, nor God himself amongst Christians never less reverenced, honoured or served. Therefore, as I said before, be in charity one with another, like brother and brother. Love, dread and serve God (to which I, as your Supreme Head and sovereign lord, exhort and require you) and then I doubt not the love and league . . . shall never be dissolved or broken between us.[57]

The King's words were an acknowledgement of failure. He had for years assumed that he could dictate what his subjects believed. He had freed them from papal diktat in order to impose his own. But he had also given them the open Bible and with it the right of appeal to a higher authority in matters of faith. He had set his bishops to produce successive drafts explaining the 'English position' on the Church's central doctrines only to discover that there were irreconcilable differences among the occupants of the episcopal bench. Much blood had been shed and flesh burned in demonstrations of what opinions were unacceptable in Henry's realm but persecution had only fertilised extremism. As he approached the end of his reign the King had to acknowledge that he was bequeathing his son a divided nation.

Those who lived above England's political snowline were already focusing their thoughts on the succession. It seemed increasingly likely that young Edward would still be a minor when he ascended his father's throne. This would invest with real power those called upon to rule in the boy-king's name. Theoretically, at least, it would provide the opportunity once and for all to settle the religious issue. Depending on which faction controlled the Council at the vital moment of transition, the English Reformation would be either overthrown or brought to a glorious conclusion. For that reason the infighting in government circles became more vicious and determined. The one place above all other where Henry's plea for peace and reconciliation went unheeded was in his own entourage.

In the final struggle the evangelicals emerged triumphant and that for a reason which can be simply stated. As we have seen over and again, access to the King's person was vital for anyone wishing to gain or retain royal favour. Henry was always susceptible to the personal approach. He could be cajoled, flattered, persuaded. Draconian decisions were always relayed via others. He found it difficult to be harsh to suitors face-to-face. In the closing years of the reign, when an ailing monarch spent more and more time in his own apartments, fewer and fewer people had regular access to him. Those who had included his wife, his physicians, his archbishop and the gentlemen of his Privy Chamber. Most of them were of the new persuasion in religion. That is why, as we shall see, the conservatives made one last desperate attack on them in 1546. Issues might be debated and policy decisions made in Council where Norfolk, Gardiner, Wriothesley and their allies wielded considerable influence but everything could be changed by a few whispered words at the royal bedside or a discussion over the card table during one of Henry's sleepless nights.

Henry's renewed warmongering and his final marriage were closely bound up together. Deprived of a Wolsey or a Cromwell to urge upon him forcefully and cogently the benefits of peace and reverting to the old policy of playing on Habsburg–Valois rivalry, he decided in the summer of 1542 to join Charles V in a mutual aggression pact against France. To prevent his enemy reactivating the 'auld alliance' he ordered a pre-emptive strike against Scotland. In October the Duke of Norfolk led an army across the border on an invasion designed to strike fear into the hearts of James V and his captains. The result was a repeat performance of some of Howard's military exploits in earlier years. All he could manage was a six-day raid and the burning of a few villages. As usual, he found other people and circumstances to blame – bad weather, illness and inadequate supplies – for his failure to deliver the dramatic blow the King had demanded. As usual, he wrote to conciliar colleagues (Wriothesley and Gardiner) to intercede with the King and assuage his disappointment. Unfortunately for the Duke, his ineffectiveness was shown up a month later when the Scots made a retaliatory raid and were, without Howard's aid, routed at Solway Moss with a vastly outnumbered force.

During the campaign one of the courtier-magnates, William, Lord Parr, had quitted himself well and Henry designated him to take over as Lord Warden of the Scottish Marches the following spring. Parr was very much upwardly mobile. He held land in Cumberland and had also recently been appointed to the post of Captain of the Gentlemen Pensioners, a prestigious personal bodyguard which came into being as part of Cromwell's household reorganisation of 1539–40. Parr was ordered to court at the end of 1542 to share the celebrations of the victory and instructed to bring his sister with him. Catherine Parr, or Lady Latimer as she was then, was about thirty and recently widowed for the second time. Almost immediately Henry began to pay court to her. Whether there was anything in his motive beyond his desire for a female companion we cannot know but cool calculation might have suggested that a mature, pious woman, not connected to one of the great noble clans, who had already cared for two aged husbands, had distinct advantages over some of Henry's earlier brides. Like the Seymours, the Parrs were his creations. They had no power base of their own and no commitment to any religious bloc. Therefore, the King could rely on their loyalty to his person. Henry and Catherine were married on 12 July 1543. William Parr had already been admitted to the Council. In December he was – somewhat ominously – created Earl of Essex.

The body of Henry's advisers was taking on a new shape. The Earl of Hertford, who soon enhanced his reputation by military exploits in Scotland, was the leader of the younger members which now included Parr and John Dudley. The latter, the stepson of Arthur Plantagenet, who died in the Tower in March 1542, was elevated to the peerage as Viscount Lisle in succession to the unfortunate Deputy of Calais. He, too, had emerged with honour from the northern campaign and was now Lord Admiral. The attendance of the 'old hands' was sporadic. Suffolk only came to the capital for short periods. Gardiner was often employed abroad. Norfolk was frequently absent on military duties and, in any case, was keeping a low profile after the Catherine Howard debacle. Matters were made worse for him early in 1543 by the behaviour of his son. Surrey and some of his cronies went on a drunken rampage through London, breaking windows and overturning market stalls. More dangerously, he allowed the beer to loosen his tongue and was reported by a serving girl as boasting of his lineage and suggesting that if anything happened to His Majesty he should become king. On this occasion he escaped with a spell in prison for hooliganism but his enemies took note of his treasonable utterances for further use. According to the Spanish ambassador the most assiduous attenders at the Council board and the ones who wielded the most influence were Wriothesley and William Fitzwilliam, Earl of Southampton. Fitzwilliam died in October 1542 and thereafter, in Chapuys's words, Wriothesley 'almost governed everything'. His plans were unfolding very satisfactorily. Now he was taking a leaf from his mentor's book and using the secretaryship as a stepping stone to the control of government business. He was intelligent enough and pragmatic enough to realise that the new-style Privy Council could not work without a strong hand to guide it. He had already emerged as more important than his colleague, Ralph Sadler, and, on 1 January 1544, he seemed to be following in Cromwell's footsteps when he was granted a peerage as Baron Wriothesley of Titchfield. Four months later, when Thomas Audley died, he took over as Lord Chancellor. Wriothesley was achieving his ambitions. The game plan was working.

All the government's efforts were now concentrated on the war and rivalries were set aside in the interests of national unity. Henry, determined to make doubly sure of Scotland, despatched Hertford and Lisle with 16,000 men and instructions to sack Edinburgh. Though doubting the political wisdom of this overkill, the commanders carried out their orders with ruthless efficiency, tearing down the walls of the city, devastating the port of Leith, harrying the land between there and the border and sowing a decade and more of ill will.

At the beginning of June embarkation for France began. The plan agreed between Henry and the Emperor was for a joint march on Paris but, as in previous combined military operations, the conflicting aims of the participants vitiated any possibility of common goals being achieved. Henry was determined to add to his mainland possessions and ordered his senior generals to invest important towns near Calais. Suffolk was assigned Boulogne and captured it with relative ease in time for Henry to stage a ceremonial entrance. Norfolk settled to the siege of Montreuil and made a hash of it. To be fair his task was difficult to the point of impossibility: the town occupied a strong position and his force was inadequate. More irritations were to follow as Howard tried to fulfil the wishes of his exacting sovereign. Henry was hugely pleased with his conquest of Boulogne and not prepared to put it at risk by leaving it undermanned in order to meet up with the Emperor for a march on Paris. Angry that his ally had reneged on their agreed strategy, Charles made a separate peace with the French King. Not a whit dismayed, Henry sailed home leaving instructions for Suffolk and Norfolk (who had just made a difficult and hazardous retreat from Montreuil) to put Boulogne in good defensive order and hold it through the winter. The Dukes were dismayed. The walls of the port were too battered to be rapidly made secure and their depleted forces were weakened by disease and malnutrition. The commanders withdrew the bulk of their forces to Calais and from there began sending them back across the Channel. The King was furious but his generals had no alternative but to ride out the storm. Once again Norfolk had to write to his master to make a grovelling confession of his failure and to beg for royal clemency. For weeks Howard and his colleagues lived in fear that the French would retake Boulogne. Had that happened Henry's generals might well have chosen to remain in exile rather than face the penalty for yielding up the King's town to the King's enemies. Fortunately for them, the Dauphin was too timid to venture an assault on Boulogne. It had all been, like Henry's earlier military adventures, expensive and unglorious but the man who had come away from it with the least honour was the Duke of Norfolk. Yet if he lacked the physical stamina and mental agility of his fellow commanders he had some excuse – he was seventy-one years of age.

The era of the new men had arrived, a fact confirmed in August 1545 by the death of that other veteran of Henry's wars, Charles Brandon. When a French fleet threatened the south coast it was Lord Lisle who chivvied them along the Channel. When the Scots proved troublesome it was the Earl of Hertford who was despatched to the border. When a commander was needed to defend Henry's French possessions the choice fell – somewhat surprisingly – upon Lord Surrey. Perhaps Henry decided that he needed a leader of panache to impress his enemy with the vigour and determination of English manhood. Young Henry Howard certainly did that. Regardless of expense he used Calais and Boulogne as bases for a series of impulsive raids into the surrounding territory. Surrey's exploits considerably cheered the King's cheerless days but they were of little comfort to his father who, in common with the civilian members of the Council, was convinced that the recent conquests were indefensible in the long run and did not want to see the Howard dynasty associated with failed policies. 'Have yourself in await that ye animate the king too much for the keeping of Boulogne; for who doth so at length shall get small thanks,' he cautioned.[58] Norfolk and his colleagues had with great difficulty been trying to persuade the King to put Boulogne on the negotiating table in order to reach a swift peace with France but, as he complained to Surrey, what progress we make in six days 'ye with your letters set back in six hours'.[59]

The King's senior advisers were in desperate straits. It seemed that the conditions which had characterised the early years of the reign were repeating themselves: a king hungry for glory and international renown was lending his support to adventurous young men who were running through all the government's ready cash at an alarming rate. In November Wriothesley and the new Secretary, William Paget, fell out because the former could not raise money that the King wanted and the latter had to report this failure to the King. Still smarting from Henry's reaction to the news, Paget wrote to the Chancellor in great anger. Yet no amount of royal or secretarial wrath could stop the nation's bankruptcy, as Wriothesley pointed out:

touching the Mint we be now so far out with that, if you take any penny more from it these three months . . . you shall utterly destroy the trade of it . . . as to the Augmentations it shall not be able to pay the £5,000 . . . yet these six days . . . And of the revenue . . . there is yet to come in . . . £15,000 or £16,000, but when we shall have it, God knoweth. As to the Tenth and Firstfruits, there remains not due above £10–12,000, which is not payable till after Christmas . . . The Exchequer shall not be able to minister above £10,000 (and that at Candlemass) of the remainder of the subsidy. The Surveyors Court owes so much that when all shall be come in that is due to it . . . they shall not be able to render up . . . more than £5,000 or £6,000; and when that shall be, God knoweth. So that, if you tarry for more money to be sent to Boulogne at this time, you may perhaps tarry too long, before you have the sum desired . . . I assure you, Master Secretary, I am at my wits' end how we shall possibly shift for three months following, and especially for the next two. For I see not any great likelihood, that any good sum will come in till after Christmas . . .[60]

The general despair in government circles was summed up by Bishop Gardiner in November:

We are at war with France and Scotland, we have enmity with the bishop of Rome, we have no assured friendship . . . with the Emperor and we have received from the Landgrave [of Hesse], chief captain of the Protestants, such displeasure that he has cause to think us angry with him . . . Our war is noisome to our realm and to all our merchants that traffic through the Narrow Seas . . . We are in a world where reason and learning prevail not and covenants are little regarded.[61]

Since religion and politics were always intertwined the national crisis had a profound effect upon the Reformation debate at all levels of society. The fear of invasion, the absence of thousands of able-bodied men on military service, the disruption of trade and the shortage of food aroused widespread discontent, much of which was channelled into xenophobic fury against the enemy and those within the country who were thought to be France's 'Catholic' supporters. Anticlericalism and, with it, evangelical fervour swept the southern counties. On 18 August, Lord Russell reported to his colleagues:

This morning I received a letter from Sir John Horsey [Sheriff of Dorset and Somerset] signifying that in divers places about Sherborne and in the town of Sherborne also commandment was brought from place to place by men of honesty, as is supposed, to the constables and tithingmen in the said parishes, that the houses of priests should be diligently searched, and all kinds of weapons, books, letters and spits (wherewith they roast their meat) should be put in safe keeping. Because this was obviously done without the commandment of the king or Council I thought it good and necessary immediately to address my letters to Sir John Horsey . . . desiring him . . . to use all diligence for the . . . finding out of those which are the beginners and setters on of the said search.[62]

In London the universal anxiety and discontent, the particular dissatisfaction of the merchants and the patriotic hatred of the leading Catholic nations disposed many, who in normal times would have disdained 'heretics', to read banned books and attend the sermons of suspect preachers. Th ex-Bishops Latimer and Shaxton had returned and were once more occupying City pulpits. Fashionable congregations gathered to hear Dr Edward Crome thunder from the pulpit of St Mary Aldermary. At St Bride's in Fleet Street, the vicar, John Cardmaker (alias Taylor), was attracting eager listeners to his doctrine of the mass and his occasional attacks on Gardiner and Bonner. The curate of St Catherine Coleman, the fiery Scot Sir William Whitehead, was one of the many outspoken priests and friars who had been forced to flee across the border by persecution in his native land. But licensed preachers were not the only – and, indeed, not the main – exponents of religious novelties in London. Throughout the city there were many groups meeting, some in secret, others more openly, for Bible study and discussion. Many of these groups were socially very mixed and for this, government legislation was in part to blame. The conservative bishops had succeeded in having an act passed forbidding men below the rank of gentleman to read the English Bible. One result was that zealous students, courtiers, lawyers and merchants had turned 'gospellers', reading and expounding the Bible to eager listeners in tavern backrooms and church crypts from Newgate to the Tower. When, in November, Wriothesley got to hear that heretical literature was being circulated, and instigated a search, he began to receive threatening letters:

> Master Secretary, I send unto you herewith a bill, which was let fall yesterday, as I was going to mass, in my dining chamber. I pray you show it to His Highness and discover his pleasure, what he would should be done about it. You know that when those naughty books were brought unto me, I could do not less than send them to His Highness, and also labour, as much as I could, to find out the author; wherein, though I have not much prevailed, yet some people be angry with my doing. Upon your answer of His Majesty's pleasure, I shall do as the same shall command me. I pray you return the bill again to me.[63]

Foreign policy, religious affairs and national well-being could not be disassociated. In October the Council persuaded Henry to make a new alliance with Charles V. At the same time Gardiner drafted a new anti-heresy bill which would make a good impression on the Emperor and show that England was no longer paying court to the German Protestant princes. In any event, such a bill was introduced into parliament during November. By then, however, Gardiner had departed to lead the English delegation at the Imperial court, and was not available to press the new legislation through. Furthermore the initial talks with Charles's representatives were going badly and it may be that Henry's enthusiasm for the alliance had temporarily waned. Certainly he made no attempt to influence the parliamentary debate. The result was that the bill was dutifully passed in the Lords but resoundingly defeated by the Commons. The frustrated conservatives on the Council felt control slipping away from them and the nation sliding into anarchy. What made their position particularly difficult was the growing dominance at court of an alliance of warlike younger men and pious evangelicals. When Henry went across the Channel on campaign in the summer of 1544 Queen Catherine was left behind as Regent, the principal members of her Council, with Wriothesley, were Cranmer and Hertford. But it was not just the leading officials with whose influence the conservative faction had to contend; many of Henry's closest attendants were tainted with opinions and attitudes that Gardiner, Norfolk and Wriothesley could only deplore.

The King's physicians were in daily attendance. They were Sir William Butts (until his death in November 1545) and Robert Huick. Both were highly respected and learned men who espoused advanced opinions. Butts, particularly, was a courtier who stood high in the King's favour and who never failed to use his influence on behalf of evangelicals. In 1543, when the Council proceedings against Cranmer were in hand and the dejected Archbishop was being carefully cold-shouldered by everyone who believed his downfall was imminent, it was Dr Butts who openly showed his continued friendship for the prelate and went in person to the King to protest at the humiliations being heaped on Cranmer by his fellow councillors. Later in the same year he sued to Henry on behalf of Richard Turner, an obscure priest of Kent, marked out by the Catholic leaders for destruction under the Act of Six Articles. Not even Cranmer, the man's diocesan bishop, dared to intercede for him. Butts, hearing of the matter from Cranmer's secretary, Ralph Morice, came to the King in his Privy Chamber, while he was being shaved by his barber. When Butts had explained the situation, Henry, without further enquiry, ordered the proceedings against Turner to be halted. Huick, a doctor equal to his colleague in learning and in boldness, was less admirable in other ways. Stubborn in all his opinions, of a biting wit and abusive in argument, he was not an easy man to get on with. He was a regular member of Dr Crome's congregation and an enthusiastic supporter of the opinions for which that cleric occasionally found himself in trouble. In religion, as in all matters, Huick was psychologically incapable of keeping his views to himself.

The King's court favourites included at least three men of advanced religious views. Sir Anthony Denny (knighted after the siege of Boulogne in September 1544), a scholar and soldier, was a man much after Henry's heart and was frequently seen in his company. He was chief gentleman of the Privy Chamber and also a privy councillor.

Another known radical was the King's 'little pig', George Blagge. He, too, was a soldier and had for many years been a comrade-in-arms of the Earl of Surrey. Perhaps it was Blagge who tempted the Earl to flirt with Lutheranism.

Yet another gentleman who, in 1544, was but newly established in the royal favour but was clearly up-and-coming was Sir William Herbert. At forty-two Herbert had put a headstrong youth behind him and, as a result of sterling military service, had already been advanced to the royal favour, before the great stroke of good fortune which befell him in 1543. He had earlier married Anne, daughter of Sir Thomas Parr. In July 1543 he therefore found himself brother-in-law to the King, when his wife's elder sister became Queen. Anne Herbert was appointed the Queen's chief lady-in-waiting, while lands and honours were showered on her husband. William Herbert and his wife were both followers of the New Learning and perhaps already had a strong leaning towards the new trends in continental Protestantism represented by John Calvin. Herbert was a patron of one of the most ardent proselytisers in Henry VIII's retinue. This was Edward Underhill, one of the band of Gentleman Pensioners and already known as a 'hot-gospeller'.

Herbert, Denny, Butts, Huick, Blagge, Underhill, Lascelles, Caradine, Hoby – these were but a few members of the King's entourage known to be infected with the new religious opinions. There were many others among the lesser court officers and satellites. The fact that the King was surrounded by so many men of the new persuasion is indicative not of a change in Henry's beliefs but of the incredibly rapid spread of a new, critical and inquisitive attitude to religion among the educated and influential classes. Henry tolerated 'heretics' at court because he liked to have around him bright young men capable of sustaining a lively academic debate. As for his own opinions, they moved slowly, and unpredictably.

The intellectual powerhouse of the royal court was to be found in the Queen's chambers. Catherine Parr did not come to her throne with any pronounced evangelical views. Henry would certainly not have selected an obviously partisan wife. She was closely related to the Catholic Throckmortons and the fact that Gardiner, rather than Cranmer, presided at her wedding to Henry may suggest that the Bishop heartily approved of her. Catherine was not the prudish bluestocking she has sometimes been presented as but she was certainly a well-read woman who inclined to humanistic studies and enjoyed stimulating debate. As a result of discussions with members of her entourage and the influence of clerics like Latimer who were engaged to preach before her, she moved, with surprising rapidity, to an evangelical position. Writing to the heads of Cambridge University in 1546, she declared, in the words of St Paul, 'I am not ashamed of the Gospel.' It is more than possible that Cranmer either inspired or encouraged the Queen's conversion seeing in her a patroness of the reformed faith who, like Anne Boleyn, would be in a position to advance the cause very considerably.

In the privileged atmosphere of the Queen's chambers religious novelties became the major topic of debate. Catherine Parr met frequently with her ladies and courtiers for Bible study and to listen to sermons from her chaplains and visiting preachers. In 1543 John Parkhurst, Charles Brandon's outspoken chaplain and a former member of Cromwell's intellectual circle, was preferred by his patroness, the Duchess of Suffolk, to the Queen's service. Parkhurst now became an important influence at court and never failed in his preaching to assert the importance of personal religion as against Catholic 'superstition'. Though Anne Herbert was the Queen's chief lady-in-waiting, it was Catherine Brandon, Duchess of Suffolk, who was the dominant personality in Catherine Parr's entourage. This vivacious twenty-five-year-old, half-Spanish *femme formidable* was quite irrepressible. She was lively and humorous in company but, as a contemporary remarked of her, 'It is a pity that so goodly a wit waiteth upon so froward a will.'[64] She was merciless in venting her sarcasm on people she disapproved of. For instance, she kept at court a pet dog, which she named 'Gardiner'. Nor had her 'victims' any redress. As wife of one of the most powerful men in the realm and as a firm favourite with the King and Queen, Catherine Brandon was hard to attack.

Most of Catherine Parr's other ladies were also evangelical sympathisers. Anne, Countess of Hertford, was a proud and quarrelsome beauty, who, as Seymour's wife and confidante of the Queen, gave herself airs and made many enemies – 'You your friends do threaten still with war,' as Surrey described her in a poem.[65] There were Lady Denny and Jane Fitzwilliam, third wife of Sir William Fitzwilliam, alderman of London, a close friend of Lord Russell. There was Anne, Countess of Sussex, whose differences of opinion with her husband, Henry Ratcliffe, on matters of religion were soon to lead to an estrangement. There were Jane Dudley, wife of the Lord Admiral and Maud Lane, widow of Sir Ralph Lane and the Queen's cousin.

The changed atmosphere at court had a direct impact on policy. Cranmer worked quietly and persistently on his reform programme. As Henry's trusted adviser on Church affairs he was able, as a result of private discussions, to obtain the endorsement of the Head of the Church to various measures. The first English-language services were introduced in 1544. The following year Cranmer issued the *King's Primer*, a vernacular devotional book, intended to replace the plethora of Catholic and Protestant manuals in circulation. Further ordinances were issued against superstitious practices, which were now redefined to include all over-elaborate worship. The composition of parliament changed and new recruits to the Commons included several evangelicals, some of them from the royal household. The Act restricting heresy prosecutions passed, despite fierce episcopal opposition, because the King's direct intervention ensured its passage through the Lords, and a new measure against banned books was defeated in December 1545.

The conservatives were losing ground on all fronts and the King's health was deteriorating. If they were to prevent the complete overthrow of the kind of England they believed in they would have to strike fast and strike boldly. There could be only one target. They dared not launch another attack on Cranmer. They would have to bring down the Queen and hope that all their high-placed enemies would fall with her. With a singular lack of imagination or with a conviction that what had worked before would work again, they relied on tactics that had been used to pluck down other men and women in whom Henry had placed trust. The principal activists in the plot were Wriothesley, Gardiner and Rich, backed up by Bishop Bonner and their determined (at times frenzied) activities involved investigations at court and in the City. It is no coincidence that this was precisely the period that Hertford and Lisle were out of the country negotiating the longed-for peace with France.

Like Thomas More before him, Lord Chancellor Wriothesley used his position to keep a close watch on suspected heretics. Among those he had arrested in recent months was Sir Peter Carew, MP for Tavistock, who had not long before been knighted for his service in the war. But the person who was to become his most famous victim was far less exalted. Anne Ayscough (married name Kyme) was the daughter of a prominent Lincolnshire gentleman who had already been in trouble for 'gospelling' – reading and commenting on the Bible to groups of illiterate enthusiasts. She had connections with heretical cells in London and also moved in court circles, for one of her brothers was a member of the Gentleman Pensioners. Wriothesley employed one Wadloe, a cursitor in Chancery, to spy on the lady and, as a result of what he discovered, Anne was arrested, tried by Bonner and, after a recantation of sorts had been extracted from her, she was sent back to the Midlands. Because of her social standing the Bishop had no desire to handle her severely. This occurred during the last days of March, a week after Gardiner's return home from a mission to the Emperor.

Gardiner was less squeamish. He decided to employ the same tactics against court evangelicals that he had used effectively against Cromwell. He had managed to associate the minister's name with that of a condemned heretic, Robert Barnes. This time the Bishop had Dr Crome, the popular and well-connected preacher, arrested and examined by the Council in early May. It was Wriothesley, by now an expert in interrogation techniques, who examined him – with gratifying results.

This Doctor Crome, after his committing, while he was in the ward at Greenwich, in the court under my Lord Chancellor, accused divers persons as well of the court as of the city, with other persons in the country, which put many persons to great trouble, and some suffered death after.[66]

Among those implicated by Crome's confession were Dr Huick and John Lascelles, who had been a marked man ever since the exposure of Catherine Howard. On 17 May they were sent to the Tower.

The hunt for heretics was swiftly taken up beyond the capital. On 15 May Bonner, who had wasted no time in holding Six Articles commissions in his diocese, reported to the King that four men and one woman had been found guilty of heresy in Essex and wished to know if public example might be made of them. But Henry refused to give the persecutors carte blanche. He ordered that two men, who had repented, were to be released. The remainder were to be burned at Colchester and two other places – but, unless 'a general infection' was apparent or any others were 'notably detected', the commissioners were to dissolve their assembly 'until a more commodious time'.[67] However, one of the radicals who was brought back for further examination was Anne Ayscough.

Meanwhile, the plotters had begun to spin the web that would, they hoped, entangle the Queen. Rumours were abroad – inevitably – that Henry VIII's latest marriage was falling apart. The Imperial ambassador, Francis van der Delft, eagerly passed on the gossip:

> Some attribute it to the sterility of the present queen, while others say that there will be no change during the present war. Madame Suffolk is much talked about and in great favour, but the king shows no alteration in his demeanour to the queen, although she is said to be annoyed by the rumour.[68]

The ambassador's assessment was almost certainly correct. Henry was an impossible man to live with and Catherine must have had to endure frequent outbursts of temper but there is no evidence of serious estrangement on the part of the royal couple. However, Henry did enjoy the company of other women, especially vivacious women like Lady Suffolk, and this encouraged Gardiner and Co. to hope – and plot. They planned to dangle some attractive woman before the King at the same time as they planted in his mind suspicions against his wife. There was no question of impugning the Queen's sexual reputation but if they could demonstrate that Catherine was a heretic, as they had done with Cromwell, that would serve just as well. The first part of the plan suffered a setback when the projected 'bait' – Norfolk's daughter, the Duchess of Richmond – screamed that she would rather cut her own throat than be a party to such villainy. But this was no reason to abandon the whole strategy and the plotters watched for their chance.

Their opportunity came one evening around 13 June. The royal couple were together in the King's chambers and Bishop Gardiner was among the others present. The conversation turned to religious matters as it often did and the Queen spoke with firmness and conviction. Abruptly Henry, 'contrary unto his manner', changed the subject. Although he gave no other sign of displeasure this action 'somewhat amazed the queen' and was well noted by Gardiner. Shortly afterwards Catherine and her companions withdrew. When she was out of earshot Henry muttered testily to his bishop of Winchester, 'A good hearing it is when women become such clerks, and a thing not much to my comfort, to come in mine old days to be taught by my wife.'

Gardiner seized his opportunity. He warmly agreed with the King and went on to point out the dangers of the opinions stubbornly maintained by the Queen and certain of her ladies. Winchester inveighed against the disruptive elements of evangelicalism:

'. . . the religion by the queen so stiffly maintained,' he said, 'did not only disallow and dissolve the policy and politic government of princes, but also taught the people that all things ought to be in common. So that what beliefs soever they pretended to hold, their opinions were indeed so odious, and for the Prince's estate so perilous that (saving the reverence they bear unto her for his Majesty's sake) the Council was bold to affirm that the greatest subject in this land, speaking those words that she did speak, and defending likewise those arguments that she did defend, had with impartial justice by law deserved death.'[69]

The Bishop had correctly judged Henry's changeable temper and caught him in one of his insecure, suspicious moods. He continued to play on Henry's vanity and apprehensions until he had received permission to make enquiries into the conduct and beliefs of the Queen, her ladies and certain others who had care of the young Prince. Hitherto, as in their examination of Crome, they had only dared to obtain information about and proceed against lesser persons connected with the court. With the King's warrant, the faction could proceed uninhibited. They were now at the height of their power. Wriothesley, Rich and Gardiner held the initiative. They continued their inquisition at all levels of society, from journeyman to courtier, from country priest to the Queen of England herself.

The conspirators first attempted an oblique attack on the Queen, through her ladies-in-waiting.

They thought it best, at first, to begin with some of those ladies, whom they knew to be great with her and of her blood. The chiefest whereof, as most of estimation, and privy to all her doings were these:

the Lady Herbert, afterwards Countess of Pembroke, and sister to the queen, and chief of her privy chamber; the Lady Lane, being of her privy chamber, and also her cousin germane; the Lady Tyrrwhit, of her privy chamber.[70]

This was where, Wriothesley suggested, Mistress Ayscough could be useful to them. Following fresh examination she had been pronounced a sacramentary and sentenced to the stake. On 29 June she was taken, not to Newgate, which was conveniently near the execution site in Smithfield, but to the Tower. There she was examined by Wriothesley, Rich and Sir John Baker, Chancellor of the Exchequer. Hour after hour they assaulted her with questions about the prominent people who had succoured her in prison. What could she tell them, they asked, of Lady Suffolk, Lady Sussex, Lady Hertford, Lady Lisle, Lady Denny and Lady Fitzwilliam? Had she received help from members of the Council? Anne remained stubbornly silent. In anger and desperation her tormentors decided to employ other methods to make Anne talk. The Lieutenant of the Tower, Sir Anthony Knyvet, was sent for and ordered to have the rack prepared.

The prisoner was strapped to the machine and Knyvet instructed the operator just to 'pinch' her, and frighten her into telling what she knew. It is no wonder that the Lieutenant was nervous. He was facing something that was not only an inhuman outrage; it was also illegal. In the interests of the state, the bounds of Tudor law were not infrequently overstepped within the stony secrecy of the Tower. The rack, however, was reserved for male felons and traitors, and they were for the most part persons of no social status. It was illegal to rack a woman and unthinkable so to torture a gentlewoman. Only some high cause of national security could possibly justify such a breach of law and human decency. Certainly it could not be excused in the interests of furthering a faction struggle. The councillors fired more questions at Anne – to no effect.

Knyvet had had enough. He signed to the gaoler to ease the pressure and release her. Angrily Wriothesley turned on him. What did the Lieutenant think he was doing? They were not finished with Mistress Ayscough yet. She must be stretched again. Knyvet anxiously pointed out that this was illegal. The Lord Chancellor's voice was raised in anger. He ordered Sir Anthony to do as he was bid. Knyvet refused. This, protested Wriothesley, was disobedience against the King who should not fail to hear of it. Sir Anthony was still not cowed. He had no authority to rack this woman and he would not be responsible for giving any such order. What happened next shocked and frightened even a seasoned soldier like Knyvet: Wriothesley and Rich, dignified, responsible members of the King's Council, laid aside their gowns, stepped across to the wheel and operated it themselves. So appalled was he that he hurried away and took a barge for Whitehall to disassociate himself from the outrage.

If the King was surprised or angry he did not show it, either then or when the councillors returned to court, still having obtained no information from their victim. Henry was only interested in results. He made his wishes known and left underlings not only to do the dirty work, but also to decide on the methods they employed. Violence was one of the pillars supporting the Henrician regime and a devoted and determined royal servant like Thomas Wriothesley did not flinch from employing it.

Henry must have encouraged his lord chancellor to proceed with his plan against the Queen if the final scene of this bizarre and distasteful episode (triumphantly recorded by John Foxe) is to be believed. A friend went to Catherine by night and told her what was afoot. She carefully chose a moment when her husband was in a good mood and cast herself on his mercy, insisting that she would never presume to offer instruction to her king. If she entered into debate with him it was only to distract him from his pain. It was the familiar story over again: anyone marked out for destruction had to be kept away from Henry. If he or she were allowed to plead in person the King would almost always forgive and forget. Catherine and her husband were reconciled and Henry's hawk-like wrath swooped on another target.

He had arranged for Wriothesley to arrest the Queen in the privy garden and he did not inform the Chancellor of his change of plan. After dinner the following afternoon, he and Catherine were wandering among the flowers and hedgerows when a gate was flung open and Lord Chancellor Wriothesley strutted into the garden, followed by forty of the King's guard. He bowed to the King and held out the warrant for Catherine Parr's arrest. To his surprise, Henry scowled and drew him aside almost (but, apparently, not quite) out of earshot of the Queen. Wriothesley fell on his knees and reminded the King of the agreed arrangements for Catherine's apprehension. He must have known something had gone very wrong before Henry opened his mouth to berate him as 'Knave! Arrant knave, beast and fool!'.

Had the Chancellor and his friends, Henry wished to know, nothing better to do than ferret out information against a lady who surpassed them all in virtue? The King swiftly terminated the brief interview with the command, 'Avaunt my sight!', turned his back on the confused Wriothesley, and returned, all smiles, to the Queen.[71] Shortly afterwards Henry extended his protection again over George Blagge when the conservatives tried to roast his 'Pig'.

Away from the court the persecution continued. A new proclamation against heretical books was published and ceremonial burnings were held. On 16 July Anne Ayscough and John Lascelles perished in the same fire along with a tailor and a priest. Alarm and despondency spread through the evangelical ranks and on 21 August an English diplomat in Flanders reported:

About 60 Englishmen have fled over here for fear of death . . . so that here are tales of persecution by the bishops, and the king is slandered for suffering it. These things are spoken by the best in the land . . . Also it is said that there are three temporal lords and one knight, with two bishops in England, which are so knit together that they have promised to burn all such as are known to be readers of the Word of God.[72]

But this was the high-water mark of the Catholic reaction. By early August Hertford and Lisle were back on the Council having successfully concluded a much-needed peace. The court had not been purged of evangelicals. Cranmer had been largely instrumental in placing humanistic tutors in Prince Edward's entourage. England's diplomatic isolation had come to an end and with it the need to stage extravagant demonstrations of orthodoxy. With that suddenness which had become the norm in Henrician politics the government's stance changed. When Sir Anthony Denny was given exclusive control of the signature stamp used for authenticating all routine documents the progressives had, to all intents and purposes, won the day. Henry's bouts of illness became more severe and prolonged and the most important political question to be asked was how long his massive ego could cling on to life.

There was, however, one more drama to be played out before the King was obliged to submit to a stronger will than his own – the downfall of the Howards. Norfolk had months before accepted the inevitability of Edward Seymour's ascendancy. Once more he offered Hertford an alliance – a sequence of marriages including that of his daughter, the Duchess of Richmond, to Thomas Seymour, the Earl's brother. Once again it was Surrey who scotched the scheme. Returning from France in June, he was enraged to discover what had been arranged in his absence. One day, in front of a crowded court, he accosted his sister and demanded to know how she dared to contemplate marriage into the upstart Seymour clan. If she wanted power that badly, he suggested, she should become the King's mistress. This embarrassing spectacle put an end to the dynastic negotiations and also to any hope of the Howards remaining a powerful political force in the next reign.

After the debacle Norfolk deliberately kept a low profile. Not so his son. Surrey simply could not conceive of another Tudor taking the throne without a Howard at his right hand. To him it was axiomatic that the only man fit to be regent was the Duke of Norfolk. He was quite incapable of keeping these hubristic views to himself and he cared not what enemies they brought him. In November he fell out with his old friend Sir George Blagge, who reported the Earl's behaviour to Hertford. Seymour grasped his opportunity to get rid of a man who could only be a liability during the reign of a minor. He gathered information and presented it to the King. It amounted to little – boasting of what the Howards would do when they had the management of affairs; quartering the royal arms of Edward the Confessor on his own escutcheon – but it was simplicity itself to dress up gaudy foolishness in the sombre accoutrements of treason. Surrey, Hertford told the King, was planning to seize the person of the Prince without waiting for Henry's death in order to ensure power for the Howards. When Norfolk, agitated beyond measure, wrote to court friends for information, his letters were intercepted and used as evidence that he was in on his son's 'plot'. On 1 December Surrey was arrested and placed in detention at Wriothesley's town mansion. The Lord Chancellor cannot have relished his guardianship of the Earl. Norfolk was his ally and for Hertford he had little but contempt. Over the ensuing days it was at Wriothesley's house that the prisoner's primary examination took place. On 12 December he was marched through the streets to the Tower. A few hours later his father joined him there, having been ceremoniously stripped of his Garter insignia and staffs of office.

Norfolk had been too often instrumental in the destruction of others to be under any illusions about his fate. He wrote desperate letters to the King: 'some great enemy of mine hath informed your Majesty of some untrue matter against me . . . If I knew that I had offended . . . in any point . . . I would declare the same to your Highness . . . whatsoever laws you have in past time made [touching religion] or hereafter shall make, I shall to the extremity of my powers stick to them.'[73] He knew it would avail him nothing. Henry Howard's 'earldom' was only a courtesy title and so he was tried by a jury of East Anglian gentlemen. They knew what was expected of them but, even so, found it hard to reach a verdict. Only when Secretary Paget confronted them with the King's demand for a guilty verdict did all the issues suddenly assume crystal clarity. Surrey was executed on Tower Hill on 19 January 1547.

Disposing of the Duke was more difficult. He was entitled to a trial by his peers and that would have presented his accusers with difficulties. He could have sworn ignorance of his son's treason and the outcome would have been far from certain. In the end he was persuaded to sign a confession and make a grovelling plea for leniency. Like Wolsey and Cromwell, he begged for mercy: 'I most humbly and with most sorrowful and repentant heart beseech his highness to have mercy, pity and compassion upon me . . .'[74] As soon as parliament assembled on 14 January, a Bill of Attainder was presented. On 27 January Wriothesley presided over a joint session of the two houses and announced the royal assent. Thomas Howard, the great survivor, had, at last, reached the end of a long career of cynical self-aggrandisement, time-serving and vindictiveness – or so it seemed.

CHAPTER 33

Long Live the King

In Shakespeare's *Julius Caesar* the eponymous ruler is murdered before the play is halfway done but his shade continues to brood over the fate of his avengers and assassins. So was it with Henry VIII and those who survived him. His children who succeeded him and those who advised them tried to fashion England to their own patterns but they could not escape the outline plan he laid down, the problems he created and the sheer personality he had imposed on Crown–subject relations. The rival dukes of Edward's reign continued the feuds which had developed since 1540. Mary failed to burn evangelicalism out of the English Church. The unfinished business of the Reformation continued to dominate Elizabeth's domestic and foreign policy. Our story is part of that continuum although it does not reach that far forward in time. The three Thomases who survived life in the lion's court were all dead within the next eight years – two of them as a direct result of the changes and chances of the second Tudor's reign.

The formalities of Thomas Howard's attainder were completed on 27 January 1547 and he prepared himself for the execution which he knew must follow within days. His mind must have gone back to his childhood when he had paid visits to his father, incarcerated in the very fortress where he now found himself. When Henry VII had come to the throne the Howard dynasty had seemed doomed. Yet it had risen from the ashes. Through six perilous decades the family's fortunes had been patiently rebuilt. Now, it had all come to nothing. Surely, Norfolk must have thought, there could be no miraculous recovery this time.

Yet, nothing happened. Three days passed and no news arrived from Whitehall. No date was fixed for the execution. Perhaps the prisoner allowed himself to hope that the King had changed his mind. Perhaps he reflected that it was typical of Henry Tudor to keep his victims pondering their fate, uncertain whether a reprieve might be despatched from the court or a token of forgiveness sent by the hand of some royal favourite. This was the way Henry had treated Wolsey, and Cromwell and other erstwhile friends whom he had turned against. Only on 31 January did Howard learn the reason for the delay.

In the early afternoon there was a great commotion outside the Tower – trumpets and cheering crowds and the sound of many horsemen. Did the prisoner guess what it all meant or did he have to wait until someone told him that Henry VIII was dead, and his nine-year-old son proclaimed king as Edward VI and now brought into the palace-fortress to prepare for his coronation in accordance with tradition? The news might not have come as a great relief, for Howard would have known that the real power in the land was vested in Edward Seymour – shortly to become Duke of Somerset – who had little reason not to carry out the sentence already passed upon the traitor. But the days lengthened into weeks and the weeks into months. Soon it was spring.

We are not told whether Norfolk wept at the news of his master's death. If he did shed tears they were probably tears of relief. We do know that the other two Thomases aired their grief in public. Cranmer was with his king at the end. He had steered clear of the political manoeuvrings at the year's end but returned to court in time to do his duty in voting on the Howard Attainder Bill. Sometime after midnight on 28 January he was sent for to come to the King's bedside. When no one else dared to mention it Sir Anthony Denny had told Henry to prepare for his end and the dying monarch had asked for the only man he had ever fully trusted and respected. He was past speech when Cranmer arrived but was able feebly to grasp the Archbishop's hand. At the end there was no master and servant, no prince and churchman; just a priest preparing a departing soul for eternity. Cranmer begged Henry to give a sign that he trusted Christ for salvation and, in response, he felt the grip on his hand tighten slightly. It was an evangelical departure: no anointing; no reading of Latin prayers; just a simple acknowledgement of the all-sufficient atoning work of Christ. Cranmer would have been glad at that.

That leave-taking goes to the heart of the relationship between the King and the Archbishop. Whatever else it was it was that of a believing sinner and his priest. When Cranmer bent to his master's will, even to the point of going against his own conscience, he displayed both weakness and pragmatism. When he adduced scriptural proofs to support marriage annulments or the claim to headship of the Church he strained intellectual honesty beyond the limit. When he indulged in the obligatory sycophancy of a courtier he came close to putting Henry in the place of God. But always he was motivated by loyalty and affection for the King which was as real as – and sometimes in competition with – his passion to purify the English Church. His grief at Henry's death was genuine. Ever afterwards he allowed his beard to grow and it was said that he did so in memory of the King.

His biographer suggests that the beard may rather have been a sign of solidarity with the continental reformers among whom hirsuitness was in fashion. However much Cranmer missed the old King, the change of regime came as a relief. With Seymour as Protector and an evangelical majority on the Council he could press ahead more rapidly with the work of reform. He and his lay supporters carried through over the next seven years 'a religious revolution of ruthless thoroughness'.[75] His domestic life also became much more agreeable. He could now live openly with his wife and his children, for one of the first tasks of Edward's first parliament was the repealing of the Act of Six Articles.

On the morning of 31 January Lord Chancellor Wriothesley had tears in his eyes when he announced the death of Henry VIII to parliament. They must have been tears of frustration and apprehension. He knew already that his career had suffered a severe, and perhaps final, setback. During the closing months of the last reign battle lines had been drawn very firmly on the Council table. Lisle was banished from the board after an incident in which he slapped Gardiner's face. But the real animosity was between Wriothesley and Hertford. They conceived for each other a hatred based on clashing ambitions. Wriothesley saw himself being outmanoeuvred: Seymour was intent on assuming power as Protector during the minority of his nephew. With the aid of his shrewd ally, Secretary Paget, who had daily access to the King, he attempted to dominate Council business. Wriothesley saw this as infringement of his position as Lord Chancellor. He opposed the Earl on every possible opportunity and he was certainly not one to mince his words. Paget referred to him as 'stout and arrogant' and Richard Grafton, the evangelical printer/publisher, referred to his 'overmuch repugning [opposing] to the rest in matters of council'.[76] He tried to persuade Henry that his brother-in-law was a dishonest schemer who, by his campaign against the Howards, had already embarked upon a plot to remove everyone who stood in the way of his own advancement to quasi-regal authority. For his part, Hertford resented the power Wriothesley possessed by virtue of his guardianship of the Great Seal. The Lord Chancellor was determined to hold on to this power. He favoured the idea of a council of regency which would not be dominated by a powerful individual. Only as an equal member of such a body could he be sure of holding on to the position he had and, by gaining the confidence of the new King, laying the foundation for further advancement.

Wriothesley was also alarmed about the religious implications of the radical faction having unchecked power in the new reign. The lurch towards religious extremism had been alarming since the last batch of persecutions the previous summer. Gardiner had stupidly got himself banished from court by needlessly annoying the King over a proposed land transaction and there was nobody of a conservative persuasion close enough to Henry to counteract the reformed propaganda being poured into his ears by Cranmer, Catherine and his chamber staff. Unscrupulous manipulators were, it seemed, taking advantage of a sick old man and were bent on gaining control of his young son. Rumour had it that in his last weeks Henry had agreed to sweeping liturgical changes, including the abolition of the mass. The mood among evangelicals in the country, if not farther afield, was buoyant. Van der Delft reported at Christmastide that the majority of the Council had swung in behind Hertford, that the upbringing of Prince Edward would be entrusted to 'heretics' and that 'the majority of the people are of these perverse sects and in favour of getting rid of the bishops and they do not conceal their wish to see Winchester and other adherents of the ancient faith in the Tower with the Duke'.[77]

Wriothesley's worst fears were swiftly realised. Seymour carried out a coup d'état so cleverly that no one except the Lord Chancellor (if we infer correctly from his later conduct) objected. The delay in announcing Henry's death was cautious rather than sinister. It enabled the leaders of government to organise themselves and agree their plans. Specifically it enabled them to consider two documents; the late King's will and a list of promotions Paget had drawn up at Henry's dictation. The will left the care of Edward and the conduct of his government in the hands of sixteen equal executors. The 'book' of promotions awarded titles and lands to those executors and other favoured individuals. Thus, for example, Seymour was to become Duke of Somerset, Lisle Earl of Warwick and Wriothesley Earl of Southampton. Although details of the 'book' were not revealed for a few days the executors knew that substantial rewards were to be announced and when they met on 31 January they were eager to settle amicably the details of their working relationship and glean the fruits of their new dignities. They readily agreed that the new Council would have to have an executive head. This was realistic as had been proved over and again in the previous reign. Two offices were created: Lord Protector of the Realm and Governor of the King's Person. The meeting agreed that both should be vested in the person of Edward Seymour. This Wriothesley objected to, even though a theoretical limitation of the Protector's power was written into the constitution to the effect that he might only act with the agreement of his fellows. Further amendments followed swiftly. By early March Somerset and his supporters had enlarged the body of councillors to twenty-six of which number the Protector had authority 'to choose, name, appoint, use and swear . . . as privy councillors such and so many as he from time to time shall think convenient'.[78] Thus Seymour had set aside Henry's will, taken absolute power for himself and made it clear that anyone who wanted a share in government would have to be loyal to him.

That patently did not include the new Earl of Southampton and Seymour swiftly disposed of him. Wriothesley had proved himself a nuisance, not only by his personal animosity towards the new chief executive, but also by calling into question the legality of the manoeuvres employed in arriving at the conciliar constitution. Somerset reacted in kind by accusing Wriothesley of legal malpractice. The Lord Chancellor was determined to continue presenting a challenge to the Protector and that meant that he had to be free to attend the Council. To this end he offloaded some of his Chancery work by commissioning four other eminent lawyers to hear cases on his behalf. He had done this in the previous reign but now, it was alleged, he had acted illegally because he had no Crown warrant for action. Somerset appointed a commission to look into the case. It was headed by Wriothesley's erstwhile colleague of the Tower dungeon, Richard Rich. There was, of course, no question of impartiality. Understandably, Southampton flew into a rage, refused to co-operate with the commission and directed some choice invective against Seymour. This only served to reinforce the opinion of his Council colleagues that Wriothesley was unruly, ambitious and untrustworthy. A courtier who knew him well observed, 'I was afraid of a tempest all the while Wriothesley was ever able to raise any . . . Most true it is I never was able to persuade myself Wriothesley would be great, but the king's majesty must be in greatest danger.'[79] On 6 March the Protector and his hand-picked body of cronies took punitive measures against their too-outspoken opponent. Wriothesley was stripped of the lord chancellorship, deprived of his seat on the Council, fined £4,000 and confined to his London house. He was specifically debarred from visiting his Hampshire estates, because the councillors feared he might raise armed support here, perhaps in collaboration with Gardiner.

If Wriothesley modelled himself on Cromwell, Seymour made Henry VIII his pattern. It took no time at all for him to reveal himself as a petty tyrant. His arrogance grew by leaps and bounds and from others he expected unquestioning obedience. When Gardiner and Bonner took exception to his religious policies they spent short spells in the Fleet and were later consigned to prison at His Majesty's pleasure (Gardiner in the Tower and Bonner in the Marshalsea). Seymour treated the Council as a rubber stamp, calling it infrequently, haranguing it when it did meet and peremptorily dismissing members who argued with him. Even the faithful Paget took him to task:

> of late your Grace is grown into great choleric fashions whensoever you are contraried in that which you have conceived in your head . . . A subject in great authority, as your Grace is, using such fashion is like to fall into great danger and peril of his own person besides that to the commonwealth . . . I beseech you . . . when the whole Council shall move you or give you advice in a matter . . . to follow the same and relent some time from your own opinion . . .[80]

In one important regard Somerset was not like his late brother-in-law. He was not bloodthirsty. Though ruthless in depriving opponents of their goods and liberty, he always hesitated to exact the ultimate penalty. He was the kind of bully who shouts and blusters but who lacks the will to make the last fatal turn of the screw. It was probably this character trait that explains Norfolk's survival, although the Protector may have reasoned that keeping the head of the Howard clan at his mercy would act as a deterrent to any of the Duke's friends and family who might have contemplated attempting anything against the new regime. This was certainly a tactic Henry had employed against papal sympathisers and members of the Pole connection. One by one, other members of Howard's family and clientage were released but, despite several pleas for his enlargement, he remained a prisoner. Whatever the motives for it, Norfolk's life was spared and the conditions of his incarceration gradually improved. He was housed in the Beauchamp Tower, adjacent to the Lieutenant's Lodging, where more distinguished prisoners were kept and where both his royal nieces had spent their last days. He was allowed access to the garden for exercise, the services of five personal attendants, visits from his family, fuel for a good fire, wall hangings to keep out the riverain draughts, a plentiful supply of books (it was his habit to read late into the night; 'unless I have books to read ere I fall asleep and after I wake again I cannot sleep,' he complained) and sufficient furniture for his modest needs. Even with these comforts containment was a severe trial, especially for a man in his seventies. It had taken its fatal toll on Arthur Plantagenet only a few years earlier. Thomas Howard, the old campaigner who had rarely been allowed the luxury of silken ease, must have had the constitution of an ox.

Wriothesley, meanwhile, was not prepared to accept exile to the political wilderness. With that political stamina all observers recognised in him, he surmounted the depression which had originally beset him when he was deprived of office. Once he had cooled down he sought rapprochement with the regime. He knew the resentments which were beginning to stir against the Protector and calculated that he only needed to bide his time and await his opportunity. He made a point of being pleasant to Somerset and he began to court the second most powerful man in the realm, the Earl of Warwick. Sometime in late 1547 he seems to have exchanged London houses with Dudley, taking Warwick's Lincoln Place in return for the more commodious Ely Place. His freedom was soon restored and his fine remitted. Probably he was permitted to attend Council meetings again, although he was not formally named as a councillor for several months.

The opportunity to ingratiate himself came at the end of 1548. While no one else was prepared to make a move against the Protector, his own younger brother, Thomas, Baron Sudeley, the Lord Admiral, conceived a hair-brained scheme to topple Somerset. Thomas had charm and audacity but he lacked the intelligence to go with it. When he approached other prominent men to join in his schemes they declined, recognising him for the lightweight that he was. Wriothesley was one of the malcontents identified by Lord Seymour as a likely ally and he made an approach in the autumn of 1548. Southampton's response is best given in the deposition he made a few months later.

> During the first session of this parliament the admiral and I were appointed with certain lords and others to dine with Sir John Gresham, then mayor of London, to consider a bill touching weirs and purprestures [illegal encroachments] in the river Thames. On the way the admiral said I had been well handled with my office. I asked him what he meant and said I was glad to be discharged of it. I told him to take heed as I had heard he would contend with his brother and make a party. He said he would have things better ordered. I warned him against attempting violence. He might say he meant well, but would show himself the king's greatest enemy. He might begin a faction and trouble, but could not end it when he would. He said he did not mean that. I said that the world believed so, and he were better buried alive than to attempt it; at which he broke off and never since looked on me. I reported this talk to the Protector.[81]

Wriothesley's declaration of the evils of faction was subtle, suggesting, as it did, that he would never stoop to such underhand activity. The reality was that he was already turning over in his mind possible moves which might put an end to the experiment of Somerset's rule and establish a government committed to less extreme religious and social courses. For the time being, he demonstrated his usefulness to the Protector. When the Lord Admiral was arrested and sent to the Tower, Wriothesley came into his own as interrogator, although he and his colleagues were unable to wring a confession from the prisoner. It was about this time that Southampton was formally reinstated as a councillor, probably at the urging of his new friend, Warwick, and because of his support of the attainder of Lord Seymour, who was duly executed in March. That summer was a disaster for the government. Real agrarian distress and widespread alarm at the accelerating pace of religious change brought about the Prayer Book Revolt in the south-west and Kett's Rebellion in East Anglia. Both had to be put down with considerable bloodshed if central authority was to be maintained. (Ironically, the situation in the eastern counties got out of hand largely because Thomas Howard's continued captivity created a power vacuum in Norfolk and Suffolk.) In the midst of these tragic events Somerset's foreign policy fell apart. Henry II of France took advantage of the disturbances to declare war and lay siege to Boulogne. At the same time the Emperor declined to be drawn into an alliance. The Protector's incompetence was starkly revealed and it was clear that drastic action was necessary to establish sound government. The personnel of the Council had changed and a conservative consensus had emerged comprising convinced Catholics and others unable to accept the headlong rush into doctrines and practices which had gone well beyond Lutheranism. Wriothesley's principal ally in this group was Henry Fitzalan, Earl of Arundel, a favourite of the late King and scion of an ancient noble house. They were in close touch with van der Delft and the main elements of their 'programme' were the appointment of Mary as Regent during the rest of her brother's minority, alliance with the Emperor and a return to the religious situation as it had been at the death of Henry. Their grouping was a rebirth of the so-called 'Aragonese faction' of the 1530s, though admittedly far less robust.

While Warwick was away quelling the East Anglian revolt and other councillors were also employed on military duties, Southampton and Arundel had plenty of opportunity to put flesh on the bones of conspiracy and it was they who took the initiative in summoning their colleagues at the beginning of October. For the next few days the capital and its environs were tremulous with activity and rumour. Messages flew back and forth between London and Windsor, where the Protector held his royal nephew virtually hostage. The rebel councillors seized the Tower. They travelled everywhere with armed escorts. Pamphlets circulated accusing the Council lords, led by Warwick, of launching a papal plot. But Dudley was not in charge of the situation. Southampton had brought some of his friends on to the Council and van der Delft was quite convinced when the crisis was over and Somerset had yielded himself into the hands of his rivals that a Catholic coup was virtually in the bag:

> The Archbishop of Canterbury still holds his place in the Council, but I do not believe they will leave him there unless he improves, and it is probable that they are now tolerating him merely that all may be done in proper order. For the same reason they are not yet making any show of intending to restore religion, in order that their first appearance in government may not disgust the people, who are totally infected. But every man among them is now devoted to the old faith, except the Earl of Warwick, who is none the less taking up the old observances again day by day, and it seems probable that he will reform himself entirely.[82]

But Warwick was very far from being converted to the 'old faith' or outmanoeuvred by the conservatives. He had been caught off guard by the tactics of Southampton and Arundel but he now showed himself to be as adept as they at intrigue. He, too, introduced supporters on to the Council to restore the balance and managed to assert his leadership of the body during November as a new form of government was hammered out. He seems to have been aided by Wriothesley's temporary absence due to a bout of illness. As soon as he recovered he made his way to the Tower and there energetically plied his old craft of interrogator. His coup was one step away from completion. Somerset was a prisoner and, as was widely assumed, destined for the block. Now, by examining the Duke and his accomplices it only remained to accumulate evidence implicating Warwick in the Protector's 'treasons', as a contemporary explained:

> my lord Wriothesley, being hot to be revenged of the both for old grudges past when he lost his office, said . . . 'I thought ever we should find them traitors both; and both is worthy to die for by my advice.' My lord of Arundel in like manner gave his consent that they were both worthy to die, and concluded there that the day of execution of the Lord Protector, the Earl of Warwick should be sent to the [Tower] and have as he had deserved.[83]

How many times in the past had Wriothesley seen men and women found guilty by association with condemned traitors and heretics and been associated with their destruction? Of course, he had had his failures, notably over Catherine Parr, and there were certainly risks involved but there was too much at stake to lose the moment and he pressed on with determination.

The scene was set for a dramatic confrontation, possibly embroidered by the contemporary who chronicled it but none the less crucial for that. One of the uncommitted councillors, deciding that Warwick was the safest man to back in a crisis, hurried from the Tower to Ely Place to warn him what was afoot. The next day the whole Council assembled in the Earl's Holborn house for a meeting. They were ushered into Warwick's bedchamber where their host lay ill but confronting them 'with a warlike visage and a long fachel [falchion, broadsword] by his side'. Wriothesley began to enumerate the Protector's offences, for which death was the only just punishment. Dudley cut him short and, with his hand on the weapon, glared at Southampton with the words, 'My Lord, you seek his blood and he that seeketh his blood would have mine also.'[84]

It was a masterstroke, not simply because it caused consternation and confusion in the Council ranks as members hastened to reconsider their loyalties, but because it signalled that Somerset was not to be attainted. The Duke had a large popular following and it was to that audience as much as the group gathered around the bed that Warwick was playing. Over the next few days the majority on the Council moved over to his side. By mid-January 1550 it was clear that Seymour would be shortly released and probably readmitted to the government where he would give his grateful support to his saviour.

Wriothesley had taken part in his last intrigue, his final attempt to reach the pinnacle of political power. His was not the kind of constitution that could suffer defeat stoically or await with patience the decisions of his enemies. He had surmounted many obstacles and braved many dangers in pursuit of his ambition. He had come from being the son of a court herald to being one of the wealthiest noblemen in the land and one of the most powerful. He had just passed his forty-fifth birthday, a man in his prime for whom fresh honours and greater influence might still have been possible. Now he looked into the future and saw that it was empty – and probably short. On 14 January he was dismissed from the court and the Council and ordered to remain in his London house. There he stayed, confined, alone but unmolested, even though Arundel was arrested on 30 January.

His adversaries had no need to take further action against him for Thomas Wriothesley was a broken man. Depression clouded his mind. When he died, on 30 July, rumour had it that he had taken poison. Potion or accidie? They can be equally toxic. A contemporary wrote thus of the Earl's passing:

> my lord Wriothesley, seeing all his heart was opened against him . . . and [thinking] this act could never be forgotten, and [because] his ambitious mind could take no [lower] place, he killed himself with sorrow in so much as he said he would not live in such misery . . . [85]

EPILOGUE

1559

. . . her majesty, being presently by the only goodness of God settled in her just possession of the imperial crown of this realm, and other dominions thereunto belonging, cannot now hide that religion, which God and the world knoweth she hath ever professed from her infancy hitherto: which as her majesty is minded to observe and maintain for herself by God's grace, during her time, so doth her highness much desire, and would be glad, the same were of all her subjects quietly and charitably embraced.

Proclamation of Queen Mary, 1553[1]

CHAPTER 34

Requiescant

One day in April 1547 Thomas Cranmer visited Thomas Howard in prison. Norfolk had asked for the interview and the Archbishop came readily. They spent two hours reminiscing about many of the joys and sorrows they had shared in the old King's reign, about past disagreements and controversies. It is said that they wept together and that Cranmer pledged himself to intercede for the Duke with the new regime. On a November day, in 1553, before a packed court at London's Guildhall, Thomas Howard presided over the trial of Thomas Cranmer for treason. It is not recorded that he sought royal clemency for the condemned Archbishop.

It would not be much of an exaggeration to say that Cranmer spent the years in between those two events creating the Church of England. He provided it with its own distinctive vernacular liturgy. He hammered out a simple statement of doctrine accessible to every literate worshipper. He provided a catechism for the instruction of the young. He licensed the complete purging of images and elaborately decked altars and the obliteration of 'idolatrous' wall paintings. He replaced the mass with the Holy Communion and exalted the ministry of the Word above the ministry of the Sacrament. The change which came over the religious life of ordinary parishioners was nothing short of revolutionary. They were now participants in rather than observers of the holy mysteries. They gathered round the Lord's 'table' set lengthwise in the chancel or nave, rather than watching clergy fussing round an 'altar' in some screened-off sanctuary. They were provided with pews to sit on so that they could listen to sermons preached from, often new, pulpits. Their churches became simplified as the 'holy clutter' of side altars and shrines was swept away and light flooded in through windows deprived of medieval stained glass to be reflected from whitewashed walls. Holy-water stoups and votive candles disappeared, to be replaced by poor boxes, intended to divert the offerings of the faithful away from the veneration of saints and towards care for the disadvantaged. With the abolition of the colourful mythology surrounding the lives of extra-biblical heroes and heroines of the Church disappeared the need for most of the traditional saints' days and festivals so that there were now fewer holy punctuation marks in the dreary prose of routine toil. Many celebratory and fund-raising events that, to the reformers, smacked of pagan survival, irreverence or 'lewdness' – plays, morris dancing, church ales, 'misrule' days, summer games – were swept away. Chantries and collegiate churches, long endowed to ensure continual prayer for the departed, were put to other uses. A beginning had been made to some of these changes during the reign of Henry VIII but with the accession of a young king brought up by humanists and evangelicals and a government controlled by men who, for whatever reasons, wholeheartedly embraced reform the cork was drawn firmly and completely from the bottle. It was more than flattery when Cranmer, in his coronation address, compared Edward VI to Josiah, the boy-king of ancient Judah who came to the throne at the age of eight, rediscovered the ancient law of Moses and devoted much of his thirty-one-year reign to purifying the religious and social life of his people.

The tragedy for Cranmer and his colleagues was that they did not have thirty-one years. Edward never enjoyed good health and he died of consumption a few weeks short of his sixteenth birthday in July 1553. The Archbishop was a man in a hurry. The Duke of Somerset and the Duke of Northumberland (formerly Earl of Warwick) who succeeded him as *de facto* king during Edward's minority were also men in a hurry. The changes they introduced were too much, too quickly. Like Henry, they aimed to dictate what the people should believe. They were much clearer in their religious programme than the old King had ever been; Cranmer provided government with a very unambiguous policy. But, like Henry, they discovered that changing the externals of popular religion was very far from changing its animus. The majority of English people could not absorb the theological niceties that informed the shift from Catholicism to Protestantism. That would take at least two generations. To a greater or lesser extent they resented being hustled along unfamiliar paths – particularly when they had to pay for the trappings of the new religion such as Bibles, pulpits, demolition work and the concomitant making good.

Deeper economic and social discontent lay beneath the so-called Prayer Book Revolt of June–July 1549 but dislike of the new service manual was the rallying cry of the Cornish rebels just as opposition to the Dissolution of the Monasteries had provided religious justification for the Pilgrims of Grace. The men of Bodmin who set the match to the stubble of anti-government sentiment insisted 'we will have our old service of matins, mass, evensong and procession in Latin as it was before'. And, as in 1536–7, the government only had one answer to insurrection: gallows and church towers festooned with the rotting corpses of peasants and priests.

Cranmer was phenomenally busy during these six years. Most of his energies were taken up with masterminding the religious reform programme but he was a conscientious Council member and one of the few to retain his place unmolested throughout the turbulent infighting between factions and individuals. He firmly supported the policies of both Somerset and Northumberland and also the draconian measures sometimes employed to enforce those policies. On 21 July 1549 he used his prerogative to preach at St Paul's before a packed cathedral which overflowed into the yard on the evils of rebellion, the benefits of the new Prayer Book and the wiles of covert papists who opposed it. Then he celebrated Communion in simple vesture rather than eucharistic vestments and episcopal fripperies. The fact that a large number of people stayed on after the service to listen to a repeat of the sermon delivered by Cranmer's chaplain from St Paul's Cross indicates that, although there were many Englishmen who resented the headlong rush of evangelical reform, there were also significant numbers who supported, and were indeed enthusiastic for, change.

Two and a half months later, in the troubled and confused days of early October, partisans of both persuasions watched with bated breath the struggle for control of King and Council. Cranmer played a crucial part in the negotiations which induced the Protector to surrender himself to his colleagues. Along with Paget and Sir Thomas Smith, Cranmer was the only Council member to obey Somerset's summons to attend him at Hampton Court and he subsequently moved with the King and his uncle to Windsor. The Archbishop was faced with difficult choices and clashing responsibilities. Uppermost in his mind will have been his loyalty to the young King. He enjoyed a special relationship of mutual affection and trust with Edward, as he had with his father and he conceived it to be his duty to be at the boy's side during these frightening days. He was also closely involved with the Duke who had provided the framework of royal and statutory support for the reforms Cranmer had proposed. It was not at all clear whether Wriothesley or Dudley held the upper hand or, indeed, what line Dudley would take if he emerged as leader of a new administration, since there was a persistent rumour that the Earl had thrown in his lot with the conservatives in order to wrest power from Somerset (he was employing gestures like Catholic observances in his household and friendly messages to the Emperor in order to keep the conservative councillors on side). For days the religious programme appeared to be in the balance. At the same time, Cranmer was aware of the justice of the charges being put forward against the Duke. He *was* arrogant and overbearing and Cranmer was among those who had felt the rough edge of his tongue. He *had*, by confused and ill-advised policies, allowed the realm to fall into near anarchy. Gradually, the Archbishop and Paget assumed the role of negotiators. Slowly, they defused what had begun as a very nasty situation. Much of the credit for the bloodless transfer of power must go to the simple, transparent Cranmer and his cunning companion.

The immediate crisis past, there remained the issue of establishing the new administration and defining its programme. It was at this moment that Cranmer's support for the evangelical cause was crucial. He aided Dudley in his endeavours to outwit the Wriothesley–Arundel faction. The Archbishop's friends from foreign reformed churches were watching anxiously and it was not until 20 October that one of them was able to report that the

> Antichrist in these difficult and perilous times is again cast down by the general decision of all the leading men in all England . . . not only have they decided that the religion adopted last year is the true one but a doubly severe penalty has now been imposed upon all who neglect it. There is nothing, therefore, for the godly to fear, and nothing for the papists to hope for, from the idolatrous mass.[2]

And ten days later a royal proclamation scotched all rumours that there was to be a return to the 'old Romish service'.

According to one contemporary chronicle, Cranmer also played a prominent part in frustrating the second conservative plot in December. What we know of Cranmer's character tends to support this suggestion that he was busy interceding for Somerset's pardon and that he talked with Dudley and others who had grudges against the ex-Protector. Warwick, the writer states, 'procured by means of the Archbishop of Canterbury great friends about the king to preserve the Lord Protector, and joined together in the same all he could for his life'.[3]

The hurdle of 1549 safely negotiated, the work of reform went on. It was rooted in Cranmer's own spiritual and intellectual pilgrimage. He ever remained the scholar grappling with old truths and their reinterpretation, studying the writings of the ancient fathers and the latest continental divines, always remaining firmly rooted in the Scriptures. In the middle years of the century, when the first ideological battles had been fought and the smoke had drifted away from the body-strewn field, academic generals across Europe were evaluating their positions and exploring their tactical options. Catholic doctrines and practices had been overthrown and new assertions made in the heat of conflict. Now it was necessary to look at the issues more closely, to define evangelical doctrine, enshrine it in treatises, pamphlets and sermons and provide it with unimpeachable biblical and patristic credentials. For example, transubstantiation had been resoundingly rejected but, that being the case, how should one interpret the words of Jesus 'This is my body; this is my blood'? With these and related issues Cranmer continued to struggle. He maintained an extensive correspondence with foreign reformers, especially those in the Swiss cantons, and he welcomed visits from continental scholars. On matters such as the mass he was much influenced by Zwingli, Oecolampadius, Bucer and

Calvin and he certainly moved beyond his earlier Lutheranism. When, in 1550, the heretic Joan Bocher was brought to trial she taunted Cranmer and his colleagues, 'It was not long ago that you burned Anne Ayscough for a piece of bread, yet came yourselves to believe the doctrine for which you burned her,'[4] the barb may well have struck home. The official doctrine of the new Church of England was more subtle than Anne Ayscough's simple rejection of the real presence but in the spectrum of belief both views were closer to each other than either was to Roman Catholic orthodoxy.

The mention of Joan Bocher alerts us to the fact that radical heretics were still burned in the reign of Edward VI. They were fewer in number than those who perished under Henry and far fewer than those who would go to the stake in the Marian reaction, but burned they were, Cranmer never questioned that this was the right and proper punishment for those who were unrepentantly wedded to heinous opinions as the basis of the faith. Like all the English Catholic and evangelical polemicists of the period he insisted that he was pursuing a middle way. When his 1549 *Prayer Book* attracted criticism from colleagues who wanted him to go further, he brought out a second, amended, edition in 1552 but made clear in a new preface 'Of Ceremonies'

whereas in this our time, the minds of men are so diverse, that some think it a great matter of conscience to depart from a piece of the least of their ceremonies, they be so addicted to their old customs; and again on the other side, some be so new-fangled, that they would innovate all things, and so despise the old, that nothing can like them, but that is new: it was thought expedient, not so much to have respect how to please and satisfy either of these parties, as how to please God, and profit them both.

In his attempts to evolve a church whose doctrine and liturgy were both pure and acceptable to a broad cross-section of the people Cranmer found himself fighting a war on two fronts. From the Tower, Gardiner sniped at him, writing a defence of transubstantiation which he managed to have published in France. On the other side stood John Hooper, champion of the evangelical extremists. Hooper became a real thorn in the flesh, partly because of his strongly held views and his bigotry in upholding them but also because he won the support of Northumberland and the King. Edward was of an age to be impressed by forthright, anti-establishment histrionics and, in 1550, he offered Hooper the bishopric of Gloucester. The zealot refused on the grounds that the vestments he would be obliged to wear were idolatrous. The Council issued a dispensation authorising Cranmer to consecrate Hooper without the offending garments. This the Archbishop staunchly refused to do. A long and extremely bad-tempered series of discussions ended with Hooper being sent to the Fleet. Only the prison environment banished the Bishop Elect's scruples and he consented to go through with the enthronement ceremony.

An intriguing corollary to this story concerns Thomas Wriothesley. In the summer of 1550 when the controversy was at its height, the embittered ex-Chancellor was making his will. In it this conservative politician nominated the ultra-evangelical John Hooper to preach his funeral sermon. It is difficult to see any other motive in this but a desire to annoy Cranmer and to have a last laugh from beyond the grave.

By the beginning of May 1553 it was clear to the inner circle of courtiers and councillors that the King was dying. By the terms of Henry VIII's will the crown was destined to pass to Princess Mary and that would spell disaster for the evangelical cause. Quite simply it would bring final victory to the successors of the 'Aragonese faction' and undo everything Cranmer had done since he had declared the annulment of Mary's mother to Henry twenty years before. Edward was adamant that this should not happen and, with either the loyal support or the sinister prompting of Northumberland he drew up a device nominating as his heir Lady Jane Grey, recently married to Northumberland's son, Guildford Dudley (a blatant piece of dynastic manoeuvring but no worse than the attempts by Thomas Howard and Edward Seymour to tie their houses to the Tudors). It was a desperate expedient but politically the only option if the Reformation impetus and the foreign and domestic policies hanging on it were not to be lost.

It was, of course, both morally and legally dubious and it was this that weighed more heavily with Cranmer than the preservation of his life's work. Dudley called his conciliar colleagues together and ordered them to sign the device. The Archbishop demurred. He asked to see Edward alone in order to dissuade him from a course of action that would be as fraught with danger for the King's conscience as it would for the nation. Permission was denied and Cranmer had to speak with his godson in the company of his peers. This reluctance to allow Cranmer to enter the bedchamber for a private conference with his godson must reveal something of the relationship between the old man and the boy, a relationship Northumberland feared. In the presence of his mentor and the other councillors, several of whom were as unhappy as Cranmer at the turn events were taking, the Archbishop was reprimanded by the King who commented that he hoped Cranmer 'would not be more repugnant to his will than the rest of the Council were'. In response to a direct command from his sovereign the Archbishop added his signature to the document. His was the last name to be written but, in accordance with convention, it appeared at the top of the list. After Edward's death on 6 July he, along with his colleagues, proclaimed Queen Jane.

Within a couple of weeks Northumberland's adventure was over. On 3 August Mary Tudor entered her capital. As she approached the Tower, bringing Dudley and other prisoners in her train, a great peal of ordnance rang out. At the entrance gate she was met by the kneeling figures of Thomas Howard and Stephen Gardiner. At last, at long last, they had triumphed over their enemies. They had come through repeated dangers and surmounted apparent failure. Only days before, they had heard the rumour that Northumberland planned to execute them but, if such a move was in his mind, he had no time to carry it out. Now, their queen, Catherine of Aragon's daughter, who had never wavered in her commitment to the Pope's church, raised them to their feet and embraced them as her loyal subjects. Their day had come and they were determined to savour it to the full.

On 14 September they were both on the Council when Cranmer was marched in to answer to the crimes of circulating seditious literature (his *Prayer Books* among other writings) and upholding the errors promulgated by Seymour and Dudley. Since those 'errors' still had the force of statute law there was, of course, no validity in this charge, but that was a mere technicality. His enemies had waited ten years since that day when they had been rapped over the knuckles for presuming to accuse the Archbishop of heresy and they were not to be balked of their prey now. Cranmer was sent off to the Tower and there remained for two months before his formal indictment before Norfolk at the Guildhall. He was charged with treason for having proclaimed Queen Jane and provided men and harness to support Dudley in his march into East Anglia to arrest Mary. The usual sentence was proclaimed against him and he returned to the Tower to await his end.

Howard was completely restored to all his lands and dignities. Or, rather, not all: about a third of the Duke's estates appropriated by the Crown had been sold off and the Duke was never able to prise them out of the hands of their new owners. He was now turned eighty and might have been expected to be allowed to enjoy in peace whatever time was left to him. It was not to be; he had one more military exploit to perform; one more military humiliation to endure. In January 1554, Sir Thomas Wyatt, son of Cromwell's ambassador, raised a minor rebellion in Kent, in a madcap attempt to seize the capital and prevent the Queen's proposed match to Philip II of Spain. Howard, apparently, was the only experienced general close to hand whom the Queen felt she could trust and he was despatched with a few hundred London levies to halt the march of the insurgents.

By the time Norfolk came within sight of the enemy Wyatt's force had grown to several thousand and had seized control of the vital Medway bridge at Rochester. The Queen's army was outnumbered but commanded higher ground and was equipped with artillery pieces. The Duke positioned his guns with the intention of creating havoc among the enemy before sending in his troops. But just as he was about to open fire some of his own men broke ranks. Anti-Spanish feeling was not confined to the rebels and the Londoners were not prepared to slaughter their fellow countrymen in furtherance of Philip's cause. With cries of 'We are all Englishmen!' they rushed towards the bridge to make common cause with Wyatt's soldiers. Norfolk and his officers extracted themselves with difficulty and fled back to London. It was a fitting end to an undistinguished military career.

Thomas Howard made his last journey home to his grand house at Kenninghall. There was work to be done in East Anglia restoring a sense of cohesion in a region which had experienced the upheaval of Kett's Rebellion and the confrontation of Northumberland's army and the Queen's supporters. But his strength was at last failing. Sometime in July he took to his bed. On 25 August he died. His had been a turbulent life, made more so by his dynastic ambition and his attempts to serve two exacting Tudor sovereigns. He had come within an ace of witnessing the destruction of his line but, in the end, it was he alone of the six Thomases who ended his life in his own home and at peace with the world.

Wyatt's Rebellion was a clear signal that the brief honeymoon was over. Mary's joy at coming to the throne and her people's joy at receiving her evaporated with the announcement of the Queen's projected marriage. Thousands of Englishmen were outraged and, when the mass was reinstated, they vented their anger on the priests. Mary had succeeded in associating Catholicism and Spanish domination in the common mind and this would make up a major strand in the national psyche for the rest of the century. The Queen had learned stubbornness from both her father and her mother and fine-honed it during long years of rejection. Now, the more her people resisted her will, the more determined she became but she was not just up against her contemporaries. She was in a head-on clash with history. She wanted everything to be back as it was before the break with Rome and her frustration, misery and hatred increased as the impossibility of her chosen position became more obvious. She married the King of Spain. She returned England to papal obedience. She replaced evangelical bishops with her own nominees. She brought Cardinal Pole in to be her Archbishop of Canterbury. She insisted that married clergy put away their wives. She ordered parish churchwardens who had just gone to the trouble and expense of reordering their churches to put everything back as it was in the 'good old days'. The more resistance she met, from her own demurring councillors down to ribald village balladiers, the harsher her reaction became. Her draconian policies forced hundreds of evangelicals who could afford to do so to flee abroad. And she sanctioned the burnings which won her the lasting reputation of 'Bloody Mary', a name she would eventually come to share with a particularly revolting aperitif.

Cranmer was the man upon whom her antipathy was primarily focused

– and not only hers; Gardiner, Bonner, Tunstall, all the ecclesiastics who had either suffered for their resistance to the Edwardine regime or submitted in order to keep their jobs, and despised themselves for doing so, funnelled their lust for revenge on the man who had been the main architect of their griefs. To the vindictiveness of a disappointed woman was added the viciousness of the ecclesiastical establishment. Cranmer had been condemned to a traitor's death but that would not suit his enemies at all. It was necessary for his heresies to be exposed in detail to the watching Catholic world, for him to acknowledge his crimes against God and the Church, and for him then to be burned to death as the arch-heretic he was.

In March 1554 he was removed to Oxford for a series of trials and examinations. His enemies feared to proceed against him in the capital because he had too many sympathisers there. The last thing the Queen wanted to do was to give the London mob and the pamphleteers any excuse for demonstrations. Thus Cranmer, who had always remained essentially a scholar, returned to an academic environment, there to be confronted by the learned men of both universities who challenged him on every aspect of his private beliefs and his public actions. His entire career and the whole process of the English Reformation were held up to scrutiny because it was vital to the regime to discredit both. All this took two years, partly because his accusers had to go through the fiction of citing him to Rome and forwarding the results of his examination thither.

At the end of it all the sixty-six-year-old cleric was pronounced a heretic, sentenced to be handed over to the secular arm, and then theatrically degraded of all his ecclesiastical offices. He was solemnly dressed in layers of imitation vestments. Then, one by one, he was stripped of the adornments of sub-deacon, deacon, priest, bishop and archbishop. He was, by this time, physically, mentally and emotionally drained but his ordeal was far from over. If Mary and Pole were to enjoy complete triumph and recompense for all the ills they had suffered at the hands of Henry VIII they had to have Cranmer's written submission, his confession that everything done in the name of Henry and his son had been wrong and that truth resided only in the Pope and the Church Catholic over which God's sole deputy presided. The exhausted old man had been subjected to intolerable pressures for two and a half years. What he endured in the Tower and Oxford's Bocardo prison, and in disputations (without the benefit of his library, long since ransacked by his enemies), and in watching friends go to the stake, and in not knowing whether the Queen intended to order his burning, was worse, for example, than anything Thomas More had endured. As well as the recorded transactions in which he was involved there were the hundreds of conversations with agents sent to badger, reason, cajole, plead and threaten the prisoner and to urge him to consider the fate of his immortal soul. Now he was presented with pre-written confessions to which he was required to set his hand and asked to amplify them with his own statements. The fact that he eventually signed a complete detailed recantation of all the convictions he held sacred, possibly in the hope of saving his life, has to be seen against the debilitating impact of all these experiences.

Mary, too, was under pressure. Popular unrest was growing throughout the country and with it demands for Cranmer's release. Even if she had ever in a moment of common humanity contemplated the possibility of a pardon, mounting support for the ex-Archbishop would have rendered that course impossible. She could not display weakness. Cranmer's execution was fixed for 21 March. It was a wet day and the old man was taken to the university church for the last formalities preceding the burning – a sermon by Dr Henry Cole, the Queen's representative, followed by a statement from the condemned man. The church was packed as Cranmer stood to speak. His adversaries had scrutinised the text, so they knew what was coming – or thought they did. The heretic would make a grovelling renunciation of all his errors and acknowledge his belief in all that Mother Church taught. They were in for a shock.

Cranmer's last moments have long since become the stuff of legend. Reaching the climax of his address the prisoner said that he repented certain of his writings but these were not his theological and liturgical works. They were statements written

> contrary to the truth which I thought in my heart, and written for fear of death . . . all such bills and papers which I have written or signed with my hand since my degradation.

Amidst sudden uproar he continued

> And as for the Pope, I refuse him, as Christ's enemy, and Antichrist, with all his false doctrine . . . and as for the sacrament, I believe as I have taught in my book against the Bishop of Winchester.

He was allowed to say no more. Angry hands pulled him from the rostrum and he was hustled to the place of execution. Or perhaps it was he who did the hustling, for observers reported that he walked with such rapid eagerness that his guards were hard put to it to keep pace with him.

He came to the stake and the fire was lit. As the flames rose around him he spoke again and the brief statement, carefully prepared, remains among the most famous of famous last words. 'Forasmuch as my hand offended, writing contrary to my heart, my hand shall first be punished there-for.' Then, as the smoke and flames engulfed him: 'Lord Jesus, receive my spirit. I see the heavens opened and Jesus standing at the right hand of God.'

The Primate of All England burned as a common heretic – there could not have been a more flagrant declaration, either literally or metaphorically, that the Reformation of Henry, Cromwell, Cranmer, Edward, Seymour and Dudley was at an end. The Archbishop's worst offence was denying the Catholic doctrine of the mass and his death re-established at the centre of English religious life both the Roman sacrament and the sacerdotal priesthood whose existence it justified. But final the change was not. A thousand days passed. Christmas 1558. A new queen was celebrating the festival in her chapel at Whitehall. At the central point of the mass the celebrant raised high the 'miraculously transubstantiated' host. Elizabeth rose in her place and stalked angrily out. There was more finality about her gesture than there was about the bonfire of March 1556 in front of Balliol College. The convoluted politics of sixteenth-century England had taken yet another twist, but thereafter the nation's road would be straighter.

When, in the dying weeks of 1558, the third of the Tudor lion's cubs entered the arena her father had earlier dominated for more than thirty-seven years, the political nation hoped, probably against hope, for an era of stability following the chaos of the mid-century decades. They were not reassured by the fact that the new ruler was another woman and the odds against an extended, peaceful reign were short indeed. No one could have foreseen that Elizabeth would be the longest ruling monarch since Edward III or that she would outlive all her sage advisers. Observers scarcely dared to peer into the cloudy future. Rather they looked back, gauging the new Queen's relations with other members of her family and hoping, each according to his own prejudices, that she would identify with the policies of Henry, Edward or Mary. Whichever she did she could not avoid alienating some sections of the population and provoking the suspicions of foreign courts. It was the Spanish ambassador, Gomez Suarez de Figueroa, Count of Feria, who made the most perceptive early judgement:

She is a very vain woman and clever woman. She must have been thoroughly schooled in the manner in which her father conducted his affairs, and I am very much afraid that she will not be well-disposed in matters of religion, for I see her inclined to govern through men who are believed to be heretics and I am told that all the women around her definitely are. Apart from this, it is evident that she is highly indignant about what has been done to her during the queen's life-time. She puts great store by the peple and is very confident that they are all on her side – which is certainly true. . . . In fact there is not a heretic or a traitor in all the kingdom who has not joyfully raised himself from the grave in order to come to her side. She is determined to be governed by no one.[5]

There was certainly something of 'resurrection' about Elizabeth I's accession. Her closest advisers were William Cecil, reared on the intellectual milk of Cambridge humanism, who had entered royal service as a protégé of Edward Seymour, and Robert Dudley, son of the executed traitor, John, Duke of Northumberland. Her first Archbishop of Canterbury, Matthew Parker, had been Anne Boleyn's chaplain, friend of Cranmer and an ardent, if scholarly, advocate of reform. Dudley had survived a spell in the Tower. Cecil and Parker had, during Mary's reign, 'laid low and said nuthin' but were now brought out of what was for the one a reluctant and for the other a welcome retirement from public affairs. They were not the only ones who had prudently kept themselves to themselves since 1553. Some of the more committed evangelicals had, out of indignation or self-preservation, lived out the years of Catholic revival in more congenial reform centres abroad. About four hundred of them now returned, many to take up leadership roles in the shires and some, like Francis Walsingham, Edward Rogers and Francis Knollys, to become royal councillors. The leadership of the Church took on a very new look. There was a clean sweep of the episcopal bench as conservatives who could not subscribe to the Elizabethan Acts of Supremacy and Uniformity were booted out in favour of progressives, many of whom had recently returned from exile.

If the central personalities had strong links with the Henrician and Edwardian ages so did the issues they had to address. The critical, interrelated problems of religion, foreign relations, finance and the succession continued to dog the government. However, the vacillations of royal policy were largely things of the past. No longer were there frequent changes of alliance: England took her place as a leading Protestant nation (and was destined to become the standard bearer against resurgent papalism) and settled to an anti-Habsburg stance. Within the nation the debate raged on between those who deplored England's renewed breach with Rome and the radicals who believed Elizabeth was compromising Gospel truth. However, the religious curriculum set up in the early months of the reign was adhered to despite the grumblings of Puritans and the plotting of Catholic recusants. Royal marriage was high on the government's agenda but was placed there by Council and parliament, not the Queen and it was the Queen who, infuriatingly, ensured that the issue was never resolved. The new monarch was determined to restore the *status quo ante* as it was before her sister's deplorable reign. All her subjects should take up the song of the Reformation being sung in 1553 – not a pennill more, not a pennill less. On religion her policy was quite clear and her decisions were frequently informed by temperament rather than by nice calculation. Thus, her own faith was a mix of biblical evangelicalism, Erasmian moderation, enjoyment of ceremonial, appreciation of visual stimuli and dislike of zealots of all stamps. It was this combination of beliefs and attitudes which was, more than anything else, responsible for the Elizabethan 'settlement'. If the Queen prevented a return to papal allegiance, she also halted the momentum for reform which had been vigorously rolling at the time of Edward's death. She resisted pressures for doctrinal advance and authorised penalties for those abstaining from adherence to the national Church but she also seldom enforced conformity with any rigour. In all this Elizabeth did not trim her theological sails to the prevailing diplomatic winds as her father had done or allow her ministers to lay forceful hands upon the ecclesiastical rudder.

It may seem bizarre to attribute consistency to a woman notorious for irresolution, prevarication and changeableness. There was not one of Elizabeth's ministers who would not at one time or another have echoed Sir Thomas Smith's words, 'I would some other man occupied my room who had more credit to get things . . . signed and things necessary resolved in time.'[6] But when Elizabeth found it hard to make choices it was not because she was the victim of short-termism, swayed back and forth by the eddies of political events at home and abroad, but because she had strong political instincts about what was best for Crown and people but could not convince herself of the most effective way to achieve her goals. Elizabeth paid close attention to the business of government and in that she was very different from her father.

This brings us to the relationships between Elizabeth and her principal officers of state and by juxtaposing these with those pertaining between Henry and his six Thomases we may reach some valid conclusions about the workings of the sixteenth-century political machine.

The most positive political result to emerge from the convolutions of four reigns was conciliar government. At the outset Elizabeth promised, 'I mean to direct all my actions by good advice and counsel.' Towards the end she asserted that she still 'did nothing without her Council and that nothing was so dangerous in affairs of states as self-opinion'.[7] Certainly there were numerous occasions when she ignored or rejected good advice but she always listened and she upheld the principle of decision-making by Crown and Council. The body that served her throughout four and a half decades was compact, had its own officials and procedures and was dominated by trained lay administrators. The overlap of court and Council, whereby the principal household officers held seats on the advisory body as of right, came to an end. Elizabeth's Council was a political body, pure and simple, on which there was no place for dynastic rivalries or competition between the temporalty and the spiritualty.

That does not mean that there were no faction fights or private feuds, nor does it mean that the Queen was not served by men who had their own agendas. The political narrative of her reign has much to do with rivalries across the Council board, behind-the-scenes intrigue, attempts to manoeuvre Elizabeth into supporting policies she had no intention of endorsing and secret negotiations of which the Queen was ignorant.

Sometimes there were furious scenes during which Elizabeth showed that she could roar as angrily as her father. Frustration and hubris drove Thomas Howard's grandson and namesake to self-destruction. Agents of the Pope and foreign princes were ever on hand to exploit divisions and rivalries for their own ends.

All this being so, it might appear that very little had changed. That was not the case. Under Elizabeth the Secretary re-emerged as the organiser of Council business and the intermediary between the Queen and her advisers. The pre-eminence which Cromwell had achieved and Wriothesley had hoped to inherit had faded away in the 1540s and 1550s and the result had been destabilisation. William Cecil restored the dignity and importance of the office and, in so doing, imparted cohesion and permanence to the whole body. The very fact that Elizabeth had furious arguments with her Council is proof of its enhanced stature. Henry VIII's advisers would never have dared stand up to him *en masse*. Yet, crucial though the Secretary's leadership was, and though he became, in effect, first minister, he was never allowed to assume that degree of independence that Wolsey and Cromwell had enjoyed. Elizabeth never abandoned important matters of state into her Secretary's hands in order to evade the tiresome drudgery of governing her country. Cecil and his successors were the *Queen*'s ministers, to be consulted when she chose, to have their wishes acceded to only when she agreed with them.

But the fundamental difference between the workings of Henry's and Elizabeth's governmental machine lies not in the structure but the personalities. The Queen and her leading servants were bound together by ties of mutual loyalty. Elizabeth's favour was constant. She never wilfully discarded a faithful adviser nor allowed her ministers to destroy each other in their faction feuds. No councillor went to the block for failing to satisfy his mistress's demands and seldom was a minister left to carry the can for the Queen's mistakes. The fear which Henry had effectively elicited to ensure the devotion of members of his inner circle was replaced, in his daughter's reign, by respect and affection. Being a woman and having a genuine aversion to violence meant that her relationships within government could not fail to be different from those of her father. It was because of the strong bonds formed between the Queen and her councillors throughout a long reign that the institution of Crown in Council became an immovable cornerstone of England's unwritten constitution.

But without the events and personalities of the years 1499–1559 that development would not have been possible. These were the sixty most creative – and, therefore, most destructive – years in the nation's history. There are many ways we can seek to come to an understanding of what was happening in this epoch which linked the medieval world to the modern. Many interpretations we can put upon the development of institutions and the shifts in social organisations. But we must never muffle the narrative in theory and certainly never dehumanise the drama. This was a turbulent age for most of which England was ruled by a turbulent king. We come closest to gaining a *feel*, a *sense* of what it must have been like to live through those painful, exciting, disturbing, fearful, inspiring years when we draw alongside the people who did just that.

The drama of the six Thomases is a tragedy of men who were destroyed not simply by a king who was a capricious monster. They were tossed to and fro by the violent gusts of social, political and religious change. Although they knew what they were doing their understanding of the perilous age in which they lived was only partial and this limited perception contributed to their destiny. Yet in the final analysis their fate must be seen as Sophoclean. They were brought down by their own vices and by their own virtues. Four of them were harried to death because they were men of principle, perhaps even vision, who pursued their own ideals and sought what they believed was best for their country. The only commitment the other two made was to themselves, their personal and dynastic ambitions. They were spared the ultimate humility of public disgrace and death. Their sufferings were internal, but who is to say that they were any the less dire for that? All six Thomases played in the lion's court and all discovered, as More warned, that it was an extremely hazardous place.

Endnotes

The place of publication is London unless stated to the contrary.

Introduction

1 A. Gilbert, *Machiavelli, The Chief Works and Others* (Durham, N. Carolina, 1965), vol. I, pp. 85–6.
2 W. Ralegh, *The History of the World*, ed. C.A. Patrides (1971), p. 56.

Part One

1 *The Letters of Marsilio Ficino* (1975), vol. I, p. 130.
2 P. Villari, *Life and Times of Girolamo Savonarola* (1888), p. 154.
3 *Ibid.* p. 518.
4 Petrarch, *Secretum Meum*, tr. W.H. Draper (1911), p. 29.
5 W.A. Pantin, *The English Church in the Fourteenth Century* (1962), pp.132–3.
6 G. Chaucer, *The Canterbury Tales, Prologue*, (Oxford, 1920), p. 423. (author's translation)
7 Cf. H.S. Bennett, *The Pastons and Their England* (Cambridge, 1922), p.166.
8 E. Hall, *The union of the two noble and illustre famelies of Lancastre and Yorke*, ed. H. Ellis (1809), p. 499.
9 E.W. Ives, *The Common Lawyers of Pre-Reformation England; Thomas Kebell: A Case Study* (Cambridge, 1983), pp. 8–9.
10 Sir John Fortescue, *De Laudibus Legem Angliae*, ed S.B. Chrimes (Cambridge, 1942), p. 8.
11 *Ibid*, p. 12.
12 *Ibid*, pp. 31–2.
13 D. Knowles, *The Religious Orders in England* (Cambridge, 1959) vol. III, p. 224.
14 *The Praise of Folly* in R.A.B. Mynors *et al.* (eds), *The Collected Works of Erasmus* (Toronto, 1986), vol. XXVII, p. 140.
15 *Rotuli Parliamentorum*, vi, p. 8; Cf. Bennett, *The Pastons and Their England*, p.183.

16 Cf. Bennett, *The Pastons and Their England*, p. 185.

17 Sir Thomas Malory, *Morte Darthur*, 1889 edn, preface.

18 Cf. C.J. Harrison, 'The petition of Edmund Dudley', *English Historical Review* (1971), pp. 82–99.

19 Hall, *Lancastre and Yorke*, p. 361. For a full discussion of Howard involvement in the events of 1483, cf. M.J. Tucker, *The Life of Thomas Howard, Earl of Surrey and Second Duke of Norfolk, 1443–1524* (The Hague, 1964), pp. 33ff; G. Brenan and E.P. Statham, *The House of Howard* (1907), vol. I, pp. 43ff.

20 Dominic Mancini, *The Usurpation of Richard III*, ed. C.A.J. Armstrong (1969), p.112.

21 *Instructions given by King Henry the Seventh to his Embassador . . .* (1761), pp.17–18.

22 Sir Francis Bacon, *History of the Reign of Henry VII*, in R. Lockyer (ed.), *Works* (1971), pp.154–5.

23 J. Burckhardt, *The Civilization of the Renaissance in Italy*, 1955 edn, p.120.

24 Plato, *The Republic*, in R.F. Allan (ed.), *The Dialogues of Plato* (Yale, 1984), vol. I, pp.749–50.

25 P.S. Allen *et al.* (eds), *Opus Epistolarum Des. Erasmi Roterodami*, (Oxford, 1906–58), vol. I, pp. 273–4.

26 J. Huizinga, *Erasmus of Rotterdam*, (1952), pp. 31–2.

27 Cf. N. Orme, *English Schools in the Middle Ages* (1973), pp.138–9.

28 J.R. Bloxam, *Register of Magdalen College Oxford* (1863), vol. III, pp. 7–9.

Part Two

1 D. Hay, (ed.), *The anglica historia of Polydore Vergil, 1485–1537*, Camden Soc., 3rd Ser., LXXIV, (1950), pp. 146–7.

2 E. Surtz and J.H. Hexter (eds), *The Complete Works of Thomas More* (New Haven) vol. III, (1965); (2) C.H. Miller *et al.* (eds), *Latin Poems* (1984), pp.101–3.

3 *Utopia*, in *The Complete Works of Thomas More*, vol. IV, pp. 91–4.

4 Cf. G.R. Elton, *The Tudor Constitution* (Cambridge, 1960), p. 61.

5 *Correspondence of Erasmus*, Mynors *et al.* (eds), *Collected Works of Erasmus* (Toronto, 1975), vol. II, p. 99.

6 *Ibid*, vol. II, p. 113.

7 *Ibid*, vol. II, p. 144.

8 J. Stow, *A Survey of London*, ed. C.L. Kingsford (Oxford, 1908), vol. I, p. 259.

9 Huizinga, *Erasmus of Rotterdam* (1952), p. 234.

10 Hall, *Lancastre and Yorke*.

11 *Correspondence of Erasmus*, in Mynors *et al.,* vol. II, p. 164.

12 Vergil, *Anglica Historia*, pp. 146–7.

13 *State Papers of the Reign of Henry VIII* (1830–52), vol. I, pp. 506–10; cf. H. Miller, *Henry VIII and the Nobility* (Oxford, 1986), p. 114.

14 *Correspondence of Erasmus*, in Mynors *et al.* vol. II, p. 148.

15 H. Ellis, (ed.), *Original Letters, illustrative of English history* (1824–1846), 3rd ser., vol. III, pp. 369–72.

16 *Calendar of State Papers Spanish*, G.A. Bergennoth and P. de Gayangos (eds), (1862–6), (Hereafter: *Cal. S.P. Span.*) vol. II, p. 71.

17 Hall, *Lancastre and Yorke*, p. 515.

18 *Ibid*, pp. 518–19.

19 Cf. A.C. Fox-Davies, *A Complete Guide to Heraldry* (1929), pp. 22, 36–7.

20 H. Noble, *History of the College of Arms* (1805), p. 123 claimed that William was York Herald but this is at odds with A. Wagner, *Heralds of England* (1967), pp. 146–7.

21 *Letters and Papers, Foreign and Domestic of the Reign of Henry VIII*, J. Gairdner, (ed.), (1861–3) (Hereafter: *L and P*), I, 880; P.S. and H.M. Allen (eds), *The Letters of Richard Fox* (1928), p. 54.

22 Report of the Deputy Keeper of the Public Records, III.ii.226; cited in D. Loades, *John Dudley Duke of Northumberland 1504–1553*, (Oxford, 1996), pp. 7–12.

23 As note 15 above.

24 Cf. G.G. Coulton, *Social Life in Britain from the Conquest to the Reformation* (Cambridge, 1926), p. 73.

25 Cf. D. MacCulloch, *Thomas Cranmer, a Life* (New Haven, 1996), p. 19.

26 *Correspondence of Erasmus*, Mynors *et al.*, vol. II, p. 249.

27 *Ibid*, vol. II, pp.186–7.

Part Three

1 C. Wriothesley, *Chronicle of England*, ed. W.D. Hamilton (Camden Soc., 1875), vol. XI, p. 8.

2 E. Hall, *The Triumphant Reign of King Henry VIII* (1904), vol. I, p. 76.

3 *Ibid*, vol. I, p. 43.

4 *Ibid*, vol. I, pp. 44–5.

5 Allen *et al.* (eds), *The Letters of Richard Fox* (1928), p. 58.

6 Hall, *Triumphant Reign*, vol. I, p. 50.

7 *Ibid*, vol. I, p. 57.

8 *Correspondence of Erasmus*, in Mynors *et al.*, vol. II, p. 278.

9 Hall, *Triumphant Reign*, vol. I, p. 59.

10 Allen *et al.* (eds), *The Letters of Richard Fox*, pp. 64–5.

11 Hall, *Triumphant Reign*, vol. I, p. 96.

12 C.J. Bates, *Flodden Field, A Collection of Some of the Earliest Evidence* (Newcastle, 1894), p. 9.

13 *Ibid*.

14 'The Flowers of the Forest', in G.F. Graham (ed.), *The Songs of Scotland* (1848), vol. I, p. 3.

15 *L and P*, I, 3001.

16 Ellis, *Original Letters*, lst ser., vol. I, pp. 116–17.

17 *Ibid*, p. 118.

18 *L and P*, I, 3376.

19 *L and P*, II, 80.

20 *L and P*, II, 106.

21 *L and P*, II, 138.

22 *L and P*, II, 113, 203.

23 Ellis, *Original Letters*, lst ser., vol. I, p. 123.

24 *L and P*, II, 80.

25 *L and P*, II, 222.

26 *L and P*, II, 224.

27 Allen *et al.* (eds) *The Letters of Richard Fox*, pp. 52–3.

28 *Ibid*, p. 63.

29 *Ibid*, p. 71.

30 *Ibid*, p. 75.

31 *L and P*, II, app. 38.

32 J.A. Guy, *The Cardinal's Court: The Impact of Thomas Wolsey in Star Chamber* (1977), pp. 60–1.

33 *Ibid*, p. 31.

34 *Ibid*, p. 73.

35 *L and P*, II: ii, 4124.

36 G. Cavendish, *The Life and Death of Cardinal Wolsey*, ed. R.S. Sylvester (1962), p. 25.

37 *Correspondence of Erasmus*, in Mynors *et al.*, vol. III, p. 233.

38 A. Ogle, *The Tragedy of Lollard's Tower* (1949), p. 152.

39 *Correspondence of Erasmus*, in Mynors *et al.*, vol. III, p. 239.

40 *L and P*, III:i, 217.

41 S. Giustinian, *Four Years at the Court of Henry VIII . . . January 12th 1515 to July 26th 1519*, ed. R. Brown (1854), vol. II, p. 17.

42 *Cal. S.P. Span., further supplement,* p. 67.

43 Giustinian, *Four Years at the Court of Henry VIII*, vol. II, pp. 74–5.

44 E. Lodge, *Illustrations of British History* (1791), vol. I, p. 34.

45 Hall, *Triumphant Reign*, vol. I, pp. 148–9.

46 Vergil, *Anglica Historia*, p. 225.

47 Cf. G. Walker, *John Skelton and the Politics of the 1520s* (Cambridge, 1988), p. 187. Walker's study argues extensively and convincingly against the Howard–Skelton connection.

48 Cf. Miller, *Henry VIII and the English Nobility*, pp. 107–8.

49 *Ibid*, pp. 108–9.

50 Surtz and Hexter, (eds), *The Complete Works of St Thomas More* (Yale, 1965), vol. IV, p. 245.

51 *Dictionary of National Biography.*

52 *L and P*, III, 1.

53 *Correspondence of Erasmus*, in Mynors *et al.*, vol. II, p. 200; vol. III, p. 239.

54 Cf. G.R. Elton, 'Thomas More, councillor' in *Studies in Tudor and Stuart Politics and Government* (Cambridge, 1974), vol. I, pp. 129ff.

55 Hall, *Triumphant Reign*, vol. I, p. 157.

56 R. Marius, *Thomas More* (1984), pp. 196f.

57 J.A. Guy, *The Public Career of Sir Thomas More* (1980), pp. 6f.

58 Erasmus, *Paraphrases on St Luke's Gospel*, Cf. J.D. Tracy, 'Ad Fontes: The humanist understanding of Scripture as nourishment for the soul', in J. Raitt (ed.), *Christian Spirituality – High Middle Ages and Reformation*, (New York, 1988), p.262.

59 D. Erasmus, *The Praise of Folly*, tr. C.H. Miller (New Haven, 1979), pp. 85–7, 95, 100.

60 *Ibid*, p. 124.

61 *Correspondence of Erasmus*, in Mynors *et al.*, vol. II, p. 203. Jerome was writing about opinions expressed in private correspondence but by the time he wrote Erasmus had just published his views in the *Encomium Moriae*, as yet unread by the author's friend.

62 *Ibid*, vol. III, pp. 18f.

63 *Ibid*, vol. III, p. 234.

64 Surtz and Hexter (eds), *The Complete Works of St Thomas More*, vol. IV, p. 281.

65 *Ibid*, p. 199.

66 *Ibid*, p. 57.

67 *Ibid*, p. 197.

68 *Ibid*, p. 241.

69 *Ibid*, p. 195.

70 *Ibid*, p. 61.

71 *Ibid*, p. 227. (My emphasis.)

72 *Ibid*, p. 229. (My emphasis.)

73 Cf. J.C. Olin, *The Catholic Reformation: Savonarola to Ignatius Loyola: Reform in the Church 1459–1540* (New York, 1971), p. 35.

74 Cf. Ogle, *The Tragedy of Lollard's Tower*, pp. 151–2.

75 *Ibid*, pp.152–3.

76 Surtz and Hexter (eds), *The Complete Works of St Thomas More*, vol. IV, p. lxxiv.

77 *Ibid*, p. 97.

78 *Ibid*, p. 103.

79 *Ibid*, pp. 100–1.

80 *The Complete Works of St Thomas More* (New Haven, 1963), vol. II, p. 5.

81 *Ibid*, (New Haven, 1984), vol. III:ii, pp. 601, 605.

82   W. Roper, *The Life of Sir Thomas More* (1935), p. 11.
83   P. More, *Selected Letters*, ed. F.F. Rogers (New Haven, 1961), p. 94.
84   Cf. T.F. Mayer, 'On the road to 1534: the occupation of Tournai and Henry VIII's theory of sovereignty', in D. Hoak (ed.), *Tudor Political Culture* (Cambridge, 1995), pp. 11ff.
85   *DNB*.
86   Cf. D. Starkey, 'Court, council and the nobility in Tudor England', in R.G. Asch and A.M. Birkie (eds), *Princes, Patronage and the Nobility. The Court at the Beginning of the Modern Age, c.1450–1650* (Oxford, 1991), pp. 175ff.
87   Cf. H.C. Porter, *Reformation and Reaction in Tudor Cambridge* (Cambridge, 1958), pp. 36–7.
88   Cf. MacCulloch, *Thomas Cranmer*, p. 22.
89   H. Noble, *History of the College of Arms* (1805), p. 123.
90   J. Foxe, *Acts and Monuments*, eds G. Townsend and S.R. Cattley (1838), vol. V, p. 363.
91   *Ibid*, p. 364.
92   Ellis, *Original Letters*, 1st ser., vol. I, p. 136.
93   Hall, *Lancastre and Yorke*, p. 597.
94   Cf. J.J. Scarisbrick, *Henry VIII* (1968), pp. 118–19.

Part Four
1   F.J. Furnivall, (ed.), *Ballads from Manuscripts* (Ballad Society, 1868–72), vol. I, pp. 93–100.
2   More, *Complete Works*, vol. III, ii (New Haven, 1984), p. 101.
3   R.H. Tawney and E. Power, *Tudor Economic Documents* (1924), vol. II, pp.176–7.
4   *Ibid*, vol. IV, pp. 64–6.
5   J. Foxe, *Acts and Monuments*, vol. IV, pp. 241–2.
6   *Ibid*.
7   Allen *et al.*, *Opus Epistolarum Des. Erasmi Roterodami*, vol. V, ep.1526.
8   Scarisbrick, *Henry VIII Original Letters*, p. 105.
9   Ellis, 1st ser., vol. I, pp. 287–92.
10   S. Anglo, *Spectacle, Pageantry, and Early Tudor Policy* (Oxford, 1969), p. 168.
11   *L and P*, III, 1213.
12   Cf. Anglo, *Spectacle, Pageantry and Early Tudor Policy*, pp. 183ff., D. Hoak, 'The iconography of the crown imperial', in D. Hoak, (ed.), *Tudor Political Culture* (Cambridge, 1995), pp. 83–4; F.A.S, Yate, *Astraea: The Imperial Theme in the Sixteenth Century* (1975).
13   J.G. Russell, *The Field of Cloth of Gold* (1969), p. 2.
14   Cf. Miller, *Henry VIII and the Nobility*, p. 49.
15   Mynors *et al.*, *Collected Works of Erasmus*, vol. IX, p. 1532.

16 W. Roper, *Life of Sir Thomas More* in *Two Early Tudor Lives* (New Haven, 1962), p. 206. Sir Henry Marney was briefly Lord Privy Seal in 1523 and elevated to the peerage soon after the events recorded here, a dignity he enjoyed for only a few weeks – he died in May. Marney had been a fixture in court and Council since the beginning of the reign. If Roper is to be trusted his defiance of Wolsey was highly significant. It may be that Sir Henry's son, John Marney, is referred to here, of whom little is known.

17 Hall, *Lancastre and Yorke*, p. 656.

18 Ellis, *Original Letters* lst ser., vol. I, pp. 220–1.

19 *Ibid*, pp. 195–6.

20 *L and P*, IV, 1212.

21 Ellis, *Original Letters*, 1st ser., vol. I, p. 222.

22 Wriothesley, *Chronicle*, pp. 14–15.

23 *L and P*, IV:i, 1241, 1371.

24 *Ibid*, IV:i, 1243.

25 *Ibid*, IV:i, 1333, 1539, etc.

26 Cf. Gilbert Burnet, *History of the Reformation of the Church of England* (Oxford, 1865), vol. VI, p. 275. Howard recalled this animosity at a time when he was under suspicion of treason and concerned to distance himself from a convicted traitor. However, there were plenty of people around who could have contradicted his version of events and it is likely that he was referring to a relationship which was well known and well remembered.

27 *State Papers of the Reign of Henry VIII*, vol. II, pp. 52–7.

28 *Ibid*, p. 62.

29 Cf. D.M. Head, *The Ebbs and Flows of Fortune: The Life of Thomas Howard, Third Duke of Norfolk* (Athens, Georgia, 1995), p. 58.

30 Ellis, *Original Letters*, 1st ser., vol. I, pp. 231–2.

31 *L and P*, III, 3608.

32 *State Papers of Henry VIII*, vol. IV, pp. 183–4.

33 *L and P*, IV, 1295, 1323, 1329, 1343.

34 *Collected Works of Erasmus*, in Mynors *et al.*, vol. VII, 1061.

35 Foxe, *Acts and Monuments*, vol. IV, p. 635.

36 Cf. A.G. Dickens, and W.R.D. Jones, *Erasmus the Reformer* (1994), p. 270.

37 H. Boehmer, *Martin Luther: Road to Reformation*, trs. J.W. Doberstein and T.G. Tappert (1957), p. 324.

38 Cf. R. Bainton, *Here I Stand: A Life of Martin Luther* (New York, 1950), p. 138.

39 *The Complete Works of St. Thomas More*, vol. V, p. 181.

40 *Ibid*, vol. III, ii, p. 205.

41 *State Papers of the Reign of Henry VIII*, vol. I, p. 20.

42 *The Complete Works of St Thomas More*, vol. V, pp. 232–3, 237.

43   Ellis, *Original Letters* 1st ser., vol. I, pp. 203–6.
44   *The Complete Works of St Thomas More*, vol. XII, p. 216.
45   Ellis, *Original Letters*, 1st ser., vol. I, p. 213.
46   Guy, *The Public Career . . .*, p. 18.
47   Sylvester and Harding (eds), *Two Early Tudor Lives* (New Haven, 1962), p. 202.
48   Ellis, *Original Letters*, 1st ser., vol. I, p. 209.
49   *Ibid*, 1st ser., vol. I, p. 204.
50   Guy, *The Public Career*, pp. 64–113 *passim*.
51   Sylvester and Harding (eds), p. 205.
52   *L and P*, IV:ii, 2544.
53   *Ibid*, IV:ii, 3105.
54   Ellis, *Original Letters*, 1st ser., vol. II, p. 20.
55   *Ibid*.
56   Hall, *Triumphant Reign*, vol. II, pp. 31–2.
57   *L and P*, IV: ii, 3360. Cf. also, Knowles, *The Religious Orders in England*, vol. III, pp. 161f.
58   Ellis, *Original Letters*, 1st ser., vol. II, pp. 19–20.
59   J.A. Guy, *The Cardinal's Court*, pp. 76–7.
60   Foxe, *Acts and Monuments*, vol. IV, p. 657.
61   D. Wilson, *Hans Holbein: Portrait of an Unknown Man* (1996), pp. 141–2.
62   *The Complete Works of St Thomas More*, vol. III, ii, p.175.
63   *Ibid*, vol. III, ii, p. 155.
64   Sylvester and Harding (eds), pp. 38, 47.
65   *L and P*, IV:ii, 3318.
66   Scarisbrick, *Henry VIII*, pp. 158–9, 162; *L and P*, IV, 3644.
67   *DNB*.
68   Scarisbrick, *Henry VIII*, p. 160.
69   Sylvester and Harding (eds), p. 39.
70   Cf. M.F. Alvarez, *Charles V – Elected Emperor and Hereditary Ruler*, trs. J.A. Lalaguna (1975), p. 76.
71   Ellis, *Original Letters*, 1st ser., vol. I, pp. 206–7.
72   *L and P*, IV:ii, 5458.
73   *Ibid*, IV: ii, 5275.
74   *State Papers of the Reign of Henry VIII*, vol. VII, p. 183; Cf. P. Gwyn, *The King's Cardinal: The Rise and Fall of Thomas Wolsey* (1990), pp. 287–9.
75   Sylvester and Harding (eds), pp. 93–4.
76   Ellis, *Original Letters*, 1st ser., vol. I, pp. 308–9.
77   Sylvester and Harding (eds), p. 183–4.
78   Foxe, *Acts and Monuments*, vol. IV, p. 657; Elton, *The Tudor Constitution*, pp. 322–3.
79   Sylvester and Harding (eds), pp. 103–4.

80 *Ibid*, p. 105.
81 D. Erasmus, *Epistolae*, vol. VIII, p. 294.
82 Ellis, *Original Letters*, 1st ser., vol. II, pp. 1–2.
83 R.B. Merriman, *The Life and Letters of Thomas Cromwell* (Oxford, 1902), vol. III, pp. 30–43.
84 Ellis, *Original Letters*, 2nd ser., vol. II, p. 20.
85 *Ibid*.
86 Knowles, *The Religious Orders in England*, vol. III, p. 163.
87 Ellis, *Original Letters*, 1st ser., vol I., pp. 185–90.
88 Sylvester and Harding (eds), pp. 108f.
89 Ellis, *Original Letters*, 2nd ser., vol. II, pp. 27–8
90 Hugh Latimer, *Sermons*, ed. G.E. Corrie (Parker Society, Cambridge, 1844), pp. 7–8.
91 T. Becon, *Works*, ed. J. Ayre (Parker Society, Cambridge, 1843), vol. I, p. 425.
92 G. Redworth, *In Defence of the Church Catholic: The Life of Stephen Gardiner* (Oxford, 1990), p. 13.
93 MacCulloch, *Thomas Cranmer*, pp. 26f.
94 *Ibid*, pp. 33–7.
95 J.G. Nichols (ed.), *Narratives of the Reformation* (Camden Soc., 1859), pp. 241–2.

Part Five

1 Elton, *The Tudor Constitution*, p. 344.
2 D. MacCulloch, *Tudor Church Militant: Edward VI and the Protestant Reformation* (1999), p. 125.
3 W. Tyndale, *Doctrinal Treatises . . .*, ed. H. Walter (Parker Soc., Cambridge, 1848), p. 255.
4 Allen *et al.*, (eds) *The Letters of Richard Fox*, vol. X, p. 2831.
5 *Ibid*, vol. VIII, p. 2228.
6 Cf. D. Wilson, *Hans Holbein*, pp. 123–80. Since writing this biography I have developed my ideas about Holbein's movements between 1526 and 1532. I now realise that there was no element of coincidence about the fact that the artist's absence from England between August 1529 and April 1532 corresponded precisely to the period when More's persecuting career was in full flood.
7 MacCulloch, *Tudor Church Militant*, p. 116.
8 *A merry jest how a Sergeant would learn to play the Friar*, cf. R.W. Chambers, *Thomas More*, 1976 edn, p. 90.
9 Cf. S.E. Lehmberg, *The Reformation Parliament 1529–1536* (Cambridge, 1970), pp. 28–9.
10 Hall, *Lancastre and Yorke*, p. 764.
11 *Parliamentary or Constitutional History of England, 1751–1762*, vol. III, pp. 42–55.

12 Edward Herbert, Lord of Cherbury, *Autobiography and History of England Under Henry VIII*, (1881 edn), p. 416.

13 Cf. Guy, *The Public Career of Sir Thomas More*, p. 206.

14 MacCulloch, *Tudor Church Militant*, p. 126.

15 Hall, *Lancastre and Yorke*, p. 764; *Cal. S.P. Span.*, IV:i, p. 324.

16 Hall, *Triumphant Reign*, vol. II, p. 167.

17 Quoted in Lehmberg, *The Reformation Parliament 1529–1536*, p. 87.

18 Foxe, *Acts and Monuments*, vol. IV, pp. 657–8.

19 Allen *et al.* (eds), *The Letters of Richard Fox*, vol. X, p. 2831.

20 *Cal. S.P. Span.*, IV:i, pp. 451–2.

21 Cf. Ellis, *Original Letters*, 1st ser., vol. II, p. 3; R.M. Warnicke, *The Rise and Fall of Anne Boleyn* (Cambridge, 1989), pp. 86–95; E.W. Ives, *Anne Boleyn* (Oxford, 1986), pp. 157–8; Sylvester and Hardy (eds), pp. 120–2.

22 Sylvester and Hardy (eds), pp. 128f; *L and P*, IV, 6295.

23 *Cal. S.P. Span.*, V, pp. 356–9.

24 Foxe, *Acts and Monuments*, vol. V, pp. 366–8.

25 *Cal. S.P. Span.*, IV:ii, 1108.

26 S. Fish, *A Supplication for the Beggars*, ed. F.J. Furnivall and J.M. Cowper (1871), p. 14.

27 Tyndale, *Doctrinal Treatises*, pp. 335–6.

28 Ellis, *Original Letters*, 3rd ser., vol I, p. 114.

29 *Ibid*, pp. 185–6.

30 Sylvester and Hardy (eds), p. 139.

31 Herbert, *Autobiography and History of England*, p. 450.

32 *L and P*, IV, 2715.

33 *Cal. S.P. Span.*, IV:i, p. 692.

34 *Ibid*, p. 354.

35 *L and P*, IV, 6688.

36 Ellis, *Original Letters*, 3rd ser., vol. II, pp. 232–3.

37 *Ibid*, 3rd ser., vol. II, pp. 187–8.

38 Merriman, *Thomas Cromwell*, vol. I, p. 237.

39 *Ibid*, vol. I, p. 327.

40 *Ibid*, vol. I, p. 328.

41 *Cal. S.P. Span.*, V:i, 228.

42 D.M. Loades, *The Papers of George Wyatt Esquire*, Camden Soc., 4th ser., V (1968), p. 29.

43 Cf. M. Dowling, 'Anne Boleyn and reform', in *The Journal of Ecclesiastical History*, XXXV, I (January 1984), 30–46.

44 Cf. S. Brigden, *London and the Reformation* (Oxford, 1989), pp. 113–15.

45 Wriothesley, *Chronicle*, pp. 16–17.

46 Foxe, *Acts and Monuments*, vol. V, p. 31.

47 M. Luther, *Works* (Philadelphia, 1943), vol. II, pp. 69, 324.

48 D. Bagchi, '"Eyn Mercklich Underscheyd": Catholic reactions to Luther's doctrine of the priesthood of all believers', in W.J. Sheils, and D. Wood (eds), *The Ministry Clerical and Lay*, Studies in Church History, XXVI (Oxford, 1989), 158. In this passage Bagchi summarises the responses of Thomas Murner and Hieronymus Emser.

49 *Cal. S.P. Span.*, IV:i, p. 719.

50 *Ibid.*

51 *State Papers of the Reign of Henry VIII*, vol. VII, p. 212.

52 *Cal. S.P. Span.*, IV:i, p. 819.

53 *L and P*, IV, 6763.

54 Sylvester and Hardy, (eds), p. 150.

55 *Cal. S.P. Span.*, IV:iii, p. 6738.

56 For Agostini's remarkable career cf. E.A. Hammond, 'Doctor Augustine, physician and Cardinal Wolsey and King Henry VIII', in *Medical History*, xix (1975), 215ff.

57 Sylvester and Hardy (eds) p. 170.

58 *Cal. S.P. Span.*, IV, p. 833.

59 Foxe, *Acts and Monuments*, vol. IV, p. 616.

60 *L and P*, V, 1661.

61 MacCulloch, *Thomas Cranmer*, pp. 62–3.

62 *Ibid*, p. 35.

63 Cf. A.G. Dickens, *The English Reformation* (1989), p. 193.

64 Cf. A.B. Chamberlain, *Hans Holbein the Younger* (1913), vol. I, pp. 340–1.

65 Ellis, *Original Letters*, 3rd ser., vol. II, pp. 192–3.

66 *L and P*, VI, 313.

67 J.E. Cox, (ed.), *The Works of Thomas Cranmer* (Parker Society, Cambridge, 1844–6), vol. II, p. 223.

68 *L and P*, VI, 10.

69 *Ibid*, V, 1452.

70 *Ibid*, V, 723.

71 *Ibid*, V, 1239.

72 *Ibid*, V, 1450.

73 *Cal. S.P. Span.*, IV:ii, p. 669.

74 Merriman, *Thomas Cromwell*, vol. I, pp. 336–7.

75 *Cal. S.P. Span.*, IV:ii, pp. 76–7.

76 Cf. A. Neame, *The Holy Maid of Kent* (1971), p.156; *L and P*, V, 941.

77 Hall, *Triumphant Reign*, vol. II, p. 209.

78 *Ibid*, pp. 209–10.

79 *Ibid*, p. 210.

80 *Cal. S.P. Span.*, IV:i, p. 445.

81 Cf. Lehmberg, *The Reformation Parliament 1529–1536*, pp. 157–8.

82 *Cal. S.P. Span.*, IV:i, pp. 295–6.

83 *L and P*, V, 1274.

84 Hall, *Triumphant Reign*, pp. ii, 215, 220.
85 *Cal S.P. Span.*, IV:i, p. 623.
86 Cf. Elton, *The Tudor Constitution*, p. 346.
87 Cf. MacCulloch, *Thomas Cranmer*, p. 88.
88 *L and P*, IV:i, 496.
89 Ellis, *Original Letters*, 3rd ser., vol. II, p. 276.
90 Wriothesley, *Chronicle*, pp. 18f; *Cal. S.P. Span.*, IV:ii, p. 700.
91 Merriman, *Thomas Cromwell*, vol. I, pp. 353–4.
92 Ellis, *Original Letters*, 3rd ser., vol. II, p. 254.
93 J. Strype, *Ecclesiastical Memorials of Archibishop Cranmer* (1816), vol. I, p. 248.
94 Ives, *The Common Lawyers*, pp. 319–21.
95 *L and P*, IV, 7.
96 Cf. Marius, *Thomas More*, p. 406.
97 More, *Works*, vol. VIII, pp. 12, 125.
98 Sylvester and Harding (eds), p. 56.
99 Hall, *Triumphant Reign*, vol. II, p. 185.
100 *Ibid.*
101 Cf. Guy, *The Public Career of Sir Thomas More*, p. 211.
102 *L and P*, V, 171.
103 H.J. Hillerbrand, (ed.), *Erasmus and His Age, Selected Letters of Desiderius Erasmus* (New York, 1970), pp. 270–1.
104 T. Wright (ed.), *Three Chapters of Letters relating to the suppression of the monasteries* (Camden Soc., XXVI, 1843), p. 29.
105 Ellis, *Original Letters*, 3rd ser., vol. II, pp. 315–18.
106 Lehmberg, *The Reformation Parliament 1529–1536*, p. 194.
107 *L and P*, VI, 1528.
108 Merriman, *Thomas Cromwell*, vol. I, p. 361.
109 E.F. Rogers (ed.), *Correspondence of Sir Thomas More* (Princeton, 1947), p. 492.
110 Elton, *The Tudor Constitution*, pp. 7–8.
111 Ellis, *Original Letters*, 3rd ser., vol. II, pp. 333, 343, 351.
112 Huizinga, *Erasmus of Rotterdam*, p. 252.
113 Cf. G.R. Elton, *Policy and Police* (Cambridge, 1972), p. 402.
114 E.F. Rogers, p. 559.
115 Elton, *The Tudor Constitution*, p. 62.
116 *L and P*, VIII, 892.
117 Rogers, p. 541.
118 Cf. Elton, *Policy and Police*, p. 411.
119 E.F. Rogers, p. 214.
120 Cf. Marius, *Thomas More*, p. 488.
121 Sylvester and Harding (eds), pp. 248f.
122 Miller, pp. 51f.
123 Wriothesley, *Chronicle*, p. 33.

124 *L and P*, VIII, 355.

125 *Cal. S.P. Span.*, V:i, p. 484.

126 Scarisbrick, *Henry VIII*, (1997 edn), p. 485.

127 Cf. Warnicke, *The Rise and Fall of Anne Boleyn*; Ives, *Anne Boleyn*; 'Stress, faction and ideology in early-Tudor England', *Historical Journal*, XXXIV (1991).

128 *L and P*, X, 615; G.W. Bernard, 'Anne Boleyn's religion', in *Historical Journal*, XXXVI (1993).

129 *Othello*, Act 1, Scene 3.

130 *Cal. S.P. Span.*, V:ii, 61.

131 *L and P*, X, 19.

132 *L and P*, X, 792.

133 *L and P*, XI, 576.

134 Elton, *The Tudor Constitution*, p. 374.

135 Ellis, *Original Letters*, 3rd ser., vol. III, pp. 168–9.

136 *L and P*, VIII:i, 995.

137 *L and P*, XI, 854.

138 *L and P*, XI, 601, 602, 603, 625.

139 *Cal. S.P. Span.*, I, pp. 463–4.

140 *L and P*, XI, 727, 773–4, 800.

141 *L and P*, XI, 816.

142 *Cal. S.P Span.*, I, pp. 495–6.

143 *L and P*, XI, 909.

144 *L and P*, XII:i, 98.

145 *L and P*, XII:i, 439.

146 *L and P*, XII:i, 478.

147 This account of the risings in Lincolnshire and the North is, of necessity, truncated. For lengthy discussions of these complex movements cf. M.H. and R. Dodds, *The Pilgrimage of Grace*, 1971 edn; M. James, *Society, Politics and Culture* (Cambridge, 1986), pp. 1888ff; S.M. Harrison, *The Pilgrimage of Grace in the Lake Counties* (1981).

148 *Cal. S.P. Span.*, II, p. 552.

149 Merriman, *Thomas Cromwell*, vol. II, pp. 20–1.

150 Ellis, *Original Letters*, 2nd ser., vol. II, p. 612.

151 Anglo, *Spectacle, Pageantry and Early Tudor Policy*, pp. 269–70.

152 W.H. Frere, and W.M. Kennedy, *Visitation Articles and Injunction* (1910) vol. II, p. 38.

153 *Ibid*.

154 M. St C. Byrne (ed.), *The Lisle Letters* (Chicago, 1980), vol. IV, p. 1001.

155 G.E. Corrie (ed.), *Sermons and Remains of Hugh Latimer* (Parker Society, Cambridge, 1845), pp. 75–7.

156 *Dictionary of National Biography*.

157 J. Ponet, *A Shorte Treatise of politike power* . . . (1556), Sig. I:iii.
158 *Cal. S.P. Foreign, Edward VI*, 471.
159 A. Wagner, *Op.cit*, p. 163.
160 Byrne (ed.), *Lisle Letters*, vol. IV, p. 420.
161 J. Stow, *Survey of London*, 1908 edn, vol. I, p. 179.
162 Ellis, *Original Letters*, 3rd ser., vol. III, pp. 85–6.
163 J. Leland, *The itinerary of John Leland* . . . (L. Toulmin Smith, edn 1907–10), vol. I, p. 281.
164 *Cal. S.P. Span.*, I:ii, p. 482.
165 Ellis, *Original Letters*, 1st ser., vol. II, pp. 87–8.
166 *L and P*, X, 134.
167 J. Kaulek, *Correspondence politique de M.M. de Castillon et de Marillac* . . . (Paris, 1885), p. 291; Cf. Byrne (ed.), *The Lisle Letters*, vol. VI, p.169.
168 *L and P*, VII, 1036.
169 *L and P*, XIII:ii, 401.
170 *S.P.*, VIII, 51–2.
171 *L and P*, XIV:i, 775.
172 Wriothesley, *Chronicle*, pp. 82–3.
173 Elton, *The Tudor Constitution*, p. 390.

Part Six

1 Cf. E.W. Ives, 'Henry VIII: The political perspective', in D. MacCulloch (ed.), *The Reign of Henry VIII: Politics, Policy and Piety* (1995), p. 31.
2 Redworth, *In Defence of the Church Catholic*.
3 Cf. W.H.St.J. Hope, 'The making of Place House at Titchfield, near Southampton, in 1538', *Archaeological Journal*, LXIII, 231f.
4 Byrne (ed.), *The Lisle Letters*, vol. VI, pp. 1086, 1108; *L and P*, XII:ii, 1187, XIII:ii, 884.
5 *L and P*, III:ii, 1188.
6 *L and P*, XIII:i, 583.
7 Byrne (ed.), *The Lisle Letters*, vol. V, pp. 152, 156.
8 Merriman, *Thomas Cromwell*, vol. II, p. 263.
9 *Ibid*, vol. I, p. 279.
10 *Ibid*, vol. II, p. 312.
11 *L and P*, XIII:ii, 979.
12 Wriothesley, *Chronicle*, pp. 95–6.
13 Merriman, *Thomas Cromwell*, vol. II, p. 295.
14 *Ibid*, vol. II, p. 291.
15 *Ibid*, vol. II, p. 301.
16 *Ibid*, vol. II, p. 298.
17 *Ibid*, vol. II, p. 287.
18 *L and P*, XIV:ii, 33.

19 Cf. Wilson, *Hans Holbein*, pp. 253–62.
20 Merriman, *Thomas Cromwell*, vol. II, p. 295.
21 *Ibid*, vol. II, p. 298.
22 *Ibid*.
23 Byrne (ed.), *The Lisle Letters*, vol. V, p. 1415.
24 Cf. Redworth, *In Defence of the Church Catholic*, p. 94.
25 Merriman, *Thomas Cromwell*, vol. II, p. 307.
26 Byrne (ed.), *The Lisle Letters*, vol. V, p. 1415.
27 Strype, *Ecclesiastical Memorials*, vol. I, ii, p. 438.
28 Wriothesley, *Chronicle*, pp. 98–9.
29 Byrne (ed.), *The Lisle Letters*, vol. V, p. 1435.
30 Nichols (ed.), *Narratives of the Reformation*, pp. 258–9.
31 Cf. MacCulloch, *Thomas Cranmer*, p. 258.
32 Byrne (ed.), *The Lisle Letters*, vol. VI, p. 1663.
33 Strype, *Ecclesiastical Memorials*, vol. I, p. 326.
34 Hall, *Lancastre and Yorke*, p. 838.
35 Cf. Byrne (ed.), *The Lisle Letters*, vol. VI, p. 226.
36 Strype, *Ecclesiastical Memorials*, vol. I, App., p. 313.
37 *State Papers of the Reign of Henry VIII*, vol. VIII, p. 349.
38 Byrne (ed.), *The Lisle Letters*, vol. V, p. 1403.
39 Merriman, *Thomas Cromwell*, vol. II, p. 345.
40 MacCulloch, *Tudor Church Militant*, pp. 5–6.
41 R. Scruton, *A Dictionary of Political Thought* (1983), p. 164.
42 *L and P*, XVI, 101.
43 The view taken here runs counter to that of E.W. Ives's: 'historians
    often write of "conservative" and "reforming" factions in the 1540s,
    but so long as on the one hand the anti-papal statutes and on the other
    the Act of Six Articles remained in force, expression of ideological
    commitment could be little more than a preference for tradition or for
    change. The use by historians of expressions such as "factional
    politics based on ideology" is incautious to say the least.' (E.W. Ives,
    'Henry VIII: The political perspective', in D. MacCulloch (ed.), *The
    Reign of Henry VIII: Politics, Policy and Piety*, 1995, p. 30) Such a
    view takes insufficient account of the degree to which religious issues
    actually mattered to the sophisticated classes in the mid-sixteenth
    century. What seems to me important is not that legislation existed
    which inhibited freedom of expression (and therefore likelihood of
    conflict) but that combatants invoked the law in their attempts to bring
    down their opponents. What then mattered was not the words in the
    statute book but the extent to which Henry could be induced to
    sanction their application. In the 1540s persecution of papists and
    evangelicals was sporadic but it was usually related to power
    struggles at the centre. Cf. also E.W. Ives, *Faction in Tudor England*
    (1979).

44 G.R. Elton, *Tudor Revolution in Government* (Cambridge, 1953), p. 213.
45 Merriman, *Thomas Cromwell*, vol. II, p. 348.
46 *Ibid*.
47 Foxe, *Acts and Monuments*, vol. V, p. 438.
48 Hall, *Lancastre and Yorke*, p. 828.
49 *L and P*, XVI, 590.
50 J.E. Cox (ed.), *The Works of Archbishop Cranmer*, vol. II, p. 401.
51 Wriothesley, *Chronicle*, pp. 130–1.
52 *State Papers of the Realm of Henry VIII*, vol. I, p. 271.
53 Foxe, *Acts and Monuments*, vol. VI, p. 578.
54 *Ibid*, vol. VIII, pp. 24–6; Nichols, *Narratives of the Reformation*, pp. 254–8; Strype, *Ecclesiastical Memorials*, vol. I, pp. xxviii, 124–6.
55 J. Foxe, *Acts and Monuments*, vol. VIII, p. 26.
56 Foxe, vol. V, p. 495.
57 Hall, *Lancastre and Yorke*, p. 865.
58 *L and P*, XX:ii, 455.
59 *Ibid*.
60 *State Papers of the Reign of Henry VIII*, vol. I:ii, p. 840.
61 J.A. Muller, *Letters of Stephen Gardiner* (Cambridge, 1933), pp. 185, 198.
62 *State Papers of the Reign of Henry VIII*, vol. I, ii, pp. 817–18.
63 *Ibid*, vol. I; vol. II, p. 840.
64 *Cal. S.P. Span.*, 1547–53, p. 101.
65 *Of a Lady that Refused to Dance with him*.
66 Wriothesley, *Chronicle*, p. 167.
67 *L and P*, XVI:i, 836, 845.
68 *Cal. S.P. Span.*, VIII, 318.
69 Foxe, *Acts and Monuments*, vol. V, pp. 553ff.
70 *Ibid*, vol. V, p. 557.
71 *Ibid*, vol. V, p. 560.
72 *L and P*, XXI:i, 1491.
73 *L and P*, XXI:ii, 540, 541.
74 Cf. Head, *The Ebbs and Flows of Fortune*, p. 227.
75 MacCulloch, *Thomas Cranmer*, p. 366.
76 S.R. Gammon, *Statesman and Schemer* (Newton Abbot, 1973), p. 134; R. Grafton, *Chronicle* (1809), vol. II, pp. 499–500.
77 *L and P*, XXI:ii, 605.
78 Cf. D.E. Hoak, *The King's Council in the Reign of Edward VI* (Cambridge, 1976), p. 39.
79 *Cal. S.P. Foreign, Edward VI*, 471.
80 Cf. Gammon, *Statesman and Schemer*, p. 151.
81 *Cal. S.P. Dom., Edward VI*, 190.
82 *Cal. S.P. Span.*, IX, pp. 462–3.

83 Cf. Hoak, *The King's Council*, p. 255.
84 *Ibid*, p. 256.
85 *Ibid*, p. 257.

Epilogue

1 Foxe, *Acts and Monuments*, vol. VI, p. 390.
2 Cf. MacCulloch, *Thomas Cranmer*, p. 448–9.
3 *Ibid*, p. 451.
4 Strype, *Ecclesiastical Memorials*, vol. II, p. 335.
5 Cf. M.J. Rodriguez-Salgado, and S. Adams (eds), 'The Count of Feria's Despatch to Philip II of 14 November 1558' in *Camden Miscellany* xxviii (1984), p. 331.
6 Cf. A. Somerset, *Elizabeth I* (1991), p. 280.
7 *Ibid*, p. 68.

Bibliography

Biographies

Readers wishing to delve further into the lives of the six Thomases will find the coverage patchy, varying from the numerous volumes available on Thomas More to the lack of anything detailed on Thomas Wriothesley. The following suggestions will, I hope, provide some useful guidance.

The starting point for all students of Wolsey is G. Cavendish, *The Life and Death of Cardinal Wolsey*. George Cavendish entered the Cardinal's service towards the end of his life and accompanied him during his final years right up until his death. His biography was written in 1557 and, though suffering from partiality and occasional lapses of memory, provides a vivid and, at times, moving picture of the great man at the height of his power and during his subsequent fall. Cavendish wrote to rescue his sometime master's reputation from the obloquy heaped upon it by most contemporaries but it was destined not to be published in full for 250 years. By that time the myth of the 'corrupt cardinal' had taken its place in the historiography of the sixteenth century. A hundred years later still, A.F. Pollard's *Wolsey* (1929), simply added colour to the picture created by Hall and other early chroniclers of the fat, vain, worldly churchman who instructed and encouraged the young King in the dubious arts of Machiavellian statesmanship. Not until 1990 was a rescue attempt made by P. Gwyn in *The King's Cardinal: The Rise and Fall of Thomas Wolsey*. Its 640 pages provided the thorough exploration and analysis the subject demanded and, despite a tendency to present the case for the defence a little too uncritically, it remains the standard work. Setting aside polemic and personality, J.A. Guy's *The Cardinal's Court: The Impact of Thomas Wolsey in Star Chamber* is a valuable, unimpassioned assessment of Wolsey's legacy as Lord Chancellor.

Thomas More is, paradoxically, poorly served by being the most written about of all the Thomases. When a man becomes a legend his character grows a nigh-impenetrable shell. When he is made a saint that carapace is burnished to a brilliance which wards off critical scrutiny. Anyone who wants to understand the real More and evaluate his place in the political and religious life of the sixteenth century must begin by forgetting all about *A Man for All Seasons* and go on to scrutinise fearlessly the propaganda images created by More's son-in-law, William Roper, and his portraitist, Hans Holbein. Roper's *The Life of Sir Thomas More, knighte* (*c.* 1557) was written at a time when a Catholic counter-attack needed *lay* heroes and martyrs (in 1535, when both men went to the block, Bishop John Fisher's death made a much greater impact on contemporaries), and when a family, afflicted by the shame of Sir Thomas's execution for treason, was seeking rehabilitation. It is a vivid biography vibrant with affectionately remembered detail but it does present us with an idealised portrait such as More himself would have wished his descendants to see, the kind of representation he instructed Holbein to make for public display. (Holbein, who knew the *real* More, significantly chose to absent himself from England during the years when his former patron was Lord Chancellor.) Roper was the prime source for Nicholas Harpsfield (*The Life and Death of Sir Thomas More, knight*) and Thomas Stapleton (*The life and illustrious martyrdom of Sir Thomas More*), both Catholic polemicists. The most interesting fact about these early studies is their lack of impact. They failed for 300 years to provide an acceptable corrective to the picture of the arch-persecutor presented by John Foxe and other Protestant apologists. Not until the nineteenth century was the image of the martyr brought out of the cupboard and dusted down with the blessing of a Vatican committed to the reconversion of England. In 1935 Professor R.W. Chambers wrote *Thomas More*, the biography that was to hold the field for several decades. A deliberately *non*-religious work, it combined the worst of both liberal historiography and confessional apologetic to offer the world a secular hagiography. By declining to involve himself in the Reformation debate Chambers was obliged to depict More as the prototype political martyr, the honest man refusing to abandon conscience at the dictate of a tyrannical monster. The major turning point in More studies came in 1963 with the publication of the first volume of *The Complete Works of St Thomas More* (New Haven, 1963). This magnificent series now permits all students an insight into More's varied output – the devotional works of his last years, the cynical Latin epigrams, the vituperative attacks on heresy, the tedious theological diatribes and the political grappling of *Utopia* and *The History of Richard III*. The first and still the best biography to make use of these sources in essaying a rounded, objective treatment of the subject was Richard Marius's *Thomas More* (1984). Read in conjunction with J.A. Guy, *The Public Career of Sir Thomas More* (1980), this still provides the most intelligible assessment of More as a man of his age.

Before leaving More and Wolsey, mention should be made of Jasper Ridley's *The Statesman and the Fanatic: Thomas Wolsey and Thomas More*, an entertaining dual biography which calls in question the stereotypes which for too long dominated popular thinking about the two men. This is thesis-driven historiography but it certainly makes one think.

Interest in Thomas Howard was, for many years, directed towards placing him in the context of his dynasty: Geral Brenan and E.P. Statham, *The House of Howard* (1907); E.M. Richardson, *The Lion and the Rose: The Great Howard Story* (New York, 1922); J.M. Robinson, *The Dukes of Norfolk: A Quincentennial History* (Oxford, 1982). Two works devoted exclusively to Thomas Howard are Neville Williams, *Thomas Howard, Fourth Duke of Norfolk* (New York, 1964) and David M. Head, *The Ebbs and Flows of Fortune: The Life of Thomas Howard, Third Duke of Norfolk* (Athens, Georgia, 1995). The latter is a frank, warts-and-all portrayal marred only by a tendency to separate Howard's political life from his family and patronage connections.

The main difficulty about getting inside the skin of Thomas Cromwell, the lynchpin of the English Reformation, is that although we know a great deal about his last momentous decade most of what went before can only be discovered from snippets of information in his letters. There is no need to emphasise again the work done by Geoffrey Elton over more than three decades in establishing Cromwell's pre-eminence in the political, religious and administrative life of the 1530s. (See below for titles.) As regards biography, the following record what facts can be known. R.B. Merriman's two volume *Life and Letters of Thomas Cromwell* (Oxford, 1902) provides a useful starting point. The correspondence gives a very good 'feel' of Cromwell's clear and clever mind when he was at the height of his power but the 'Life' is marred by the prejudice which the very name of Cromwell all too frequently conjures up. A.G. Dickens, *Thomas Cromwell and the English Reformation* (1959), relates in brief compass what can be known about the minister and allots him a place in the religious life of the period. B.W. Beckingsale, *Thomas Cromwell: Tudor Minister* (1978), struggles manfully to make the slender evidence reveal a believable character. Ultimately, the student's best means of obtaining a rounded impression of this central figure is through the eyes of the other people with whom he had dealings, as revealed in individual biographies and the documents brought together in the collections of state papers and diplomatic correspondence.

With Thomas Cranmer the reader is on surer ground. John Foxe gathered a considerable amount of documentary and verbatim evidence for his pages about the Archbishop in *Acts and Monuments of these latter and perilous days touching matters of the Church* (G. Townshend and S.R. Cattley, eds., 1837–41). Foxe's material and manuscripts came into the hands of John Strype towards the end of the seventeenth century and formed the basis of *Memorials of the Most Reverend Father in God, Thomas Cranmer, Archbishop of Canterbury* (P.E. Barnes, ed. 1853) and *Ecclesiastical Memorials relating chiefly to religion . . .* (Oxford, 1822).

These were, of course, hagiographical in intent. Early Catholic vituperation appeared in Nicholas Harpsfield's *Bishop Cranmer's Recantacyons*. Controversy was fanned anew by the Victorian evangelical and Anglo-Catholic revivals. The best outcome of this ecclesiastical spat was *The Works of Archbishop Cranmer* (J.E. Cox, ed., Parker Society, 1844–6). Various 'lives' dating from the nineteenth and earlier twentieth century can still be found, all more or less marred by that animus in which Christian polemicists are uniquely gifted. Hillaire Beloc's *Cranmer* (1931) is laughable. A.F. Pollard wrote the first non-partisan biography, *Thomas Cranmer and the English Reformation, 1489–1556* (1905). The post-World War II period produced *Thomas Cranmer* (1955) by G.W. Bromiley and a companion work. *Thomas Cranmer, Theologian* (1956) by the same author, a useful, brief introduction to the reformer's thinking. Jasper Ridley's *Thomas Cranmer* (Oxford, 1962) held the ring for several years and is still probably the best way in for new readers. It could be coupled with *The Work of Thomas Cranmer* (G.E. Duffield, ed., Appleford, 1964), which offers a selection of the Archbishop's correspondence and theological writings. However, since 1996 the subject has been dominated by Diarmaid MacCulloch's monumental *Thomas Cranmer, A Life*. This balanced and scholarly re-examination of all the available evidence, coupled with fresh research on the reformer's library, provides a step-by-step account of Cranmer's intellectual and religious development. MacCulloch's book is indispensable but, for this reader at least, the man behind the mass of accumulated material remains an enigma.

Thomas Wriothesley still awaits a serious biographer. A huge volume of correspondence is available in the Public Record Office, much of it catalogued and abstracted in *Letters and Papers Foreign and Domestic of the Reign of Henry VIII*. A.L. Rowse offered a brief biographical sketch in *History Today*, XV (1965), 382–90, 468–74, and A.J. Slavin's article 'The fall of Lord Chancellor Wriothesley: a study in the politics of conspiracy', *Albion*, VII, IV (1975), 265ff. is useful on events *c.* 1536–50, though not without flaws.

Printed and Early Sources

Allen, P.S. and H.M. (eds.), *The Letters of Richard Fox, 1486–1527* (Oxford, 1928).

Allen, P.S. *et al.* (eds.), *Opus Epistolarum Des. Erasmi Roterodami* (Oxford, 1906–58).

Bacon, Sir Francis, *History of the Reign of Henry VII* in R. Lockyer (ed.), *Works* (1971).

Bain, J. (ed.), *Hamilton Papers: Letters and Papers Illustrating the*

Political Relations of England and Scotland in the Sixteenth Century (Edinburgh, 1890).

Becon, T., *Works*, ed. J. Ayre (Parker Society, Cambridge, 1843).

Bergenroth, G.A. and de Gayangos, P. (eds.), *Calendar of State Papers, Spanish* (1862–6).

Brown, R., Bentinck, C. and Brown, H. (eds.), *Calendar of State Papers, Venetian* (1864–98).

Byrne, M. St C. (ed.), *The Lisle Letters* (Chicago, 1980).

Cavendish, G., *The Life and Death of Cardinal Wolsey* in R.S. Sylvester and D.P. Harding (eds.), *Two Early Tudor Lives* (New Haven, 1962).

Corrie, G.E. (ed.), *Sermons and Remains of Hugh Latimer . . .* (Parker Society, Cambridge, 1844, 1845).

Cox, J.E. (ed.), *The Works of Archbishop Cranmer* (Parker Society, Cambridge, 1844–6).

Dasent, J.R. (ed.), *Acts of the Privy Council of England* (1890–1907).

Dowling, M. (ed.), 'William Latymer's chronickille of Anne Bulleyne', *Camden Miscellany 30*, Camden Society, 4th series, XXXIX (1990), 23–66.

Ellis, H. (ed.), *Original Letters, illustrative of English history* (1824–46).

Elton, G.R. (ed.), *The Tudor Constitution, Documents and Commentary* (Cambridge, 1960).

Erasmus, D., *The Praise of Folly*, trs. C.H. Miller (New Haven, 1979).

Fish, S., *A Supplication for the Beggars*, eds. F.J. Furnivall and J.M. Cowper (1871).

Fortescue, J., *The Governance of England*, ed. C. Plummer (Oxford, 1885).

Foxe, J., *Acts and Monuments*, G. Townsend and S.R. Cattley, eds., (1838).

Frere, W.H. and Kennedy W.M., *Visitation Articles and Injunction* (1910).

Gairder, J. (ed.), *Letters and Papers, Foreign and Domestic, of the Reign of Henry VIII* (1861–3).

(ed.), *Paston Letters, AD 1422–1509* (1904).

Giustinian, S., *Four Years at the Court of Henry VIII . . . January 12th 1515 to July 26th 1519, ed. R. Brown (1854).*

Gough Nichols, J. (ed.), *Chronicle of the Grey Friars of London*, Camden Society, 1st series, LIII (1852).

Documents of the English Reformation, X (Cambridge, James Clarke and Co., 1994).

Hall, E., *The union of the two noble and illustre famelies of Lancastre and Yorke*, ed. H. Ellis (1809), p. 499.

Hardyng, J. and Grafton, R., *Chronicle of John Hardyng . . .*, ed. H. Ellis (1812).

Hay, D., (ed.), *The anglica historia of Polydore Vergil, 1485–1537*, Camden Soc., 3rd ser., LXXIV, (1950).

Herbert, E., Lord Cherbury, *The Life and Rayne of Henry VIII* (1872).

Hillerbrand, H.J. (ed.), *Erasmus and His Age, Selected Letters of Desiderius Erasmus* (New York, 1970).

Hughes, P.L. and Larkin, J.F. (eds.), *Tudor Royal Proclamations* (New Haven, 1964, 1969).

Kaulek, J., *Correspondence politique de M.M. de Castillon et de Marillac . . .* (Paris, 1885).

Knighton, C.S. (ed.), *Calendar of State Papers, Domestic, Edward VI, 1547–1553* (1992).

Latimer, Hugh, *Sermons*, ed. G.E. Corrie (Parker Society, Cambridge, 1844).

Letters and Papers, Foreign and Domestic of the Reign of Henry VIII, J. Gairdner, ed., (1861–3).

Loades, D.M. (ed.), *Papers of George Wyatt Esquire . . .*, Camden Society, 4th series, V (1968).

Luther, M., *Works* (Philadelphia, 1943).

Mancini, D., *The Usurpation of Richard III*, ed. C.A.J. Armstrong (1969).

Merriman, R.B., *The Life and Letters of Thomas Cromwell* (Oxford, 1902).

More, Thomas, *Selected Letters*, ed. F.F. Rogers (New Haven, 1961).

Muller, J.A. (ed.), *Letters of Stephen Gardiner* (Cambridge, 1933).

Mynors, R.A.B. *et al* (eds.), *Correspondence of Erasmus* in *The Collected Works of Erasmus* (Toronto, 1975).

Nichols, J.G. (ed.), *Narratives of the Reformation*, Camden Society, old series, LXXVII (1859).

Nott, G.F. (ed.), *Works of Henry Howard* (New York, 1965).

Reynolds, E.E. (ed.), *The Life and Illustrious Martyrdom of Sir Thomas More by Thomas Stapleton*, trs. P.E. Hallett (New York, 1966).

Rogers, E.F. (ed.), *Correspondence of Sir Thomas More* (Princeton, 1947).

Roper, W., *The Life of Sir Thomas More* in R.S. Sylvester and D.P. Harding (eds.), *Two Early Tudor Lives* (New Haven, 1962).

Starkey, Thomas, *A Dialogue between Pole and Lupset*, ed. T.F. Mayer, Camden Society, 4th series, XXXVII (1989).

State Papers published under the authority of His Majesty's Commission, King Henry VIII, (11 vols, 1830–52).

Stow, J., *Annales* (1615).

A Survey of London, ed., C.L. Kingsford, (Oxford, 1908).

Strype, J., *Memorials . . . of Thomas Cranmer* (1853).

Tawney, R.H. and Power, E., *Tudor Economic Documents* (1924).

The Complete Works of St Thomas More (New Haven, 1963).

Tyndale, W., *Doctrinal Treatises . . .*, ed. H. Walter (Parker Society, Cambridge, 1848).

   Expositions and Notes on Sundry Portions of the Holy Scriptures together with the Practices of Prelates . . ., ed. H. Walter (Parker Society, 1849).

Answer to Sir Thomas More's Dialogue, the Supper of the Lord . . . and William Tracy's Testament Expounded . . ., ed. H. Walter (Parker Society, Cambridge, 1850).

Vergil, P., *Anglica Historia*, ed. D. Hay, Camden Society, new series, LXXIV (1950).

White, B. (ed.), *Eclogues of Alexander Barclay* (Early English Text Society, Oxford, 1928).

Wright, T. (ed.), *Three Chapters of Letters relating to the suppression of the monasteries*, Camden Society, XXVI (1843).

Wriothesley, C., *A Chronicle of England during the Reigns of the Tudors*, ed. W.D. Hamilton, Camden Society, new series, XI, XX (1875–7).

Secondary Works – Books and Articles

Ackroyd, P., *The Life of Thomas More* (1998).

Allen, J.W., *A History of Political Thought in the Sixteenth Century* (1960 edn.)

Alvarez, M.F., *Charles V – Elected Emperor and Hereditary Ruler*, trs. J.A. Lalaguna (1975).

Anglo, S., *The Great Tournament Roll of Westminster* (1968).
Spectacle, Pageantry and Early Tudor Policy (Oxford, 1969).

Aston, M., *England's Iconoclasts. I. Laws Against Images* (Oxford, 1988).
The King's Bedpost, Reformation and Iconography . . . (Cambridge, 1993).

Bagchi, D., '"Eyn Mercklich Underscheyd": Catholic reactions to Luther's doctrine of the priesthood of all believers' in W.J. Sheils and D. Wood (eds.), *The Ministry Clerical and Lay Studies in Church History*, XXVI (Oxford, 1989).

Bainton, R., *Here I Stand: A Life of Martin Luther* (New York, 1950).

Bates, C.J., *Flodden Field, A Collection of Some of the Earliest Evidence* (Newcastle, 1894).

Beckingsale, B.W., *Thomas Cromwell: Tudor Minister* (1978).

Beer, B.L., *Northumberland: The Political Career of John Dudley, Earl of Warwick and Duke of Northumberland* (Kent State University Press, 1973).
Rebellion and Riot: Popular Disorder in England during the Reign of Edward VI (Kent State University Press, 1982).

Bennett, H.S., *The Pastons and Their England* (Cambridge, 1922).

Bernard, G.W., 'The fall of Anne Boleyn', *English Historical Review*, CVI (1990).
'Anne Boleyn's religion', *Historical Journal*, XXXVI (1993).

Block, J., *Factional Politics in the English Reformation, RHS Studies in History*, LXVI (1993).

Boehmer, H., *Martin Luther: Road to Reformation*, trs. J.W. Doberstein and T.G. Tappert (1957).

Bowker, M., *The Henrician Reformation: The Diocese of Lincoln under John Longland 1521–1547* (Cambridge, 1981).

Bradshaw, B. and Duffy, E., (eds.), *Humanism, Reform and the Reformation: The Career of Bishop John Fisher* (Cambridge, 1989).

Brenan, G. and Statham, E.P., *The House of Howard* (1907).

Brigden, S., *London and the Reformation* (Oxford, 1989).

Bromiley, G.W., *Thomas Cranmer, Theologian* (1956).

Burckhardt, J., *The Civilization of the Renaissance in Italy* (1955 edn.)

Burnet, Gilbert, *History of the Reformation of the Church of England* (Oxford, 1865).

Bush, M.L., *The Government Policy of Protector Somerset* (1975).

Cameron, E., *The European Reformation* (Oxford, 1991).

Chamberlain, A.B., *Hans Holbein in the Younger* (1913).

Chambers, R.W., *Thomas More* (1976 edn.)

Chapman, H.W., *The Sisters of Henry VIII* (1969).

Chrimes, S.B., *Henry VII* (1972).

Coleman, C. and Starkey, D., *Revolution Reassessed* (1986).

Condon, M., 'Ruling elites in the reign of Henry VII' in C. Ross (ed.), *Patronage, Pedigree and Power in Late Medieval England* (Gloucester, 1979).

Connell-Smith, G., *Forerunners of Drake* (1954).

Cornwall, J., *Revolt of the Peasantry, 1549* (1977).

Coulton, G.G., *Social Life in Britain from the Conquest to the Reformation* (Cambridge, 1926).

Cross, C., *Church and People, 1450–1600: The Triumph of the Laity* . . . Henocks, 1976).

Cross, C., Loades, D. and Scarisbrick, J.J., 'Law and government under the Tudors', essays presented to Sir Geoffrey Elton, Cambridge, 1988.

De Molen, R.L. (ed.), *Leaders of the Reformation* (Selinsgrove, 1984).

Demaus, R., *Hugh Latimer. A Biography* (1869).
  William Tyndale: A Biography (1904).

Dickens, A.G., *Thomas Cromwell and the English Reformation* (1959).
  Lollards and Protestants in the Diocese of York 1509–1558 (1982, revised edn.).
  The English Reformation (1989).
  Later Monasticism and the Reformation (1994).

Dickens, A.G. and Jones, W.R.D., *Erasmus the Reformer* (1994).

Dickens, A.G. and Tonkin, J.M., with Powell, K., *The Reformation in Historical Thought* (Oxford, 1985).

Dodds, M.H. and R., *The Pilgrimage of Grace and the Exeter Conspiracy* (Cambridge, 1971 edn.)

Dowling, M., 'Anne Boleyn and reform', *The Journal of Ecclesiastical History*, XXV, I (January 1984), 30–46.

Duffy, E., *The Stripping of the Altars: Traditional Religion in England 1400–1580* (New Haven, 1992).

Elton, G.R., *The Tudor Revolution in Government: Administration Changes in the Reign of Henry VIII* (Cambridge, 1953).

'King or minister? The man behind the English Reformation', *History*, new series, XXXIX (1954), 216–32.

England Under the Tudors (1955).

The Tudor Constitution (Cambridge, 1960, 2nd edn. 1982).

Policy and Police: The Enforcement of the Reformation in the Age of Thomas Cromwell (Cambridge, 1972).

Reform and Renewal: Thomas Cromwell and the Common Weal (Cambridge, 1973).

'Sir Thomas More and the opposition to Henry VIII', *Studies in Tudor Politics and Government*, I (1974) 129–56.

'Thomas More, councillor', *Studies in Tudor and Stuart Politics and Government* (1974).

Studies in Tudor and Stuart Politics (1974–84).

'Tudor government: the points of contact', *Royal Historical Society* trs (1976), 211f.

Reform and Reformation (1977).

Thomas Cromwell, ed. J. Loades, *Headstart History Papers* (1991).

Emmison, F.G., *Tudor Secretary: Sir William Petre at Court and Home* (1961).

Erickson, C., *Bloody Mary* (New York, 1978).

Fleisher, M., *Radical Reform and Political Persuasion in the Life and Writings of Thomas More* (1973).

Fox, A., *Thomas More: History and Providence* (Oxford, 1982).

Fox, A. and Guy, J., (eds.), *Reassessing the Henrician Age: Humanism, Politics and Reform, 1500–1550* (Oxford, 1986).

Fox-Davies, A.C., *A Complete Guide to Heraldry* (1929).

French, K.L. *et al.*, *The Parish in English Life, 1400–1600* (Manchester, 1997).

Furnivall, F.J. (ed.), *Ballads from Manuscripts* (Ballad Society, 1868–72) vol. I.

Gammon, S.R., *Statesman and Schemer: William, First Lord Paget – Tudor Minister* (Newton Abbot, 1973).

Garrett, C.H., *The Marian Exiles: A Study in the Origins of Elizabethan Puritanism* (Cambridge, 1938).

Gilkes, R.K., *The Tudor Parliament* (1969).

Gunn, S.G. and Lindley, P.G. (eds.), *Cardinal Wolsey: Church, State and*

Art (Cambridge, 1991).

Gunn, S.J., *Charles Brandon, Duke of Suffolk, c. 1484–1545* (Oxford, 1988).

Guy, J.A., *The Cardinal's Court: The Impact of Thomas Wolsey in Star Chamber* (1977).

The Public Career of Sir Thomas More (Brighton, 1980).

Haigh, C. (ed.), *The English Reformation Revisited* (Cambridge, 1987).

English Reformations: Religion, Politics and Society Under the Tudors (Oxford, 1993).

Hammond, E.A., 'Doctor Augustine, physician to Cardinal Wolsey and King Henry VIII', *Medical History*, XIX (1975), 215–49.

Harris, B.J., *Edward Stafford, Third Duke of Buckingham, 1478–1521* (Stanford, 1986).

Harrison, C.J., 'The petition of Edmund Dudley', *English Historical Review* (1971), 82–99.

Harrison, S.M., *The Pilgrimage of Grace in the Lake Counties* (1981).

Haugaard, W.J., 'Katherine Parr: the religious convictions of a Renaissance queen', *Renaissance Quarterly*, XXII (1969), 346–59.

Head, D.M., *The Ebbs and Flows of Fortune: The Life of Thomas Howard, Third Duke of Norfolk* (Athens, Georgia, 1995).

Heal, F. and O'Day, R., *Church and Society in England, Henry VIII to James I* (1977).

Herbert, Edward, Lord of Cherbury, *Autobiography and History of England Under Henry VIII* (1881 edn.)

Higgs, L.M., *Godliness and Governance in Tudor Colchester* (Michigan, 1998).

Hoak, D., 'The iconography of the crown imperial' in D. Hoak (ed.), *Tudor Political Culture* (Cambridge, 1995).

The King's Council in the Reign of Edward VI (Cambridge, 1976).

Hope, W.H. St J., 'The making of Place House at Titchfield, near Southampton, in 1538', *Archaelogical Journal*, LXIII.

Hoskins, W.G., *The Age of Plunder: King Henry's England, 1500–1547* (1976).

Howarth, D., *Images of Rule, Art and Politics in the English Renaissance 1485–1649* (1997).

Hudson, W.S., *The Cambridge Connection and the Elizabethan Settlement of 1559* (Durham, North Carolina, 1980).

Huizinga, J., *Erasmus of Rotterdam* (1952).

Hunt, E.W., *Dean Colet and His Theology* (1956).

Hutton, R., *The Rise and Fall of Merry England* (Oxford, 1994).

Ives, E.W., *Faction in Tudor England, Historical Association Appreciations, VI* (1979).

'Faction at the court of Henry VIII', *History*, LVII (1972), 69f.

The Common Lawyers of Pre-Reformation England; Thomas Kebell: A

Case Study (Cambridge, 1983).

Anne Boleyn (Oxford, 1986).

'Anne Boleyn and the early Reformation in England: the contemporary evidence', *Historical Journal*, XXXVII (1994), 389–400.

'The queen and the painters: Anne Boleyn, Holbein and Tudor royal portraits', *Apollo* (July 1994), 36–45.

'Henry VIII: the political perspective' in D. MacCulloch (ed.), *The Reign of Henry VIII: Politics, Policy and Piety* (1995).

James, M. (ed.), *Society, Politics and Culture, Studies in Early Modern England* (Cambridge, 1986).

'Obedience and dissent in Henrician England: the Lincolnshire rebellion, 1536', *Past and Present*, XLVIII (1970), 1–72.

Jordan, W.K., *Edward VI: The Young King* (1968).

Edward VI: The Threshold of Power (1970).

Knowles, D.E., *The Religious Orders in England* (Cambridge, 1948–59).

Lake, P. and Dowling, M. (eds.), *Protestantism and the National Church in Sixteenth-Century England* (1987).

Lehmberg, S.E., *The Reformation Parliament 1529–1536* (Cambridge, 1970).

The Later Parliaments of Henry VIII 1536–1547 (Cambridge, 1977).

Loach, J. and Tittler, R., *The Mid-Tudor Polity, c. 1540–1560* (1980).

Loades, D., *John Dudley, Duke of Northumberland, 1504–1553* (Oxford, 1996).

Two Tudor Conspiracies (Cambridge, 1965).

The Papers of George Wyatt Esquire, Camden Society, 4th series, V (1968).

The Reign of Mary Tudor: Politics, Government and Religion in England 1553–1558 (1979).

The Tudor Court (1987).

Lodge, E., *Illustrations of British History* (1791).

MacCulloch, D., 'Two dons in politics: Thomas Cranmer and Stephen Gardiner, 1503–1533', *Historical Journal*, XXXVII (1994), 1–22.

(ed.), *The Reign of Henry VIII, Politics, Policy and Piety* (1995).

Thomas Cranmer, A Life (New Haven, 1996).

Tudor Church Militant: Edward VI and the Protestant Reformation (1999).

Marius, R., *Thomas More* (1984).

Martienssen, A. *Queen Katherine Parr* (1973–).

Mattingley, G., *Catherine of Aragon* (1942).

Renaissance Diplomacy (1955).

Mayer, T.F., 'On the road to 1534: the occupation of Tournai and Henry VIII's theory of sovereignty' in D. Hoak (ed.), *Tudor Political Culture* (Cambridge, 1995).

McConica, J.K., *English Humanists and Reformation Politics Under*

Henry VIII and Edward VI (Oxford, 1965).

Miller, H., *Henry VIII and the English Nobility* (Oxford, 1986).

Moat, D. (ed.), *Tudor Political Culture* (Cambridge, 1995).

Mozley, J.F., *Coverdale and His Bibles* (1953).

    William Tyndale (1937).

Neame, A., *The Holy Maid of Kent: The Life of Elizabeth Barton 1506–1534* (1971).

Noble, H., *A History of the College of Arms* (1804).

Oberman, H.A., *Masters of the Reformation: The Emergence of a New Intellectual Climate in Europe* (Cambridge, 1981).

Ogle, A., *The Tragedy of Lollard's Tower* (1949).

Olin, J.C., *The Catholic Reformation: Savonarola to Ignatius Loyola: Reform in the Church 1459–1540* (New York, 1971).

Orme, N., *English Schools in the Middle Ages* (1973).

Pantin, W.A., *The English Church in the Fourteenth Century* (1962), pp. 132–3.

Pollard, A.F., *Thomas Cranmer and the English Reformation, 1489–1556* (1905).

Porter, H.C., *Reformation and Reaction in Tudor Cambridge* (Cambridge, 1958).

Porter, H.C. and Thomson, D.F.S., *Erasmus and Cambridge* (Toronto, 1963).

Read, C., *Mr Secretary Cecil and Queen Elizabeth* (1955).

Redworth, G., *In Defence of the Church Catholic: The Life of Stephen Gardiner* (Oxford, 1990).

Reynolds, E.E., *The Life and Death of St Thomas More* (1978).

Richardson, W.C., *Stephen Vaughan, Financial Agent of Henry VIII* (Baton Rouge, Louisiana State University, 1953).

Ridley, J.G., *Thomas Cranmer* (Oxford, 1962).

    The Statesman and the Fanatic: Thomas Wolsey and Thomas More (1982).

    Henry VIII (1984).

Riehl Leader, D., *A History of the University of Cambridge I: The University to 1546* (Cambridge, 1988).

Rowlands, J. and Starkey, D., 'An old tradition reasserted: Holbein's portrait of Queen Anne Boleyn', *The Burlington Magazine*, CXXV (February 1983), pp. 88–92.

Rowse, A.L., 'Thomas Wriothesley, First Earl of Southampton', *History Today*, XV (1965), 382–90, 468–74.

Rupp, E.G. *Studies in the Making of the English Protestant Tradition* (Cambridge, 1947).

Russell, J.G., *The Field of Cloth of Gold: Men and Manners in 1520* (1969).

Scarisbrick, J.J., *The Reformation and the English People* (Oxford, 1984).

Henry VIII (New Haven, 1968; 2nd edn. 1997).

Simon, J., *Education and Society in Tudor England* (Cambridge, 1966).

Slavin, A.J., *Politics and Profit: A Study of Sir Ralph Sadler, 1507–1547* (Cambridge, 1966).

'The fall of Lord Chancellor Wriothesley: a study in the politics of conspiracy', *Albion*, VII (1975), 265–85.

'Cromwell, Cranmer and Lord Lisle, a study in the politics of reform', *Albion*, IX (1977), 316–36.

Smith, L.B., *Tudor Prelates and Politics* (1953).

A Tudor Tragedy: The Life and Times of Catherine Howard (1961).

Somerset, A., *Elizabeth I* (1991).

Starkey, D., 'Court, council and the nobility in Tudor England' in R.G. Asch and A.M. Birkie (eds.), *Princess Patronage and the Nobility. The Court at the Beginning of the Modern Age, c. 1450–1650* (Oxford, 1991).

(ed.), *Henry VIII: A European Court in England* (1991).

Tawney, R.H. and Power, E., *Tudor Economic Documents* (1924).

The Collected Works of Erasmus (Toronto, 1986).

Thomas, K., *Religion and the Decline of Magic* (1971).

Tjernagel, N.S., *Henry VIII and the Lutherans: A Study in Anglo-Lutheran Relations from 1521 to 1547* (St Louis, 1965).

Tracy, J.C., 'Ad Fontes: the humanist understanding of Scripture as nourishment for the soul' in J. Raitt (ed.), *Christian Spirituality – High Middle Ages and Reformation* (New York, 1988).

Tucker, M.J., *The Life of Thomas Howard, Earl of Surrey and Second Duke of Norfolk, 1443–1524* (The Hague, 1964).

Villari, P., *Life and Times of Girolamo Savonarola*, trs. L. Villari (1888), p. 154.

Wagner, A., *Heralds of England* (1967).

Walker, G., *John Skelton and the Politics of the 1520s* (Cambridge, 1988).

Warnicke, R.M., *The Rise and Fall of Anne Boleyn* (Cambridge, 1989).

Wegg, J., *Richard Pace, Tudor Diplomat* (1937).

Wernham, R.B., *Before the Armada: The Emergence of the English Nation, 1485–1558* (1966).

Williams, N., *Thomas Howard, Fourth Duke of Norfolk* (New York, 1964).

Henry VII and His Court (1971).

Wilson, D., *A Tudor Tapestry: Men, Women and Society in Reformation England* (1972).

England in the Age of Thomas More (1978).

Hans Holbein: Portrait of an Unknown Man (1996).

Yates, F.A.S., *Astraea: The Imperial Theme in the Sixteenth Century* (1975).

Index

Compiled by John Noble

Boleyn, Sir Thomas, Viscount Rochford
(later Earl of Wiltshire and Ormond),
76, 78, 206, 237, 241, 248, 254, 257,
276, 284, 295, 312, 319, 333, 343,
429
Bonner, Edmund, Bishop of London, 298,
321, 467–8, 472, 488, 489, 499, 515
books
banned by More and Tunstall, 312–13,
357–8
burning of, 177, 179, 272–3, 281, 492
Borgia, Rodrigo *see* Alexander VI, Pope
Bosch, Hieronymous, 12, 151
Bosworth Field, Battle of (1485), 25, 32,
33, 113, 115
Botolf, Gregory, defector to Rome, 453
Boulogne
capture of (1544–45), 481, 482, 485
siege of (1492), 39
siege of (1549), 501
Bourbon, Duke of, 230
Bourbon, Nicholas, 353
Bourchier, Henry, Earl of Essex, 107
Bourchier, John, Lord Berners, 114, 191
Bowker, George *see* Damplip, Adam
Brackenbury, Sir Thomas, 32
Brandon, Catherine, Duchess of Suffolk,
487, 489
Brandon, Charles, Viscount Lisle (later
Duke of Suffolk), 202, 254, 260, 269,
351, 404, 437, 446, 471, 480, 482
Amicable Grant and, 198, 199, 210–11,
227
anti-annulment/divorce position, 295,
338, 340
anticlericalism of, 284
diplomatic missions, 114, 118, 119, 250
Eltham Ordinance and, 227–8, 241
friend of Henry VIII, 71, 78, 98, 100,
103, 115, 226, 328
made Earl Marshal, 209, 351
marriages of, 115–16, 120–2, 243, 471
Mary Tudor (Henry's sister) and,
116–22, 135, 354

military service in France, 103, 105,
107, 113, 195, 207, 481
parliament and, 290
part of the Howard/Boleyn clique, 241,
248, 294
Pilgrimage of Grace and, 398, 399, 471
President of the Council, 294
Wolsey and, 120–2, 136, 235, 241, 250,
259, 284, 288
Brant, Sebastian, 11, 133
Ship of Fools, 145
Bray, Edmund, 294–5
Bray, John, Prior, treason trial, 55–6
Brereton, William, 303, 389
Brest, naval blockade of (1513), 104–5
Brixius (de Brie), Germanus (French
scholar), 159–60, 216
Browne, Anne (wife of Brandon), 115
Browne, Anthony, Observant friar,
413–14
Browne, Sir Anthony, 447, 448
Bruges, 93
anti-French treaty (1521), 212
Bryan, Francis, 163
Bucer, Martin, 434, 510
Buckingham, Duke of *see* Stafford,
Edward
Bullinger, Heinrich (Swiss reformer),
405
Burckhardt, Georg (known as Spalatin),
Solace and Consolation of Princes,
434
Burghley *see* Cecil, William
Burkhardt, Jacob, 43
Butler, James, 206
Butler, John, Commissary at Calais,
447
Butler, Piers, Earl of Ormond, 203, 205,
206, 207
Butts, Sir William, King's physician, 314,
344, 353, 460, 485, 486

Cabot, John, 11, 36
Cabral, Pedro Alvarez, 11

Index

College of Arms, 72–4
Colt, Sir John, 58
Colt, William, 140
Columbus, Christopher, 11
common law
  in England, 21–2
  versus canon law, 151, 153–5, 316,
    363–4
  see also law
Compton, Sir William, 78, 79, 227
conservative Catholics, 336, 353–5,
  404–5, 454
  attempt to destroy Catherine Parr,
    488–92
  attempt to destroy Cranmer, 473–5
  attempt to halt the Reformation, 472–6,
    513–17
  opposition to Cromwell, 442, 443–4,
    451–2, 454–5, 456–7
  in parliament, 443–6
  a recognisable faction at court, 459–60,
    502
  removal of clergy by Elizabeth, 518
  support for Catherine of Aragon, 181–2,
    305, 306–7, 318, 329, 332–4, 338,
    339, 341, 344, 345, 349, 352, 360–1,
    362, 365–6, 368–9, 379, 414, 435,
    459
  support for Princess Mary, 395–6,
    414–16
  see also Pilgrimage of Grace
Constable, Sir Marmaduke, 111
Constable, Sir Robert, 222
Constantine, George, 362
Cordoba, Gonzalo de, 91
Cornish rebellion (1497), 38, 47
Corpus Christi College (Cambridge), 90
Council Attendant, to Henry VIII, 163,
  425–6, 450, 452–3, 464–5
Council (to Edward VI)
  confrontation between Wriothesley and
    Dudley, 503
  conservative Catholic consensus,
    502

Cranmer's membership of, 508–9
  and Lady Jane Grey, 512
  Somerset as executive head, 498
  split between conservatives and
    evangelicals, 509
Council (to Elizabeth I), 519–20
Council (to Henry VIII), 62–3, 64, 68–71,
  76, 79–81, 84, 98, 120, 122–3, 163,
  260, 317–18, 336, 352, 459
  after Cromwell, 460–1
  alliance with Charles V called for,
    484–5
  anticlericalism, 288
  Cromwell and, 334–6, 452–3
  discusses Catherine Howard scandal,
    469
  Erastian leanings, 288, 289
  evangelical ascendancy, 498
  examines prominent evangelicals,
    473–5
  factions, 457–8, 461
  Gardiner and, 442, 450, 466
  Henry's distrust of, 295
  Henry's divorce and, 318, 319
  Holy Maid of Kent and, 367–8
  hostility to Wolsey, 240, 253, 286–8,
    294
  Howard, 3rd Duke of Norfolk and, 294,
    295, 306, 380–1, 450, 467, 482
  More and, 291–2, 294, 374–5
  Pilgrimage of Grace and, 400–1
  proceeds against Cranmer for heresy,
    474–5, 485
  rapprochement with Charles V and the
    papacy favoured, 388
  split between conservatives and
    evangelicals, 479, 485
  war with France and, 482
  Wriothesley and, 409, 466
  see also King's Council Learned in the
    Law (to Henry VII); Star Chamber
Council (to Mary I), Cranmer indicted for
  treason and heresy, 513
Council of Trent, 375

557